Encyclopaedia of
# Boxing

# Encyclopaedia of
# BOXING

**MAURICE GOLESWORTHY**

**ROBERT HALE · LONDON**

© MAURICE GOLESWORTHY 1960, 1961,
1965, 1970, 1971, 1975, 1979, 1983 and 1988

*First edition 1960*
*Second edition 1961*
*Third edition 1965*
*Fourth edition 1970*
*Reprinted (with corrections) 1971*
*Fifth edition 1975*
*Sixth edition 1979*
*Seventh edition 1983*
*Eighth edition 1988*

Golesworthy, Maurice
Encyclopaedia of boxing.——8th ed.
1. Boxing. Encyclopaedias
I. Title
796.8'3'0321

ISBN 0-7090-3323-0

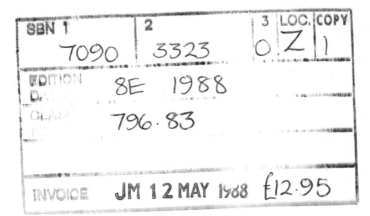

Robert Hale Limited
Clerkenwell House,
45/47 Clerkenwell Green,
London EC1R OHT

PRINTED AND BOUND IN GREAT BRITAIN BY
WBC BRISTOL AND MAESTEG

# Contents

# Acknowledgments

I would like to acknowledge with gratitude the valuable assistance given me by so many boxing enthusiasts, as well as the fighters themselves, who provided information and helped settle innumerable queries.

In particular I would like to acknowledge the assistance of the late Mr. J. M. Knowles, of Aberdeen, who, during the course of his travels in 52 different countries of the world, was on friendly terms with many of the old stars, including such famous fighters as Jim Jeffries, Jim Corbett, Tommy Burns, Jack Johnson, Jim Driscoll and Freddie Welsh. Mr. Knowles was a real boxing fanatic, and his first-hand knowledge of big boxing occasions, which began for him with the Burns-Johnson fight, enabled him to provide me with much useful information.

I also had a lot of help from the late Mr. John S. Salak, of Freeport, New York, who was well known on both sides of the Atlantic as a sports writer and former Assistant Managing Editor of *The Ring* magazine. Mr. Salak took a great deal of trouble to try and disentangle some of the confusion caused through the duplication of certain world titles by the old N.B.A. and the N.Y.A.C.

Special acknowledgment is also due to *Boxing News*, not only for allowing me to use the tabulated lists of European champions from their *Annual* as a basis for the information about title-holders which appears in this book, but because it has kept me in touch with the fight game as a regular reader since 1942.

Thanks also to the British Boxing Board of Control and the Amateur Boxing Association for kindly allowing me to quote their official rules, and to the European Boxing Union, for certain valuable information.

MAURICE GOLESWORTHY

# Introduction

When I started my first boxing scrapbooks as a young schoolboy I little dreamed that some 25 years later I would still have those books and they would prove of such immense value in helping me to compile an Encyclopaedia of Boxing.

In those days it was not only my enthusiasm for boxing which persuaded me to start my collection but that ever-growing thirst for knowledge. Nothing pleased me more than to be able to settle a sporting argument or to be able to reel off to my school chums a list of world champions in proper chronological order.

Often, when I haven't known the answer to a certain question, I have spent hours searching through my collection of books, papers and magazines, and it was my experience on those occasions that indicated the need for a comprehensive reference book.

My experience as a newspaper librarian and as respondent of readers' questions for national sports magazines emphasised the need to have all the necessary information in proper order for easy access, and I sincerely hope that in this book I have now been able to produce something which will prove of interest and value to the many boxing enthusiasts who, like myself, like to have the facts at their finger-tips.

During more than 12 months in the preparation of the first edition of this book I was surprised to find that many facts which I had always taken as gospel did not stand up under closer investigation. It is amazing to see the different dates and figures given in print about the same occasions. I have found as many as four different dates for the same fight, or different times given for knock-outs.

I can assure the reader that I have been at great pains to track down the correct figures in every case, but I am bound to admit that even now I would not be so bold as to say that every figure in this book is correct. If one finds contradictions in contemporary publications what chance have we got to find the right answers 30, 40 or 50 years later?

When I compiled the first edition of this book in 1960, I was already complaining about the difficulty in establishing boxing records because of the tangle over world titles. Sadly the situation has deteriorated rapidly ever since and it is only my enthusiasm for boxing rather than record keeping that has made me persevere.

In 1960 we had 10 weight divisions with only two of these world titles in dispute (i.e. 12 champions). Today there are no fewer than 17 divisions with the possibility of 48 champions! If that isn't enough chaos there are more divisions in the offing. At the lighter end of the scale there are already 5 divisions spread over 14 lbs where there used to be only two!

Look at the World Heavyweight Championship which to many of us is something almost sacred. Its importance has slipped to such an extent that we have had as many as 13 men who have held the various titles since October 1979. In the previous eight years there were only five claimants to this supreme title.

Despite this confusion, further aggravated by the introduction of the International Boxing Federation in 1983, when compiling lists of world champions I have still tried to hold to the sensible premise that a champion can only lose his title in the ring. However, I must confess that this has become extremely difficult and some duplication is unavoidable, but it should be made clear that while not entirely ignoring the I.B.F. I have generally not included their champions in these lists. The names of more widely recognised champions appear in capital letters in these lists, but, alas, such champions are becoming increasingly rare.

In giving the results of championship fights I have also tried to be as precise as possible in stating how a fight ended when it did not go the distance. Some boxing authorities record almost every ending inside the distance as a knock-out, but I feel that I am being more helpful and informative in giving the actual ending, i.e. whether the referee stopped the bout, or the boxer retired, or whether the boxer was knocked out of time.

Boxing, or prize fighting as it used to be called, has been popular for more than 200 years, and the problem has been to know what to include and what to omit in producing a single volume which could be made available at a price which would keep it within range of the majority of fight fans. That problem applied particularly to the number of biographies of the fighters. No matter how many were included certain favourites were bound to be missed.

I have decided, therefore, to include every fighter who ever won a British title plus the majority of undisputed world champions. However, to keep the size of the book within reasonable proportions I have had to be more selective with world champions in more recent editions. Even so there are well over 400 biographies.

Apart from these, however, the reader will find that this Encyclopaedia contains information about several other fighters, either under the various countries, or in the other data. These can all be traced through the index.

If a champion lost his title and later regained it in the same year then this is clearly shown in the following way. Jack Bloggs, champion 1923-27, 27-31.

Before leaving you to peruse this book at your leisure let all of us boxing enthusiasts join together in the hope that those politicians and other busy-bodies who are doing their utmost to abolish our favourite sport will in future, direct their energies towards preventing fights between nations. God gave the lion his teeth and claws to fight with; He gave us our fists for the same purpose, but I am not so sure about nuclear missiles.

MAURICE GOLESWORTHY

# Illustrations

# A

## ABANDONED:

An indoor bout between Dal Hawkins and Fred Bogan at San Francisco, June 3, 1889, was abandoned after 75 rounds because of bad light.

It was resumed the following day and Hawkins won by a knockout in the 90th round, so gaining recognition as world featherweight champion.

When Johnny Reagan met Jack Dempsey (Nonpareil) for the world middleweight title, Long Island, December 13, 1887, the fight had to be abandoned soon after the start as the tide came in and flooded the ring. It was resumed later the same day at another spot several miles away and Dempsey won in 45 rounds.

## AGE:

According to the rules of the B.B.B. of C. all professional boxers must be over the age of 18 years. Boxers between 18 and 19 years of age are limited to contests of no more than 24 minutes; 19 and 20, a limit of 30 minutes; over 20 any distance up to 45 minutes actual boxing.

In America no boxer under 20 can take part in a 10-round contest. The limit is six rounds at 18 and eight rounds at 19.

## Oldest:

The oldest boxer to win the world heavyweight title was Jersey Joe Walcott. He was 37 years 5 months when he knocked out Ezzard Charles at Pittsburgh, July 18, 1951.

Bob Fitzsimmons was 34 years 9 months when he won the title in March 1897.

The oldest title winners in the other divisions have been:

Light-heavy—Bob Fitzsimmons, 41 years 5 months.
Middle—Ray Robinson, 37 years 10 months.
Junior Middle—Freddie Little, 32 years 11 months.
Welter—Jack Britton, 33 years 5 months.
Junior Welter—Duilio Loi. 33 years 8 months.
Light—Rocky Kansas and Carlos Teo Cruz, both 30 years 7 months but with Cruz the elder by nine days.
Junior Light—Kuniaki Shibata, 25 years 11 months.
Feather—Eder Jofre, 37 years 1 month.
Bantam—Johnny Buff, 33 years 3 months.
Fly—Dado Marino 33 years 11 months.
*Note:* Ages given above are at the time of winning the title.

The oldest world champion at any weight was Archie Moore. He may have been 48 when finally deprived of his light-heavyweight title in 1962, although he only admitted to being 45.

Before Moore, the oldest man ever to hold a world title was Bob Fitzsimmons. He retained the light-heavyweight title until he was 43 years 6 months.

Several first-class boxers engaged in exhibition bouts at a surprisingly old age. Jack Johnson was 65 and Joe Jeannette 66 when they sparred with each other in 1945. But probably the oldest professional boxer ever to engage in a real contest was Walter Edgerton "The Kentucky Rosebud." He was 65 when he knocked out John Henry Johnson in four rounds, 1916. As Johnson was then 45 this contest also represents what is probably the highest age aggregate.

Jem Mace, one-time world champion, was 58 years 10 months when he was beaten in three rounds by Charlie Mitchell at Glasgow, February 7, 1890.

Another old-timer, Daniel Mendoza, was one day short of his 56th birthday when he lost to Tom Owen in 12 rounds on Banstead Downs, July 4, 1820.

Bobby Dobbs, a Tennessee negro welterweight who was well known in many parts of the world during the early part of the century, was believed to have been 56 years of age when he engaged in his last contests in Europe in 1914.

Bill Richmond was 55 when he beat Jack Carter in his last prize fight, November 12, 1818.

Tom Faulkner (Deptford) was 54 when he defeated Bill Thornton at Studley in 50 minutes, March 21, 1791.

George Maddox was 54 when he was defeated in 52 rounds by Bill Richmond, August 9, 1809.

Bob Fitzsimmons was 51 years 7 months when he went six rounds with K. O. Sweeney in a "No Decision" bout at Williamsport, Philadelphia, January 29, 1914.

Jack Johnson was 50 when knocked out by Bill Hartwell at Kansas City in six rounds, May 15, 1928.

Bep van Klaveren of Holland, who was European lightweight champion in 1931-32, was 48 when he attempted a come-back and won his way through to a European welterweight title fight with Idrissa Dione in November 1955. The Dutchman was beaten on points over 15 rounds.

Those already mentioned are among the oldest. Others whose age at the time of their last contest may be of interest are:

Kid Azteca 45, Jack Dempsey 45, Walter Neusel 45, Tancy Lee 44, Jack Britton 44, Tiger Jack Fox 43, Max Schmeling 43, Sam Langford 43, Pedlar Palmer 42, Nel Tarleton 41, Jess Willard 41, Jersey Joe Walcott 39, Tommy Farr 39, Larry Gains 39.

The oldest fighter ever to make his professional debut was Dr. Herbert Odom, a Chicago welterweight, who was 46 when he beat Eddie Partee (aged 19), r.s.f. 2, University of Illinois, July 20, 1979. Odom had given up amateur boxing in 1956.

Sam Minto, a West Indian who settled in Britain, fought as a featherweight/ lightweight from 1910 to 1948 when he was reputed to be over 60 years of age. He did, however, fight mostly in booths.

## Youngest:

The youngest boxer ever to win the world heavyweight title is Floyd Patterson. He was 21 years 10 months when he knocked out Archie Moore, November 30, 1956.

However, allowing for the confusion caused by the authorities, Mike Tyson may be regarded by many as becoming champion when he was only aged 21 years 32 days (i.e. when he added the I.B.F. version to the W.B.A. and W.B.C. versions already held by beating Tony Tucker, August 1, 1987.

The youngest title holders in other divisions have been:

Light-Heavy—John Henry Lewis, 21 years 5 months.

Middle—Al McCoy, 19 years 6 months.

Junior or Light Middle—Sandro Mazzinghi, 24 years 11 months.

Welter—Dixie Kid, 20 years 4 months.

Junior or Light Welter—Wilfredo Benitez, 17 years 6 months.

Light—Mando Ramos, 20 years 3 months.

Junior Light—Ben Villaflor, 19 years 5 months.

Feather—Dal Hawkins, 18 years 1 month.

Abe Attell was 17 years 8 months when he outpointed George Dixon, October 20, 1901, but his claim to the title at that time was not generally recognised.

Abe Attell was universally acknowledged as champion after his knockout win over Harry Forbes, February 1, 1904. Then Attell was 21 days short of his 20th birthday.

Bantam—Terry McGovern was 19 years 6 months when he knocked out Pedlar Palmer to become undisputed champion.

Pedlar Palmer was only 19 years 6 days when he claimed the title after beating Billy Plimmer but this was not given universal recognition.

Fly—Masahiko Harada, 19 years 6 months.

The youngest boxer to win a British title was Ted "Kid" Lewis. He was 18 days short of his 19th birthday when he gained the British featherweight championship by beating Alec Lambert in 17 rounds at the N.S.C., London, October 6, 1913.

Jack "Kid" Berg was only 16 years 4 months when he outpointed the British featherweight champion, Johnny Curley, over 15 rounds, October 29, 1925, in a non-title fight at Premierland, London.

Eric Boon was 13 days short of his 19th birthday, when he won the British lightweight title from Dave Crowley, December 15, 1938.

Georges Carpentier was 15 years 11 months when he claimed the French lightweight title outpointing Paul Til over 10 rounds, Paris, December 22, 1909.

Carpentier holds the record among European title holders for he was only 17 years 9 months when he gained the welterweight title from Young Joseph at Earls Court, London, October 23, 1911.

It is possible that George Taylor of London was only 16 years of age when he claimed the Bare Knuckle Championship in 1734.

## AKINS, Virgil:

American negro, born St. Louis. Started his professional career in 1948 as a lightweight. In eliminators for the world welterweight title, Akins stopped Tony DeMarco in 12 rounds, and Isaac Logart in six rounds before winning the title with a victory over Vince Martinez, June 6, 1958. Akins had Martinez down nine times before the referee stopped the contest in the fourth round.

Akins lost the title when he was outpointed over 15 rounds by Don Jordan, Los Angeles, December 5, 1958.

## ALI, Muhammad:

Although it is open to argument as to whether or not this American negro was the greatest heavyweight boxer of all-time there is no doubt that he did more for the fight game than any other fighter at any weight. Apart from being a determined and talented boxer he proved to be a great personality and world-wide coverage by the media made him the best known boxer in ring history.

After first winning the world title from Sonny Liston in 1964 he joined the American Black Muslim movement, gave up his real name—Cassius Clay—and became known as Muhammad Ali. Thereafter he took part in 24 world title bouts and became the first man ever to have regained the heavyweight crown on two occasions. He was first deprived of the title by the authorities in 1967 after refusing to be inducted into the U.S. Armed Forces. But in 1971, and after being out of the ring for more than three years, he made a come-back and although failing in his first bid to recapture the title, being outpointed by Joe Frazier in March 1971, he again became champion after demolishing Frazier's successor, the formidable George Foreman, in eight rounds in Zaire, October 1974. This was after he had avenged his defeat by Frazier and another at the hands of Ken Norton.

Ali was 36 years of age when he suffered the third defeat of his professional career, being surprisingly outpointed by the comparatively unknown Leon Spinks in February 1978. Exactly seven months later he regained the crown in a return bout by literally dancing his way to a points victory over a fighter 12 years his junior. A truly astonishing performance from this fighter with an inimitable style.

That was the last fight in which this once great fighter showed anything of his real class, but unfortunately, after another long lay-off, he chose to continue fighting even though he was nearly 38 years of age. His career, therefore, ended on a sad note with convincing defeats by Larry Holmes and Trevor Berbick, the last in December 1981.

## ALBERT HALL, LONDON:

The Royal Albert Hall has been a popular venue for boxing for many years.

In December 1918 the Inter-Service Boxing Association held their competition at the Albert Hall and the King's Trophy was won by Bombardier Billy Wells who outpointed Joe Beckett over three rounds.

On Boxing Day 1919 the first "big fight" ever to be seen at the Albert Hall took place. In this contest Ted "Kid" Lewis stopped Matt Wells in 12 rounds.

It was soon after this that boxing really took a firm hold on the Albert Hall and in July 1920 the former world heavyweight champion, Tommy Burns, appeared there when trying to make a come-back. He was stopped in seven rounds by Joe Beckett.

About the same period Bombardier Billy Wells made at least four appearances at the Albert Hall including the final contest of his career when he was knocked out in three rounds by Jack Stanley, April 30, 1925.

Important fights which have taken place at the Albert Hall since then are too numerous to list here but they have included such stars as Len Harvey, Jack Petersen, Larry Gains, George Cook, Ernie Roderick, Al Phillips, Brian Curvis, Howard Winstone, Alan Rudkin, Johnny Clark, Alan Minter and Charlie Magri.

## ALDRIDGE, George:

A good stand-up style boxer born London but fighting out of Market Harborough, George Aldridge won both the Midland and Southern Area middleweight titles and had a brief spell as British champion.

When Terry Downes was deprived of the British championship by the B.B.B.C. Aldridge was matched with John McCormack and captured the vacant title by knocking out the Scot in six rounds.

That was in November 1962, but it was only six months later that he was beaten in sensational fashion by Mick Leahy, the referee stopping the fight in only 1 minute 45 seconds of the 1st round.

## ALLEN, Terry:

Born Islington, London, 1924, Allen, whose real name is Edward Albert Govier, started boxing when he was nine and won a schoolboy championship. As an amateur he won 102 of 107 contests.

A two-handed fighter, the Islington barrow boy was not long in coming to the fore when he turned professional soon after leaving school.

In December, 1943, he created quite a stir by stopping Billy Hazlegrove in nine rounds at Blackpool. However, he suffered a setback when knocked out by Alec Murphy in May, 1946, and had his biggest disappointment in March, 1947. It was then he stepped into the gap to meet Rinty Monaghan after Emile

Famechon had dropped out. Unfortunately Allen had not long been out of hospital and he was beaten in one round.

That was not the real Terry Allen and he proved this by going on to a 15-round draw with world flyweight champion, Rinty Monaghan, in September, 1949. When the Irishman relinquished his title, Allen became world champion by outpointing Honore Pratesi over 15 rounds, April 25, 1950.

Allen lost his world title to Dado Marino on points at Honolulu, August 1, 1950.

On June 11, 1951, he won the vacant British flyweight title with a decision over Vic Herman at Leicester; lost it to Teddy Gardner, March 1952, but when Gardner retired Allen again became British champion by stopping Eric Marsden in six rounds at Harringay.

Terry Allen retired undefeated British champion in 1954.

## ALLEN, Tom:

Born Birmingham, 1840. Allen won a number of fights in this country and fought a draw with Joe Goss before going to America in 1868.

There he won the American championship in beating Bill Davis in 43 rounds in January, 1869. Exactly five months later, however, he lost the title when, although he had Mike McCoole well beaten, gunmen persuaded the referee to give the decision in the Irishman's favour.

In 1870 the English champion Jem Mace visited America and in a contest billed as for the world championship Allen was beaten by him in 10 rounds.

When Mace relinquished the world title Allen claimed it and confirmed it by stopping Mike McCoole in 20 minutes, St. Louis, September 23, 1873.

Allen lost his title to Joe Goss, September 7, 1876. This contest, which was fought in two rings in Kenton and Boone counties, Kentucky, lasted 21 rounds. According to all accounts Allen was having the better of the milling but he was again threatened by gunmen and threw away the fight by fouling Goss and so being disqualified.

## AMATEUR BOXING ASSOCIATION:

The A.B.A. is a non-profit making organisation which was founded in 1880 to encourage, develop, and control amateur boxing in England.

Its government and control is vested in a National Committee composed of the Honorary Officers of the Association and the elected representatives of the three Service Boxing Associations and the various National, London, Provincial and County Associations affiliated to the A.B.A.

The head office is at Francis House, Francis Street, London SW1 1DE.

## AMATEUR CHAMPIONS:
### Most titles:

The highest number of title wins in each division of the A.B.A. Championships are as follows:

Super-heavyweight 2: J. Oyebola, 1986-87.

Heavyweight 5: F. Parks, 1899, 1901-02, 1905-06.

Light-heavy 4: H. J. Mitchell, 1922-23-24-25.

Middle 5: R. C. Warnes, 1899, 1901, 1903, 1907, 1910. H. W. Mallin, 1919, 1920-21-22-23. F. Mallin, 1928-29-30-31-32.

Light-middle 3: R. Douglas, 1983-84-85.

Welter 3: N. Gargano, 1954-55-56. T. Waller, 1970, 1973-74.

Light-welter 2: D. Stone, 1956-57. R. Kane, 1958-59. B. Brazier, 1961-62. R. McTaggart, 1963, 1965. A. Willis 1980-81.

Light 4: M. Wells, 1904-05-06-07. F. Grace, 1909, 1913, 1919-20. G. Gilbody, 1977, 1979-80-81.

Feather 5: G. R. Baker, 1912-13-14, 1919, 1921.

Bantam 4: W. W. Allen, 1911-12, 1914, 1919.

Fly 5: T. Pardoe, 1929-30-31-32-33.

Light-fly 4: J. Lyon, 1981-82-83-84.

No boxer has won more than five A.B.A. championships in any division.

The record for the most A.B.A. titles was set up by J. Steers (Belsize) who won six—heavyweight, 1890, 1892-93, Middleweight, 1891-92-93.

This record was equalled in 1987 by J.

Lyon (St. Helens)—Light-fly 1981-82-83-84, and Flyweight 1985, 1987.

The record for the most national amateur title wins is held by A. Watson (Leith). He won the Scottish Heavyweight championship 1938, 1942-43, and the light-heavyweight championship 1937-38-39, 1943-44-45, 1947. Ten in all. He also won the A.B.A. light-heavyweight title 1945 and 1947.

The highest number of title wins in each division of the other National amateur championships of the home countries:

*Irish Championships:*

Heavyweight 7: G. O'Colmain, 1946-47-48-49-50-51-52.

Light-heavy 5: W. J. Murphy, 1927-28-29-30, 1932. R. Hearns, 1933-34-36-37-38. O. Byrne, 1957-58-59, 1961, 1967.

Middle 7: J. J. Chase, 1926-27-28-29-30-31-32.

Light-middle 4: E. McCusker, 1965, 1967-68-69; B. Byrne, 1976-77-78-79.

Welter 5: H. Perry, 1956, 1958, 1960-61-62.

Light-welter 5: J. McCourt, 1966-67-68-69, 1972.

Light 7: E. Smyth, 1933-34-35-36-37-38, 1940.

Feather 3: W. Gifford, 1943-44-45. B. McCarthy, 1969-70-71.

Bantam 8: M. Dowling, 1968-69-70-71-72-73-74-75.

Fly 3: P. Connolly, 1933, 36, 38, B. McCarthy, 1966-67-68. N. McLaughlin, 1971-72, 1974. D. Larmour, 1973, 1975-76.

Light-fly 3: B. Dunne, 1974-75-76.

*Scottish Championships:*

Super-heavyweight 2: R. Nagle, 1986-87.

Heavyweight 6: J. Rafferty, 1974-75-76-77-78-79.

Light-heavy 7: A. Watson, 1937-38-39, 1943-44-45, 1947.

Middle 3: C. Calderwood, 1955-56-57.

Light-middle 5: T. Imrie, 1966-67-68-69-70.

Welter 3: S. Cooney, 1974, 1976, 1978.

Light-welter 4: J. Douglas, 1974-75-76-77.

Light 6: J. Gillan, 1970-71-72-73-74-75.

Feather 4: A. Lyons, 1927-28-29, 31.
Bantam 3: A. Murphy, 1941-42-43; S.
Ogilvie, 1970, 1974, 1975. J. Bambrick,
1976-77-78.
Fly 5: A. McHugh, 1966-67-68-69-70.
Light-fly 2: A. Docherty, 1984-85. W.
Docherty, 1986-87.

*Welsh Championships:*
Heavyweight 3: W. H. Walters, 1936-
37, 1939.
Light-heavy: 5: R. Howells, 1926-27-
28-29-30.
Middle 4: F. Hatto, 1926-27-28-29.
Light-middle 2: D. Hinder, 1956-57.
A. Couch, 1965, 67; D. Brewster, 1979-
80.
Welter 3: J. Davies, 1921-22-23. A.
Anthony, 1928-29-30. W. Teague, 1983-
84-85.
Light-welter 5: P. Ahmed, 1977-78-79-
80-81.
Light 4: I. R. Lloyd, 1921-22, 24, 29; E.
Pritchard, 1975-76, 1977, 1980.
Feather 5: M. M. Williams, 1920-21-
22-23, 1925. F. Perry, 1924, 1926-27-28-
29.
Bantam 4: A. Barnes, 1933-34-35-36.
Fly 4: M. O'Sullivan, 1970, 1972-73-
74.
Light-fly 2: R. Regan, 1986-87.

## Consecutive title wins:
The highest number of consecutive

National Amateur title wins for each
country are:
IRELAND—8 by M. Dowling, bantamweight 1968-69-70-71-72-73-74-75.
SCOTLAND—8 by A. Bell, middleweight
1930-31, light-heavyweight 1932, middleweight and light-heavyweight 1930-31,
light-heavy and heavyweight 1932,
heavyweight 1933, light-heavy and
heavyweight 1934.
WALES—8 by R. Howells, middleweight 1923-24-25, light-heavyweight
1926-27-28-29-30.
QUEENSBERRY and A.B.A.—5 by H.
Chinnery, middleweight 1867-68-69,
heavyweight 1870-71. H. Mallin, middleweight 1919-20-21-22-23. F. Mallin,
middleweight 1928-29-30-31-32. T.
Pardoe, flyweight 1929-30-31-32-33.

One of the most remarkable records in
Amateur boxing is that of H. Pat Floyd
(London Polytechnic). He last won the
A.B.A. heavyweight title 17 years after
his first success. He was champion in
1929, 1934, 1935, 1946.

## AMATEUR to PROFESSIONAL
Amateur champions who subsequently
turned professional and won British
titles (Empire and Commonwealth titles
only mentioned when no British title
won):—

| | Amateur Title | British Professional Title |
|---|---|---|
| Avoth, E. A. | Welsh (L.M.) 1963. | British (L.H.) 1969-71. |
| Barton, R. | A.B.A. (M.) 1953. | British (L.H.) 1956. |
| Bodell, J. | A.B.A. (L.H.) 1961. | British (H.) 1969-70, 1971-72. |
| Brown, J. | A.B.A. (Fly) 1958. | British (Fly) 1962-63. |
| Buchanan, K. | A.B.A. (Fe.) 1965. | British (L.) 1968-70, 1973-74 |
| Calderwood, C. | Scottish (M.) 1955-56-57. | British (L.H.) 1960-63, 1964-66. |
| Caldwell, J. | Irish (Fly) 1956-57. | British (Fly) 1960-61, (B.) 1964-65 |
| Charnley, D. | A.B.A. (Fe.) 1954. | British (L.) 1957-65. |
| Clark, J. | A.B.A. (B.) 1966. | British (B.) 1973-74 |
| Conteh, J. | A.B.A. (M.) 1970. A.B.A. (L.H.) 1971. | British (L.H.) 1973-74 |
| Cooper, H. | A.B.A. (L.H.) 1952-53. | British (H.) 1959-69, 1970-71 |
| Cowdell, P. | A.B.A. (B.) 1973, (L.) 1975, (Fe.) 1976-77. | British (Fe.) 1979-82, (Jnr. L.) 1986, 1987- |

| | | |
|---|---|---|
| Curvis, B.‡ | A.B.A. (W.) 1958 | British (W.) 1960-66. |
| Diamond, A. | A.B.A. (L.) 1883-84-85. | British (M.) 1893* |
| Dickie, R. | Welsh (B.) 1982. | British (Fe.) 1986- |
| Dickson, Alex | A.B.A. (L.) 1984. | British (L.) 1987- |
| Dower, D. | A.B.A. (Fly) 1952. | |
| | Welsh (Fly) 1952. | British (Fly) 1954-56. |
| Erskine, J. | A.B.A. (H.) 1953. | British (H.) 1956-58. |
| Finnegan, C. | A.B.A. (M.) 1966. | |
| | Olympic (M.) 1968. | British (L.H.) 1973-74 |
| Gardner, J. | A.B.A. (H.) 1948. | British (H) 1950-52. |
| Gilbody, R. | A.B.A. (B.) 1982. | British (B.) 1985-87. |
| Gilroy, F. | Scottish (B.) 1966-67. | British (Fe.) 1972-73 |
| Glencross, T. | Irish (B.) 1956. | British (B.) 1959-63. |
| Graham, H. | A.B.A. (M.) 1978. | British (Lt.M.) 1981-83, |
| | | (M.) 1985-86. |
| Hall, H. | A.B.A. (W.) 1944. | British (W.) 1948-49. |
| Hill, C. | Scottish (B.) 1951. | |
| | Scottish (Fe.) 1953. | British (Fe.) 1956-59. |
| Hill, J. | Scottish (Fly) 1925-26. | |
| | A.B.A. (Fly) 1926. | British (Fly) 1927-29. |
| Ireland, A. | A.B.A. (W.) 1921. | British (M.) 1928-29. |
| Jones, C. | Welsh (W.) 1976-77. | British (W.) 1980-82. |
| Kaylor, M. | A.B.A. (M.) 1980. | British (M.) 1983-84. |
| Keenan, P. | Scottish (Fly) 1948. | British (B.) 1951-53, 54-59. |
| Lewis, P. | A.B.A. (Fe.) 1952-53. | British Emp. (Fe.) 1957-60. |
| London, B.† | A.B.A. (H.) 1954. | British (H.) 1958-59. |
| Magri, C. | A.B.A. (L.Fly) 1974, (Fly) 1975- | British (Fly) 1977-81 |
| | 76-77. | |
| Marriott, R. | A.B.A. (L.) 1912, 14. | British (L.) 1919-20. |
| McAlinden, D. | Irish (H.) 1967. | British (H.) 1972-75. |
| McAuley, D. | Irish (Fly) 1980. | British (Fly) 1986- |
| McCleave, D. | A.B.A. (L.) 1931. | |
| | A.B.A. (W.) 1932, 34. | British (W.) 1936. |
| McCluskey, J. | A.B.A. (Fly) 1964-65. | British (Fly) 1967-77. |
| McCormack, J. | A.B.A. and Scottish (L.M.) 1956. | British (M.) 1959. |
| McGowan, W. | A.B.A. (Fly) 1961 | British (Fly) 1963-66, |
| | | (B.) 1966-68. |
| McGuigan, B. | Irish (B.) 1978. | British (Fe.) 1983-84. |
| McKenzie, C. | A.B.A. (L.W.) 1976. | British (L.W.) 1978- |
| McKenzie, G. | A.B.A. (B.) 1920. | British (Fe.) 1924-25. |
| Marsh, T. | A.B.A. (W.) 1980-81. | British (Lt.W.) 1984-86. |
| Meade, N. | A.B.A. (H.) 1974. | British (H.) 1981-83. |
| Minter, A. | A.B.A. (M.) 1971. | British (M.) 1975-77, |
| | | 1977-78. |
| Mizler, H. | A.B.A. (B.) 1930. | |
| | A.B.A. (Fe.) 1932. | |
| | A.B.A. (L.) 1933. | British (L.) 1934. |
| Nash, C. | Irish (L.) 1970-71-72-73, 1975. | British (L.) 1978-79. |
| Needham, D. | A.B.A. (Fly) 1969-70. | British (B.) 1974-75, |
| | | (Fe.) 1978-79. |
| Notice, H. | A.B.A. (H.) 1983. | British (H.) 1986- |
| O'Sullivan, D. | A.B.A. (B.) 1947. | British (B.) 1949-51. |
| Paul, L. | A.B.A. (L.M.) 1972. | British (L.M.) 1973-74 |
| Petersen, J. | A.B.A. (L.H.) 1931. | |
| | Welsh (H.) 1931. | British (L.H.) 1932. |
| | | British (H.) 1932-33, 34-36 |
| Pritchett, J. | A.B.A. (W.) 1962-63 | British (M.) 1965-69. |

| | | |
|---|---|---|
| Pyatt, C. | A.B.A. (W.) 1982. | British (Lt.M.) 1986. |
| Richardson, A. | A.B.A. (Fe.) 1969. | British (Fe.) 1977-78. |
| Singleton, J. | A.B.A. (L.) 1971. | British (L.W.) 1974-76 |
| Smith, R. | A.B.A. (H.) 1912-13. | British (L.H.) 1914-16, 18 19. |
| Spinks, T. | A.B.A. (Fly) 1956. | British (Fe.) 1960-61. |
| Stracey, J. | A.B.A. (L.W.) 1969. | British (W.) 1973-75. |
| Straughn, A. | A.B.A. (L.H.) 1979-80-81. | British (C.) 1986-87. |
| Thomas, E. | A.B.A. (L.) 1946. | |
| | Welsh (L.) 1946. | British (W.) 1949-50. |
| Thompson, W. | A.B.A. (L.) 1944. | British (L.) 1947-51. |
| Turpin, R. | A.B.A. (W.) 1945. | British (L.H.) 1955, 1956-58. |
| | A.B.A. (M.) 1946. | British (M.) 1950-54. |
| Wallace, K. | A.B.A. (Fly) 1980-81 | British Comm. (Fly) 1983-84. |
| Waterman, P. | A.B.A. (L.W.) 1952. | British (W.) 1956-58. |
| Watt, J. | A.B.A. (L.) 1968 | British (L.) 1972-73, 1975-77. |
| Webster, F. | A.B.A. (B.) 1926. | |
| | A.B.A. (Fe.) 1927. | |
| | A.B.A. (L.) 1928. | British (L.) 1929-30. |
| Wells, M. | A.B.A. (L.) 1904-05-06-07. | British (W.) 1914. |
| Willis, T. | A.B.A. (L.W.) 1980-81 | British (L.) 1985- |
| Wilshire, N. | A.B.A. (M.) 1979. | British Comm. (Lt.M.) 1985-87. |
| Winstone, H. | A.B.A. (B.) 1958 | British (Fe) 1961-69. |
| Woodcock, B. | A.B.A. (L.H.) 1939. | British (H.) 1945-50. |

    * Not recognised by the N.S.C.
  † Boxed under the name of Brian Harper as an amateur.
  ‡ Boxed under the name of Brian Nancurvis as an amateur.

**Former Olympic champions who won world professional titles:**

| | *Olympic champion* | *World title(s)* |
|---|---|---|
| Ali, M. (as Clay C.) | L.H. 1960. | H. 1964-70, 74-78, 78-79. |
| Benvenuti, G. | W. 1960. | Jnr.M. 1965-66. M. 1967, 68-70. |
| Breland, M. | W. 1984. | W. 1987 (W.B.A.). |
| Fields, J. | Fe. 1924. | W. 1929-30. |
| Foreman, G. | H. 1968. | H. 1973-74. |
| Frazier, J. | H. 1964. | H. 1970-73. |
| Genaro, F. | Fly. 1920. | Fly. (N.B.A.) 1928-29. |
| La Barba, F. | Fly. 1924. | Fly. 1925-27. |
| Leonard, R. | L.Welter. 1976. | W. 1979-80, 80-82. L.M. 1981. M. 1987. |
| Oliva, P. | L.Welter. 1980. | L.Welter (W.B.A.) 1986-87. |
| Patterson, F. | M. 1952. | H. 1960-62. |
| Pavlov, M. | L.H. 1972. | L.H. (W.B.C.) 1978. |
| Perez, P. | Fly. 1948. | Fly. 1954-60. |
| Randolph, L. | Fly. 1976. | Jnr.Fe. (W.B.A.) 1980. |
| Spinks, L. | L.H. 1976. | H. 1978. |
| Spinks, M. | M. 1976. | L.H. 1983-85 (W.B.A.) 1985. H. 1985- |

## AMBERS, Lou:

An Italian-American, born New York, 1913. In May 1935, he was matched with Tony Canzoneri for the vacant world lightweight title but was outpointed. In a return contest Ambers took the title with a 15-round points victory, September 3, 1936.

Ambers successfully defended his crown in a third meeting with Canzoneri but lost it to Henry Armstrong, August 17, 1938. The negro got the decision after 15 rounds.

In a return contest with Armstrong in August, 1939, Lou Ambers reversed the decision to regain the title, but he finally lost it to Lew Jenkins, who stopped him in three rounds. This was the first time in his career that Ambers had been knocked out, but when these two met for a second time in February, 1941, Jenkins again won inside the distance, Ambers being knocked out in seven rounds. This was Lou Ambers' last contest.

## ANDERSON, Brian:

Despite a good run as a light-middleweight this Sheffield-born fighter did not come close to winning the British title in that division, but soon after moving up to middleweight in 1983 he got more power into his punching and followed stable-mate Herol Graham as British middleweight champion when he stopped Tony Burke in eight rounds in Belfast in October 1986. He had then been boxing professionally for over six years. Showed good all-round skill but retired from the game soon after losing title to Tony Sibson in September 1987.

## ANDERSON, Jimmy:

When the B.B.B.C. decided to recognise Junior weight classes Jimmy Anderson, a hard hitting fighter from Waltham Cross who had won 20 of his first 27 fights inside the distance, became the first man to win the British junior-lightweight title by stopping Jimmy Revie in nine rounds. That was in February 1968.

Anderson successfully defended his title twice before the division was abolished in 1970.

## ANDREETTI, Vic:

Won a British title at his fourth attempt when he outpointed Des Rea, the junior-welterweight champion, in an all-action contest at Nottingham in February 1969. Vic was then aged 27 and he retired undefeated champion just over a year later after stopping Des Rea in four rounds in a return bout.

Earlier in his career Andreetti had twice failed to lift the lightweight title from Maurice Cullen and had also been outpointed by Rea for the junior title.

## ANDRIES, Dennis:

Born Guyana and brought up in Hackney, Andries is a no-frills fighter who has shown great strength and powers of endurance. In his early days he was often careless but kept fighting back and won the British light-heavyweight title at the third attempt, outpointing Tom Collins in January 1984. After confirming his superiority over Collins in a return match Andries fought a draw with the European champion Alex Blanchard before capturing the W.B.C. version of the world title by surprisingly outpointing American J. B. Williamson. So Andries had reached the top after many setbacks. Alas he was well beaten by Thomas Hearns in his second defence of the title, taking a lot of punishment before the referee intervened in the 10th of their fight in Detroit in March 1987.

## ANGOTT, Sammy:

An Italian-American lightweight who won the world title, as recognised by N.B.A., when he beat Davey Day in May, 1940. At that time, however, Lou Ambers, and subsequently Lew Jenkins were the more generally acknowledged title-holders of the lightweight division.

Nicknamed "The Clutch," Angott, whose style was said to resemble a boxing octopus, went on to gain world-wide recognition as lightweight champion by outpointing Lew Jenkins over 15 rounds, December 19, 1941.

Angott confused the championship of the lightweight division by relinquishing his title in November, 1942, although he still continued to fight. Then, in October, 1943, he again became recognised by the N.B.A. as champion by outpointing

Slugger White. He finally lost this title to Juan Zurita in March, 1944, and despite a declared intention to retire he continued his career until 1950.

Angott's peculiar style made him a difficult man to handle in the ring, and the outstanding performance of his career was probably his victory over world featherweight champion, Willie Pep, in an overweight match, March, 1943.

It always took a good man to beat Pep, and at that time this was the featherweight champion's only defeat in a run of 136 victories.

## APOSTOLI, Fred:

This Italian-American never had the satisfaction of gaining world-wide recognition as middleweight champion, although there is little doubt that he earned the title.

Apostoli had been a Golden Gloves champion in his amateur days, and three years after turning professional he became a leading contender for the world title.

At that time I.B.U. recognised Marcel Thil as middleweight champion, while in America, Freddie Steele held the title.

In September, 1937, Fred Apostoli stopped Marcel Thil in 10 rounds in New York. That should have been enough to gain him the title, but the fighters had signed an agreement that this was not a title fight.

However, Thil resigned the championship after his defeat, and less than four months later Apostoli beat the American claimant to the title, Freddie Steele, in an overweight match. Apostoli scored a k.o. in the ninth round. The date—January 7, 1938.

Apostoli was unable to secure a return match with Steele at the weight, but on April 1, 1938, he strengthened his claim to the crown by outpointing Glen Lee over 15 rounds in a contest billed as for the world title.

Still N.B.A. would not recognise this Italian-American but named Al Hostak as champion. However, N.Y.A.C. supported Apostoli's claim and he held the title until October 2, 1939, when he was beaten in seven rounds by Ceferino Garcia.

## ARCHIBALD, Joey:

Claimed world featherweight title in October, 1938, when he outpointed Mike Belloise. The N.B.A. recognised Leo Rodak as champion of this division but Archibald settled this confusion by beating Rodak, April 18, 1939.

Despite the claims of Pete Scalzo, who had beaten Archibald in December, 1938, in an overweight bout, the Irish-American was almost universally accepted as champion until he was beaten by Harry Jeffra, May 20, 1940.

A year later Archibald regained the title from Jeffra, but he finally lost it in September, 1941, when he was knocked out in 11 rounds by Chalky Wright.

## ARGENTINE:

Pascual Perez and Carlos Monzon are probably the finest boxers ever to come out of the Argentine, but in ring history their names are overshadowed by a heavyweight. This giant never won a world title but his name will go down to posterity for his part in the most sensational contest ever fought in America. This Argentinian's name— Luis Angel Firpo.

After going to the States in 1922 Firpo had less than 20 fights before retiring but he certainly made a name for himself.

Firpo's big day was September 14, 1923, when he met the world champion, Jack Dempsey, at the New York Polo Grounds before 82,000 spectators. They saw less than two rounds of fighting but it was something they never forgot. It was in this epic that Dempsey was knocked out of the ring in the first round after he had floored the South American seven times.

There have since been endless arguments as to whether Dempsey was out of the ring for more than ten seconds or whether he was helped back inside the ropes. The argument cannot be settled here. Suffice to say that Dempsey certainly did get back into the ring and, after putting Firpo down for one more count, early in the second round, he knocked him out with a right to the jaw.

So much has been said and written about that particular contest that many people are liable to forget that Firpo beat such men as Bill Brennan, Jess

Willard and Ermino Spalla (Italian and European heavyweight champion). Firpo had a terrific round-house right-hand punch. He also proved that he could take punishment, and if he had taken his training more seriously he might have done better.

After being out of the ring for 10 years Firpo tried to make a come-back in 1936 but he was knocked out by the Chilean heavy-weight, Arturo Godoy, in three rounds.

## Champions:

World: Light-heavyweight, Victor Galindez (W.B.A. version) 1974-78; Miguel Cuello (W.B.C.) 1977-78; Hugo Corro 1978-79. Middleweight, Carlos Monzon, 1970-77; J. Welterweight, Nicolino Loche, 1968-72; Ubaldo Sacco (W.B.A.) 1985-86; Juan Martin Coggi (W.B.A.) 1987-; Super-flyweight, Santos Laciar 1987. Flyweight, Pascual Perez, 1954-60.

Olympic: Heavyweight, Rodriguez Jurado, 1928; Santiago Alberto Lovell, 1932; Rafael Iglesis, 1948.

Light-heavyweight: Vittorio Avendano, 1928.

Featherweight: Carmelo Ambrosio Robledo, 1932; Oscar Casanovas, 1936.

## ARGUELLO, Alexis:

One of the elite of fighters to have won world titles in as many as three divisions, this hard-hitting Nicaraguan, who now lives in Florida, won the featherweight title from Ruben Olivares in November 1974; the W.B.C. version of the Junior lightweight title from Alfredo Escalara in January 1978, and the W.B.C. light-weight title with a comfortable points win over Britain's Jim Watt in 1981.

He voluntarily gave up these titles as he put on weight, but then failed in a bid for the light-welterweight crown when he was stopped in 14 rounds by Aaron Pryor in 1982.

Tall and fast Arguello won the vast majority of his fights inside the distance. He was known as "The Explosive Thin Man."

## ARIZMENDI, (Baby) Alberto:

This Mexican was involved in the mix-up among title claimants in the feather-weight division during the 1930's.

After Battling Battalino relinquished the featherweight title in 1932, Tony Paul, and subsequently Freddie Miller, were acknowledged as champions by the N.B.A., but Kid Chocolate became the N.Y.A.C. champion.

Arizmendi came into the picture as successor to Kid Chocolate, for when the Cuban negro relinquished his claim to the title in 1934, Arizmendi beat Mike Belloise on points to gain N.Y.A.C. recognition.

Soon after this the Mexican beat Henry Armstrong on two occasions (he had already beaten Armstrong once before winning the title), but in 1935 he was fast gaining weight and he had to give up his claim to the featherweight crown.

By this time Henry Armstrong had gained the world welterweight title, but when Arizmendi met the American negro for the sixth time he was out-pointed over 10 rounds.

## ARMSTRONG, Evan:

They don't come any tougher than this former builder's labourer from Ayrshire who had been fighting profes-sionally for nearly eight years, mostly as a bantamweight, before taking the British featherweight title from Jimmy Revie in July 1971.

He failed in bids for the Common-wealth and European titles, losing respectively to Toro George and Joe Legra, and then lost his British crown to Tommy Glencross in September 1972.

A year later, at the age of 30 years 7 months, Evan recaptured the British title and made the Lonsdale Belt his own property before retiring undefeated British champion in February 1975.

He captured the Commonwealth title in April 1974 when he beat Bobby Dunne in 8 rounds, but lost it to David Kotey before the year was out.

## ARMSTRONG, Henry:

This American negro, who was born in Columbus, Mississippi, and is now a Baptist minister, is the only man ever to hold three world boxing titles simul-taneously.

Henry Armstrong had this remarkable

distinction for about four months during 1938, when he was universally recognised as king of the featherweights, light-weights and welterweights. It was not until the end of 1938 that due to difficulty in getting down to nine stone (126 lbs.) he relinquished his feather-weight title.

He first entered the championship field in October, 1936, when he beat the N.Y.A.C. claimant to the world feather-weight title, Mike Belloise. About five months later he again got the better of the Italian-American, but it was not until October 29, 1937, that Armstrong gained world-wide recognition as featherweight champion, knocking out Petey Sarron in six rounds.

This remarkable fighter, who was the nearest thing to perpetual motion ever seen in the ring, next won the world welterweight title. He achieved this by outpointing another fighting machine. Barney Ross, May 31, 1938.

With two world titles under his belt, Armstrong just had to gain the one in between—the lightweight crown—and he accomplished this August 17, 1938, by outpointing Lou Ambers over 15 rounds in New York City.

As already mentioned, Armstrong relinquished his featherweight title at the end of 1938. In August, 1939, he lost his lightweight crown in a return with Lou Ambers, and on October 4, 1940, he was outpointed by Fritzie Zivic for the welterweight title.

The "Sepia Slayer" gave one of his most courageous displays in trying to regain the title from Zivic in January, 1941, but one of the largest crowds ever to witness a boxing contest in the Madison Square Garden saw him blinded and battered to a stand-still before the referee stopped the fight in the twelfth round.

Armstrong announced his retirement at the end of that fight, but he came back a few months later, and although defeats by Willie Joyce, Beau Jack and Ray Robinson prevented him from gaining another world title fight he kept going until 1945.

## ARTHUR, Bobby:

A cagey fighter who used his brains as well as his fists, Arthur took over the vacant British welterweight title when he gained a controversial victory over John Stracey on a disqualification.

That was in October 1972, but in a return bout in June 1973 this Coventry-born fighter was k.o'd by Stracey in four rounds.

In his next contest, Arthur tried for the newly created Light-middleweight title but was stopped in 10 rounds by Larry Paul.

## ATTELL, Abe:

If this Jewish-American's original claim to the featherweight title is accepted then he was one of the youngest men ever to win a world title.

Born at San Francisco in February, 1884, Attell started boxing profession-ally at the age of 16 and was only 17 years 8 months when outpointing the re-doubtable George Dixon over 15 rounds at St. Louis, October 28, 1901.

This was Attell's second meeting with Dixon, for he had gained a draw with the coloured man only a week before.

Attell claimed the title because cham-pion Terry McGovern was having weight trouble at that time and it seemed that he had abandoned the feather-weight division.

However, McGovern was really the champion until he was beaten by Young Corbett in November, 1901, but when Corbett relinquished the crown, Attell gained recognition by defeating Harry Forbes in five rounds.

That was February 1, 1904, and although a few people still recognised Young Corbett as champion because he had not lost his title in the ring, this muddle was eventually cleared up when Corbett was beaten by Tommy Sullivan and Attell then beat Sullivan in four rounds.

That great Welsh boxer, Jim Driscoll, gave him one of his hardest fights in February, 1909, and although it was a "No Decision" bout, Driscoll was reckoned to have had the better of things after 10 rounds.

A terrific hitter, Attell held on to his

featherweight title until February, 1912, when he was outpointed over 20 rounds by Johnny Kilbane. He retired in 1917.

## ATTENDANCES:

The world record attendance for a boxing match is 135,132. That was the number of people at the Fraternal Order of Eagles' free show at Milwaukee, Wisconsin, U.S.A., when Tony Zale knocked out Billy Prior in nine rounds. The date—August 18, 1941.

The world record to pay—120,757. Gene Tunney v. Jack Dempsey, Sesqui Centennial Stadium, Philadelphia, U.S.A., September 23, 1926.

The world record indoor attendance 63,350, Muhammad Ali v. Leon Spinks, Superdome, New Orleans, September 15, 1978.

The British record—82,000. Len Harvey v. Jock McAvoy, White City, London, July 10, 1939.

The British record indoor attendance—18,197. Freddie Mills v. Joey Maxim, Earl's Court, London, January 24, 1950.

The world record paid attendance at a contest other than between heavyweights is 61,370. Ray Robinson v. Randolph Turpin, for the world middleweight title, Polo Grounds, New York, September 12, 1951.

Attendances at some other important contests (not record attendances):

104,943: Gene Tunney v. Jack Dempsey, Soldiers' Field, Chicago, U.S.A.. September 22, 1927.

80,183: Jack Dempsey v. Georges Carpentier, Boyle's 30 Acres, Jersey City, July 2, 1921.

70,043: Joe Louis v. Max Schmeling, Yankee Stadium, New York, June 23, 1938.

50,000: Bruce Woodcock v. Lee Savold, White City, London, June 6, 1950.

44,000: Freddie Mills v. Gus Lesnevich, White City, London, July 26, 1948.

20,000: Jack Dempsey v. Jess Willard, Bay View Park, Toledo, Ohio, July 4, 1919.

20,000: Jack Johnson v. Tommy Burns, Rushcutters Bay, Sydney, Australia, December 26, 1908.

15,000: J. L. Sullivan v. Charlie Mitchell, Madison Square Garden, New York, May 30, 1884. This fight never took place because Sullivan arrived at the stadium too ill to fight.

41: J. L. Sullivan v. Charlie Mitchell, Chantilly, France, March 10, 1888.

In the days of the old prize ring there were some remarkably large attendances. Obviously any figures published were only estimates, but the record for bare fist contests may well have been set up at Odiham, Hampshire, January 9, 1788, when Richard Humphries met Daniel Mendoza in the second of their three contests and beat him in 29 minutes. The attendance was reported to have been in the region of 60,000.

Attendances at some other important prize fights:

35,000: Tom Spring v. Bill Neate, Hinckley Downs, Near Andover, May 20, 1823.

25,000: Tom Cribb v. Tom Molineux, Thistleton Gap, Leicestershire, September 28, 1811.

12,000: Tom Sayers v. J. C. Heenan, Farnborough, Kent, April 17, 1860.

Only 2,434 attended the second Muhammad Ali v. Sonny Liston contest at Lewiston, Maine, U.S.A., May 25, 1965. This is a record low for a world heavyweight title fight.

## AUSTRALIA:

Boxing was introduced to Australia by Jem Mace, who opened a school of instruction in the noble art in Sydney and found a skilful and willing pupil in Larry Foley.

Foley continued where Mace left off. He set up a training establishment in George Street, Sydney, and it was there that he taught such great fighters as Bob Fitzsimmons, Jem Hall, Peter Jackson, Frank Slavin and Young Griffo.

The greatest Australian boxer among these was undoubtedly Young Griffo. Those who saw him proclaimed him as a genius. Many rate him to have been the most skilful natural boxer ever known. Such a claim would be difficult to establish, but he was certainly a difficult man to hit, for he had a most uncanny defence. Griffo's career is detailed elsewhere in this volume.

Another outstanding exponent of the noble art was Peter Jackson. He was not an Australian but a West Indian negro. However, he settled in Australia, had his first contests there, and is generally accepted as being an Australian boxer.

In his prime, which would be about 1888 to 1892, he was undefeated in England, Ireland, Australia and the United States. How he would have fared in a contest with champion John L. Sullivan can only be left to the imagination, for Sullivan avoided such a meeting, giving the reason that he would not fight a coloured man.

When Jackson came to England for the first time in 1889, he beat eight of our best men. In May, 1892, he returned to London and beat Frank Slavin in 10 rounds at the N.S.C.

Jackson's most important contest was that with Jim Corbett in San Francisco, May 21, 1891. Here were two of the finest boxers ever known among heavyweights and they gave a remarkable display of their skill with neither being able to establish a real advantage. It developed into a marathon and was abandoned as a draw after 61 rounds.

Jackson developed tuberculosis when still a young man and was feeling the effects of this disease when he was knocked out in three rounds by Jim Jeffries in 1898.

One of the true gentlemen of the ring, Peter Jackson died in 1901 at the age of 40.

James Leslie Darcy may be ranked alongside Young Griffo as Australia's outstanding boxer. But he died at the age of 21 before he had really established his greatness and before he was able to fight for the world middleweight title.

Another Australian whose outstanding ring career was cut short by the Grim Reaper was Dave Sands. He won three Australian titles and the Empire middleweight championship before he was killed in a road accident near Sydney in August, 1952.

Apart from Peter Jackson, Australia produced other men who made their mark in the heavyweight division. Chief among these was probably Bill Squires. Three times he met world champion, Tommy Burns, but three times he was beaten inside the distance. These fights took place in Colma, California, Paris and Sydney.

Bill Lang was another Australian to meet champion Tommy Burns. Lang was beaten in six rounds, Melbourne, September, 1908.

It was Lang who marked finis to the long career of Bob Fitzsimmons, but it took him 12 rounds to stop the 47-year-old Cornishman.

Rugged Frank Slavin, known as the "Sydney Cornstalk," was highly ranked among the world's heavyweights in the 1890's. In December, 1889, he fought a 14-round draw for the championship of England with Jem Smith. This contest took place at Bruges, Belgium.

Among others, Slavin later beat Jake Kilrain and Frank Craig, but he was knocked out by Peter Jackson and Jem Hall.

Hugh D. McIntosh staged the first really "big fight" in Australia when he built the Rushcutter's Bay Stadium, Sydney, and persuaded Tommy Burns to defend his title against Bill Squires. That was in August, 1908. Four months later the stadium was again filled to capacity when Burns lost his title to Jack Johnson. In those days this stadium was an open-air arena, but it has since been covered.

The first Australian to win an undisputed world title was Jimmy Carruthers. His career is detailed elsewhere in this volume.

## Champions:

World:—

Middleweight: Les Darcy, 1915-16 (recognised only in Australia).

Featherweight: Johnny Famechon, 1969-70.

Junior featherweight: Jeff Fenech (W.B.C.) 1987-

Bantamweight: Jimmy Carruthers, 1952-54. Lionel Rose, 1968-69.

Empire and Commonwealth:—

Heavyweight: Peter Jackson, 1892.

Light-heavyweight: Bob Dunlop, 1968-70; Steve Aczel, 1975; Tony Mundine, 1975-78.

Middleweight: Ron Richards, 1940-41; Dave Sands, 1949-52; Tony Mundine, 1972-75.

Junior or Light-middleweight: Charkey Ramon, 1972–75; Ken Salisbury, 1984–85; Troy Waters, 1987-

Welterweight: George Barnes, 1954-56, 1956-58, 1958-60; Darby Brown, 1956; Clyde Gray, 1973-80; Brian Janssen, 1987; Wilf Gentzen, 1987-

Junior or Light-welterweight: Hector Thompson, 1973-77; Lachie Austin, 1977-78; Jeff Malcolm, 1978-79.

Lightweight: Pat Ford, 1953-54, 1954; Barry Michael, 1981-82, 1985-86; Graeme Brooke, 1984-85.

Junior lightweight: Billy Moeller, 1975-77; Lester Ellis, 1984-85.

Featherweight: Johnny Famechon, 1967-69; Bobby Dunne, 1972-74.

Super-bantamweight: Paul Ferreri, 1977-78.

Bantamweight: Jimmy Carruthers, 1952-53. Lionel Rose, 1969. Paul Ferreri, 1972-76, 1981-86.

Flyweight: Henry Nissen, 1971-74; Jim West, 1974-76.

## AVOTH, Eddie:

A Welshman who was unlucky to be stopped with a cut eye when meeting Young McCormack for the vacant British light-heavyweight crown in 1967 but won the title in a return fight, forcing McCormack to retire, also with a cut eye, after eleven hard-fought rounds at the World Sporting Club in January 1969.

Five months later Avoth failed in a bid for the vacant European title, being outpointed by Yvan Prebeg.

After successfully defending his British title in another meeting with McCormack, and winning the vacant Commonwealth championship by stopping Trevor Thornberry, Avoth lost these titles in a hard-fought bout with Chris Finnegan in January 1971, the referee calling a halt less than a minute from the end of the 15th round.

# B

## BAER, Max:

The story is that Max Baer took up boxing when he discovered his punching power after knocking a farm labourer through a shop door. That unfortunate fellow had made an insulting remark as Baer walked his girlfriend home.

Max Baer certainly was a hard hitter, and he also had the natural ability and the physique to have become one of the ring's all-time greats, but he was also a clown, and although everyone loved him for this, it prevented him from taking the game seriously enough.

He won the world heavyweight title from Primo Carnera, the referee stopping the fight in the 11th round, at Long Island, June 14, 1934, but was beaten in his first defence of the title one day short of a year later. Then it was that veteran James J. Braddock outpointed him over 15 rounds at Long Island.

Known as "The Livermore Larruper," Max Baer floored the giant Carnera 11 times in their title fight, a fair enough indication of his punching power when one remembers that he was conceding the Italian 53¼lbs.

Despite being recognised as a playboy of the ring, Baer was really a fine fighter. He beat King Levinsky three times, Max Schmeling, Ben Foord and Tony Galento, and while he lost to Tommy Farr on points in London, April 15, 1937, he reversed the decision in New York, March 15, 1938.

In a come-back Baer suffered badly in the hands of Lou Nova.

## BALDOCK, Teddy:

Born Poplar, East London, Baldock started his career as a flyweight but made his mark in the bantamweight division.

In 1927 the bantamweight class was in a state of confusion as to the true champion. Charlie Rosenberg had been deprived of the title through his inability to make the weight, and although the crown was claimed by Bud Taylor he was not given universal recognition.

Baldock was not even British champion at that time, but he claimed the world title after outpointing one of America's leading bantamweights, Archie Bell, May 5, 1927.

The Poplar boy's claim did not carry much weight, however, at least not until he had beaten the British champion.

In August, 1928, Baldock found himself the centre of another disputed title claim. He beat Johnny Brown (St. George's) in less than two rounds and was acknowledged in some quarters as the new British bantamweight champion. However, he had no right to this title for it was not a beltmatch, and Brown had previously relinquished his titles after his defeat by Kid Pattenden.

Still, Baldock did eventually clinch the British title by outpointing Kid Pattenden at Olympia, London, in one of the hardest bantamweight fights on record. The date was May 16, 1929.

Baldock relinquished his crown in 1931 when he had difficulty in getting down to 118 lbs. He retired following defeats by Panama Al Brown (world featherweight champion), and by Dick Corbett (British bantamweight champion).

## BARE KNUCKLES:

See also under GLOVES.

The last heavyweight championship fight to be contested with bare knuckles was when John L. Sullivan beat Jake Kilrain in 75 rounds, 136 minutes, Richburg, Mississippi, July 7, 1889.

The last bare knuckle fight for the British heavyweight championship took place December 17, 1885, London. Jem Smith beat Jack Wannop in 10 rounds.

Bare knuckle prize fights were not entirely abandoned for the gloved contests until around 1895.

A list of bare knuckle champions appears under WORLD CHAMPIONS (Prize Ring).

## BARRY, James:

An Irish-American, born Chicago, Illinois, Jimmy Barry laid claim to the world bantamweight title after he had beaten Casper Leon in 28 rounds September, 1894.

However, this claim was not recognised on this side of the Atlantic where Billy Plimmer was champion.

Plimmer was subsequently beaten by Pedlar Palmer, but when Barry came to London towards the end of 1897 he was not matched with our champion but with Walter Croot. This was billed as for the world title although Croot had previously been well beaten by Pedlar Palmer.

Nevertheless, Barry was a notable bantamweight for he was undefeated throughout his career and he k.o'd our Walter Croot in 19 rounds.

Unfortunately Croot died after this contest but Barry was cleared of all charges when the magistrates decided that this had been a "contest" in the true sense of the world and not a "fight."

## BARTON, Ronald:

This West Ham, London, boy had a notable career as an amateur before he turned professional in 1954.

While serving in the R.A.F. he won their middleweight title in 1952 and again in 1953. In that second year he also gained the Imperial Services and A.B.A. titles.

After only 22 professional fights Barton won the vacant British light-heavyweight championship by stopping Albert Finch. The Croydon boxer was forced to retire in the eighth round with a badly cut eye.

Barton retired undefeated champion later in 1956. He made a come-back in 1959, but finally retired in 1961.

## BASHAM, Johnny:

A former British, Empire and European welterweight champion, Johnny Basham was born Newport, Mon., 1890.

He was the first man to win a Lord Lonsdale Belt outright in the welterweight division, for after winning the title from Johnny Summers in December, 1914, he beat another claimant to the title, Tom McCormick, and followed this with a victory over Eddie Beattie. All three of these men were beaten inside the distance.

Basham successfully defended his titles once more, outpointing Matt Wells, before losing them to Ted "Kid" Lewis in June, 1920.

Ted "Kid" Lewis was always a stumbling block to Johnny Basham, for they met on three further occasions and the Welshman was never able to last the distance.

Basham's second defeat by Lewis took place followed in October, 1921 in a contest for the British middleweight title.

Basham had claimed this title after he had outpointed Gus Platts at the Albert Hall, London, in May, 1921, but he could not gain the recognition of the N.S.C.

This ruling body subsequently acknowledged Lewis as the middleweight title-holder, and, as already mentioned, Basham failed to relieve him of this championship.

The Welshman's fourth meeting with Ted "Kid" Lewis was not until more than eight years later. Then, on December 13, 1929, Lewis won inside three rounds.

## BASILIO, Carmen:

Born Canastota, New York, one of a family of ten children, Basilio turned professional in 1948 but it was not until he beat Al Andrews in May, 1952 that people began to sit up and take notice of this onion farmer.

An aggressive fighter with a good left hook, Basilio went on to take the world welterweight title from Tony DeMarco, June 10, 1955, the referee stopping the fight in the twelfth round.

Nine months later he lost the title to Johnny Saxton but regained it in a return bout with the referee calling "enough" in the ninth round.

That was September, 1956. Twelve months later he relinquished this title on becoming middleweight champion by outpointing Ray Robinson over 15 rounds. This was probably Basilio's finest display.

Basilio and Robinson met again in March, 1958, and the coloured man was able to reverse the decision in another hectic battle.

In his last fight Basilio was outpointed by Paul Pender in a bid for the middleweight crown.

## BASS, Benny:

Born in Russia of Jewish parents, Benny Bass was taken to the United States as a child and there enjoyed a boxing career spanning more than 20 years.

Bass started as an amateur soon after World War I and his professional career did not close until well into World War II.

When Kid Kaplan relinquished the world featherweight title in 1927, Bass gained the recognition of the N.Y.A.C. by outpointing Red Chapman, September 19, 1927. Bass had previously beaten Chapman on a first round disqualification.

Bass lost his title on points to Tony Canzoneri, February 10, 1928.

From December, 1929, until July, 1931, he was recognised in America as holder of the world's Junior lightweight title.

## BASSEY, Hogan "Kid" M.B.E.

Born Calabar, Nigeria, 1932, Bassey won the Nigerian flyweight title when he was only 17. In 1950 he became Nigerian bantamweight champion and gained the West African bantamweight crown in the following year.

Hogan, or to give him his proper name, Okon, came to England at the end of 1951 and made his home in Liverpool where he soon earned a big reputation in the ring.

Fighting mostly in Liverpool and Manchester, Bassey worked his way up to an Empire featherweight title bout in November, 1955. His opponent was Billy Kelly and this time the Nigerian boxer reversed an earlier defeat at the hands of the Irishman by stopping him in eight rounds.

In 1957, Sandy Saddler announced his retirement from the ring and so left the world featherweight title vacant. Bassey was matched with the European champion, Cherif Hamia, for this title and beat the Algerian, the referee stopping the fight in the tenth round.

Bassey lost his world championship to Davey Moore in Los Angeles, March 18, 1959, being forced to retire with cut eyes at the end of the thirteenth round.

He failed to regain it in a return match with Moore five months later, giving up at the end of the tenth round.

## BATTALINO, Christopher "Battling":

An Italian-American born Hartford, Connecticut, in 1908, Battling Battalino won the world featherweight title in his home-town on September 23, 1929, when he outpointed the Frenchman, Andre Routis.

Battalino successfully defended his title against such celebrated opponents as Kid Chocolate, Fidel La Barba and Freddie Miller, but a second meeting with Miller in January, 1932, was declared "No Contest" after three rounds and Battalino was deprived of his title by the N.B.A.

As often happens in a situation like this the matter was disputed but in any event the Hartford boy was himself forced to relinquish the title soon afterwards through weight difficulties.

## BATTEN Jimmy:

After a noted amateur career this Millwall fighter turned professional in 1974 and captured the vacant British light-middleweight title by forcing Albert Hillman to retire in seven rounds at the Royal Albert Hall in February 1977. That was this stylish boxer's nineteenth professional bout.

Batten won a Lonsdale Belt in this division before losing the title to Pat Thomas at Wembley Conference Centre in September 1979, when he was temporarily blinded in his right eye and the referee stopped it in the 9th round.

Batten failed to lift the vacant European crown when he was surprisingly k.o'd in three rounds by Frenchman, Gilbert Cohen, in November 1978.

## BECKETT, Joseph:

Born Southampton, 1892, this two-fisted fighter learnt his trade in the boxing booths where he was in the ring at the age of 12.

Beckett was one of Britain's most under-rated heavyweight champions. Not a fast mover but possessing a really good left-hook, Beckett's reputation suffered because of his two quick defeats at the hands of Georges Carpentier.

The Frenchman knocked Beckett out in 73 seconds when they first met in December 1913. The knockout in their second meeting in October, 1923 has been variously estimated as anything from 15 to 35 seconds.

Despite these defeats, however, Beckett should be ranked well up the list of English heavyweights. He came into the public eye just before World War I and after doing well in Service competitions he met Dick Smith for the vacant British light-heavyweight title. This was in February, 1918, and Beckett was beaten on points over 20 rounds.

Moving into the heavyweights division Beckett next beat Harry Reeve in five rounds and followed this by stopping the British heavyweight champion Bombardier Billy Wells, in the same distance, February 27, 1919.

Naturally, Beckett claimed the championship, but he was not officially recognised by the N.S.C. until he had beaten Frank Goddard in two rounds at Olympia, London, June 17, 1919.

Beckett subsequently proved the right to the crown by knocking out Billy Wells in three rounds at Olympia as well as making short work of Dick Smith at the Albert Hall, London.

In 1920, when the former world champion, Tommy Burns, visited London, he fancied his chance of making a come-back against Beckett, but the Southampton man proved the Canadian a super optimist by battering him to defeat in seven rounds.

Beckett retained his British title until he retired in 1923.

## BELCHER, Jem:

Born Bristol, England, 1781, Belcher is considered to have been the first bare-knuckle prize fighter to introduce any science into the sport.

When barely 17 years of age he beat a tough fighter named Bob Britton. He followed this with a good win over another notable pugilist, Paddington

Jones, and after drawing with and beating Jack Bartholomew in successive battles, Belcher was already reckoned to be the best man in the country.

The championship had not been claimed by a worthy man since Gentleman John Jackson had retired in 1795, but when Belcher beat Andrew Gamble in only five rounds on Wimbledon Common, December 22, 1800, he was acknowledged as Champion of England.

In July, 1803, he suffered the misfortune which was to hasten the end of a brilliant career. While playing rackets he was injured and blinded in one eye.

Belcher relinquished his title and did not fight again for more than two years, but then, like so many champions since his day, he thought he could make a come-back and regain the championship.

So, on December 6, 1805, he met his successor to the championship, a fellow Bristolian, Hen Pearce. Who could blame Belcher for trying to make a come-back, after all, he was, even then, not yet 25, but the handicap of having a blind side, and, no doubt, the handicap of the long lay-off was too much for him and he had to give up after 18 rounds.

Still Belcher would not admit that there was a better man than he inside the ring and in April, 1807, he again tried to regain the public's favour.

His opponent this time was Tom Cribb. Belcher made rings around him but for the greater part of the fight he could not use his right hand which he had injured in one of the earlier rounds. He had to give up after 41 rounds.

Belcher was a stubborn man who would not admit to being second best, and when Cribb claimed the championship Belcher challenged him to another meeting in February, 1809. However, it seemed that Lady Luck had deserted Belcher for ever. Again he smashed his right hand and was beaten in 31 rounds.

Jem Belcher fought no more after that and he was only 30 when he died in 1811.

## BELGIUM:

This country has not yet succeeded in producing a world champion but there have been several first-class Belgian fighters and they have done especially well in the welterweight division.

Probably the best known of all Belgian ring-men is Jean Sneyers. This remarkable little fighter retired in 1958 after winning European titles at flyweight, bantamweight, and featherweight.

As a flyweight he was only beaten once—by Peter Keenan. The only man to beat him in the bantamweight division was the Tunisian, Gaetano Annaloro, but Sneyers was subsequently able to reverse that decision. As a featherweight he was defeated 10 times in 37 fights.

Another popular Belgian fighter was their former heavyweight champion, Pierre Charles, who weighed over 14 stone (196 lbs.) and stood 6ft. 2½ins. in his socks.

Charles gained the European heavyweight title by outpointing the German, Carl Hayman, in February, 1929. He eventually lost this title to another German, Hein Muller, but again became champion when he beat Muller in a return contest.

In May, 1933, Charles was beaten by Paolino Uzcudun, but after the Spanish champion had lost the title to Primo Carnera, and he in turn, relinquished it, Pierre Charles became European champion for the third time by outpointing another German, Vincenz Hower, June 21, 1935.

Charles appears to have spent most of his time fighting Germans for it was yet another boxer from that country who finally relieved Charles of the title in March, 1937. This time it was Arno Koeblin.

Gustav Roth deserves special mention not only because he was recognised in Europe (not including Britain) as World light-heavyweight champion 1936-38, but because he was European champion at heavyweight, light-heavyweight and welterweight. He never met the more widely recognised world light-heavyweight champion of his day—John Henry Lewis.

## Champions:

EUROPEAN:

Heavyweight—Pierre Charles, 1929-31, 32-33, 35-37; Karl Sys 1943-44; Jean-Pierre Coopman, 1977.

Light-heavyweight—Fernand De-large, 1926-27; Gustav Roth, 1936-38.

Middleweight—Rene Devos, 1926-27; Gustav Roth, 1933-34; Cyrille Delannoit, 1948-49.

Welterweight—Piet Hobin, 1923-25; Leo Darton, 1928; Alfred Genon, 1928-29; Gustav Roth, 1929-31; Adrien Anneet, 1933; Felix Wouters, 1936-38.

Lightweight—Francois Sybille, 1929-30, 1930-31, 1932-33, 1934; Kid Dussart, 1947, 1949; Fernand Roelands, 1976-77.

Junior lightweight—Jean-Marc Renard, 1984, 1986-87.

Featherweight—Arthur Wyns, 1920-22; Henri Hebrans, 1924-25; Phil Dolhem, 1939; Jean Sneyers, 1953-54.

Bantamweight—Henri Scillie, 1924-27; Nicolas Biquet, 1932-35, 1937; Jean Sneyers, 1952; Pierre Cossemyns, 1961-62.

Flyweight—Michel Montreuil, 1923-25; Émile Degand, 1929-30; Kid David, 1935; Raoul Degryse, 1946-47; Jean Sneyers, 1950.

OLYMPIC:

Welterweight—Jean Delarge, 1924.

## BELLOISE, Mike:

After Battling Battalino relinquished the world featherweight title in 1932 there was no undisputed champion for more than five years. Mike Belloise was one of several men who claimed the title during that period.

An Italian-American born New York City, Belloise first came into the championship picture when he was matched with Baby Arizmendi for the N.Y.A.C's version of the title. Belloise was outpointed on this occasion but soon afterwards Arizmendi relinquished the title and when the N.Y.A.C. matched Belloise with Everette Rightmire he beat the French-German in 14 rounds.

In October, 1936, Belloise was beaten by Henry Armstrong in a non-title bout, but although "Homicide Hank" then went on to gain worldwide recognition as featherweight champion, Belloise clung to his claim backed by the N.Y.A.C. until he was beaten on points by Joey Archibald, October, 1938.

## BENDIGO, William Thompson:

Born Nottingham, England, October 11, 1811, he was undefeated until meeting Ben Caunt in April, 1838. This was Bendigo's second match with Caunt who outweighed him by nearly 3 stone (42lbs.). Their first meeting had ended after 22 rounds when Caunt was disqualified for hitting Bendigo as he sat in his corner. Caunt had found that he couldn't catch up with his nimbler opponent and this made him wild enough to commit this foul between rounds.

The second meeting between these two lasted 75 rounds and also ended in a disqualification. This time it was Bendigo who was ruled out for going down without being hit. He claimed that he had slipped.

The deciding contest did not take place until more than seven years later, September 9, 1845. That too had an unsatisfactory ending for Caunt was disqualified for going down without being hit in the 93rd round. Truth is, however, that Caunt was unable to keep his feet at that stage.

Bendigo, who, as one might imagine, had two brothers named Shadrach and Meshach, became Champion of England when he beat Deaf James Burke in 24 minutes at Heather, Leicestershire, February 12, 1839.

He retired soon afterwards but regained the championship in 1845 in his third fight with Ben Caunt as related above.

Bendigo, who is believed to have been the first prize fighter to adopt a southpaw stance, had only one more contest, beating Tom Paddock in 49 rounds.

After retiring from the ring he became an evangelist and a memorial was erected at Nottingham following his death in 1880.

### BENITEZ, Wilfredo:

Undoubtedly one of the most naturally talented and graceful boxers of the post-war era, Wilfredo Benitez, one of a family of eight children born in the New York Bronx, became the youngest fighter ever to win a world title when he captured the light-welter crown in 1976 at the age of 17 years 6 months.

He won a 2nd world title before the age of 22, outpointing Carlos Palomino for the welterweight championship in January 1979.

A master tactician, Benitez was stripped of his light-welter title by the W.B.A. and lost his welter title to Sugar Ray Leonard in November 1979, when the referee stopped their contest with only six seconds remaining. That was his first defeat in 39 bouts.

In May 1981 Benitez joined the elite of fighters by winning a third world title—the W.B.C. version of the light-middle crown, by knocking out Britain's Maurice Hope in 12 rounds. In this fight he really proved his punching power.

After two successful defences Benitez finally lost his third world title when outpointed by Thomas Hearns in December 1982—only his second defeat in 46 bouts to that date.

### BENVENUTI, Nino:

A stylish boxer always on the move, this Italian Insurance agent won the Olympic welterweight title in 1960 and turned professional soon afterwards.

A credit to boxing throughout his career, Benvenuti won the world junior-middleweight title in 1965 from Sandro Mazzinghi and the world middleweight title with a surprise points win over Emile Griffith in New York in April 1967.

The coloured American turned the tables on the Italian in a return bout later the same year, but when these two met for a third time in March 1968, at the opening of the New Madison Square Garden, Benvenuti regained the title with a unanimous points decision.

After successfully defending the crown against Don Fullmer, Fraser Scott, Luis Rodriguez, and Tom Bethea, this son of an Adriatic fisherman, was beaten by Argentinian Carlos Monzon in November 1970.

### BERG, Jack "Kid":

Born Whitechapel, London, 1909, this tough fighter is one of the most celebrated names in British ring history. No boxer ever did more to uphold the prestige of this country in the American ring.

Berg never became a fully-fledged world title-holder, although he was recognised in America as Junior welterweight champion. He was, however, one of the outstanding lightweights of his time, and he might well have become the champion of this division had he been able to secure a match with the title-holder at the right time.

When Sammy Mandell held the title Berg was unable to secure a fight with him. Then, when Al Singer took the crown from Mandell a match between Berg and Singer was an obvious one but it never materialised. Some time previously the "Whitechapel Whirlwind" had refused to meet Singer because he was such a close friend.

When Berg did eventually get his chance against Tony Canzoneri, who had beaten Singer, he had an off-day against a man he had already beaten in a non-title fight, and Canzoneri retained his crown with a third round knockout. Five months later Berg lost to Canzoneri on points.

Jack "Kid" Berg had his first fight at Premierland, London, when only 14. By the time he was 16 he was fighting some of the best men in Europe—Johnny Cuthbert, Johnny Curley, Andre Routis, Harry Corbett, etc.

He was only 16 years 4 months when he outpointed the British featherweight champion, Johnny Curley, over 15 rounds in a non-title fight.

Berg did not become a British champion until he was 25 and had spent nearly five years fighting the best men on the other side of the Atlantic. Then, on October 29, 1934, he took the British lightweight title from Harry Mizler, forcing him to retire in the tenth round at the Albert Hall, London.

In April, 1936, Berg lost his British title to Jimmy Walsh at Liverpool, the referee stopping the contest in the ninth round.

## BERLENBACH, Paul:

Born New York of German parentage, Berlenbach was an amateur wrestling champion before taking up boxing and turning professional in 1923. He was a terrific hitter and won his first ten contests inside the distance.

In March, 1925, he knocked out the former world light-heavyweight champion, Battling Siki, in ten rounds, and won that title in his next fight by outpointing Mike McTigue, May 30, 1925.

Berlenbach successfully defended his crown against Jim Slattery, Jack Delaney and Young Stribling, but he lost it in a return with Delaney, July 26, 1926. Delaney got the decision at the end of a hard fight in which Berlenbach had taken a great deal of punishment.

In 1929 Berlenbach turned to wrestling once more. He made a boxing comeback in 1931 but retired two years later.

## BERRY, Tom:

This English light-heavyweight was a veteran of 35 years of age when he was matched with the Yorkshireman, Syd Pape, for the vacant British light-heavyweight title in March, 1925.

Pape was a good fighter but Berry knew too much for him, and despite his age he was able to outlast Pape and earn the referee's decision at the end of 20 rounds.

Nearly two years later the amazingly fit Berry outpointed the Irish champion, Dave Magill, in a contest which was considered to be for the Empire light-heavyweight championship.

Berry had also claimed the European crown with his victory over Pape, but in April, 1927, he lost all these titles when outpointed by Gipsy Daniels at the N.S.C.

## BEYNON, Bill:

This quiet spoken Welsh miner was one of the best bantamweights in Europe about the time of the First World War.

On June 2, 1913, at the N.S.C., London, he outpointed Digger Stanley over 20 rounds, to take the British bantamweight title, but it was a decision which caused one of the biggest uproars in the club's history, and the two men were quickly rematched.

Their second meeting at the N.S.C. took place on October 27, 1913, and Beynon lost the title when the decision went to Stanley at the end of 20 rounds.

Beynon had a third meeting with Digger Stanley more than four years later, but the gipsy fighter again got the better of him, winning in only five rounds.

Age overtakes another master boxer as Ernie Roderick (*left*), nearly 35 years of age, loses his British welterweight title in a hard fought battle with Henry Hall, at Harringay in November 1948

British lightweight champion, Ronnie James proves no match for American world title holder Ike Williams and is k.o'd in the ninth round at Cardiff in September 1946

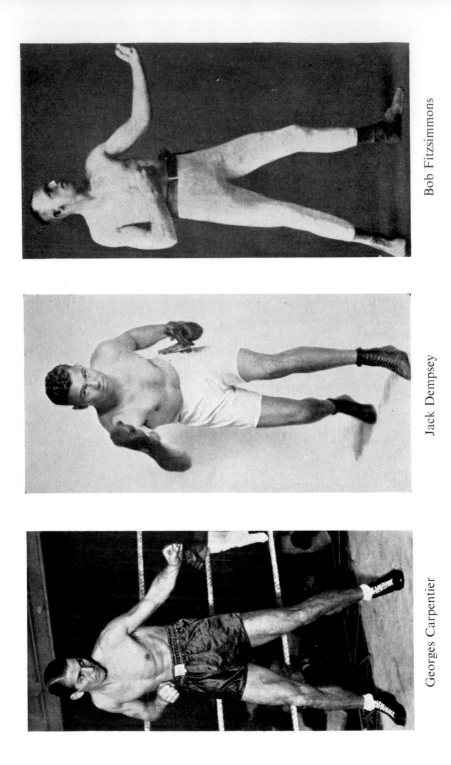

Bob Fitzsimmons

Jack Dempsey

Georges Carpentier

Three of Beynon's most important contests were with that great French battler, Charles Ledoux. They first met at the American Skating Rink, Cardiff, in December, 1913, and Ledoux got the decision when Beynon was retired by his corner with a badly cut eye as bell sounded for the eighth round. In their return match Beynon retired at the end of the ninth round.

Beynon's third match with the European champion took place in Paris seven years later. This time the Frenchman landed a knockout in the fourth round.

Beynon was killed in a colliery disaster in 1932.

## BLACK BOXERS:

The first black man to take part in a prize fight was probably Bill Richmond, a negro from Richmond, Staten Island, New York.

Richmond was brought to this country in 1777 by General Earl Percy (Duke of Northumberland). General Percy had been in command of British troops occupying New York.

Richmond's first fight in England was against George "Docky" Moore at York in 1804. He won in 25 minutes.

In October, 1805, he met the up and coming champion, Tom Cribb, at Hailsham, Sussex, but was beaten in 1 hour 30 minutes.

The next black fighter of note, and one who made a greater impression on the fancy, was Tom Molineux from Virginia. Molineux had been given his freedom from slavery in America after winning a fight in which he had been heavily backed by his master.

Bill Richmond took Molineux under his wing when Tom subsequently decided to try his luck in England, and the Virginian made such progress that in 1810 he was matched with the reigning champion, Tom Cribb.

According to the rules of the game Molineux should have been proclaimed champion after this memorable battle with Cribb at Coptall Common, near East Grinstead, but racial prejudice was much in evidence on this occasion.

Molineux knocked Cribb out in the 28th round and after the regulation half-minute break the champion could not respond to three successive calls to scratch. As one can imagine, there was terrific excitement. The fancy were dismayed at the prospect of having a nigger as champion, and thereupon Molineux was accused of fighting with lead shot in his hands. This false accusation was eventually disposed of but the delay was enough to allow Cribb to recover.

After that the negro showed more ill effects from the weather—it was raining and freezing—than from the blows of his opponent, and he collapsed from sheer exhaustion after 39 rounds, Cribb being declared the winner.

Molineux had a return match with Cribb nine months later but it was a much improved champion on this occasion, for Cribb had undergone a course of intensive training and the negro was beaten in less than 20 minutes.

In more modern times there have been many famous black fighters and several of these won world titles. Only two of the 13 heavyweight champions in the post-war period have not been coloured men, while in the lighter divisions we have had such outstanding coloured champions as Panama Al Brown, Dick Tiger, Emile Griffith, Tiger Flowers, but there have been other great black fighters who never gained world titles.

Outstanding among these was Peter Jackson, a West Indian, who settled in Australia and is still considered by many good judges to be one of the best half dozen heavyweights of all time. One thing is certain. There has never been a more highly respected, more modest and courteous fighter than this negro.

Three other negro heavyweights of merit who never won world titles were Sam Langford, Joe Jeannette and Sam McVey.

For the greater part of his career Langford was really little more than a middleweight, but he gave weight to many of the best men in the world and beat them. His remarkable career extended over 21 years, 1902-23. Among those he defeated were Young Peter Jackson, Joe Gans, Joe Jeannette, "Fireman" Jim Flynn, Iron Hague, Dixie Kid, Philadelphia Jack O'Brien,

Gunboat Smith, Harry Wills, and Tiger Flowers.

After 1919 Langford was considered to be the black heavyweight champion of the world.

Known as the "Boston Tar Baby," Langford was beaten on points over 15 rounds by Jack Johnson in 1906, but after Johnson won the world title he held Langford in such great respect that he would not allow his fellow negro to meet him again in the ring, although Langford persistently challenged "Little Artha" for a crack at the title.

Langford spent the last 32 years of his life in blindness.

Sam Langford's contemporary, Joe Jeannette, met Jack Johnson on several occasions, mostly in "No Decision" bouts.

Less than 12 months before Johnson beat Tommy Burns for the world championship, Jeannette fought a draw with the Texas negro in New York. Thereafter, Jeannette was also missing from the list of fighters Johnson agreed to meet.

One of the most gruelling contests ever fought was that between Joe Jeannette and Sam McVey, a 14 stone (196 lbs.) negro from California.

This fight took place in Paris in April, 1909. McVey dropped Jeannette in the first round and then proceeded to batter him for another 37 rounds. By then Jeannette had been down 21 times but he was still coming back fighting and he sent McVey down for the first time in the 39th round. Thereafter McVey was floored another 18 times, although not without putting Jeannette on the canvas on a further half dozen occasions, making 28 times in all.

So the bloody battle went on until, when the gong sounded for the 49th round, McVey got off his stool only to collapse and be counted out.

McVey had two contests in England in 1911, beating George Rodel in one round and Alf Langford in seven. He died penniless in New York at the age of 36 in 1921.

## Firsts among Black Boxers:

The first black man to fight for the championship—Tom Molineux, who met Tom Cribb at Coptall Common, Sussex, December 18, 1810.

The first black man to win world championships in each division:—

Heavyweight—Jack Johnson, negro from Galveston, Texas, 1908.

Light-heavyweight—Battling Siki, West African negro, 1922.

Middleweight—Theodore (Tiger) Flowers, Georgia negro, 1926.

Welterweight—Joe Walcott, West Indian negro, 1901.

Lightweight—Joe Gans, Baltimore negro, 1902.

Featherweight—George Dixon, Canadian negro, 1891.

Bantamweight—George Dixon, Canadian negro, 1890.

The first occasion on which two black men fought for the world heavyweight title was when Joe Louis knocked out John Henry Lewis in one round, New York City, January 25, 1939.

When Jack Johnson held the title he met another negro named Jim Johnson. However, the fight, which took place in Paris and was declared a draw at the end of 10 rounds, was not a championship contest.

The first black fighter to be recognised as a British title-holder was Andrew Jeptha, a South African, who knocked out the British welterweight champion, Curley Watson, in four rounds at Wonderland, London, March 25, 1907.

Jeptha claimed the British title until he was beaten by Watson in November, 1907.

The first black fighter to win a British title under B.B.B.C. rules was Dick Turpin (Leamington), who became middleweight champion in 1948.

The first black man to referee a world title fight was Zack Clayton. He was third man when Jersey Joe Walcott successfully defended his heavyweight title by outpointing Ezzard Charles, Municipal Stadium, Philadelphia, June 5, 1952.

## BLACKFRIARS, The Ring:

For about 30 years this was one of the most popular boxing arenas in London. A peculiar octagonal building situated in Blackfriars Road, it was originally a

Nonconformist chapel but fell into disuse until it was taken over by the former lightweight champion, Dick Burge, and his partner, Tom Pritchard.

That was in 1910, and they promoted boxing shows two or three times a week. Their Sunday afternoon programmes soon became particularly popular with London's East Enders.

Dick Burge died tragically during World War I but for another 22 years his widow carried on her husband's work. In fact, Mrs. Burge was for many years the only woman boxing promoter.

The building was destroyed by German bombs during the Second World War at a time when efforts were being made to recapture some of its old glory as a top-line boxing arena.

### BLAKE, Jack:

Born Great Yarmouth, 1891, Bandsman Blake sprang into the boxing limelight on New Year's Day, 1914, when he outpointed the great Dixie Kid over 20 rounds at The Ring, Blackfriars. It is true that the Dixie Kid was then well past his best, but he was still a "name" in the boxing world and a victory over him was a notable achievement.

In March, 1914, Blake challenged Bombardier Billy Wells for the British heavyweight title but was knocked out by the heavier man in four rounds.

Bandsman Blake became British middleweight champion when he outpointed Pat O'Keefe at the N.S.C., May 22, 1916. On that occasion Blake was somewhat fortunate as he was almost knocked out in the final round.

In a return match at the N.S.C., fought during an air raid, January 28, 1918, Blake was knocked out in the second round.

### BLOOMFIELD, Jack:

Started boxing towards the end of World War I while serving in the R.A.F. He soon developed into an excellent prospect and was tipped as a probable contender for world honours before an internal injury cut short his career.

In 1921 this Islington, London, boy was matched with the experienced Ted "Kid" Lewis for the vacant British middleweight title, but was beaten on points.

On May 1, 1922, Bloomfield was officially acknowledged by the N.S.C. as British light-heavyweight champion following his victory over Harry Drake in nine rounds. At that time the title was also claimed by Ted "Kid" Lewis.

Bloomfield relinquished his claim to the crown in 1923 and was matched with Frank Goddard for the vacant British heavyweight championship.

Although giving away more than two stone (28 lbs.) Bloomfield was getting the better of the ex-Guardsman before he lost his temper and was ruled out for a foul in the second round.

In his last fight, on August 9, 1924, Bloomfield was knocked out in the third round by Tom Gibbons, the high-ranking Irish-American heavyweight.

### BODELL, Jack:

Another British heavyweight champion who never quite made world class although this willing fighter from Swadlincote, Derbyshire, had a good run at home.

His bulldozing style earned him the vacant British title in October 1969 when he outpointed Carl Gizzi, but he lost it five months later to Henry Cooper.

One of "Honest Jack's" best displays was in beating Joe Bugner in September 1971 to regain the British and Commonwealth titles and also annex the European crown, but then followed devastating defeats in three bouts totalling less than five rounds of fighting against Jerry Quarry, Jose Urtain (European title) and Danny McAlinden (British and Commonwealth titles), before Bodell decided to call it a day.

### BOON, Eric:

Hard-hitting son of a Chatteris, Cambridgeshire, blacksmith, Boon sprang right to the top of the tree when, only a little over 18 years of age, he outpointed the British lightweight champion, Jimmy Walsh, in a non-title fight.

That was in May, 1938, and soon afterwards Walsh lost his title to Dave Crowley. Then, after winning seven more fights inside the distance, "Boy" Boon was matched with Crowley for the championship on December 15, 1938.

Boon still had 13 days to go for his 19th birthday, but he became one of the youngest men ever to win a British title by knocking out the experienced Londoner in the 13th round.

In February, 1939, Boon engaged in the memorable contest with Arthur Danahar at Harringay, London. This was one of the classics of British ring history. On the one hand the tough, aggressive, crouching fighter, and on the other, Arthur Danahar, the stylish, upstanding scientific boxer. Danahar piled up the points in the earlier rounds but eventually he was caught by some of Boon's vicious left hooks, and although by that time Boon himself looked a sorry sight with one eye closed, the Chatteris boy went on to pound Danahar into defeat, the referee stopping the contest in the 14th round.

Boon eventually experienced difficulty in making the lightweight limit and he lost his title to Ronnie James in August, 1944.

In December, 1947, Boon met Ernie Roderick for the British welterweight title but was outpointed.

## BOOTHS:

Today travelling fairground boxing booths can be numbered on the fingers of one hand, but in the past the booth has been an ideal nursery for up-and-coming champions. The booth proprietor's troupe of boxers is paraded "out front" and a challenge issued for any member of the audience to come inside, put on the gloves, and try to last three or four rounds with any one of the proprietor's fighters. There is a cash prize on the end of it for any member of the public who can "go the distance." No points decisions are given, the challenger simply has to be still on his feet when the final bell sounds.

Such contests have not only proved a fine attraction with the spectators who enjoy cheering on their local hero, but they provide first-class schooling for the professionals. Fighting regularly every evening and meeting such a variety of challengers is excellent experience for the aspiring champion.

Apart from this benefit to the individual boxers the booths have also been immeasurable value to the game as a whole. Many a keen local fighter has had a chance which he may never have got but for the arrival of the booth in his village miles away from the nearest boxing club, gymnasium or promoter.

Men like Jimmy Wilde, Jim Driscoll, Joe Beckett and Freddie Mills, to mention but a few, owed much of their prowess to the experience they obtained in the old fairground boxing booths.

For a while after the Second World War the B.B.B.C. banned licensed boxers from appearing in fairground booths when some booth proprietors were abandoning the old form of challenge bouts and staging advertised contests between professionals. The Stewards of the Board felt that these booth proprietors were thus competing with their own licensed promoters.

However, an agreement was reached whereby the Board allowed licensed boxers to operate in booths which are owned by members of the Showman's Guild of Great Britain.

Under this agreement the booth proprietors must not advertise the names of the boxers outside the fairground by boards or display cards, and the names of all challengers for bouts to take place in the booth must be issued from the platform of the booth.

## BOWKER, Joe:

During the early part of the 20th century there were few better fighters under nine stone (126 lbs.) than this Manchester man.

Bowker got his early experience in the boxing booths and at the age of 20 he won a novice bantamweight competition at the N.S.C., London.

In a very short time he was rated the best bantamweight in Britain and he proved this by beating Andrew Tokell for the championship of that division in May, 1903.

However, it was not until he had beaten Owen Moran on points over 20 rounds at the N.S.C. that this Lancashire lad was officially ranked as the British bantamweight champion.

At that time the world title was held by

Frankie Neil, of San Francisco. The N.S.C. invited him to London, and there, on October 17, 1904, he was outpointed by Bowker over 20 rounds.

Bowker next scored two victories over the redoubtable Pedlar Palmer. "The box o' tricks" was then a little past his best but the fact that Bowker managed to catch up with this will-o'-the-wisp and knock him out in their second meeting says much for the boxing ability and powers of concentration of the Manchester man.

One who was his master was Jim Driscoll. The Welsh genius outpointed Bowker over 15 rounds in May, 1906, when Bowker substituted for Johnny Summers, and he knocked him out in their second meeting in June, 1907. That last contest was for the British featherweight title. Bowker had claimed the championship of this division after his second win over Pedlar Palmer but he never gained official recognition.

Despite this official attitude Bowker should be listed among the British featherweight champions, for although Johnny Summers beat Spike Robson in a title fight in January, 1906, it must be remembered that Bowker had himself beaten Robson only three months previously, and therefore the Northumberland man had no right to be fighting for the title at that time.

After he had fought so much in the featherweight division Bowker's claim to the world bantamweight title was forgotten after 1905.

He was, however, still British and European bantamweight champion until he was knocked out in eight rounds by Digger Stanley at the N.S.C., October 17, 1910.

Joe Bowker died in London in October, 1955, aged 72.

## BOZA-EDWARDS, Cornelius:

Began fighting in Uganda at the age of 11 before coming to England and settling down in Harrow to turn professional in 1976. He subsequently moved to Las Vegas but not before he won the W.B.C. version of the world junior-lightweight title in a bruising points victory over Rafael Limon in March 1981. After only five months he lost this title when surprisingly k.o.'d by Rolando Navarette. The following year he captured the European crown with a convincing win over Carlos Hernandez but soon relinquished this title to go after the world crown. The W.B.C. champion at this time was Bobby Chacon whom Boza-Edwards had previously beaten, but this time (in May 1983) the Californian won a blood-bath despite needing 40 stitches to cuts around his eyes. In his last fight in 1987, he was k.o.'d by Luis Ramirez when bidding for the W.B.C. world lightweight title.

## BRADDOCK, James J.:

Known as the "Cinderella Man," this Irish-American worked his way up to a crack at Tommy Loughran's light-heavyweight title in 1929 but was outpointed. He slipped badly after that, hand injuries being part of the trouble, until in 1934 he was penniless and out of work.

In June, 1934, he came back to start a meteoric rise to the top with a third round k.o. win over Corn Griffin. Twelve months later he was world heavyweight champion!

On that June day in 1935 when Braddock, known as only an average fighter for so many years, entered the ring against champion Max Baer, it was easy to get odds of 10-1 against Braddock taking the title. But he shocked the critics with a fine display of boxing to earn a points victory at the end of 15 rounds.

Unfortunately, Braddock was not a busy champion. He did not defend his title until June 22, 1937, when he was knocked out in the eighth round by Joe Louis.

## BRAIN, Benjamin:

Big Ben Brain was one of the several famous bare-knuckle prize fighters who hailed from Bristol.

Although known as Big Ben, he was under six feet tall, but he weighed something in the region of 14 stone (196 lbs.), and when he came to London in 1786 he proved his strength and durability by beating "The Fighting Grenadier," John Boone, in under 40 minutes' actual fighting.

Brain became Champion of England when he defeated Tom Johnson in 18 rounds at Wrotham, Kent, January 17, 1791. He died three years later of a liver complaint without having defended his title.

## BRAZIL:

The first fighter to really put Brazilian boxing on the map by winning a world title was the brilliant bantamweight Eder Jofre (q.v.).

Another who laid claim to be world champion was Miguel de Oliveira. He was recognised by W.B.C. as light-middleweight title-holder 1975-76.

Brazilian fly-weight, Jose Severino, got a chance for the vacant world title (W.B.A. version) in 1969 but was outpointed by Hiroyuki Ebihara, while Brazil's leading heavyweight of recent years, Luiz Pires, has been stopped three times inside the distance by the better known Argentinian, Oscar Bonavena.

## BRITISH BOXING BOARD OF CONTROL, The:

The B.B.B. of C., as it is now constituted, was formed in 1929 by a number of boxing enthusiasts who considered that the game would benefit from stricter control under regulations primarily concerned with the well-being of all professional boxers in this country.

The original suggestion for such a Board had been made some 20 years earlier by the *Sporting Life*, but it had not materialised due to the friction between some sides of the boxing fraternity and the National Sporting Club, whose leading light, "Peggy" Bettinson, wanted to retain the greater part of the control of any such organisation.

A Board of Control was formed in 1919 but it was largely under the influence of the N.S.C.

Subsequently members of the N.S.C. developed a more diplomatic attitude toward the scheme and in 1929 most of the men who formed the new Board and elected the Stewards to draw up regulations were members of the old N.S.C.

In fact, the N.S.C. was immediately given a permanent seat on the new Board of Control.

The N.S.C. retained this privilege until 1937, when it ceased to function as a club but began to promote contests for the general public, and therefore came into competition with other boxing promoters.

The Stewards of the B.B.B.C. are men who have the best interests of the game at heart. They do not receive any payment for their services.

Everyone connected with professional boxing in the United Kingdom and Northern Ireland, whether he be boxer, manager, promoter, referee or time-keeper, is licensed by the Board, and they also provide inspectors who attend all contests to see that everything is properly conducted.

One of the most important aspects of the Board's work is on the medical side. Everything possible has been done to safeguard the health of all boxers with proper regulation and control, and the Board also keeps a wary eye open to see that boxers do not come to harm by being overmatched.

The Board derives its income from the issue of licences and from a tax levied on the takings of all boxing promotions.

To facilitate the proper control of boxing over the whole of the United Kingdom and Northern Ireland the Board has formed eight Area Councils as follows: Scottish, Northern Ireland, Welsh, Northern, Central, Southern, Western and Midlands.

The address of the B.B.B.C. is 70 Vauxhall Bridge Road, London SW1.

## BRITISH CHAMPIONS:

Len Harvey and Ted "Kid" Lewis are the only two men who have held British titles at three different weights.

Len Harvey was middleweight champion 1929-33, light-heavyweight 1933-34, 1938-42, heavyweight 1933-34, 1938-42.

Ted "Kid" Lewis was featherweight champion 1913-14, welterweight 1920-24, middleweight 1920 (unofficial), 1921-23.

Johnny Summers also claimed British

titles at three different weights but not all these claims were generally accepted. He claimed featherweight title 1906 (disputed), lightweight 1908-09, welterweight 1912-14.

## Titleholders:

### Heavyweight

Charlie Mitchell bt. Jack Knifton, pts. 3, St. George's, London, Dec. 22, 1882. Mitchell went to America in March, 1883, and was away for five years.

Jem Smith bt. Jack Wannop, pts. 10, London, Sept. 30, 1889.

Ted Pritchard bt. Smith, 3 rnds., New Cross, London, July 27, 1891.

Jem Smith bt. Pritchard, k.o. 2, Holborn, London, May 10, 1895.

George Crisp bt. Smith, disq. 5, Newcastle, Feb. 19, 1897.

Crisp no longer acknowledged as champion following his defeat by Frank Craig, the American negro, Nov., 1898.

Jack Palmer bt. Ben Taylor, k.o. 12, Newcastle, May 2, 1903.

Gunner Moir bt. Palmer, disq. 9, N.S.C., London, Oct. 29, 1906.

Iron Hague bt. Moir, k.o. 1, N.S.C., London, Apl. 19, 1909.

Billy Wells bt. Hague, k.o. 6, N.S.C., London, Apl. 24, 1911.

Joe Beckett bt. Wells, k.o. 5, Holborn, London, Feb. 27, 1919. (Not recognised by N.S.C.).

Frank Goddard bt. Jack Curphey, k.o. 10, London, May 26, 1919.

Joe Beckett bt. Goddard, k.o. 2, Olympia, London, June 17, 1919. Beckett retired October, 1923.

Frank Goddard bt. Jack Bloomfield, disq. 2, Albert Hall, London, Nov. 21, 1923.

Phil Scott bt. Goddard, k.o. 3, London, Mar. 18, 1926. Scott relinquished title June, 1931.

Reggie Meen bt. Charlie Smith, pts. 15, Leicester, Nov. 16, 1931.

Jack Petersen bt. Meen, k.o. 2, Wimbledon, London, July 12, 1932.

Len Harvey bt. Petersen, pts. 15, Albert Hall, London, Nov. 30, 1933.

Jack Petersen bt. Harvey, rtd. 12, White City, London, June 4, 1934.

Ben Foord bt. Petersen, r.s.f. 3, Leicester, Aug. 17, 1936.

Tommy Farr bt. Foord, pts. 15, Harringay, London, Mar. 15, 1937. Farr relinquished title Aug., 1938.

Len Harvey bt. Eddie Phillips, disq. 4, Harringay, London, Dec. 1, 1938. Harvey retired November, 1942.

Jack London bt. Freddie Mills, pts. 15, Manchester, Sept. 15, 1944.

Bruce Woodcock bt. London, k.o. 6, Tottenham, London, July 17, 1945.

Jack Gardner bt. Woodcock, rtd. 11, Earl's Court, London, Nov. 14, 1950.

Johnny Williams bt. Gardner, pts. 15, Earl's Court, London, Mar. 11, 1952.

Don Cockell bt. Williams, pts. 15, Harringay, London, May 12, 1953. Cockell retired July, 1956.

Joe Erskine bt. Johnny Williams, pts. 15, Cardiff, Aug. 27, 1956.

Brian London bt. Erskine, k.o. 8, White City, London, June 3, 1958.

Henry Cooper bt. London, pts. 15, Earl's Court, London, Jan. 12, 1959. Cooper relinquished title June 1969.

Jack Bodell bt. Carl Gizzi, pts. 15, Nottingham, Oct. 13, 1969.

Henry Cooper bt. Bodell, pts. 15, London, Mar. 24, 1970.

Joe Bugner bt. Cooper, pts. 15, Wembley, Mar. 16, 1971.

Jack Bodell bt. Bugner, pts. 15, Wembley, Sept. 27, 1971.

Danny McAlinden bt. Bodell, k.o. 2, Birmingham, June 27, 1972.

Bunny Johnson bt. McAlinden, k.o. 9, W.S.C., London, Jan. 13, 1975.

Richard Dunn bt. Johnson, pts. 15, Wembley, Sept. 30, 1975.

Joe Bugner bt. Dunn, k.o. 1, Wembley, Oct. 12, 1976. Bugner relinquished title Mar. 1977.

John L. Gardner bt. Billy Aird, rtd. 5, Albert Hall, London, Oct. 24, 1978. Gardner relinquished title 1981.

Gordon Ferris bt. Billy Aird, pts. 15, Birmingham, Mar. 30, 1981.

Neville Meade bt. Ferris, k.o. 1, Birmingham, Oct. 12, 1981.

David Pearce bt. Meade, r.s.f. 9, Cardiff, Sept. 22, 1983. Pearce relinquish title 1985.

Hughroy Currie bt. Funso Banjo, pts. 12, Alexandra Pavilion, London, Sept. 18, 1985.

Horace Notice bt. Currie, r.s.f. 6, Isle of Man, Apl. 12, 1986.

## Cruiserweight

Sam Reeson bt. Stewart Lithgo, pts. 12, Latchmere Leisure Centre, London, Oct. 31, 1985. Reeson relinquished title Oct. 1896.

Andrew Straughn bt. Tee Jay, pts. 12, Stevenage, Oct. 25, 1986.

Roy Smith bt. Straughn, pts. 12, Alfreton, Feb. 17, 1987.

Tee Jay bt. Smith, r.s.f. 1, Battersea, May 9, 1987.

## Light-heavyweight

Dick Smith bt. Dennis Haugh, pts. 20, N.S.C., London, Mar. 9, 1914.

Harry Reeve bt. Smith, pts. 20, N.S.C, London, Oct. 30, 1916. Reeve relinquished title 1917.

Dick Smith bt. Joe Beckett, pts. 20, N.S.C., London, Feb. 25, 1918. Smith relinquished title 1918.

Boy McCormick bt. Harold Rolph, disq. 11, London, Apl. 28, 1919.

Ted "Kid" Lewis bt. McCormick, r.s.f. 14, London, Nov. 17, 1921. Not recognised by the N.S.C. McCormick relinquished official title 1921.

Jack Bloomfield bt. Harry Drake, r.s.f. 9, N.S.C., London, May 1, 1922. Bloomfield relinquished title 1923.

Tom Berry bt. Syd Pape, pts. 20, N.S.C., London, Mar. 9, 1925.

Gipsy Daniels bt. Berry, pts. 20, Holland Park, London, Apl. 25, 1927. Daniels relinquished title 1928.

Frank Moody bt. Ted Moore, pts. 20, N.S.C., London, Nov. 27, 1927.

Harry Crossley bt. Moody, pts. 15, N.S.C., London, Nov. 25, 1929.

Jack Petersen bt. Crossley, pts. 15, Holborn, London, May 23, 1932. Petersen relinquished title 1932.

Len Harvey bt. Eddie Phillips, pts. 15, Olympia, London, June 13, 1933. Harvey relinquished title 1934.

Eddie Phillips bt. Tommy Farr, pts. 15, Mountain Ash, Feb. 4, 1935.

Jock McAvoy bt. Phillips, k.o. 14, Wembley, London, Apl. 27, 1937.

Len Harvey bt. McAvoy, pts. 15, Harringay, London, Apl. 7, 1938.

Freddie Mills bt. Harvey, k.o. 2, Tottenham, London, June 20, 1942. Mills retired 1950.

Don Cockell bt. Mark Hart, k.o. 14, Harringay, London, Oct. 17, 1950.

Randolph Turpin bt. Cockell, r.s.f. 11, White City, London, June 10, 1952. Turpin relinquished title 1952.

Dennis Powell bt. George Walker, rtd. 11, Liverpool, Mar. 26, 1953.

Alex Buxton bt. Powell, r.s.f. 10, Nottingham, Oct. 26, 1953.

Randolph Turpin bt. Buxton, k.o. 2, Harringay, London, Apl. 26, 1955. Turpin relinquished title 1955.

Ron Barton bt. Albert Finch, rtd. 8, Harringay, Mar. 13, 1956. Barton retired 1956.

Randolph Turpin bt Alex Buxton, r.s.f. 5, Leicester, Nov. 26, 1956. Turpin retired 1958.

Chic Calderwood bt. Arthur Howard, r.s.f. 13, Paisley, Jan. 28, 1960.

Calderwood forfeited title Nov. 1963, but regained it by beating Bob Nicholson, r.s.f. 7, Paisley, Nov. 11, 1964. Calderwood killed in car accident Nov. 1966.

Young McCormack bt. Eddie Avoth, r.s.f. 7, London, June 19, 1967.

Eddie Avoth bt. McCormack, rtd. 11, London, Jan. 13, 1969.

Chris Finnegan bt. Avoth, r.s.f. 15, London, Jan. 24, 1971.

John Conteh bt. Finnegan, pts. 15, London, May 22, 1973. Conteh relinquished title Dec. 1974.

Johnny Frankham bt. Chris Finnegan, pts. 15, London, June 3, 1975.

Chris Finnegan bt. Frankham, pts. 15, London, Oct. 14, 1975. Finnegan retired Feb. 1976.

Tim Wood bt. Phil Martin, pts. 15, London, Apl. 28, 1976.

Bunny Johnson bt. Wood k.o. 1, Wolverhampton, Mar. 8, 1977. Johnson relinquished title Dec. 1981.

Tom Collins bt. Dennis Andries, pts. 15, London, Mar. 15, 1982.

Dennis Andries bt. Collins, pts. 12, Lyceum Ballroom, London, Jan. 16, 1984. Andries relinquished title 1986.

Tom Collins bt. John Moody, r.s.f. 10, Albert Hall, London, March 11, 1987.

## Middleweight

Ted Pritchard bt. Dick Burge, k.o. 2, London, Nov. 26, 1894. Pritchard was no longer considered to be champion after his defeat by Frank Craig, the

American negro, Holborn, Nov. 26, 1894. Dan Creedon, a New Zealander, subsequently beat Craig in a contest billed as for the middleweight championship of England, but the author does not consider Craig qualified to fight for this title.

Anthony Diamond bt. Dido Plumb, pts. 12, Birmingham, Feb. 25, 1898.

Dido Plumb bt. Jem Ryan, k.o. 8, N.S.C., London, Mar. 17, 1900. Plumb lost his hold on the title following defeats by the Americans, Charles McKeever and Philadelphia Jack O'Brien.

Jack Palmer claimed title in 1902 but almost immediately moved up into the heavyweight class.

Pat O'Keefe bt. Mike Crawley, pts. 15, N.S.C., London, Mar. 19, 1906.

Tom Thomas bt. O'Keefe, pts. 15, N.S.C., London, May 23, 1906.

Jim Sullivan bt. Thomas, pts. 20, N.S.C., London, Nov. 14, 1910. Sullivan relinquished title 1911.

Jack Harrison bt. Pte. McEnroy, pts. 20, N.S.C., London, May 20, 1912 Harrison relinquished title 1913.

Pat O'Keefe bt. Harry Reeve, pts. 20, N.S.C., London, Feb. 23, 1914.

Bandsman Blake bt. O'Keefe, pts. 20, N.S.C., London, May 22, 1916.

Pat O'Keefe bt. Blake, k.o. 2, N.S.C., London, Jan. 28, 1918. O'Keefe relinquished title 1919.

Tom Gummer bt. Jim Sullivan, r.s.f. 14, N.S.C., London, Mar. 29, 1920.

Gus Platts bt. Gummer, k.o. 6, Sheffield, Mar. 28, 1921.

Johnny Basham bt. Platts, pts. 20, Albert Hall, London, May 31, 1921. Neither Platts nor Basham were acknowledged by the N.S.C.

Ted "Kid" Lewis bt. Jack Bloomfield, pts. 20, Holland Park, London, June 27, 1921.

Roland Todd bt. Lewis, pts. 20, Albert Hall, London, Feb. 15, 1923. Lonsdale Belt not presented. Lewis was subsequently deprived of Lonsdale Belt by the N.S.C. Todd was deprived of title by the N.S.C. 1925.

Tommy Milligan bt. George West, r.s.f. 14, Holland Park, London, July 12, 1926. Milligan was subsequently beaten by Alex Ireland and Frank Moody, but although neither of these was accepted as champion by the N.S.C. they were forced to declare the title vacant.

Len Harvey bt. Alex Ireland, k.o. 7, Olympia, London, May 16, 1929.

Jock McAvoy bt. Harvey, pts. 15, Manchester, Apl. 10, 133. McAvoy relinquished title 1945.

Ernie Roderick bt. Vince Hawkins, pts. 15, Albert Hall, London, May 29, 1945.

Vince Hawkins bt. Roderick, pts. 15, Albert Hall, London, Oct. 28, 1946.

Dick Turpin bt. Hawkins, pts. 15, Birmingham, June 28, 1948.

Albert Finch bt. Turpin, pts. 15, Nottingham, Apl. 24, 1950.

Randolph Turpin bt. Finch, k.o. 5, Harringay, London, Oct. 17, 1950. Turpin relinquished title 1954.

Johnny Sullivan bt. Gordon Hazell. k.o. 1, Harringay, London, Sept. 14, 1954.

Pat McAteer bt. Sullivan, disq. 9, Liverpool, June 16, 1955. McAteer relinquished title 1958.

Terry Downes bt. Phil Edwards, r.s.f. 13, Harringay, London, Sept. 30, 1958.

John McCormack bt. Downes, disq. 8, Wembley, London, Sept. 15, 1959.

Terry Downes bt. McCormack, r.s.f. 8, Wembley, London, Nov. 3, 1959.

Downes forfeited title Nov. 1962.

George Aldridge bt. John McCormack, k.o. 6, Manchester, Nov. 26, 1962.

Mick Leahy bt. Aldridge, r.s.f. 1, Nottingham, May 28, 1963.

Wally Swift bt. Leahy, pts. 15, Nottingham, Dec. 14, 1964.

Johnny Pritchett bt. Swift, r.s.f. 12, Nottingham, Nov. 8, 1965.

Pritchett retired June 1969.

Les McAteer bt. Wally Swift, rtd. 11, Nottingham, July 14, 1969.

Mark Rowe bt. McAteer, r.s.f 14, London, May 12, 1970.

Bunny Sterling bt. Rowe, r.s.f. 4, London, Sept. 8, 1970.

Kevin Finnegan bt. Sterling, pts. 15, London, Feb. 11, 1974.

Finnegan relinquished title Aug. 1974.

Bunny Sterling bt. Maurice Hope, r.s.f. 8, London, June 10, 1975.

Sterling relinquished title 1975.

Alan Minter bt. Kevin Finnegan, London, Nov. 4, 1975.

B.B.B.C. deprived Minter of title.

Kevin Finnegan bt. Frankie Lucas, r.s.f. 11, London, May 31, 1977.

Alan Minter bt. Finnegan, pts. 15, London, Nov. 8, 1977.

Minter relinquished title Nov. 1978.

Tony Sibson bt. Frankie Lucas, r.s.f. 5, Albert Hall, London, Apl. 10, 1979.

Kevin Finnegan bt. Sibson, pts. 15, Albert Hall, London, Nov. 6, 1979.

Finnegan retired Sept. 1980.

Roy Gumbs bt. Howard Mills, r.s.f.3, Cafe Royal, London, Feb. 2, 1981.

Mark Kaylor bt. Gumbs, k.o. 5, Alexandra Pavilion, London, September 14, 1983.

Tony Sibson bt. Kaylor, pts. 12, Wembley, Nov. 27, 1984.

Sibson relinquished title 1984.

Herol Graham bt. Jimmy Price, k.o. 1, Britannia L.C., London, Apl. 24, 1985.

Graham relinquished title 1986.

Brian Anderson bt. Tony Burke, r.s.f. 8, Belfast, Oct. 29, 1986.

Tony Sibson bt Anderson, r.s.f. 7, Albert Hall, London, Sept. 16, 1987.

*Light-middleweight*

Larry Paul bt. Bobby Arthur, k.o. 10, Wolverhampton, Sept, 25, 1973.

Maurice Hope bt. Paul, k.o. 8, Wolverhampton, Nov. 5, 1974.

B.B.B.C. deprived Hope of title 1977.

Jimmy Batten bt. Albert Hillman, rtd. 7, London, Feb. 1, 1977.

Pat Thomas bt. Batten, r.s.f. 9, Wembley, London, Sept. 11, 1979.

Herol Graham bt. Thomas, pts. 15, Sheffield, Mar. 24, 1981.

Graham relinquished title 1983.

Prince Rodney bt. Jimmy Batten, r.s.f. 6, Albert Hall, London, Oct. 11, 1983.

Rodney relinquished title 1984.

Jimmy Cable bt. Nick Wilshire, pts. 12, Albert Hall, London, Feb. 22, 1984.

Prince Rodney bt. Cable, k.o. 1, Hastings, May 11, 1985.

Chris Pyatt bt. Rodney, k.o. 9, Albert Hall, London, Feb. 19, 1986.

Pyatt relinquished title October 1986.

Lloyd Hibbert bt. Nick Wilshire, pts. 12, Albert Hall, London, Mar. 11, 1987. 1987.

Hibbert relinquished title 1987.

*Welterweight*

Charlie Knock bt. Curley Watson, Wonderland, London, rtd. 17, May 21, 1906.

Curley Watson bt. Knock, pts. 10, Wonderland, London, Dec. 17, 1906.

Andrew Jeptha bt. Watson, k.o. 4, Wonderland, London, Mar. 25, 1907.

Joe White bt. Jeptha, pts. 15, Merthyr, Aug. 8, 1907. White was not recognised by the N.S.C.

Curley Watson bt. Jeptha, pts. 15, N.S.C., London, Nov. 18, 1907. White next defeated Watson at Liverpool but was still not recognised by the N.S.C.

Jack Goldswain bt. Watson, pts. 6, Wonderland, London, May 22, 1909.

Curley Watson bt. Goldswain, rtd. 6, Wonderland, London, June 11, 1909. Watson died 1909.

Young Joseph bt. Jack Goldswain, disq. 11, N.S.C., London, Mar. 21, 1910.

Arthur Evernden bt. Joseph, disq. 3, London, Jan. 23, 1911.

Johnny Summers bt. Evernden, r.s.f. 13, N.S.C., London, June 17, 1912.

Johnny Basham bt. Summers, k.o. 9, N.S.C., London, Dec. 14, 1914.

Ted "Kid" Lewis bt. Basham, k.o. 9, London, June 9, 1920.

Tommy Milligan bt. Lewis, pts. 20, Edinburgh, Nov. 26, 1924. Milligan relinquished title 1925.

Hamilton Johnny Brown bt. Harry Mason, pts. 20, Albert Hall, London, Oct. 8, 1925.

Harry Mason bt. Brown, pts. 20, Albert Hall, London, Nov. 19, 1925.

Jack Hood bt. Mason, pts. 20 Holland Park, London, May 31, 1926. Hood relinquished title 1934.

Harry Mason bt. Len Smith, disq. 14, Birmingham, June 11, 1934.

Pat Butler bt. Mason, pts. 15, Leicester, Dec. 17, 1934. Butler relinquished title 1935.

Dave McCleave bt. Chuck Parker, pts. 15, Earl's Court, London, Apl. 23, 1936.

Jake Kilrain bt. McCleave, k.o. 8, Glasgow, June 2, 1936.

Ernie Roderick bt. Kilrain, k.o. 7, Liverpool, Mar. 23, 1939.

Henry Hall bt. Roderick, pts. 15, Harringay, London, Nov. 8, 1948.

Eddie Thomas bt. Hall, pts. 15,

Harringay, London, Nov. 14, 1949.
Wally Thom bt. Thomas, pts. 15, Harringay, London, Oct. 16, 1951.
Cliff Curvis bt. Thom, k.o. 9, Liverpool, July 24, 1952. Curvis retired 1953.
Wally Thom bt. Peter Fallon, pts. 15, Liverpool, Sept. 24, 1953.
Peter Waterman bt. Thom, rtd. 5, Harringay, London, June 5, 1956. Waterman relinquished title 1958.
Tommy Molloy bt. Jimmy Newman pts. 15, Streatham, London, July 15, 1958.
Wally Swift bt. Molloy, pts. 15, Nottingham, Feb. 1, 1960.
Brian Curvis bt. Swift, pts. 15, Nottingham, Nov. 21, 1960.
Curvis relinquished title.
Johnny Cooke bt. Brian McCaffrey pts. 15, Manchester, Feb. 13, 1967.
Ralph Charles bt. Cooke, pts. 15, London Feb. 20, 1968.
Charles relinquished title.
Bobby Arthur bt. John Stracey, disq. 7, London, Oct. 31, 1972.
John Stracey bt. Arthur, k.o. 4, London, June 5, 1973.
Stracey relinquished title in 1975.
Pat Thomas bt. Pat McCormack, k.o. 13, London, Dec. 15, 1975.
Henry Rhiney bt. Thomas, r.s.f. 8, Luton, Dec. 7, 1976.
Kirkland Laing bt. Rhiney, r.s.f. 10, Birmingham, Apl. 4, 1979.
Colin Jones bt. Laing, r.s.f. 9, Wembley, London, Apl. 1, 1980.
Jones relinquished title Dec. 1982.
Lloyd Honeyghan bt. Cliff Gilpin, pts. 12, Albert Hall, London, Apl. 5, 1983.
Honeyghan relinquished title 1985.
Kostas Petrou bt. Rocky Kelly, r.s.f. 9, Darlington, Apl. 13, 1985.
Sylvester Mittee bt. Petrou, pts. 12, Alexandra Pavilion, London, Nov. 27, 1985.
Lloyd Honeyghan bt. Mittee, r.s.f. 7, Alexandra Pavilion, London, Nov. 27, 1985.
Honeyghan relinquished title 1986.
Kirkland Laing bt. Mittee, r.s.f. 5, Southwark, London, Mar. 14, 1987.

*Light-welterweight*
Des Rea bt. Vic Andreetti, pts. 15, London, Feb. 27, 1968.

Vic Andreetti bt. Rea, pts. 15, Nottingham, Feb. 17, 1969.
Andreetti retired March 1970.
Division abolished in 1970 but reestablished in 1973 although the title "Light" is now preferred to "Junior".
Des Morrison bt. Joe Tetteh, pts. 15, London, Nov. 27, 1973.
Pat McCormack bt. Morrison, k.o. 11, London, Mar. 26, 1974.
Joey Singleton bt. McCormack, pts. 15, Liverpool, Nov. 21, 1974.
Dave Green bt. Singleton, r.s.f. 6, London, June 1, 1976.
Green relinquished title 1977.
Colin Power bt. Des Morrison, r.s.f. 10, London, Oct. 19, 1977.
Power relinquished title June 1978.
Clinton McKenzie bt. Jim Montague, r.s.f. 10, Belfast, Oct, 11, 1978.
Colin Power bt. McKenzie, pts. 15, Wembley, London, Feb. 6, 1979.
Clinton McKenzie bt. Power, pts. 15, Wembley, London, Sept. 11, 1979.
Terry Marsh bt. McKenzie, pts. 12, Britannic L.C., London, Sept. 19, 1984.
Marsh relinquished title 1986.
Tony Laing bt. McKenzie, pts. 12, Albert Hall, London, May 7, 1986.
Laing relinquished title 1986.
Tony McKenzie bt. Clinton McKenzie, r.s.f. 3, Hemel Hempstead, Sept. 20, 1986.
Lloyd Christie bt. Clinton McKenzie, r.s.f. 3, Croydon, Jan. 28, 1987.

*Lightweight*
Dick Burge bt. Jem Carney, disq. 11, London, May 25, 1891.
Tom Causer bt. Burge, disq. 7, London, May 31, 1897.
Dick Burge bt. Causer, k.o. 1, London, Oct. 8, 1897. Burge became overweight.
Jabez White bt. Harry Greenfield, k.o. 8, N.S.C, London, Nov. 20. 1899.
†Jack Goldswain claimed title after beating White at 10 stone, pts. 20, N.S.C., London, Apl, 23, 1906.
Young Joseph bt. Goldswain, pts. 20, Wonderland, London, June 20, 1908. Not recognised by N.S.C.
Johnny Summers bt. Goldswain, r.s.f. 14, N.S.C., London, Nov. 23, 1908.
Freddie Welsh bt. Summers, pts. 20, N.S.C., London, Nov. 8, 1909.
Matt Wells bt. Welsh, pts. 20, N.S.C.,

London, Feb. 27, 1911.
Freddie Welsh bt. Wells, pts. 20, N.S.C., London, Nov. 11, 1912. Welsh relinquished title 1917.
Bob Marriott bt. Johnny Summers, disq. 10, N.S.C., London, June 23, 1919. Marriott relinquished title 1920.
Ernie Rice bt. Ben Callicott, k.o. 7, N.S.C., London, Apl. 11, 1921.
Seaman Hall bt. Rice, pts. 20, Liverpool, Sept. 18, 1922.
Harry Mason bt. Hall, disq. 13, Olympia, London, May 17, 1923. Mason went to America and was deprived of title by N.S.C.
Ernie Izzard bt. Jack Kirk, pts. 20, N.S.C., London, Nov. 24, 1924.
Harry Mason bt. Izzard, r.s.f. 9, Holland Park, London, June 22, 1925. Mason relinquished title 1926.
Sam Steward bt. Ernie Rice, k.o. 12, London, Sept. 17, 1928.
Fred Webster bt. Steward, pts. 15, London, May 2, 1929.
Al Foreman bt. Webster, k.o. 1, Premierland, London, May 21, 1930. Foreman deprived of title by B.B.B.C. March, 1932.
Johnny Cuthbert bt. Jim Hunter, r.s.f. 10, Glasgow, Aug. 11, 1932.
Harry Mizler bt. Cuthbert, pts. 15, London, Jan. 18, 1934.
Jack "Kid" Berg bt. Mizler, rtd. 10, Albert Hall, London, Oct. 29, 1934.
Jimmy Walsh bt. Berg, r.s.f. 9, Liverpool, Apl. 24, 1936.
Dave Crowley bt. Walsh, pts. 15, Liverpool, June 23, 1938.
Eric Boon bt. Crowley, k.o. 13, Harringay, London, Dec. 15, 1938.
Ronnie James bt. Boon, k.o. 10, Cardiff, Aug. 12, 1944. James forfeited title June, 1947—overweight.
Billy Thompson bt. Hawthorne, r.s.f. 3, Liverpool, Oct. 16, 1947.
Tommy McGovern bt. Thompson, k.o. 1, Wandsworth, London, Aug. 28, 1951.
Frank Johnson bt. McGovern, pts. 15, Manchester, July 25, 1952. Johnson forfeited title June, 1953—overweight.
Joe Lucy bt. McGovern, pts. 15, Earl's Court, London, Sept. 29, 1953.
Frank Johnson bt. Lucy, pts. 15, Harringay, London, Apl. 26, 1955.
Joe Lucy bt. Johnson, r.s.f. 8,

Manchester, Apl. 13, 1956.
Dave Charnley bt. Lucy, pts. 15, Harringay, London, Apl. 9, 1957.
Charnley retired January 1965.
Maurice Cullen bt. Dave Coventry, pts. 15, Liverpool, Apl. 8, 1965.
Ken Buchanan bt. Cullen, k.o. 11, London, Feb. 19, 1968.
Buchanan relinquished title.
Willie Reilly bt. Jim Watt, r.s.f. 10, Nottingham, Feb. 1, 1972.
Reilly stripped of title by B.B.B.C.
Jim Watt bt. Tony Riley, r.s.f. 12, Solihull, May 3, 1972.
Ken Buchanan bt. Watt, pts. 15, Glasgow, Jan. 29, 1973.
Buchanan relinquished title Sept., 1974.
Jim Watt bt. Johnny Cheshire, r.s.f. 7, Glasgow, Jan. 27, 1975.
Watt relinquished title 1977.
Charlie Nash bt. Johnny Claydon, t.k.o. 12, Derry, Feb. 28, 1978.
Nash relinquished title July 1979.
Ray Cattouse bt. Dave McCabe, r.s.f. 8, Glasgow, Mar. 24, 1980.
George Feeney bt. Cattouse, r.s.f. 14, Albert Hall, London, Oct. 12, 1982.
Feeney relinquished title 1984.
Tony Willis bt. Ian McLeod, pts. 12, Digbeth, May 16, 1985.


†There is some confusion in the division of the different weight classes at this time, and although this was billed as for the lightweight championship it is generally agreed that the limit in 1906 was either 9st. 7 or 8lbs. (133-134lbs.).

White refused to relinquish his title, having been defeated at 10st. (140lbs.) but an acknowledged contemporary authority, the Editor of the *Mirror of Life*, declared that Goldswain was the proper lightweight champion. Goldswain strengthened his claim by beating another man who considered himself to be lightweight champion about the same time, Pat Daly, Goldswain k.o.'d Daly in five rounds, N.S.C., London, February 11, 1907.


*Junior Lightweight*
Jimmy Anderson bt. Jimmy Revie, r.s.f. 9, Albert Hall, London, Feb. 20, 1968.

Division abolished 1970 but revived 1986.

John Doherty bt. Pat Doherty, pts. 12, Preston, Jan. 16, 1986.

Pat Cowdell bt. Doherty, r.s.f. 6, Bradford, Apl. 17, 1986.

Najib Daho bt. Cowdell, k.o. 1, Manchester, May 24, 1986.

Pat Cowdell bt. Daho, r.s.f. 9, Birmingham, Oct 26, 1987.

*Featherweight*

Fred Johnson bt. Charlie Beadling, k.o. 4, Newcastle, Apl. 29, 1895.

Harry Greenfield bt. Johnson, k.o. 13, London, Jan. 11, 1897. Greenfield was not acknowledged by the N.S.C.

Ben Jordan bt. Fred Johnson, k.o. 13, N.S.C., London, Feb. 22, 1897.

Ben Jordan bt. Greenfield, k.o. 9, N.S.C., London, May 29, 1899. Jordan relinquished title 1905.

Joe Bowker bt. Pedlar Palmer, r.s.f. 12, N.S.C., London, Mar. 20, 1905.

The above match was made at 8st. 12lbs. (124lbs.) and declared to be for the championship, but the N.S.C. later confused the issue by making the following fight at 9st. (126lbs.) and announcing this as a title fight:

Johnny Summers bt. Spike Robson, pts. 15, N.S.C., London, Jan. 29, 1906.

Subsequently:—

Spike Robson bt. Summers, disq. 4, N.S.C., London, Dec. 17, 1906.

Jim Driscoll bt. Bowker, k.o. 17, N.S.C., London, June 1, 1907. Driscoll beat the other claimant, Spike Robson, in April, 1910, and again in January, 1911. Driscoll retired February, 1913.

Ted "Kid" Lewis bt. Alec Lambert, r.s.f. 17, N.S.C., London, Oct. 6, 1913. Lewis relinquished title 1914—overweight.

Llew Edwards bt. Owen Moran, disq. 10, N.S.C., London, May 31, 1915. Edwards relinquished title 1916.

Charlie Hardcastle bt. Alf Wye, k.o. 1, N.S.C., London, June 4, 1917.

Tancy Lee bt. Hardcastle, k.o. 4, N.S.C., London, Nov. 5, 1917. Lee relinquished title 1919.

Mike Honeyman bt. Bill Marchant, pts. 20, N.S.C., London, Jan. 26, 1920.

Joe Fox bt. Honeyman, pts. 20, N.S.C., London, Oct. 31, 1921. Fox relinquished title 1923.

George McKenzie bt. Harry Leach, pts. 20, Holland Park, London, June 2, 1924.

Johnny Curley bt. McKenzie, pts. 20, N.S.C., London, Mar. 30, 1925.

Johnny Cuthbert bt. Curley, pts. 20, N.S.C., London, Jan. 24, 1927.

Harry Corbett bt. Cuthbert, pts. 20, N.S.C., London, Mar. 12, 1928.

Johnny Cuthbert bt. Corbett, pts. 15, N.S.C., London, May 16, 1929.

Nel Tarleton bt. Cuthbert, pts. 15, Liverpool, Oct. 1, 1931.

Seaman Watson bt. Tarleton, pts. 15, Liverpool, Nov. 10, 1932.

Nel Tarleton bt. Watson, pts. 15, Liverpool, July 26, 1934.

Johnny McGrory bt. Tarleton, pts. 15, Liverpool, Sept. 24, 1936. McGrory forfeited title 1938—overweight.

"Spider" Jim Kelly bt. Benny Caplan, pts. 15, Belfast, Nov. 23, 1938.

Johnny Cusick bt. Kelly, r.s.f. 12, Belfast, June 28, 1939.

Nel Tarleton bt. Cusick, pts. 15, Liverpool, Feb. 1, 1940. Tarleton relinquished title February, 1947.

Ronnie Clayton bt. Al Phillips pts. 15, Liverpool, Sept. 11, 1947.

Sammy McCarthy bt. Clayton, rtd. 8, White City, London, June 1, 1954.

"Spider" Billy Kelly bt. McCarthy, pts. 15, Belfast, Jan. 22, 1955.

Charlie Hill bt. Kelly, pts. 15, Belfast, Feb. 4, 1956.

Bobby Neill bt. Hill, r.s.f. 9, Nottingham, Apl. 13, 1959.

Terry Spinks bt. Neill, r.s.f. 7, Albert Hall, London, Sept. 27, 1960.

Howard Winstone bt. Spinks, rtd. 10, London, May 2, 1961.

Winstone relinquished title Feb. 1969.

Jimmy Revie bt. O'Brien, r.s.f. 5, W.S.C., London, Mar. 24, 1969.

Evan Armstrong bt. Revie, k.o. 12, London, July 5, 1971.

Tommy Glencross bt. Armstrong, pts. 15, London, Sept. 25, 1972.

Evan Armstrong bt. Glencross, r.s.f. 3, Glasgow, Sept. 17, 1973.

Armstrong retired Feb. 1975.

Vernon Sollas bt. Jimmy Revie, k.o. 4, London, Mar. 25, 1975.

Alan Richardson bt. Sollas r.s.f. 8, Leeds, Mar. 15, 1977.

Dave Needham bt. Richardson, pts. 15, London, Apl. 20, 1978.

Pat Cowdell bt. Needham, pts. 15, Albert Hall, London, Nov. 6, 1979.

Cowdell relinquished title Apl. 1982.

Steve Sammy Sims bt. Terry McKeown, k.o. 12, Glasgow, Sept. 20, 1982.

Sims relinquished title Jan. 1983.

Barry McGuigan bt. Vernon Penprase, r.s.f. 2, Belfast, Apl. 12, 1983.

McGuigan relinquished title 1985.

Robert Dickie bt. John Feeney, pts. 12, Albert Hall, London, Apl. 9, 1986.

*Bantamweight*

Billy Plimmer bt. Jem Stevens, rtd. 15, N.S.C., London, April 2, 1891.

Pedlar Palmer bt. Plimmer, disq. 14, N.S.C., London, Nov. 25, 1895.

Harry Ware bt. Palmer, pts. 20, N.S.C., London, Nov. 12, 1900.

Joe Bowker bt. Ware, pts. 15, N.S.C., London, Dec. 15, 1902. Not always recognised as an official title fight.

Joe Bowker bt. Owen Moran, pts. 20, N.S.C., London, May 30, 1904. Bowker can be accepted as champion from this date, for Owen Moran had beaten another title-claimant, Andrew Tokell, who had in turn also beaten Harry Ware.

Digger Stanley bt. Bowker, k.o. 8, N.S.C., London, Oct. 17, 1910.

Bill Beynon bt. Stanley, pts. 20, N.S.C., London, June 2, 1913.

Digger Stanley bt. Beynon, pts. 20, N.S.C., London, Oct. 27, 1913.

Curley Walker bt. Stanley, disq. 13, N.S.C., London, Apl. 20, 1914. Walker relinquished title 1915.

Joe Fox bt. Jimmy Berry, r.s.f. 16, N.S.C., London, Nov. 22, 1915. Fox relinquished title 1918.

Tommy Noble bt. Joe Symonds, pts. 20, N.S.C. London, Nov. 25, 1918.

Walter Ross bt. Noble, r.s.f. 10, N.S.C., London, June 30, 1919. Ross relinquished title 1919.

Jimmy Higgins bt. Harold Jones, r.s.f. 13, N.S.C., London, Feb. 23, 1920.

Tommy Harrison bt. Higgins, k.o. 13, Liverpool, June 26, 1922.

Harry Lake bt. Harrison, pts. 20, N.S.C., London, Feb. 26, 1923.

Johnny Brown (St. George's) bt. Lake, pts. 20, N.S.C., London, Nov. 26, 1923. Brown relinquished title 1927

following defeat by Kid Pattenden in non-title fight.

Kid Pattenden bt. Kid Nicholson, k.o. 12, N.S.C., London, June 4, 1928.

Teddy Baldock bt. Pattenden, pts. 15, Olympia, London, May 16, 1929. Baldock relinquished title 1931—overweight.

Dick Corbett bt. Johnny King, pts. 15, Manchester, Dec. 21, 1931.

Johnny King bt. Corbett, pts. 15, Manchester, Oct. 10, 1932.

Dick Corbett bt. King, pts. 15, Manchester, Feb. 12, 1934. Corbett relinquished title 1934—overweight.

Johnny King bt. Len Hampston, pts. 15, Manchester, May 27, 1935.

Jackie Paterson bt. King, k.o. 7, Manchester, Feb. 10, 1947.

Stan Rowan bt. Paterson, pts. 15, Liverpool, Mar. 24, 1949. Rowan relinquished title Nov. 1949—overweight.

Danny O'Sullivan bt. Teddy Gardner, rtd. 9, Albert Hall, London, Dec. 13, 1949.

Peter Keenan bt. O'Sullivan, k.o. 6, Glasgow, May 9, 1951.

John Kelly bt. Keenan, pts. 15, Belfast, Oct. 3, 1953.

Peter Keenan bt. Kelly, k.o. 6, Paisley, Sept, 21, 1954.

Freddie Gilroy bt. Keenan, r.s.f. 11, Belfast, Jan. 10, 1959. Gilroy relinquished title Nov., 1963.

Johnny Caldwell bt. George Bowes, r.s.f. 7, Belfast, Mar. 5, 1964.

Alan Rudkin bt. Caldwell, r.s.f. 10, Nottingham, Mar. 22, 1965.

Walter McGowan bt. Rudkin pts. 15, Wembley, London, Sept. 6, 1966.

Alan Rudkin bt. McGowan, pts. 15, Manchester, May 13, 1968.

Rudkin relinquished title.

Johnny Clark bt. Paddy Maguire, pts. 15, London, Feb. 20, 1973.

Clark relinquished title.

Dave Needham bt. Paddy Maguire, pts. 15, Nottingham, Dec. 10, 1974.

Paddy Maguire bt. Needham r.s.f. 14, London, Oct. 20, 1975.

Johnny Owen bt. Maguire, r.s.f. 11, London, Nov. 29. 1977.

Owen died Nov. 1980.

John Feeney bt. Dave Smith, r.s.f. 8, London, Sept. 22, 1981.

Hugh Russell bt. Feeney, disq. 13,

Belfast, Jan. 25, 1983.
Davy Larmour bt. Russell, pts. 12, Belfast, Mar. 2, 1983.
John Feeney bt. Larmour, r.s.f. 3, Belfast, Nov. 16, 1983.
Ray Gilbody bt. Feeney, pts. 12, Hartlepool, June 13, 1985.
Billy Hardy bt. Gilbody, r.s.f. 3, St. Helens, Feb. 19, 1987.

*Flyweight*
*Sid Smith bt. Joe Wilson, pts. 20, N.S.C., London, Dec. 4, 1911. Smith relinquished title following defeat by Bill Ladbury, k.o. 11, Blackfriars, London, June 2, 1913. This was at catchweights.
Percy Jones bt. Ladbury, pts. 20, N.S.C., London, Jan. 26, 1914.
Joe Symonds bt. Jones, k.o. 18, Plymouth, Apl. 15, 1914. Symonds was not officially recognised because Jones was overweight in this match. Jones, however, forfeited his title.
Jimmy Wilde bt. Symonds, pts. 15, N.S.C., London, Nov. 16, 1914. This was a non-title fight.
Tancy Lee bt. Wilde, r.s.f. 17, N.S.C., London, Jan. 25, 1915.
Joe Symonds bt. Lee, rtd. 16, N.S.C., London, Oct. 18, 1915.
Jimmy Wilde bt. Symonds, r.s.f. 12, N.S.C., London, Feb. 14, 1916. Wilde relinquished title 1923.
Elky Clark bt. Kid Kelly, r.s.f. 19, N.S.C., London, Mar. 31, 1924. Clark relinquished title 1927.
Johnny Hill bt. Alf Barber, r.s.f. 14, N.S.C., London, May 23, 1927. Hill died Sept., 1929.
Jackie Brown bt. Bert Kirby, k.o. 3, West Bromwich, Oct. 13, 1929.
Bert Kirby bt. Brown, k.o. 3, Holborn, London, Mar. 3, 1930.
Jackie Brown bt. Kirby, pts. 15, Manchester, Feb. 2, 1931.
Benny Lynch bt. Brown, r.s.f. 2, Manchester, Sept. 9, 1935. Lynch relinquished title 1938—overweight.
Jackie Paterson bt. Paddy Ryan, k.o. 13, Glasgow, Sept. 30, 1939.
Rinty Monaghan bt. Paterson, k.o. 7, Belfast, Mar. 23, 1948. Monaghan retired 1952.
Terry Allen bt. Eric Marsden, r.s.f. 6, Harringay, London, Oct. 21, 1952. Allen retired 1954.

Dai Dower bt. Eric Marsden, pts. 15, Harringay, London, Feb. 8, 1955. Dower relinquished title 1957.
Frankie Jones bt. Len Reece, k.o. 11, Porthcawl, July 31, 1957.
Johnny Caldwell bt. Jones, k.o. 3, Belfast, Oct. 8, 1960. Caldwell relinquished title 1961.
Jackie Brown bt. Brian Cartwright, pts. 15, Birmingham Feb. 27, 1962.
Walter McGowan bt. Brown, k.o. 12, Paisley, May 2, 1963. McGowan relinquished title 1966.
Johnny McCluskey bt. Tony Barlow, k.o. 8, Manchester, Jan. 16, 1967. McCluskey retired Sept. 1977.
Charlie Magri bt. Dave Smith, r.s.f. 7, London, Dec. 6, 1977. Magri relinquished title Aug. 1981.
Kelvin Smart bt. Dave George, k.o. 6, Wembley, London, Sept. 14, 1982.
Hugh Russell bt. Smart, rtd. 7, Belfast, Jan. 25, 1984. Russell relinquished title Apl. 1985.
Duke McKenzie bt. Danny Flynn, r.s.f. 4, Albert Hall, London, June 5, 1985. McKenzie relinquished title Aug. 1986.
Dave McAuley bt. Joe Kelly, r.s.f. 9, Glasgow, Oct. 20, 1986.

*The flyweight division was not established until 1909. Before that men under 8st. 4lbs. (116lbs.) were usually recognised as bantamweights.

Sid Smith was the first man to win a Lonsdale Belt contest in the flyweight division.
See WORLD CHAMPIONS (Prize Ring) for the earliest British bare-knuckle champions.

## BRITTON, Jack:

This busy Irish-American fighter had a remarkable career which extended over 26 years. He started as a lightweight in 1904 and did not retire until 1930 when he was in his 45th year. Then he became a boxing instructor.

Britton was recognised as a clever counter-puncher and within four years of the start of his professional career he had fought his way into the front rank of American welterweights.

At that time the championship of the

welterweight division was hotly disputed and no one had a clear-cut claim to the title. Britton was one of those who staked a claim for the championship and in June, 1915, he outpointed another claimant, Mike Glover. However, later in the same year he was twice beaten in Boston by Ted "Kid" Lewis.

Britton and Lewis became two of the keenest rivals in ring history. First Britton took the title from Lewis in April, 1916, then Lewis won it back in June, 1917, only for Britton to regain it in March, 1919. Altogether these two fought each other on at least 20 different occasions.

Britton retained his title until November, 1921, when he was beaten by Mickey Walker.

# BROADCASTING:

See also TELEVISION:

Radio was first used to broadcast the result of a fight in 1919, when on July 4, Jack Dempsey beat Jess Willard in three rounds at Toledo, Ohio.

The first boxing commentary was broadcast from Boyle's Thirty Acres, Jersey City, July 2, 1921. It commenced in the closing round of an eight-round "No Decision" bantamweight bout between Packey O'Gatty and Frankie Burns, and continued through the main event which was Jack Dempsey's world title defence against Georges Carpentier.

The first broadcast to be made of any part of a boxing contest in Great Britain was on March 29, 1926, when Johnny Curley met Harry Corbett at the N.S.C., London.

The first complete running commentary to be broadcast in Great Britain was of a contest between Teddy Baldock and Willie Smith, at the Royal Albert Hall London, October 6, 1927.

# BROOME, Harry:

Born at Birmingham in 1826, Broome was one of the lesser lights among this country's earliest bareknuckle champions.

He claimed the title after beating Willie Perry (The Tipton Slasher) on a foul in 15 rounds at Mildenhall, Suffolk, September 29, 1851.

When Perry challenged Broome to a return contest four months later, the Birmingham man did not accept and so forfeited the title.

In October, 1856, he met Tom Paddock in a bid to regain the championship but was beaten in 51 rounds, Bentley, Suffolk.

Broome, who started fighting when he was only 16, died at the age of 39.

# BROTHERS:

See under FAMILIES.

# BROUGHTON, Jack:

Known as the "Father of boxing" Jack Broughton was probably the greatest bare-knuckle prize fighter in history.

Born in Gloucestershire, Broughton was discovered by James Figg and encouraged to come to London and try his luck in the ring.

Broughton's name has gone down indelibly in the history of the ring not only for his prowess as a fighter but because he invented boxing gloves (then known as "mufflers") and because it was he who wrote the first code of rules governing boxing.

Broughton's Rules were drawn up in 1743 and were recognised until being superseded by the London Prize Ring Rules in 1838. See elsewhere in this volume under RULES.

It was said that Broughton was moved to produce these rules following the death of George Stevenson a month after being badly beaten by Broughton in April, 1741.

Jack Broughton became Champion of England when he defeated George Taylor in 20 minutes, at Tottenham Court Road, London. Authorities differ as to the date of this contest but it was probably in 1734 or a little later.

It would appear that Broughton was champion for so long that he became a little too sure of himself. When he met Jack Slack in April, 1750, he had been backed by his patron, the Duke of Cumberland, with a bet of £10,000 but Broughton was under-trained and was beaten by the younger man in only 14 minutes.

The Duke of Cumberland did everything in his power to ruin Broughton after this defeat, but the Gloucester man survived his patron's wrath to die a rich land-owner at the ripe old age of 85.

## BROUILLARD, Lou:

A southpaw, this French-Canadian won the world welterweight title from Young Jack Thompson on points over 15 rounds in Boston, October 23, 1931.

Bouillard lost this championship title to Jackie Fields in January, 1932, but twenty months later he was recognised by N.Y.A.C. as world middleweight champion following his seventh round k.o. victory over Ben Jeby.

In October, 1933, Brouillard lost his middleweight title when outpointed by Vince Dundee.

A tough body puncher, Brouillard beat Bob Olin in April, 1934, which was only seven months before that fighter became world light-heavyweight champion.

Around this time Marcel Thil had the strongest claim to recognition as world middleweight champion and Brouillard met the Frenchman on three occasions.

The first time, in November, 1935, Brouillard was outpointed over 12 rounds, but on the second and third occasions he was disqualified, in the fourth and sixth rounds respectively.

## BROWN, "Panama" Al:

Panamanian negro who was well known on this side of the Atlantic during the 1930's for he had several contests in London, Paris, and other European cities.

A very fine boxer, Brown had the advantage of height and reach over the majority of his opponents, for although nearly six foot tall he was only a bantamweight.

He won the vacant world bantamweight title by outpointing Vidal Gregorio in New York, June 18, 1929, although, at that time, he was not accorded world-wide recognition. However, he proved his right to the title when he came to Europe and beat the leading bantams and feathers including Knud Larsen, the Dane, and Eugene Huat of France.

In this country in 1931 Brown beat Willie Farrell, Jack Garland and Teddy

Baldock, but lost on a foul to the British featherweight champion, Johnny Cuthbert.

He came to England again in 1932 and 1933, drawing with Nel Tarleton, and beating Dick Burke, Johnny Peters, Tommy Hyman, Art Boddington, Dave Crowley and Johnny King.

The Americans deprived Brown of his world title in 1934 while he was on this side of the Atlantic, but it was not until June 1935 that he lost his championship in the ring. Then he was outpointed by Baltazar Sangchilli.

He was still fighting top-line men at the age of 41 when he met Chalky Wright and Mike Belloise in 1944.

## BROWN, Jackie (Manchester):

The flyweight division is renowned for speedy men and Jackie Brown of Manchester was one of the most agile of them all.

He won the vacant British flyweight title when he knocked out Bert Kirby in three rounds at West Bromwich in October, 1929; lost it in a return match by another third round k.o. five months later but regained it in another meeting with the Birmingham boxer in February, 1931. On that occasion Brown won on points.

In May, 1931, Brown outpointed Lucien Popesco for the European title but his greatest honour was yet to come.

On October 31, 1932, he met the world champion, Young Perez, at Belle Vue, Manchester, and in one of the fastest and most thrilling contests ever seen at that arena, Brown gained the crown when the towel came fluttering in from the Tunisian's corner in the thirteenth round.

Brown lost his titles to Benny Lynch in the same arena on September 9, 1935. The referee stopping the contest in the second round.

## BROWN, Jackie (Edinburgh):

This hard-hitting flyweight was an A.B.A. and Empire Games champion before turning professional and going on to win the British and Empire titles.

When these titles became vacant Brown was matched with Brian Cartwright in February, 1962. He had previously outpointed the Birmingham boy and he repeated this victory in their second meeting, although, of course, this was over the full title fight distance of 15 rounds.

Jackie Brown annexed the vacant Empire title with a victory over Orizu Obilaso in December, 1962, but when he met fellow Scot, Walter McGowan, in May, 1963, he was knocked out in the 12th round.

## BROWN, Joe:

An American negro from New Orleans, Joe Brown had passed his 30th birthday before he won the World lightweight title from Wallace Bud Smith in August, 1956.

Brown had beaten Smith quite easily in a non-title fight three months earlier, and when they met for the championship in Brown's home-town, the 30-year-old negro was able to gain another convincing victory over 15 rounds.

When these two met for a third time, in February, 1957, Brown outpunched Smith and the fight was stopped after the end of the tenth round.

Brown lost his title when outpointed by Carlos Ortiz in April, 1962, and was subsequently k.o.'d in 6 rounds by British champion, Dave Charnley.

## BROWN, Johnny (St. Georges):

Took the British and Empire bantamweight titles from Harry Lake with a 20-round points victory at the N.S.C., London, November 26, 1923.

Brown also claimed the European title with this victory but he was not generally recognised on the continent.

Brown successfully defended his British title against Harry Corbett and Mick Hill to make the Lonsdale Belt his own property, but after losing to Kid Pattenden in a non-title fight, he gave up his claim to the crown.

In August, 1928, Brown was also beaten by another title claimant, Teddy Baldock. The referee stopped this fight in the second round.

## BROWN, Johnny (Hamilton):

A Scotsman who first came to the fore as a lightweight but he failed to lift the British title when he met the champion

Seaman James Hall, in January, 1923.

Four months later Brown became Scottish welterweight champion but he lost this title to Tommy Milligan in September, 1924.

In a bid for the British welterweight title in July, 1924, Brown went 20 rounds with Ted "Kid" Lewis but lost on points.

Brown was more successful in his second effort to win the British welterweight championship, for in October, 1925, he decisioned the new champion, Harry Mason.

His glory was shortlived, however, for only 42 days later he was beaten in a return match with Mason.

## BRUNO, Frank:

Although, up to the present time, this London heavyweight has never won a British title he is included here because of the amount of interest, and, indeed, controversy, he has created since turning professional in 1982 after winning the A.B.A. heavyweight championship two years earlier. He is, of course, Britain's top heavyweight, having captured the European title with a convincing fourth round k.o. of giant Swede Anders Eklund in October 1985. Prior to this Bruno had lost only one of his 26 professional fights, being k.o.'d by James Bonecrusher Smith in the 10th round after leading the American on points. After two more quick wins, including a first round k.o. of world-ranked Gerrie Coetzee, Bruno's ambitions were again dented when he was k.o.'d by another top-class American, Tim Witherspoon in July 1986. At the time of writing we are left with the question as to whether Bruno will follow in the tradition of his British heavyweight predecessors in not being quite world class. He needs greater mobility.

## BUCHANAN, Ken:

One of Britain's classiest boxers, this ex-carpenter from Edinburgh, who punched with bewildering speed and had a terrific left-hook was A.B.A. featherweight champion before turning professional in 1965.

After winning his first 23 fights Buchanan defeated the British lightweight champion Maurice Cullen in 11 rounds, putting the champion down five times before applying the finisher.

Buchanan suffered a slight set-back when he suffered his first defeat in his 34th fight—being outpointed by Miguel Velasquez in a bid for the vacant European title, but he went on to win the world lightweight title in September 1970 by outpointing Ismael Laguna in one of his finest exhibitions of boxing.

With Laguna under suspension this victory did not bring the brilliant Scotsman world-wide recognition, but that came in February 1971 when he beat the Mexican, Ruben Navarro, on points in Los Angeles.

The stylish Buchanan successfully defended his title against Ismael Laguna, but lost it in New York in June 1972 in a controversial ending to his fight with Roberto Duran, the referee stopping the contest in the Panamanian fighter's favour as the buzzer sounded before the start of the 14th round.

Buchanan came home to re-capture the British lightweight title from fellow Scot, Jim Watt, in January 1973, and in the following year he took the European title by battering Antonio Puddu for five rounds before knocking him out in the sixth.

After a dispute with the B.B.B.C. he relinquished his British title in September 1974 and retired undefeated European champion the following year.

Buchanan returned to the ring in 1979 but failed to lift the European lightweight title from Charlie Nash in December that year. He then rounded off his career with a brief spell as a lightwelter.

## BUFF, Johnny:

Born in the United States of Polish extraction, Johnny Buff (real name Lesky) started boxing while serving in the U.S. Navy in World War I and won the American flyweight title in 1921.

In September, 1921, he took the world bantamweight title from Pete Herman with a 15-round points win, but in a return fight in July, 1922, Buff was stopped in 14 rounds.

Buff could still make the flyweight limit and in September, 1922, he was matched with Pancho Villa for the American version of the world 8 stone championship but was halted in 11 rounds.

At that time Johnny Buff was 34 years of age. At 33 he had been the oldest man ever to win the world bantamweight title.

## BUGNER, Joe:

Despite winning the British and Commonwealth heavyweight titles twice and the European crown three times this Hungarian-born fighter, who was brought up in England from the age of seven, had to endure a lot of criticism from the fans and was something of an enigma. Unfortunately his punching power seldom seemed to match his physical attributes and his tendency to be rather defensive did not endear him to all the boxing fraternity.

He first won the British, Commonwealth and European heavyweight titles only three days after his 21st birthday with a controversial points victory over veteran Henry Cooper in 1971, but before the year was out Jack Bodell highlighted Bugner's limitations in depriving the youngster of these titles.

However, with youth on his side Bugner was expected to develop into a world-beater. He enjoyed a winning streak in 1972 and gave one of his finest displays in stopping Jurgen Blin in eight rounds to recapture the European title. Although on the losing end his defeats by Muhammad Ali and Joe Frazier in 1973 earned Bugner a lot more respect, but when still not 26 years of age he retired in 1976 as undefeated European champion.

In October that year he made a comeback and again surprised his critics with one of his most belligerent displays, demolishing Richard Dunn inside one round to regain the British, Commonwealth and European titles. If only he had produced more of this style throughout his career! After only one more fight Bugner again retired undefeated champion in 1977. He made three more comebacks, most recently after emigrating to Australia and then ended his career earning over £¼m. by going eight rounds with Frank Bruno before being rescued.

## BURGE, Dick:

Acknowledged by several historians at Britain's cleverest boxer of the late 19th century, Dick Burge, who was born at Cheltenham in 1865, won the British lightweight title and also fought for the middleweight and heavyweight crowns as well as for the world lightweight championship.

It was in May, 1891 that Burge, who had acquired his skill in the boxing booths, won the British lightweight title from Jem Carney who was disqualified in the eleventh round.

While he still retained the lightweight crown, Burge met Ted Pritchard for the middleweight title in November, 1894, but was beaten by the heavier man in two rounds. Despite this defeat Burge fought for the heavyweight title twelve months later when he met Jem Smith. On that occasion he was beaten in nine rounds.

In June, 1896, Burge fought Kid Lavigne for the world lightweight title at the N.S.C., but, weakened by his efforts to make the weight, he was well beaten, the referee stopping the contest in the seventeenth round.

He lost his lightweight title to Tom Causer on a seventh round disqualification, May 31, 1897.

In 1910, Dick Burge opened the Blackfriars Ring in London's East End. He promoted regular shows there until his death during World War I when his wife succeeded him as head of that famous boxing arena.

## BURKE, "Deaf" James:

Born London, 1809, the son of a Thames Waterman, Burke had his first prize fight when he was only 18 and his last when he was 33—a lengthy career and a full one too, for he had at least 20 contests.

That number doesn't seem much today but it meant that he was one of the busiest of all our leading bare knuckle prize fighters.

Burke was the Max Baer of his day for he was something of a clown and he was often joking with his opponents during the most hectic part of a contest.

He became recognised as Champion of England following his hard fight with Simon Byrne in May, 1833. This took place near St. Albans. It lasted 3 hours 6 minutes before the Irishman was beaten and he died three days later.

Burke was tried but acquitted of a charge of having caused the death of Simon Byrne.

It is said that Burke was not in the best of condition when he met William Thompson, "Bendigo," in February, 1839, and he was beaten in ten rounds.

When "Bendigo" retired, Burke again claimed the championship but he lost it to Nick Ward on a foul when the crowd broke into the ring after 16 rounds to save Ward from further punishment. That was at Lillingstone Level, Oxfordshire, September 22, 1840.

Burke subsequently became a stage actor but he died of consumption when he was only 34.

## BURNS, Tommy:

This French-Canadian has not always been accorded the credit he deserves as an outstanding heavyweight champion. Everyone knows how he was beaten by Jack Johnson who was one of the all-time "greats" if not the greatest heavyweight, so it was no disgrace to lose to him, but so many people forget that Burns beat such men as Jim Flynn, Jack O'Brien, Bill Squires, Gunner Moir, Jack Palmer, Jem Roche, Jewey Smith and Bill Lang.

Burns was the smallest man ever to win the heavyweight title for he was only 5 feet 7 inches tall, although he had an exceptionally long reach for a man of that height.

A clever boxer and a fast mover, Burns took the title from Marvin Hart at Los Angeles, February 23, 1906.

Shortly after this he set off on a world tour which included a visit to London where he knocked out Gunner Moir at the N.S.C. and Jack Palmer at Wonderland.

Some say Burns was dodging Johnson but that wasn't true. Before he met the negro in Sydney, December 26, 1908, Burns admitted that he didn't think he could beat Johnson, "but I'll give him the fight of his life."

Burns didn't quite do that but he did put up a remarkably stout-hearted display, refusing to acknowledge defeat before the fight was stopped by the police in the fourteenth round and Johnson awarded the decision.

Unofficially Burns could be regarded as the first man to hold both the world heavyweight and light-heavyweight titles simultaneously. This would be around 1906-08. However, he never took much interest in the lighter title even though he was still regarded as light-heavyweight champion after losing the heavyweight crown in 1908. Indeed, Thomas S. Andrews continued listing him as light-heavyweight champion in his American annual as late as the 1912 issue.

Tommy Burns came to England again in 1920 and fancied his chance of staging a come-back against Joe Beckett. However, age was against him (he was 39) and he was beaten in seven rounds.

## BUTLER, Pat:

In December, 1934, Pat Butler of Leicester took the British welterweight title from Harry Mason in a close fight before his home-town crowd. Butler got the decision at the end of fifteen rounds.

Unfortunately, Butler was forced to relinquish the title without defending it a few months later because of ill health.

## BUXTON, Alex:

Born at Watford, the son of a West Indian, Alex Buxton first made a name for himself in the ring when he was serving in the Royal Marines and was stationed in Australia.

One of three boxing brothers, Alex turned professional in 1942 and subsequently had one run in which he won twelve consecutive contests inside the distance. He had one of the longest careers in recent times, continuing to fight until 1963.

Buxton was really a middleweight but it was in the light-heavy division that he won the British title. This was in October, 1953, when he defeated Dennis Powell at Nottingham, the referee stopping the contest in the tenth round.

Buxton lost his British title to Randolph Turpin, being knocked out in the second round, April, 1955, and when he was matched with Turpin for the vacant light-heavy title, following the retirement of Ron Barton in 1956, he was again beaten by the Leamington fighter, this time in five rounds.

# C

## CABLE, Jimmy:

A fighter who has never lacked courage in an up and down career, Jimmy Cable from Orpington recovered from a defeat by Jimmy Batten in 1983 to go on and win both the British light-middle and the European light-middle titles in 1984. On these occasions he beat favourites Nick Wilshire and French champion Said Skouma respectively. He failed to move into world title contention when beaten by Buster Drayton in 85 seconds and lost his British crown to Prince Rodney in another first round k.o. Cable's European title went to Georg Steinherr when the German outpointed a below form champion in September 1984. Cable subsequently moved up into the middleweight class.

## CALDERWOOD, Chic:

This ill-fated fighter who was the first Scotsman to win the British light-heavyweight title when he stopped Arthur Howard in thirteen rounds, January 1960, never lost that title in the ring. He was, however, deprived of the crown when he had to serve a prison sentence in 1963 after being charged with assault, but no-one took over in his absence and he quickly regained his crown in November 1964 by stopping Bob Nicholson in seven rounds.

He was still champion in November 1966 when he met his death in a car crash.

## CALDWELL, Johnny:

A two-fisted Belfast-born fighter who won the world bantamweight title before he became British champion at that weight.

Turning professional as a flyweight he won 17 fights in a row before capturing the British crown by stopping Frankie Jones in October, 1960.

Caldwell was only half a pound inside the limit for that fight and when, eight months later, he put on enough weight to challenge and beat the world bantamweight title-holder (European version) Alphonse Halimi, he had still not defended his flyweight crown and very soon after decided to relinquish it and concentrate on gaining undisputed recognition as world bantam champion.

However, Caldwell failed to achieve this in January, 1962, being k.o'd by America's world champion, Eder Jofre.

The Belfast southpaw then failed in his first attempt at the British bantamweight title, losing to Freddie Gilroy, but when that fighter relinquished the crown, Caldwell won it by stopping George Bowes.

Caldwell lost this title to Alan Rudkin in March, 1965, one of only five defeats in 35 professional bouts.

## CAMPI, Eddie:

An American of Irish-French parentage, Eddie Campi fought as a bantamweight and for a short time just before the first World War he claimed the world championship of that division but he was never accorded universal recognition.

It was in June, 1913, that Campi outpointed Charles Ledoux over 20 rounds at Vernon. At that time the Frenchman was recognised in Europe as the world champion but Campi did not rate a world title in America because only four months prior to this contest he had been beaten by another leading contender, the Dane, Kid Williams.

After Williams had also beaten Ledoux he again beat Campi by a k.o. in twelve rounds, January 31, 1914, and later in the same year Campi was put right out of the running when he was outpointed by Pete Herman.

Campi met his death in an accident while hunting in June 1918.

## CANADA:

Canada has produced six world champions. Their names are listed below and details of their careers can be found elsewhere in this volume, but there have been more first-class Canadian boxers who didn't quite achieve the distinction of a world title.

Outstanding among these was Larry Gains the Toronto-born Negro who was well known in Britain. A real craftsman, Gains won the Empire heavyweight title from Phil Scott in 1931 and held it until 1934 when he was beaten by Len Harvey.

Gains may not have won a world title but he beat two men who did, namely Max Schmeling and Primo Carnera, and he also fought a draw with Mike McTigue.

Another notable Canadian boxer to do well in Britain was Arthur King. In 1948 he stopped the British lightweight champion, Billy Thompson in seven rounds to win the Empire title, but he subsequently forfeited this crown when he became an American citizen.

## Champions:

WORLD:

Heavyweight—Tommy Burns, 1906-08.

Light-heavyweight—Jack Delaney, 1926-27. Donny Lalonde (W.B.C.) 1987-

Middleweight—Lou Brouillard, 1933 (N.Y.A.C. only).

Featherweight—George Dixon, 1891-97, 1898-1900; Jackie Callura, 1943 (N.B.A. only).

Bantamweight—Johnny Coulon, 1911-14.

EMPIRE AND COMMONWEALTH:

Heavyweight—Tommy Burns, 1910; Larry Gains, 1931-34.

Light-heavyweight—Gordon Wallace, 1956-57; Yvon Durelle, 1957-59. Gary Summerhays, 1978-79; Willy Featherstone, 1987-

Middleweight—Wilf Greaves, 1960. Blair Richardson, 1966-67.

Welterweight—Clyde Gray, 1973-79, 79-80; Chris Clarke, 1979.

Lightweight—Arthur King, 1948-51.

OLYMPIC:

Welterweight—T. Schneider, 1920.

Bantamweight—H. Gwynne, 1932.

## CANNON, Tom:

Known as the "Great Gun of Windsor," Tom Cannon was acknowledged as Champion of England following the retirement of Ned Painter in 1824.

Up to that time Cannon was undefeated and he clinched the championship by two victories over Josh Hudson.

Like a number of champions since his day, Cannon also made several appearances in the theatre. In 1825 he starred with another bruiser, Peter Crawley, in a drama entitled *The Fight at Warwick*.

He lost the Championship to Jem Ward in a hard battle at Stony Stratford, Warwickshire, July 19, 1825. Near the end it seemed as if a puff of wind would blow either man down but Ward just managed to summon enough strength to apply the finisher.

## CANZONERI, Tony:

One of the busiest and best American fighters between the two world wars, Tony Canzoneri fought for the world championship in three divisions and won in two of them.

Canzoneri reached his peak as a lightweight, but it was as a bantamweight that he began his career.

In 1927, Canzoneri, who had put his age on to start boxing as a professional, was matched with Bud Taylor for N.B.A.'s version of the world bantamweight title. He was not yet 19 but he earned a draw with the more experienced Taylor.

Canzoneri lost the return bout but then he moved up into the featherweight division and gained his first world title by outpointing Benny Bass, February, 1928.

This Italian-American who stood only 5 feet 4 inches and had his own peculiar style of fighting without a guard, lost the title on a points decision to Andre Routis after only seven months. He then turned lightweight.

He failed in his first effort to lift the world championship crown of this division, being outpointed by Sammy Mandell. That was in August 1929. In January, 1930, he was beaten by our own Jack "Kid" Berg in New York but by the end of 1930 he had won the world lightweight title from Al Singer with a k.o. in 66 seconds of the first round—a record for the division.

Canzoneri lost this title on points to Barney Ross in June, 1933, but when Ross relinquished the championship Canzoneri again became title-holder by outpointing Lou Ambers, May 10, 1935.

In a return bout with Ambers, Canzoneri was beaten, September 3, 1936, and when these two met for a third time in May, 1937, Ambers again got the decision.

Canzoneri retired at the end of 1939. He died at the age of 51 in December, 1959.

## CARNERA, Primo:

This giant Italian was regarded as something of a freak when he first took up boxing in 1928. He stood nearly 6 feet 6 inches in his socks and weighed around 19 stone (266lbs.) but these figures were greatly exaggerated in the ballyhoo and publicity which preceded his first appearance in London in 1929.

Carnera had worked in a marble quarry before becoming a circus wrestler and strong man, and it was in the circus that he was discovered by the French heavyweight boxer, Paul Journee.

On that first appearance in London, Carnera k.o.'d Jack Stanley in the opening round and followed this with a victory over Young Stribling on a foul in the fourth round and a sixth round win over a German, Franz Diener.

Carnera didn't make much of an impression as a boxer at that time but he was a real trier and he soon developed into quite a useful performer. A fast mover for his size he might have been a great champion but for one drawback— he had a "glass" jaw.

As is so often true with really big men, Carnera was soft-hearted. He was probably the most exploited champion of all time for he was swindled almost from start to finish of his boxing career. Fortunately, Carnera had better luck later in life as a professional wrestler, and made a small fortune at that game.

As a boxer he won the world heavyweight title by finishing Jack Sharkey with a right uppercut in the sixth round, Long Island Bowl, June 28, 1933.

Carnera successfully defended his title against Paolino Uzcudun and Tommy Loughran but lost it to Max Baer, June 14, 1934. The "Man Mountain" was floored eleven times in that contest before the referee stopped the fight in the eleventh round.

Apart from his fights in London in 1929, Carnera made four other boxing appearances in this country.

In December, 1930, he stopped Reggie Meen in two rounds. In March and April, 1932, he knocked out George Cook in four and outpointed Don McCorkindale over ten rounds.

Carnera's only defeat in this country was at the hands of the Canadian negro, Larry Gains, who got a ten round points decision over him at the White City, May 30, 1932.

## CARNEY, Jem:

Claimed the lightweight championship of England in 1886 and went to Boston, America, in November, 1887 to meet the American champion, Jack McAuliffe, in a fight for the world title.

This was one of the most gruelling contests ever fought at that weight in the United States. It lasted for 3 hours 40 minutes. Fought with driving gloves it was declared a draw when McAuliffe's friends invaded the ring as their man was getting the worst of it.

Jem Carney was a remarkable old character. One of the last of this country's leading boxers to fight without gloves, he lived long enough to be well remembered and greatly respected by many contemporary boxing personalities.

Carney, who was born in Birmingham, lost his lightweight title when he was beaten by Dick Burge, May 25, 1891. He was disqualified in the eleventh round.

## CARPENTIER, Georges:

Born Liévin, Pas de Calais, France, Carpentier is undoubtedly the most famous boxer that that country has ever produced.

Carpentier won titles at almost every weight, the first when he was still a month short of his 16th birthday. That was the French lightweight title, in December, 1909. In June, 1911, he became his country's welterweight champion and went on to win the European title when still under 18 years of age.

The handsome "Orchid Man," who was a special favourite of the ladies, had one of the fastest right hands in the business. It was also one of the most lethal, and there is little doubt that had he been a heavier man he would have won the top honour in boxing.

As it was Carpentier was never afraid to concede weight to good men but although he was the terror of British heavyweights, stopping Bombardier Billy Wells, Dick Smith, George Cook and Joe Beckett, he was out of his reach when he met Jack Dempsey for the world title. This contest which took place at Boyle's Thirty Acres, Jersey City, July 2, 1921, drew the first-ever million-dollar gate.

Carpentier probably conceded the champion 24 lbs. and although he caught Dempsey with his lethal right hand and shook the "Manassa Mauler" he couldn't match the heavier man's ferocity and was knocked out in the fourth round.

In his own class Carpentier won the world light-heavy title by knocking out Battling Levinsky in October, 1920, and lost it to Battling Siki with a surprise sixth round defeat in Paris in September, 1922.

Carpentier was never quite the same fighter after that defeat, although he was still too good for our champion, Joe Beckett.

In July, 1924, he failed to come out fighting at the start of the 15th round of a contest against Gene Tunney after receiving what his manager, Francois Descamps, claimed was a low blow, and the result was given as a T.K.O.

Apart from the titles already mentioned Carpentier won the European middle-weight championship by stopping the former British title-holder, Jim Sullivan, in two rounds. He won the European heavyweight title with his fourth round k.o. of Billy Wells in June, 1913, and was, of course, heavyweight champion of his own country.

Carpentier, who had his first fight at the age of 14 when he weighed only 7 stone 2 lbs. (100 lbs.), retired at the age of 33. He died in 1974.

## CARRUTHERS, Jimmy:

Born New South Wales, Australia, in 1929, Carruthers became the first man from that continent to win an undisputed world title.

He started boxing as a professional in 1950 and was undefeated up to the time of his retirement in May, 1954. He was, however, beaten when he attempted a come-back seven years later.

A southpaw, Carruthers won the world bantamweight title by knocking out Vic Toweel in 2 minutes 19 seconds of the first round at Johannesburg, November 15, 1952.

He successfully defended this championship against Vic Toweel, Henry Gault, and Chamrern Songkitrat, before relinquishing it in 1954.

## CARTER, Jimmy:

This American negro was the first fighter to win the world lightweight title on three different occasions.

He started as an amateur when only 14 and turned professional after his demob from the army in 1946.

Carter first won the lightweight title in May, 1951, when he surprised the critics with a victory over Ike Williams. The referee stopped this contest in the fourteenth round.

Carter lost the crown to Lauro Salas in May, 1952, but regained it from the Mexican in October the same year.

Paddy DeMarco was next to relieve him of the title in March, 1954, but he regained it for the third time by stopping DeMarco in fifteen rounds, November, 1954.

This time Carter held on to the championship until June, 1955, when he finally lost it to Wallace Bud Smith on a points decision.

In October, 1957, Jimmy Carter was outpointed by the British Empire lightweight champion, Willie Toweel, at the Albert Hall, London.

## CASUALTIES:
## Fatal:

When a boxer dies through injury

sustained in a contest there is usually a hue and cry raised by the anti-boxing fraternity. The truth is, however, that the proportion of ring deaths is infinitesimal when compared to the number of contests fought and is smaller than the number in some other sports.

Since the beginning of World War II the total of deaths caused by injury in the ring is nearly 400, but that includes every country in the world. The average is something like 8 or 9 deaths a year.

The B.B.B.C. has done everything in its power to safeguard the health of its licensed boxers. In addition to the normal medical examination before each fight there are inspectors at all tournaments to report on the various contestants, noting such information as whether a boxer took a lot of punishment. If a boxer is stopped inside the distance he is automatically suspended for at least 21 days and is not permitted to take part in another contest until he has passed a special medical examination and a doctor's certificate declaring him fit has been received by the Board. He may also be suspended if he loses four consecutive contests. In America a boxer who is knocked out is automatically suspended for at least 60 days.

Headguards were first introduced into the Olympic Games boxing tournament in 1984.

In many parts of the world in recent years responsibility for stopping a fight because of injury has been taken out of the referee's hands and become that of the ring doctor.

Listed below are a few of the fatal casualties in ring history. The first name in each case was the casualty.

Apl. 24, 1741. George Stevenson v. Jack Broughton, London.

June 2, 1830. Sandy McKay v. Simon Byrne, Selcey Forest.

May 30, 1833. Simon Byrne v. James Burke, St. Albans.

Sept. 13, 1842. Tom McCoy v. Chris Lilly, Hastings, New York.

Dec. 14, 1894. Andy Bowen v. Kid Lavigne, New Orleans.

Dec. 6, 1897. Walter Croot v. Jimmy Barry, N.S.C., London.

Nov. 7, 1898. Tom Turner v. Nat Smith, N.S.C., London.

Jan. 29, 1900. Mike Riley v. Matt Precious, N.S.C., London.

Apl. 24, 1901. Billy Smith (Murray Livingstone) v. Jack Roberts, N.S.C., London.

May 24, 1913, Luther McCarty v. Arther Pelkey, Calgary, Canada. (McCarty had injured his spine the previous day when diving into shallow water).*

Aug. 22, 1913. Bull Young v. Jess Willard, Vernon, California.

Aug. 25, 1930. Frankie Campbell v. Max Baer, San Francisco.

Feb. 10, 1933. Ernie Schaaf v. Primo Carnera, New York.

†June 24, 1947. Jimmy Doyle v. Ray Robinson, Cleveland, Ohio.

Feb. 2, 1948. Sam Baroudi v. Ezzard Charles, Chicago.

Sept. 20, 1949. Archie Kemp v. Jack Hassen, Sydney.

Oct. 4, 1949. Enrico Bertola v. Lee Oma, Buffalo, New York.

June 26, 1950. Jan Rennie v. Jan Nicolaas, Rotterdam, Holland.

Feb. 23, 1950. Laverne Roach v. George Small, New York.

Aug. 29, 1951. George Flores v. Roger Donoghue, New York.

Jan. 20, 1952. Mutapha Mutstaphaoui v. Pierre Greef, Roubaix, France.

Aug. 28, 1952. Mickey Johnson v. Tommy Banabas, Morecambe, Lancs.

Oct. 1, 1952. Jimmy Taylor v. Charley Joseph, New Orleans.

†Nov. 4, 1952. Honore Pratesi v. Jake Tuli, London.

†Dec. 8, 1953. Ray Grassi v. Mohamed Chickhaoui, Marseilles, France.

May 4, 1957. Jimmy Elliott v. Pat McAteer, Johannesburg, South Africa.

‡May 28, 1957. Jackie Tiller v. Eric Brett, Doncaster.

†Mar. 24, 1962. Benny Paret v. Emile Griffith, New York.

†Mar. 21, 1963. Davey Moore v. Sugar Ramos, Los Angeles.

July 19, 1978, Angelo Jacopucci v. Alan Minter.

†Sept. 19, 1980, Johnny Owen v. Lupe Pintor.

June 14, 1982, Young Ali v. Barry McGuigan.

†Nov. 13, 1982, Deuk-Koo Kim v. Ray Mancini.

Sept. 9, 1983, Francisco "Kiko" Bejines v. Albert Davila.

Mar. 13, 1986, Steve Watt v. Rocky Kelly.

*Some reports say McCarty was injured falling from a horse.

†These are the only eight of the above-mentioned contests in which the beaten boxer was not counted out. Pratesi was outpointed, Doyle, Grassi and Moore retired, and the referee stopped Tiller-Brett, Paret-Griffith, Owen-Pintor and Kim-Mancini contests.

‡Tiller did not die until April 15, 1958. He was in a coma for 10 months, then returned home slightly improved but had a relapse.

## CATTOUSE, Ray:

Considering his run of success this lightweight from Balham, London was not a crowd-puller. His loose-limbed style was efficient but unexciting, despite his aggressiveness. His heart was certainly in the right place and in March 1980 he won the vacant British title by stopping Dave McCabe in eight rounds.

In February 1982 he held European champion Joey Gibilisco to a draw in Italy, recovering from a bad start to batter the champion towards the end of the contest.

In October 1982 Cattouse lost his British title when stopped in 14 rounds by George Feeney and only fought two more contests.

## CAUNT, Benjamin:

Standing 6 ft. 2½ inches and weighing around 15 stone (210 lbs.) Caunt won the Championship of England by beating Nick Ward in 47 minutes at Long Marsden, Warwickshire, May 11, 1841.

His most notable fights however were the three he had with Bendigo (William Thompson).

Caunt lost the first of these in July, 1835 in 22 rounds. In their second meeting Bendigo was disqualified in the 75th round for going down without a blow (Bendigo claimed that he had slipped). But in their third meeting Bendigo regained the championship he had previously handed in when announcing his retirement, by beating Caunt in 93 rounds. This time it was Caunt who was disqualified for going down without being hit. The date— September 9, 1845.

## CAUSER, Tom:

In October, 1896, at Birmingham, Tom Causer was beaten in five rounds by Eddie Connelly of America in a fight billed as for the 9 stone 4 lbs. (130 lbs.) championship of the world.

However, neither man was light-weight champion of his country at that time, although Causer did possess a 9 stone 8 lbs. (134 lbs.) championship belt for a victory over Arthur Lock.

Causer could not be recognised as British lightweight champion until May, 1897, when he beat Dick Burge on a foul in seven rounds. He lost this title only a little over four months later when Burge stopped him in the first round.

## CERDAN, Marcel:

French-Algerian who was a born fighter. He had a lethal left-hook which travelled only a few inches but which stopped most of his opponents when it connected properly.

Cerdan won the French middleweight title in February, 1938, and the European crown in February, 1947.

He suffered his first defeat for nearly six years when he was out-pointed for the European middleweight champion-ship by Cyrille Delannoit in May, 1948, but two months later Cerdan won the return bout.

On September 21, 1948, Cerdan took the world middleweight title from Tony Zale in Jersey City. He outpunched the veteran champion, forcing him to retire in the interval between the eleventh and twelfth rounds.

In June, 1949, the former butcher from Casablanca defended his world title against the tough Italian-American known as the "Bronx Bull," Jake La Motta.

Cerdan injured his shoulder in the first round of that contest. Fighting a man like La Motta with one arm was an impossible task, but Cerdan stuck it out for nine rounds before he retired.

Cerdan and his manager, Jo Longman, were killed in an air crash at the Azores,

October 28, 1949, when *en route* to the States for a return bout with Jake La Motta.

## CHAMBERS, Arthur:

Born Salford, Lancashire, in 1847, Arthur Chambers is now generally recognised as the first lightweight champion of the world.

Chambers had about a dozen fights in this country before going to America and lost only one, but his most important piece of work before making that trip across the Atlantic in 1872 was to sit on the committee which drew up the original Queensberry Rules of Boxing.

On September 4, 1872, Chambers beat the American champion, Billy Edwards in 35 rounds. The fight which took place on Squirrel Island, Canada, had an unsatisfactory ending when Edwards was disqualified after Chambers claimed that he had been bitten. It was this contest which is now considered to have been the first for the world title, although, at that time it was only ranked as an American lightweight title fight.

Chambers was actually presented with a world title belt after he had beaten George Seddons in 39 rounds on Long Island, New York, August 3, 1873.

In March, 1879, Chambers met Johnny Clark in a gruelling battle which lasted for 2 hours 23 minutes (136 rounds) before Clark succumbed. Both men finished in a terrible state, and Clark nearly died. Chambers never fought again after this.

## CHARLES, Ezzard:

This American negro has not been highly rated among the former world heavyweight champions but that is probably because he was not an aggressive fighter who pleased the crowd.

The truth is, however, that Charles, though cautious, was a clever boxer whose style has been compared to that of Gene Tunney.

Charles was a Golden Gloves champion in his amateur days when he fought as a welter and as a middleweight. He turned professional in 1940 and some idea of his ability can be gauged from the names of a few of the men he defeated. These included Lloyd Marshall, Archie

Moore, Jimmy Bivins, Elmer Ray, Joe Baksi, Joey Maxim, Gus Lesnevich, Joe Louis and Joe Walcott.

When Joe Louis first announced his retirement in March, 1949, Charles was matched with Jersey Joe Walcott for the vacant title as recognised by the N.B.A. Charles gained a unanimous points decision, June 22, 1949.

However, it was not until he had beaten Joe Louis on points over 15 rounds, September 27, 1950, that Charles was really established as world champion.

Ezzard Charles lost his title to Jersey Joe Walcott when he was knocked out in the seventh round, Pittsburgh, July 18, 1951, and he failed to regain it when outpointed in a return match.

In 1954 Charles again fought for the title, meeting Rocky Marciano twice in three months. In the first contest he proved that he was game and could take punishment when he went 15 rounds before losing on points. In the second match he was stopped in the eighth round.

## CHARLES, Ralph:

A West Ham printer who always displayed terrific fire-power and won three-quarters of his fights inside the distance.

The only time he went a full 15 rounds was in February 1968 when he emerged as the new British and Commonwealth welterweight champion after outpointing Johnny Cooke.

A sensational k.o. over Johann Orsolics in Vienna in November 1970 brought him the European crown but he lost this when stopped by Roger Menetrey in June 1971.

Charles relinquished his British title to go after the world crown, but in March 1972 he was k.o'd by Jose Napoles in seven rounds. He retired the following year.

## CHARNLEY, Dave:

Born Dartford, Kent, 1935, Charnley learnt boxing as a member of the Dartford A.B.C. and the London Fitzroy Lodge B.C.

He was a Kent Schoolboy champion in 1950-51, A.B.A. featherweight champion in 1954, and also represented Britain in the Empire Games of 1954.

A southpaw with an aggressive all-action style of fighting which pleased the average fan, Charnley won the British lightweight title from Joe Lucy with a 15-round points victory at Harringay, April 9, 1957.

On May 12, 1959, he annexed the Empire title by knocking out Willie Toweel in the tenth round at Wembley Pool, and in March, 1960, he added the European title to his collection.

Charnley failed in two attempts to wrest the world title from Joe Brown, although he did succeed in stopping Brown in a third meeting after the coloured American had lost his title.

In August, 1962, Charnley lost his Empire crown to Bunny Grant and forfeited his European title in the following year, but he retained the British championship until retiring in January, 1965.

## CHIONOI, Chartchai:

Coming from a poor family in Bangkok, Chionoi became the first man to regain the world flyweight title twice after losing it.

He first won the crown from Walter McGowan in nine rounds in December, 1966, but after having trouble making the weight he was beaten in eight rounds by Efren Torres in February, 1969.

In March 1970 he regained the title in a return bout with Torres but lost it again when hammered into defeat in two rounds by Erbito Salavarria in December that year.

Salavarria was deprived of the W.B.C. version of the title in 1971 for allegedly using an illegal stimulant and the W.B.C. champion, Masao Ohba, was killed in a car crash. Chionoi then became W.B.A. champion by stopping Fritz Chervet in 4 rounds, but he lost this title when he failed to make the weight for a defence against Susumu Hanagata in October 1974 and was beaten by the Jap in 6 rounds.

## CHIP, George:

Born in America of Lithuanian extraction, George Chip started boxing professionally in 1909. Most of his

contests were "No Decision" bouts.

When Chip was at his peak there was some dispute as to the rightful holder of the world middleweight title, but Chip generally became accepted as the champion of this division following his sixth round k.o. of Frank Klaus in 1913.

In a return bout Chip finished the Pittsburgh fighter in five rounds but in April, 1914, he was surprisingly relieved of his title.

His younger brother, Joe, was due to fight Al McCoy, a not very highly rated southpaw from New Jersey, but at the last minute he had to stand down. Brother George agreed to substitute and was knocked out in the first round.

George Chip twice tried to regain the title from McCoy but failed to knock him out (that was the only way to win a title in "No Decision" bouts).

## CHOCOLATE, KID:

This Cuban negro was one of the finest boxers ever to win a featherweight title. A real treat to watch in the ring he was known as the "Cuban Bon Bon."

Kid Chocolate had many contests as an amateur before entering the paid ranks in 1927 and when he went to America the following year he soon chalked up a long string of victories.

In 1931 he took the world Junior lightweight from Benny Bass and was declared world featherweight champion by the N.Y.A.C. following his k.o. victory over Lew Feldman in October, 1932.

This was not recognised by the N.B.A. and in December, 1933, when he lost his Junior lightweight title to Frankie Klick, Kid Chocolate relinquished his claim to the world featherweight crown and moved up into the lightweight division.

Kid Chocolate is a national hero in his own country and the Cuban government awarded him a pension on his retirement from the ring in 1938.

## CHRISTIE, Lloyd:

Hard-hitting Wolverhampton welterweight who came up the hard way and packed in a great deal of experience before getting himself in line for a title shot. A dangerous fighter who won nearly half of his bouts inside the distance before stopping Leicester's Tony McKenzie inside three rounds to win the British light-welterweight crown in January 1987. That was Christie's 38th contest in six years as a professional and his first chance at the title. His younger brother Errol boxes as a middleweight.

## CHRISTOFORIDIS, Anton:

The only Greek fighter ever to win a world title, Christoforidis started his career as a middleweight but was a light-heavyweight when he went to America in 1940.

Soon after the Greek fighter's arrival in the States, Billy Conn relinquished his world light-heavyweight title to go after the bigger boys, and in January, 1941, Christoforidis gained N.B.A. recognition as Conn's successor by outpointing Melio Bettina over 15 rounds in Cleveland.

Christoforidis lost this title when he dropped a points decision to Gus Lesnevich, May 22, 1941.

He became an American citizen and served in the U.S. Army and the U.S. Navy during the war.

## CLARK, Elky:

Born Glasgow, 1898, Elky Clark had passed his 20th birthday before he took a serious interest in boxing.

However, he went on to win the Scottish flyweight and bantamweight titles, and in March, 1924, the N.S.C. matched him with Kid Kelly for the vacant British flyweight championship.

Clark won the title when the referee stopped this contest in the twentieth round.

In September, 1924, the little Scot was recognised as British Empire champion following a k.o. victory over Jim Hanna, and in January, 1925, he annexed the European flyweight crown by outpointing Michel Montreuil.

Clark retained all these titles until he retired because of ill health in 1927, which was soon after he had been beaten by Fidel La Barba in Madison Square Garden when making a bid to gain the world championship.

## CLARK, Johnny:

A sharp-hitting bantamweight from Walworth who overcame illness and injury to win the British and European titles.

Alan Rudkin stood between him and the British crown and Clark was twice beaten by the rugged Liverpudlian in memorable battles before Rudkin retired and Clark took over as champion after outpointing Paddy Maguire in February 1973. Clark had then been fighting professionally for nearly seven years.

In his next fight Clark, a printer by trade, captured the vacant European championship by gaining a unanimous points decision over Franco Zurlo at the Albert Hall.

In January 1974 he relinquished his British title to concentrate on his European crown, but within six months eye trouble forced his retirement at the age of 26, having suffered only three defeats in 43 professional fights.

## CLAYTON, Ron:

Born Blackpool, 1923, Ron Clayton turned professional in 1941 and became one of only six men ever to win two Lonsdale Belts outright.

In September, 1947, at Liverpool, he outpointed the Empire and European featherweight champion, Al Phillips, in a contest which was also for the vacant British title.

Clayton lost his European title to Ray Famechon in 1948 at Nottingham; his Empire title to Roy Ankrah in 1951 at Earl's Court, London, and his British title to Sammy McCarthy at the White City in June, 1954. In this contest with McCarthy, Clayton was forced to retire at the end of the eighth round.

Ron Clayton was forced to give up boxing in June, 1954, after suffering persistent eye trouble.

## COCHRANE, Freddie "Red":

Born Elizabeth, New Jersey, Cochrane had Irish blood in his veins. He started fighting in his home-town in 1933 and had mixed success until about 1939 when he came into the world class as a welterweight.

In July, 1941, he won the world welterweight championship from Fritzie Zivic at Newark, getting the decision at the end of fifteen rounds.

During the war, Cochrane served in the U.S. Navy, then, in 1945, he was twice beaten by the leading middleweight title contender, Rocky Graziano, before losing his welterweight crown to Marty Servo. Cochrane was k.o'd by Servo in the fourth round, February 1, 1946, and did not take part in another contest after this.

## COCKELL, Don:

Born Battersea, London, 1928, this ex-blacksmith turned professional as soon as he was 18 and was not long in making his mark in the light-heavyweight division.

On October 17, 1950, he won the vacant British light-heavy title by knocking out Mark Hart in the fourteenth round, but he lost this title to Randolph Turpin at a time when his form was badly affected by ill-health. The referee stopped this contest with Turpin in the eleventh round to save Cockell from further punishment.

That was in June, 1952, and it was about this time that Cockell was putting on weight so fast that in a comparatively short time he went from 12 stone to 14 stone.

Many critics wrote Cockell off when he was having this weight trouble but he shocked them all and upset the odds by taking the British and Empire heavyweight crown from Johnny Williams in May, 1953.

Although Cockell's career as a heavyweight was a short one—he retired in July, 1956—he became one of the most successful of all British heavyweights in recent years in the international field.

Before giving up the game he paid three visits to America. In the first two he defeated the rated U.S. heavyweight Harry Matthews, and on the third visit he gave a lion-hearted display of courage before going down to the world champion, Rocky Marciano, the referee stopping the contest in the ninth round.

## COHEN, Robert:

An Algerian-Hebrew, Robert Cohen won the French bantamweight crown in November, 1953, the European title in February, 1954, and the world title in September, 1954.

Cohen gained the world championship by outpointing Chamrern Songkitrat in Bangkok before a record crowd (for bantamweight division) of 69,962. This title claim was not recognised in America.

After being badly injured in a car crash in 1954 Cohen recovered to fight a draw with Willie Toweel but he lost his world title to Mario D'Agata, retiring in the sixth round, Rome, June 29, 1956.

## COLLINS, Tom:

Coloured fighter born in Netherlands Antilles but settled in Leeds. Won the vacant British light-heavyweight title by outpointing Dennis Andries (a fighter who had previously beaten him on two occasions), in March 1982.

Collins is an easy-going type of boxer who normally does little pressurising, but he has a good left jab and a swinging right which can really hurt.

Collins' career has been very much wrapped up with Dennis Andries for he lost his British title to the Londoner from Guyana in their fourth meeting in January 1984 and lost another points decision to him less than three months later.

He regained the vacant British title by stopping John Moody and before 1987 was out achieved his greatest triumph by knocking-out the 6ft 6in Dutchman Alex Blanchard with one punch to take the European light-heavyweight championship at the age of 32.

## COLOUR BAR:

In the past colour prejudice has existed to a high degree in the boxing world. Several notable coloured boxers who might well have become world champions never even got a chance to fight for the title. It is also a well known fact that many of the coloured men who did achieve world honours had to be satisfied with smaller purses than their challengers.

Quite often it was most convenient for the reigning champion to draw the colour bar. For instance, John L. Sullivan refused to meet any coloured men after he had become well established as champion, although he did fight Herbert Slade, a Maori, in 1883, and arrangements were also made for him to fight an American negro, George Godfrey, but this fight was called off. After that, however, Sullivan constantly drew the colour bar, and, in particular, he refused to meet the great Peter Jackson.

James J. Jeffries was another heavyweight champion to draw the colour bar. There was an important exception in his case, for after six years in retirement, he was persuaded to try and rescue the white man's cause by meeting the hated Jack Johnson, the fighter who is considered to have prolonged the history of the colour bar in boxing.

The colour prejudice crept in again during Jack Dempsey's reign as heavyweight champion. In 1926 he was expected to defend his title against the New Orleans negro, Harry Wills, and the New York Athletic Commission threatened to ban Dempsey from the State if he refused to meet Wills.

A lot of complications arose, some political some otherwise but the outcome of it was that Tex Rickard preferred to match Dempsey Gene Tunney. So New York was denied this attraction which subsequently took place in Philadelphia.

The colour bar was in existence for many years in Britain. It is a well known fact that coloured boxers were prevented by the B.B.B.C. from competing for any British titles and these men usually had to be content with fighting for Empire titles.

This ban was lifted by the Board in September, 1947, and the first coloured man to win a British title under B.B.B.C. rules was Dick Turpin (Leamington) who outpointed Vince Hawkins over 15 rounds at the Aston Villa Football ground, June 28, 1948, to become middleweight champion. Turpin had previously won the Empire title.

## COLOURED BOXERS:

See under BLACK BOXERS.

## COME-BACK:

For details of world champions who regained their titles after losing them in the ring see under *World Championship* (Regained title).

Many well-known fighters have changed their minds after retirement and decided to try and make a come-back in the ring. Most of these have failed dismally; some have met with moderate success, but very few have been able to regain the respect they may have held in their original ring career.

When they attempted to come back many of these men were doomed to failure because they refused to acknowledge the plain fact that they were too old for the task.

Here are details of come-backs made by some of the best-known fighters.

John L. Sullivan decided to make a come-back at the age of 46 when he weighed nearly 20 stone (280lbs.) and he succeeded in knocking out Jack McCormick inside two rounds. Despite this victory, however, Sullivan had second thoughts and never fought again.

James J. Jeffries was persuaded to come out of retirement after six years and meet Jack Johnson in the hope that a white man may again become world heavyweight champion. Jeffries was knocked out in the 15th round, Reno, July 4, 1910.

Tommy Burns was another world champion who still fancied his chance after hanging up his gloves. At the age of 39 he met the British champion, Joe Beckett, but had to retire in the seventh round. Burns never fought again.

Max Schmeling made his come-back at the age of 42, but defeats by Walter Neusel, another fighter making a come-back, and by the German lightheavyweight champion, Richard Vogt, put an end to Schmeling's ring career.

Primo Carnera was beaten in his first come-back fight at the age of 40, so he decided to change to wrestling and in that sport he met with great success.

Sugar Ray Robinson made one of the most successful come-backs of any fighter in modern times. He announced his retirement in December, 1952, and went on the stage. Two years later he decided to return to the ring and after winning five out of six fights he regained the world middleweight title in December, 1955. After that Robinson twice lost and twice regained this title.

Another fighter who met with some success after deciding to return to the

Sugar Ray Leonard ties up Marvin Hagler as he relieves him of the world middleweight title in one of the richest fights ever — Las Vegas, April 1987

Georges Carpentier leans into Jack Dempsey in the first fight to draw a million-dollar gate, Jersey City, July 1921. Dempsey won inside four rounds

Mike Tyson's intense ferocity can be seen here as the 21-year-old throws a right hand at Tony Tucker in the fight which brought the hard-hitting youngster recognition as undisputed world heavyweight champion — Las Vegas, August 1987

James J. Jeffries comes out of retirement to try and win back the world heavyweight title for the white man from Jack Johnson. In this contest, fought at Reno in July, 1910, Jeffries was knocked out in the 15th round

ring was Benny Leonard. In 1925 he retired undefeated world lightweight champion. Six years later, at the age of 35, Leonard decided to make a come-back, and, after a number of warming-up exhibition bouts, he was undefeated in 19 contests before his come-back ended with a six-round defeat at the hands of Jimmy McLarnin, then a leading contender for the world welter-weight crown. This fight took place October 7, 1932.

Tommy Farr attempted a come-back in 1950 after 10 years' absence from the ring. He was then 36 years of age but he was able to win the Welsh heavyweight title, a distinction he had first gained 14 years earlier. Altogether Farr had 15 fights on the come-back trail before landing a British heavyweight title final eliminator with Don Cockell. This contest took place March 9, 1953, and Farr was beaten, the referee stopping the contest in the seventh round. Farr announced his retirement two months later.

Luis Angel Firpo, famous as the fighter who knocked Jack Dempsey out of the ring in their world title bout of 1923, was another man to make a return to the ring after 10 years' absence. He was 40 years of age when he again put on the gloves but although he won his first comeback fight with a third round knockout, he was himself knocked out in three rounds when he met Arturo Godoy in his second bout. Firpo did not fight again after that.

Muhammad Ali can certainly claim to have made one of the most successful come-backs, although his retirement in 1967 was forced on him by the authorities after he had refused military service. He was then out of action for more than $3\frac{1}{2}$ years before resuming his career and twice regaining the world heavyweight title.

Pedlar Palmer returned to the ring to have one more fight at the age of 42 after an absence of nearly seven years. He was beaten by Jim Driscoll in four rounds, March 10, 1919.

Jim Driscoll attempted a come-back after being out of the ring more than six years. In March, 1919, he beat Pedlar Palmer—also making a come-back as

already mentioned—then drew with Francis Rossi, but in his final contest he was knocked out by the hard-hitting Charles Ledoux after giving a remarkable exhibition and outwitting the French-man for most of the contest. Driscoll was then nearly 38.

Possibly the greatest come-back of all time was that made by Sugar Ray Leonard in 1987. After holding the world welterweight and junior middleweight titles, this talented American retired from the ring with eye trouble in November 1982. During a spell of over five years he had only one fight (in May 1984), but in April 1987, and without any warm-up fight, he came back to take on and beat one of the greatest middleweight champions of the post-war era, Marvin Hagler, before retiring once more.

## COMMONWEALTH TITLES:

See under EMPIRE AND COMMONWEALTH TITLES:

## CONLEY, Frankie:

Born in Italy but brought up in America, Frankie Conley claimed the world bantamweight title in February, 1910.

The previous champion, Jimmy Walsh, had become overweight. Digger Stanley claimed the title on this side of the Atlantic but Conley was recognised in America following his 42-round k.o. victory over Monte Attell at Vernon, February 22, 1910.

Twelve months later Conley was outpointed by Johnny Coulon. He failed to regain the title in a return bout.

## CONN, Billy:

This Irish-American is best remem-bered as the man who probably went closest to lifting the world crown from Joe Louis before the negro first an-nounced his retirement.

Although conceding the champion $25\frac{1}{2}$lbs., Conn gave one of the best displays of his career and appeared to be well on the way to a points victory until he made the mistake of trying to mix it with Louis and was knocked out a couple of seconds before the bell ended the 13th round.

Conn got another chance against Louis in June, 1946, but on this occasion the champion stopped him in eight rounds.

Billy Conn, who beat three ex-world champions when still in his teens, gained American recognition as world light-heavyweight champion by outpointing Melio Bettina over 15 rounds, New York, July 13, 1939.

He successfully defended this title against Bettina and Gus Lesnevich, before relinquishing it in 1941 to enter the heavyweight division and go after a fight with Joe Louis.

## CONTEH, John:

One of Britain's most talented post-war fighters John Conteh also proved to be a determined and single-minded individualist when he stood up for what he believed to be right and refused to be pushed around by boxing's establishment. Walking out on a defence of his W.B.C. light-heavyweight title against Miguel Cuello in Monte Carlo in May 1977 cost him his crown and brought him much criticism, but there were also those who admired the Liverpool fighter for making such a stand.

When he eventually came back after 12 months out of the ring he convincingly defeated Joe Cokes but then lost a controversial split decision when trying to regain the world title from Mate Parlov in Belgrade in June 1978. He subsequently failed in two more attempts to regain the title, being beaten by Matthew Saad Muhammad on both occasions.

A former A.B.A. middle and light-heavyweight champion this exciting combination puncher won the European light-heavyweight title in his 19th professional contest, beating Rudiger Schmidtke inside 12 rounds at Wembley in March 1973. In his next fight he added the British and Commonwealth titles to his collection by outpointing Chris Finnegan in a great contest.

Conteh displayed all of his considerable talents when outpointing Argentinian, Jorge Ahumada, to capture the vacant W.B.C. light-heavyweight title in October 1974. He automatically relin-

quished his European crown after this victory and also gave up his British and Commonwealth titles.

The fact that he twice broke his right hand, and his love of night club life, probably stood between this talented fighter and even greater successes.

## CONTESTS:
### Fewest:

Among the men who won world titles with gloves the boxer who fought the fewest real contests was probably James J. Corbett who had only 19, including no more than six after winning the heavyweight title.

Not including exhibition bouts James J. Jefferies had only 21 contests. After winning the heavyweight championship from Bob Fitzsimmons in June, 1899 he fought only eight times.

Although Gene Tunney had more contests than Jeffries he only fought twice after winning the world heavyweight title and then retired undefeated.

The Australian bantamweight, Jimmy Carruthers, who was world champion 1952-54, had many contests as an amateur but fought only 25 times as a professional. He won the world crown in his 15th contest.

Vic Toweel, the South African bantamweight won the world title in his 14th contest. He had 32 bouts.

Ingemar Johansson fought only 28 professional contests.

Charlie Magri won the British fly-weight title in 1977 in only his third professional fight.

See also WORLD CHAMPIONSHIP (Fewest fights).

### Most Contests in Career:

Abe the Newsboy (Abraham Hollandersky) who was one of the most widely travelled boxers of all time, is generally considered to have had most contests.

His career extended from 1905 to 1918 and during this time he is reputed to have taken part in 1,309 contests. However, a large number of these were exhibitions and many others were with nonentities and therefore this claim cannot be taken seriously.

The man who had the most real

contests was probably Bobby Dobbs, an American negro born in slavery in Knoxville, Tennessee, in 1858. He is believed to have started his fighting career at the age of 17 and gone on fighting regularly until he was 56. During those 39 years he is reckoned to have fought over 1,000 bouts, and very few were exhibitions. No wonder he was nicknamed the "Master Teacher." His claim has, however, never been clearly substantiated as few of his fights in the first 20 years of his career were accurately recorded.

Scottish bantamweight Frank Parkes from Dundee, who fought between the two World Wars, has been credited with around 700 fights, but most of these were in fair ground booths and not recorded.

Sam Langford, the Canadian negro who fought all weights from welter to heavy, reckoned to have had 640 contests from the age of 15 until he retired in 1926 at the age of 43.

The famous Welsh flyweight, Jimmy Wilde, claimed a total of 864 bouts including those he fought in fairground booths. Most record books credit him with around 150 bouts.

Another fighter who travelled around the world was Jeff Smith. In fact, he was known as "The Globe Trotter." A reliable estimate of his total number of bouts would be between 600 and 650. An American born in New York, Jeff Smith fought as a welterweight from 1909 to 1927.

The former British champion, Len Harvey, had 418 contests during his 23 years in the ring. He retired in 1942.

Other British fighters who had more than 400 contests were Ted "Kid" Lewis and Len Wickwar. Lewis was fighting regularly at least once a week at Wonderland, London, around 1910, and his career in the ring lasted 20 years. Wickwar once had 8 contests in a month and his career total is about 460.

## Most Contests in a Day:

Battling Levinsky, the Jewish-American light-heavyweight, once fought three contests totalling 32 rounds in a single day. The date was January 1, 1915, and Levinsky met Bartley Madden in a 10-round "No Decision" bout in Brooklyn,

Soldier Kearns in another 10-round "No Decision" bout in New York, and Gunboat Smith, in a 12-round draw at Waterbury.

Jack McAuliffe, the former world lightweight champion, won three contests in one night. Two of these contests were of three rounds and the other was four rounds. This was in New York City, April 15, 1885.

Tony Galento, an Italian-American heavyweight, beat three men in one night, all inside the distance. The date was August 6, 1931, and Galento stopped two of his opponents in the first round and the other in three rounds.

The American welterweight, Kid McCoy, beat three men in one night at Wonderland, London, December 2, 1901. He k.o.'d Jack Scales and Dave Barry, while another opponent, Sandy Fergusson, was disqualified.

Former lightweight champion Freddy Welsh, also k.o.'d three men in one night. At Pontypridd, April 17, 1907, he stopped Evan Evans in one round, Charlie Weber in two rounds, and Gormer Organ in three rounds.

Dick Hyland, Californian lightweight, beat Young Erlenborn and Jack Haley, each in five rounds, and Young Sullivan in three rounds, Denver, February 1, 1906.

Tommy Burns defended his world title twice in one day and won both contests with first round knock-outs. The victims were Jim O'Brien and Jim Walker, San Diego, March 28, 1906.

Lamar Clark, Cedar City, Utah, heavyweight, knocked out six opponents in one night December 1, 1958. However, these were not first-class opposition.

## Most Contests with Same Opponent:

The record among first-class professionals is probably held by two welterweights, Ted "Kid" Lewis and Jack Britton. They met at least 20 times, no one is quite sure of the actual figure, but they once met four times in five weeks in places as far apart as Toronto, St. Louis, New York City and Dayton.

Others who met on several occasions include:—

Sam Langford and Harry Wills, 23

times.
Sam Langford and Sam McVey, 15 times.
Sam Langford and Joe Jeannette, 14 times.

## COOKE, Johnny:

Turned professional in 1960 after an outstanding amateur career but did not achieve his ambition until he was 32. Then he became British welterweight champion by outpointing Brian McCaffrey after Brian Curvis had retired from the ring. Cooke had earlier failed to take the title from Curvis.

A much travelled fighter from Bootle, Cooke won the vacant Empire title with a points victory over Lennox Beckles, but he lost both titles to Ralph Charles in February 1968.

## COOPER, Henry, O.B.E.:

In a professional career spread over more than 16 years (55 fights) Henry Cooper established himself as one of the most popular personalities in British ring history.

He created a record by holding the British heavyweight title for 10 years 5 months, winning it in January 1959 by outpointing Brian London, and successfully defending the crown eight times (becoming the first man to win three Lonsdale belts), before relinquishing the title in January 1969 because the B.B.B.C. had refused to recognise a proposed fight with Jimmy Ellis as being for the world title. Cooper, however, regained the title at the first attempt in March 1970, showing his class in outpointing Jack Bodell.

One of boxing twins born Bellingham, London, Henry Cooper had three spells as European heavyweight champion without losing that title in the ring until narrowly outpointed by Joe Bugner in March 1971.

With this defeat Cooper also lost his British and Commonwealth titles and immediately announced his retirement being then only two months short of his 37th birthday.

Like so many British heavyweights the genial Cooper never quite made it in world class. Defeats by Zora Folley, Roger Rischer and Amos Johnson kept him out of that bracket and he was also beaten on two occasions by Cassius Clay and once by Floyd Patterson. But Cooper had a terrific left hook and this nearly caused a major upset in June 1963 when it floored Cassius Clay just before the bell.

## CORBETT, Dick:

Born Bethnal Green, London, Corbett started boxing in 1926. He won the vacant Empire bantamweight title in May, 1930, by outpointing Willie Smith, of South Africa, and after beating the former British bantam champion, Teddy Baldock, he went on to win the British title by outpointing Johnny King at Manchester, December 21, 1931.

The auburn-haired Corbett was beaten by Johnny King in a return bout, October 10, 1932, but he challenged King again in February, 1934, and regained the British and Empire titles with another points win.

These two men subsequently fought two draws, before Corbett became overweight and was forced to relinquish his titles in December, 1934.

## CORBETT, Harry:

Elder brother of Dick Corbett, Harry won the British featherweight title from Johnny Cuthbert, on points, at the N.S.C., March 12, 1928, but lost it in a return bout, May 16, 1929.

Before this Harry Corbett had failed to take the British bantamweight title from Johnny Brown, the referee stopping the contest in the 16th round. That was in February 1925.

Corbett eventually lost the sight of his left eye and was forced to retire in 1936.

## CORBETT, James J.:

James J. Corbett is considered to have been the first scientific gloved boxer as distinct from bare-knuckle prize fighters.

He was originally employed as a bank clerk in San Francisco and gained a big reputation as an outstanding amateur boxer.

He first made a name for himself as a professional when he knocked out Joe Choynski in June, 1889, and he followed this with another good win in February, 1890, this time stopping Jake Kilrain in six rounds.

In May, 1891, he fought his remarkable contest with the heavier Peter Jackson. Neither could get the better of the other and it was stopped and declared "No contest" after 61 rounds.

When John L. Sullivan visited San Francisco in June 1891, he engaged in a four-round exhibition bout with the local hero, and although the champion only sparred in full evening attire, Corbett learnt enough to make him feel that he had the beating of the big Irish-American.

Corbett got his chance on September 7, 1892, at the Olympic Club, New Orleans. He conceded the champion 34lbs. but he upset the odds by winning the title with a k.o. in the 21st round.

Corbett lost the title to Bob Fitzsimmons, at Carson City, March 17, 1897, when he was knocked out in the 14th round.

In 1900, and again in 1903, Corbett tried to regain the world title from Jim Jeffries. In the first contest he was leading all the way with his clever boxing and fine ring generalship, but he was stopped in the 23rd round. The second contest went only 10 rounds before Jeffries got in with his k.o. punch.

Corbett never fought again after his second defeat by Jeffries for he was then 37. He died in 1933.

## CORBETT, Young:

The real name of this American featherweight was William Rothwell.

In November, 1901, he taunted the world featherweight champion, Terry McGovern, so much before they met in the ring that McGovern lost his head and was surprisingly knocked out in the second round.

Corbett proved that this was no accident by stopping McGovern in 11 rounds when they met again in March, 1903, but later that year both these men moved up into the lightweight division and left the featherweight title vacant.

At the heavier weight, Corbett again beat McGovern and also Dave Sullivan, but was prevented from going for the lightweight title when defeated by Jimmy Britt and Battling Nelson.

## CORBETT III, Young:

Born in Italy but brought up in America, Young Corbett III started boxing soon after World War I in California and sprang into the limelight in 1926 by drawing with another much-fancied Californian fighter, Young Jack Thompson.

A hard-hitting southpaw, Corbett again beat Thompson in 1928 and also won and lost to another leading welterweight, Sammy Baker.

In 1930 Corbett beat Jackie Fields in a non-title fight, and gained another victory over Thompson, but he was to remain on the verge of the welterweight title for more than three years.

It was not until February 22, 1933, that Corbett achieved his ambition by outpointing Jackie Fields in a title fight, but then his reign was short lived, for he lost the crown in his next fight, May 29, 1933, being knocked out in the first round by Jimmy McLarnin.

Following this defeat, Corbett moved up into the middleweight division, and after beating Lou Brouillard, Gus Lesnevich, Fred Apostoli and Glen Lee, he was right in line for a crack at this title.

Apostoli was already claiming the championship when Corbett beat him in February, 1938, but the Italian-American was not named as title holder. Then, when a return match was arranged with the title label on it, Corbett was beaten in eight rounds.

## CORCORAN, Peter:

This Irishman from Galway fought at a time when the prize ring was having one of its bad spells around the 1760's.

Indeed, history has it that when Corcoran won the championship by knocking out Bill Darts in only one round at Epsom, May 10, 1771, Darts had been paid £100 to throw the fight. As this was probably the shortest bare-knuckle prize-fight on record it seems more than likely that the story is true.

Corcoran was eventually relieved of the championship by Harry Sellars, who beat him in 38 rounds, Staines, Middlesex, October 16, 1775.

## COULON, Johnny:

Born Canada in 1889, Johnny Coulon started fighting about 1905. He was recognised in America as the first world flyweight champion in 1910, but this claim was not accepted on this side of the Atlantic.

Coulon was also involved in a disputed world bantamweight championship, for although he was recognised in America as the title-holder at this weight following his victory over Frankie Conley at New Orleans, in 1911, he was not rated as champion in Britain.

Coulon forfeited his claim to the bantamweight title after his defeat by Kid Williams in three rounds, June 9, 1914.

## COUNT, The:

See also under KNOCK-DOWNS (Rules).

In the original rules of prize fighting, "Broughton's Rules" of 1743, a fighter was allowed half a minute to come up to scratch after being knocked down.

In the London Prize Ring Rules, which were first produced in 1838 and revised in 1853, a fighter was allowed 38 seconds to come up to scratch.

It was not until the Queensberry Rules were produced in about 1864 that mention was made of the ten-second count as we know it today.

For many years it was only in professional contests that an audible count was made. The amateur was given no such assistance in learning the length of time he had been down and it was therefore a risky business for him to try and remain down to take a rest. This rule was not altered by the Amateur Boxing Association until 1951, when the audible count was adopted as in professional boxing.

## Long Count:

In some important contests a boxer has, for one reason or another, been allowed more than 10 seconds to rise after he had been knocked down.

The most famous of these so-called "long counts" was that which occurred in the second Gene Tunney-Jack Dempsey contest at Chicago, September 22, 1927.

Tunney was leading all the way until in the seventh round it happened. Dempsey got Tunney against the ropes and dropped him with at least two hooks to the jaw.

No man had previously survived this sort of punching from Dempsey in his prime and there is no doubt that when Tunney went down the "Manassa Mauler" thought that he had finished the fight.

After some hesitation Dempsey moved back towards the ropes. The count had been started but it was ignored by the referee until, quite correctly, he had succeeded in getting Dempsey to move into a neutral corner. Then the count was restarted and Tunney got up when it reached "nine" and back pedalled for the remainder of the round in order to recover.

The official timekeeper reckoned that Tunney had been down for 14 seconds, but other estimates put it at 16 or 18 seconds. At any rate, many considered it doubtful whether Tunney could have beaten 10 seconds had it been counted from the time he went down. On the other hand it could be said that Tunney deliberately stayed down as long as possible. The argument will never be settled.

Another occasion when a champion might have lost his title but for a "long count" was the first meeting between Bombardier Billy Wells and Dick Smith at The Ring, Blackfriars, London, May 31, 1915.

Much to everyone's surprise Smith put Wells down with what looked like a "finisher." Even referee Tom Dunning seemed taken aback. He was officiating from outside the ring and did not commence his count until he had climbed through the ropes. This gave Wells at least another six seconds in which to recover, and he came back to win with a k.o. in the ninth.

Bombardier Billy Wells was involved in what was considered at the time to have been another "long count." This was at Ghent, near Brussels, June 1, 1913, on the occasion of his first meeting with Georges Carpentier. Some eye witnesses believed that the Frenchman was down for longer than nine seconds when he had been floored by Wells in the first round. However, Wells failed to take advantage of his groggy opponent and Carpentier recovered to k.o. the Englishman in the fourth round.

It is sometimes asserted that Jack Dempsey was out of the ring for more than 10 seconds when Luis Angel Firpo sent him through the ropes in the first round of their historic battle in 1923.

World featherweight champion, Terry McGovern, also figured in a "long count" incident. He was put down in the second round of a contest with Oscar Gardner, New York, March 9, 1900. Some witnesses alleged that McGovern was allowed a count of 18 or 20 seconds. However, he recovered to knock out Gardner in the next round.

In the eighth round of a world lightweight title bout between Joe Brown and Ralph Dupas at Houston, May 7, 1958. Dupas was counted out by the official "counter" but the referee stopped his count at "nine" because Brown had not remained in a neutral corner.

This made little difference to the outcome, for when Dupas rose after about 11 or 12 seconds he was dropped twice more before the referee stopped the contest later in that round.

The second Cassius Clay—Sonny Liston title bout in May 1965 was one of the ring's biggest fiascos. Liston was down for 12 seconds, before regaining his feet, but the contest proceeded for at least 10 more seconds before it was stopped.

The longest count ever timed was one of 32 seconds. This was at Madison Square Garden, March 12, 1948. Marcel Cerdan floored Lawrence Roach with a right but the Texan pulled the French Moroccan down with him. Cerdan quickly regained his feet but an argument then ensued between Referee Arthur Donovan, who reckoned it was a knockdown and wanted to begin a count, and Timekeeper, Jack Watson, who refused to count because he believed that Roach had slipped. Roach had been on the canvas for 24 seconds before the count began and he got up at 8. He was subsequently stopped in the eighth round when the referee intervened.

When Harry Mason regained the British lightweight title from Ernie Izzard at the Holland Park Rink, London, June 22, 1925, there were amazing scenes in the eighth round.

Mason put Izzard down. After what must have been a lapse of 10 seconds he lifts his opponent up and props him against the ropes in his corner. Mason fully expected to hear the announcement of his k.o. victory, but the referee did not leave his seat outside the ring. Mason, obviously dismayed, promptly returned to action and again put Izzard on the canvas. This time Izzard got up quickly only to be sent down once more. Recovering his feet again Izzard was sent down for the fourth time. By now, however, the timekeeper was signalling the end of the round while fighting broke out among spectators who thought the time-keeper was signalling the end of the fight. This debacle was eventually stopped in Mason's favour in the next round.

## COWDELL, Pat:

After an outstanding amateur career, winning the A.B.A. bantamweight title in 1975, and the featherweight title in 1976 and 1977, as well as a bronze medal at the 1976 Olympics, this polished fighter from Warley fought professionally from 1977. Over a period of ten years he has lost five times in 40 contests and four of those defeats were in title fights.

Cowdell failed in his first bid for the British featherweight title, losing a controversial points decision to Dave Needham, but he took the crown in a return in 1979.

A brave effort to win the world W.B.C. title from Salvador Sanchez in Houston in December 1981 ended in a split decision going against him, but in his next fight he lifted the European title from Salvatore Melluzzo.

This skilful boxer relinquished his British title and also his European crown when he prematurely retired in 1983, but in his second come-back fight in 1984 he won the European junior-lightweight title by outpointing Jean Marc Renard but was stopped in the first round by Azumah Nelson in a bid for the W.B.C. world featherweight title.

Still Cowdell's career was not finished. In 1986 when nearly 33 years of age he won the British junior-lightweight title by stopping champion John Doherty in six rounds but lost it when he was apparently counted out as the ring was invaded after he had been floored four times by Najib Daho and the bell sounded to end the first round. This quick defeat hurt Cowdell's pride and he gained revenge in October 1987 by hammering Daho almost to a standstill in nine rounds to regain the title.

## CRAWLEY, Peter:

A Londoner who was one of England's leading prize fighters for more than ten years but as soon as he had won the championship by beating Jem Ward in 11 rounds, lasting 26 minutes, Royston Heath, Herts, January 2, 1827 he announced his retirement from the ring.

Crawley was also something of an actor. He appeared in "The Fight at Warwick" on the London stage.

## CRIBB, Tom:

One of the most highly respected of all bare-knuckle pugilists, Tom Cribb was born in 1781.

In 1807 he beat the former champion, Jem Belcher, in 41 rounds, and after the reigning champion, John Gully, had announced his retirement, Cribb claimed the title.

He really clinched his right to the championship by beating Bob Gregson in 23 rounds, October 25, 1808.

In February, 1809, he again beat Jem Belcher, this time in 31 rounds, and he subsequently beat the American negro, Tom Molineux, on two occasions.

These contests with Molineux are sometimes considered to have been the first world championship fights.

To be quite fair, Cribb was really beaten in his first meeting with Molineux, December 18, 1810, being unable to resume after the 28th round. However, his second cleverly gained respite by claiming that the negro was fighting with lead in his hands. By the time the excitement had died down Cribb had recovered and he went on to win in 39 rounds.

Cribb did not fight again after his second victory over Molineux. He eventually gave up his claim to the championship in 1818.

After his death in 1848, an imposing monument was erected in Woolwich cemetery. It consists of a lion standing on a rock with its right paw resting on an urn over which is draped the belt which Cribb received as Champion of England.

## CRIQUI, Eugene:

One of the hardest right-hand punchers of his day, this Frenchman won his country's flyweight title in 1912, the featherweight crown in 1921, and the European featherweight title in 1922, before becoming world featherweight champion in June, 1923, by knocking out Johnny Kilbane in the sixth round.

Criqui lost his world title 54 days later on points over 15 rounds to Johnny Dundee at New York Polo Grounds, July 26, 1923.

Criqui was known as the man with the iron jaw. During the First World War he had been wounded with a bullet which smashed his jaw. It was patched up with wire and plates and when he had made a complete recovery they said that he couldn't be knocked out. However, as a matter of fact he was stopped by Tommy Noble, Pat Moore and Danny Frush.

The first two of these defeats took place in England, but on another occasion when he visited this country he beat the British featherweight champion, Joe Fox, in 12 rounds at Holland Park. That was in May, 1922.

## CRISP, George:

This Newcastle man was really only a welterweight but in February, 1897, he claimed the heavyweight championship of England after gaining a surprise win over Jem Smith in five rounds.

His claim was not taken too seriously however, especially after his defeat by the American negro, Frank Craig, in November, 1898.

On that occasion Crisp was beaten in 13 rounds and very little was heard of him after that.

## CROSSLEY, Harry:

Born Swinton, Yorkshire, and brought up at Mexborough, Harry Crossley was one of a family of boxers. One of his two brothers, Herbert, was a fine heavyweight prospect, but died in America at an early age.

Harry Crossley was a pit boy and he took up boxing in 1924. In November, 1929, he won the British light-heavyweight title by outpointing Frank Moody over 15 rounds.

He lost this title when outpointed by Jack Petersen at the Stadium Club, London, May 23, 1932.

Harry Crossley was only 47 when he died in December, 1948.

## CROWLEY, Dave:

Dave Crowley was one of the gamest little fighters ever seen in a London ring. He was born at Clerkenwell of Irish parents and started boxing at the Gainsford B.C. in Drury Lane.

In 1933 he went the distance with that brilliant world bantamweight champion, Panama Al Brown, and the following year he gave the world featherweight champion, Freddie Miller, one of the hardest fights of his career.

In 1936 he was stopped in 9 rounds by Mike Belloise in a bid for the world featherweight title as recognised by N.Y.A.C. although many ringsiders believed that it was only the "no foul" rule that saved Belloise from disqualification.

Dave Crowley was steered to the top by Harry Levene. An aggressive fighter, the Clerkenwell boy won the British lightweight title by outpointing Jimmy Walsh at Liverpool in June, 1938. He lost it six months later when he was knocked out by Eric Boon in the thirteenth round of a hard battle at Harringay, London.

## CULLEN, Maurice:

Born Shotton, Co. Durham, this stylish boxer who was noted for his clever left-handed work, won the vacant British lightweight title by outpointing Dave Coventry at Liverpool, April 8, 1965.

Cullen had three successful defences of the title before losing it to Ken Buchanan in January 1968. He had trouble in making the weight for this bout and was k.o.'d in the eleventh round.

## CURLEY, Johnny:

This red-haired boy from Lambeth was encouraged by his elder brother, Harry, to take up boxing. Harry was a useful fighter himself and eventually got Johnny started on the fistic ladder with a couple of bouts at the old N.S.C.

It was in this club that Johnny took the British featherweight title from George McKenzie with a 20-round points decision in March, 1925.

He successfully defended his crown against Harry Corbett and Bill Hindley before losing it to Johnny Cuthbert in a close fight at the N.S.C. in January, 1927.

## CURRAN, Petty Officer "Nutty":

A hard hitting heavyweight who would have been British champion had he been able to get a fight with the titleholder, Iron Hague, at the N.S.C.

As it was, P.O. Curran knocked Hague out in the fifteenth round when they met in February, 1910, but because this contest took place at the old Cosmopolitan Rink, Plymouth, instead of at the N.S.C., he was never officially recognised as champion.

However, Curran did gain recognition as British Empire Champion when he beat the Australian, Bill Lang, on a disqualification in the first round, January 18, 1911.

Curran had another crack at a British heavyweight champion, in March, 1916. Then the title-holder was Billy Wells, but when they met at Plymouth, Curran was knocked out in the fifth round.

During his career, Curran had two victories to his credit over another former British heavyweight champion, Gunner Moir. He beat the Gunner on a foul in two rounds at Mountain Ash in 1910, and knocked him out in the first round of a bout at the Blackfriars Ring in 1912.

## CURRIE, Hughroy:

This Jamaican-born heavyweight brought up in London has shown erratic form but captured the vacant British title in a most unentertaining 12-round brawl with Funso Banjo which ended with Currie gaining the narrowest of points wins.

Only seven months later, in April 1986, Currie lost his title in a much livelier contest with Horace Notice and both fighters had been floored before the referee intervened in the sixth round to save Currie from further punishment.

## CURVIS, Brian:

In 1964 this brilliant Welsh southpaw, younger brother of Cliff (q.v.) became the first man to win two Lonsdale belts in the welterweight division, and he defended his British crown six times before retiring undefeated champion in October 1966.

At the time of his retirement Curvis was also Empire title-holder, having held that crown since taking it from George Barnes in May 1960.

Curvis suffered only four defeats in 41 fights. Before turning professional he had won the A.B.A. welterweight title.

## CURVIS, Cliff:

This Swansea southpaw started boxing when he was only eight. He won a schoolboy title at 14 and turned professional two years later as a featherweight.

In 1946 he was knocked out in two rounds by Al Phillips in an eliminator for the British featherweight title and was beaten by Harry Hughes in 1949 in a final eliminator for the British lightweight title.

However, Curvis won national honours in the welterweight division, for he took the British and Empire titles from Wally Thom with a ninth round k.o. at Liverpool, July 24, 1952.

The following year Curvis left his Empire title in South Africa when he was outpointed there by Gerald Dreyer.

Curvis retired from the ring in disgust when he learnt that his end of the purse

for a proposed return bout with Wally Thom would be only £510.

## CUSICK, Johnny:

Known as "Nipper" Cusick, this Manchester boy won the Northern Area bantamweight title in 1937, then defeated a leading featherweight of the day, "Spider" Jim Kelly.

However, in the final eliminator for the British featherweight title, Cusick was beaten by Benny Caplan.

That was in 1938. Later that same year "Spider" Jim Kelly took the title from Caplan, and in June, 1939, Cusick won the championship with another victory over Kelly.

Cusick was only champion for seven months. On February 1, 1940, he was outpointed by Nel Tarleton at Liverpool.

## CUTHBERT, Johnny:

A stylish boxer from Sheffield, Cuthbert won the British title in both the featherweight and the lightweight divisions.

He took the featherweight title from Johnny Curley in January, 1927. Lost it to Harry Corbett in March, 1928, but after holding Corbett to a draw in a return match, he regained the British title by beating him in a third meeting May 16, 1929.

Cuthbert finally lost the featherweight crown to Nel Tarleton in October, 1931.

In the lightweight division Cuthbert had already fought a 15-round draw with the champion, Al Foreman, and when that boxer relinquished the title, Cuthbert was matched with Jim Hunter for the vacant championship.

They met at Glasgow in August, 1932 and Cuthbert stopped Hunter in the tenth round.

The Sheffield fighter was not called upon to defend this title until January, 1934, when he was beaten on points by Harry Mizler.

## DADE, Harold:

American negro who was a Golden Gloves champion before turning professional in 1942.

He won the world bantamweight title by outpointing Manuel Ortiz in San Francisco, January 6, 1947, but lost it in a return contest a little over two months later.

Dade then moved up into the featherweight division and got into line for a world title fight but in December, 1949, he was beaten by Willie Pep during the interval between that fighter losing and regaining his world crown.

Harold Dade retired in 1955 and died prematurely of asthma in 1962 when only 37.

## D'AGATA, Mario:

An Italian who won the world bantamweight title from Robert Cohen in Rome in June, 1956. D'Agata, a deaf-mute, had the Frenchman well and truly beaten, forcing him to retire at the end of the sixth round.

D'Agata lost his title on a points decision to Alphonse Halimi in Paris, April 1, 1957.

There was a remarkable incident in this contest which may have affected the result.

In the third round the lighting apparatus over the ring burst into flames. The contest had to be stopped while the fire was extinguished, but D'Agata had received a slight burn on one shoulder from falling debris and there is no doubt that proved something of a handicap to him in the remaining 12 rounds.

## DAHO, Najib:

Born Morocco but based in Manchester this fighter has shown plenty of stamina throughout a career which has been, for the most part, in the lightweight division. However, it was after dropping down to junior-lightweight that he really made the fans sit up and take notice. After nine years as a professional and at the age of 27 he upset the odds by battering British junior-lightweight champion Pat Cowdell into defeat in one round. That was in May 1986. Later the same year he failed in bids for the I.B.F. world junior-lightweight title and also the European crown, being outpointed by Barry Michael in Manchester and having to pull out in the fifth round with a tooth forced into his gum in a tough fight with Jean Marc Renard in Belgium.

## DALY, Pat:

Born in London of Irish parents, Pat Daly spent some time in America where he took up boxing.

In this country Daly claimed the lightweight title following a victory over Johnny Hughes in February, 1901, but at that time the championship of this division was more firmly held by Jabez White.

Daly clung to his claim until February, 1907, when he was knocked out in five rounds by Jack Goldswain.

## DANIELS, "Gipsy" Bill:

One of Britain's busiest cruiserweights back in the 1920s this Welshman from Llanelli beat several top class men.

In October, 1924, when Phil Scott was on the way to the top of Britain's heavyweights, Gipsy Daniels conceded him two stone (28 lbs.) and outpointed him over 15 rounds at Liverpool.

1927 was a good year for Daniels. He outpointed fellow Welsh cruiserweight, Frank Moody, fought two draws with the 14 stone 8 lbs. (204 lbs.) Belgian heavyweight champion, Pierre Charles, and took the British light-heavyweight title from Tom Berry with a twenty-round points victory.

Daniels' best performance, however, was in February, 1928, when he went to Germany and knocked out Max Schmeling in the first round. Schmeling was then the European cruiserweight champion, but Daniels did not claim that title.

Daniels relinquished his British championship in 1928.

## DARCY, Les:

Considered to have been the finest middleweight ever born in Australia, Les Darcy might well have been able to gain an undisputed world title but just when he seemed on the verge of attaining this goal he died of blood poisoning. Darcy was then only 21.

Darcy claimed the world middleweight title after beating Jeff Smith on a foul in two rounds in Sydney, May 23, 1915, and strengthened his claim later the same year by stopping American, Eddie McGoorty, in 15 rounds and again in 8 rounds.

In September, 1916, Darcy took all the punishment George Chip could hand out and then knocked out the Lithuanian-American in the ninth round.

Chip had been recognised in America as world middleweight champion a little over two years before that fight, but the man who had the Americans' backing as title-holder at that time was Al McCoy, so Darcy set off for the United States to secure a fight with him and clear up the championship dispute.

It was while he was training and still negotiating for a match with McCoy in 1917 that he developed an abscess after one of his teeth had been knocked out in a spar with the heavyweight, Fred Fulton. In a few days he was dead.

## DARTS, Bill:

This old bare-knuckle prize fighter is not very highly rated among the champions of his period. He won the championship by beating Tom Juchau in 40 minutes at Guildford, Surrey, May, 1766, but according to the historians he finished Juchau with a blow below the belt.

In June, 1769, Darts was beaten in 45 minutes by Tom Lyons, the Waterman, but as Lyons did not fight again after this Darts was matched with the Irishman, Peter Corcoran for the championship, May 10, 1771.

Darts was beaten with one punch and it was alleged that he had been bribed with £100 to "throw" this fight.

There ended a none too inspiring career.

## DEATHS:

See under CASUALTIES (FATAL).

## DEBUTS:

The only two men ever to fight for a world title when making their debut as professionals were Jack Skelly in 1892 and Pete Rademacher in 1957.

Jack Skelly was the New York Amateur bantamweight champion when he fought George Dixon for the world featherweight title at New Orleans, September 6, 1892. He was knocked out in the eighth round.

Pete Rademacher's professional debut was an even shorter one. He won the Olympic heavyweight title at Melbourne in 1956 but when he met the world heavyweight champion, Floyd Patterson, at Seattle, August 22, 1957, he was knocked out in the sixth round.

## DEFEATS:
### Fewest:

See also under UNDEFEATED.

Several fighters have completed their ring careers with only a single defeat, but the finest record among these, considering the large number of contests fought, was that of Packey McFarland, the Irish-American lightweight. He had over 100 contests but lost only once, and that early in his career when he was only 16 years of age.

Other fighters who suffered only one defeat in a completed professional career include:—

Arthur Chambers (Lancashire lightweight), Gene Tunney and James J. Jeffries (American heavyweights), Luther McCarty (American heavyweight), John L. Sullivan (American heavyweight). Miguel Angel Cuello (Argentinian light-heavyweight), Johnny Hill (British flyweight).

Fighters with only two defeats in a completed professional career include:—

Luis Angel Firpo (Argentine heavyweight), and Frank Klaus (American middleweight). Raul Marcias (Mexican bantamweight), George Foreman

(American heavyweight), Harry Harris (American bantamweight), Eder Jofre (Brazilian bantamweight), Ingemar Johansson (Swedish heavyweight), Ben Jordan (British featherweight).

Jimmy Wilde suffered only four defeats in a record of 864 bouts including several hundred fought in fairground booths.

## Most:

Of all the world heavyweight champions since John L. Sullivan the man who lost most contests in proportion to the number fought was James J. Braddock. He is known to have been defeated 25 times in just under 90 contests.

Among all the men who ever attained world championship honours in all divisions under Queensberry Rules, the fighter who had the highest proportion of defeats in his career was the Irish-American featherweight, Joey Archibald. He was defeated 41 times in 106 contests.

## DELANEY, Jack:

A French-Canadian, whose real name was Ovila Chapdelaine, Delaney was a fast punching cruiserweight with a good right hook.

In December, 1925, he met Paul Berlenbach for the world light-heavyweight title but lost on points.

Delaney turned the tables on Berlenbach in a return match at Brooklyn in July, 1926, and retained the championship for about twelve months before moving into the heavyweight division.

Amongst the heavier men Delaney was kept out of reach of a world title fight owing to defeats by Tom Heeney and Jack Sharkey.

## DEMPSEY, Jack

One of the most colourful characters in ring history, William Harrison, who later took the name of Dempsey, started as a penniless and hungry fighter but went on to earn some of the biggest purses ever.

There is an old boxing adage which says that hungry fighters are the best fighters and in his early days Dempsey developed a "killer" instinct in the ring which was to be the hallmark of his career.

Dempsey very nearly gave up fighting when he went to work in the Seattle shipyards, but when his brother died, Dempsey returned to the ring because he needed the money for funeral expenses.

It is ironic that such a tragedy in the Harrison household should have provided boxing with its biggest crowd puller.

A rugged, non-stop fighter, who always pleased the spectators, Dempsey went on to win the world heavyweight title from Jess Willard in three rounds, at Toledo, Ohio, July 4, 1919.

Prior to this Dempsey had won five consecutive fights in the first round and although he conceded the giant Willard nearly 4 stone (56 lbs.) he proved himself one of the hardest hitters of all time by flooring the Kansas cowboy seven times in the first round.

Willard was on the canvas when the bell ended that opening stanza and Dempsey started on his way back to the dressing-room thinking he had won on a knock-out. But amid the uproar the bell had not been heard as it sounded in time to save Willard from the fatal "10" count.

Dempsey was recalled to the ring and in the next two rounds he so battered one of the biggest men ever to have held the world title that Willard's second threw in the towel at the end of the third round.

Dempsey made the mistake of not being a fighting champion. He knocked out a lot of men in exhibition bouts but they were not championship contests, and when he met Gene Tunney in September, 1926, the "Manassa Mauler" had fought only two title fights in the previous four years.

This lack of real contests showed up in the ring and Tunney beat him over ten rounds.

After that Dempsey knocked out Jack Sharkey in seven rounds, and he was in better form when he met Tunney for the second time. It was on this occasion that Dempsey put the champion down in the seventh round and might have regained the title but for the famous "long count" which allowed Tunney valuable extra seconds in which to shake off the effects of Dempsey's punches.

Jack Dempsey figured in five of the 13 contests that have drawn million-dollar gates. The first of these was his title defence against Georges Carpentier at Jersey City, July 2, 1921. The others were his two contests with Tunney, the one with Firpo and that with Sharkey.

After hanging up his gloves Jack Dempsey became one of the highest paid boxing referees in the history of the game. The man who had earned 3 dollars and 50 cents for winning his first fight received 10,000 dollars for refereeing the Ceferino Garcia—Glen Lee middle-weight title bout in 1939.

## DEMPSEY, Jack "Nonpareil":

Born in Ireland and emigrated to Brooklyn as a child, Jack Dempsey started his ring career as a wrestler.

When he took up boxing he was a lightweight and in 1882 he claimed the championship of this division. He beat two or three good men at this weight but after putting on a few pounds he passed his title over to Jack McAuliffe in 1884 and moved into the middleweight class.

In July, 1884, he won the middleweight title by knocking out George Fulljames in 22 rounds at Toronto. He was the first undisputed champion of this division under Queensberry Rules.

On August 27, 1889, Dempsey was knocked out in 32 rounds by George La Blanche, but although the referee awarded the decision to La Blanche, it caused such a furore that this fighting Marine was never recognised as champion. The reason was that he had finished Dempsey with a pivot blow and it was decided to make this an illegal punch.

Dempsey eventually lost his middle-weight title to Bob Fitzsimmons, January 14, 1891, at New Orleans. In this contest the "Nonpareil" proved that he had a great fighting heart. He took terrific punishment for 13 rounds and Fitzsimmons pleaded in vain with the referee to stop the contest before he was able to knock Dempsey out.

## DENMARK:
## Champions:
World:—

Lightweight: Battling Nelson, 1908-10.

Bantamweight: Kid Williams, 1914-17.

European:—

Light-heavyweight: Tom Bogs, 1968-69.

Middleweight: Chris Christensen, 1962. Tom Bogs, 1969-70, 1973. Ayub Kalule, 1985.

Welterweight: Jorgen Hansen, 1978, 79-82. Hans Henrik Palm, 1982.

Lightweight: Jorgen Johansen, 1952-54. Borge Krogh 1966-67. Gert Bo Jacobsen, 1986-

Featherweight: Knud Larsen, 1929.

Olympic:—

Lightweight: H. Nielson, 1924.

## DIAMOND, Anthony:

This Birmingham publican won the A.B.A. lightweight title three years in succession, 1883-84-85, and when prevailed upon not to compete in this class the following year, he entered for the heavyweight title and won that.

Having run out of opposition in the amateur ranks Diamond turned professional and he claimed the British middleweight title following his 12-round victory over Dido Plumb, February 25, 1898, but he was never recognised by the N.S.C.

## DICKIE, Robert:

A Welshman from Carmarthen who possesses real punching power and uses it well to the body. Dickie is a former Welsh A.B.A. bantamweight champion who won 10 of his first 13 professional fights inside the distance before capturing the vacant British featherweight title with a disputed points decision over John Feeney. In his next fight Dickie demolished former champion Sammy Sims in five rounds and then won a Lonsdale belt in a record 203 days while clearing up any doubt about his superiority over Feeney with another points victory at Ebbw Vale in October 1986.

## DICKSON, Alex:

After winning the A.B.A. lightweight title in 1984 and representing Britain in the Olympic Games, this stylish Scottish

southpaw from Bellshill narrowly outpointed Tony Willis for the British
lightweight title in his third year as a
professional. Although badly cut about
the face in this September 1987 contest
Dickson showed non-stop aggression.

## DILLON, Jack:

A hard-hitting American who had
Scottish and Irish blood in his veins,
Jack Dillon met most of the best men of
his day. He just lacked the avoirdupois
to win a world heavyweight title but he
was one of the best cruiserweights of all
time and was not afraid to concede
weight to any fighter.

Dillon was not known as "Jack the
Giant Killer" for nothing. One of his
outstanding achievements was to concede 2st. 7lbs. (35lbs.) to Frank Moran
and beat him decisively over 10 rounds
in a "No Decision" bout, Brooklyn,
June 29, 1916.

With Philadelphia Jack O'Brien and
Tommy Burns both concentrating on
the heavyweight division, Jack Dillon
claimed the light-heavyweight championship in 1909 but he was not accorded
world-wide recognition at that time.

When O'Brien retired in 1912 Dillon's
claim to the title was undisputed and he
gained official recognition by defeating
Al Norton over 10 rounds, April 28,
1914.

Dillon lost his title to Battling
Levinsky at Boston, October 24, 1916.

## DIXIE KID:

An American negro, his real name was
Aaron L. Brown. He fought many times
in England, and although at his best he
weighed under 10 stone (140lbs.) he was
always willing to fight anyone from
welterweight to heavyweight.

In April, 1904, he beat the redoubtable
Joe Walcott on a foul in 20 rounds, and
subsequently fought a draw with the
West Indian negro. But although Walcott
was recognised as world welterweight
champion at that time, this honour was
never passed on to the Dixie Kid.

The Kid himself never pressed the
matter, the title didn't bother him, and
when he came to Europe in 1905 he left
his championship claim behind him in
America.

In this country the Dixie Kid beat
three of our welterweight champions
inside the distance, namely Arthur
Evernden, Johnny Summers, and Jack
Goldswain.

## DIXON, George:

A Canadian negro, born at Halifax,
Nova Scotia, George Dixon was one of
the most skilful coloured boxers ever,
and although at times his claim to the
world featherweight crown was in dispute, he may well have fought more
world title contests than any other boxer
in history.

Dixon was the first man to be
recognised as world bantamweight
champion following his victory over
Nunc Wallace at the Pelican Club,
London, in June, 1890, but he soon put
on weight and relinquished his claim to
the title.

In March, 1891, he knocked out Cal
McCarthy in 22 rounds at Troy, New
York, and claimed the world feather-
weight crown.

Dixon lost this title to Solly Smith on
points over 20 rounds at San Francisco
in October, 1897, but he regained it from
Dave Sullivan just over a year later.

He finally lost the featherweight
championship to Terry McGovern in
New York, January 9, 1900. Dixon took
a terrible beating in this fight before his
manager threw in the sponge in the
eighth round. He was never the same
fighter again afterwards.

## DOHERTY, John:

It was when the B.B.B.C. decided to
re-activate the junior-lightweight division
in 1986 that this Yorkshireman from
Bradford was given a chance to become
a champion. He came in as a late
substitute for the injured Najib Daho
and outpointed Croydon Irishman Pat
Doherty to become the first British 9st.
4lbs. title-holder for nearly 16 years.

John showed plenty of class in that
victory but only 91 days later he could
not match the experience, class and
strength of veteran Pat Cowdell who
lifted his crown by stopping him inside
six rounds.

## DOWER, Dai:

Born Abercynon, Wales, 1933, Dai Dower lost only four bouts in a distinguished amateur career. He was Welsh amateur and A.B.A. flyweight champion in 1952 and also represented Great Britain at the Olympic Games of that year.

In 1953 he turned professional and in October, 1954, he became Empire flyweight champion by outpointing Jake Tuli over 15 rounds.

Dower won the vacant British flyweight championship with a points decision over Eric Marsden at Harringay, February 8, 1955.

A month later he gained the European flyweight title with a victory over Nazzareno Gianelli, of Italy, but he lost this to the Spaniard, Young Martin, when he was stopped in the 12th round, October 3, 1955.

In March, 1957, Dower went to Buenos Aires to meet Pascual Perez for the world flyweight title but he was knocked out in the first round.

Dower relinquished his British title soon afterwards.

## DOWNES, Terry:

Born London, 1936, Downes became one of the most colourful characters in British boxing and went on fighting for the sheer love of it long after becoming one of the game's richest men.

He first took up boxing seriously when serving in the U.S. Marines, and won U.S. All-Services titles. But for his tendency to cut easily he might have had even more successes in the ring, but as it was he won the British middleweight title over 17 months after his first professional fight in Britain and the world title just over two years later in January, 1961.

Downes collected the British title by stopping Phil Edwards in 13 rounds. He lost it to John McCormack on a foul but regained the crown by stopping the Scotsman in a return bout.

Another of those bad cuts forced the referee to stop the fight when Downes first attempted to wrest the world title from Paul Pender, but the aggressive British fighter achieved his ambition in a return.

Pender outpointed Downes in a third meeting in 1962 and at the end of that year the B.B.B.C. deprived Downes of his British title for refusing to defend it against John McCormack within a certain time.

Downes was a fighter who always gave value for money and so it was shortly before his retirement, when in November, 1964, he tried to capture the world light-heavyweight title but was beaten in 11 rounds by Willie Pastrano.

## DRAWS:

Of all the world champions, George Dixon and Young Griffo are the men who were concerned in the most drawn contests. The precise figures are difficult to ascertain with certainty but each had between 40 and 50.

Dixon fought 39 contests in Britain in 1890 and 1902-05, and 16 of these were draws.

There has been only one drawn contest for the world heavyweight title under Queensberry Rules. That was in 1906 when Tommy Burns, the holder, was held to a draw by Philadelphia Jack O'Brien.

Another contest involving a world heavyweight champion also ended in a draw. That was the occasion when Jack Johnson met another negro, Jim Johnson, in Paris in December, 1913. This was declared a draw at the end of 10 rounds when Jack was unable to continue because of a broken hand. However, this is not normally ranked as a championship contest.

The following are the only drawn contests where a British title has been at stake:—

Len Harvey (holder) v. Jack Hood, Dec. 18, 1929. Middleweight.

Harry Mason (holder) v. Len Harvey, Apl. 29, 1926. Welterweight.

Al Foreman (holder) v. Johnny Cuthbert, Dec. 15, 1930. Lightweight.

Jabez White (holder) v. Jim Curran, Dec. 23, 1901. Lightweight.

Jim Driscoll (holder) v. Owen Moran, Jan. 27, 1913. Featherweight.

Harry Corbett (holder) v. Johnny Cuthbert, Mar. 18, 1929. Featherweight.

Johnny Cuthbert (holder) v. Nel Tarleton, Nov. 6, 1930. Featherweight.

Dick Corbett (holder) v. Johnny King, Aug. 20, 1934. Bantamweight.
Rinty Monaghan (holder) v. Terry Allen, Sept. 30, 1949. Flyweight.

## DRISCOLL, Jim:

This handsome Welshman, born at Cardiff in 1880, was one of the real masters of the noble art of self defence. He was an exponent of the true straight left delivered as a scoring punch and as adept at ducking and slipping punches as any boxer who ever lived.

Quiet and unassuming, Jim Driscoll endeared himself to the hearts of all Welshmen. He was inclined to be temperamental, however, and one occasion when this was most noticeable was when he was disqualified for butting Freddy Welsh in a contest at Cardiff in December, 1910.

Still, it was a rare occurrence to see Driscoll lose his temper in the ring, for he was a really scientific boxer in the best tradition of the game.

Driscoll took the British feather-weight title from Joe Bowker with a k.o. in the 17th round, N.S.C., June 1, 1907.

He held on to this British crown until retiring in 1913 soon after he had been held to a draw by Owen Moran.

In February, 1910, Driscoll won the first Lonsdale Belt match in the feather-weight division by stopping Seaman Hayes in six rounds, and he went on to make the belt his own property with two victories over Spike Robson.

During his distinguished career Jim Driscoll also won the European feather-weight title by knocking out Jean Poesy, of France, in 12 rounds at the N.S.C. in June, 1912.

In 1909 Driscoll went to America and there met the world featherweight cham-pion, Abe Attell, over 10 rounds in New York. The Welshman was considered by most judges to have had the better of this contest but it was a "no decision" bout and Attell could not lose the title without being knocked out.

Driscoll attempted a come-back in 1919 when he beat Pedlar Palmer and drew with Francis Rossi, but in his next contest, after outboxing the hard-hitting Frenchman, Charles Ledoux, for 14 rounds, Driscoll's seconds threw in the towel in the 16th round when the Welshman had been caught by some of Ledoux's murderous punches and was in a bad way. Afterwards Ledoux referred to Jim Driscoll as "my master at boxing."

Jim Driscoll died of consumption, January, 1925.

## DUFFY, Paddy:

An Irish-American from Boston, Paddy Duffy was the first man to be recognised as world welterweight cham-pion when he beat Bob Lyons, of England, in a bare-knuckle contest at Boston, April, 1884.

The welterweight limit was then set at 142lbs. and Duffy confirmed his right to the title by stopping Billy McMillan in 17 rounds at Fort Foote, Vancouver.

Duffy died of consumption when only in his twenties, July 19, 1890.

## DUNDEE, Joe:

An Italian-American welterweight, Joe Dundee got himself in line for a crack at the world title when he beat the former champion, Mickey Walker, in eight rounds, June 24, 1926.

In December of the same year he was halted in one round by Eddie Roberts, but that fighter had come in slightly over the weight. In any event, Dundee won the return match.

Dundee gained the world title by outpointing Pete Latzo in New York, June 3, 1927. In August, 1928, he was beaten by Jack Thompson in an over-weight match, and lost his title to Jackie Fields at Detroit, when he was dis-qualified in the second round, July 25, 1929.

## DUNDEE, Johnny:

This great-hearted fighter was born in Italy, went to America at an early age and started his ring career there about 1910. He went on fighting until 1932 and was one of the busiest featherweights of his day.

His real name was Giuseppe Carrora and a remarkable aspect of his career was that he would often take off as much as 15lbs. for a fight. He was extremely fast and won the world junior light-weight (130lbs.) title with a victory over

George Chaney in November, 1921.

He lost this title to Jack Bernstein in May, 1923, but two months later he became world featherweight champion by decisioning Eugene Criqui and before the end of the year regained the Junior lightweight title from Bernstein. He lost this lightweight crown to Kid Sullivan in June 1924 and resigned the featherweight title through weight difficulties the same year.

## DUNDEE, Vince:

Brother of the former world welterweight champion, Joe Dundee, Vince was recognised by the N.Y.A.C. as world middleweight title-holder following his points defeat of Lou Brouillard in October, 1933.

At this time Marcel Thil, of France, was more widely recognised as titleholder in this division, although the N.B.A. named Teddy Yarosz as their number one middleweight.

Eventually the N.B.A. and the N.Y.A.C. champions came together and Dundee was beaten. This was at Pittsburgh September 11, 1934.

In 1931 Dundee met two British champions. He twice outpointed Len Harvey in New York early in the year, and in July he came to London and was held to a draw by Jack Hood.

## DUNN, Richard:

A Bradford scaffolder whose boxing career was getting him nowhere until early in 1975 when at the age of 30 he came under the management of veteran George Biddles. He revitalised Dunn and the heavyweight, whose assets were gameness and a knock-out punch, made more money in the last two years of his career than most of his predecessors in much more extensive careers.

Despite having been previously k.o.'d by Bunny Johnson in a final eliminator for the British title Biddles immediately got Dunn a fight with Johnson. This time Dunn outpointed the coloured champion to take the British and Commonwealth crowns. He then defended these titles with a fine demolition job against Danny McAlinden in two rounds; flattened Texan Terry Krueger in three, and won the vacant European

title by battering Bernd August into defeat in three rounds. All this from a fighter who had lost four of his last seven fights before being managed by Biddles!

The big pay day for the 6ft 4in southpaw came in his next bout when he got a crack at the world title, but although showing gameness was well beaten by Muhammad Ali inside five rounds.

Joe Bugner then came out of retirement to prove Dunn's limitations by knocking him out in only 2 min 14 secs. All of Dunn's titles went in that fight and he ended his career by being knocked out in five by South African Kallie Knoetze in September 1977. It was the eleventh time in his career that Dunn had been stopped inside the distance but he laughed all the way to the bank.

## DURAN, Roberto:

At his peak this hard-hitting Panamanian fighter was one of the most feared opponents in the lightweight division. A former street-fighter he became known as "Stone Fist" in the 1970s when very few men could go the distance with him.

After winning the world lightweight title by stopping our own Ken Buchanan at the age of 21 in 1972, Duran successfully defended his crown on 12 occasions before relinquishing it in 1979 to move up into the welterweight division. He then had two memorable battles with Sugar Ray Leonard, outpointing him over 15 rounds to become World champion again in June 1980, but losing in a most shocking manner five months later and destroying his own reputation for toughness by turning his back and quitting in the eighth round.

However, those who thought his career finished were sadly mistaken for he came back to join the élite of men who have held three world titles, capturing the W.B.A. version of the Junior middleweight crown from Davey Moore in 1983.

Duran proved his greatness by going the distance with world middleweight champion Marvin Hagler in November 1983 and emerging virtually unscathed before officially relinquishing his junior middleweight title and then losing a title fight to Thomas Hearns with a second round k.o. in June 1984.

At the time of writing, this great little fighter has lost only seven of his 88 bouts, five of those defeats coming after his 30th birthday, but he has still not hung up his gloves.

# E

## EARL'S COURT, LONDON:

Earl's Court is a well-known venue for boxing in London. The Empress Hall was closed in 1958 but the Exhibition Hall now has a capacity of 18,000.

World flyweight champion, Peter Kane, beat the former bantamweight title-holder, Balthazar Sangchilli, at Earl's Court in April 1939.

Another great flyweight, Benny Lynch, fought his last important contest at this arena in 1938 when he was k.o.'d by Aurel Toma.

At the other end of the scale, Jack Petersen appeared once at Earl's Court, and that was when he successfully defended his British and Empire heavyweight titles against Jock McAvoy in April, 1936.

Two of the most important contests to be staged there since the last war were those between Randolph Turpin and Sugar Ray Robinson in 1951, when Turpin took the world middleweight title; Joe Brown and Dave Charnley nearly 10 years later, when the former retained his world lightweight crown, and when Muhammad Ali retained his world heavyweight title with a third round k.o. of Brian London in August 1966.

## EBIHARA, Hiroyuki:

This Japanese flyweight won the world title in sensational fashion in September, 1963, knocking out Pone Kingpetch in only 2 minutes 7 seconds.

Prior to this Ebihara, a southpaw, had suffered only one defeat in 38 professional fights, and that by another Jap who was to win the world flyweight title, Mashiko Harada.

Ebihara's title-winning fight was a short one, but so was his reign as champion, for it was only four months later that Kingpetch regained the crown, beating Ebihara on points.

## EDWARDS, Llew:

An outstanding boxer who maintained the true Driscoll tradition, this Welshman from Porth came to the fore in 1914 and won the vacant British featherweight title with a victory over Owen Moran at the N.S.C., May 31, 1915. Moran was disqualified in the 10th round.

Six months later Edwards went to Australia and there he collected the Empire title by stopping Jimmy Hill in 13 rounds at Sydney.

Edwards remained in Australia and relinquished his British title in 1916.

In September, 1917, he won the Australian lightweight crown and held this until April, 1921.

## EMPIRE and COMMONWEALTH TITLES: Title Holders since World War I:

*Heavyweight.*

Joe Beckett bt. George Cook, disq. 6, London, Apl. 10, 1922. Beckett relinquished title.

Phil Scott bt. George Cook, disq. 17, Edinburgh, Jan. 27, 1926.

Larry Gains bt. Scott, k.o. 2, Leicester, June 13, 1931.

Len Harvey bt. Gains, pts. 15, London, Feb. 8, 1934.

Jack Petersen bt. Harvey, rtd. 12, London, June 4, 1934.

Ben Foord bt. Petersen, r.s.f. 3, Leicester, Aug. 17, 1936.

Tommy Farr bt. Foord, pts. 15, London, Mar. 15, 1937. Farr deprived of title by B.B.B.C.

Len Harvey bt. Larry Gains, rtd. 13, London, Mar. 10, 1939. Harvey relinquished title.

Jack London bt. Freddie Mills, pts. 15, Manchester, Sept. 15, 1944.

Bruce Woodcock bt. London, k.o. 6, London, July 17, 1945.

Jack Gardner bt. Woodcock, rtd. 11, London, Nov. 14, 1950.

Johnny Williams bt. Gardner, pts. 15, London, Mar. 11, 1952.

Don Cockell bt. Williams, pts. 15, London, May 12, 1953. Cockell relinquished title.

Joe Bygraves bt. Kitione Lave, pts. 15, London, June 26, 1956.

Joe Erskine bt. Bygraves, pts. 15, Leicester, Nov. 25, 1957.

Brian London bt. Erskine, k.o. 8, London, June 3, 1958.

Henry Cooper bt. London, pts. 15, London, Jan. 12, 1959.

Joe Bugner bt. Cooper, pts. 15, London, Mar. 16, 1971.

Jack Bodell bt. Bugner, pts. 15, London, Sept. 27, 1971.

Danny McAlinden bt. Bodell, k.o. 2, Birmingham, June 27, 1972.

Bunny Johnson bt. McAlinden, k.o. 9, London, Jan. 13, 1975.

Richard Dunn bt. Johnson, pts. 15, London, Sept. 30, 1975.

Joe Bugner bt. Dunn, k.o. 1, London, Oct. 12, 1976.

Bugner relinquished title March 1977.

John L. Gardner bt. Billy Aird, rtd. 5, London, Oct. 24, 1978.

Gardner retired 1981.

Trevor Berbick bt. Conroy Nelson, r.s.f. 2, Halifax, Canada, July 21, 1981.

Berbick deprived of title Jan. 1986.

Horace Notice bt. Hughroy Currie, r.s.f. 6, Isle of Man, Apr. 12, 1986.

### Cruiserweight

Stewart Lithgo bt. Steve Aczel, k.o. 11, Brisbane, May 14, 1984.

Chisanda Mutti bt. Lithgo, r.s.f. 9, Dusseldorf, W. Germany, Dec. 1, 1984.

Glenn McCrory bt. Mutti, pts 12, Gateshead, Sept. 4, 1987.

### Light-heavyweight.

Jack Bloomfield bt. Soldier Jones, rtd. 5, London, Mar. 26, 1923. Bloomfield relinquished title.

Tom Berry bt. Dave Magill, pts. 20, Manchester, Jan. 31, 1927.

Gipsy Daniels bt. Berry, pts. 20, London, Apl. 25, 1927. Daniels relinquished title.

Len Harvey bt. Jock McAvoy, pts. 15, London, July 10, 1939.

Freddie Mills bt. Harvey, k.o. 2, London, June 20, 1942. Mills relinquished title.

Randolph Turpin bt. Don Cockell, r.s.f. 11, London, June 10, 1952. Turpin relinquished title.

Gordon Wallace bt. Ron Barton, pts. 15, London, June 19, 1956.

Yvon Durelle bt. Wallace, k.o. 2, Moncton, May 30, 1957. Durelle retired 1959.

Chic Calderwood bt. Johnny Halafihi, r.s.f. 12, Glasgow, June 9, 1960.

Calderwood forfeited title Nov. 1963.

Bob Dunlop bt. John (Young) McCormack, r.s.f. 7, Sydney, Feb. 12, 1968.

Dunlop relinquished title.

Eddie Avoth bt. Trevor Thornberry, rtd. 6, Brisbane, Oct. 23, 1970.

Chris Finnegan bt. Avoth, r.s.f. 15, London, Jan. 24, 1971.

John Conteh bt. Finnegan, pts. 15, London, May 22, 1973.

Conteh relinquished title 1974.

Steve Aczel bt. Maxie Smith, r.s.f. 3, Manchester, Feb. 19, 1975.

Tony Mundine bt. Aczel, k.o. 12, Blacktown, Australia, Oct. 30, 1975.

Gary Summerhays bt. Mundine k.o. 11, Melbourne, Feb. 27, 1978.

Lottie Mwale bt. Summerhays, r.s.f. 5, Lusaka, Zambia, Mar. 31, 1979.

Leslie Stewart bt. Mwale, pts. 12, Trinidad, Aug. 4. 1985.

Stewart relinquished title May 1987.

Willy Featherstone bt. Enoch Chama, pts. 12, Sydney, Nova Scotia, Sept. 12, 1987.

### Middleweight

Ted "Kid" Lewis bt. Frankie Burns, k.o. 11, London, June 19, 1922.

Roland Todd bt. Lewis, pts. 20, London, Feb. 15, 1923. Todd relinquished title.

Tommy Milligan bt. George West, r.s.f. 14, London, July 12, 1926. Milligan deprived of title by N.S.C.

Len Harvey bt. Alex Ireland, k.o. 7, London, May 16, 1929.

Jock McAvoy bt. Harvey, pts. 15, Manchester, Apl. 10, 1933. McAvoy relinquished title.

Ron Richards bt. Fred Henneberry, disq. 11, Sydney, Feb. 26, 1940. Richards relinquished title.

Bos Murphy bt. Vince Hawkins pts. 15, London, Jan. 26, 1948.

Dick Turpin bt. Murphy, k.o. 1,

Coventry, May 18, 1948.

Dave Sands bt. Turpin, k.o. 1, London, Sept. 6, 1949. Sands was killed August, 1952.

Randolph Turpin bt. George Angelo, pts. 15, London, Oct. 21, 1952. Turpin relinquished title.

Johnny Sullivan bt. Gordon Hazell, k.o. 1, London, Sept. 14, 1954.

Pat McAteer bt. Sullivan, disq. 9, Liverpool, June 16, 1955.

Dick Tiger bt. McAteer, k.o. 9, Liverpool, Mar. 27, 1958.

Wilf Greaves bt. Tiger, pts. 15, Edmonton, June 22, 1960.

Dick Tiger bt. Greaves, r.s.f. 9, Edmonton, Nov. 30, 1960.

Tiger relinquished title Sept. 1963.

Gomeo Brennan bt. Mick Leahy, pts. 15, London, Oct. 22, 1963.

Tuna Scanlan bt. Brennan, pts. 15, Auckland, Mar. 14, 1964. Scanlan retired.

Gomeo Brennan bt. Earl Nikova, pts. 15, Auckland, Nov. 12, 1964.

Blair Richardson bt. Brennan pts. 15, Glace Bay, Canada, Mar. 26, 1966.

Richardson relinquished title.

Johnny Pritchett bt. Milho Calhoun, rtd. 8, Manchester, Oct. 9, 1967.

Pritchett retired June 1969.

Les McAteer bt. Wally Swift, rtd. 11, Nottingham, July 14, 1969.

Mark Rowe bt. McAteer, r.s.f. 14, London, May 12, 1970.

Bunny Sterling bt. Rowe, r.s.f. 4, London, Sept. 8, 1970.

Tony Mundine bt. Sterling, r.s.f. 15, Brisbane, Apl. 14, 1972.

Mundine relinquished title May 1975.

Monty Betham bt. Carlos Mark, pts. 15, Wellington, N.Z. July 24, 1975.

Alipate Korovou bt. Betham, k.o. 12, Fiji, Mar. 18, 1978.

Ayub Kalule bt. Korovou, r.s.f. 14, Copenhagen, May 25, 1978.

Kalule deprived of title Jan. 1980.

Tony Sibson bt. Chisanda Mutti, pts. 15, Wembley, Mar. 4, 1980.

Sibson relinquished title 1983.

Roy Gumbs bt. Ralph Hollett, r.s.f. 5, Nova Scotia, Feb, 8, 1983.

Mark Kaylor bt. Gumbs, k.o. 5, Alexandra Pavilion, London, Sept. 14, 1983.

Tony Sibson bt. Kaylor, pts. 12,

Wembley. Nov. 27, 1984.

*Light-middleweight*

Charkey Ramon bt. Pat Dwyer, r.s.f. 8, Melbourne, Oct. 30, 1972.

Ramon retired 1975.

Maurice Hope bt. Tony Poole, r.s.f. 12, London, Apl. 20, 1976.

Hope relinquished title Mar. 1979.

Kenny Bristol bt. Pat Thomas, pts. 15, Georgetown, July 29, 1979.

Herol Graham bt. Bristol, pts. 15, Sheffield, Nov. 25, 1981.

Graham relinquished title 1984.

Ken Salisbury bt. Nelson Bosso, pts. 12, Sydney, Australia, Aug. 21, 1984.

Nick Wilshire bt. Salisbury, r.s.f. 2, Albert Hall, London, June 5, 1985.

Lloyd Hibbert bt. Wilshire, pts. 12, Albert Hall, London, Mar. 11, 1987.

Troy Waters bt. Hibbert, t.k.o. 4, Hobart, Aug. 16, 1987.

*Welterweight*

Johnny Basham bt. Matt Wells, pts. 20, London, Nov. 13, 1919.

Ted "Kid" Lewis bt. Basham, k.o. 9, London, June 9, 1920.

Tommy Milligan bt. Lewis, pts. 20, Edinburgh, Nov. 26, 1924. Milligan relinquished title.

Eddie Thomas bt. Pat Patrick, k.o. 13, Johannesburg, Jan. 27, 1951.

Wally Thom bt. Thomas, pts. 15, London, Oct. 16, 1951.

Cliff Curvis bt. Thom, k.o. 9, Liverpool, July 24, 1952.

Gerald Dreyer bt. Curvis, pts. 15, Johannesburg, Dec. 8, 1952.

Barry Brown bt. Dreyer, r.s.f. 7, Wellington, Jan. 15, 1954.

George Barnes bt. Brown, k.o. 11, Sydney, Nov. 24, 1954.

Darby Brown bt. Barnes, pts. 15, Sydney, Aug. 6, 1956.

George Barnes bt. Brown, pts. 15, Sydney, Nov. 12, 1956.

John Van Rensburg bt. Barnes, pts. 15, Salisbury, May 17, 1958.

George Barnes bt. Van Rensburg, r.s.f. 13, Sydney, Aug. 18, 1958.

Brian Curvis bt. Barnes, pts. 15, Swansea, May 9, 1960.

Curvis retired October 1, 1966.

Johnny Cooke bt. Lennox Beckles, pts. 15, Liverpool, Oct. 16, 1967.

Ralph Charles bt. Cooke, pts. 15, London, Feb. 20, 1968.

Charles stripped of title by B.B.B.C.

Clyde Gray bt. Eddie Blay, pts. 15, Toronto, Feb. 12, 1973.

Chris Clarke bt. Gray, r.s.f. 10, Halifax, Canada, Aug. 28, 1979.

Clyde Gray bt Clarke, r.s.f. 10, Halifax, Canada, Nov. 13, 1979.

Gray retired 1980.

Colin Jones bt. Mick Harris, r.s.f. 9, Wembley, Mar. 3, 1981.

Jones relinquished title 1984.

Sylvester Mittee bt. Fighting Romanus, Britannia L.C., London, Oct. 10, 1984.

Lloyd Honeyghan bt. Mittee, r.s.f. 8, Alexandra Pavilion, London, Nov. 27, 1985.

Honeyghan relinquished title 1986.

Brian Janssen bt. Judas Clottey, pts, 12, Brisbane, Australia, Apl. 6, 1987.

Wilf Gentzen bt. Janssen, pts. 12, Melbourne, Australia, Aug. 28, 1987.

*Light-welterweight*

Joe Tetteh bt. Joe Santos, r.s.f. 10, Wellington, Sept. 21, 1972.

Hector Thompson bt. Tetteh, pts. 15, Brisbane, Mar. 26, 1973.

Lachie Austin bt. Thompson, r.s.f. 15, Perth, Australia, Apl. 28, 1977, but owing to dispute over fighters' weights title declared vacant.

Hector Thompson bt. Austin, pts. 15, Perth, Australia, June 6, 1977.

Lachie Austin bt. Thompson, pts. 15, Perth, Sept. 15, 1977.

Jeff Malcolm bt. Austin, Melbourne, Sept. 24, 1978.

Obisia Nwankpa bt. Malcolm, pts. 15, Lagos, Mar. 3, 1979.

Billy Famous bt. Nwankpa, pts. 12, Lagos, Nigeria, May 28, 1983.

Famous relinquished title 1986.

Tony Laing bt. David Chibuye, r.s.f. 11, Tottenham, Oct. 24, 1987.

*Lightweight*

Laurie Stevens bt. Jack "Kid" Berg, pts. 12, Johannesburg, Jan. 11, 1936.

Stevens relinquished title.

Arthur King bt. Billy Thompson, rtd. 7, Manchester, Oct. 1, 1948. King Forfeited title 1951.

Frank Johnson bt. Frank Flannery, r.s.f. 10, Melbourne, Jan. 23, 1953.

Pat Ford bt. Johnson, pts. 15, Melbourne, Aug. 28, 1953.

Ivor Germain bt. Ford, pts. 15, Melbourne, Apl. 9, 1954.

Pat Ford bt. Germain, pts. 15, Melbourne, July 2, 1954. Ford relinquished title.

John Van Rensburg bt. Joe Lucy, Johannesburg, Feb. 12, 1955.

Willie Toweel bt. Van Rensburg, pts. 15. Johannesburg, June 16, 1956.

Dave Charnley bt. Toweel, k.o. 10, Wembley, London, May 12, 1959.

Bunny Grant bt. Charnley, pts. 15, Jamaica, Aug. 4, 1962.

Manoel Santos bt. Grant pts. 15, Wellington, Mar. 15, 1967.

Santos retired 1967.

Love Allotey bt. Bunny Grant, pts. 15, Accra, Oct. 7, 1967.

Percy Hayles bt. Allotey, pts. 15, Kingston, Jamaica, July 27, 1968.

Hayles deprived of title for failing to defend against nominated contenders 1975.

Jonathan Dele bt. Jimmy Watt, pts. 15, Lagos, May 3, 1975.

Lennox Blackmore bt. Dele, pts. 15, Lagos, Sept. 30, 1977.

Hogan Jimoh bt. Blackmore, k.o. 5, Lagos, Oct. 25, 1978.

Langton Tinago bt. Jimoh, r.s.f. 7, Lagos, Dec. 7, 1980.

Barry Michael bt. Tinago, pts. 15, Melbourne, May 6, 1981.

Claude Noel bt. Michael, pts. 15, Melbourne, Australia, July 22, 1982.

Graeme Brooke bt. Noel, pts. 12, Melbourne, Australia, Nov. 2, 1984.

Barry Michael bt. Brooke, pts. 12, Melbourne, Australia, Feb. 22, 1985.

Michael deprived of title 1986.

Langton Tinago bt. Graeme Brooke, k.o. 5, Manchester, Aug. 23, 1986.

Mo Hussein bt. Tinago, k.o. 12, Basildon, Mar. 4, 1987.

*Junior Lightweight*

Billy Moeller bt. Jimmy Bell, pts. 15, Sydney, May 13, 1975.

Johnny Abba bt. Moeller, pts., 15, New Guinea, Dec. 1, 1977.

Abba relinquished title (rtd.) Dec. 1982.

Langton Tinago bt. Safui Okebaden, pts. 12, Zimbabwe, May 7, 1983.

John Sichula bt. Tanago, k.o. 5, Zimbabwe, Feb. 4, 1984.

Lester Ellis bt. Sichula, pts. 12, Melbourne, Australia, Nov. 16, 1984. Ellis relinquished title 1985.

John Sichula bt. Hans Sankisa, k.o. 3, Zambia, June 8, 1985.

Sam Akromah bt. Sichula, pts. 12, Accra, Oct. 26, 1986.

John Sichula bt. Akromah, pts. 12, Lusaka, Aug. 29, 1987.

### Featherweight.

Johnny McGrory bt. Willie Smith, pts. 12, Johannesburg, Dec. 26, 1936. McGrory relinquished title.

"Spider" Jim Kelly bt. Benny Caplan, pts. 15, Belfast, Nov. 23, 1938.

Johnny Cusick bt. Kelly, pts. 15, Belfast, June 28, 1939.

Nel Tarleton bt. Cusick, pts. 15, Liverpool, Feb. 1, 1940. Tarleton relinquished title.

Al Phillips bt. Cliff Anderson, pts. 15, London, Mar. 18, 1947.

Ronnie Clayton bt. Phillips, pts. 15, Liverpool, Sept. 11, 1947.

Roy Ankrah bt. Clayton, pts. 15, London, Apl. 30, 1951.

Billy Kelly bt. Ankrah, pts. 15, Belfast, Oct. 2, 1954.

Hogan Bassey bt. Kelly, k.o. 8, Belfast, Nov. 19, 1955. Bassey relinquished title.

Percy Lewis bt. Charlie Hill, r.s.f. 10, Nottingham Dec. 9, 1957.

Floyd Robertson bt. Lewis, pts. 15, Belfast, Nov. 26, 1960.

John O'Brien bt. Robertson, pts. 12, Accra, Feb. 3, 1967.

Johnny Famechon bt. O'Brien, r.s.f. 11, Melbourne, Nov. 24, 1967. Famechon relinquished title 1969.

Toro George bt. Ken Bradley, r.s.f. 6, Canberra, Dec. 12, 1970.

Bobby Dunne bt. George, pts. 15, Melbourne, Nov. 3, 1970.

Evan Armstrong bt. Dunne, r.s.f. 8, Brisbane, Apl. 5, 1974.

David Kotey bt. Armstrong, k.o. 10, Accra, Dec. 7, 1974. Kotey relinquished title 1975.

Eddie Ndukwu bt. Alan Richardson, r.s.f. 12, Lagos, June 17, 1977.

Pat Ford bt. Ndukwu, rtd. 9, Lagos, Aug. 1, 1980.

Ford relinquished title 1981.

Azuma Nelson bt. Brian Roberts, r.s.f. 5, Accra, Sept. 26, 1981. Nelson relinquished title 1985.

Tyrone Downes bt. Snake Mandeya, pts. 12, Trinidad, Feb. 28, 1986.

### Super-bantamweight

Paul Ferreri bt. Brian Roberts, r.s.f. 15, Perth, Australia, Sept. 15, 1977. Division abandoned 1978.

### Bantamweight

Jimmy Higgins bt. Vince Blackburn, pts. 20, London, Apl. 26, 1920.

Tommy Harrison bt. Higgins, k.o. 13, Liverpool, June 26, 1922.

Harry Lake bt. Harrison, pts. 20, London, Feb. 26, 1923.

Johnny Brown (St. George's) bt. Lake, pts. 20, London, Nov. 26, 1923.

Teddy Baldock bt. Brown, r.s.f. 2, London, Aug. 29, 1928. Baldock relinquished title.

Dick Corbett bt. Willie Smith, pts. 15, London, May 22, 1930.

Johnny King bt. Corbett, pts. 15, Manchester, Oct. 10, 1932.

Dick Corbett bt. King, pts. 15, Manchester, Feb. 12, 1934. Corbett relinquished title.

Jim Brady bt. Kid Tanner, pts. 15, Dundee, Jan. 1, 1941.

Jackie Paterson bt. Brady, pts. 15. Glasgow, Sept. 12, 1945.

Stan Rowan bt. Paterson, pts. 15, Liverpool, Mar. 24, 1949.

Vic Toweel bt. Rowan, pts. 15, Johannesburg, Nov. 12, 1949.

Jimmy Carruthers bt. Toweel, k.o. 1, Johannesburg, Nov. 15, 1952. Carruthers relinquished title.

Peter Keenan bt. Bobby Sinn, pts. 15, Sydney, Mar. 28, 1955.

Freddie Gilroy bt. Keenan, r.s.f. 11, Belfast, Jan. 10, 1959. Gilroy relinquished title Nov. 1963.

Johnny Caldwell bt. George Bowes, r.s.f. 7, Belfast, Mar. 5, 1964.

Alan Rudkin bt. Caldwell, r.s.f. 10, Nottingham, Mar. 22, 1965.

Walter McGowan bt. Rudkin, pts. 15, Wembley, Sept. 6, 1966.

Alan Rudkin bt. McGowan, pts. 15, Manchester, May, 13, 1968.

Lionel Rose bt. Rudkin, pts. 15, Melbourne, Mar. 8, 1969.
Rose relinquished title.
Alan Rudkin bt. Johnny Clark, r.s.f. 12, London, Apl. 21, 1970.
Rudkin retired.
Paul Ferreri bt. John Kellie, pts. 15, Melbourne, Sept. 16, 1972.
Sully Shittu bt. Ferreri, pts. 15, Accra, Jan. 29, 1977.
Shittu deprived of title by Commonwealth Committee July 1978.
Johnny Owen bt. Ferreri, pts. 15, Ebbw Vale, Nov. 2, 1978.
Owen died Nov. 1980.
Paul Ferreri bt. Mike Irungu, pts. 15, Copenhagen, May 21, 1981.
Ferreri deprived of title July 1986.
Ray Minus bt. Ferreri, t.k.o. 10, Nassau, Sept. 27, 1986.

*Flyweight*
Jackie Paterson bt. Kid Tanner, pts. 15, Manchester, Mar. 11, 1940.
Rinty Monaghan bt. Paterson, k.o. 7, Belfast, Mar. 23, 1948. Monaghan relinquished title.
Teddy Gardner bt. Terry Allen, pts. 15, Newcastle, Mar. 17, 1952.
Jake Tuli bt. Gardner, r.s.f. 12, Newcastle, Sept. 8, 1952.
Dai Dower bt. Tuli, pts. 15, London, Oct. 19, 1954. Dower relinquished title.
Frankie Jones bt. Len Reece, k.o. 11, Porthcawl, July 31, 1957.
Dennis Adams bt. Jones, k.o. 3, Glasgow, Oct. 23, 1957.
Adams forfeited title 1962.
Jackie Brown bt. Orizu Obilaso, pts. 15, London, Dec. 10, 1962.
Walter McGowan bt. Brown, k.o. 12, Paisley, May 2, 1963.
McGowan relinquished title 1966.
John McCluskey bt. Harry Hayes, pts. 15, Melbourne, July 16, 1970.
Henry Nissen bt. McCluskey, rtrd. 8, Melbourne, Aug. 6, 1971.
Jim West bt. Nissen, r.s.f. 4, Melbourne, Mar. 14, 1974.
West relinquished title 1975.
Patrick Mambwe bt. Gwyn Jones, r.s.f. 9, Lusaka, July 3, 1976.
Title declared vacant June 1979.
Ray Amoo bt. Neil McLaughlin, pts. 15, Lagos, Feb. 8, 1980.
Stephen Muchoki bt. Amoo, r.s.f. 12, Copenhagen, Oct. 17, 1980.
Keith Williams bt. Muchoki, r.s.f. 9, Bloomsbury Crest Hotel, London, Feb. 3, 1983.
Williams relinquished title 1985.
Richard Clarke bt. Wayne Mulholland, k.o. 4, Jamaica, Apr. 26, 1986.
Clarke deprived of title 1987.
Nana Yaw Konadu bt. Albert Musankabala, k.o. 6, Accra, Oct. 10, 1987.

## ENGLAND:
## Champions:
World:—
Heavyweight: Bob Fitzsimmons, 1897-99.
Light-heavyweight: Bob Fitzsimmons, 1903-05; Len Harvey, 1939-42 (not recognised in America); Freddie Mills, 1942-50 (not recognised in America until 1948); John Conteh (W.B.C. version) 1974-77.
Middleweight: Bob Fitzsimmons, 1891-94; Randolph Turpin, 1951, 1953 (European version); Terry Downes, 1961-62; Alan Minter, 1980.
Welterweight: Ted "Kid" Lewis, 1914-16, 1917-19; John H. Stracey (W.B.C.), 1975-76.
Lightweight: Arthur Chambers, 1872-79.
Featherweight: None.
Bantamweight: Billy Plimmer, 1892-95; Pedlar Palmer, 1895-99; Joe Bowker, 1904-05; Digger Stanley, 1909-12.
Flyweight: Sid Smith, 1912-13; Jackie Brown, 1932-35; Peter Kane, 1938-43; Terry Allen, 1950; Charlie Magri, 1983.
European:—
Heavyweight: Bruce Woodcock, 1946-50; Jack Gardner, 1951; Dick Richardson, 1960-62; Henry Cooper, 1964, 1968-69, 1970-71; Joe Bugner, 1971, 1972-75, 1976-77; Jack Bodell, 1971; Richard Dunn, 1976; John L. Gardner, 1980-81; Frank Bruno 1985-86.
Cruiserweight: Sammy Reeson, 1987-
Light-heavyweight: Freddie Mills, 1947-50; Don Cockell, 1951-52; Chris Finnegan, 1972; John Conteh, 1973-74.
Middleweight: Gus Platts, 1921; Ted "Kid" Lewis, 1921-23; Roland Todd,

1923-24; Len Harvey, 1929-32 (disputed); Randolph Turpin, 1951-54; Kevin Finnegan, 1974-75, 1980; Alan Minter, 1978-79; Tony Sibson, 1980-82, 1984-85; Herol Graham 1986-87.

Light-middleweight: Herol Graham 1983-84; Chris Pyatt 1986-87.

Welterweight: Young Joseph, 1910-11; Arthur Evernden, 1911 (disputed); Ted "Kid" Lewis, 1920-23; Billy Mack, 1923; Jack Hood, 1933; Ernie Roderick, 1946-47; Wally Thom, 1954-55; Ralph Charles, 1970-71; John Stracey, 1974-75; Dave Green, 1979.

Light-welterweight: Dave Green, 1976-77; Colin Power, 1978; Clinton McKenzie, 1980-82; Terry Marsh 1985-86

Lightweight: Matt Wells, 1911-12; Bob Marriot, 1919; Ernie Rice, 1921-22; Harry Mason, 1923-24; Alf Howard, 1930; Billy Thompson, 1948-49; Dave Charnley, 1960-63.

Junior Lightweight: Pat Cowdell, 1984-85.

Featherweight: Ted "Kid" Lewis, 1913-14; Billy Matthews, 1922; Al Phillips, 1947; Ron Clayton, 1947-48; Pat Cowdell, 1982-83; Jimmy McDonnell, 1985-86.

Bantamweight: Joe Bowker, 1910; Digger Stanley, 1910-12; Tom Harrison, 1921-22; Harry Lake, 1923; Johnny Brown, 1923-24; Teddy Baldock, 1928-29; Peter Kane, 1947-48; Alan Rudkin, 1971; Johnny Clark, 1973-74.

Flyweight: Sid Smith, 1913; Bill Ladbury, 1913-14; Jackie Brown, 1931-32; Terry Allen, 1950; Teddy Gardner, 1950-53; Charlie Magri, 1979-83, 1984-85, 1985-86; Duke McKenzie, 1986-

Empire and Commonwealth:-
Heavyweight: Billy Wells, 1914-19; Joe Beckett, 1920-22; Phil Scott, 1926-31; Len Harvey, 1934, 1939-42; Jack London, 1944-45; Bruce Woodcock, 1945-50; Jack Gardner, 1950-52; Don Cockell, 1953-54; Brian London, 1958-59; Henry Cooper, 1959-71; Joe Bugner, 1971, 1976-77; Jack Bodell, 1971-72; Richard Dunn, 1975-76; John L. Gardner, 1978-81; Horace Notice, 1986-

Cruiserweight: Stewart Lithgo, 1984; Glenn McCrory, 1987-

Light-heavyweight: Jack Bloomfield, 1923-24; Tom Berry, 1927; Len Harvey,

1939-42; Freddie Mills, 1942-50; Randolph Turpin, 1952-55; Chris Finnegan, 1971-73; John Conteh, 1973-74; Stewart Lithgo, 1984.

Middleweight: Ted "Kid" Lewis, 1922-23; Roland Todd, 1923-24; Len Harvey, 1929-33; Jock McAvoy, 1933-40; Dick Turpin, 1948-49; Randolph Turpin, 1952-53; Johnny Sullivan, 1954-55; Pat McAteer, 1955-57; Johnny Pritchett, 1967-69; Les McAteer, 1969-70; Mark Rowe, 1970; Tony Sibson, 1980-83, 1984-; Mark Kaylor 1983-84.

Light-middleweight: Maurice Hope, 1976-79; Herol Graham, 1981-84; Nick Wilshire 1985-87; Lloyd Hibbert, 1987

Welterweight: Johnny Summers, 1913-14; Matt Wells, 1914-19; Ted "Kid" Lewis, 1920-23; Wally Thom, 1951-52; Johnny Cooke, 1967-68; Ralph Charles, 1968-72.

Lightweight: Frank Johnson, 1953; Mo Hussein, 1987-

Featherweight: Johnny Cusick, 1939-40; Nel Tarleton, 1940-45; Al Phillips, 1947; Ronnie Clayton, 1947-51.

Bantamweight: Tommy Harrison, 1922-23; Harry Lake, 1923; Johnny Brown, 1923-28; Teddy Baldock, 1928-29; Dick Corbett, 1930-32, 1934-35; Johnny King, 1932-34; Stan Rowan, 1949; Teddy Gardner, 1952; Alan Rudkin, 1965-66, 1968-69, 1970-72.

Flyweight: Teddy Gardner, 1952; Keith Wallace, 1983-85.

British:—

As the vast majority of British champions have been Englishmen this list would be almost a repetition of that which appears under the heading BRITISH CHAMPIONS. Therefore, to save valuable space, the list has been omitted from this section.

The country or town of birth of all British champions is given under their respective biographies.

Olympic:—
Heavyweight: A. L. Oldham, 1908; R. R. Rawson, 1920.

Light-heavyweight: H. J. Mitchell, 1924.

Middleweight: J. W. H. T. Douglas, 1908; H. W. Mallin, 1920 1924; C Finnegan, 1968.

Lightweight: F. Grace, 1908.

Featherweight: R. K. Gunn, 1908.

Bantamweight: H. Thomas, 1908.
Flyweight: T. Spinks, 1956.

See under *West Indies* for champions born in those islands but brought up in England.

## ENTRANCE CHARGES:

The highest charge made for tickets in Britain before World War II was 25 guineas. That was the top price for seats at Holborn Stadium to see Joe Beckett fight Georges Carpentier, December 4, 1919.

It is interesting to note that when Daniel Mendoza met Richard Humphries at Doncaster, September 29, 1790, spectators were charged half a guinea.

The entrance charge for spectators at the Lambeth School of Arms, Paradise Street, London, around 1860, was one sovereign.

As regards black-market prices for fight tickets. When Frank Slavin met Peter Jackson at the N.S.C., London, May 30, 1892, tickets were said to have fetched as much as £25 each.

The same price was paid for tickets for Olympia, London, to see Ted "Kid" Lewis and Georges Carpentier, May 11, 1922.

Ringside seats for Tyson v. Smith fight at Las Vegas in March 1987 were £500 each.

## ERNE, Frank:

Frank Erne was the only Swiss-born fighter to win a world title.

After fighting a 20-round draw with George Lavigne in September, 1898, he took the lightweight title from the Saginaw Kid in a return match, July. 1899.

In July, 1900, he agreed to get down to 128lbs, and meet the world featherweight champion, Terry McGovern. That was a mistake, for Erne had nothing to gain from such a match, and on this occasion even his skilful defence could not keep off the hard-hitting McGovern and he was knocked out in the third round.

In September, 1901, Erne tried for the world welterweight title but was stopped in nine rounds by the heavier Rube Ferns.

Erne lost his lightweight crown when he was knocked out in $1\frac{1}{2}$ minutes by the clever negro, Joe Gans, May 12, 1902.

## ERSKINE, Joe:

This soft-spoken Welshman from Tiger Bay, Cardiff, was encouraged to take up boxing by his father, who had also been a fighter, and his grandmother, who was a real boxing enthusiast.

In 1952 he was Welsh A.B.A. heavyweight champion and was the A.B.A. champion the following year.

On August 27, 1956, he won the vacant British heavyweight title by outpointing former champion, Johnny Williams, at Cardiff.

Erskine annexed the Empire title with a victory over Joe Bygraves at Leicester in November, 1957, but on June 3, 1958, he lost both these titles when he was knocked out in the eighth round by Brian London.

Erskine did not punch hard enough for a heavyweight, but he was a skilful boxer, and when he decided to try and make a come-back he outpointed Max Brianto in Cardiff and then jumped right back into the top bracket by gaining a decision over one of the leading American heavyweights, Willie Pastrano, February 24, 1959.

However, he failed in three subsequent attempts to regain the British title, being stopped inside the distance on each occasion by Henry Cooper.

## ESCOBAR, Sixto:

Born Barcelona, Puerto Rico, Escobar was acknowledged by the N.B.A. as world bantamweight champion following his nine-round victory over Baby Casanova, Montreal, June 26, 1934. The N.B.A. had previously deprived Al Brown of this honour.

Escobar lost the championship to Lou Salica in August, 1935, but regained it in a return bout in November the same year.

It was not until he defeated Tony Marino in New York, with a 13th round k.o., August 31, 1936, that this Puerto Rican gained world-wide recognition, for Marino had previously beaten Baltazar Sangchili, the man recognised as champion on this side of the Atlantic.

Escobar lost his title a second time in August, 1936, when he was beaten by

Harry Jeffra, but he again became champion when he reversed the decision in a return bout in 1938.

Weight trouble caused Escobar to relinquish his crown in 1939 and he retired the following year.

## EUROPEAN BOXING UNION:

The European Boxing Union, as at present constituted, was founded in 1948. Seventeen countries are affiliated: France, Great Britain, Belgium, Italy, Switzerland, Greece, Spain, Portugal, Austria, Denmark, Turkey, Germany, Sweden, Holland, Luxembourg, Norway and Finland.

## Champions:

*Heavyweight.*

Bruce Woodcock bt. Albert Renet, k.o. 6, Manchester, July 29, 1946. Woodcock deprived of title by E.B.U.

Jo Weidin bt. Stephane Olek, pts. 15, Manchester, June 3, 1950.

Jack Gardner bt. Weidin, pts. 15, London, Mar. 27, 1951.

Hein Ten Hoff bt. Gardner, pts. 15, Berlin, Sept. 23, 1951.

Karel Sys bt. Hein Ten Hoff, ps. 15, Brussels, Jan. 12, 1952.

Heinz Neuhaus bt. Sys, pts. 15, Dortmund, Mar. 9, 1952.

Franco Cavicchi bt. Neuhaus, pts. 15, Bologna, June 26, 1955.

Ingemar Johansson bt. Cavicchi, k.o. 13, Bologna, Sept. 30, 1956.

Dick Richardson bt. Hans Kalbfell, r.s.f. 13, Dortmund, Mar. 27, 1960.

Ingemar Johansson bt. Richardson, k.o. 8, Gothenburg, June 17, 1962. Johannson forfeited title 1963.

Henry Cooper bt. Brian London, pts. 15, London, Feb. 24, 1964. Cooper forfeited title 1964.

Karl Mildenberger bt. Sante Amonti, k.o. 1, Berlin, Oct. 17, 1964.

Henry Cooper bt. Mildenberger, disq. 8, Wembley, London, Sept. 18, 1968. Cooper relinquished title 1969.

Peter Weiland bt. Bernard Thebault, k.o. 1, Kiel, Dec. 12, 1969.

Jose Urtain bt. Weiland, k.o. 7, Madrid, Apl. 3, 1970.

Henry Cooper bt. Urtain, r.s.f. 9, London, Nov. 10, 1970.

Joe Bugner bt. Cooper, pts. 15, London, Mar. 16, 1971.

Jack Bodell bt. Bugner, pts. 15, London, Sept. 27, 1971.

Jose Urtain bt. Bodell, r.s.f. 2, Madrid, Dec. 17, 1971.

Jurgen Blin bt. Urtain, pts. 15, Madrid, June 9, 1972.

Joe Bugner bt. Blin, k.o. 8, London, Oct. 10, 1972.

Bugner relinquished title 1975.

Richard Dunn bt. Bernd August, r.s.f. 3, London, Apl. 6, 1976.

Joe Bugner bt. Dunn, k.o. 1, London, Oct. 12, 1976.

Bugner deprived of title by E.B.U. 1977.

Jean-Pierre Coopman bt. Jose Urtain, k.o. 4, Antwerp, Mar. 12, 1977.

Lucien Rodriguez bt. Coopman, pts. 15, Antwerp, May 7, 1977.

Alfredo Evangelista bt. Rodriguez, r.s.f. 11, Madrid, Sept. 9, 1977.

Lorenzo Zanon bt. Evangelista, pts. 12, Turin, Apl. 18, 1979. Zanon relinquished title 1979.

John L. Gardner bt. Rudi Gauwe, rtd. 9, Albert Hall, London, Apl. 22, 1980. Gardner retired 1981.

Lucien Rodriguez bt. Felipe Rodriguez, pts. 12, Paris, Nov. 26, 1981.

Steffen Tangstad bt. Rodriguez, pts. 12, Copenhagen, Nov. 9, 1984.

Anders Eklund bt. Tangstad, r.s.f. 4, Copenhagen, Mar. 9, 1985.

Frank Bruno bt. Eklund, Wembley, London, Oct. 1, 1985. Bruno relinquished title 1986.

Steffen Tangstad bt. John Westgarth, pts. 12, Randers, Apl. 18, 1986. Tangstad deprived of title Oct. 1986.

Alfredo Evangelista bt. Andre Van Den Oetelaar, r.s.f. 5, Bilbao, Jan. 8, 1987.

Anders Eklund bt. Evangelista, k.o. 7, Copenhagen, Mar. 28, 1987.

*Cruiserweight*

Sammy Reeson bt. Manfred Jassman, pts. 12, Albert Hall, London, Apl. 22, 1987.

*Light-heavyweight.*

Freddie Mills bt. Pol Goffaux, rtd. 4, London, Sept. 8, 1947. Mills relinquished title.

Albert Yvel bt. Renato Tontini, disq.

10, Algiers, July 9, 1950.

Don Cockell bt. Yvel, r.s.f. 6, London, Mar. 27, 1951. Cockell relinquished title.

Connie Rux bt. Willie Schagen, k.o. 12, Berlin, July 26, 1952. Rux relinquished title.

Jacques Hairabedian bt. Renato Tontini, pts. 15, Rome, July 12, 1953.

Gerhard Hecht bt. Hairabedian, pts. 15, Hamburg, Apl. 9, 1954.

Willi Hoepner bt. Hecht, rtd. 2, Hamburg, Mar. 11, 1955.

Gerhard Hecht bt. Hoepner, k.o. 13, Dortmund, June 12, 1955.

Artenio Calzavara bt. Hecht, pts. 15, Milan July 12, 1957.

Willi Hoepner bt. Calzavara, disq. 6, Hamburg, May 30, 1958.

Erich Schoeppner bt. Hoepner, k.o. 5, Hamburg. Dec. 12, 1958. Schoeppner forfeited title 1962.

Giulio Rinaldi bt. Chic Calderwood, pts. 15, Rome, Sept. 28, 1962.

Gustav Scholz bt. Rinaldi, disq. 8, Dortmund, Apl. 4, 1964. Scholz relinquished title 1965.

Giulio Rinaldi bt. Peter Gumbert, rtd. 13, Rome, July 8, 1965.

Piero del Papa bt. Rinaldi, pts. 15, Rome, Mar. 12, 1966.

Lothar Stengel bt. del Papa, k.o. 5, Frankfurt, Dec. 2, 1967.

Tom Bogs bt. Stengel, r.s.f. 1, Copenhagen, Sept. 11, 1968.

Bogs relinquished title.

Yvan Prebeg bt. Eddie Avoth, pts. 15, Zagreb, June 28, 1969.

Piero del Papa bt. Yvan Prebeg, pts. 15, Milan, Feb. 6, 1970.

Conny Velensek bt. del Papa, pts. 15, Berlin, Jan. 22, 1971.

Chris Finnegan bt. Velensek, pts. 15, Nottingham, Feb. 1, 1972.

Rudiger Schmitdke bt. Finnegan, r.s.f. 12, London, Nov. 14, 1972.

John Conteh bt. Schmitdke, r.s.f. 12, London, Mar. 13, 1973.

Conteh relinquished title Oct. 1974.

Domenico Adinolfi bt. Karl-Heinz Klein, r.s.f. 1, Campione, Italy, Dec. 4, 1974.

Mate Parlov bt. Adinolfi, r.s.f. 11, Belgrade, July 10, 1976.

Parlov relinquished title July 1977.

Aldo Traversaro bt. Bunny Johnson, r.s.f. 11, Genoa, Nov. 26, 1977.

Rudi Koopmans bt. Traversaro, rtd. 6, Rotterdam, Mar. 7, 1979.

Richard Caramonolis bt. Koopmans, rtd. 8, Marseilles, Feb. 2, 1984.

Alex Blanchard bt. Caramonolis, r.s.f. 6, Amsterdam, May 28, 1984.

Tom Collins bt. Blanchard, k.o. 2, Usk, Gwent, Nov. 11, 1987.

*Middleweight.*

Marcel Cerdan bt. Leon Fouquet, k.o. 1, Paris, Feb. 2, 1947.

Cyrille Delannoit bt. Cerdan, pts. 15, Brussels, May 23, 1948.

Marcel Cerdan bt. Delannoit, pts. 15, Brussels, July 10, 1948. Cerdan relinquished title.

Cyrille Delannoit bt. Lucien Van Dam, pts. 15, Brussels, Nov. 6, 1948.

Tiberio Mitri bt. Delannoit, pts. 15, Brussels, May 7, 1949. Mitri forfeited title.

Randolph Turpin bt. Lucien Van Dam, k.o. 1, London, Feb. 27, 1951.

Tiberio Mitri bt. Turpin, r.s.f. 1, Rome, May 2, 1954.

Charles Humez bt. Mitri, r.s.f. 3, Milan, Nov. 13, 1954.

Gustav Scholz bt. Humez, rtd. 12, Berlin, Oct. 4, 1958. Scholz relinquished title 1961.

John McCormack bt. Harko Kokmeyer, pts. 15, London, Oct. 17, 1961.

Chris Christensen bt. McCormack, disq. 4, Copenhagen, Feb. 8, 1962.

Lazlo Papp bt. Christensen, r.s.f. 7, Vienna, May 16, 1962. Papp retired 1965.

Nino Benvenuti bt. Luis Folledo, k.o. 6, Rome, Oct. 15, 1965. Benvenuti relinquished title.

Carlos Duran bt. Luis Folledo, r.s.f. 12, Turin, Nov. 17, 1967.

Tom Bogs bt. Duran, pts. 15, Copenhagen, Sept. 11, 1969.

Carlos Duran bt. Bogs, pts. 15, Rome, Dec. 4, 1970.

Jean-Claude Bouttier bt. Duran, pts. 15, June 9, 1971.

Bouttier stripped of title by E.B.U.

Tom Bogs bt. Fabio Bettini, pts. 15, Copenhagen, Jan. 18, 1973.

Bogs relinquished title.

Elio Calcabrini bt. Bunny Sterling, pts. 15, San Remo, Nov. 7, 1973.

Jean-Claude Bouttier bt. Calcabrini, rtd. 12, Paris, Mar. 2, 1974.

Kevin Finnegan bt. Bouttier, pts. 15,

Paris, May 27, 1974.
Gratien Tonna bt. Finnegan, pts. 15, Monte Carlo, May 7, 1975.
Tonna relinquished title Oct. 1975.
Bunny Sterling bt. Frank Reiche, r.s.f. 13, Hamburg, Feb. 23, 1976.
Angelo Jacopucci bt. Sterling, pts. 15, Milan, June 4, 1976.
Germano Valsecchi bt. Jacopucci, pts. 15, Milan, Oct. 1, 1976.
Alan Minter bt. Valsecchi, k.o. 5, Milan, Feb. 4, 1977.
Gratien Tonna bt. Minter, r.s.f. 8, Milan, Sept. 21, 1977.
Tonna deprived of title by E.B.U. May 1978.
Alan Minter bt. Angelo Jacopucci, k.o. 12, Bellaria, Italy, July 19, 1978.
Minter relinquished title 1979.
Kevin Finnegan bt. Gratien Tonna, pts. 12, Paris, Feb. 7, 1980.
Matteo Salvemini bt. Finnegan, pts. 12, San Remo, Sept. 10, 1980.
Tony Sibson bt. Salvemini, k.o. 7, London, Dec. 8, 1980.
Sibson relinquished title 1982.
Louis Acaries bt. Frank Wissenbach, r.s.f. 6, Paris, Dec. 3, 1982.
Tony Sibson bt. Acaries, pts. 12, Paris, Feb. 25, 1984.
Sibson deprived of title 1985.
Ayub Kalule bt. Pierre Joly, r.s.f. 8, Copenhagen, June 20, 1985.
Herol Graham bt. Kalule, r.s.f. 10, Sheffield, Feb. 5, 1986.
Sambu Kalambay bt. Graham, pts. 12, Wembley, London, May 26, 1987.
Kalambay relinquished title Oct. 1987.

*Light-middleweight*
Bruno Visintin bt. Yoland Leveque, pts. 15, Turin, May 22, 1964.
Bo Hogberg bt. Visintin, rtd. 6. Copenhagen, Jan. 1, 1966.
Yolande Leveque bt. Hogberg, pts. 15, Stockholm, Feb. 12, 1966.
Alessandro Mazzinghi bt. Leveque, k.o. 12, Rome, June 17, 1966.
Mazzinghi relinquished title.
Remo Golfarini bt. Jo Gonzales, pts. 15, Rome, Nov. 30, 1968.
Gerhard Piaskowy bt. Golfarini, pts. 15, Vibo Valentia, July 16, 1969.
Jose Hernandez bt. Piaskowy, r.s.f. 14, Barcelona, Sept. 11, 1970.
Carlos Duran bt. Hernandez, pts. 15,

San Remo, July 5, 1972.
Jacques Kechichian bt. Duran, r.s.f. 9, Lignano, July 4, 1973.
Jose Duran bt. Kechichian, pts. 15, Madrid, June 7, 1974.
Eckhard Dagge bt. Duran, rtd. 9, Berlin, June 24, 1975.
Vito Antuofermo bt. Dagge, pts. 15, Berlin, Jan. 16, 1976.
Maurice Hope bt. Antuofermo, r.s.f. 15, Rome, Oct. 1, 1976.
Hope relinquished title Sept. 1978.
Gilbert Cohen bt. Jimmy Batten, k.o. 3, Wembley, Nov. 21, 1978.
Marijan Benes bt. Cohen, k.o. 4, Banja Luka, Mar. 17, 1979.
Louis Acaries bt. Benes, pts. 12, Paris, Mar. 19, 1981.
Luigi Minchillo bt. Acaries, pts. 12, Fornia, July 1, 1981.
Minchillo retired 1983.
Herol Graham bt. Clemente Tshinza, k.o. 2, Sheffield, May 23, 1983.
Graham relinquished title 1984.
Jimmy Cable bt. Said Skouma, r.s.f. 11, Toulouse, May 25, 1984.
Georg Steinherr bt. Cable, pts. 12, Munich, Sept. 28, 1984.
Steinherr deprived of title 1985.
Said Skouma bt. Enrico Scacchia, k.o. 6, Geneva, Nov. 30, 1985.
Skouma relinquished title Aug. 1986.
Chris Pyatt bt. Jan von Elteran, r.s.f. 1, Albert Hall, London, Sept, 7, 1986.
Gianfranco Rosi bt. Pyatt, pts. 12, Perugia, Italy, Jan. 28, 1987.

*Welterweight.*
Ernie Roderick bt. Omar Kouidri, pts. 15, London, June 4, 1946.
Robert Villemain bt. Roderick, rtd. 9, Paris, Feb. 1, 1947. Villemain relinquished title.
Livio Minelli bt. Giel de Roode, r.s.f. 11, The Hague, Mar. 4, 1949.
Michele Palermo bt. Minelli, pts. 15, Milan, July 14, 1950.
Eddie Thomas bt. Palermo, pts. 15, Carmarthen, Feb. 19, 1951.
Charles Humez bt. Thomas, pts. 15, Porthcawl, June 13, 1951. Humez relinquished title.
Gilbert Lavoine bt. Cliff Curvis, disq. 10, Paris, Mar. 22, 1953.
Wally Thom bt. Lavoine, r.s.f. 10, Liverpool, Aug. 26, 1954.

Idrissa Dione bt. Thom, pts. 15, Liverpool, June 23, 1955.

Emilio Marconi bt. Dione, pts. 15, Grosseto, Feb. 12, 1956.

Peter Waterman bt. Marconi, r.s.f. 14, London. Jan. 28, 1958. Waterman relinquished title.

Emilio Marconi bt. Jacques Herbillon, pts. 15, Milan, Dec. 26, 1958.

Duilio Loi bt. Marconi, pts. 15, Milan, Apl. 19, 1959. Loi retired 1964.

Fortunato Manca bt. Francois Pavilla, rtd. 6, Rome, Oct. 9, 1964. Manca retired.

Jean Josselin bt. Brian Curvis, rtd. 13, Paris, April 25, 1966.

Carmelo Bossi bt. Josselin, pts. 15, San Remo, May 17, 1967.

Fighting Mack bt. Bossi, r.s.f. 9, Lignano, Aug. 14, 1968.

Silvano Bertini bt. Mack, k.o. 13, Bologna, Jan. 18, 1969.

Jean Josselin bt. Bertini, r.s.f. 8, Paris, May 5, 1969.

Johann Orsolics bt. Josselin, k.o. 4, Vienna, Sept. 25, 1969.

Ralph Charles bt. Orsolics, k.o. 12, Vienna, Nov. 20, 1970.

Roger Menetrey bt. Charles, k.o. 7, Geneva, June 4, 1971.

John H. Stracey bt. Menetrey, r.s.f. 8, Paris, May 27, 1974.

Stracey relinquished title Dec. 1975.

Marco Scano bt. Pat Thomas, k.o. 2, Caglieri, Italy, Apl. 9, 1976.

Jorgen Hansen bt. Scano, k.o. 5, Randers, Denmark, June 2, 1977.

Jorg Eipel bt. Hansen, disq. 13, Berlin, Aug. 6, 1977.

Alain Marion bt. Eipel, k.o. 15, Creil, France, Dec. 17, 1977.

Jorgen Hansen bt. Marion, k.o. 6, Randers, Denmark, Apl. 27, 1978.

Josef Pachler bt. Hansen, disq. 8, Villach, Austria, Aug. 18, 1978.

Henry Rhiney bt. Pachler, k.o. 10, Dornbirn, Austria, Dec. 2, 1978.

Dave Green bt. Rhiney, r.s.f. 5, London, Jan. 23, 1979.

Jorgen Hansen bt. Green, k.o. 3, Randers, June 28, 1979.

Hansen relinquished title Jan. 1982.

Hans Henrik Palm bt. Georges Warusfel, r.s.f. 2, Copenhagen, Feb. 26, 1982.

Colin Jones bt. Palm, r.s.f. 2, Copen-

hagen, Nov. 5, 1982.

Jones relinquished title 1983.

Gilles Elbilia bt. Frankie Decaestecker, pts. 12, Paris, Oct. 10, 1983.

Elbilia deprived of title May 1984.

Gianfranco Rosi bt. Perico Fernandez, Perugia, Italy, July 7, 1984.

Lloyd Honeyghan bt. Rosi, k.o. 3, Perugia, Italy, Jan. 5, 1985.

Honeyghan relinquished title Sept. 1986.

Jose Varela bt. Brahim Messaoudi, rtd. 5, Russelheim, Oct. 10, 1986.

Alfonso Redondo bt. Varela, rtd. 9, Dusseldorf, Apr. 4, 1987.

Mauro Martelli bt. Redondo, pts. 12, Geneva, June 25, 1987.

*Light-welterweight*

Olli Maki bt. Conny Rudhof, pts. 15, Helsinki, Feb. 14, 1964. Maki forfeited title Feb, 1965.

Juan Sombrita bt. Sandro Lopopolo pts. 15, Santa Cruz, July 17, 1965.

Willi Quatuor bt. Sombrita, pts. 15, Berlin, Dec. 26, 1965. Quatuor relinquished title 1966.

Conny Rudhof bt. Olli Maki, pts. 15, Frankfurt, Feb. 1, 1967.

Johann Orsolics bt. Rudhof, pts 15, Vienna, June 6, 1967.

Bruno Arcari bt. Orsolics, r.s.f. 12, Vienna, May 7, 1968. Arcari relinquished title.

Rene Roque bt. Sandro Lopopolo, pts. 15, Montecatini Terme, Italy, Apl. 22, 1970.

Pedro Carrasco bt. Roque, pts. 15, Madrid, May 21, 1971.

Carrasco relinquished title.

Roger Zami bt. Sandro Lopopolo, pts. 15, Paris, Feb. 28, 1972.

Cemal Kamaci bt. Zami, pts. 15, Istanbul, Oct. 1, 1972.

Toni Ortiz bt. Kamaci, pts. 15, Istanbul, June 16, 1973.

Perico Fernandez bt. Ortiz, k.o. 12, Madrid, July 26, 1974.

Fernandez relinquished title Sept. 1974.

Jose Fouz bt. Walter Blaser, pts. 15, Zurich, Mar. 8, 1975.

Cemal Kamaci bt. Fouz, r.s.f. 7, Cologne, Oct. 31, 1975.

Kamaci retired.

Dave Green bt. Jean-Baptiste Pied-

vache, rtd. 9, London, Dec. 7, 1976.
Green relinquished title 1977.
Primo Bandini bt. Piedvache, disq. 6,
Rimini, Aug. 10, 1977.
Jean-Baptiste Piedvache bt. Bandini,
k.o. 5, Paris, Dec. 5, 1977.
Colin Power bt. Piedvache, r.s.f. 11,
Paris, June 5, 1978.
Fernando Sanchez bt. Powers, r.s.f.
12, Miranda De Ebro, Spain, Sept. 9,
1978.
Jose Luis Heredia bt. Sanchez, pts. 12,
Malaga, Mar. 3, 1979.
Jo Kimpuani bt. Heredia, r.s.f. 3,
Dunkirk, May 19, 1979.
Kimpuani deprived of title by E.B.U.
July 1980.
Giuseppe Martinese bt. Clinton
McKenzie, rtd. 10, Sengalia, Aug. 27,
1980.
Antonio Guinaldo bt. Martinese, k.o.
3, Sengalia, Dec. 17, 1980.
Clinton McKenzie bt. Guinaldo, pts.
12, London, Oct. 13, 1981.
Robert Gambini bt. McKenzie, disq.
2, Albert Hall, London, Oct. 12, 1982.
Patrizio Oliva bt. Gambini, pts. 12,
Forio D'Ischia, Italy, Jan. 5, 1983.
Oliva relinquished title 1985.
Terry Marsh bt. Alessandro Scapecchi,
k.o. 6, Monte Carlo, Oct. 26, 1985.
Marsh deprived of title Nov. 1986.
Thomas "Tek" N'Kalankete bt. Tony
Laing, t.k.o. 9, Antibes, Feb. 6, 1987.

*Lightweight.*
Roberto Proietti bt. Bruno Bisterzo,
rtd. 6, Rome, May 26, 1946. Proietti
relinquished title.
Emile Dicristo bt. Joseph Preys, pts.
15, Brussels, Dec. 4, 1946.
Kid Dussart bt. Dicristo, pts. 15,
Brussels, Mar. 29, 1947.
Roberto Proietti bt. Dussart, rtd. 13,
Brussels, May 21, 1947.
Billy Thompson bt. Proietti, pts. 15,
London, Feb. 17, 1948.
Kid Dussart bt. Thompson, disq. 6,
London, July 5, 1949.
Roberto Proietti bt. Dussart, pts. 15,
Brussels, Dec. 17, 1949. Proietti re-
linquished title.
Pierre Montane bt. Billy Thompson,
k.o. 12, Manchester, Feb. 23, 1951.
Elis Ask bt. Montane, k.o. 12,
Helsinki, Aug. 17, 1951.

Jorgen Johansen bt. Ask, pts. 15,
Copenhagen, Jan. 4, 1952.
Duilio Loi bt. Johansen, pts. 15,
Milan, Feb. 6, 1954. Duilio Loi relin-
quished title April, 1959.
Mario Vecchiatto bt. Laouari Godih,
disq. 8, Milan, Oct. 24, 1959.
Dave Charnley bt. Vecchiatto, rtd. 10,
Wembley, Mar. 29, 1960. Charnley
forfeited title 1963.
Conny Rudhof bt. Giordano Campari,
pts. 15, Russelsheim, Sept. 29, 1963.
Rudhof relinquished title 1964.
Willi Quatuor bt. Michele Gullotti,
k.o. 14, Berlin, May 8, 1964. Quatuor
relinquished title 1965.
Franco Brondi bt. Leon Zadourian,
rtd. 3, Cannes, Mar. 13, 1965.
Maurice Tavant bt. Brondi, k.o. 3,
Lyons, Oct. 9, 1965.
Borge Krogh bt. Tavant, pts. 15,
Copenhagen, Nov. 3, 1966.
Pedro Carrasco bt. Krogh, r.s.f. 8,
Madrid, June 30, 1967.
Carrasco relinquished title 1969.
Migue! Velazquez bt. Ken Buchanan,
pts. 15, Madrid, Jan. 29, 1970.
Antonio Puddu bt. Velazquez, k.o. 4,
Cagliari, July 31, 1971.
Ken Buchanan bt. Puddu, k.o. 6,
Cagliari, May 1, 1974.
Buchanan retired 1975.
Fernand Roelands bt. Holyk pts. 15,
Bruges, Feb. 6, 1976.
Perico Fernandez bt. Roelands, r.s.f.
1, Zaragoza, July 9, 1976.
Fernandez relinquished title 1977.
Jim Watt bt. Andre Holyk, r.s.f. 1,
Glasgow, Aug. 5, 1977.
Watt relinquished title Apl. 1979.
Charlie Nash bt. Andre Holyk, pts.
12, Derry, June 27, 1979.
Nash relinquished title Feb. 1980.
Francisco Leon bt. Giancarlo Usai,
r.s.f. 9, Tarras, June 1, 1980.
Charlie Nash bt. Leon, pts. 12,
Dublin, Dec. 14, 1980.
Joey Gibilisco bt. Nash, k.o. 6,
Dublin, May 10, 1981.
Lucio Cusma bt. Gibilisco, rtd. 11,
Cape D'Orlando, Italy, Mar. 17, 1983.
Rene Weller bt. Cusma, pts. 12,
Frankfurt, Mar. 9, 1984.
Gert Bo Jacobsen bt. Weller, r.s.f. 8,
Randers, Jan. 10, 1986.

Len Harvey

Ted Lewis

Dido Plumb

Benny Lynch

A new world heavyweight champion is born. Joe Louis finishes
James J. Braddock in the eighth round, Chicago, June 22nd, 1937

Exit Primo Carnera, the last
European world heavyweight
champion for 25 years, battered
into defeat by Max Baer in 1934

Tommy Farr surprised champion Joe Louis with his speed in
1937. The finest display this
century by a Britisher in a world
heavyweight title fight

### Junior-lightweight

Tommaso Galli bt. Luis Aisa Marin, pts. 15, Ladispoli, Jan. 13, 1971.

Domenico Chiloiro bt. Galli, pts. 15, Lignano, Aug. 16, 1972.

Lothar Abend bt. Chiloiro, pts. 15, Hamburg, Oct. 13, 1972.

Sven Erik Paulsen bt. Abend, k.o. 3, Oslo, May 7, 1974.

Paulsen relinquished title 1976.

Roland Cazeaux bt. Rudi Haeck, pts. 15, St. Nazaire, Feb. 27, 1976.

Natale Vezzoli bt. Cazeaux, r.s.f. 11, Milan, Sept. 24, 1976.

Carlos Hernandez bt. Vezzoli, r.s.f. 4, Valladolid, Mar. 10, 1979.

Rodolfo Sanchez bt. Hernandez, pts. 12, Miranda de Ebro, Mar. 1, 1979.

Carlos Hernandez bt. Sanchez, pts. 12, Valladolid, Dec. 21, 1979.

Cornelius Boza-Edwards bt. Hernandez, rtd. 4, London, Mar. 17, 1982.

Boza-Edwards relinquished title July 1982.

Roberto Castanon bt. Daniel Londas, rtd. 9, Leon, Nov. 6, 1982.

Alfredo Raininger bt. Castanon, pts. 12, Caserta, Dec. 14, 1983.

Jean-Marc Renard bt. Raininger, pts. 12, Casavatore, April 12, 1984.

Pat Cowdell bt. Renard, pts. 12, Birmingham, July 7, 1984.

Cowdell deprived of title 1985.

Jean-Marc Renard bt. Marco Gallo, r.s.f. 8, Catanzano, Jan. 29, 1986.

Renard relinquished title Mar. 1987.

Salvatore Curcetti bt. Daniel Londas, r.s.f. 1, Reims, May 16, 1987.

### Featherweight

Al Phillips bt. Raymond Famechon, disq. 8, London, May 27, 1947.

Ronnie Clayton bt. Phillips, pts. 15, Liverpool, Sept. 11, 1947.

Raymond Famechon bt. Clayton, pts. 15, Nottingham, Mar. 22, 1948.

Jean Sneyers bt. Famechon, pts. 15, Brussels, Oct. 17, 1953.

Raymond Famechon bt. Sneyers, rtd. 3, Paris, Sept. 20, 1954.

Fred Galiana bt. Famechon, r.s.f. 6, Paris, Oct. 3, 1955. Galiana relinquished title.

Cherif Hamia bt. Sneyers, pts. 15, Paris, Jan. 21, 1957. Hamia relinquished title.

Sergio Caprari bt. Sneyers, rtd. 11, San Remo, Aug. 18, 1958.

Gracieux Lamperti bt. Caprari, pts. 15, San Remo, Aug. 15, 1959.

Alberto Serti bt. Lamperti, pts. 15, San Remo, Aug. 19, 1962.

Howard Winstone bt. Serti, rtd. 14, Cardiff, July 9, 1963.

Winstone forfeited title 1967.

Jose Legra bt. Yves Desmarets, r.s.f. 3, Madrid, Dec. 22, 1967. Legra relinquished title.

Manuel Calvo bt. Nevio Carbi, pts. 15, Barcelona, Dec. 17, 1968.

Tommaso Galli bt. Calvo, r.s.f. 15, Barcelona, Aug. 20, 1969.

Jose Legra bt. Galli, pts. 15, June 26, 1970.

Legra relinquished title.

Gitano Jiminez bt. Tommy Glencross, pts. 15, Gijon, May 12, 1973.

Elio Cotena bt. Jiminez, r.s.f. 11, Naples, Feb. 12, 1975.

Nino Jiminez bt. Cotena, rtd. 12, Madrid, Dec. 3, 1976.

Manuel Masso bt. Jiminez, r.s.f. 10, Madrid, Sept. 16, 1977.

Roberto Castanon bt. Masso, k.o. 11, Barcelona, Dec. 16, 1977.

Castanon relinquished title June 1981.

Salvatore Melluzzo bt. Laurent Grimbert, r.s.f. 7, Marsala, July 22, 1981.

Pat Cowdell bt. Melluzzo, r.s.f. 10, Wembley, London, Mar. 30, 1982.

Cowdell relinquished title Jan. 1983.

Loris Stecca bt. Steve Sims, r.s.f. 5, Sassari, Apl. 7, 1983.

Stecca relinquished title Sept. 1983.

Barry McGuigan bt. Valerio Nati, k.o. 6, Belfast, Nov. 16, 1983.

McGuigan relinquished title 1985.

Jim McDonnell bt. Jose Luis Vicho, Wembley, London, Nov. 5, 1985.

McDonnell relinquished title Jan. 1987.

Valerio Nati bt. Marc Amand, r.s.f. 2, Forli, March 13, 1987.

Nati relinquished title Oct. 1987.

### Bantamweight.

Jackie Paterson bt. Theo Medina, disq. 8, London, Mar. 19, 1946.

Theo Medina bt. Paterson, k.o. 4, Glasgow, Oct. 30, 1946.

Peter Kane bt. Medina, pts. 15,

Manchester, Sept. 19, 1947.
Guido Ferracin bt. Kane, pts. 15, Manchester, Feb. 20, 1948.
Luis Romero bt. Ferracin, k.o. 7, Barcelona, Aug. 10, 1949.
Peter Keenan bt. Romero, pts. 15, Glasgow, Sept. 5, 1951.
Jean Sneyers bt. Keenan, k.o. 5, Glasgow, May 21, 1952. Sneyers relinquished title.
Keenan bt. Maurice Sandeyron, pts. 15, Glasgow, June 17, 1953.
John Kelly bt. Keenan, pts. 15, Belfast, Oct. 3, 1953.
Robert Cohen bt. Kelly, k.o. 3, Belfast, Feb. 27, 1954. Cohen relinquished title.
Mario D'Agata bt. Andre Valignat, disq. 5, Milan, Oct. 29, 1955.
Piero Rollo bt. D'Agata, pts. 15, Cagliari, Oct. 15, 1958.
Freddie Gilroy bt. Rollo, pts. 15, Wembley, London, Nov. 3, 1959. Gilroy forfeited title 1960.
Pierre Cossemyns bt. Gilroy, rtd. 9, Brussels, May 27, 1961.
Piero Rollo bt. Cossemyns, k.o. 5, Brussels, Apl. 13, 1962.
Alphonse Halimi bt. Rollo, pts. 15, Tel Aviv, June 26, 1962.
Piero Rollo bt. Halimi, pts. 15, Cagliari, Oct. 28, 1962.
Amed Mimun Ben Ali bt. Rollo, pts. 15, Madrid, July 19, 1963.
Risto Luukkonen bt. Ben Ali, pts. 15, Helsinki, Dec. 9, 1963. Luukkonen forfeited title 1964.
Amed Mimum Ben Ali bt. Pierre Vetroff, pts. 15, Barcelona, Feb. 4, 1965.
Tommaso Galli bt. Ben Ali, pts. 15, San Remo, Aug. 19, 1965.
Amed Mimun Ben Ali bt. Galli, pts. 15, Barcelona, June 17, 1966.
Salvatore Burruni bt. Ben Ali, pts. 15, Naples, Jan. 10, 1968.
Burruni relinquished title.
Franco Zurlo bt. Ben Ali, pts. 15, Taurianova, Dec. 17, 1969.
Alan Rudkin bt. Zurlo, rtd. 11, London, Feb. 16, 1971.
Agustin Senin bt. Rudkin, pts. 15, Bilbao, Aug. 10, 1971.
Senin retired undefeated.
Johnny Clark bt. Franco Zurlo, pts 15, Apl. 17, 1973.
Clark retired undefeated.

Bob Allotey bt. Guy Caudron, pts. 15, Madrid, Oct. 4, 1974.
Daniel Trioulaire bt. Allotey, r.s.f. 9, Notre Dame de Bondeville, France, Feb. 9, 1975.
Salvatore Fabrizio bt. Trioulaire, pts. 15, Ospedaletti, Italy, Aug. 14, 1976.
Franco Zurlo bt. Fabrizio, pts. 15, Fasano, Italy, Feb. 23, 1977.
Juan Francisco Rodriguez bt. Zurlo, pts. 15, Vigo, Spain, Sept. 16, 1978.
Johnny Owen bt. Rodriguez, pts. 12, Ebbw Vale, Feb. 28, 1980.
Owen died Nov. 1980.
Valerio Nati bt. Juan Francisco Rodriguez, pts. 12, Forli, Dec. 3, 1980.
Guiseppe Fossati bt. Nati, pts. 12, Lignano Sabbiadoro, Apl. 28, 1982.
Walter Giogetti bt. Fossati, pts. 12, Sciacca, July 9, 1983.
Giogetti deprived of title Oct. 1984.
Ciro de Leva bt. John Feeney, pts. 12, Salerno, Nov. 14, 1984.
Leva relinquished title Sept. 1986.
Antoine Montero bt. Ray Gilbody, r.s.f. 1, Paris, Oct. 27, 1986.
Louis Gomis bt. Montero, pts. 12, La Seyne Sur-mer, May 22, 1987.

*Flyweight.*

Raoul Degryse bt. Emile Famechon, pts. 15, Brussels, Oct. 9, 1946.
Maurice Sandeyron bt. Degryse, pts. 15, Brussels, May 21, 1947.
Rinty Monaghan bt. Sandeyron, pts. 15, Belfast, Apl. 5, 1949. Monaghan relinquished title.
Terry Allen bt. Honore Pratesi, pts. 15, London, Apl. 25, 1950.
Jean Sneyers bt. Allen, pts. 15, Nottingham, Oct. 30, 1950. Sneyers relinquished title.
Teddy Gardner bt. Louis Skena, k.o. 6, Newcastle, Feb. 18, 1952. Gardner relinquished title.
Louis Skena bt. Young Martin, r.s.f. 14, Madrid, June 12, 1953. Skena relinquished title.
Nazzareno Giannelli bt. Terry Allen, pts. 15, Milan, Sept. 10, 1954.
Dai Dower bt. Giannelli, pts. 15, London, Mar. 8, 1955.
Young Martin bt. Dower, k.o. 12, Nottingham, Oct. 3, 1955.
Risto Luukkonen bt. Martin, pts. 15, Helsinki, Sept. 4, 1959.

Salvatore Burruni bt. Luukkonen, pts. 15, Alghero, June 29, 1961. Relinquished title 1965.

Rene Libeer bt. Paul Chervet, rtd. 15, Lille, June 13, 1965.

Fernando Atzori bt. Libeer, pts. 15, Florence, Jan. 25, 1967.

Fritz Chervet bt. Atzori, rtd. 11, Berne, Mar. 3, 1972.

Chervet stripped of title by E.B.U.

Fernando Atzori bt. Dominque Cesari, k.o. 12, Novara, June 28, 1973.

Fritz Chervet bt. Atzori, k.o. 7, Zurich, Dec. 26, 1973.

Chervet relinquished title.

Franco Udella bt. Pedro Molledo, k.o. 5, Milan, Oct. 25, 1974.

Charlie Magri bt. Udella, pts. 12, Wembley, London, May 1, 1979.

Magri relinquished title 1983.

Antoine Montero bt. Mariano Garcia, rtd. 8, La Roche, June 17, 1983.

Montero deprived of title July 1984.

Charlie Magri bt. Franco Cherchi, r.s.f. 1, Cagliari, Aug. 24, 1984.

Magri relinquished title 1985.

Franco Cherchi bt. Alain Limarola, pts. 12, Lucca, Sept. 27, 1985.

Charlie Magri bt. Cherchi, k.o. 2, Alessandria, Oct. 30, 1985.

Duke McKenzie bt. Magri r.s.f. 5, Wembley, London, Aug. 20, 1986.

The following British fighters have won European titles in more than one weight division—Johnny Basham, welter 1919-20, middle 1921; Pat Cowdell, feather 1982-83, junior-light 1984-85; Dave Boy Green, light-welter 1976-77, welter 1979; Herol Graham, light-middle 1983-84, middle 1986-87; Ted Kid Lewis, feather 1914, welter 1920, middle 1921-23.

Roberto Proietti, of Italy, created a record by winning the European lightweight title on four different occasions.

The first European title bout to be fought in Britain with the approval of the International Boxing Union was Alf Howard's win over the Belgian, Francois Sybille, at Liverpool Stadium, January 16, 1930.

### EVERNDEN, Arthur:

Born Chatham, Kent, January 19, 1886, Arthur Evernden took the British welterweight title from Young Joseph on January 23, 1911. Joseph was disqualified in the third round.

With this victory Evernden also claimed the European championship but he was not recognised on the Continent.

Evernden lost his British title to Johnny Summers at the N.S.C., June 17, 1912, the referee stopping the contest in the 13th round.

F

## FAMECHON, Johnny:

A member of the well-known French family of boxers, Johnny, who was born in Paris but emigrated to Australia, is a son of André and nephew of Emile and Ray Famechon. The latter once fought for the world featherweight title which Johnny won with a surprise points win over Jose Legra in a very close contest, January 21, 1969.

In his first defence against Fighting Harada in July 1969 the points decision in his favour was hotly disputed, but Johnny left no doubt of his superiority in a return bout six months later when he stopped the Jap in fourteen rounds.

However, he lost his crown when outpointed by Vicente Salvidar in Rome, May 9, 1970, and announced his retirement the following day.

## FAMILIES:
## Brothers:

The only brothers ever to win world titles:—

Bruce Curry, world light-welterweight champion (W.B.C.) 1983-84.

Don Curry, world welterweight champion 1983-84; (W.B.A.) 1985-86.

Joe Dundee, world welterweight champion 1927-29.

Vince Dundee, world middleweight champion 1933-34.

Leon Spinks, world heavyweight champion 1978.

Michael Spinks, world light-heavyweight champion 1981-85.

The Spinks brothers also won light-heavyweight and middleweight Olympic Gold medals respectively in 1976.

The Attell brothers, Abe and Monte, also came close to this achievement. Abe was world featherweight champion 1901-1912, and Monte claimed the bantamweight title in 1909 but he never gained universal recognition.

Brothers who have won British titles are:—

Harry Corbett, British featherweight champion 1928-29.

Dick Corbett, British bantamweight champion 1931-32, 1934.

Cliff Curvis, British welterweight champion, 1952-53.

Brian Curvis, British welterweight champion, 1960-66.

George Feeney, British lightweight champion, 1982-85.

John Feeney, British bantamweight champion, 1981-83.

Chris Finnegan, British light-heavyweight champion, 1971-73.

Kevin Finnegan, British middleweight champion, 1974.

Tony Laing, British light-welterweight champion, 1986.

Kirkland Laing, British welterweight champion, 1979-80, 1987-

John McCormack, British light-heavyweight champion, 1967-69.

Pat McCormack, British light-welterweight champion, 1974.

Dick Turpin, British middleweight champion 1948-50.

Randolph Turpin, British middleweight champion 1950-51, light-heavyweight 1952-53, 1955, 1956.

The Famechon family, of France, is probably the only one to have as many as three brothers, each of whom won a national title. They were all French champions:—

Andre, Lightweight champion, 1943-44.

Emile, Flyweight champion 1946-47.

Raymond, Featherweight champion 1945-49.

In the old bare-knuckle prize ring days the brothers Nick and Jem Ward each won the championship. Jem was champion 1825-27. Nick 1840-41.

Among the amateurs the outstanding brothers were Harry W. and Frederick G. Mallin. Each won the A.B.A. middleweight title five times, Harry in 1919-20-21-22-23, and Frederick in 1928-29-30-31-32.

In Scottish amateur boxing in 1913 the brothers J. and R. Whiteford both reached the finals of the heavyweight division but refused to box each other.

The Finazzo brothers of Baltimore, U.S.A. created a record when six of them boxed on the same bill, Baltimore, Aug. 5, 1938.

When Jack "Kid" Berg fought and beat each of the Perlick brothers (Herman and Henry) within a month in 1930 these identical twins were finger-printed before the second contest just to make sure which brother entered the ring.

## Father and son:

No fighter who has won a world title has ever had a son who also achieved that distinction, but two families have so far had father and son as British champions.

"Spider" Jim Kelly was British and Empire featherweight champion 1938-39. His son, Billy, was British featherweight champion 1955-56, and Empire champion 1954-55.

Jack London was British and Empire heavyweight champion 1944-45. His son, Brian, held the same title 1958-59.

In bare-knuckle days Jack Slack was Champion of England 1750-60, and his grandson, Jem Belcher, held the title 1799-1803.

In America, Jacob Hyer claimed the championship of that country in 1816 and was succeeded by his son, Tom, in 1841.

## FARR, Tommy:

Many good judges rate Tommy Farr as the best British heavyweight of modern times. He went closer to winning the world title than any other British heavyweight since Bob Fitzsimmons, but it was not only Farr's fight wth Joe Louis in August, 1937, which earned him such a high rating among all British heavyweights. His performance in that contest overshadowed everything else he ever did, but his other achievements should not be overlooked.

Tommy Farr didn't have the punch of a heavyweight, otherwise he might have come world champion, but he was a really "brainy" fighter who was always very cool and unflustered in the ring.

His crouching style foxed a lot of his opponents and it certainly gave Joe Louis a headache. The "Brown Bomber" was at his peak when Farr met him and it was his first defence of the world title. At the end of 15 rounds one judge had given nine rounds to Louis and six to Farr. The other judge eight to Louis, five to Farr and two even, and the referee awarded 13 to Louis, one to Farr and one even.

So Tommy Farr was one of only three men ever to go the distance with Louis as champion.

When one considers the excellent boxing reputation which Farr built up in the late 1930's it is difficult to understand why he took so long to reach the top.

Born Clydach Vale, South Wales, March 12, 1914, Farr started fighting professionally in 1926 and boxed as a middleweight and later as a cruiserweight for several years without attracting much attention.

He won the Welsh light-heavyweight title in 1933, but after that he lost to Eddie Phillips, Jack Casey, Charlie Berlanger and Dave Carstens, and it was not until 1935 that the boxing fans began to sit up and take notice of this miner from South Wales.

Then Farr embarked on a run of 18 contests in which he was undefeated, and these included winning the Welsh heavyweight title and his victory over Ben Foord for the British heavyweight championship in March, 1937.

Even then we had not seen the best of Tommy Farr. It was in his next fight, on April 15, 1937, that this Welshman reached his peak. Then he outpointed Max Baer at Harringay, and in so doing gave a performance which has never been bettered by a British heavyweight in a London ring.

Farr had one more fight before meeting Louis. In this he knocked out Walter Neusel in the third round, another first-rate performance, for no other British heavyweight had been able to get the better of that German.

After losing to Louis, Farr remained in America in the hope of getting a return, but a surprising decision which gave victory to Jim Braddock in his next fight took some of the fighting heart out of him, and after that he had trouble with managers, trainers and sparring partners, and was beaten by Max Baer, Lou Nova and Red Burman.

When Farr returned to London he had been deprived of his British title by the B.B.B.C. He had four more contests, including a victory over Red Burman, and then retired.

Young men who had never seen Farr in his original career had the opportunity of watching him perform again when he decided to make a come-back in 1950 at the age of 36.

In this come-back Farr suffered only four defeats in 15 fights before he was stopped in eight rounds by Don Cockell, March 9, 1953. He never fought again after that and died in 1986.

### FEARNS, Duggan:

One of the lesser known champions of the old prize ring, Duggan, sometimes referred to as Jack, claimed the title after beating Harry Sellars in only 1½ minutes at Slough, Bucks, September 25, 1779.

Quick finishes were unheard of in those days of long enduring contests and this was said to have been a "cross."

That was probably true for this was one period in the history of the prize ring when the game had fallen into disrepute. So much so that boxing historians have since paid little heed to the champions around that time.

### FEENEY, George:

In his last fight George Feeney paid the penalty for a slow start and was outpointed over 12 rounds in his effort to wrest the European lightweight title from the German Rene Weller. George had the German going towards the end but it was not enough. A cautious fighter the Hartlepool lightweight proved that punches could hurt when he stopped Ray Cattouse in 14 rounds to capture the British title in his 23rd professional fight in 1982. He also stopped Tony Willis inside a round in his first defence of that title but had to wait two years for his European chance. He retired undefeated British champion. Elder brother of John (q.v.).

### FEENEY, John:

Crafty bantamweight from Hartlepool who was outpointed by Johnny Owen in bid for British and Commonwealth title in June 1980, but, after Owen's tragic death, became the British champion by stopping Dave Smith inside 8 rounds in September 1981.

A respected but cautious fighter John Feeney lost his British title to Hugh Russell when disqualified for use of the head, but regained it in November 1983 by stopping Davy Larmour inside three rounds.

After this John Feeney had weight problems and lost his crown when outpointed by Ray Gilbody in June 1985. Moving into the featherweight division he was beaten by Robert Dickie in a bid for the vacant British title in April 1986.

John Feeney made four unsuccessful bids for the European bantamweight title having to go abroad on each occasion and losing on points.

### FERNS, James R. (Rube):

The Kansas Rube was twice holder of the world welterweight title.

He first won the crown by handing out a thoroughly good beating to Mysterious Billy Smith on January 15, 1900, Smith was disqualified for fouling in the 21st round.

Nine months later Ferns was outpointed by Matty Matthews, but he regained the title by knocking out Matthews in a return bout, May 24, 1901.

Ferns finally lost the welterweight championship to the West Indian negro, Joe Walcott, who knocked him out in five rounds in December, 1901.

### FERRIS, Gordon:

Former Irish heavyweight champion from Inniskillen who was a good boxer with a hard left jab and won the vacant British heavyweight title in a close hard-fought contest with Billy Aird at Birmingham in March 1981. Unfortunately for him he lost the title in his first defence less than seven months later when k.o'd in the 1st round by Neville Meade.

## FIELDS, Jackie:

Born Jacob Finkelstein in Chicago this Jewish-American is recognised as one of the most aggressive welterweight fighters of all time.

He won the Olympic Games featherweight title in 1924 and turned professional the following year.

In February, 1928, he was outpointed by Sammy Mandell the world lightweight champion, but in the same year he twice got the better of one of the leading welterweights in the country at that time, Vince Dundee.

In October, 1928, Fields sprang right to the top of the line of welterweight title contenders by outpointing Young Jack Thompson in Chicago.

Thompson had already beaten the champion, Joe Dundee, in an overweight match, and on the strength of this Fields was declared champion by the N.B.A.

Fields really established himself as welterweight title-holder when he defeated Joe Dundee at Detroit, July 25, 1929.

In a third meeting with Young Jack Thompson, May, 1930, Fields was outpointed and lost the championship.

However, in January, 1932, he regained the crown by outpointing Lou Brouillard over ten rounds in Chicago, and this time he held it for just over twelve months before being outpointed by Young Corbett III at San Francisco, February 22, 1933. Fields retired from the ring soon afterwards.

## FIGG, James:

Champion with the broadsword and at cudgelling, James Figg who was born at the village of Thame, Oxfordshire, is acknowledged as the first champion of the English prize ring.

Figg opened a school of arms in London known as Figg's Amphitheatre and his principal challenger for the championship was a pipe-maker from Gravesend one Ned Sutton.

These two met on three different occasions and Figg confirmed his right to the title by defeating Sutton every time.

It is difficult to establish precisely the beginning and end of Figg's reign as champion but it would be approximately from 1719 until he retired undefeated in 1730, which was four years before his death.

It was Figg who discovered the "Father of Boxing" Jack Broughton and brought him to London.

## FILMS:

It was at the Edison Laboratories, Orange, New Jersey, June, 1894, that the first moving pictures of a boxing match were made.

Mike Leonard and Jack Cushing gave an exhibition on this occasion, but the principals were more in earnest three months later. This time they were James J. Corbett and Peter Courtney and they fought for six rounds before Corbett landed the knock-out punch.

These, however, were little more than experiments and the first contest to be filmed for display to the public was that between Bob Fitzsimmons and Jim Corbett at Carson City, Nevada, March 17, 1897.

It had been intended to film an earlier fight between Fitzsimmons and Peter Maher, February 21, 1896, but the film was a failure and in any case Fitzsimmons saw to it that there wasn't much chance of a film by dispatching his opponent with almost the first punch of the fight.

The first contest to be filmed in the British Isles is believed to have been that between Jack Johnson and Ben Taylor at the Cosmopolitan Club, Plymouth, July 31, 1908, when Johnson won by a k.o. in eight rounds.

The first sound film of a boxing match was one made of the first Sharkey-Schmeling contest, June 12, 1930, New York City. However, there was a "live" sound introduction made to a film of the Mickey Walker v. Tommy Milligan fight at the N.S.C., London, in June 1927.

## FINCH, Albert:

Born Croydon, May 16, 1926. Albert Edward Finch started as an amateur with the Croydon A.B.C. and later the Fitzroy-Lynn B.C. He turned professional in August, 1945.

Albert Finch took the British middleweight title from Dick Turpin in April, 1950, at the second attempt. In an earlier meeting Finch had been outpointed but in the return contest at Nottingham, Finch was awarded the decision at the end of 15 rounds.

Back in 1948, Finch had been the first professional to defeat Dick Turpin's brother, Randolph, but when these two met again at Harringay in October, 1950, the Leamington boxer knocked Finch out in the fifth round to capture his middleweight title.

Finch subsequently put on weight and in October, 1951, he tried for Don Cockell's British and European light-heavyweight titles but was knocked out in the seventh round.

The Croydon boxer had two more tries for the British light-heavyweight title but was beaten on both occasions.

## FINLAND:
## Champions:
WORLD:
None.
EUROPEAN:
Lightweight: Elis Ask, 1951-52.
Flyweight: Risto Luukkonen, 1959-61.
OLYMPIC:
Welterweight: Sten Suvie, 1936.
Light-welterweight: Olli Maki, 1964-65.
Bantamweight: Peni Hamalainen, 1952; Risto Luukkonen, 1963-64.

## FINNEGAN, Chris, M.B.E.:
After winning an Olympic Gold medal in Mexico in 1968 this bricklayer from Iver, Bucks, turned professional at the age of 24 and in a career that lasted only seven years proved to be a credit to the fight game. He always gave the fans their money's worth and conducted himself in a sportsmanlike manner. Lack of a real k.o. punch was the only thing that prevented him from rising to even greater heights.

As it was he won the British and Commonwealth light-heavyweight titles from Eddie Avoth in 1971, and after losing these in a classic ring battle with John Conteh in 1973 he regained the British crown in another great contest, this time with Johnny Frankham in 1975.

In 1972 he beat Conny Velensek to take the European crown, but lost this

title when beaten on a cut by Rudiger Schmitdke in November 1972, just six weeks after a gruelling contest with World champion, Bob Foster, which obviously took a lot out of the British fighter. Finnegan was k.o.'d by Foster in the fourteenth round after a great display.

Shortly after regaining his British title with the win over Johnny Frankham, Finnegan had to give up fighting following an eye operation.

## FINNEGAN, Kevin:
After a long spell in the shadow of elder brother Chris, this speedy middleweight from Cowley simply rocketed into the world ratings with two fine victories in 1974.

He won the British middleweight title from Bunny Sterling and the European title, causing a major upset in Paris, by gaining a unanimous points victory over one of France's boxing heroes, Jean-Claude Bouttier.

A talented fighter, Finnegan subsequently relinquished the British title and lost his European crown to another Frenchman, Gratien Tonna.

Alan Minter proved a major stumbling block to Finnegan for he was three times beaten by this Crawley man in British middleweight title bouts. Once after regaining the title by stopping Frankie Lucas in May 1977.

Still Finnegan regained this title for a third time in 1979 by outpointing Tony Sibson and so won a Lonsdale Belt outright. He also regained the vacant European crown by again beating Tonna, but lost this title in September 1980 to the Italian Matteo Salvemini. Kevin retired soon afterwards.

## FITZSIMMONS, Bob:
This Cornishman, who was brought up in New Zealand, was the only English-born fighter ever to win the world heavyweight title under Queensberry Rules. Indeed, he did more than that, he won three world titles, the other two being at middleweight and at light-heavyweight.

Bob Fitzsimmons was a man of iron constitution who was, if necessary, able to absorb a lot of punishment. However, it was very rare, except towards the end of his career, that he was on the receiving end, for he had one of the hardest punches ever for a man of his weight and most of his opponents were stopped inside the distance.

During his ring career which lasted from 1880 to 1914, Fitzsimmons earned many distinctions. He was the oldest man to win the world's light-heavyweight title, which he did at the age of 41, and he was the first fighter to win three world titles.

Bob Fitzsimmons left England for New Zealand when he was only about two years old and made his earliest ring appearances in Timaru in about 1880.

After several contests there and in Australia, Bob went to America in 1890 and after winning two more fights he met Jack Dempsey the "Nonpareil" for world middleweight title at New Orleans, Fitzsimmons won by a k.o. in the 13th round.

Bob then turned his attention to the heavyweights. He was barely 12 stone (168 lbs.) but in those days there was no light-heavyweight division. He gave away nearly three stone to Irishman, Peter Maher, and finished him in the 12th round.

Fitzsimmons continued undefeated for another four or five years and in some circles was considered to be the heavyweight champion, Jim Corbett having announced his retirement, but on March 17, 1897, Gentleman Jim put the gloves on again and proceeded to give Fitzsimmons a boxing lesson. Corbett demonstrated his skill for 12 rounds, while the Cornishman bided his time waiting for the chance. It came in the 14th and that was the end of Corbett, Bob Fitzsimmons was undisputed world heavyweight champion.

By this time Bob Fitzsimmons was a naturalised American. He did not defend his title until three years later when the challenger was 24-years-old James J. Jeffries, one of the toughest and strongest men ever seen in the ring.

This massive fighter from Ohio stood over six feet and weighed nearly 16 stone (224 lbs.) but nevertheless the spindly, bald-headed, 37-year-old champion was the favourite.

Fitzsimmons got in many of his best punches in this contest which took place at San Francisco, June 9, 1899, but they had little effect against the "Boilermaker" and although he was able to outbox Jeffries for several rounds, he was himself knocked out in the 11th.

Bob's career did not end there, however. He won his next five fights, all inside the distance, and then, in July, 1902, when he had passed his fortieth birthday, he made a bid to regain the heavyweight crown from Jeffries but was knocked out in eight rounds.

The light-heavyweight division was created in 1903 and Bob became the second man to win the championship, outpointing George Gardner over 20 rounds.

He lost this title to Philadelphia Jack O'Brien, being knocked out in the 13th round, December, 1905, but he did not have his last fight until he was in his 52nd year when he fought a six-round "no decision" bout with Dan Sweeney at Williamsport, Pennsylvania.

This true gladiator of the ring died of pneumonia in Chicago in October, 1917.

## "FIXED FIGHTS"

See under "THROWING A FIGHT."

## FLOWERS, Theodore "Tiger":

An American negro who was deacon in a Georgia church before he took up boxing, hence his ring nickname, the "Georgia Deacon."

When this good natured, God fearing man was in his prime very few fighters got the better of him in the ring. Mike McTigue was one man who gained a decision over him but that verdict became something of a joke in American boxing circles for 90% of the people in the Garden that night thought the coloured boy had won by the proverbial mile.

Flowers won the world middleweight title by outpointing Harry Greb in the Madison Square Garden, February 26, 1926. He lost it to the former world welterweight champion, Mickey Walker, who got the decision at the end of ten rounds, December 3, 1926.

The "Georgia Deacon" died in New

York, November, 1927, following an eye operation.

## FOORD, Ben:

Born in South Africa in 1913, Ben Foord started fighting professionally in 1931, and came to this country soon afterwards.

In November, 1933, he beat Jack London on points at the Crystal Palace but in an eliminator for the British heavyweight title in March, 1934, he was stopped by Jack Petersen in 13 rounds.

Petersen went on to regain the British and Empire titles from Len Harvey, but when Foord challenged him again in August, 1936, the South African caused a big surprise by beating the Welshman. Despite a fractured right hand, Foord had Petersen in so much trouble in the third round that the referee stopped the contest.

Ben Foord lost his British and Empire titles when outpointed by Tommy Farr, March 15, 1937. He returned to South Africa and died there, tragically, in 1942.

## FORBES, Harry:

An Irish-American who first attempted to win the world bantamweight title in December, 1899, but was stopped in two rounds by Terry McGovern.

In September, 1900, he fought a draw with Caspar Leon for the title which had then become vacant, and in April, 1901 he won the crown by outpointing Leon over 15 rounds at Memphis.

After successfully defending the championship against Dan Dougherty, Tommy Feltz, and Andrew Tokell, Forbes was knocked out in two rounds by Frankie Neil, at San Francisco, August, 13, 1903.

## FOREMAN, Al:

Born London in 1904, Al Foreman took up boxing when he was hungry and out of work. When he was only 16 he fought a 15-round draw with Johnny Brown (St. George's) at Premierland, London. At that time Brown held the British bantamweight title.

Foreman who originally fought under the name of Bert Harris, emigrated to Canada, and, at Montreal in 1928, he created a record (since broken) by knocking out Ruby Levene of Boston in 11½ seconds.

He returned to England in 1930 and challenged Fred Webster for the British lightweight championship. When no one offered to stage this contest Foreman took charge of the promotion himself, and on May 21, 1930, at Premierland, he knocked out Webster in the first round.

The following year Foreman was deprived of his title by the B.B.B.C. after he had refused a small purse to meet Johnny Cuthbert.

## FOREMAN, George:

This powerful negro from the ghettos of Houston, Texas, may go down in history as the ring's greatest enigma.

To begin with he was surprisingly under-rated for despite 37 wins in a row very few expected him to beat Joe Frazier when they met for the heavyweight title in January 1973. But Foreman did not merely beat the favourite—he demolished him, putting the champion down six times before the referee called a halt in the 2nd round.

After this Foreman was acclaimed as invincible and strengthened this view by the ruthless manner in which he made such short work of Ken Norton, but in October 1974 he surprised everyone again when he was outclassed by Muhammad Ali, and lost his title after being k.o'd in the 8th round.

## FOSTER, Bob:

A coloured American who recovered from early set-backs when he was overmatched and went on to win the world light-heavy title by knocking out Dick Tiger with a solid left-hook in the fourth round of their contest in New York, May 24, 1968.

One of the hardest punchers ever seen in the light-heavyweight division he jabbed his way through 14 successful defences of his title, stopping most opponents inside the distance before announcing his retirement in September 1974 soon after the W.B.C. had deprived him of his crown. Foster returned to the ring 9 months later but was unable to get a title fight.

Like so many light-heavies before him

he failed in an attempt on the heavy-weight title being k.o.d inside 2 rounds by Joe Frazier in November 1970.

## FOUL:

In this country, either in professional or amateur boxing it is a foul to hit below the belt, on the back of the head or neck or on the kidneys, for using the pivot blow, for hitting with the open glove, the inside or butt of the hand, or with the wrist or elbow. It is also a foul to hold, butt, shoulder, wrestle or engage in roughing tactics, remain in a clinch unnecessarily, or hit on the break. A boxer can also be disqualified for not trying, for persistently ducking below the waist line, intentionally falling without being hit, for hitting an opponent when he is down, for careless use of the head, or for ungentlemanly conduct.

There have been only eight world title contests from which a new champion has emerged through a disqualification.

Heavyweight: Max Schmeling beat Jack Sharkey on a foul in four rounds, New York, June 12, 1930.

Middleweight: Frank Klaus beat Billy Papke, 15 rounds, Paris, March 5, 1913.

Marcel Thil beat Gorilla Jones, 11 rounds, Paris, June 11, 1932.

Welterweight: Rube Ferns beat Mysterious Billy Smith, 21 rounds, Buffalo, January 15, 1900.

Dixie Kid beat Joe Walcott, 20 rounds, San Francisco, April 30, 1904.

Lightweight: Arthur Chambers beat Billy Edwards, 35 rounds, Squirrel Island, October 6, 1872.

Willie Ritchie beat Ad Wolgast, 16 rounds, Daly City, California, November 28, 1912.

Junior-lightweight: Johnny Dundee beat George Chaney, 5 rounds, New York, November 18, 1921.

In September 1922 when Battling Siki relieved Georges Carpentier of the world light-heavyweight title by knocking him out in the sixth round, the contest was originally awarded to the Frenchman, the referee claiming that Siki had been guilty of a foul. There was nearly a riot before the judges revoked the referee's decision.

## Foul-proof protector:

These are believed to have been adapted for boxing from a protector invented by "Foulproof" Taylor after he had been injured in a fight scene in Grand Opera.

In America the protector was made compulsory by J. A. Farley of the N.Y.A.C. in 1930, at the same time as the introduction of the no-foul rule.

On January 1, 1950, the B.B.B.C. also made it compulsory for protectors to be worn in all contests.

## No-foul Rule:

In 1930 the N.Y.A.C. decided that it would no longer be possible for a fighter to win a decision simply because he had been struck a low blow.

This became known as the "no-foul rule" and the idea was conceived at a time when racketeers and gangsters were getting such a big hold on the game and protecting their betting interests by forcing a fighter to foul and therefore lose a contest as soon as he realised that he would be unable to win.

The gamblers' money was safe-guarded in this way because they had an understanding that no bets would be paid-off on any contest ending in a disqualification.

Since the introduction of this rule in America, it has become the practice for the referee to have the option of awarding the round to the contestant who has been fouled.

Technically, however, it is still possible for a fight to end in a disqualification in America, for while it is true that a fighter cannot be ruled out of a contest because of a single low blow, he can be disqualified for hitting an opponent when he is down; for using the knee; purposely going down without being hit; or for failure to obey the referee, or any physical action which may injure a contestant except by fair sportsmanlike boxing. Low blows are excluded from the latter.

For many years there have been several people who consider that the "no-foul rule" should be introduced in this country, but the suggestion never has been accepted by the authorities.

In the first place, because of our

system of scoring with points over a whole contest rather than by rounds won, it would be difficult to decide what number of points a boxer should lose for committing such a foul.

## FOX, Joe:

Leeds bantamweight who was well known on both sides of the Atlantic during and after the first World War.

An exponent of the straight left style of boxing, Fox first went to America in 1914. On his return the following year he won the vacant British bantamweight title with a victory over Jimmy Berry at the N.S.C., November 22, 1915. The referee stopped the contest in the 16th round to save Berry from further punishment.

Fox won the Lonsdale Belt outright by defeating Tommy Harrison and Joe Symonds before relinquishing the title in 1918 and paying another visit to America where he had several "no decision" bouts.

In October, 1921, Fox won the British featherweight title from Mike Honeyman at the N.S.C., getting the referee's nod at the end of 20 rounds.

At Holland Park, London, in May, 1922, Fox met the European featherweight champion, Eugene Criqui, but after outboxing the hard hitting Frenchman for several rounds, Fox got into trouble and the referee was forced to stop the contest in the 12th round when the Frenchman had Fox well and truly beaten.

Joe Fox relinquished his featherweight title in 1923 and made yet another trip to the United States and Canada before retiring in 1926.

## FRANCE:

The first French prize fighter to appear in Britain was a giant by the name of Pettit. He was a circus strong man who stood 6 feet 3 inches tall and weighed around 16 stone.

In 1751 this Frenchman challenged the reigning champion, Jack Slack. When they met at Harlston, Norfolk, on July 29, 1751, Pettit was beaten in 25 minutes.

Turning to more modern times the man who put French boxing on the map

was Francois Descamps. This shrewd Frenchman started by running a boys' gymnastic class. He discovered the youthful Georges Carpentier fighting in the street, encouraged him to join his class, and from thereon the fame of both these great personalities was assured.

## Champions:

WORLD:

Light-heavyweight: Georges Carpentier, 1920-22.

Middleweight; Marcel Thil, 1932-37. Marcel Cerdan, 1948-49.

Featherweight: Andre Routis, 1928-29; Eugene Criqui, 1923.

Bantamweight: Robert Cohen, 1954-56; Alphonse Halimi, 1957-59, 1960-61 (European recognition only).

Flyweight: Victor (Young) Perez, 1931-32.

EUROPEAN:

Heavyweight: Georges Carpentier. 1913-22; Battling Siki; 1922-23; Lucien Rodriguez, 1977, 1981-84.

Light-heavyweight: Georges Carpentier, 1913-22; Battling Siki, 1922-23; Emile Morelle, 1923; Raymond Bonnel, 1923-24; Marcel Thil, 1934-35; Albert Yvel, 1950-51; Jacques Hairabedian, 1953-54; Richard Caramonolis, 1984.

Middleweight: Georges Carpentier, 1912-14. Ercole Balzac, 1920-21; Barthelemey Molina, 1928; Marcel Thil, 1929-30, 1932-33, 1934; Edouard Tenet, 1938, 1939; Marcel Cerdan, 1947-48, 1948; Charles Humez, 1954-58; Jean-Claude Bouttier, 1971, 1974; Gratien Tonna, 1977-78; Louis Acaries, 1982-84.

Junior or Light-middleweight: Yolande Leveque, 1966; Jacques Kechichian, 1973-74; Gilbert Cohen, 1978-79; Louis Acaries, 1981; Said Skouma, 1985-86.

Welterweight: Georges Carpentier, 1911-12; Marcel Cerdan, 1939-40; Robert Villemain, 1947-48; Charles Humez, 1951-52; Gilbert Lavoine, 1953-54; Idrissa Dione, 1955-56; Jean Josselin, 1966-67, 1969; Roger Menetrey, 1971-74; Alain Marion, 1977-78; Gilles Elbilia, 1983-84.

Junior or Light-welterweight: Rene Roque, 1970-71; Roger Zami, 1972; Jean-Baptiste Piedvache, 1977-78; Jo Kimpuani, 1979-80; Robert Gambini, 1982-83.

Lightweight: Fred Bretonnel, 1924; Lucien Vinez, 1924-27; Aime Raphael, 1928-29; Maurice Arnoult, 1937; Gustave Humery, 1937; Emile Dicristo, 1946-47; Pierre Montane, 1951; Maurice Tavant, 1965-66.

Junior-lightweight: Roland Cazeaux, 1976.

Featherweight: Louis de Ponthieu, 1919-20; Eugene Criqui, 1922-23; Edouard Mascart, 1923-24; Charles Ledoux, 1924-25; Maurice Holtzer, 1935-38; Raymond Famechon 1948-53, 1954-55; Cherif Hamia, 1957-58; Gracieux Lamperti, 1959-62.

Bantamweight: Charles Ledoux, 1912-21, 1922-23; Joseph Decico, 1936-37; Theo Medina, 1946-47; Robert Cohen, 1954-55; Alphonse Halimi, 1962; Daniel Trioulaire, 1975-76; Antoine Montero, 1986-87; Louis Gomis, 1987-

Flyweight: Emile Pladner, 1928; Eugene Huat, 1929; Kid Oliva, 1930; Praxille Gyde, 1932-35; Valentin Angelmann, 1936-38; Maurice Sandeyron, 1947-49; Louis Skena, 1953-54; Rene Libeer, 1965-67; Antoine Montero, 1983-84.

France has produced more European Champions than any other country outside of Great Britain.

OLYMPIC:

Light-heavyweight: R. Michelot, 1936.

Middleweight: J. Despeaux, 1936.

Featherweight: R. Fritsch, 1920.

## FRANKHAM, Johnny:

Even this fighter himself admitted that he often did not pay as much attention as he should have done to his training and his form in the ring was erratic, but at his best this light-heavyweight from Reading was a clever and fast-moving boxer. He was certainly at his best when he outpointed Chris Finnegan for the vacant British title in June 1975. The decision was a controversial one but in a great contest Frankham displayed coolness in picking his punches.

A former A.B.A. light-heavyweight champion Frankham turned professional in 1970 and won the British title in his 37th contest, 27 of them victories. His reign, however, was short-lived, for in a return four months later Chris Finnegan turned the tables in another exciting contest.

## FRAZIER, Joe:

This tough slugger from Philadelphia clearly established himself as undisputed world heavyweight champion in March 1971 when he gained a unanimous points verdict over the previously undefeated title-holder, Muhammad Ali in a fight which drew a million-dollar gate at the Madison Square Garden.

Ali was only the third man to go the distance with the relentless, all-action Frazier, the others being Oscar Bonavena (twice) and George Johnson, and Frazier's victory in that "Fight of the century" was his 27th win in 27 bouts since turning professional after winning the Olympic heavyweight competition in 1965.

When Ali was deprived of the world title by the authorities Frazier first won N.Y.A.C. recognition by stopping Buster Mathis inside 11 rounds in April 1968 and then annexed the W.B.A. version of the crown in February 1970 by giving their champion, Jimmy Ellis, such a hammering that he did not leave his stool for the 5th round.

Frazier was freely referred to as "undestructible," but like many others before him who were considered unbeatable he met his master. George Foreman not only beat him but did so surprisingly easily, the referee intervening in the 2nd round after Frazier had been down six times—January 1973.

## FREEMAN, Thomas J.:

An Irish-Scotch-American who was born at Hot Springs, Arkansas in 1904 and started fighting soon after World War I.

However, it was not until September 1930 that he got a long-awaited shot at a world title, and then he won a return bout with Young Jack Thompson to become welterweight champion.

In April, 1931, Freeman was again in the same ring as Thompson and this time he received a hammering. He was unable to come up for the 12th round and so lost the championship.

## FULLMER, Gene:

American middleweight from West

Jordan, Utah, who was an all-action fighter known in boxing circles as the "Cyclone."

In January, 1957, he caused a surprise by the manner in which he clearly outpointed Ray Robinson to win the world middleweight title, but he was k.o'd in a return match four months later.

After the N.B.A. had deprived Robinson of the title Fullmer won it by stopping Carmen Basilio in 14 rounds, Aug. 29, 1959, and he retained this version of the world championship until outpointed in a rugged fight at San Francisco, Oct. 23, 1962.

## GANS, Joe:

An American negro, Joe Gans was one of the most skilful boxers of all time. Known as "The Old Master" he was something of a genius in the ring and a great counter-puncher.

Joe Gans came to the fore in 1895 when he drew with that other boxing master, Young Griffo, over 10 rounds, a performance he was able to repeat two years later.

Gans first fought for the world lightweight title in March, 1900, but on that occasion he was severely criticised and even called a coward. For 11 rounds he was outpointing the champion, Frank Erne, but in the 12th round, immediately he sustained a cut eye, Gans gave up.

Near the end of that year he was knocked out inside two rounds by Terry McGovern and it was alleged that the negro had "thrown" this contest.

After that, however, Gans quickly regained the public's confidence. He took the lightweight title from Frank Erne in May, 1902, stopping the champion in only 1½ minutes' fighting and was only beaten once in the next eight years. That was when he conceded weight to Sam Langford and went 15 rounds.

Gans often went out of his division to meet the best welterweights and middleweights in the world. In September, 1904 he tried to wrest the welterweight crown from Joe Walcott and got a draw at the end of 20 rounds. On two occasions he knocked out that top ranking welterweight Mike Twin Sullivan.

In September, 1906, he fought the epic battle with Battling Nelson at Goldfield, Nevada. It was scheduled for 45 rounds

and it went 42 round before Nelson was disqualified for striking a low blow.

It was in their return fight in July, 1908 that Gans lost his title, being knocked out in the 17th round. In a third meeting, September, 1908, Gans, now 34 years of age and a veteran of nearly 20 years in the ring, was stopped in 21 rounds.

The strain of making the weight for these meetings with Nelson hastened the "Old Master's" death. Tuberculosis got the better of him and he passed away in August, 1910.

## GARCIA, Ceferino:

Filipino who met Barney Ross for the world welterweight championship in September, 1937, but was outpointed.

He later failed to take the title from Henry Armstrong but had more success when he moved up into the middleweight division.

In this class Garcia won the recognition of N.Y.A.C. as world champion when he stopped Fred Apostoli in seven rounds in October, 1939.

He subsequently held Henry Armstrong to a draw in defence of this crown but on May 23, 1940, he was beaten by Ken Overlin.

## GARDNER, George:

Born County Clare, Ireland, in 1877, the son of a bare-knuckle prize fighter, George Gardner went to America when still a youngster.

In 1901 and again the following year he was outpointed by the great Joe Walcott. He also went 20 rounds before losing on points to Jack Johnson in 1902.

A rugged fighter, Gardner was the second man to hold the world lightheavyweight title when he knocked out Jack Root in 12 rounds at Fort Erie, July 4, 1903.

Unfortunately for Gardner he came up against the redoubtable Bob Fitzsimmons in his next fight and was relieved of the championship by a points decision at the end of 20 rounds.

## GARDNER, Jack:

Born Market Harborough, Leicestershire, November 6, 1926, Jack Gardner was a sergeant in the Grenadier Guards when he won the Army, Imperial Services and the A.B.A. heavyweight titles in 1948. In that same year he also represented Great Britain in the Olympic Games but was beaten by a Swiss.

Gardner turned professional in November, 1948, and won his first 13 fights inside the distance before losing to the Canadian heavyweight, Vern Escoe, in July, 1949. He was again beaten by Escoe in February, 1950, but he went on to defeat Johnny Williams in a British and Empire heavyweight title eliminator and then took these titles from Bruce Woodcock in November, 1950. Gardner forced the champion to retire in the 11th round.

Jack Gardner was rather a slow mover but he had a good left hand and this helped him to take the European title from the Austrian, Joe Weidin, in March, 1951.

Gardner later disappointed his supporters by losing to the German, Hein Ten Hoff. That was in September, 1951, and cost Gardner his European title. In March, 1952, he also lost his British and Empire titles when he was outpointed by Johnny Williams.

The Market Harborough boxer expressed disapproval at the verdict which gave Williams victory on that occasion and he retired soon afterwards.

However, in 1954-55 Gardner made a come-back. He avenged his previous defeat by Williams, knocking him out inside five rounds in a British and Empire title eliminator, but he was beaten in two rounds by the Empire champion, Joe Bygraves, in April, 1956.

### GARDNER, John L.:

All-action heavyweight who won the vacant British and Commonwealth titles in October 1978 in typical fashion by crowding and punching Billy Aird non-stop for five rounds at the end of which Aird signalled his retirement.

That was Gardner's 28th professional contest, all of them fought in London, and he had suffered only one defeat, a surprise one punch k.o. in 2 min. 20 secs. by comparatively unknown American, Dale Arrington, in September 1977.

Not noted for a k.o. punch this

Hackney, London fighter with an aggressive style won the vacant European heavyweight title in 1980 by forcing Rudi Gauwe to retire inside 9 rounds.

He relinquished his Commonwealth title in October 1980, and his British title the following year, during which a defeat by American Mike Dokes prevented him from becoming a world title contender.

### GARDNER, Teddy:

Born West Hartlepool, County Durham, in 1922, Gardner started boxing at the age of 12 and turned professional when he was only 16.

He sprang to the top in August, 1948, when he outpointed the British bantamweight champion, Jackie Paterson, in a non-title bout fought at 8 stone 8 lbs. (120 lbs.).

Later, when Paterson had been beaten by Stan Rowan and Rowan had relinquished the championship, Teddy Gardner was matched with Danny O'Sullivan for the vacant title. This was in December, 1949. Gardner was forced to retire in the ninth round.

Teddy Gardner got his British title in the flyweight division in March 1952, when he outpointed Terry Allen at Newcastle. This was only three weeks after he had won the vacant European flyweight championship by stopping Louis Skena of France in six rounds.

Gardner retired undefeated champion in September, 1952.

### GAVILAN, Kid:

A coloured Cuban welterweight, Gavilan, who was known as the "Cuban Hawk" gave up working in the sugar fields to turn professional in 1943. His career extended over 15 years and during that time he was never knocked out.

Gavilan was an exponent of the "bolo" punch, and after Ray Robinson relinquished the welterweight title in 1951, the Cuban gained the recognition of the N.B.A. as the negro's successor by outpointing Johnny Bratton, May 18, 1951.

He was accorded more general recognition in July, 1952, after he had defeated Gil Turner. The referee intervening in the 11th round.

Gavilan defended his title against Billy Graham, Chuck Davey, Carmen Basilio and Johnny Bratton, before losing it to Johnny Saxton in October, 1954.

While he held this title Gavilan made a bid for the middleweight crown but was outpointed by Bobo Olson.

## GENARO, Frankie:

This stylish flyweight won the Olympic Games title in 1920. He turned professional the same year and had reached the top line of flyweight contenders in March, 1923, when he defeated the reputable Pancho Villa.

Still it was Villa who got a title fight with Jimmy Wilde three months later and captured the world championship.

When Pancho Villa died in 1925 Genaro claimed the title on the strength of his victory over the Filipino but he was not universally recognised at that time. Then, when he was beaten by Fidel La Barba in August, 1925, his title hopes lapsed for the time being.

In February, 1928, this Italian-American staked another claim to the hotly disputed flyweight championship when he beat the N.B.A. title-holder, Albert Berlanger, but when he came to Paris in 1929 he was knocked out in 59 seconds by Emile Pladner.

Genaro got the decision over Pladner on a disqualification in a return bout and then regained N.B.A. recognition as flyweight king-pin by outpointing Berlanger a second time in June, 1930.

However, Paris wasn't a happy hunting ground for Genaro and when he returned there in October, 1931, it was to be finally eliminated from the flyweight championship with a second round k.o. by Young Perez.

## GERMANY:

Apart from their amateurs the Germans had never won an international title in any of the lighter weight divisions until Rudhof and Quatuor each captured the European lightweight crown in the 1960s. In fact they have produced very few outstanding men in even the welter or middleweight divisions, but when it comes to heavies and light-heavyweights

it is then that you find the Fatherland well to the fore.

The best known German heavyweight was, of course, Max Schmeling the "Black Uhlan." But Schmeling never fought in this country and if you were to ask a Britisher to name a German heavyweight the chances are that he would recall another who paid several visits here before the last war—Walter Neusel.

Neusel, 6 foot 2½ inches and weighing around 14 stone (196 lbs.) was a real stumbling block to ambitious British and Empire heavyweights and cruiser-weights during the 1930's. In fact, there were only two Britishers able to beat him, and they were Tommy Farr, who knocked him out in the third round, and the South African, Don McCorkindale, who beat him on a foul. In another meeting Neusel and McCorkindale fought a 12-round draw.

Britishers whom Neusel defeated included Gipsy Daniels, Larry Gains, George Cook, Ben Foord, Reggie Meen, Jack Pettifer, and, of course, Jack Petersen.

Three times the British champion, Jack Petersen, tried to get the better of this tough German, but on each occasion he was out-slogged by the heavier man. Three defeats which probably took more out of the Welshman than any other half dozen contests and hastened his retirement from the ring.

Since the war two other British heavyweight champions have been beaten by Germans. Jack Gardner lost to Hein Ten Hoff in March, 1951, and Johnny Williams was beaten by Heinz Neuhaus in February, 1953.

## Champions:

WORLD:
Heavyweight: Max Schmeling, 1930-32.

EUROPEAN:
Heavyweight: Hein Muller, 1931-32; Arno Koeblin, 1937-38; Adolf Heuser, 1939; Max Schmeling, 1939; Hein Ten Hoff, 1951-52; Heinz Neuhas, 1952-55; Karl Mildenberger, 1964-68; Peter Weiland, 1969-70; Jurgen Blin, 1972.

Light-heavyweight: Max Schmeling, 1927-28; Ernst Pistulla, 1931-32; Adolf

Heuser, 1932-33, 1938-39; Connie Rux, 1952-53; Gerhard Hecht, 1954-55, 1955-57; Willi Hoepner, 1955, 1958; Erich Schoeppner, 1958-62; Gustav Scholz, 1964-65; Lother Stengel 1967-68, Conny Velensek, 1971-72; Rudiger Schmitdke, 1972.

Middleweight: Hein Domgoergen, 1931-32; Josef Besselmann, 1942-43; Gustav Scholz, 1958-61.

Light-middleweight: Gerhard Piaskowy, 1969-70; Eckhard Dagge 1975-76; Georg Steinherr, 1984-85.

Welterweight: Gustave Eder, 1934-35; Jose Varela, (born Spain but a German citizen) 1986-87.

Junior-welterweight: Willie Quatuor, 1965-66; Conny Rudhof, 1967.

Lightweight: Conny Rudhof, 1963-64; Willie Quatuor, 1964-65; Rene Weller, 1984-86.

Junior-lightweight: Lothar Abend, 1972-74.

OLYMPIC:

Heavyweight: H. Runge, 1936.

Light-middleweight: Dieter Kottysch, 1972.

Welterweight: M. Wolke (E. Germ.), 1968; J. Bachfeld (E. Germ.), 1976.

Bantamweight: W. Behrendt, 1956.

Flyweight: W. Kaiser, 1936.

## GIARDELLO, Joey:

A really tough champion who came up the hard way and never gave up trying although it took him 15 years to achieve his ambition and become world middleweight champion.

Born in Brooklyn but brought up in Philadelphia, Giardello was fighting professional at 18 years of age and had had over 100 bouts before he got a match with the world champion (N.B.A's version) Gene Fullmer.

A lot of people, including Giardello, thought that he had won that fight but the official decision was a draw, and after more defeats than victories in his next half-dozen bouts many believed that the Philadelphia veteran was on the way out.

Joey Giardello was far from that, however, and he proved it in December, 1963, completely upsetting the odds and capturing the world title by outpointing Dick Tiger.

In a return bout nearly two years later Giardello was well and truly beaten by the Nigerian and fought only four more contests before retiring.

## GILBODY, Ray:

After a brilliant amateur career, winning the A.B.A. flyweight title in 1979 and the bantamweight title in 1980 and 1982, this fast-moving fighter had a fairly short professional career in which his stand-up style with chin out often got him into trouble with the stronger hitters.

He outpointed the experienced John Feeney for the British bantamweight title in 1985 but lost two bids for the European crown, being stopped inside a round by Antoine Montero in Paris. In his next fight the Warrington fighter was saved from further punishment by the referee in the third round of a fight with Billy Hardy and announced his retirement soon afterwards.

## GILROY, Freddie:

Born Belast, 1936, Freddie Gilroy learnt the game from the age of nine with the St. John Bosco A.B.C. in the Northern Ireland capital.

He turned professional in 1957 and an undefeated run culminated in him winning the British and Empire bantamweight championship from Peter Keenan in Belfast, January 10, 1959. The referee stopped the contest in the 11th round.

Eleven months later this two-fisted fighter hammered his way to the European bantamweight title in his 19th professional contest with a points victory over Piero Rollo of Italy.

In October, 1960, Gilroy was matched with Alphonse Halimi for the world title (European version) but was beaten on points, a defeat that cost him his European crown.

After successfully defending his British and Empire titles against Billy Rafferty (twice) and Johnny Caldwell, Gilroy relinquished them in November, 1963, because of difficulty in making the weight.

## GLENCROSS, Tommy:

This Scottish southpaw, who was his country's amateur bantamweight champion in 1967, got a crack at the European featherweight crown in March 1972 but was outpointed by Jose Legra.

Four months later he took the British title from Evan Armstrong with a points victory, but had to take heavy punishment when he made another attempt at the European title in May 1973. On this occasion he was beaten by the Spaniard, Gitano Jiminez.

In September that year he lost his British title in a return with Evan Armstrong, the fight being stopped in the third round because of his cut eye.

## GLOVES:

Forgetting the days of the ancient Greeks and Romans (who fought with their hands encased in gloves of leather and iron covered with spikes or thongs) and accepting the fact that boxing was really first popularised by James Figg (1695-1734) it is a well known fact that gloves were invented and introduced by Jack Broughton, Champion of England, 1729–50.

Broughton produced these gloves, or as they were then known—mufflers, so that the gentry, who were so inclined, could enjoy the sport at his gymnasium without suffering any serious injury to face or hands.

This would be in about 1734 when the "mufflers" were probably about ten ounces.

At that time, however, these gloves were reserved for use in gymnasiums and in training bouts. All proper contests before the public were fought with the bare knuckles.

Gloves were first mentioned in the rules of boxing in 1864, the year in which the Queensberry Rules are generally considered to have been published. Then, however, they were rarely more than five ounces, and more often than not, if gloves were worn at all (they were not worn in championship bouts), they were only two-ounce or skin-tight kid gloves.

Skin-tight gloves remained popular until the turn of the century and were worn in some important contests up until 1902-03, although the first man to win the world heavyweight title in a gloved contest, James J. Corbett, beat Sullivan back in 1892 and wore five-ounce gloves on that occasion.

Although John L. Sullivan won the American championship by beating Paddy Ryan in a bare knuckle contest he fought most of his contests with gloves and is considered to have been the first champion to popularise the wearing of these.

In Britain today gloves must be of a standard weight of six ounces for welterweights and under, and eight ounces for middleweights and over. In Amateur bouts it is eight ounces for boxers below 67 kgs. (147 lbs.), and 10 ounces above that weight. Both to wear 10 ounce if one contestant is over 67 kgs (147 lbs.). While in the greater part of America the minimum is also eight ounces at all weights.

In January 1982 New York State made thumbless gloves mandatory for fights not involving world titles. They also excluded amateurs from this rule which soon proved most unpopular with the majority of fighters. The idea was to help prevent eye injuries.

## GODDARD, Frank:

A well-built London heavyweight who lacked the skill to take him into the world class but was a tough fighter.

The men he defeated included Joe Beckett, Billy Wells, Jack Bloomfield, Tom Gummer, Dick Smith, Harry Curzon and Jack Curphey.

When he stopped Jack Curphey in 10 rounds on May 26, 1919, Goddard claimed the British heavyweight title, but at that time Joe Beckett also claimed this championship, having beaten Billy Wells in February, 1919. Beckett, however, was not recognised by the N.S.C. until he had met and knocked out Goddard at Olympia, June 17, 1919. Goddard went out in the second round.

Goddard was matched with Jack Bloomfield for the vacant title in November, 1923, after Beckett had retired, and he got the decision on a disqualification in the second round.

He successfully defended his crown against Jack Stanley in April, 1924, but he lost it to Phil Scott, who knocked him out in the third round, March 18, 1926.

## GOLDSWAIN, Jack:

This Bermondsey fighter caused a surprise by outpointing Jabez White over 20 rounds at the N.S.C. in April, 1906.

This match was made at 10 stone (140lbs.) but it was billed as being for the British lightweight title. White, however, refused to relinquish the crown, claiming that he had been beaten in an overweight bout, and there is some confusion as to who was the rightful title-holder about this time.

The Editor of the *Mirror of Life* eventually declared that Goldswain was the lightweight champion, and he held on to this honour until November, 1908, when he was beaten in 14 rounds by Johnny Summers, the referee stopping the contest.

Goldswain also claimed the welter-weight title during his career. He earned this distinction by outpointing Curley Watson at Wonderland in May, 1909, but even this claim to the championship is a doubtful one, and in any case. Goldswain was beaten only 20 days later in a return with Watson.

## GOMEZ, Wilfredo:

At his peak this Puerto Rican fighter enjoyed a run of 32 wins inside the distance. Obviously he was one of the most ferocious punchers of the post-war era and is numbered among the élite of fighters to win world titles in three divisions—super-bantamweight, feather-weight and junior lightweight. After capturing the first title in May 1977 he successfully defended it 17 times before relinquishing the crown in April 1983.

The all-action Gomez won and lost the W.B.C. featherweight title and the junior-lightweight championship in his last four fights. Indeed, he fought to the last gasp when stopped by Alfredo Layne in nine rounds in May 1986. Gomez always gave the fans their money's worth.

## GONG:

A gong was first used to sound time at the beginning and end of each round during the heavyweight championship contest between James J. Corbett and John L. Sullivan at the Olympic Club,

New Orleans, September 7, 1892.

## GOODRICH, Jimmy:

An Irish-German-American, Jimmy Goodrich started boxing soon after World War I. His real name is James Edward Moran.

By the time Benny Leonard had retired undefeated lightweight champion in 1925, Goodrich was one of the leading contenders.

Eliminating tournaments were run to find a successor to Leonard, and Goodrich won the one arranged by the N.Y.A.C.

In this tournament Goodrich clinched the title with a knock-out victory over Stanislaus Loayza in Italy, 1925, but he only retained the championship for five months before he was outpointed by Rocky Kansas.

After that Goodrich dropped quickly from the top rank, losing to Mushy Callahan, Jack Bernstein and Baby Joe Gans. He retired in 1930.

## GOSS, Joseph:

When trying to establish the identity of the first heavyweight champion of the world, Joe Goss, of Northampton, England, is one of the fighters who must be taken into consideration.

In this country he was twice beaten by Jem Mace, but between these two defeats he also fought a draw with the English champion.

In 1870 Mace went to America and there defeated another Englishman, Tom Allen, in what was considered at the time to be a fight for the world championship. Mace retired in 1871 and Allen claimed the title.

Now Goss had fought a draw with Allen in England, and when he followed the Birmingham fighter to America he challenged him for the world champion-ship and they met in Kentucky, September 7, 1876.

According to contemporary reports Allen was the better man for most of the contest, but when a section of the crowd adopted a threatening attitude towards him he decided that it was better to "foul out" rather than go on to victory, and he was disqualified in the 21st round.

Goss lost his title, either American or

world, in his next fight, a really hard battle with Paddy Ryan at Collier Station, West Virginia, May 30, 1880.

He was a cleverer fighter than Ryan but after fighting for 87 rounds, lasting 1 hour 27 minutes (some say 1 hour 24 minutes) age began to tell and Goss was unable to continue. Goss was then 41, Ryan 27.

Goss settled in America and died there in 1885.

## GRAHAM, Bushy:

Angelo Geraci was born in Italy but emigrated to America, and there, when he took up boxing, he adopted the name of Bushy Graham.

He claimed the world bantamweight title for a time in 1928 but was never accorded general recognition at a time when this championship was in a state of chaos.

Graham met the rightful champion, Charlie Rosenburg, in New York, February 4, 1927. Rosenburg emerged the victor on points, but he had come in overweight and so forfeited his title. In addition to this both fighters were suspended for 12 months.

During this period of suspension, Bud Taylor gained the recognition of the N.B.A. as bantamweight champion, but when Graham returned to the ring he ignored this and gained some support in New York State for his claim as title-holder following his points win over Corporal Izzy Schwartz, May 23, 1928.

Soon after this, however, Graham was forced to move up into the featherweight division and his claim to the title lapsed.

## GRAHAM, Herol:

Turning professional in 1978, shortly after winning the A.B.A. middleweight championship, this Nottingham-born fighter defied his critics who considered him too cautious by going on to win the British light middleweight title in his 17th fight (all of them wins) outpointing Pat Thomas before his Sheffield home-town crowd in March 1981. He added the Commonwealth title eight months later, and in May 1983, the European title. The secret of his success is sharp reflexes which keep him out of trouble.

In 1985 he moved up into the middle-weight division to capture the vacant British crown with a win inside 100 seconds over Jimmy Price, and then added the European title by stopping Ayub Kalule in 10 rounds, again in front of his Sheffield fans. Graham has certainly revived boxing in the steel city.

## GRAZIANO, Rocky:

Born of Italian parents in a New York East Side tenement flat, his real name was Rocco Barbella but he had it legally changed to Graziano.

A really tough kid, Graziano couldn't keep out of trouble in his younger days, but when he made the grade in the ring he became one of the highest paid fighters of modern times, and since retiring has made a lucrative living as a television actor.

Graziano was always a big draw because he was an all-action fighter with a punch that was liable to finish a contest at any time.

In the ring Graziano had the "killer" instinct like Jack Dempsey, and his style has been likened to that of another famous middleweight, Stanley Ketchell.

As an amateur Graziano was a Golden Gloves champion. He turned professional in 1942 and in four years, during which he won the majority of his fights by knock-outs, he worked his way up to a world middleweight title fight with Tony Zale. He gave the champion a difficult time but was knocked out in the sixth round.

In a return meeting in July, 1947, Graziano turned the tables on Zale by knocking him out in the same round, but in a third meeting, in June, 1948, Zale regained the championship with a knock-out in round three.

These three fights were among the bloodiest battles seen in America since the last war.

After several more victories Graziano made another bid for the middleweight crown in April, 1952, but he was stopped in three rounds by Ray Robinson.

This hard-hitting middleweight had only one more fight after that before hanging up his gloves.

## GREB, Harry:

Harry Greb, of Pittsburgh, was one of the most ferocious fighters of modern times. From the first gong he would come out fighting like a wild cat and his non-stop tearaway style with arms flaying in all directions earned him the nickname of "The Flying Dutchman" or "The Human Windmill."

Greb was the only man ever to beat Gene Tunney, although he was beaten on two other occasions by the more scientific and heavier man. Still, although it is often mentioned, Greb's victory over Tunney was by no means his only claim to fame.

No indeed, Harry Greb had a busy 13 years in the ring and during that time he fought most of the best middleweights, cruiserweights, and even heavyweights, in the world. A lot of his fights were "no decision" affairs, but during his career he beat six men who at one time or another were themselves world champions. These were Frank Mantell, Gene Tunney, Tommy Loughran, Johnny Wilson, Jimmy Slattery and Mickey Walker.

It was even suggested that Greb could beat Jack Dempsey. This idea got around after the two had met in a hectic training spar which was stopped after Dempsey had sustained a cut eye.

Of course, these two never met in a proper contest, but Greb had a good win over another leading heavyweight, Bill Brennan, only a few months before that fighter went 12 rounds with Dempsey for the title.

Greb won the world middleweight title by outpointing Johnny Wilson in August, 1923, and lost it in a close fight with Tiger Flowers, Feb, 26, 1926.

Towards the close of his career Greb suffered with eye trouble, and it is believed that he fought many of his later contests when he was actually blind in one eye.

Greb was a great fighter and he might have been even better if he had taken his training seriously. Instead, he preferred a gay life, and it was cut short when he died at the age of 32.

## GREEN, Dave "Boy":

One of Britain's most exciting and aggressive post-war fighters who hails from Chatteris, Cambridgeshire, the same place as that other great puncher of yesteryear—Eric Boon.

Dave Green won all of his first 15 professional fights inside the distance before relieving Joey Singleton of the British light-welterweight title in six rounds in June 1976. Before the year was out Green captured the vacant European title by forcing Frenchman, Jean-Baptiste Piedvache, to retire at the end of nine bloody rounds.

Green, who proved that he can box as well as fight, relinquished these titles to concentrate on a bid for the world welterweight crown, but he was stopped in 11 rounds by the W.B.C. champion Carlos Palomino at the Albert Hall in June 1977.

In January 1979, after recovering from a spell out of action with a broken hand, the powerful "Fen Tiger" took the European welterweight crown by halting Henry Rhiney in five rounds, but only five months later, when fighting abroad for the first time, he was surprisingly k.o'd in 3 rounds by Jorgen Hansen to lose his European title.

Despite this defeat, however, Dave Green got his long awaited crack at the world title in March 1980, but he was k.o'd in 4 rounds by Sugar Ray Leonard.

After a brief come-back as a light-middleweight Green retired in November 1981.

## GREENFIELD, Harry:

Born Camden Town, London, in 1871, Harry Greenfield claimed the British featherweight championship when he knocked out Fred Johnson in 13 rounds in January, 1897.

This claim was not recognised by the N.S.C. and Greenfield eventually lost to their champion, Ben Jordan, being knocked out in the ninth round, May 29, 1899.

In November, 1899, Greenfield met Jabez White at the N.S.C. for the lightweight title but this time he was stopped in eight rounds.

## GRIFFITH, Emile:

A credit to the fight game who never refused to meet any opposition, this coloured Virgin Islander based in New Jersey won no less than five world titles and is the greatest come-back specialist in boxing history.

He twice regained the world welterweight crown in return bouts with opponents who had previously beaten him (see under list of World Champions) and after moving up into the middleweight division he won that world title by beating Dick Tiger in April 1966; lost it to Benvenuti a year later, but regained it from the Italian in September 1967.

Benvenuti finally deprived Griffith of this title when they met for a third time in March 1968, taking a unanimous decision.

He has since attempted to regain both the middle and welterweight titles and went the distance with Eckhard Dagge, the W.B.C. light-middleweight champion in 1976. He did not finally retire until the following year when he was 39 years of age.

## GRIFFO, Young:

Albert Griffiths, born Sydney, Australia, in 1871, is considered to have been one of the finest defensive boxers of all time.

Even though he never bothered to train, Young Griffo was too good for most of his opponents because he had a natural ability for the game which has probably never been surpassed by any other boxer.

Griffo first claimed the world featherweight title after outpointing Billy Murphy in Sydney in September, 1890. Murphy had already been to America and beaten their leading featherweight, Ike Weir, but the Americans still refused to acknowledge Griffo as world champion. Griffo beat Murphy again in July, 1891, but his claim to the championship faded after he turned down a challenge from the New Zealander for another match.

Young Griffo went to America in 1893 and was unbeaten in about a dozen fights until he met the heavier Jack McAuliffe shortly after that fighter had resigned the world lightweight title. By all accounts this fight should have gone to the Australian, but the referee awarded the decision to the Irish-American.

During 1894 and 1895 Griffo met the American claimant to the world featherweight title, George Dixon, three times, and each fight was declared a draw. These fights were ring epics and probably the finest displays of the true art of self defence ever seen in the ring.

Sad to relate, this genius of the ring took to drink. He ended up in an asylum and died in New York, 1927.

## GULLY, John:

One of the most celebrated figures of the old prize ring, John Gully, who was born at Bristol in 1783, was bought out of a debtor's prison to become a prize fighter after he had been befriended by a fellow Bristolian, Hen Pearce, the "Game Chicken."

He later met Pearce in the ring but was beaten in 64 rounds lasting 1 hour 17 minutes.

When Pearce retired in 1807 Gully became recognised as his successor to the title, although some say that Gully refused the championship.

However, he was certainly the best man in England at the time, for he twice beat his principal challenger, Bob Gregson, once in 36 rounds and the second time in 24 rounds.

After his second victory over Gregson, Gully did not fight again. He became mine host of the Plough Inn, Carey Street, London, and eventually won a fortune as a gambler on horse racing and prize fighting.

Gully served as a Member of Parliament, owned a colliery, and was a successful horse breeder. He won the Derby three times. In 1854 he won the Two Thousand Guineas as well as the Derby.

Respected in the ring as a scientific fighter, Gully was evidently well respected after he gave up fighting. Indeed, he was offered a knighthood but he did not accept this honour.

## GUMBS, Roy:

A tall and muscular West Indian from Tottenham, London, who proved to be a powerful puncher noted for his right uppercuts. His early career was undistinguished but he showed his punching power when winning the vacant British middleweight title by stopping Howard Mills inside three rounds in February 1981. He made a Lonsdale Belt his own before winning the Commonwealth title and was in line for a crack at the European crown when losing his titles in September 1983 before a capacity crowd at Muswell Hill when outpunched and k.o.'d in five rounds by Mark Kaylor.

## GUMMER, Tommy:

Born Rotherham in 1894, Tommy Gummer won the vacant British middleweight title by stopping Jim Sullivan in 14 rounds at the N.S.C., March 29, 1920.

Twelve months later he was beaten in six rounds by Gus Platts at Sheffield. The N.S.C. did not recognise this as a title fight but it forced Gummer to relinquish his claim to the championship.

While he held the British title Gummer met the French middleweight champion, Ercole Balzac, for the European crown, but was beaten in nine rounds.

## GUM SHIELD:

The gum shield, or mouth guard, as used in modern times, is said to have been invented by a London dentist, Mr. Jack Marks, in 1902.

The first boxer who regularly wore a gum shield is believed to have been Ted "Kid" Lewis. The former world welterweight champion started wearing one of these mouth guards in 1912.

Mouth guards are known to have been worn by the ancient Hellenic boxers about 1200 B.C.

# H

## HAGLER, Marvin:

Raised in Newark, New Jersey but later moved to Brockton, Mass., the shaven-skulled middleweight earned the name "Marvellous" because he was one of the most efficient boxing-machines of the post-war era. His sheer efficiency meant that he never did more than required and possibly because of this he lacked charisma.

With his southpaw stance and tremendous punching power he came to Wembley in September 1980 and showed such precision that he cut Britain's world middleweight champion Alan Minter to ribbons before the referee intervened after 1 minute 45 seconds of the third round. Sadly many of the fans behaved diabolically that night showering the ring with missiles.

A dedicated champion, Hagler successfully defended his title 12 times, including two remarkable wins over Thomas Hearns and John Magabi, indeed his 3-round demolition of Hearns in April 1985 has been described as one of the most exciting 3-rounds of fighting ever seen.

In view of his record his defeat by Sugar Ray Leonard in Las Vegas in April 1987 was a shock. Leonard was also recognised as a brilliant boxer but he had had only one fight in the previous five years. This richest fight ever ended in a controversial split decision and brought Hagler's championship reign to a much discussed finish after well over six years.

## HAGUE, William Ian "Iron":

A Yorkshireman born at Mexborough in 1885, "Iron" Hague started boxing about 1904.

He was a really strong man with a terrific punch but unfortunately he never took his boxing seriously.

During a ring career which lasted about nine years, Hague only had around 30 fights, but he won more than half of these by knock-outs.

Hague came to the fore in 1908 by stopping Frank Craig in four rounds at Sheffield, and he went on to win the British heavyweight title by knocking out Gunner Moir in the first round of a contest at the N.SC., April 19, 1909.

Shortly after this he was matched with the renowned Sam Langford at the N.S.C., but Hague was not clever enough for the negro who put him out in the fourth round.

Hague was subsequently beaten by P.O. Curran, Jewey Smith and Sergeant Sunshine, but as these bouts were fought outside the jurisdiction of the N.S.C. his victors were never recognised as champions and Hague continued to claim the title.

When the N.S.C. presented their first Lonsdale Belt for competition in the heavyweight division in 1911, Hague was matched with Bombardier Billy Wells for the title and was knocked out in six rounds, April 24, 1911.

## HALIMI, Alphonse:

Before turning professional in 1955, Halimi had won the French amateur bantamweight title.

On April 1, 1957, in his 19th professional contest, he took the world bantamweight crown from Mario D'Agata with a points victory in Paris.

At that time the N.B.A. recognised Raton Macias as bantamweight champion, but Halimi settled this dispute by defeating him in Los Angeles, November, 1957.

Unfortunately for Halimi, when he met Mexican Jose Becerra at Los Angeles in July, 1959, he chose to fight rather than box, and was outpunched and knocked out by the Mexican in the eighth round.

In October, 1960, Halimi again became recognised as world bantamweight champion on this side of tle Atlantic by outpointing Freddie Gilroy. But he was deprived of this title seven months later when outpointed by Johnny Caldwell.

Halimi later lost to Caldwell in a return bout but in 1962 he held the European Bantam title for a short spell.

## HALL, Henry:

Learnt the finer points of the game as an amateur with the Hillsborough Boys' Club in his home town of Sheffield, and had about 300 bouts before turning professional in 1945.

Hall was unbeaten in his first 13 professional contests before losing to Ginger Stewart on points at Manchester.

On November 8, 1948, he took the British welterweight title from the experienced Ernie Roderick at Harringay. Hall got the referee's verdict at the end of 15 rounds.

This Sheffield fighter lost the crown in his first defence on November 14, 1949, being outpointed by Eddie Thomas.

## HALL, James:

Seaman James "Nobby" Hall, of Peebles, Scotland, had a ring career which extended over 20 years.

A good defensive boxer who liked to counter punch, Hall, who was Imperial Services welterweight champion in 1920, 1921 and 1922, won the British and European lightweight title from Ernie Rice with a 20-round points victory at Liverpool, September 18, 1922.

He successfully defended his titles against Hamilton Johnny Brown in January, 1923, but lost them four months later when he was disqualified in the 13th round of a contest with Harry Mason at Olympia, London.

## HARADA, Masahiko:

This Japanese, nicknamed "Fighting" Harada, was the youngest man ever to win the world flyweight title when, in October, 1961, he stopped Pone Kingpetch in 11 rounds.

Harada was then only aged 19 years 6 months, but like his compatriot, Hiroyuki Ebihara, his reign was short-lived, for it was only three months later that Harada was outpointed in a return bout with Kingpetch.

However, after moving up among the bantamweights he caused an upset in

May 1965 by outpointing previously unbeaten Eder Jofre and so gain his second world title.

Harada successfully defended this title four times, incuding a defeat of Alan Rudkin, but he had weight problems before losing his crown to Lionel Rose in February 1968.

Before retiring in 1970 Harada made two unsuccessful attempts to take the featherweight crown from Johnny Famechon.

## HARDCASTLE, Charlie:

Born Barnsley, 1894, Charlie Hardcastle won the vacant British featherweight title by knocking out Alf Wye in the first round of a contest at the N.S.C., June 4, 1917.

On July 9, 1917, Hardcastle beat the durable Louis Ruddick on a foul in 14 rounds, but only four months later he lost the championship to Tancy Lee, being knocked out in the fourth round at the N.S.C.

## HARDY, Billy:

One of a family of 14 children from Sunderland the redhead who turned professional in 1983 soon became popular as an all-action bantamweight with a straight-right style and won the British title at the age of 22 by smashing Ray Gilbody into defeat inside 3 rounds in February 1987.

## HARRINGAY ARENA, LONDON:

Many "big fights" were staged at this North London arena between 1936 and 1958.

The first was that between Ben Foord and Walter Neusel, November 18, 1936. The South African appeared there again only four months later when he lost his British heavyweight title to Tommy Farr.

After that, two more British heavyweight champions were crowned at this arena, Len Harvey in 1938, and Don Cockell in 1953.

Both these fighters were well known at Harringay, for Harvey also won the British light-heavyweight title there in 1938, and Cockell gained the same title at Harringay in 1950.

The hall at Harringay had a capacity of just under 11,000. The last contests to be staged there took place on October 28, 1958, after which it was sold as a warehouse.

## HARRIS, Harold:

Born Chicago, Harold Harris was boxing professionally at the age of 16. His build was so frail that he became known as the "Human Hairpin."

After Terry McGovern had relinquished the world bantamweight title, Harris claimed the championship on the strength of a points victory over Pedlar Palmer, March 18, 1901, and another over the British champion, Harry Ware, April 15, 1901. Both contests were fought in London.

Harris was not accorded world-wide recognition, however, and eventually he put on weight and was forced to give up his claim to this championship.

## HARRISON, Jack:

This middleweight from Rushden, Northants, claimed to be a descendant of the old prize ring champion, Tom Sayers.

He won the vacant British middleweight title by outpointing Pte. Pat McEnroy at the N.S.C., May 20, 1912, but he relinquished it the following year.

## HARRISON, Tom:

A bantamweight who was born at Hanley, Stoke-on-Trent, August 17, 1892, Tom Harrison failed in his first attempt to win the British title, being outpointed by Joe Fox at the N.S.C., April 17, 1916.

He actually became European champion before he gained the British title, for on October 24, 1921, in his home town, he gave the best display of his career in outpointing the famous Charles Ledoux. However, less than six months later he lost the European title in a return with the Frenchman at Liverpool.

It was not until two months after this, June 26, 1922, that Harrison won the British and Empire bantamweight titles by knocking out Jimmy Higgins in the 13th round at Liverpool.

Harrison lost these titles to Harry Lake, being outpointed over 20 rounds

at the N.S.C., February 26, 1923.

## HART, Marvin:

An American who started fighting as a middleweight in 1899, and during his career, which lasted something like 11 years, he was scarcely ever more than a light-heavyweight, yet he is listed among the heavyweight champions of the world.

Hart only held that title for a little over six months and some chroniclers do not even bother to accord him the honour. That is because he did not win the title from the reigning champion nor did he beat many top-class heavyweights in any form of elimination competition.

What happened was that when James J. Jeffries decided to retire in 1905 mainly because he had run out of worthwhile opposition, he agreed to referee a match between Marvin Hart and Jack Root, and to award his title to the winner.

Now, Hart is often underrated as a fighter. The fact is that he was not heavy enough to be a top-class heavyweight, but he had most certainly held his own among the men around 160 to 175lbs. Indeed, he had also been able to outpoint Jack Johnson over 20 rounds early in 1905. The negro was then still maturing, but it was a good performance, for no other man ever went that distance with Johnson and gained a points decision over him.

The title match between Hart and Root was fought at Reno, Nevada, July 3, 1905, and Hart won on a knock-out in the 12th round.

The first time Hart defended the championship he was beaten. His victor was another comparatively light heavyweight, Tommy Burns. The date was February 23, 1906, and Burns got a points decision at the end of 20 rounds.

## HARVEY, Len:

Born at Stoke Climsland, near Callington, Cornwall, July 11, 1907, Len Harvey fought his first professional fight at the age of 12½. When he retired in 1942 he had fought 418 contests and earned the admiration and respect of everyone connected with the game.

Len Harvey was, without doubt, one

of the brainiest boxers ever to hold a British title. He had no punch to speak of, but he relied on sheer boxing skill and tactics, and was guided by an ice-cool brain in defeating the vast majority of his opponents.

When Harvey was at the peak of his career, from about 1928 to 1939, only two British fighters were able to get the better of him. They were Jock McAvoy and Jack Petersen, but Harvey also won decisions over both these fighters.

During his very full career in the ring Len Harvey won three British and Empire titles, heavyweight, light-heavyweight and middleweight, and also claimed the world light-heavyweight championship.

Before winning these titles Harvey went very close to taking the British welterweight crown. That was in April, 1926, when he fought a 20-round draw with champion Harry Mason.

Harvey won the British middleweight title by stopping Alex Ireland in seven rounds, May 16, 1929. He lost it to Jock McAvoy in April, 1933, but two months later he won the vacant light-heavywight championship by outpointing Eddie Phillips.

Harvey met Marcel Thil for the world middleweight title at the White City in July, 1932, but was beaten over 15 rounds.

In November, 1933, Harvey gave one of the best displays of his career and caused quite a shock by relieving Jack Petersen of the British heavyweight title at the Albert Hall.

This Cornishman displayed his ring-craft to the full that evening and got the referee's verdict at the end of 15 rounds.

In February, 1934, Harvey added the Empire heavyweight title to his collection by outboxing another ring-wise fighter, Larry Gains, at the Albert Hall.

Len Harvey lost his heavyweight titles in a return with Jack Petersen, being forced to retire in the 12th round, and was outpointed in a third meeting with the Welshman.

In 1938 he regained the British light-heavyweight title which he had relinquished in 1934, outpointing Jock McAvoy, and he also became heavyweight champion once again when, in a match for the vacant crown, his opponent, Eddie Phillips, was disqualified in the fourth round.

When the world light-heavyweight championship became vacant just before World War II, the B.B.B.C. agreed to nominate the winner of a match between Harvey and Jock McAvoy as successor to John Henry Lewis. Harvey had been outpointed by the coloured American in November, 1936, but he made no mistake against McAvoy and got the referee's nod at the end of 15 rounds. The date, July 10, 1939.

Harvey did not fight again until June 20, 1942, when he met Freddie Mills and was knocked out for the first time in his career, losing his light-heavyweight titles.

That was the Cornishman's last contest. Five months later he announced his retirement and relinquished his British and Empire heavyweight titles.

## HAWKINS, Dal:

Dal Hawkins is generally considered to have been the first world featherweight champion. He met Fred Bogan at San Francisco in June, 1889. After 75 rounds they had to stop the fight because of bad light. It was restarted the next morning and Hawkins knocked Bogan out in the 16th round.

Hawkins was probably only 18 years of age when he beat Bogan to claim the championship and was still putting on weight. Very soon he had to abandon the featherweight division and compete with the lightweights.

He remained in the top class for a number of years and in March, 1899, he met the world lightweight champion, Frank Erne, but was stopped in seven rounds.

The following year Hawkins was twice beaten by another leading lightweight, the redoubtable Joe Gans.

Probably the finest display in this American's career was in boxing a 20-round draw with the remarkable George Dixon at San Francisco in July, 1897.

## HAWKINS, Vince:

This broad-shouldered middleweight was born at Salisbury but lived at Eastleigh, Hants. He learnt boxing with the Basingstoke B.C.

After turning professional Hawkins enjoyed a run of 74 fights without defeat before being outpointed by Ernie Roderick in a match for the vacant British middleweight title, May, 1945.

Hawkins got a return fight with Roderick in October, 1946, and this time he got the verdict and the championship.

In January, 1948, Hawkins met Bos Murphy, of New Zealand, for the vacant Empire middleweight title but lost on points.

Six months later this Eastleigh middleweight lost his British crown to Dick Turpin, who got the referee's verdict at the end of 15 rounds at Birmingham.

## HEARNS, Thomas:

A legend in his own time this big-hitter from Detroit is the first fighter to claim world titles in four different divisions. After a run of 28 fights without defeat (all but two inside the distance) he won the W.B.A. version of the world welterweight title by stopping Pipino Cuevas in two rounds in 1980. He added the W.B.C. version of the super welterweight crown in December 1982 by outpointing the indomitable Wilfred Benitez, and in June 1984 k.o.'d another all-action fighter, Roberto Duran in two rounds to capture the vacant W.B.C. junior middleweight championship. His only defeat up to that point was by Sugar Ray Leonard for his welterweight title in 1981. In April 1985 he became rather too ambitious and failed to capture his fourth world title when beaten in three rounds by Marvin Hagler but he took the W.B.C. version of the vacant middleweight title in October 1987, by knocking out Argentina's Juan Domingo Roldan inside four rounds.

## HEENAN, John Carmel:

When John C. Heenan went prospecting for gold in California he found none of that yellow stuff but he did build himself a big reputation as a fighter among the toughest men in the area.

Heenan, who was known as "The Benecia Boy," claimed the American championship following the retirement of John Morrissey in 1859, and, the following year, he came to England to meet our champion, Tom Sayers, in what is considered to have been the first international heavyweight championship contest ever fought.

It took place at Farnborough, Hants, April 17, 1860, and opinions differ as to which man was having the better of things before the ring was broken and the fight declared a draw after 42 rounds lasting 2 hours 20 minutes.

Heenan returned to England once more in 1863 to meet another of our champions, Tom King. This time he was clearly beaten in 24 rounds. The "Benecia Boy" did not fight again after that.

## HEIGHT:
### Shortest:

The shortest fighters ever to win world titles were Pascual Perez, the Argentine flyweight—4 foot 11 inches, and Johnny Coulon, the Canadian bantamweight— 4 foot 11¼ inches.

The shortest fighter ever to win the world heavyweight title under Queensberry Rules was Tommy Burns, of Canada—5 foot 7 inches.

### Tallest:

The tallest professional fighters ever were probably Gogea Mitu of Rumania, who had a number of contests during the 1930s, and Jim Culley, the Tipperary Giant, who appeared both as a boxer and a wrestler during the 1940s. Both were 7ft. 4ins.

Charles Freeman of Michigan, who claimed to be Champion of America in 1820, stood 7ft. 3ins. tall.

Another of the tallest was Henry Johnson, a Canadian negro known as "The Human Skyscraper." He fought around the turn of the century and stood 7ft. 2ins., weighing 19 stone (266lbs.).

Johnson's height is equalled by the South African, Ewart Potgieter, who had three fights in London in 1955. Potgieter weighed around 23 stone (322lbs.).

The tallest man ever to win a world title was Primo Carnera, heavyweight champion 1933-34. He stood 6ft. 5½ins. Some records claim that Jess Willard was taller but it is doubtful whether this fighter was more than 6ft. 5¼ins.

Ernest Terrell, who won the W.B.A.

version of the world heavyweight title in 1965, stood 6ft. 6ins.

Panama Al Brown, who held the world bantamweight crown from 1929 to 1935, was 5ft. 11ins., one of the tallest of the lighter weight fighters.

Britain's tallest champion was Richard Dunn, heavyweight title-holder 1975-76. 6ft. 4ins.

One of the tallest men ever to compete in British amateur boxing was Roger Hunter, 6ft. 7ins., and over 18 stone (252lbs.). He was Metropolitan Police champion 1937, R.A.F. (Officers), and Imperial Services (Officers) champion, 1938.

## HERMAN, Pete:

An Italian-American, Pete Herman won the world bantamweight championship from Kid Williams in New Orleans January 9, 1917.

He lost the title to Joe Lynch in December, 1920, but regained it in a return fight with Lynch seven months later.

Herman finally lost the bantamweight championship when he was outpointed by Johnny Buff in September, 1921.

Herman came to London in January, 1921, and, weighing over the bantamweight limit, he stopped Jimmy Wilde, who was then past his best, in 17 rounds.

He returned to London in July, 1921, and knocked out Jimmy Higgins, the British bantamweight champion.

Failing eyesight forced Pete Herman to retire from the ring in 1922. He eventually went blind, but an operation partially restored his sight.

## HIBBERT, Lloyd:

Accidents and lack of activity did not prevent this Birmingham fighter from winning the vacant British light middleweight title with a close points victory over Nick Wilshire at the Albert Hall in March 1987. This win also made Hibbert Commonwealth champion. Immediately prior to this, the stylish Hibbert had fought only three contests in a period of 3 years 11 months and he was nearly 28 years of age.

## HIGGINS, Jim:

This miner from Hamilton, Scotland,

had a meteoric rise to the top immediately after World War I.

He started boxing in 1919, and in February of the following year he won the vacant British bantamweight title with a victory over Harold Jones at the N.S.C. The referee intervened in the 13th round.

Two months later Higgins added the Empire title to his record by outpointing the Australian, Vince Blackburn.

Higgins tried for the European championship in May, 1920, but he was knocked out by Charles Ledoux in 11 rounds at Holland Park, London.

In July, 1921, this Scotsman was beaten by Pete Herman the American bantamweight, only two weeks before that fighter was to regain the world title.

Higgins lost his British and Empire titles in June, 1922, when he was knocked out in 13 rounds at Liverpool by Tommy Harrison.

## HILL, Charlie:

A Scotsman from Cambuslang, Charlie Hill won his home country's featherweight title in December, 1954, and took the British title from "Spider" Bill Kelly in February 1956.

He made the Lonsdale Belt his own property by defeating Jimmy Brown and Chic Brogan, but in April, 1959, he was relieved of his British championship by fellow Scot, Bobby Neill.

Hill was down 10 times in that contest at Nottingham before the referee stopped it in the ninth round.

Hill had previously failed to add the Empire title to his record when he was stopped in 10 rounds by Percy Lewis.

## HILL, Johnny:

Born at Edinburgh, Johnny Hill won the A.B.A. flyweight championship before turning professional in 1926.

On May 23, 1927, he became the British flyweight champion by stopping Alf Barber in the 14th round of a contest at the N.S.C.

Hill annexed the European title in March, 1928, with a win over Emile Pladner, and he also beat a leading American flyweight, Newsboy Brown.

In October, 1929, this Scot was due for his big chance. He was matched with

America's Frankie Genaro for the world title. The contest was booked for the Albert Hall, but shortly before it was due to take place Hill collapsed in training and in a few days he was dead.

So the career of a brilliant flyweight was cut short. He had only been beaten once (by Emile Pladner) in 23 professional contests.

## HOLBORN STADIUM, LONDON:

Built by promoter Jack Callaghan, this was a well-known venue for boxing during the years between the two world wars.

The first contest staged there was for the world flyweight championship, Jimmy Wilde beating the Zulu Kid in 11 rounds, December 18, 1916.

Jack Petersen sprang into the limelight when he made his first appearances at the Holborn Stadium in 1931. It was there during the following year that the Welshman took the British light-heavyweight title from Harry Crossley.

Probably the biggest boxing attraction ever staged at this London stadium was the first meeting between the reigning British heavyweight champion, Joe Beckett, and the European heavyweight and light-heavyweight title-holder, Georges Carpentier. This took place December 4, 1919, and the hall, which had a capacity of 5,000, could have been filled four times over. The fight went to the Holborn because at the time Olympia was being renovated.

## HOLLAND:
## Champions:

World:—
None.

European:—
Light-heavyweight: Herman Van T'Hof, 1926; Rudi Koopmans, 1979-84; Alex Blanchard 1984-87.

Middleweight: Bep Van Klaveren, 1938.

Welterweight: Fighting Mack, 1968-69.

Lightweight: Bep Van Klaveren, 1931-32.

Olympic:—
Featherweight: L. Van Klaveren, 1928.

## HOLMES, Larry:

One of a Georgia family of 11 children this giant 6ft. 3in. negro succeeded Muhammad Ali as the most widely recognised World heavyweight champion, although officially he was only W.B.C. title-holder.

Not colourful, but a fighter who always showed great stamina and powers of recovery, he became noted for his left jab. He won the W.B.C. title by outpointing Ken Norton in June 1981, and after beating Alfredo Evangelista, Osvaldo Ocasio, Mike Weaver, Ernie Shavers, Lorenzo, Zanon, Leroy Jones and Scott LeDoux, all inside the distance, he earned world-wide acclaim as champion by stopping former title-holder Muhammed Ali in 11 rounds at Las Vegas in October 1980.

Holmes was one of the busiest of heavyweight champions, defending his title 20 times before, at the age of 35, he was outpointed by Michael Spinks in September 1985. This defeat prevented Holmes from equalling Rocky Marciano's record of 49 straight wins. Holmes should have called it a day but his pride made him take on Spinks again seven months later. This time he lost only on a split decision but it was evident that Father Time had intervened.

## HONEYGHAN, Lloyd:

A flashy type of fighter whose superb confidence and great skill has taken him to the top since winning the vacant British welterweight title with a points victory over Cliff Gilpin in April 1983.

Showed real power in knocking out European welterweight champion Gianfranco Rosi in three rounds on the Italian's home ground in 1985, and shook the boxing world in September 1986 by battering the undisputed world welterweight champion Don Curry into defeat in six rounds. This was Curry's first professional defeat in a run of 26 fights and one of the finest-ever wins by a British fighter in America.

Honeyghan, born in Jamaica and brought up in Bermondsey, relinquished the W.B.A. version of his title because he did not wish to meet any South African fighters but he stopped former junior welterweight champions Johnny Bumphus in two rounds and Gene Hatcher in only a few seconds of all-out aggression. However, he was not in his best form when losing his W.B.C. title to Jorge Vaca at Wembley in October 1987.

## HONEYMAN, Mike:

Born Woolwich, London, in 1896, Mike Honeyman was an attractive boxer but not a hard hitter.

He won the vacant British featherweight title by outpointing Bill Marchant, of Manchester, over 20 rounds at the N.S.C. in January, 1920.

Honeyman successfully defended his title against the former champion, Tancy Lee, stopping the Scot in 19 rounds, but when he met Joe Fox in October, 1921, he was beaten over 20 rounds.

After a couple of years Honeyman made a come-back as a lightweight but was eventually stopped by Alf Simmons.

## HOOD, Jack:

Jack Hood started boxing professionally in 1921. Born at Birmingham, he was one of the brainiest boxers ever to win the British welterweight crown.

Hood took this title from Harry Mason in 1926, and went on to make the Lonsdale Belt his own property with another victory over Mason and a win over Alf Mancini.

Before the end of 1926 Jack Hood had two fights in America, drawing one and going 12 rounds with Jack McVey in a "no decision" bout.

Hood challenged Len Harvey three times for the Cornishman's British middleweight crown. He lost the first at Holborn, drew the second at Olympia, and lost the third at the Albert Hall.

In July, 1931, Hood fought a 10-round draw with the leading American middleweight contender, Vince Dundee, the man who had twice outpointed Len Harvey in New York earlier that same year.

Hood won the European welterweight title from the Belgian, Adrien Anneet, at Birmingham in May, 1933.

This class boxer relinquished his titles when he announced his retirement in 1934. Actually, he did have two more fights after this but he did not appear in the ring again after February, 1935.

## HOPE, Maurice:

A graduate of the Repton A.B.C. this hard-hitting Antiguan born fighter who was brought up in Hackney, London, showed tremendous power and precision when he battered British light-middleweight champion, Larry Paul, into defeat with an eighth round k.o. in November 1974.

A fine counter-puncher with a southpaw stance, this quiet-spoken coloured man made a Lonsdale Belt his own property before winning the European title in October 1976, stopping Vito Antuofermo in 15 rounds. In March 1977 he should have been proclaimed W.B.C. light-middleweight champion after 15 gruelling rounds with the German champion, Eckhard Dagge, but the best he could get out of this fight in Berlin was a draw.

After relinquishing the European title this elegant and gifted southpaw won the W.B.C. version of the world title at his second attempt, stopping Rocky Mattioli inside 8 rounds in March 1979, but he lost this crown when k.o'd in 12 rounds by the brilliant Wilfred Benitez in May 1981.

Maurice Hope was also Commonwealth light-middleweight champion from April 1976 until relinquishing the title after winning the world championship. He retired after failing to regain the European title from Luigi Minchillo in March 1982 and Britain lost one of her finest active sporting gentlemen.

## HUNGARY:

Hungary's best-known fighter is Laszlo Papp, although Billy Soose, who made a name for himself in America as a middleweight, had Hungarian blood in his veins. Soose, however, was born in America of Hungarian parents.

A native born Hungarian, Papp, whose various titles can be seen below, never had a chance to contest the world championship. He was not permitted to turn professional until the age of 31, and because of the Communist régime's attitude to professionalism he was "persuaded" to quit in 1965 when he became Hungary's national coach. He was undefeated in a professional career of 29 bouts.

This is where the foundations of modern British boxing were laid. A scene at the old National Sporting Club in Covent Garden. In the ring Sam Longford and Iron Hague. The date—May 24th, 1909

Jimmy Wilde

Phil Scott

Dick Turpin ducks under right swing of world middle-weight champion Marcel Cerdan at Earls Court, London, March 28th, 1949, but is k.o'd in the seventh round. The talented Cerdan was killed in an air crash seven months later

Randolph Turpin (*right*) seen winning the world middleweight title from Sugar Ray Robinson at Earls Court, London, July 10th, 1951

## Champions:

## HURST, Sam:
This 6ft. 3in. prize fighter, who weighed around 17 stone (238lbs.) was known as "The Stalybridge Infant."

He held the British championship for a short time following the retirement of Tom Sayers, winning it by stopping Tom Paddock in less than 10 minutes, November 5, 1860, but losing it only seven months later when he was beaten in 40 minutes by the famous Jem Mace.

## HYER, Tom:
This New York butcher, son of Jacob Hyer, the first American prize fighter of note, became the first white American to hold the championship of his country.

Yankee Sullivan, an Irishman, was champion of America in 1848 when he was challenged by Tom Hyer. Some time elapsed before these two could be got together in the same ring, although they clashed in a drunken tavern brawl. Eventually, Sullivan agreed to the match, and it took place at Rock Point, Maryland, February 7, 1849, Hyer winning in 16 rounds.

An attempt was then made to match Hyer with the British champion, William Perry, but the contest never materialised and Hyer retired without fighting again.

## IMPERIAL SERVICES BOXING ASSOCIATION:

This Association was formed in 1919 to organise and control boxing in the Royal Navy, Army and R.A.F.

All Auxiliary and volunteer forces, including the Territorial Army and the pre-Service training units, are affiliated direct to the A.B.A., and do not come under the control of I.S.B.A., which is concerned with the regular forces only.

Each of the three fighting Services take it in turn to nominate the president, chairman, honorary secretary and honorary treasurer of the Association for one year.

The A.B.A. provide one of their members to sit on the I.S.B.A. committee without the power to vote. On the other hand, the I.S.B.A. is affiliated to the A.B.A., and three members of each of the three Services sit on the national committee of the A.B.A., each with the power to vote.

Professionals are not permitted to box in the Services except against other professionals, and then only in contests limited to six rounds. Professionals can, of course, box outside the Service when given "leave of absence."

The three regular Services each hold individual championships and there is also an inter-Service team championship. The individual winners of these champions qualify for the semi-final stage of the A.B.A. championships.

Boxing championships in the Army and the Royal Navy commenced in 1892. After the First World War these two Services each organised their own championships and the R.A.F. also commenced their competition in 1919.

Three of the most outstanding Service boxing records are those of Sub. Lt. E. H. G. Gregson, R.N., Capt. D. A. C. Shephard, R.M., and Cpl. J. Jones, Royal Welch Fusiliers.

Sub. Lt. Gregson won the Royal Navy and Marine (Officers) heavyweight championship 1925-26-27-28-29-30-31; Imperial Services (Officers) 1930-31.

Capt. Shephard was Royal Navy and Marines (Officers) middleweight champion 1921-22-23-24-25-26-29-31-34; Imperial Services (Officers) 1923-24-25-29-34.

Cpl. Jones was Army featherweight champion 1930-31-32-33; Imperial Services featherweight champion 1930-31-32.

## INTERNATIONAL BOXING:

The first international title fight was that between Tom Molineux (American negro) and Tom Cribb (England) at Copthall Common, near East Grinstead, Sussex, December 18, 1810. Cribb was declared the winner when Molineux was unable to continue after 33 rounds lasting 55 minutes.

Cribb again beat Molineux at Thistleton Gap, Leicestershire, in 11 rounds, September 28, 1811.

The first international fight is believed to have been that between Bob Whitaker (England) and an Italian gondolier whose name has been given as Tito Alberto di Carini. This took place at Figg's Amphitheatre, London, in 1733. The Englishman won.

## INTERNATIONAL BOXING FEDERATION:

This organisation was formed in 1983 and has its headquarters Newark, New Jersey. Without understanding the politics of boxing in America it is difficult to justify the formation of a third world-wide organisation such as the I.B.F. which has unwittingly cheapened world championships merely by introducing more title-holders. However, this organisation has gained recognition in many quarters, particularly in Australia and the Far East, although their champions are not listed in this volume. The I.B.F. introduced the super-middleweight division at 168 lbs in 1984, but their first champions were Joo-do Chun and Dodie Penalosa, bantamweight and junior-fly-weight respectively after a promotion in Japan. Their first widely known champion, Marvin Camel, won their version of the cruiserweight title only three days later in December 1983. They have since tried to introduce still more junior weight classes.

## IRELAND:

Every Irishman loves a fight. That is certainly borne out by their record in international boxing, for if one includes all those fighters who were born in America of Irish immigrants then they have produced more world champions than any other country with the exception of the United States.

The fighters who were actually born in Ireland and won world titles number seven, but another 33 world champions who were born in America had Irish blood from either one or both parents.

### Champions:

World:—

Light-heavyweight: George Gardner, 1903; Mike McTigue, 1923-25.

Middleweight: Jack Dempsey (Non-pareil), 1884-91.

Welterweight: Jimmy McLarnin, 1933-34, 1934-35.

Lightweight: Jack McAuliffe, 1886-96.

Featherweight: Barry McGuigan (W.B.A.) 1985-86.

Bantamweight: Johnny Caldwell, 1961-62 (European recognition only).

Flyweight: Rinty Monaghan, 1948-50.

In addition to those mentioned above the following world champions who were born outside of the Emerald Isle had Irish blood in their veins:—

Heavyweight: John L. Sullivan, James J. Corbett, Jack Dempsey, Gene Tunney, James J. Braddock.

Light-heavyweight: Philadelphia Jack O'Brien, Jack Dillon, Tommy Loughran, Billy Conn, Jim Slattery.

Middleweight: Mike O'Dowd, Mickey Walker, Harry Greb; Paul Pender.

Welterweight: Mysterious Billy Smith, Matty Matthews, Mike Twin Sullivan, Jack Britton, Mickey Walker, Freddie Cochrane, Honey Mellody.

Lightweight: Jimmy Goodrich, Lew Jenkins.

Featherweight: Billy Murphy, Terry McGovern, Johnny Kilbane, Joey Archibald, Dave Sullivan.

Bantamweight: Jimmy Barry, Harry Forbes, Frankie Neil, Terry McGovern, Jimmy Walsh, Johnny Coulon, Joe Lynch.

European:—

Lightweight: Charlie Nash, 1979-80, 1980-81.

Featherweight: Barry McGuigan, 1983-85.

Bantamweight: John Kelly, 1953-54; Freddie Gilroy, 1959-60.

Flyweight: Rinty Monaghan, 1949-50.

Empire and Commonwealth:—

Heavyweight: Petty Officer Curran, 1911-12; Danny McAlinden, 1972-75.

Welterweight: Tom McCormick, 1914.

Featherweight: Jimmy Kelly, 1938-39; Billy Kelly, 1954-55.

Bantamweight: Freddie Gilroy, 1959-60; Johnny Caldwell, 1964-65.

Flyweight: Rinty Monaghan, 1948-50.

## IRELAND, Alex:

Born Edinburgh, Alex Ireland was A.B.A. welterweight champion the year before he turned professional in 1922.

In March, 1923, he won the Scottish welterweight title by outpointing Bob Lowrie, but he lost this championship only two months later to Johnny Brown.

Ireland subsequently moved up into the middleweight division and it was at this weight that he really made a name for himself.

On March 14, 1928, he beat another famous Edinburgh fighter, Tommy Milligan, on a disqualification in the ninth round. Milligan was then holding the European, British and Empire middleweight titles, but although Ireland claimed these titles he was never granted official recognition.

However, Ireland proved himself the best middleweight in Britain or the Empire at that time by defeating another man with a victory over Milligan, the rugged Welsh fighter, Frank Moody.

In May, 1929, the B.B.B.C. agreed to a match between Ireland and Len Harvey for the official British title and Lonsdale Belt, and this took place at Olympia,

Ireland being knocked out in the seventh round.

In his last fight, April 14, 1930, Alex Ireland was outpointed by Steve McCall for the Scottish middleweight championship.

## ITALY:

Probably the best known Italian fighter was Primo Carnera, the "Ambling Alp," but it is among the medium-weight fighters, the lightweights and featherweights, that the Italians have excelled.

One of the finest lightweight fighters ever seen on the Continent was an Italian, his name Roberto Proietti, and he created a record by winning the European title on four separate occasions from 1942 to 1949.

Unfortunately, Proietti did not do so well on the few occasions he left the Continent, for he lost two fights in London, one to Tommy Barnham, and another to Billy Thompson, and he was beaten by Johnny Williams in his only visit to America.

## Champions:

World:—

Heavyweight: Primo Carnera, 1933-34.

Middleweight: Vince Dundee (N.Y.S.A.C. only) 1933-34; Nino Benvenuti, 1967, 1968-70.

Junior or Light-middleweight: Nino Benvenuti, 1965-67; Sandro Mazzinghi, 1968-69; Carmelo Bossi, 1970-71; Miguel Angel Castellini, 1976-77; Gianfranco Rosi (W.B.A.) 1987-

Welterweight: Young Corbett III, 1933-34; Joe Dundee, 1927-29.

Junior-welterweight: Duilio Loi, 1962-63; Sandro Lopopolo, 1966-67; Rosario Oliva, (W.B.A.) 1986-

Featherweight: Johnny Dundee, 1923-24.

Junior-featherweight: Loris Stecca, (W.B.A.) 1984; Salvatore Bottigilieri, 1987-

Bantamweight: Frank Conley (American recognition only) 1910-11; Bushy Graham (N.Y.S.A.C. only) 1928-29; Mario D'Agata (except N.B.A.), 1956-57.

Flyweight: Salvatore Burruni, 1965.

Light-flyweight: Franco Udella, 1975.

In addition to those mentioned above who were born in Italy, the following world champions were born in America of Italian parents (one or both):—

Heavyweight: Rocky Marciano.

Light-heavyweight: George Nichols, Melio Bettina, Joey Maxim.

Middleweight: Johnny Wilson, Vince Dundee, Fred Apostoli, Rocky Graziano, Sammy Mandell, Jake La Motta, Joe Dundee, Carmen Basilio.

Welterweight: Marty Servo, Carmen Basilio, Tony De Marco.

Lightweight: Rocky Kansas, Sammy Mandell, Tony Canzoneri, Lou Ambers, Sammy Angott, Paddy De Marco.

Featherweight: Battling Battalino. Harry Jeffra, Petey Scalzo, Phil Terranova, Sol Bartolo, Willie Pep, Tony Canzoneri, Tommy Paul, Mike Belloise.

Bantamweight: Pete Herman, Eddie Martin, Lou Salica, Harold Dade, Tony Marino.

Flyweight: Frankie Genaro, Fidel La Barba, Midget Wolgast.

Note: Not all these American-born fighters were undisputed world champions.

European:—

Heavyweight: Ermino Spalla, 1923-26; Primo Carnera, 1933-34; Francho Cavicchi, 1955-56; Lorenzo Zanon, 1979-80. Francisco Damiani, 1987-

Light-heavyweight: Michel Bonaglia, 1929; Merlo Preciso, 1935; Luigi Musina, 1942; Artenio Calzavara, 1957; Giulio Rinaldi, 1962-64; Giulio Rinaldi, 1965-6; Piero Del Papa, 1966-67, 1970-71; Demenico Adinolfi, 1974-76; Aldo Travesaro, 1977-79.

Middleweight: Bruno Frattini, 1924-25; Mario Bosisio, 1928, 1930-31; Leone Jacovacci, 1928; Tiberio Mitri, 1949-50, 1954; Nino Benvenuti, 1965-67; Carlos Duran, 1966-67, 1970-71; Elio Calcabrini, 1973-74; Matteo Salvemini, 1980.

Junior or Light-middleweight: Bruno Visintin, 1964-66, Allessandro Mazzinghi, 1966-68; Remo Golfarini, 1968-69; Carlos Duran, 1972-73, 1974; Vito Antuofermo, 1976; Luigi Minchillo, 1981-83; Gianfranco Rosi, 1987.

Welterweight: Mario Bosisio, 1925-26; Salverio Turiello 1938-39; Livio Minelli, 1949-50; Michele Palermo, 1950-

51; Emilio Marconi, 1956-59; Duilio Loi, 1959-64; Fortunato Manca, 1964-65; Carmelo Bossi, 1967-68; Silvano Bertini, 1969; Marco Scano, 1976-77; Gianfranco Rosi; 1984-85.

Junior or Light-welterweight: Bruno Arcari, 1968-70; Primo Bandini, 1977; Giuseppe Martinese, 1980; Patrizio Oliva, 1983-85.

Lightweight: Anacleto Locatelli, 1932, 1933; Carlo Orlandi, 1934-35; Enrico Venturi, 1935-36; Vittorio Tamagnini, 1936-37; Aldo Spoldi, 1938-39; Bruno Bisterzo, 1941 (twice), 1943-46; Ascensio Botta, 1941, 1942; Roberto Proietti, 1942-43, 1946, 1947-48, 1949-50; Duilio Loi, 1954-59; Mario Vecchiatto, 1959-60; Franco Brondi, 1965; Antonio Puddu, 1971-74; Joey Gibilisco, 1981-83; Lucio Cusma, 1983-84.

Junior-lightweight: Tommaso Galli, 1971; Domenico Chiloiro, 1972; Natale Vezzoli, 1976-79; Alfredo Raininger, 1983-84; Salvatore Curcetti, 1987-.

Featherweight: Luigi Quadrini, 1928-29; Gino Bondavalli, 1941-44; Fedrico Cortonesi, 1944-45; Pasquino Bonetti, 1945-46; Sergio Caprari, 1958-59; Alberto Serti, 1962-63; Tommaso Galli, 1965-66; Salvator Burruni, 1968-69; Tommaso Galli, 1969-70; Elia Cotena, 1975-76; Salvatore Melluzzo, 1981-82; Loris Stecca, 1983; Valerio Nati, 1987.

Bantamweight: Dominique Bernasconi, 1927-28, 1929, 1932-33; Gino Cattaneo, 1939-41; Gino Bondavalli, 1941-42; Guido Ferracin, 1948-49; Mario D'Agata, 1955-58; Piero Rollo, 1958-59; Franco Zurlo, 1969-71; Salvatore Fabrizio, 1976-77; Franco Zurlo, 1977-78; Valerio Nati, 1980-82; Giuseppe Fossati, 1982-83; Walter Giorgetti, 1983-84; Ciro de Leva, 1984-86.

Super-flyweight: Jiro Watanabe, 1984-86.

Flyweight: Enrico Urbinatti, 1938-39; Nazzareno Giannelli, 1954-55; Salvatore Burruni, 1961-65; Fernando Atzori, 1967-72, 1973; Franco Udella, 1974-79; Franco Cherchi, 1985.

Olympic:—
Heavyweight: F. DePiccoli, 1960.
Light-heavyweight: C. Pinto, 1964.
Middleweight: Pietro Toscani, 1928.
Welterweight: G. Benvenuti, 1960.
Lightweight: Carlo Orlandi, 1928; Aureliano Bolognesi, 1952.
Featherweight: Ernesto Formenti, 1948; F. Masso, 1960.
Bantamweight: Vittorio Tamagnini, 1928; Underico Sergo, 1936; M. Stecca, 1984.
Flyweight: F. Atzori, 1964.

## IZZARD, Ernie:

In 1924 Harry Mason was deprived of his British lightweight title by the Boxing Board while he was away in America, and Ernie Izzard, of Herne Hill, and Jack Kirk were selected to fight for the vacant championship.

Izzard was a clever boxer and he outpointed Kirk over 20 rounds on November 24, 1924, but Mason, back from America, challenged Izzard and they met at the Holland Park Rink, London, June 22, 1925.

There was nearly a riot that evening when the referee stopped the contest at the beginning of the ninth round, awarding the decision to Mason, because Izzard's seconds would not leave the ring and Izzard had not come out of his corner.

Izzard starting fighting as a flyweight at the age of 15 soon after World War I when he was known as the Herne Hill Hairpin and became a frequent performer in the London rings until his retirement.

# J

## JACKSON, John:

Although "Gentleman" John Jackson had only three important fights he is one of the most celebrated figures in the history of the British prize ring.

He was, without doubt, a most capable fighter and a man of great strength, but he made his mark in the fistic world because he was unusually intelligent for a bare-knuckle prize fighter and he was a particularly good instructor who numbered many peers of the realm among his pupils.

Jackson opened a boxing school in Bond Street, London, and it was here that he made so many influential friends and revived the interest of the "Fancy" in the Noble Art of Self Defence.

One of his most celebrated pupils was Lord Byron.

Such was the respect in which Jackson was held by the nobility that when George IV was crowned in 1820 the former champion was chosen to head a bodyguard of famous prize fighters.

In his three main contests Jackson beat William Fewterell in 67 minutes; lost to George Inglestone when he had to give up with a broken leg, and then beat Daniel Mendoza in 10½ minutes.

It was this last contest, fought at Hornchurch, Essex, April 15, 1795, which gave him the right to call himself Champion of England, a title he retained for about four years.

"Gentleman" Jackson was one of the founder members of the old Pugilistic Club, which was formed in 1814.

When he died in 1845 an imposing monument was erected to his memory in Brompton cemetery.

## JAMES, Ronnie:

This Swansea lightweight started fighting professionally when he was only 16. That was back in 1933. The war was to delay his chance of a British title fight until 1944, but in that year, at Cardiff on August 12, he became champion by knocking out Eric Boon in the 10th round.

James never defended his title and when there was some doubt about his ability to make the weight after a lapse of nearly three years, the B.B.B.C. stipulated that he should make 9 stone 12 lbs. (only 3 lbs. over the lightweight limit) for a contest with Cliff Curvis in June, 1947. James failed to do this and was deprived of the title.

In September, 1946, James met the N.B.A. world champion, Ike Williams, at Cardiff, but he was outclassed and knocked out in the ninth round.

## JAPAN:

The first world champion from Japan was Yoshio Shirai in 1952, but the post-war boxing boom in this country has since produced many more world title holders among the smaller men, including two who won titles at more than one weight.

### Champions:

WORLD:

Junior or Light-middleweight: Koichi Wajima, 1971-74, 1975, 1976; Masashi Kudo (W.B.A.), 1978-79; Tadashi Mirhara, (W.B.A.) 1981-82.

Light-welterweight: Tsuyoshi Hamada, (W.B.C.), 1986-

Junior-lightweight: Yoshiaki Numata, 1967; Hirashi Koboyashi, 1967-71; Kuniaki Shibata, 1973; Yasatsune Uehara, 1980-81.

Featherweight: Kuniaki Shibata, 1970-72.

Bantamweight: Masahiko Harada, 1965; Takuya Muguruma, 1987.

Flyweight: Yoshio Shirai, 1952-54; Masahiko Harada, 1962-63; Hiroyuki Ebihara, 1963-64; Shoji Oguma (W.B.C.), 1974-75, 1980-81; Koji Kobayashi, (W.B.C.) 1984.

Light-flyweight: Yoko Gushiken (W.B.A.), 1976; Shigeo Nakajima, 1980;

Tadashi Tomori, 1982.
OLYMPIC:—
Bantamweight: T. Sakurai, 1964.

## JAY, Tee:

Born Ghana and settled in Clapham. London, Tee Jay is a well-built cruiserweight who boxed in his country's Olympic team before having his first professional fight in England in 1985.

An aggressive fighter, real name Taju Akay, he dropped a close points decision to Andy Straughn when making his first bid for the vacant British cruiserweight in October 1986. That was only his sixth professional fight and only one fight later, in May 1987, he won one of the fastest British title contests on record, taking the title from Roy Smith in only 90 seconds.

## JEBY, Ben:

After Mickey Walker relinquished the world middleweight crown in 1931 Ben Jeby of New York was nominated as successor to the championship by the N.Y.A.C. following his points victory over Chuck Devlin in November, 1932.

At this time Gorilla Jones was recognised as middleweight champion by the N.B.A. and Marcel Thil by the I.B.U. Jeby met Jones in April, 1933, but it was declared "no contest" after six rounds.

In August, 1933, Jeby lost all claim to the world title when he was knocked out in seven rounds by Lou Brouillard.

Before winning the N.Y.A.C. title Jeby had been one of the men to put a stop to Len Harvey's world championship aspirations by outpointing the Cornishman when he was in America in 1931.

## JEFFRA, Harry:

During his career which extended from 1933 to 1951, Harry Jeffra, an Italian-American whose real name is Guiffi, won the world bantamweight title and also claimed the featherweight crown.

He lost only three fights before taking the bantamweight championship from Sixto Escobar in September, 1937 but he held on to the title for only five months before losing it in a return with the Puerto Rican.

Jeffra put on weight after this and in September, 1939, he met the world featherweight champion, Joey Archibald, in a 15-round title fight but was outpointed.

He again lost to Archibald 12 months later after the Irish-American had been deprived of his crown by the N.B.A. and the championship was in a state of confusion.

Jeffra laid claim to the title and was acknowledged as champion by a small minority in his home state of Maryland during 1941 following a victory over Lou Transparenti and one over Archibald.

By this time Chalky Wright was generally acknowledged as world number one featherweight and when these two met at Baltimore, June 19, 1942, Jeffra was stopped in 10 rounds.

## JEFFRIES, James J.:

This powerfully built American went from novice to world champion in only 11 fights. Indeed, he had fewer contests than any other Queensberry champion apart from J. J. Corbett.

A man of great strength, Jeffries developed a crouching style which made him a difficult man to combat and although he was not an outstanding boxer he possessed a remarkable left hook which could cave in a man's ribs.

Tom Sharkey was one man who could vouch for the power of Jeffries' punching. When they met for the world title in 1899, there were many at the ringside who disputed the referee's verdict in favour of Jeffries, but there was no disputing the fact that Sharkey ended up in hospital with broken ribs.

Jeffries weighed around 16 stone (224lbs.) when he was in his prime. He proved too powerful a hitter for the crafty Bob Fitzsimmons when they met at Coney Island, June 9, 1899, and he relieved the Cornishman of the world championship with a knock-out in the 11th round.

After that Jeffries defended his title against Tom Sharkey, Jack Finnigan, Jim Corbett (twice), Gus Ruhlin, Bob Fitzsimmons and Jack Munroe, before announcing his retirement from the ring in 1905.

In 1910 "The Boilermaker" was persuaded to put on the gloves again in an effort to rescue the white man's cause by winning back the championship from Jack Johnson. The venture was ill-advised and Jeffries was knocked out by the negro in the 15th round.

That was the only defeat the "California Grizzly Bear" ever sustained in the ring. He died in 1953.

## JENKINS, Lew:

An Irish-American lightweight with the big punch who started fighting in 1934.

In May, 1940, he took the world title from Lou Ambers, knocking him out in the third round, and successfully defended his title by stopping Ambers in seven rounds in a return bout.

In July, 1940, Jenkins met Henry Armstrong the reigning welterweight champion in a fight made at 140 lbs. Armstrong's title was not at stake but in any case Jenkins was well beaten by the end of six rounds when the referee stopped the contest.

Jenkins lost his world crown when he was outpointed by Sammy Angott at Madison Square Garden, December 19, 1941.

## JEPTHA, Andrew:

South African negro who came to England in 1902 and became the first coloured man to win a British title.

In February, 1907, he met the British welterweight champion, Curley Watson, at Wonderland, and was beaten over 20 rounds. That was his second defeat by the Chatham fighter, but when they came together again at Wonderland, March 25, 1907, Jeptha scored a fourth round knock-out.

Less than five months later, when already suffering from eye trouble, he was outpointed by Joe White at Merthyr but the authorities would not recognise the Welshman as champion and Jeptha continued to claim the title until he was outpointed by Watson at the N.S.C. in November 1907.

Even after that Jeptha still considered himself champion for that contest had not been fought over the championship distance of 20 rounds, but by 1910 his sight had deteriorated so badly that he was forced to retire. He went blind soon afterwards.

## JEWISH BOXERS:

The first Jew to win the championship was Daniel Mendoza, who was born at Aldgate, London, July 5, 1764, and succeeded Big Ben Brain as Champion of England in 1794.

Since then only one Jewish fighter has won the Heavyweight championship of the world. That was Max Baer, the jovial American, who beat Primo Carnera in June, 1934.

Another outstanding Jewish heavyweight who fought the best men in the world around the turn of the century, but never won the world championship, was Joe Choynski. This Californian fighter's best display was probably his 20-round draw with the powerful Jim Jeffries some 18 months before the "Boilermaker "won the title.

Arguably the most famous British Jew in ring history was Ted "Kid" Lewis (q.v.). Others who won British titles include such stars as Young Joseph, Jack Bloomfield, Harry Reeve, Harry Mason, Al Foreman and Harry Mizler, each of whom have separate biographies in this volume.

## JOFRE, Eder:

Generally acclaimed as one of the greatest bantamweight champions in boxing history, this hard-hitting Brazilian became the first fighter from that country to win a world title when he k.o'd Eloy Sanchez in six rounds in November, 1960, although it was not until after he had beaten Piero Rollo and Johnny Caldwell, both in 10 rounds, that he really settled the title muddle in this division and gained world-wide recognition.

Jofre suffered only two defeats in 53 contests as a bantamweight both at the hands of the Jap, Masahiko Harada. His world title went with the first defeat in May, 1965, and the other, in June, 1966, persuaded him to retire.

After more than three years out of the ring, Jofre began a come-back as a featherweight in 1969, and gained the world title in that division by out-pointing Jose Legra in May 1973. Jofre was then 37 years of age and the oldest man ever to win this title, but he finished the stronger man despite suffering cuts over both eyes.

The W.B.C. deprived him of this title in June 1974 for failing to sign for defence against Alfredo Marcano.

## JOHANSSON, Ingemar:

Johansson put Swedish boxing on the map when he knocked out Eddie Machen, then rated No. 1 contender for the world heavyweight title, in 2 minutes 16 seconds before 50,000 spectators at Gothenburg in 1958.

That was the Swede's 22nd pro-fessional contest and his 22nd victory. He had previously won the European heavyweight title by knocking out Franco Cavicchi in 13 rounds, and had also stopped Henry Cooper and Joe Erskine inside the distance.

Johansson's shock victory over Machen earned him a crack at Floyd Patterson for the world title and these two met at the Yankee Stadium, New York, June 26, 1959.

Most of the critics did not give Johansson much chance of beating Patterson, but the Swede had every confidence that his terrific right-hand punch would win him the title.

In training he hid this right hand from the American critics but he brought it into use in the third round of the title fight and Patterson was dropped seven times before the referee intervened to award the contest to Johansson, the first European to win the crown since Primo Carnera.

However, it was only 12 months later that Patterson turned the tables on Johansson, and the American champion completely erased that first defeat with another k.o. victory over the Swede in a third meeting in March, 1961.

After this Johansson regained the European title by stopping Dick Richardson in eight rounds, but he was deprived of this crown for failing to defend it, and announced his retirement soon after outpointing Brian London in April, 1963.

## JOHNSON, Bunny:

Born in Jamaica but brought up in Birmingham Bunny Johnson was the first immigrant to win British titles at two different weights. He had been boxing professionally for nearly seven years when he won the British and Commonwealth heavyweight titles by knocking out Danny McAlinden in 1975 (his seventeenth successive victory), but after another four wins in a row he lost the titles when outpointed by Richard Dunn in September 1975. Johnson later dropped down a weight division and won the British light-heavyweight title by knocking out Tim Wood with a right to the jaw in only 1 min. 43 secs., the fastest k.o. in a British light-heavyweight title fight. This was at Wolverhampton in March 1977.

Johnson gave a disappointing display when making a bid for the vacant European light-heavyweight title and the referee stopped the fight in favour of the Italian, Aldo Traversaro, in the eleventh round in Genoa, November 1977.

After moving to Australia he relin-quished his British title in December 1981.

## JOHNSON, Frank:

A tough fighter he took the British lightweight crown from Tommy McGovern at Manchester in July, 1952, and then went to Australia where he collected the Empire title by stopping Frank Flannery.

Johnson, a Mancunian, did not take his fighting too seriously and in June, 1953, he was deprived of his titles by the B.B.B.C. after failing to make the weight for a contest with Joe Lucy.

The Mile End boxer outpointed him on that occasion, but after another trip to Australia Johnson came back to turn the tables on Lucy and regain his British titles in April, 1955.

Around this time Johnson began to experience more weight difficulties and he was not at his best in a third meeting with Lucy in April, 1956. In the eighth round the referee intervened and awarded the contest to Lucy.

Johnson subsequently made a come-back as a welterweight and in December,

1956, he took part in one of the hardest contests seen in Birmingham for several years. His opponent was the British welterweight champion, Peter Waterman. Johnson suffered a badly cut eye in the first round but would not give up until the end of the tenth round when that eye was completely closed.

## JOHNSON, Fred:

Most historians name Fred Johnson from Hackney, London, as the first featherweight champion of England, and although he was never officially referred to as such he certainly was the outstanding fighter in this country between 8 stone 8 lbs. and 8 stone 12 lbs. (120 lbs.—124 lbs.) during the 1880's and the early 1890's.

In April, 1888, he won an 8 stone 10 lbs. (122 lbs.) competition open to all England at the Agricultural Hall, Islington, London. Johnson won a number of these competitions about that time, and on April 29, 1895, he beat another leading featherweight of the day, Charlie Beadling, in four rounds at Newcastle.

Johnson was stopped in 13 rounds by Harry Greenfield in January, 1897, but this was not recognised by the N.S.C. and it was not until he was beaten in 13 rounds by Ben Jordan in February 1897, that the Hackney fighter gave up his claim to the British championship.

## JOHNSON, Harold:

An American negro from Pennsylvania who was rated among the world's top light-heavyweights for around 15 years, a remarkable achievement.

It was unfortunate for Johnson that the great Archie Moore was at the peak of his career at the same time for he didn't quite have the weight necessary to make a real show among the heavyweights, although it should be noted that Johnson beat such notable heavies as Eddie Machen, Nino Valdes, Arturo Godoy and Jimmy Bivins.

Johnson was beaten in 14 rounds by Archie Moore when he made his first bid for the light-heavyweight title in 1954. But he gained New York recognition in 1961 (after Moore had been deprived of the crown) by stopping Jesse Bowdry, and world-wide recognition followed

when he outpointed Doug Jones in May, 1962.

In June, 1963, Johnson lost his title when narrowly outpointed by Willie Pastrano.

## JOHNSON, Jack:

Several books have been devoted to the career of this famous negro fighter from Galveston, Texas, and it is difficult to do him justice in a brief biography.

Most writers have acknowledged his greatness although there are a few who say that he was over-rated as a champion. There have been endless discussions as to whether or not he was the greatest heavyweight of all time.

This writer is prepared to accept the word of one of the greatest authorities on boxing, the American, Nat Fleischer, who rated Jack Johnson as the king-pin of all the heavyweight champions. It should be pointed out, however, that this was before another contender for this title, Muhammad Ali, had reached his peak.

In his book *Fifty Years at Ringside*, Fleischer not only described Johnson as the Best All-Around heavyweight, but also as the fighter with the best defence, the best uppercut, the best counter-puncher, best at feinting, and the most crafty.

The claim that Johnson was the greatest heavyweight champion is often criticised on the grounds that he did not defend his title against any outstanding men. He beat Jim Jeffries, but then Jeffries had been six years out of the ring. However, it is not fair to try and belittle Johnson because of the lack of first-class opposition. That was no fault of his.

Johnson's genius as a defensive boxer has never been disputed. No man was ever his master at milling on the retreat and he had an uncanny knack of stopping opponents' punches in mid-air or almost before the other man had really set them going.

Son of a former knuckle-fighter, Johnson ran away from home at the age of 12 and worked in racing stables.

At 17 he got a job as a sparring partner to Joe Walcott the Barbados Demon, but it was not until a couple of years later, after he had returned home to Galveston and won a fight in a fair booth, that he decided to make boxing his career.

He started fighting seriously in 1899 but did not earn enough to keep himself and for a while he continued working as a painter.

It was a victory over Frank Childs in Los Angeles in 1902 that really put him on the fistic map.

Jack Johnson followed the champion, Tommy Burns, to England in 1908, hoping for a title fight, but the Canadian had departed for Australia.

The negro fighter stayed here long enough to dispose of Al McNamara and Ben Taylor in a couple of contests at Plymouth and then moved on to the Antipodes.

At Sydney on Boxing Day, 1908, he finally caught up with Burns and although the Canadian was game he proved no match for the crafty negro who was declared the winner when the police stopped the fight in the 14th round.

After this Johnson parted from his manager Sam Fitzpatrick and his manner and bearing outside the ring as he flaunted around the world made him the most unpopular champion of all time.

His first wife committed suicide in 1912. He was subsequently sentenced to prison in America but escaped with his second wife to Europe. However, he did eventually return to the States and served his prison sentence.

Johnson's behaviour so incensed the white people that a big campaign was set under way in several parts of the globe to search for a "white hope" to wrest the championship from the negro.

It was not until 1915 that the man was found who proved capable of doing this. That man was Jess Willard the giant cowboy from Kansas, and he took the championship crown from Johnson with a knock-out in the 26th round at Havana, Cuba, April 5, 1915.

Johnson fought a number of contests after this, not really retiring until 1928. Even after that he appeared in many exhibition bouts right up until he was 66. He died in a car crash in 1946.

## JOHNSON, Tom:

Acknowledged as Champion of England following his victory over Jack Jarvis in 15 minutes in September, 1783, this Derbyshire prize-fighter's real name was Jackling.

He confirmed his claim to the title by beating the "Croydon Drover," and Stephen Oliver in 1784.

Johnson held the championship until 1791, beating several good men, but he took to drink and gambling, and on January 17 of that year he met his master in Big Ben Brain, being beaten in 18 rounds lasting 20 minutes.

After that Johnson quickly deteriorated both in health and social stature and he died in 1797 at the age of 47.

## JONES, Colin:

Hard-hitting Welsh welterweight from Gorseinon who had three world title fights before continued back trouble interrupted his career.

Jones likes to pick his punches rather than rush the job and it was this that cost him a decision over the faster punching Milton McCrory in their W.B.C. world title fight in Las Vegas in March 1983. However, Jones still earned a draw in one of the best displays by a British fighter in America since the war.

In a return five months later Jones lost a split decision favouring McCrory, and a third world title attempt in January 1985 saw the fiercely competitive Welshman beaten by the classy W.B.A. champion Don Curry when the referee had to call a halt in the fourth round because of Jones' badly split nose.

After winning the A.B.A. welterweight title in 1976 and 1977 he took the British welterweight title by stopping Kirkland Laing in April 1980 and continued his unbeaten run by adding the Commonwealth title with another inside-the-distance win over Mark Harris. Apart from a disqualification he was still unbeaten when in his 25th fight he lifted the European title from Hans Henrik Palm in Copenhagen.

## JONES, Frank:

Born Plean, Scotland, Frank Jones won the Scottish flyweight title in September, 1956 and the vacant British and Empire titles in July, 1957. His opponent in the latter contest was Len Reece of Cardiff. The Scot won by a k.o. in the 11th round.

Jones lost his Empire title to Dennis Adams of South Africa when he was knocked out in the third round at Glasgow, October, 1957.

In November, 1960, he lost his British title to Johnny Caldwell.

## JONES, Percy:

This brilliant Welsh flyweight from Porth in the Rhondda had his career cut short during the first World War when he was gassed and lost a leg while serving in France and died in 1922 after a long illness.

A really tough little fighter, Percy Jones won the vacant British and European flyweight titles by outpointing Bill Ladbury at the N.S.C., January 26, 1914.

Jones showed amazing durability in this contest for Ladbury went all out for a knock-out in the last few rounds but Jones stayed the distance to earn the referee's decision.

Jones also claimed the world title after this victory and although he was not recognised in America where it was being disputed by Johnny Coulon and Kid Williams, Jones gained everyone's favour on this side of the Atlantic by outpointing Eugene Criqui over 20 rounds at Liverpool in March, 1914.

However, Jones soon became overweight and he relinquished his claim in October of the same year shortly after being knocked out by Joe Symonds at Plymouth.

## JONES, William "Gorilla":

After Mickey Walker relinquished the world middleweight title in 1931 to go after the heavyweight crown. "Gorilla" Jones was acknowledged as champion by N.B.A. following his victory over Tiger Thomas in August that year and Oddore Piazzo in January, 1932.

In June, 1932, Jones, an American negro, was beaten by Marcel Thil in Paris, being disqualified in the 11th round, and although the Americans would not acknowledge Thil as champion they did deprive Jones of the crown.

The N.B.A. thought fit to restore this to him after his victory over Sammy Slaughter in January 1933, but their decision did not carry much weight on this side of the Atlantic where Marcel Thil really established himself as the rightful title-holder.

Jones eventually lost all claim to the world title following defeats by Emilio Martinez and Oscar Rankin in 1934.

## JORDAN, Ben:

Born Bermondsey, London, April 1, 1873, Ben Jordan was one of this country's finest featherweights in the early part of this century.

In February, 1897, he won the British featherweight title by stopping Fred Johnson in 13 rounds at the N.S.C., and he followed this by beating both Tommy White and Eddie Curry inside the distance.

He then went to America and there gave his finest display by outpointing the renowned George Dixon over 25 rounds in New York, July 1, 1898.

Jordan claimed the world title after that but the truth is that Dixon was not holding the championship at that time for he had previously been defeated by Solly Smith and did not regain the crown until four months after losing to the Bermondsey fighter.

On his return from America Jordan confirmed his right to the British title by defeating Harry Greenfield, Jordan stopped his man in the ninth round with a kidney punch. This fight took place at the N.S.C., May 29, 1899, and it was after this that the N.S.C. decided to ban kidney punching.

Jordan clung to his claim to the world championship but when he again crossed the Atlantic in October, 1899, he was decisively beaten by Eddie Santry who had already fought a draw with Dixon. Santry stopped Jordan in the 16th round.

When Dixon came to England in 1903 he beat Jordan in six rounds.

In December, 1904, he gave another fine display in outpointing Pedlar Palmer, but early in the following year he relinquished the featherweight championship and retired.

## JORDAN, Don:

In January, 1958, Don Jordan came to London and was outpointed by the British lightweight champion, Dave Charnley. At that time this American negro from Los Angeles was not rated among the world title contenders, but he made such rapid progress that before the year had ended he had won eight contests and then taken the world welterweight title from Virgil Akins with a 15-round points decision in front of his home-town crowd.

That victory was a surprise to the fistic fraternity but Jordan proved his superiority beyond any shadow of doubt when he clearly outpointed Akins in a return match at St. Louis, April 24, 1959.

Following defeats in two non-title bouts Jordan lost his crown to Benny Paret in May, 1960.

## JOSEPH, Aschel "Young":

Born Aldgate, London, 1885, this Jewish fighter won the first Lonsdale Belt put up for competition in the welterweight division.

Before that, however, in June, 1908, he beat the British lightweight champion, Jack Goldswain, over 20 rounds at Wonderland, but this was not recognised as a title-fight.

Joseph did not have much of a punch but he was a very clever boxer, and in March, 1910, he became the British welterweight champion by beating Jack Goldswain again, this time on a disqualification in 11 rounds at the N.S.C.

Later in 1910, Joseph claimed the European title after beating Battling Lacroix of France, but in January, 1911, in his first defence of his titles, he was beaten on a third round disqualification when meeting Arthur Evernden.

In October, 1911, Young Joseph was knocked out in the 10th round in a contest with Georges Carpentier for the European welterweight title at the King's Hall, London.

## JUCHAU, Tom:

Some historians do not even bother to mention Tom Juchau as Champion of England. He won the title in that dismal period during the 1760's and 1770's following the defeat of Jack Slack and the advent of Tom Johnson.

Known as "Disher the Paviour" Juchau claimed the title after beating George Milsom in 70 minutes at St. Albans, August 27, 1765, but lost it only nine months later to Bill Darts who got the better of him in 40 minutes' bruising at Guildford.

## KANE, Peter:

Born at Golborne, Lancashire, in 1918, Peter Kane, the fighter with the Eddie Cantor eyes, had the urge to become a boxer long before he left school.

He made his earliest appearances in the roped square when the fairground booth came around to his district and as soon as he reached the age of 16 he took out a professional licence.

Kane soon proved his punching power for he won 23 of his first 27 professional contests inside the distance and then got right into the top bracket by outpointing the French champion, Valentin Angelmann, over 12 rounds at Liverpool in November, 1936.

By October, 1937, Kane had worked his way up to a fight with Benny Lynch for the world flyweight title. This contest which took place at Shawfield Park, Glasgow, was one of the finest flyweight battles of all time. Lynch won by a knock-out in the 13th round.

Kane got his return match five months later but Lynch failed to make the weight. The result was a draw.

In September, 1938, Peter Kane won the vacant world flyweight title by outpointing the American, Jackie Jurich, at Liverpool.

The Golborne fighter subsequently fought most of his contests as a bantamweight, although, in June, 1943, he did make the flyweight limit in order to defend his world title and was knocked out in the first round.

Many thought that that was the finish of Kane's ring career but they were soon proved wrong. This determined fighter won many more contests as a bantamweight and in September, 1947, became the European champion of that division by outpointing the Frenchman, Theo Medina, at Belle Vue, Manchester. Kane had beaten the Frenchman three months earlier in a non-title fight.

Peter Kane lost his European title to the Italian, Guido Ferracin in February, 1948, and retired at the end of that year.

## KANSAS, Rocky:

This Italian-American whose real name was Rocco Tozze, had been fighting for 15 years when he won the world lightweight title from Jimmy Goodrich in 1925. He was then 30 years of age and the oldest man ever to win the championship of this division.

Kansas had twice been beaten by Benny Leonard when he had tried to gain the lightweight title in 1922.

Once he had reached the top, however, this veteran fighter's reign was short-lived. Only six months after winning the title he was beaten in Chicago by Sammy Mandell. That was his last important fight.

## KAPLAN, Louis "Kid":

When Johnny Dundee resigned his world featherweight title it was the aggressive slugger, Louis Kaplan, who emerged as champion from the N.Y.A.C. elimination tournament. Kaplan, a Jewish-American, clinched the title by stopping Danny Kramer in nine rounds in January, 1925.

By 1927 Kaplan was forced by increasing weight to relinquish his claim to the crown and he fought as a lightweight until retiring in 1933.

## KAYLOR, Mark:

A.B.A. middleweight champion in 1979 Kaylor was soon showing his punching power among the professionals. All but three of his first 24 fights were won inside the distance, including a fifth round k.o. of Roy Gumbs in September 1983 which brought him the British and Commonwealth titles. Suffered his first set-back when disqualified for hitting American Tony Cerda after the bell, and the West Ham fighter lost his British and Commonwealth titles when outpointed by Tony Sibson at Wembley in November 1984. A subsequent bid for the European crown failed when he was pulled out by

his corner at the end of eight gruelling rounds against Herol Graham in
November 1986.

## KEENAN, Peter:

Peter Keenan of Glasgow is one of
only six fighters who have won two
Lonsdale Belts outright.

He was a Scottish A.B.A. flyweight
champion before turning professional
and it was not long before he got among
the leading bantamweights in the country.

In May, 1951, Keenan knocked out
Danny O'Sullivan to become the British
champion and before that year was out
he had added the European title to his
record by outpointing Luis Romero.

These victories put him right in line
for a world title bout and he got this in
January, 1952, when he went to South
Africa to meet Vic Toweel. Keenan lost
on points.

Four months later he lost his European
title when he was knocked out by Jean
Sneyers, but he regained this crown in
June, 1953, by defeating Maurice
Sandeyron.

Once again this Scot was on the verge
of a world title fight but then he was
surprisingly beaten by John Kelly in
October, 1953, losing his British and
European titles.

Keenan made amends for this defeat
by turning the tables on Kelly in a return
bout and he subsequently won the
Empire title from the Australian, Bobby
Sinn.

Keenan retained his British and
Empire titles until January 10, 1959,
when he was defeated by another
Irishman, Freddie Gilroy, the referee
stopping the fight in the 11th round. The
Scotsman announced his retirement that
same night before leaving the ring.

## KELLY, Johnny:

A Belfast southpaw who upset the
odds in October, 1953, when he outpointed Peter Keenan for the British and
European bantamweight titles.

A cool fighter, Kelly was undefeated
in 21 professional bouts before losing his
European crown with a third round k.o.
by Robert Cohen in February, 1954.

Until then Kelly had looked a particularly good prospect for world honours
but this fight and his subsequent k.o. by
Peter Keenan, which cost him the British
title, indicated that he could not take a
punch on the chin.

## KELLY, "Spider" Jim:

This Irishman from Derry won his
country's featherweight title in September,
1936, and then sprang right up among
the top rankers in February, 1937, by
outpointing Nel Tarleton.

In November, 1938, he won the vacant
British and Empire featherweight titles
with a victory over Benny Caplan at
Belfast but he lost these titles in June,
1939, when well beaten by Johny Cusick,
the referee intervening in the 12th round.

## KELLY, "Spider" Billy:

Son of Jim Kelly, the former featherweight champion, Billy took the Empire
featherweight championship from Roy
Ankrah of the Gold Coast in a contest at
Belfast in October 1954.

He added the British title to his record
with a points victory over Sammy
McCarthy in Belfast, January 1955.

Kelly lost his Empire crown to Hogan
Bassey in November, 1955, and his
British title went to Charlie Hill in a
close contest at Belfast in February,
1956. The referee's decision in the Hill
fight nearly caused a riot.

## KETCHEL, Stanley:

Rated by most knowledgeable boxing
critics as the greatest middleweight of all
time, Stanley Ketchel, or to give him his
real name, Stanislaus Kiecal, was a
natural born fighter.

Ketchel had no time for defence for he
was an all-out attacker. Outside the ring
he was pleasant enough with a good
sense of humour but once inside the
Squared Circle he showed no mercy but
had the "killer" instinct which is the
essential part of the mental make-up of
all truly great champions.

Known as the "Michigan Assassin"
Ketchel usually weighed around 11 stone
4 lbs. (158 lbs.) but he never worried
about taking on heavier men.

In October, 1909, he met the world
heavyweight champion Jack Johnson,
and indeed, was the first man to floor the
Black Panther.

Ketchel conceded Johnson 2 stone 7 lbs. (35 lbs.) on that occasion, an impossible handicap against such a renowned fighter and when the Polish-American was knocked out in the 12th round the negro hit with such force that Ketchel's front teeth were found embedded in Johnson's glove.

After Tommy Ryan retired in 1907, Ketchel became world middleweight champion by knocking out Mike Twin Sullivan in less than two minutes' fighting at Colma, February 22, 1908.

He lost his crown when surprisingly beaten in 12 rounds by Billy Papke at Los Angeles, September 7, 1908. In the first round of that bloody battle Ketchel was floored four times after he had been taken by surprise by Papke, who, instead of offering the preliminary handshake, hit the champion with all his might.

In the return fight 11 weeks later Ketchel got his revenge and regained the championship by knocking out Papke in the 11th round.

The career of this colourful personality was cut short on October 15, 1910, when he was shot and killed by a jealous farmhand.

## KILBANE, Johnny:

An aggressive, two-fisted fighter, Johnny Kilbane, who was born at Cleveland, Ohio, of Irish stock, won the world featherweight title from Abe Attell in February, 1912, and held on to it for nearly 11 years.

Kilbane was not a hard puncher but he was clever and had a good defence.

Most of his bouts were "no decision" contests, in which he could only lose his title by a knock-out, but that defensive ability kept him out of trouble until June, 1923, when he was stopped in the sixth round by Eugene Criqui.

Kilbane did not fight again after that. He became a referee and a respected politician who served as a State Senator in the Ohio Assembly.

## KILRAIN, Jake:

This Scotman's real name is Harry Owens but when he took up boxing he decided to call himself after the famous old bare-knuckle prize fighter.

Kilrain started fighting professionally in 1931. In June, 1936, he took the British welterweight championship from Dave McCleave with a knockout in the eighth round. He successfully defended the title against Jack Lord at Manchester, but in March, 1939, he was knocked out by Ernie Roderick at Liverpool.

This Glasgow fighter was subsequently beaten on two occasions by Arthur Danahar and also suffered two defeats at the hands of Eric Boon. He retired in 1950.

## KING, Johnny:

Born at Manchester, Johnny King started as a flyweight at the age of 14.

He took the British and Empire bantamweight titles from Dick Corbett in October, 1932, lost the return match in February, 1934, and subsequently fought two draws with Corbett before the London fighter became overweight and gave up the title.

Then King regained the crown by outpointing Len Hampston and he went on to make the belt his own property with a victory over fellow Mancunian, Jackie Brown.

In 1935, King twice fought Nel Tarleton, the British featherweight champion, in non-title contests, beating the Liverpool favourite in the first bout and drawing the second.

King retained his bantamweight title until February, 1947, when he was knocked out in seven rounds by Jackie Paterson.

## KING, Tom:

Born Stepney, London, in 1835, Tom King first interested himself in the art of fisticuffs while serving in the Royal Navy.

His three principal contests were with Jem Mace whom he met on two occasions, and another with the American, John C. Heenan.

King first met Mace at London Bridge, January 28, 1862, but was beaten in 43 rounds lasting 68 minutes. It is obvious from this that King was a man of some merit and he proved this beyond a shadow of doubt when at their second meeting, he was able to beat the scientific Mace by a knockout in the 21st round.

This victory gave King the Championship of England, a title which he retained until his retirement in 1864, shortly after he had beaten John C. Heenan in 24 rounds at Wadhurst.

## KINGPETCH, Pone:

The first man ever to regain the world flyweight title this fighter from Thailand actually won the crown on three separate occasions.

In April 1960 he outpointed veteran Pascual Perez in Bangkok to become a national hero. He lost the title in October 1962 to Fighting Harada but turned the tables on the Jap in a return bout three months later.

In September 1963 he again lost the crown, this time in sensational fashion, being k.o'd in 2 minutes 7 seconds by another Jap, Hiroyuki Ebihara, but he won yet another return bout in January 1964.

A long lay-off followed and the effects of this were in evidence when he was beaten by Salvatore Burruni in April 1965.

## KIRBY, Bert:

The highlight of this hard hitting Birmingham flyweight's career concerns one other fighter—Jackie Brown of Manchester.

In October, 1929, these two were matched in a British flyweight eliminator but shortly before the contest was due to take place, the champion, Johnny Hill, died, and the Board of Control announced that the Kirby—Brown bout would be for the vacant title.

It took place on a Sunday morning in Birmingham and Brown won with a knock-out in the third round.

Five months later these two fought the return at the Holborn Stadium, London, and this time Kirby completely turned the tables on the Manchester fighter by knocking him out in the third round.

Their third meeting was at Manchester in February, 1931, and Kirby lost his title when Brown got the referee's nod at the end of 15 rounds.

## KLAUS, Frank:

Known as "The Pittsburgh Bear" this German-American is considered to have been one of the roughest and toughest fighters of all time, and an all-out attacker who proved on many occasions that he could absorb terrific punishment and still keep going forward.

He first claimed the world middleweight title in 1912 and added some strength to his claim by beating the European champion, Georges Carpentier. The Frenchman was disqualified in the 19th round when his Manager, Francois Descamps, entered the ring. The truth is, however, that Klaus was 3 lbs. over the weight limit for that bout.

Klaus re-established his claim to the world title in March, 1913, when he beat Billy Papke on a foul in 15 rounds in Paris, but he did not remain undefeated really long enough to confirm his right to the title. In October that same year, at Pittsburgh, he was knocked out in six rounds by George Chip.

## KNOCK, Charlie:

Stratford, Essex, welterweight who was one of the first men to be recognised as British champion at that weight.

He claimed the title in May, 1906, after he had stopped Curley Watson in 17 rounds at Wonderland. The contest was actually billed as being for the 10 stone 4 lbs. (144 lbs.) Championship of England.

Knock lost this title in a return with Watson who beat him in 10 rounds at Wonderland, December, 1906.

Knock had something of a reputation for a right hand punch under the heart which finished many of his contests in quick time including one with Iron Hague who later became British heavyweight champion. On this occasion he conceded Hague over 4-stone (56lbs.).

## KNOCK-DOWNS:
## Most in a single contest:

Remembering that under the old Prize Ring rules a round ended every time one of the contestants went down then the record for the most knock-downs in a fight must be the same as that for the record number of rounds—276.

That was the total number of knock-downs when Jack Jones beat Patsy Tunney at Cheshire, England, 1825.

In more recent contests under Queensberry Rules the record probably belongs to the meeting between Battling Nelson and Christy Williams at Hot Springs, Arkansas, U.S.A., December 26, 1902. Nelson had Williams down 41 times before putting him down for the full count in the 17th round. Nelson was down seven times.

The record for scoring the most knock-downs in a world heavyweight title fight with gloves probably belongs to Max Baer. He put the giant Italian, Primo Carnera, down 11 times in 11 rounds when winning the title, June 14, 1934.

Some other contests with a large number of knock-downs:—

Joe Grim "The Iron Man," an Italian cruiserweight who settled in America and earned a reputation as one of the toughest men in the ring was down 17 times in a fight with Bob Fitzsimmons at Philadelphia in 1903, and at least 17 times (some say 30) when he met Jack Johnson nearly two years later.

Jack Dempsey floored Jess Willard seven times in the first round of their world title fight, July 4, 1919. The "Manassa Mauler" also put Luis Angel Firpo down nine times in two rounds in their famous fight of 1923.

Bruce Woodcock put Jock Porter down nine times before the referee intervened in the third round, November 27, 1945.

Charlie Hill was floored 10 times by Bobby Neill before the referee intervened in the ninth round of their British featherweight title contest, April 13, 1959.

Floyd Patterson put Pete Rademacher down seven times when winning by a sixth round knock-out, August 22, 1957.

The record for a world title fight at any weight goes to Vic Toweel of South Africa. When defending his bantamweight crown against Danny O'Sullivan in Johannesburg, December 2, 1950, he had the Englishman down 14 times before forcing him to retire in the tenth round.

When scoring a first-round knock-out, Jock McAvoy floored Eddie Risko six times in 2 minutes 28 seconds actual fighting, New York, December 20, 1935.

Peter Keenan, British bantamweight champion, put challenger Frankie Williams (Birkenhead) down 11 times before the referee stopped the fight in the seventh round, January 28, 1953.

Olle Tandberg floored Jock Porter 21 times before the referee intervened in the seventh round, Stockholm, January 8, 1946.

Benny Lynch scored ten knock-downs over Jackie Brown (Manchester) to win the world flyweight title, September 9, 1935. Brown retired in the second round.

Pat Kelly (Derry) floored Johnny O'Callaghan (Dagenham) 14 times in a featherweight contest before the referee stopped the fight in the fourth round, Belfast, September 20, 1958.

## Rules:

It is mandatory for a fighter to take a count of "eight" every time he is knocked down. And since 1963, in most parts of the world it has been a generally accepted rule that the count should continue at the end of any round, except the last, until the fighter rises or is counted out.

In most states of the United States of America the referee should stop a contest immediately a fighter has been knocked down three times in any one round.

## Knocked out of the ring:

This has occurred many times in big fights but undoubtedly the most famous occasion was the Jack Dempsey—Luis Angel Firpo contest on the New York Giants' baseball ground, September 14, 1923.

In the first round Dempsey put the giant South American down seven times but once Firpo sent Dempsey flying through the ropes to land among the Press men in the front row.

Dempsey scrambled back into the ring in a daze (some reports say that he was pushed back) but Firpo failed to press home his advantage and in the second round Dempsey landed a knock-out. The fight lasted 3 minutes 57 seconds.

Another world heavyweight champion to be knocked out of the ring but who was able to come back and win was Joe Louis. Buddy Baer sent him through the ropes in the first round of a fight at Washington, May 23, 1941. Louis was back at the count of "four" and went on to win when Baer was disqualified in the seventh round.

World bantamweight champion, Vic Toweel, was knocked out of the ring in the first round of his contest with Jimmy Carruthers, November 15, 1952, at Johannesburg. He got back but was knocked out in 2 minutes 19 seconds.

Len Harvey was knocked out of the ring in the second round by Freddie Mills at the Tottenham Hotspur football ground, June 20, 1942. Harvey was unable to beat the count and so lost his British and Empire light-heavyweight titles.

When flyweight Jimmy Wilde sportingly agreed for his fight with the former world bantamweight champion Pete Herman to go ahead at the Albert Hall in December 1920, despite the fact that the Italian-American was well over the bantamweight limit, the Welshman was knocked out of the ring three times.

## KNOCK-OUT:

The hardest knock-out punch ever delivered is often credited to the negro heavyweight, Jack Johnson.

Oddly enough, the victim on this occasion was another of the hardest hitters the ring has ever known, the middleweight, Stanley Ketchel.

They met at Colma, California, October 16, 1909. In the 12th round Ketchel surprised Johnson and put him down. The negro appeared more annoyed than hurt and he sprang up to knock Ketchel flat on his back with a right to the chin.

By the time Ketchel had fully recovered, Johnson had left the arena and two of the white man's teeth were found embedded in Johnson's glove.

Another remarkable knock-out was that scored by Georges Carpentier over the Australian heavyweight George Cook, at the Albert Hall, London, January 22, 1922.

The speed with which Carpentier executed the final punch makes this a knock-out to remember. Milling on the retreat, the Frenchman caught Cook with a right hand which might well have been the "finisher," but even as Cook was falling Carpentier stooped and hit

him full on the jaw with another right hand.

There was some dispute as to whether or not Carpentier had committed a foul by hitting Cook when he was down, but dispute or not, it was certainly quick action on the Frenchman's part.

Another noteworthy knock-out took place at San Francisco, November 15, 1901. Then Gus Ruhlin was actually counted out while sitting on his stool after the end of the fifth round. He had taken a terrific hammering from Jim Jeffries.

## Double knock-outs:

No boxer of world championship class has ever figured in a double knock-out, but only the action of the referee prevented this from happening in a world lightweight title contest at Vernon, California, July 14, 1912.

The champion, Ad Wolgast, and the challenger, Joe Rivers, connected simultaneously in the 13th round and both dropped to the canvas. It appeared that neither would be able to rise but referee Jack Welch lifted Wolgast onto his feet and supported him while he counted Rivers out.

## Fewest knock-outs:

Several fighters with lengthy careers have escaped being knocked out but probably the most famous fighter who achieved this distinction as well as winning a world title was the American negro, William "Gorilla" Jones.

Jones, who won the N.B.A. version of the middleweight title in 1931, had a career extending over 16 years, during which he had around 200 contests and was never knocked out.

"Sugar" Ray Robinson was never counted out in a career of over 200 fights but he was once stopped inside the distance by Joey Maxim who forced him to retire in the 14th round.

Len Harvey was only counted out once in 418 professional contests and that was in the last of them when he was defeated by Freddie Mills.

Other men with outstanding records in this respect include Ted "Kid" Lewis, knocked out only three times in more than 250 contests; Joe Grim (The Iron

Man) three times in over 300 contests; Jack Britton, only once in over 300 contests, and Harry Greb, only twice in nearly 300 contests.

Joe Grim conceded the great Jack Johnson about 70lbs. in July, 1905, but although Johnson floored him at least 17 times in a six-round bout he could not knock him out.

## Most knock-outs:

This record is difficult to establish as there are a large number of boxers who fought in fair-ground booths and most of their fights have never been chronicled. In addition there are globe-trotting fighters like Abe the Newsboy (Abraham Hollandersky) who also took on all comers as well as men like Bobby Dobbs who was fighting before the turn of the century.

However, among the records that are fairly accurately established the fighter who knocked-out most opponents would be the American William Lawrence "Young" Stribling, one of the finest fighters who never won a world title.

In examining his record we come up against the difficulty that many wins were set down as a k.o. when the opponent was merely stopped inside the distance and not actually counted out. But it would appear from careful research that at least 119 of Stribling's opponents were actually counted out.

Commencing as a bantamweight in 1921 Stribling fought right through to heavyweight before meeting his death in a motor-cycle accident in 1933.

Next to Stribling, if only because we have to accept the fact that no more than a quarter of his fights have ever been traced, comes our own Jimmy Wilde. Only about a quarter of his fights are accurately recorded and of these he k.o.'d 101 opponents. There is no doubt that this figure could be trebled if all of his fair-ground bouts were traced. On the other hand, of course, many of these opponents were nonentities and not to be taken seriously.

A more recent record which can be established with more certainty (although, again, not complete certainty) is that of the former light-heavyweight champion Archie Moore. He stopped at least 128 opponents inside the distance and of these at least 94 were actually counted out. Moore's professional career extends from 1935 and 1965 and includes over 200 bouts.

Jack Dempsey created the record for the most one-round knock-outs with at least 30 including exhibition bouts. After he became world champion most of his bouts were exhibitions but even before that he had registered about 20 one-round knock-outs.

Mike Tyson created a record by winning his first 19 professional fights inside the distance (including 8 k.o.'s) before being made to go 10 rounds for a points win over James Tillis in May 1986.

Meeting only second-rate fighters, Lamar Clark, Cedar City, Utah, heavyweight, knocked out six opponents in one night, December 1, 1958. Around this time he ran up a record total of 44 consecutive wins inside the distance.

## Quickest knock-outs:

The world record for the quickest knock-out is held by Al Couture, a French-American, who stopped Ralph Walton in $10\frac{1}{2}$ seconds including the count, Lewiston, Maine, U.S.A., September 26, 1946.

Couture was half-way across the ring as the bell sounded and he landed his big punch as Walton was putting in his gumshield.

This record is also claimed by Ross Cleverley of the Royal New Zealand Air Force. But when he stopped D. Emerson (Pahiatua) in under 10 seconds in an open class middleweight bout at Palmerston, New Zealand, July 8, 1952, he did not score a knock-out. The referee stopped the contest without bothering to count immediately Emerson, had been floored with the first punch. In a Golden Gloves tournament at Minneapolis, U.S.A., November 4, 1947. Mike Collins dropped Pat Brownson with a single punch and the contest was stopped in only four seconds.

In Britain we have another claimant for this record in Teddy Barker, Swindon lightweight. But his contest with Bob Robert (Nigeria), at Maesteg, September 2, 1957, was also stopped by the referee without a count as Roberts got to his feet after being dropped with the first punch. Time—10 seconds.

Another contest similarly stopped after only one punch was when Al Carr beat Lew Massey, New Haven, April 3, 1936.

The British record is shared by two fighters at 11 seconds including the count. Jack Cain, Notting Hill, beat another Notting Hill boxer, Harry Deamer, in a lightweight novices competition at the N.S.C., London, February 20, 1922, and Hugh Kelly, Blantyre lightweight, k.o.'d Steve Cook (Southend), Normandy Hotel, Glasgow, May 14, 1984.

The quickest knock-out in each division in a world title contest is as follows:—

Heavyweight: 56 seconds, James J. Jeffries k.o.'d Jack Finnigan, Detroit, April 6, 1900.

Light-heavyweight: 118 seconds, Gus Lesnevich k.o'd Billy Fox, New York, March 5, 1948.

Middleweight: 45 seconds, Al McCoy k.o'd George Chip, New York, April 7, 1914.

Welterweight: 45 seconds, Lloyd Honeyghan stopped Gene Hatcher, Marbella, Aug. 30, 1987.

Light-welterweight: 127 seconds, Roberto Cruz k.o'd Battling Torres, Los Angeles, March 21, 1963.

Lightweight: 66 seconds, Tony Canzoneri k.o'd Al Singer, New York, November 14, 1930.

Junior-lightweight: 116 seconds, Ben Villaflor k.o'd Kuniaki Shibata, Honolulu, October 17, 1973.

Featherweight; 150 seconds, Freddie Miller k.o'd Jose Girones, Barcelona, February 17, 1935. (Not recognised by N.Y.A.C.).

Bantamweight: 75 seconds, Terry McGovern k.o'd Pedlar Palmer, New York, September 12, 1899.

Flyweight: 58 seconds, Emile Pladner k.o'd Frankie Genaro, Paris, March 2, 1929. (Not recognised by N.Y.A.C.).

The record for a British title fight is 40 seconds. Dave Charnley k.o'd Darkie Hughes for the European, British and Empire lightweight titles, Nottingham, November 20, 1961.

One-round knock-outs have been far too numerous to list here, but appended below are a few knock-outs scored in under one minute including the count:—

11 secs. Elroy Sparks k.o'd Bill Nickerson, Yarmouth, Nova Scotia, May 24, 1958. Willard Dean k.o'd Claude Allen, Corpus Christi, Texas. May 12, 1940. Rudy Zymeck k.o'd Alex Luke, Newark, New Jersey, October 9, 1939. Joe Jakes k.o'd Al Foreman (negro), Brooklyn, January 13, 1942. Irish Jimmy Pierce k.o'd Tommy Jessup, Holyoke, Mass., March 9, 1942. Al Massey k.o'd Mike Cortez, Philadelphia, Nov. 9, 1967.

11½ secs. Al Foreman (London) k.o'd Ruby Levene, Montreal, April 25, 1928.

12 secs. Battling Nelson k.o'd William Rossler, Harvey, Illinois, April 5, 1902. Eddie Vann k.o'd George Stern, London November 15, 1949. Jack Petersen k.o'd Charlie Smith, Cardiff, January 29, 1934. J. L. Sullivan k.o'd William Fleming, Memphis, Tennessee, May 1, 1884.

14 secs. Dal Hawkins k.o'd Martin Flaherty, Carson City, Nevada, March 17, 1897. Packey O'Gatty k.o'd Shimakado, Yokohama, Japan, January 12, 1928. (O'Gatty boxer v. ju-jitsu wrestler).

15 secs. Augustin Argote (Bilbao) k.o'd Javier Lirio (Goipuzcoa), San Sebastian, Spain, February 2, 1952.

24 secs. Jack Dempsey k.o'd Carl Morris, New Orleans, December 16, 1918.

25 secs. Jack Petersen k.o'd Hein Muller, Cardiff, May 16, 1933.

26 secs. Jackie Paterson k.o'd Eric Jones, Glasgow, August 15, 1939. Joe Louis k.o'd Eddie Simms, Cleveland, December 14, 1936.

27 secs. Jack Dempsey k.o'd Fred Fulton, Harrison, New Jersey, July 27, 1918. Some records say 23 seconds.

35 secs. Georges Carpentier k.o'd Joe Beckett, London, October 1, 1923. Don Cockell k.o'd Lloyd Marshall, London, February 27, 1951.

40 secs. Dave Charnley k.o'd Darkie Hughes, Nottingham, November 20, 1961.

45 secs. Tommy McGovern k.o'd Billy Thompson, London, August 28, 1951.

47 secs. Mike DeJohn k.o'd Charley

Powell, Syracuse, November 6, 1959.

48 secs. Randolph Turpin k.o'd Luc Van Dam, London, February 27, 1951.

54 secs. Lee Savold k.o'd Gino Buonvino, New York, March 19, 1948.

59 secs. Gus Lesnevich k.o'd Melio Bettina, New York, May 23, 1947.

The record among bare-knuckle prize fighters in a championship contest may well have been set up by Peter Corcoran, of Ireland, who beat the reigning champion, Bill Darts, in less than a minute, May 10, 1771.

In America, Tom Dow is said to have delivered a knock-out punch in seven seconds against Ned Kelly, Leavenworth, Kansas, January 4, 1868. This could not be ranked as a world record, however, for at best, when comparing it with contests under Queensberry Rules it could only be rated as a 17-second knock-out if one included the count.

## LA BARBA, Fidel:

One of the intellectuals of the ring, La Barba was a well-educated man. In 1924 he won the Olympic flyweight championship and turned professional soon afterwards.

Following the death of Pancho Villa, the world flyweight champion, in July, 1925, there was some confusion as to the Filipino's rightful successor.

La Barba beat another leading claimant to the title, Frankie Genaro, on points over 10 rounds, in August, 1925, and he was recognised in America as champion of this division until his retirement in August, 1927.

After 12 months in Stanford University La Barba returned to the ring and continued to fight as a featherweight until 1933.

## LADBURY, Bill:

This hard-punching flyweight from Deptford, London, knocked out Sid Smith, the British and European flyweight champion, in a catch-weight match on June 2, 1913.

Smith relinquished these titles and in January, 1914, Ladbury was matched with Percy Jones at the N.S.C. for the British championship, but he was outpointed over 20 rounds.

Ladbury lost his life during World War I.

## LAGUNA, Ismael:

An exceptionally fast puncher from Panama who surprised Carlos Ortiz with his speed and captured the world lightweight title with a points decision over the Puerto Rican in April 1965.

Ortiz regained the title in a return bout

seven months later and again got the better of the Panamanian in a third meeting in 1967, but Laguna became the fifth man to regain this crown when he forced the new champion, Mando Ramos, to retire in nine rounds with cut eyes, March 1970.

It was Ken Buchanan who finally deprived Laguna of the title in September 1970, and after being defeated again by the clever Scot in a return bout Laguna retired.

## LAING, Kirkland:

Jamaican born Nottingham fighter who won the A.B.A. featherweight title in 1972 and began his professional career in 1975 as a light-middleweight before dropping back to welterweight.

A gifted stylist he has had two spells as British welterweight champion, first winning the title by beating Henry Rhiney inside 10 rounds in 1979; losing it almost exactly a year later to Colin Jones, but regaining it nearly six years later at the age of 32 when he was matched with Sylvester Mittee for the vacant crown and beat the former welterweight champion in five rounds.

Arguably Laing's greatest triumph was to earn a split decision over that boxing legend Roberto Duran in Detroit in September 1982. Admittedly Duran was then aged 31, but the Panamanian fighter subsequently won the W.B.A. junior middleweight title.

## LAING, Tony:

Young brother of Kirkland who turned professional in 1977 and had only 13 fights in the first seven years of his career, but that 13th fight saw him gain a split points decision over veteran Clinton McKenzie to capture the vacant British light-welterweight title. This decision was widely disputed, although it was Laing's second points victory over the former British champion.

A gifted fighter with a good style, Laing relinquished his British title to go after the European crown but he had difficulty in making the weight and Thomas "Tex" N'Kalankete proved too strong for him, winning the vacant title when Laing was stopped in the ninth round after two knockdowns. However, before the end of 1987 he had captured the vacant Commonwealth title by stopping Zambian David Chibuye in 11 rounds.

## LAKE, Harry:

Bugler Lake, of the Royal Marines, took the British bantamweight title from Tommy Harrison in a 20-round contest at the N.S.C. in February, 1923.

Five months later Lake won the European title by outpointing Charles Ledoux, but in November, 1923, he lost both these titles to Johnny Brown, of St. George's, and subsequently fought as a featherweight until 1933.

## LAMOTTA, Jake:

Known as "The Bronx Bull," Jake Lamotta started fighting professionally in 1941.

A tough, rugged fighter, Lamotta won the world middleweight title with a surprise victory over Marcel Cerdan in June, 1949.

The Frenchman suffered a shoulder injury in the first round and was no match for the squat Italian-American who gave one of his finest all-action displays and forced Cerdan to retire between the 9th and 10th rounds.

Lamotta successfully defended his crown against Tiberio Mitri and Laurent Dauthille, but in February, 1951, he was beaten by Ray Robinson.

In his contest with the Detroit negro Lamotta retired in the 13th round.

Lamotta had two successive defeats after this which prevented him from getting a return bout for the title, and he retired in 1954 after taking part in very few more bouts.

## LARMOUR, Davy:

Belfast bantamweight who had only 18 professional contests between 1977 and 1983 but won the British title with a shock points win over Hugh Russell in March 1983, which was five months after he had lost to the same fighter.

Larmour was nearly 31 years of age when he won the title and he lost it to John Feeney eight months later when referee Harry Gibbs intervened in the third round with the Irishman half-way through the ropes.

## LATZO, Pete:

When Latzo started fighting in 1919 he used the name of Young Clancy. Most of his earliest contests were "no decision" affairs but he won several inside the distance.

In May, 1926, he took the world welterweight title from Mickey Walker with a clear points victory over 10 rounds, but he lost it to Joe Dundee a little over 12 months later.

This Slav-America from Pennsylvania then moved up into the middleweight and light-heavyweight classes.

He beat ex-world middleweight champion Tiger Flowers, and both won and lost to Maxie Rosenbloom, who was then still working his way up to the world light-heavyweight crown.

In June, 1928, Latzo met the world light-heavyweight champion, Tommy Loughran, but was beaten on points. He got a return bout but was again defeated.

Latzo remained among the leading middleweights for several more years until he retired following a fourth round knock-out at the hands of Teddy Yarosz in June, 1934.

## LAVIGNE, George:

When Jack McAuliffe relinquished the world lightweight title in 1893 he nominated George Lavigne as his successor.

This two-handed fighter was unbeaten at that time, and he went on to establish his right to the world championship by stopping the British title-holder, Dick Burge, in 17 rounds at the N.S.C., June 1, 1896.

"The Saginaw Kid," as Lavigne was known lost his title when outpointed by Frank Erne over 20 rounds at Buffalo, July 3, 1899.

## LAW, The, and Boxing:

Fighting, of course, is illegal in this country, but boxing, if it is properly organised and controlled, is acceptable in law because it is considered to be an exhibition of skill rather than a fight.

By "properly organised and controlled" one could take it to mean any contest run under the auspices of the British Boxing Board of Control or the Amateur Boxing Association. The former has had its authority recognised in law* and as far as amateur boxing is concerned its legality has never been questioned, for it has always been assumed that amateurs when engaging in contests are giving nothing more than an exhibition. A professional, on the other hand, is thought to be more likely to be trying to subdue his opponent in his efforts to win a money prize. The fact that amateurs also box for prizes seems not to have been considered.

In the old prize ring days the sport survived not only because there were not enough police to subdue it but because it was supported by so many influential people. Indeed, the position was slightly ludicrous, for although the sport was banned by law and scorned upon by the church it was never surprising to see a few church dignitaries or Parliamentarians at the ringside.

In those days championship fights were held at places in the country where no one would dream of staging a contest today. But these lonely venues were chosen of necessity to avoid the Bow Street Runners. Despite this threat of prosecution and the distances to be covered in reaching the scene of the contest, many of these events were exceedingly well attended even by present-day standards.

Even when the law caught up with the offenders it is on record that many magistrates, who were probably fight fans themselves, treated the law-breakers leniently.

However, when a fighter died as a result of a contest it was a different matter, although even in this respect the law has given the accused the benefit of the doubt for there is no record of a prize fighter being given a heavy sentence following a charge of manslaughter.

Indeed, when George Stevenson died in a contest with Jack Broughton in 1741, the champion was not even arraigned on a charge of manslaughter. This was a case where the influence of a V.I.P. may have been used to override the law, for Broughton's backer was the Duke of Cumberland, third son of George II.

It is sometimes supposed that the advent of gloves and the Queensberry

Rules brought the sport into line with the law, but such is not the case.

There is no doubt that these innovations helped to influence the men who enforce the law to look upon the sport more favourably, but the essential difference to be proved in a court of law still remains the same—are the combatants engaged in a fight, which is a breach of the peace, or in a boxing match, which may be an exhibition of skill?

Even spectators of a boxing contest may not be certain of escaping the attention of the law. Lord Brampton once ruled that if two people fought to subdue each other they were committing a misdemeanour, and the spectators of that fight, as well as the promoters and officials taking part, or assisting, were aiding and abetting.

On the other hand, another English Judge, Lord Bramwell (1802-1892), considered that a sparring match with gloves, fairly conducted, was not unlawful, but that it might become unlawful if the men fought on till they were so weak that a dangerous fall or blow was likely to be the result.

In 1897 Walter Croot (Leytonstone) died after being knocked out by Jimmy Barry (Chicago, U.S.A.) in a contest for the bantamweight championship of the world at the N.S.C., London.

Barry was brought before Sir James Vaughan, who made the point that there is a "thin partition" between what may be termed a "fight" and a "contest." The magistrate decided that in this case the two men were engaged in a contest.

Probably the most important case in which the legality of boxing was under examination was that which followed the death of one Murray Livingstone in 1901. Boxing under the name of Billy Smith, he had died after falling and striking his head during a contest with Jack Roberts at the N.S.C., April 24, 1901.

Roberts, together with nine leading members of the club, were committed to the Old Bailey charged with "feloniously killing and slaying Livingstone."

The case came before Mr. Justice Grantham, and the leading counsel for the prosecution, Mr R. D. Muir, let it be known that the case was being brought in an effort to stop boxing competitions rather than to exact punishment upon the accused. So this was indeed a test case.

One of the defending counsel had this to say to the jury. "Because there is an inseparable risk in this noble English art of boxing, is it to be stopped? Is it to be stopped by the judicial interference of well-meaning busybodies, or by a set of alternative rules more applicable to children at a Dame's School than to British manhood holding world-wide Empire?"

This is how the learned Judge summed up for the jury.

"Now I cannot help saying that I am afraid, if my charges to juries were looked at, it would be found that I had on many occasions advised the people to use their fists instead of the what—instead of using the knife . . . It is much better for a man to use the weapon that God has given him, namely his fists, because it is not so dangerous, and that is why it is that a great number of people are fond of boxing. On the other hand, it is very desirable that proper boxing under proper rules should be kept up; all people should not be afraid of using their fists when necessary . . . Therefore the counsel for the prosecution are as right as the counsel for the defence are, to keep up the sport of England."

The jury's verdict in this case was one of accidental death. They found that it was a boxing contest and the defenders were "Not guilty."

Prize fighting was also illegal in the United States for many years and fights were held in out-of-the-way places. Indeed, several important fights took place on barges moored off-shore out of reach or beyond the jurisdiction of the law.

In 1889, after John L. Sullivan defeated Jake Kilrain over 75 rounds at Richburg, Mississippi, the contestants were charged with assault and battery. The American champion was sentenced to 12 months' imprisonment and Kilrain got two months. Sullivan was released on bail, obtained a re-trial, and ended up with a fine of $1,000.

In 1896 the Horton Law became effective in New York State and this allowed boxing although with the police having discretionary power to intervene. This was succeeded only four years later by the Lewis Law banning the sport except in properly constituted clubs for members only.

This situation lasted until 1911 when yet another new law, the Frawley Law, allowed bouts of up to 10 rounds each, but they were to be considered as merely exhibitions because no official decisions as to the winner were to be permitted.

This law was revoked in 1917, and boxing was illegal in New York State until an Englishman, W. A. Gavin, started a movement which resulted in the Walker Law coming into force in 1920.

This is the law which still holds good today, and it allows bouts of up to 15 rounds with a decision, all to be controlled by a boxing commission.

California was the first State of America to legalise boxing, although between 1914 and 1924 contests of more than four rounds' duration were not permitted in that State.

Today boxing in New York State and most other States of America is on a better legal footing than boxing in this country, where no law has yet been passed in favour of this sport.

Other countries where boxing is a legalised sport include New Zealand, Australia and Canada. These are mentioned in particular because they were among the first to pass such laws.

Among the more recent occasions when the law was exercised to prevent a boxing contest from taking place in this country was that in 1911.

In Birmingham Jim Driscoll and Owen Moran were due to meet in a British featherweight title fight, but the day before the contest they were brought into court and bound over to keep the peace.

In London the same year Mr. C. B. Cochran was hoping to promote a fight between the world champion, Jack Johnson, and our own champion, Bombardier Billy Wells. The fight was booked for Earl's Court, but the coloured man had whipped up such racial hatred since winning the title and feeling ran so high that the London

County Council stepped in and managed to secure an injunction which prevented the free-holders of the arena from holding this contest on their premises. *The B.B.B.C. won its case on an appeal when, in 1933, it was sued by Jack Doyle, the Irish heavyweight boxer. Doyle had had his purse withheld by the Board after being disqualified in the second round of a contest with Jack Petersen at the White City, July 12, 1933.

## LEAHY, Mick:

A naturalised British subject born in Eire, Mick Leahy won the British middleweight title in sensational fashion when he battered champion, George Aldridge, into defeat in only 1 minute 45 seconds of the 1st round at Nottingham in May, 1963. Referee, Ike Powell, stopped the fight to save Aldridge from further punishment.

An all-action fighter, the red-haired ex-Irishman failed in a bid to wrest the European crown from Lazlo Papp, losing on points in Vienna in October 1964, and two months later he lost his British title via a points decision to Wally Swift.

Mick Leahy gave up boxing in 1965 after losing the sight of one eye as the result of a car accident.

## LEDOUX, Charles:

This dynamic French fighter was almost as well known in this country, just before and after World War I, as he was in his own.

In 1912 he beat Joe Bowker in London and also came over to meet the British bantamweight champion, Digger Stanley. Ledoux was outpointed on that occasion.

Ledoux also made at least three visits to Cardiff, where he beat Bill Beynon twice, and knocked out Johnny Hughes.

There was also his memorable contest at the N.S.C. in 1916 when he marked finis to the career of the veteran Jim Driscoll by stopping him in 16 rounds.

In October, 1921, Ledoux was beaten by Tommy Harrison in a European bantamweight title fight at Hanley, but he took that title from the Hanley boxer in a return contest at Liverpool in April, 1922, and confirmed his superiority by stopping Harrison in a third meeting in

the English boy's home town in October, 1922. On that occasion, however, Harrison had considerably weakened himself in his efforts to make the weight.

Charles Ledoux lost his European bantamweight title in another contest on this side of the Channel when he was outpointed by Bugler Harry Lake.

An aggressive two-handed fighter noted for his power and skill inside, Ledoux claimed the world bantamweight crown following his seven-round knock-out of Digger Stanley at Dieppe in June, 1912, but when he went to America he was beaten by Eddie Campi in a 20-round contest at Vernon, June 24, 1913.

## LEE, James "Tancy":

The greatest triumph of this Scotsman from Leith, Edinburgh, was his victory over Jimmy Wilde for the British and European flyweight titles in January, 1915.

Tancy Lee made his mark in the professional ranks rather late in life, for he was well past 30 when he stopped Wilde in 17 rounds at the N.S.C. That was Wilde's first defeat in an important contest.

Lee was a clever little fighter with a right swing that felled a lot of his opponents, but he met his match in Joe Symonds, the Plymouth flyweight, who relieved him of his titles in October, 1915. The game Scot's seconds threw in the towel.

That wasn't the end of this Scot's championship career, however, for in November, 1917, at the N.S.C., he knocked out Charlie Hardcastle in four rounds to become British featherweight title-holder, and he went on to win the Lonsdale Belt outright in this division by defeating Joe Conn and Danny Morgan before relinquishing the title in 1919.

Lee was still fighting at the age of 44.

## LEGRA, Jose:

A self-exiled Cuban and former shoeshine boy who came to the fore after emigrating to Spain.

He won the vacant European featherweight title, forcing Yves Desmarets to retire in three rounds in Madrid in December 1967, and came to Britain the following July to capture the world crown by defeating Howard Winstone in five rounds at Porthcawl.

A dedicated, non-drinking, non-smoking fighter, Legra lost his world title in London in January 1969 when outpointed by Johnny Famechon. This was only his second defeat since leaving Cuba in 1963—the other had been by Howard Winstone in 1965.

After only three more defeats in another 25 fights Legra regained the world title when nearly 30 years of age by beating a 3lbs. overweight Clemente Sanchez in 10 rounds in December, 1972, but he lost it only 5 months later to another veteran, Eder Jofre.

## LEONARD, Benny:

A Jewish-American whose real name was Benjamin Leiner, this fighter is generally acknowledged as one of the greatest lightweights of all time.

Leonard sprang into prominence in 1916 when he met Freddie Welsh, the world lightweight champion, in New York. At that time only "no decision" bouts were allowed but Leonard was considered to have outpointed the Welshman in their 10-round contest.

When these two met again in May, 1917, Leonard really went for Welsh and the referee stopped the contest in the ninth round after the champion had been floored three times in quick succession. So Leonard became champion and he held on to this title until he retired undefeated in 1925.

During the eight years he was champion Leonard took all challengers in his stride. In July, 1917, he beat the world featherweight champion Johnny Kilbane, in three rounds. In June, 1922, he met Jack Britton for the world welterweight title, but in the 13th round, when he had Britton down, he struck him a light punch and was immediately disqualified. That was Leonard's only defeat in a spell of nearly 11 years up to the time of his retirement.

Leonard attempted a come-back in 1931, and although he was then past his 35th birthday his great skill and ringcraft took him through 19 contests without defeat. Then, in October, 1932, he met one of the leading challengers for the welterweight title, Jimmy McLarnin, and was knocked out in six rounds. Leonard never fought again after that. He died in April, 1947.

## LEONARD, Sugar Ray:

American from Wilmington, S. Carolina, who must be ranked among the finest ring tacticians of the post-war era if not over a far greater period. Apart from the fact that he won world titles at three weights—welter, light-middle and middle, he was beaten only once in 35 bouts from 1977 to 1987 and that by no less a star than Roberto Duran who outpointed Leonard in June 1980 to relieve him of the welterweight title he had won from Wilfredo Benitez in 1979. Leonard avenged that defeat only five months later to regain the title which he held until his initial retirement in 1982. He had won the light-middle crown in 1981 but relinquished it before the year was out.

Leonard's most remarkable achievement was to come back from a lay-off of nearly three years, and without even a warm-up fight (he had had only one fight in the previous five years), beat the much vaunted middleweight champion Marvellous Marvin Hagler in one of the richest fights on record—Las Vegas, April 1987. Leonard retired again immediately after this points win.

## LESNEVICH, Gus:

Russian-American light-heavyweight who is well remembered in Great Britain for his two great battles with Freddie Mills for the world title, and also for a gallant stand against our heavyweight champion, Bruce Woodcock.

A former Golden Gloves champion, Lesnevich gained American recognition as world light-heavyweight champion by outpointing Anton Christoforidis in May, 1941.

In Britain, Len Harvey was still considered to hold this world title, but in 1942 he was beaten by Freddie Mills.

To settle this disputed championship Lesnevich came over to meet Mills in London on May 14, 1946, and stopped the Englishman in 10 of the most gruelling rounds seen over here since the war.

A return fight was a "must" and this

took place on July 26, 1948, Mills winning on points after 15 rounds.

Between these two meetings with Mills, Lesnevich came over to meet Bruce Woodcock and was knocked out in the eighth round.

In August, 1949, Lesnevich made a bid for N.B.A.'s world heavyweight title but he was stopped inside the distance by Ezzard Charles. He did not fight again after this defeat.

## LEVINSKY, Battling:

A Jewish-American whose real name was Barney Lebrowitz, Levinsky won the world light-heavyweight title by defeating Jack Dillon at the second attempt in October, 1916.

One of the busiest fighters of his generation, Levinsky fought most of the toughest men around at that time. Billy Miske, Tommy Gibbons, Harry Greb, Bill Brennan and Jack Dempsey were some of his opponents. The up-and-coming Dempsey knocked Levinsky out.

In October, 1920, Levinsky lost his world title when he came up against that brilliant Frenchman, Georges Carpentier. The "Orchid Man" scored a knock-out in the fourth round.

Battling Levinsky's career lasted for nearly 20 years before he retired in 1929. He died in Philadelphia 20 years later.

## LEWIS, Harry:

An aggressive type of fighter, this Jewish-American was well known on this side of the Atlantic in the years immediately preceding World War I.

He was one of several top-line welter-weights who claimed the world title during that period when the championship of this division was hotly disputed following the eclipse of Joe Walcott in 1906 and the rise of Ted "Kid" Lewis in 1915.

Lewis established a strong claim to the title by defeating Honey Mellody in April, 1908. That Irish-American fighter had previously defeated Joe Walcott.

Lewis continued to claim the championship until he was beaten by Leo Houck in May, 1911.

Only Private Palmer and Johnny Mathieson were able to get decisions over Lewis in his many fights in England. He was particularly well-known at Wonderland, and there he was often seen to enter the ring smoking a cigar.

While in England he stopped the following men, all inside the distance: Young Joseph, Johnny Summers, Private Harris, Seaman Hull, Jimmy Horman, Dixie Kid, Johnny Mathieson, Jimmy Thompson and Jack Harrison. He also outpointed Harry Mansfield.

## LEWIS, John Henry:

A well-built, scientific boxer with a good right-hand punch, this American negro won the world light-heavyweight title from Bob Olin in one of the hardest fights ever seen in that division. The date was October 31, 1935, and Lewis got the decision at the end of 15 rounds.

Lewis was a busy champion, for he fought 57 times after winning the title until he was forced to relinquish it in 1939 when suffering from eye trouble.

At that time he was due to meet Len Harvey in a return bout, but the B.B.B.C. doctor would not let the negro fight. He had previously outpointed Harvey over 15 rounds in London in November, 1936.

After Lewis had won the title in 1935 the first man he defended it against was another Englishman, Jock McAvoy. Lewis won on points in New York.

In January, 1939, he challenged Joe Louis for the heavyweight title, the first time two coloured men had met for this crown, but he was beaten inside a round.

## LEWIS, Ted "Kid":

Born in London in October, 1894, Ted "Kid" Lewis developed into one of the all-time greats of British ring history. He is also remembered as one of the most successful British fighters ever to compete in America. Over there Lewis is considered to have made nearly £150,000, for he was a great favourite with the Americans because of his fighting heart and tear-away all-action style.

A Jewish boy whose real name was Gershon Mendeloff, Lewis started fighting when he was only 14, and before he had retired at the age of 35 in 1929 he had won three British titles, two Empire titles, three European titles, and a world championship.

In his early days at Wonderland, young Lewis was fighting more than once a week, and before he reached his 19th birthday, he had won the British featherweight title by stopping Alec Lambert in 17 rounds at the N.S.C.

Lewis also claimed the European championship of this division early in 1914, but he relinquished both titles soon afterwards as he put on weight.

In 1914 Lewis went to Australia, and from there on to the United States, where, inside 12 months, he established himself as the first undisputed world welterweight champion for about nine years.

Lewis really clinched the title by outpointing Jack Britton for the second time in September, 1915. He lost the championship to Britton in April, 1916, won it back in June, 1917, and finally lost it to the same fighter in March, 1919.

Lewis returned to America for another bout with Britton in February, 1921, but was outpointed over 15 rounds. That was the last of at least 20 meetings between these two fighters.

Back in this country this colourful fighter won the British Empire and European welterweight crown in June, 1920, and the British and European middleweight championships in 1921.

In June, 1922, he added the Empire middleweight title to his collection.

This celebrated fighter had so many thrilling victories that it would be difficult to name his greatest win, but among the men he beat were Mike Glover, Matt Wells, Frank Moody, Gus Platts, Johnny Basham, Jack Bloomfield, Boy McCormick, Ronald Todd, Johnny Brown, and, of course, Jack Britton.

## LISTON, Charles (Sonny):

A powerful Negro who was an enigma of the ring. When he became champion in September 1962, after knocking out Floyd Patterson in only 2 mins. 6 secs., he seemed invincible and was heralded as one of the all-time greats.

This view was strengthened by his second decisive win over Patterson in only 2 mins. 10 secs. But then came his disappointing display against Cassius Clay—a 7 to 1 underdog. In that February 1964 fight Liston failed to come up for the 7th round because of a torn shoulder tendon, and when they met again in May 1965 he was even more innocuous, being stopped in the first round.

A truly astonishing come-down for the fighter who had built up such a fine ring reputation with only one defeat in 36 bouts before meeting Clay, winning 25 inside the distance.

Liston died at home on December 30, 1970, although his body was not discovered until 6 days later.

## LIVERPOOL STADIUM:

Today boxing does not draw the packed houses it used to do in Liverpool but for many years this city was one of the strongest centres of the boxing game in this country, and the two Liverpool Stadiums, the old stadium in Pudsey Street and its successor were the scene of many of the finest contests this side of the Atlantic.

Boxing was started at the old Liverpool Stadium in 1911 by Mr. Arnold Wilson, who later became one of the country's leading promotors in London. In those early days the place was known as the Albert Hall and had been used as a skating rink.

There boxing flourished until the mid 1920's when interest in Liverpool appeared to lag. Liverpool Stadium was then under the direction of "Pa" Taylor, and when things became too bad he was forced to close down in 1928.

A year later there stepped upon the scene one of the leading fight promotors of all time. Mr. Johnny Best. He took over the Stadium and reopened it for boxing in 1929.

To begin with, Mr. Best had a tough time whipping up enthusiasm for his regular Thursday shows, but soon the crowds began rolling back.

In 1931, however, Mr. Best had to close again when the site was purchased for the erection of a new cinema, but enthusiasm for the sport was then running so high on Merseyside that Mr. Best formed a company and a new boxing stadium, the present, was built adjoining St. Paul's station. Lord

Lonsdale laid the foundation stone and it was opened in October, 1932.

Mr. Best did a fine job in keeping the sport alive with his regular weekly shows amid the air-raids of the hectic war years.

In 1956 Johnny Best passed away, and his son, Johnny Best Junior, carried on for a number of years, until failure to continue drawing big crowds forced him to give up these promotions.

Promotions continued at Liverpool Stadium until 1985 and it was finally closed two years later.

Because of the many surprise reversals which have befallen title-holders at the Liverpool Stadium it became known as the "Graveyard of Champions," but many champions have also made their reputations in the old and new stadiums. Men like Nel Tarleton Johnny Cuthbert, Peter Kane and Ernie Roderick were firm favourites there, and that greatest of all flyweights, Jimmy Wilde, fought several of his earliest contests at Liverpool, when he first ventured outside the Principality.

Several American stars have appeared at Liverpool Stadium, and two of them, the Dixie Kid and Harry Lewis, once met there in what was considered to have been a contest for the world welterweight title. Lewis won that fight with a knock-out in the eighth round. The date was January 18, 1912.

## LONDON, Brian:

Born West Hartlepool in 1934, Brian is son of the former British heavyweight champion, Jack London.

Boxing under his real name, Brian Harper, he won the A.B.A. heavyweight title in 1954 before turning to the professional ranks in the following year.

He took the British and Empire heavyweight titles from Joe Erskine with an eighth round knock-out in June, 1958, but he was outpointed by Henry Cooper in his first defence of these titles in January, 1959.

Despite this defeat, London got a world title fight with Floyd Patterson on May 1, 1959, but he proved no real match for the champion.

London's finest display up to that time was his victory over the highly rated American, Willie Pastrano, whom he stopped in five rounds in September, 1958. The American had previously outpointed London in a 10-round contest.

He subsequently failed in two attempts to gain the European title, being k.o'd by Dick Richardson and outpointed by Henry Cooper. The latter bout, which was also for the British title, was London's third defeat by Cooper.

London got a second crack at the world title in 1966 but was k.o'd inside 3 rounds by Muhammad Ali.

## LONDON, Jack:

This bulky West Hartlepool heavyweight, started fighting in 1931, and was on the fringe of the top class for several years. Defeats by Gipsy Daniels, Ben Foord and Larry Gains prevented him from getting a title fight but he eventually came to the top during the war when he notched two victories over an ageing Larry Gains and then beat Tom Reddington and Tommy Martin in an Empire heavyweight eliminator.

Jack London lost to Freddie Mills in December, 1941, but he beat the Bournemouth fighter on points when they met for the vacant British and Empire heavyweight titles in September, 1944.

London was then 31, and when he made his first defence of these titles, against Bruce Woodcock in July, 1945, he was knocked out in the sixth round.

## LONG FIGHTS:

The longest contest on record was one in which gloves were worn. It was fought at the Olympic Club, New Orleans, April 6-7, 1893, between Andy Bowen and Jack Burke. After 110 rounds lasting 7 hours 19 minutes it was declared "no contest."

Here are some of the longest bouts on record:—

(G—gloves, K—knuckles).

6 hrs. 40 mins. Dan Needham v. Patsy Kerrigan, San Francisco, Feb. 27, 1890. G.

6 hrs. 15 mins. James Kelly v. Jonathan Smith, Dalesford, Victoria, Australia, Dec. 3, 1855. K.

6 hrs. 3 mins. Mike Madden v. Bill

Hayes, Edenbridge, Kent, July 17, 1849. K.

5 hrs. 45 mins. Mike Madden v. Jack Grant, Woking, Surrey, Dec. 12, 1848. K.

5 hrs. 8 mins. Harry Sharpe v. Frank Crosby, Nameski, Illinois, Feb. 2, 1892. G.

5 hrs. 3 mins. William Sheriff v. Jack Welsh, Philadelphia, Apl. 4, 1884. K.

4 hrs. 30 mins. Jack Jones v. Patsy Tunney, Cheshire, 1825. K.

4 hrs. 20 mins. Jack Fitzpatrick v. James O'Neil, Berwick, Maine, Dec. 4, 1860. K.

3 hrs. 49 mins. Michael Donovan v. W. C. McClellan, San Francisco, Aug. 18, 1879, K.

3 hrs. 40 mins. Jem Mace v. Joe Coburn, St. Louis, Nov. 30, 1871. K.

3 hrs. 30 mins. Benjamin Brain v. Wm. Hooper, Newbury, Berks., Aug. 30, 1790. K.

3 hrs. 20 mins. Ned Price v. Joe Coburn, Stoneham, Mass., May 1, 1856. K.

3 hrs. 16 mins. ‡James "Deaf" Burke v. Simon Byrne, St. Albans, Herts., May 30, 1833. K.

3 hrs. 12 mins. †Joe Jeanette v. Sammy McVey, Paris, Apl. 17, 1909. G.

3 hrs. 10 mins. J. L. Sullivan v. Charlie Mitchell, Chantilly, France, Mar. 10, 1888. K.

3 hrs. 8 mins. Tom Sayers v. Harry Poulson, Appledore, Kent, Jan. 29, 1856. K.

3 hrs. 2 mins. Aaron James v. Tom Sayers, Canvey Island, June 26, 1857. K.

3 hrs. James "Deaf" Burke v. Bill Fitzmaurice, Harpenden Common, Herts., June 9, 1829. K.

The longest world title fight this century was when lightweight champion Battling Nelson was stopped in the 40th round by Ad Wolgast, Port Richmond, Feb. 22, 1910. This contest was scheduled for 45 rounds.

†Longest contest this century.

‡Longest championship fight ever.

## LONGEST CAREER:

Bobby Dobbs, an American negro born in slavery in Knoxville, Tennessee, is believed to have started fighting when he was 17. That being true, then his career extended over a period of 39 years, for he had his last contest in 1914 when he was in his 56th year.

Among world champions the longest boxing career was that of Bob Fitzsimmons. He had his earliest fights in Timaru, New Zealand, in 1880, and his last in Sydney, New South Wales, in December, 1909. However, if one includes an exhibition bout with K.O. Sweeney at Williamsport, Pennsylvania, in January, 1914, then his career lasted 34 years.

Among post-war fighters the record belongs to the Mexican, Kid Azteca, who had his first fight at the age of 14 and whose career extended over 32 years until 1961.

Kenny Lane, born Michigan, April 9, 1932, began fighting professionally in 1953 and did not have his last contest until over 32 years later in November 1985. Lane, however, only fought four times after 1965.

Among the old-time prize fighters the record was set up by Jem Mace. His career lasted nearly 35 years, October, 1855, to February, 1890. Like Fitzsimmons, Mace also took part in an exhibition bout several years later. This was in 1895 when he boxed with Dick Burge at the N.S.C.

## LORD LONSDALE BELTS:

The first of these belts was presented to the National Sporting Club by the 5th Earl of Lonsdale in 1909. It was awarded to Freddie Welsh when he took the British lightweight title from Johnny Summers at the club in November that year.

Since then, with the exception of the war years, it has been the practice to award one of these belts to the winners of all British title fights in each weight division. The recipient holds the belt for as long as he is champion and if he wins three title fights in the same division the belt becomes his property.

By issuing these belts the N.S.C. strengthened their control over the game in this country. They wanted to make sure that all championship contests were

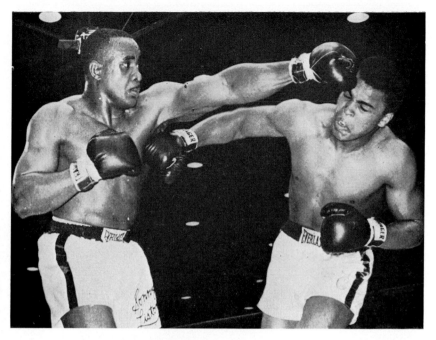

Cassius Clay (Muhammad Ali), 7–1 underdog, taking the world title from Sonny Liston, Miami, February 1964

With a knock-out left-right to Foreman's head, Muhammad Ali regains world title, Kinshasa, October 1974

Bruce Woodcock suffers in an unsatisfactory ending to world heavyweight title eliminator with Lee Savold in December 1949, but Savold is disqualified for a low blow

British middleweight champion Terry Downes, outpointing the fabulous black fighter, Sugar Ray Robinson, in 1962. At that time Robinson was aged 41 and Downes 26

John Conteh (*left*) captures WBC version of light-heavyweight title with victory over Jorge Ahumada, October 1974

fought at the club and only men who held a Lonsdale Belt would be considered as champions.

A total of 22 Lonsdale Belts were issued by the N.S.C. and of these 20 were won outright.

The winners of the original belts were as follows:—

Flyweight—Sid Smith, 1911.
Bantamweight—Digger Stanley, 1910.
Featherweight—Jim Driscoll, 1910.
Lightweight—Freddie Welsh, 1909.
Welterweight—Young Joseph, 1910.
Middleweight—Tom Thomas, 1909.
Light-heavyweight—Dick Smith, 1914.
Heavyweight—Billy Wells, 1911.

All except the flyweight, welterweight and middleweight belts were won outright by the original holders. The remaining three belts were subsequently taken out of circulation by Jimmy Wilde (flyweight), Johnny Basham (welterweight), Pat O'Keefe (middleweight).

When the N.S.C. became defunct the British Boxing Board of Control carried on the tradition of awarding Lonsdale Belts. The original holders of B.B.B.C. belts were:—

Flyweight—Benny Lynch, 1936.
Bantamweight—Johnny King, 1937.
Featherweight—Johnny McGrory, 1936.
Lightweight—Jimmy Walsh, 1936.
Welterweight—Jake Kilrain, 1938.
Middleweight—Jock McAvoy, 1937.
Light-heavyweight—Jock McAvoy, 1937.
Heavyweight—Tommy Farr, 1937.

One of the bantamweight Lonsdale Belts was presented to Joe Louis after he had defeated Tommy Farr in 1937.

Henry Cooper is the only man ever to win three Lonsdale belts outright.

In addition to Cooper five men have so far won two Lonsdale Belts outright. They are Nel Tarleton (featherweight), Ronnie Clayton (featherweight), Peter Keenan (bantamweight), Howard Winstone (featherweight), Brian Curvis (welterweight), and Clinton McKenzie (light-welterweight).

In 1978 the B.B.B.C. decided that they would no longer award any fighter more than one belt in the same weight division.

The shortest time taken for any fighter to win a Lonsdale Belt outright is 203 days by Robert Dickie (featherweight) in 1986.

## LOUGHRAN, Tommy:

Tommy Loughran started fighting professionally soon after World War I. It soon become evident that he was something of a genius in the ring, and he gave many dazzling displays which quickly earned him a big reputation beyond his native Philadelphia.

In those early days Loughran was a middleweight but he eventually moved up into the light-heavyweight division, and in January, 1923, he met that tough fighter, Harry Greb, for the American cruiserweight title.

Here was contrast in style, Greb the rough-and-tumble fighter, Loughran a first-class boxer with a great left hand. The fighter won on this occasion, and indeed, Greb was something of a stumbling block in Loughran's early career. They met six times in all, two were "no decision" bouts, one was drawn, Greb won two and Loughran one.

Because he was such a difficult man to hit, Tommy Loughran became known as the "Phantom of Philly," but his skilful boxing was not appreciated by a lot of the customers and it was some time before he was able to get himself a championship contest.

Then, in 1927, after Delaney had relinquished the light-heavyweight title, Loughran won it by outpointing Mike McTigue at Madison Square Garden.

At this time the N.B.A. recognised Jim Slattery as champion, but Loughran cleared up this dispute by defeating Slattery in December, 1927.

After more than three years without a defeat Loughran relinquished his title in 1929 to go after the heavyweight crown. There is no doubt that this Irish-American was clever enough to have become world heavyweight champion but unfortunately he didn't carry enough weight nor did he have a really hard punch.

Loughran's title hopes were dashed by Jack Sharkey, who stopped him in 27 seconds of the third round, but he still remained in the top bracket and beat such men as King Levinsky, Max Baer, Ernie Schaaf, Johnny Risko and Paolino Uzcudun, and in 1933 he worked his way into line for another crack at the heavyweight title by outpointing Jack Sharkey.

He got his title fight on March 1, 1934, against Primo Carnera. Loughran conceded the champion 86lbs. but went the distance before losing on points.

After that Loughran was beaten by Walter Neusel, Johnny Risko, and, when well past his best, he came to England, beat Maurice Strickland and Jack London, but lost to Tommy Farr and Ben Foord.

## LOUIS, Joe:

Born Lexington, Alabama, in May, 1914, this negro's real name was Joseph Barrow.

He was a Golden Gloves champion in the light-heavyweight division in 1934 and turned professional in July of the same year.

In no time at all his fame had spread throughout the United States. His style was deceptive, for he looked slow as he shuffled around the ring, but he punched with such terrific speed and power that he was undefeated in his first 27 fights and won all but four of them inside the distance. A future world champion was on the way.

But then, in his 28th fight, something went wrong. This is still one of the most talked about contests in Louis's illustrious career. It was on June 19, 1936, that he met the former world champion, Max Schmeling, and was surprisingly knocked out in the 12th round. Schmeling had apparently found a flaw in the coloured man's armour.

Still, Louis more than made amends for that defeat, for no one will ever forget what he did to the German in their return fight on June 22, 1938. Schmeling must have thought that all hell had been let loose upon him in that ring and he was knocked out in only 2 minutes 4 seconds.

Between those two meetings with Schmeling, Louis had won the world title by stopping James J. Braddock in eight rounds, June 22, 1937, and he was to become the busiest heavyweight champion of all time.

From the day he won the title until he first announced his retirement in March, 1949, Joe Louis defended his crown 25 times.

During that time only three men went the distance with him, Tommy Farr, Arturo Godoy and Jersey Joe Walcott. Louis never had a return fight with Farr but he subsequently stopped Godoy in eight rounds and Walcott in 11 rounds.

After Louis had announced his retirement, Ezzard Charles was recognised as champion by the N.B.A. Louis continued to give exhibition bouts until September, 1950, when he was persuaded to meet Charles for the title. The man that Charles outpointed on that occasion was but a shadow of the real Louis.

Still Louis began to recover some of his old form and he was still good enough to beat Lee Savold, the man the B.B.B.C. had agreed to nominate as world champion after his victory over Bruce Woodcock. Louis stopped him in six rounds.

Louis looked like getting a chance to win back the world title but in October, 1951, his career was brought to an end with an eighth round knockout by Rocky Marciano.

During that career, Louis had knocked out five world heavyweight champions. They were Max Schmeling, Jack Sharkey, Primo Carnera, Max Baer and Jimmy Braddock. He also knocked out Jersey Joe Walcott before that negro won the title.

## LUCY, Joe:

Born Mile End, London, this clever southpaw won the vacant British lightweight title by outpointing a former champion, Tommy McGovern, at Earl's Court in September, 1953.

He lost the championship to Frank Johnson in April, 1955, but regained it in a return bout twelve months later. Then, after defending it successfully against Sammy McCarthy, he was beaten by another southpaw, Dave Charnley, at Harringay, April, 1957.

## LYNCH, Benny:

Who had the most devastating punch,

Jimmy Wilde or Benny Lynch? That question has started many arguments. It is safe to say that whether you favour the Welshman or the Scot there is very little to choose between them, and there have certainly been no harder punching flyweights.

The story of Benny Lynch is a tragic one. No fighter ever had a better sense of balance than this little Scot, and therein lay the secret of his punching power. But, when he was at the height of his fame, he took to drink and he fell from grace as quickly as he had risen. Only eight years after he relinquished the world title he died poor and heart-broken at the age of 33.

Benny Lynch started fighting in 1931. Three years later he won the Scottish flyweight title, and in September, 1935, he took the world title from Jackie Brown in sensational fashion at Belle Vue, Manchester. Brown never had a chance against the all-out onslaughts of the little Scot, and after he had been floored 10 times before the end of the second round the referee intervened.

At that time the Americans favoured Small Montana as world champion, so to settle this dispute the Filipino came to London in January, 1937. Lynch was still at his peak and he was the undoubted points winner after 15 rounds.

There was still no signs of his decline when he met Peter Kane in October, 1937, although it was rumoured that the Scot was not paying as much attention to his training as he should have done. Nevertheless, this fight was one of the most thrilling ever seen in the flyweight division and Lynch scored a knock-out in the 13th round.

In June, 1938, Lynch was matched to defend his title against the American, Jackie Jurich, but the Scot weighed in 6½lbs. over the limit. He knocked out the Californian in the 12th round but he forfeited his world title.

The end of Lynch's career came in October, 1938, when, sadly out of training and in very poor condition, he was knocked out in three rounds by the Roumanian, Aurel Toma.

## LYNCH, Joe:

Known as the "Californian Peach," this Irish-American who had the advantage of height and reach also had a winning right hook.

In December, 1920, he took the world bantamweight title from Pete Herman at Madison Square Garden. In July, 1921, he lost his crown in a return bout with Herman but he regained it from Johnny Buff 12 months later.

Although N.Y.A.C. deprived Lynch of his title in October, 1923, he was generally recognised as champion until March, 1924, when he was outpointed by Abe Goldstein.

Joe Lynch had three fights in London, 1918-19. He was knocked out in three rounds by Jimmy Wilde, then outpointed Tommy Noble before losing a points decision in a return with Wilde.

## LYONS, Tom:

One of the lesser known champions of the old prize ring, Lyons the Waterman took the title from Bill Darts at Kingston, Surrey, June 27, 1769. Lyons won in 45 minutes.

There is no record of him ever having fought again after this.

## MACE, Jem:

Jem Mace was the last genius of the old school of prize fighting but he was also the father of modern scientific boxing. He lived long enough to see the transition from bare knuckles to gloves and his expert knowledge of the noble art was passed on through his star pupil, Larry Foley, to such famous gloved fighters as Bob Fitzsimmons, Peter Jackson, Young Griffo, and Jem Hall.

Mace came from Norwich. He was known as "The Swaffham Gipsy" and although there is some dispute as to whether or not he was a Romany, there is no doubt that he was one of the cleverest boxers who stepped into the roped square.

When he was 64 he was still fit and nimble enough to give an exhibition of boxing which held the connoisseurs of the National Sporting Club entranced. That was in 1895 when he sparred with the British lightweight champion, Dick Burge.

For the greater part of his career Mace was little more than a welterweight but he was a powerful hitter with either hand and he showed no respect for heavier opponents.

Mace first won the championship by beating Sam Hurst in June, 1861. He lost his title to Tom King in November, 1862, but he become champion again in 1866 when he stopped Joe Goss in 21 rounds.

In May, 1870, he crossed the Atlantic and beat the American champion, Tom Allen, in a world title fight at Kennerville, Louisiana.

Mace was then nearing his 40th birthday and after fighting a draw with Joe Coburn at St. Louis, he decided to retire and devote his time to teaching others the noble art.

## MADISON SQUARE GARDEN:

The present Madison Square Garden is the third sports arena of this name. It stands on Seventh Avenue, New York City, between 31st and 32nd Street, and staged its first boxing show in March 1968. Like its predecessor it is designed to stage shows of all kinds, not only boxing.

It was the old sports arena on Eighth Avenue which established the name Madison Square Garden in boxing history. This was built by that enterprising promoter, Tex Rickard, who was backed by circus owner John Ringling and a group of Wall Street financiers.

When it opened in November, 1925, the first event was not boxing but a six-day bicycle race, but there is no doubt that Rickard really built it for boxing and the first big fight was staged there on December 11, 1925.

This was a world light-heavyweight title contest between Paul Berlenbach and Jack Delaney. Over 17,000 people saw Berlenbach retain his title on points over 15 rounds.

After that many world title contests were fought in this arena promoted by the biggest names in the business. Tex Rickard was succeeded by William F. Carey in 1930, and then came James J. Johnston. In 1937 Mike Jacobs, who had worked with Rickard when the plans for the building were originally tied up, took over and reigned until 1949, when the Garden came under the control of James D. Norris, Truman Gibson took over in 1958 and was succeeded in 1960 by Harry Markson.

The original Madison Square Garden on Madison Avenue staged its first prize fight back in 1882 when the Leicestershire middleweight, Joe Collins, better known as Tug Wilson won $1,000 by lasting a stipulated distance of four rounds with John L. Sullivan.

That arena was rebuilt in 1890 and it was not until May 5, 1925, that the last fight took place in the old Garden, Syd Terris beating Johnny Dundee over 12 rounds.

## MAGRI, Charlie:

An exciting fighter who put life back into the flyweight division when he won the British title in only his third professional bout. This was in December 1977, when he showed typical non-stop aggression against Dave Smith who was on the canvas five times before the referee intervened.

Before turning professional Magri had enjoyed a brilliant amateur career, winning the A.B.A. light-fly title in 1974 and the flyweight title in 1975-76-77.

A two-handed puncher who did not care much for defence he was soon out on his own, winning his first 23 professional fights, including capturing the European title, before being surprisingly stopped by low-ranked Mexican, Juan Diaz in six rounds in October 1981. Despite this and another defeat by Jose Torres in May 1982, a defeat he subsequently avenged, Magri, who was born in Tunisia, went on to become world flyweight champion by typical non-stop aggression which overwhelmed Eleoncio Mercedes at Wembley in March 1983, with the referee calling a halt in the seventh round. Alas, the popular Hackney fighter lost his crown to a comparatively unknown Filipino, Frank Cedeno, in his first defence, being stopped in the sixth round after giving it all he had.

Despite this set-back Magri subsequently regained the European title he had relinquished, his fight with Franco Cherchi being stopped in Magri's favour after a clash of heads had left Cherchi with a badly cut eyebrow, but lost this crown when beaten by the British champion, Duke McKenzie, in five rounds in May 1986 with manager Terry Lawless throwing in the towel as Magri was rising from a count of nine.

## MAGUIRE, Paddy:

Big-hearted Irishman who won the British bantamweight title at the third attempt in a tremendous battle with Dave Needham at the World Sporting Club in October 1975. The referee was forced to call a halt in the fourteenth round with Needham bleeding from a cut over his right eye. Many thought that Needham just had the edge at this stage of a really exciting contest.

Maguire subsequently made two attempts to lift the European title, forcing a draw with Daniel Trioulaire and having to retire with a bad cut in the eighth against Franco Zurlo. In his last contest before announcing his retirement in November 1977 Maguire lost his British crown when the referee stopped his defence against Johnny Owen because the Brixton Irishman was cut.

## MANAGERS:

A boxer's career is just as dependent upon the adroitness of his manager as it is upon his own skill in the ring. An astute manager can take even an average boxer a long way towards the top, while a bad manager could halt the progress of the best boxer in the world.

The most obvious side of a manager's job is the financial one, for it is up to him to get the best terms he can for his fighter. But probably the most important part of a manager's task is to select the right type of opposition. This is particularly so in the case of a boxer just starting on his way up the fistic ladder.

In the early days, fighters had patrons rather than managers and it was not until the end of the 19th century that it became the fashion for the leading pugilists to have their own managers.

Among the first fighters to have a manager was Jem Smith, a Londoner who claimed the British heavyweight title in 1885. The man who took charge of his affairs in about 1887 was John Fleming, later to become matchmaker at the old N.S.C.

Since Mr. Fleming adopted the management of a prize fighter as a profession, there have been many outstanding managers far too numerous to mention here.

However, while it may be dangerous to give the names of so few and risk the omission of the reader's particular star manager, here are a few men who can truly be said to be representative of the best in their profession:—

Barrett, Mike: Manager of Ray Gilbody.

Berlinger, Victor: Manager of British champions Harry Mizler and Dave McCleave.

Black, Julian: Who, with John

Roxborough, managed Joe Louis.

Broadribb, Ted: As a fighter he was the only Englishman ever to stop Georges Carpentier. In those days Broadribb fought under the name of Young Snowball. Outstanding among the men he managed were Tommy Farr, Nel Tarleton, Jack Hood, Harry and Dick Corbett.

Brady, William A.: The only man to manage two world heavyweight champions—James J. Corbett and James J. Jeffries.

Caplan, Hymie: Managed five world champions, Ben Jeby, Al Singer, Lou Salica, Solly Krieger and Lew Jenkins.

Descamps, Francois: The excitable Frenchman who discovered the great Georges Carpentier and guided him to a world title.

Duff, Mickey: Manager of Lloyd Honeyghan, Cornelius Boza-Edwards and Kirkland Laing.

Engel, George: Managed two world middleweight champions, Frank Klaus and Harry Greb.

Gibson, Billy: Managed three world champions, Benny Leonard, Gene Tunney and Kid Kaplan.

Hernandez, Arturo "Cuyo": Managed five world champions—Manuel Ortez, Ruben Olivares, Juan Zurita, Carlos Zarate and Alfonso Zamora.

Johnston, Jimmy: Managed Mike McTigue, Ted "Kid" Lewis, Pete Latzo, Johnny Dundee and Bob Pastor. Died in 1946.

Jacobs, Joe: In partnership with Bill McCarney he managed world champions Max Schmeling, Frankie Genaro, Jack Delaney and Andre Routis. One of the most astute managers of all time it was Joe Jacobs who made famous the saying "We wuz robbed." The way in which he steered the beer drinking heavyweight Tony Galento, into a world title fight with Joe Louis is a lesson in boxing management.

Kearns, Jack "Doc": Manager of world champions Jack Dempsey, Mickey Walker, Joey Maxim, Abe Attell, Benny Leonard, Archie Moore.

Lawless, Terry: Manager of John H. Stracey, Maurice Hope, Charlie Magri and Frank Bruno.

Lewis, Nate: Managed Packey McFarland, Charley White, Abe Attell, and Leo Rodak, and was matchmaker at the Chicago Stadium.

Rose, Charles: Journalist and manager who once guided the fistic affairs of such men as Len Harvey, Frank Goddard, George Cook and Phil Scott.

O'Rourke, Thomas: Famous in America around the turn of the century. He managed world champions Joe Walcott and George Dixon.

Sullivan, Dan: Matchmaker at the Blackfriars Ring for many years. Managed Len Harvey, Jack Doyle, Johnny Curley, Mike Honeyman and Gipsy Daniels.

Thomas, Eddie: Former British and European welterweight champion who steered Howard Winstone and Ken Buchanan to world titles.

Weill, Al: Managed world champions Rocky Marciano, Marty Servo, Joey Archibald and Lou Ambers.

## MARCIANO, Rocky:

An Italian-American whose real name was Rocco Marchegiano, he fought as an amateur in New England while working in a shoe factory and turned professional in 1947.

Al Weill eventually took him under his management and steered him to the world heavyweight title.

Marciano always trained hard and successfully defended his title six times. In his first 42 contests, this tough fighter who had a rather crude style but carried a k.o. punch in either fist, was not even knocked off his feet.

Marciano won all 42 of those fights and in all but five of them he finished his opponent inside the distance.

His next bout was a world title contest with Jersey Joe Walcott. The veteran negro succeeded in putting Marciano down for a count of "three" in the first round and built up a good lead in the earlier stages, but then Marciano came from behind and won with a remarkable right-hand punch which finished Walcott in the 13th round.

Marciano successfully defended his title six times before he announced his retirement in 1956. During his professional career he had fought 49 times without defeat and had knocked out three world champions, Joe Louis, Joe Walcott and Ezzard Charles.

He was killed in an air crash in August 1969, the day before his 46th birthday.

## MARINO, Salvador Dado:

Born Honolulu, Dado Marino first fought outside of his native islands in 1947 when he came to England to meet Jackie Paterson for the world flyweight title.

Paterson was unable to make the weight, however, and the fight was postponed, the Scot being deprived of his title.

Marino fought Rinty Monaghan instead and won on a foul in nine rounds at Glasgow, but a month later he was outpointed by Peter Kane at Manchester.

In October, 1947, Marino returned to this country to meet Rinty Monaghan in a contest which was recognised by the N.B.A. and Eire as being for the world flyweight title. Monaghan got the referee's decision at the end of 15 rounds.

Marino eventually won the title from Terry Allen at Honolulu in August, 1950, but after losing to Yoshio Shirai in a non-title bout, the Jap deprived him of his crown with a points victory in Tokyo in May, 1952.

## MARINO, Tony:

An American bantamweight who had only a short career. Marino started fighting professionally in 1931, but in February, 1937, he died tragically of a brain haemorrhage following a contest at Brooklyn. He was then only 24 years of age. Marino claimed the world bantamweight championship in 1936 after he had stopped Baltazar Sangchilli, but the Spaniard had not been very widely recognised as title-holder. In any event Marino's reign did not last long for he was beaten in his very next fight by the N.B.A. champion, Sixto Escobar.

## MARRIOTT, Bob:

This Bermondsey, London, lightweight, won the A.B.A. title in 1912 and again in 1914.

He turned professional in 1915 and won the vacant British lightweight championship in a match with Johnny Summers at the N.S.C. two years later.

Summers was disqualified in the tenth round for persistent holding.

He also claimed the European title after beating Raymond Vittet on a third round disqualification in 1919.

Marriott, however, was really an amateur at heart. Apparently he had no real interest in making boxing his career and soon after losing his European title to Georges Papin in 1920, he relinquished his British crown and retired.

## MARSH, Terry:

An intelligent fighter whose boxing career ended in dramatic fashion. He won the A.B.A. welterweight title in 1980 and 1981 before turning professional and winning the British light-welter crown from Clinton McKenzie in 1984. Marsh gave a dazzling display of boxing on the retreat as well as guts and determination to outpoint the more experienced champion.

Although not noted for his punching power the likeable Marsh won the vacant European light-welter title officially by a sixth round k.o. of Alessandro Scapecchi, although the Italian had regained his feet and turned his back on Marsh. In any event the loser had had enough.

Marsh was shockingly deprived of his European crown but went on to snatch the IBF version of the world light-welter title from their champion Joe Louis Manley with an all-action display in front of his home-town crowd in March 1987. The referee had to rescue the battered American in the 10th round. Six months later, shortly after signing for a second defence of his title, Marsh announced his retirement when an epileptic condition was diagnosed.

## MARTIN, Eddie:

Known as "Cannonball" Martin, this Italian-American from Brooklyn won the world bantamweight title from Abe Goldstein in December, 1924.

His reign lasted only three months for in his first defence of the title he was outpointed by Charlie Rosenburg in New York.

Martin had comparatively few contests after this although he did not retire until 1932.

## MASON, Harry:

Harry Mason was winning boys' competitions in Leeds when he weighed under six stone. He eventually won the British lightweight title and the welterweight title, each on two separate occasions, but he was never quite able to make a Lonsdale Belt his own property.

He first won the British and European lightweight title on a disqualification from Seaman Hall at Olympia in May, 1923, but after that he went to America to try and get a contest with Benny Leonard and while he was away he was deprived of his titles.

Mason did not succeed in gaining a world title fight although he won six out of seven contests on the other side of the Atlantic.

Ernie Izzard was declared British lightweight champion following a victory over Jack Kirk, but when Mason returned from the States he regained the British championship by stopping Izzard in eight rounds at the Holland Park Rink. Izzard actually failed to come up for the ninth round.

Mason now moved up into the welterweight division and in November, 1925, he took the British title at that weight from Hamilton Johnny Brown. He then relinquished his lightweight crown and later lost his welterweight title to Jack Hood.

After Hood relinquished the welterweight championship in 1933, Mason regained it with a victory over Len "Tiger" Smith in June, 1934. But before the year was out he had been beaten by Pat Butler over 15 rounds at Leicester, a decision which was hotly disputed at the time.

## MATTHEWS, William R.:

Matty Matthews first fought for the world welterweight crown in 1898, but was beaten by Mysterious Billy Smith.

In October, 1900, he took the championship from Rube Ferns but lost it in a return bout when he was knocked out in ten rounds.

Matthews was a clever boxer but Rube Ferns was his biggest stumbling block. They met at least five times and the "Kansas Rube" got the better of Matthews on three occasions.

Matthews twice beat the former world welterweight champion, Tommy Ryan. He retired in 1905.

## MAXIM, Joey:

A Golden Gloves champion before he turned professional, this Italian-American won the vacant American light-heavyweight title by outpointing Gus Lesnevich in May, 1949.

In January, 1950, he came to London and relieved Freddie Mills of the world crown, knocking him out in the tenth round.

Immediately after this victory Maxim went after the heavyweight championship. He got a match with Ezzard Charles in May, 1951, but was beaten on points.

In June, 1952, he stopped Ray Robinson in 14 rounds in defence of his light-heavyweight title, but he lost this to Archie Moore on points in December, 1952.

Joey Maxim, whose real name is Berardinelli, was the only man to beat Floyd Patterson in a professional bout before the negro became world champion.

Maxim outpointed Patterson in June 1954, over eight rounds, but after that he dropped out of favour with defeats by Bobo Olson, Willie Pastrano, and Eddie Machen.

## McALINDEN, Danny:

The first Irishman to win the British heavyweight title, this colourful fighter achieved that distinction in June, 1972, when he battered Jack Bodell before flattening him with a right to the jaw in the second round.

A real crowd pleaser, McAlinden had more than his share of problems with injuries and postponed fights, and like so many in the heavyweight division who are prepared to take punches while landing his own, he suffered some surprising defeats. He lost his British and Commonwealth titles to Bunny Johnson in 1975 and failed to regain them later that year when knocked out inside two rounds by Johnson's successor, Richard Dunn.

## McATEER, Les:

A nephew of former middleweight

champion Pat McAteer, Les won the British and Empire titles at that weight when he beat Wally Swift in a hard battle at Nottingham in July 1969. Swift retired with a cut eye after eleven rounds.

This good-looking Birkenhead boxer with an upright style failed in a bid for the European title in April 1970 being outpointed by Tom Bogs.

He lost his British and Empire titles the following month when beaten in 14 rounds by Mark Rowe.

## McATEER, Pat:

This Birkenhead middleweight won a Lonsdale Belt outright. He took the British and Empire titles from Johnny Sullivan in June, 1955, at Liverpool, the Preston fighter being disqualified in the ninth round.

McAteer successfully defended his titles against Lew Lazar and Martin Hansen, but in March, 1958, he lost his Empire crown to Dick Tiger, and then, following his defeat by Terry Downes in a non-title bout three months later, he announced his retirement from the ring.

McAteer had fought 57 professional contests, losing only six times.

## McAULEY, Dave:

Part-time chef from Larne who was Irish A.B.A. flyweight champion in 1980 and took the vacant British flyweight title in October 1986, when he k.o.'d local boy Joe Kelly in nine rounds in Glasgow. That was this tall Irishman's 13th professional fight.

A typical all-action flyweight, McAuley came close to winning the W.B.A. version of the world title, flooring champion Fidel Bassa a number of times before being stopped in the 13th round of a thrilling encounter in Belfast in April 1987.

## McAULIFFE, Jack:

An Irishman born at Cork, but emigrated to Brooklyn as a child, McAuliffe became known as the "Napoleon of the Ring."

In a career which lasted for about 12 years he was undefeated although he came very close to it in 1887 when he met the British lightweight champion, Jem Carney, at Revere, Massachusetts. Carney was getting the better of things in the 74th round when McAuliffe's supporters broke into the ring and the referee was forced to abandon the fight as a draw.

McAuliffe started as bantamweight but by the time Nonpareil Jack Dempsey relinquished his world lightweight title in 1884, the Irishman was the best man in America at that weight and Dempsey nominated him as his successor.

McAuliffe quickly confirmed his right to the crown by beating several other top liners and his claim was beyond dispute by the time he had stopped Bill Frazier in 21 rounds at Boston in October, 1886.

A cooper by trade, McAuliffe must have been a first-rate boxer, for apart from Carney, no one came anywhere near relieving him of his lightweight title and he retired undefeated in 1896 and went on the stage.

When he was 48 he gave a three-round exhibition with Dick Burge at the N.S.C., January 15, 1914.

## McAVOY, Jock:

Born at Burnley but settled in Rochdale, McAvoy was another man who took to fighting when he was hungry and out of work. In a lengthy career he lost only 14 out of 148 fights.

He won the British and Empire middleweight titles from Len Harvey at Manchester in April, 1933, made the Lonsdale Belt his own property, and held on to the British title until he relinquished it 12 years later.

McAvoy went to America in 1935-36 and there he beat Al McCoy, Babe Risko (at a time when Risko was recognised in America as world middleweight champion), Jimmy Smith and Anson Green.

McAvoy really proved his punching power against Risko for he had the Syracuse fighter down six times in a first round victory.

In March, 1936, McAvoy was matched with John Henry Lewis for the world light-heavyweight title but was beaten on points.

He also had a crack at the British heavyweight title that same year but lost to Jack Petersen.

McAvoy won the British lightheavyweight title during the following year when he knocked out Eddie Phillips in the 14th round but he lost it to Len Harvey in April, 1938, and was again beaten by the Cornishman in July, 1939, in a contest which was claimed on this side of the Atlantic to be a world title bout.

One of McAvoy's most thrilling contests took place in Paris in January, 1935. It was at 1 lb. over the middle-weight limit and was for the European light-heavyweight title. Marcel Thil was the Rochdale fighter's opponent and this Frenchman got the referee's nod at the end of 15 rounds.

In July, 1945, at the age of 36, Jock McAvoy beat George Howard in two rounds at the Tottenham Hotspur Football Ground, but he retired soon afterwards.

## McCARTHY, Sammy:

A good boxer with an attractive style, Sammy McCarthy, of Stepney, took the British featherweight title from Ronnie Clayton, who was forced to retire in the eighth round at the White City, June, 1954.

He lost this title in his first defence against Spider Billy Kelly at Belfast, in January, 1955, and then moved into the lightweight division.

In June, 1956, McCarthy met Joe Lucy for the lightweight title at Wembley Pool but the referee intervened in the 13th round when Lucy was leading by a wide margin of points.

## McCLEAVE, Dave:

A London Meat Market porter, Dave McCleave of Lambeth was A.B.A. lightweight champion in 1931, welter-weight champion in 1932 and 1934, and Empire Amateur welterweight cham-pion in 1934.

After turning professional, he won the vacant British welterweight title by outpointing Chuck Parker at Earls Court in April, 1936, but lost it only six weeks later to Jake Kilrain, who knocked him out in the eighth round at Glasgow.

## McCLUSKEY, John:

A clever boxer who hails from Hamilton, the same Scottish town as that other brilliant flyweight, Walter McGowan, and who actually took over McGowan's British title after that fighter had relinquished it.

McCluskey won the title in a thrilling battle with Tony Barlow at Manchester in January 1967, stopping the local fighter in eight rounds. That was only McCluskey's eighth professional bout, but he had been an outstanding amateur winning the A.B.A. flyweight title in 1964 and retaining it the following year.

Lack of opposition prevented Mc-Clusky from making real money out of his title and for the most part he fought bantamweights.

After two years of inactivity he officially retired in August 1977.

## McCORMACK, John:

In 1956 this southpaw from Glasgow won the A.B.A. and the Scottish Amateur light-middleweight titles. That same year he also won a bronze medal at the Olympics in Melbourne.

McCormack turned professional in February, 1957, and after winning 13 of his first 14 bouts he became Scottish middleweight champion with a victory over Len Mullen.

In September, 1959, McCormack was matched with Terry Downes for the latter's British middleweight title. The result was rather unsatisfactory for after being outpointed and floored eight times the Scot got the decision in the eighth round when Downes was disqualified for an alleged low blow.

A return was immediately arranged but although McCormack gave a better account of himself he was still no match for the tearaway Downes and lost in eight rounds.

In 1961 McCormack met Harko Kokmeyer for the vacant European middleweight title and he outpointed the Dutch champion in an uninspiring contest. Only four months later he lost the crown to Chris Christensen follow-ing a controversial 4th round disquali-fied which caused an uproar.

## McCORMACK, Pat:

A younger brother of Young John McCormack, Pat fought far and wide before achieving his ambition by winning a British title in March 1974.

Pat was only a month short of his 28th birthday when he took the lightwelterweight title by stopping Des Morrison in the 11th round with a good left hook to the head. This was in March 1974.

However, in November that same year the title went to Joey Singleton when he outpointed McCormack in a close fight.

## McCORMACK, Young John:

Born Dublin but fighting out of Brixton, London, this rugged twohanded fighter became a naturalised British subject so that he could try for a British title. He achieved his ambition in June 1967 when matched with Eddie Avoth for the British light-heavyweight crown, the referee stopping the contest in the seventh round when Avoth suffered a cut eye.

McCormack failed to annex the Empire title, losing to Bobby Dunlop in seven rounds in Sydney in February 1968, and he lost his British crown when he was also handicapped by a cut eye in his return with Avoth in January 1969, retiring at the end of eleven gruelling rounds.

## McCORMICK, Noel (Boy):

Born in India of Irish parents in December, 1899, McCormick made his home in Manchester and began to attract attention during the first World War as a bulldog type of fighter.

In his 13th professional contest he won the vacant British light-heavyweight title when his opponent, the Canadian, Harold Rolph, was disqualified in the 11th round. This match took place on April 28, 1919.

McCormick went to America after this and was undefeated in four bouts which included a points victory over "Gunboat" Smith.

On his return to this country he was beaten in 12 rounds by the British heavyweight champion, Joe Beckett, and in November, 1921, Ted "Kid" Lewis relieved him of his light-heavyweight crown when forcing him to retire in the 14th round.

However, no Lonsdale Belt was presented at this contest and according

to the N.S.C. McCormick was still champion until he relinquished the title.

In April, 1926, he had another try for the British heavyweight crown but was stopped in ten rounds by Phil Scott.

## McCOY, Al:

German-American who fought most of his bouts in New York State during the time of the Frawley Law which did not allow decisions to be made.

He was the first southpaw to win a world title when at Brooklyn in April, 1914, he surprised everyone by knocking out George Chip in the first round. The middleweight champion had come in as a last minute substitute for his brother Joe.

After that McCoy was considered to have been beaten on several occasions but as these were "no decision" bouts he could only lose his title by the knock-out route.

So he remained champion until November, 1917, when he was stopped in six rounds by Mike O'Dowd.

## McCOY, Charles "Kid":

A really skilful boxer, this American came to England in 1895 and was surprisingly outpointed by the former Amateur champion, Ted White.

However, in a later visit he made amends by beating three men in one night at Wonderland when he did not even bother to change into boxing gear but fought in his street clothes.

After learning all of Tommy Ryan's methods while acting as a sparring partner, he relieved him of the world welterweight title in March, 1896, by knocking him out in the 15th round.

McCoy then put on weight fast and although he relinquished his welterweight title in 1897 and claimed the middleweight championship he was never seriously considered for the heavier crown for he passed, almost immediately, into the heavyweight division.

At the top weight he beat such men as Joe Choynski, Peter Maher, Steve O'Donnell, Gus Ruhlin (McCoy conceded the Akron Giant nearly 28 lbs.) and Dan Creedon.

A defeat by Tom Sharkey prevented him from getting a title fight.

McCoy, who made a name for himself in films following his retirement from the ring, has been rated by Nat Fleischer as the best light-heavyweight ever and by another American boxing authority, Alexander Johnston, as one of the most skilful boxers ever produced by that country.

"Kid" McCoy committed suicide in 1940.

## McDONNELL, Jim:

Clever box-fighter from Stepney, London, who was A.B.A. lightweight champion in 1982 and as a professional turned featherweight and went on to win the European crown in that division after it had been left vacant by Barry McGuigan. The tall McDonnell k.o.'d Jose Luis Vicho in the fourth round at Wembley in November 1985. After one successful defence McDonnell relinquished the title to move into the junior lightweight division in 1987. He never fought for the British featherweight crown.

## McGOVERN, Terry:

A Brooklyn Irishman, Terrible Terry McGovern was one of the most colourful fighters of all time.

When he started fighting as an amateur at the age of 16 he knocked out all opposition and within 12 months he had entered the professional ranks.

A wicked puncher who won half his fights inside the distance, McGovern gained the world bantamweight title by knocking out Pedlar Palmer in 2 minutes 32 seconds at Tuckahoe, New York, September 12, 1899.

He relinquished this title soon afterwards when he began to put on weight, and then, almost immediately, won the featherweight championship, giving the redoubtable George Dixon such a hammering that the negro's manager threw in the sponge in the eighth round. This was at the Broadway A.C. January 9, 1900.

In July, 1900, McGovern, who was a tearaway fighter, stopped the world welterweight champion, Frank Erne, in three rounds, but this was not for that title because the Swiss-American had agreed to get down to 128 lbs. or five pounds under the welterweight limit for this contest.

McGovern lost his featherweight crown to Young Corbett who knocked him out in the second round of a contest fought at Hartford, Connecticut, November 28, 1901.

So McGovern's reputation as an unstoppable "killer" came to an end and to prove it was no fluke, Young Corbett gave McGovern a return bout and knocked him out in 11 rounds in March, 1903.

McGovern died in 1918 at the age of only 37.

## McGOVERN, Tommy:

Tommy McGovern turned professional in 1946, and had his earliest fights in America.

He returned to this country in 1948 and after winning the Southern Area lightweight title he went on to take the British championship by knocking out Billy Thompson in only 45 seconds of a contest at Wandsworth, August 28, 1951.

McGovern lost his crown to Frank Johnson who got the referee's nod at the end of 15 rounds in July, 1952.

The Bermondsey fighter had a chance to regain the title when he was matched with Joe Lucy after Johnson had become overweight, but Lucy won on points.

## McGOWAN, Walter M.B.E.:

A delightful boxer who always displayed brilliant footwork McGowan was only 20 years of age when he knocked out fellow Scot, Jackie Brown, to become British and Empire flyweight champion in May 1963.

That was only McGowan's 10th professional bout but he had always shown great skill as an amateur and won the A.B.A. flyweight title in 1961.

In June 1966 he became World champion by clearly outpointing Salvatore Burruni at Empire Pool, and in the following September he moved up a class to beat Alan Rudkin for the British and Empire bantam crown.

That was a controversial decision and when these two met again in May 1968 Rudkin regained his titles.

Between those bouts the Hamilton-born boxer lost his world title in a closely fought contest with Chartchai Chionoi when he was forced to retire with a badly cut nose, and he subsequently lost a return bout when suffering from cuts.

## McGRORY, Johnny:

This skilful Scottish boxer with a classic style took the British feather-weight title from Nel Tarleton at Liverpool in September, 1936.

Before the end of that year he had gained the Empire title by outpointing Willie Smith of South Africa at Johannesburg.

Born at Glasgow, McGrory has been described as a second Jim Driscoll. He was certainly a delightful boxer to watch.

He seemed certain to get a chance of a world title bout but when he was practically signed up to meet Pete Sarron he was surprisingly beaten by Ginger Foran in March, 1937. In this bout McGrory received a fractured jaw and was knocked out in the seventh round. However, while it lost him a chance of a world championship bout, it did not cost him his title for it was an overweight match.

McGrory forfeited his title the following year when he could not make the weight but although he outpointed the British lightweight champion, Dave Crowley in a non-title bout, he never got a chance to fight for that title.

## McGUIGAN, Barry:

One of the most talented of Britain's fighters in recent years this terrific hitter won the vacant British featherweight title by stopping Vernon Penprase inside two rounds in April 1983 and then took the vacant European title with another devastating show, stopping Valerio Nati in six rounds.

An Irishman born Monaghan, the moustached McGuigan relinquished his British and European title to concentrate on a bid for the world title. His chance came in June 1985 when he met the W.B.A. champion Eusebio Pedroza at Shepherd's Bush and he made no mis-take. It was one of the finest fights seen in London for many years with McGuigan ending the 7-year reign of the Panamanian champion with a 15-round points win.

McGuigan lost his title in the searing heat of Las Vegas, being outpointed over 15 gruelling rounds by substitute Steve Cruz. Ahead for a long spell the gutsy McGuigan collapsed after the final bell ended a last round in which he had been floored twice.

## McKENZIE, Clinton:

Croydon southpaw and elder brother of Duke McKenzie, Clinton had a distin-guished career first winning the British light-welterweight crown in 1978 and regaining it in 1979 from Colin Power who had previously relieved him of the crown. His first bid for the European title failed in 1980 when stopped inside the distance by Giuseppe Martinese, but in October 1981 was successful when he showed real class in beating champion Antonio Guinaldo at the Albert Hall.

Clinton was, unfortunately, careless enough to be disqualified for a low punch in two successive fights in 1982, the second of these costing him his European crown with Robert Gambini floored in the second round.

After retaining his British title in four bouts he lost it when outpointed by Terry Marsh in a fight which saw both men punch themselves almost to a standstill.

Clinton McKenzie announced his retirement in September 1986 when he was beaten in three rounds in a fight with Tony McKenzie for the title vacated by Marsh.

## McKENZIE, Duke:

This tall flyweight from Croydon, London, had a good grounding after turning professional in 1982 with five of his earliest fights fought in America—winning all of them. It was no surprise when he gained the British title, vacated on retirement by Hugh Russell, by outclassing Danny Flynn at the Albert Hall in June 1985. McKenzie had the Scotsman down six times before the fight was stopped in the fourth round.

Duke McKenzie won the European title from Charlie Magri with a fifth round stoppage at Wembley in May 1986—only Duke's 14th professional fight, all of them wins.

## McKENZIE, George:

Born at Leith, Edinburgh, George McKenzie won the A.B.A. bantamweight title in 1920, and when he turned professional he became the British featherweight champion by outpointing Harry Leach over 20 rounds at Holland Park, June 2, 1924.

McKenzie beat Leach in a return bout six months later, but in March, 1925, he lost his title when outpointed by Johnny Curley.

## McKENZIE, Tony:

Leicester-born light-welterweight (no relation to the other McKenzies mentioned here) who won the vacant British title by stopping Clinton McKenzie inside three rounds in September 1986. Tony put a second notch on a Lonsdale belt only five weeks later when he beat Michael Harris by a 10th round k.o. at Stevenage. However, his bid to win a Lonsdale Belt in record time ended in disaster when he was relieved of his title, being battered and stopped inside three rounds by Lloyd Christie.

## McLARNIN, Jimmy:

A popular fighter with a big following Jimmy McLarnin was born in Belfast but was taken to Canada when still a baby and settled in Vancouver.

A powerful hitter with a really fast right hand, McLarnin started as a bantamweight in 1920, and before he retired in 1937 he had defeated no less than 13 world champions and won nearly a third of his contests inside the distance.

McLarnin came to the fore as a lightweight in 1926. In May, 1928, he met the world champion, Sammy Mandell, but was beaten over 15 rounds. Soon after this he was forced to move up into the welterweight division and it was at this weight that he gained world honours.

1930-31-32-33 were McLarnin's peak years. During that time he beat Sammy Mandell, Young Jack Thompson, Al Singer, Billy Petrolle, Lou Brouillard, Benny Leonard, and Sammy Fuller, before taking the welterweight crown from Young Corbett with a one round knock-out in Los Angeles, May 29, 1933.

Twelve months later almost to the day, May 28, 1934, McLarnin lost the championship to Barney Ross, but in a return match he regained the crown on September 17, 1934.

This Irishman finally lost the title in a third meeting with Ross, May 28, 1935.

## McTIGUE, Mike:

Born County Clare, Ireland, Mike McTigue had 12 brothers and sisters. He emigrated to America when he was 16.

McTique was a good boxer although he lacked a really heavy punch. Nevertheless, he won the world light-heavyweight title at La Scala Theatre, Dublin, March 17, 1923, when he proved too good for Battling Siki in a 20-round contest.

McTigue lost the championship when he took a lot of punishment and was outpointed by Paul Berlenbach in New York, May 30, 1925.

A little over two years later, after Jack Delaney had relinquished the title he had taken from Berlenbach, McTigue was given a chance to regain the crown in a match with Tommy Loughran, but it was the "Phantom of Philly" who got the referee's decision and the title at the end of 15 rounds.

By the time McTigue retired in 1930 he had been fighting for more than 20 years and had taken part in about 250 contests.

## MEADE, Neville:

A likeable character from Jamaica who fought out of Swansea. Unfortunately his career as a heavyweight was handicapped by injuries and the fact that he was 26 years of age before turning professional after winning the A.B.A. title in 1974. Probably the best win of his career was a third round stoppage of Lucien Rodriguez who won the EBU title 18 months later and also went the distance with Larry Holmes. The powerfully-built Meade won the British title in dramatic fashion knocking out champion Gordon Ferris in only 2 mins. 45 secs., but lost in his first defence when stopped in nine rounds by Dave Pearce in

September 1983.

## MEEN, Reggie:

This Desborough, Northants, heavyweight had a meteoric rise to fame but he faded almost as quickly. The main reason for his decline was that he lacked the "killer" instinct to finish off a beaten opponent. He was also inclined to be slow, but he had a good left hook.

He disappointed his supporters with a poor showing against Primo Carnera at the Albert Hall in December, 1930, when he was knocked out in the second round, but in November, 1931, he won the vacant British heavyweight title by outpointing Charlie Smith at Leicester.

Eight months later he lost the championship when he was knocked out in the second round by Jack Petersen at Wimbledon.

## MEGGS, George:

Meggs the Collier is not rated very high in the list of British champions. He won the title by defeating Bill Stevens in 17 minutes, London, March 2, 1761.

By all accounts this was a very poor fight and Stevens later confessed that he had "thrown' the contest having been persuaded to do this by a former champion, Jack Slack.

In 1762 Meggs was twice defeated by George Milsom.

## MELLODY, Billy "Honey":

An Irish-American, Honey Mellody claimed the world welterweight title after beating Joe Walcott on points over 15 rounds at Chelsea, Massachusetts, October 16, 1906.

He confirmed his superiority over the ex-champion by beating him again in a return match only six weeks later, but there was still some dispute as to Mellody's right to the title because Walcott had never actually beaten the Dixie Kid but had simply re-claimed the championship because the Kid seemed uninterested in defending it and went to Europe.

In any event, Mellody was beaten by Mike Twin Sullivan in April, 1907.

## MENDOZA, Daniel:

Born at Aldgate, London, in 1764, this Jewish boy won his first fight at the age of 16 when he beat a carrier in a street set-to.

One who saw that fight was Richard Humphries, a famous pugilist of that time, and he took Mendoza under his wing for a while but they eventually fell out.

These two subsequently met on four occasions in the ring. Mendoza lost the first two but won the remaining two contests.

Mendoza claimed the championship after beating Bill Warr in 17 minutes at Bexley Heath, November 12, 1794, but he lost it to John Jackson in nine rounds lasting only 10½ minutes, at Hornchurch, Essex, April 15, 1795.

## MEXICO:

In recent years Mexican boxing has gained popularity on a par with bull-fighting and they have produced many first-class men.

The first Mexican-born fighter to gain an undisputed world title was Lauro Salas. He took the lightweight crown from Jimmy Carter in 1952.

Another Mexican, Manuel Ortiz, had won the bantamweight title back in 1942 but Ortiz was actually born in California.

### Champions:

WORLD:

Lightweight: Juan Zurita, 1944-45 (N.B.A. only); Lauro Salas, 1952; *Mando Ramos, 1969-70; Jose Luis Ramirez, (W.B.C.) 1984-85.

Welterweight: Carlos Palomino (W.B.C.), 1976-79; Jorge Vaca (W.B.C.), 1987-

Light-welterweight: Rene Arredondo (W.B.C.), 1986, 1987.

Featherweight: Baby Arizmendi, 1934 (N.Y.A.C. only); Chalky Wright, 1941-42 (N.Y.A.C. only); Vicente Salvidar, 1964-67, 1970; Clemente Sanchez, 1972; Ruben Olivares (W.B.A.) 1974; Salvador Sanchez, 1980-82.

Junior-featherweight: Juan Meza (W.B.C.), 1984-85; Lupe Pintor, (W.B.C.), 1985-86.

Bantamweight: *Manuel Ortiz, 1942-47, 1947-50; Raton Macias, 1955-57 (N.B.A. only); Jose Becerra, 1959-60; Ruben Olivares, 1969-70, 1971-72; Chuco

Castillo, 1970-71; Rafael Herrera, 1972; Romeo Anaya, 1973; Alfonso Zamora, 1975-77.

Super-flyweight: Gilberto Roman, 1986-87.

Flyweight: Efren Torres, 1969-70; Miguel Canto (W.B.C.), 1975; Guty Espadas (W.B.A.), 1976-78; Antonio Avelar, 1981-82; Freddy Castillo, 1982; Gabriel Bernal, 1984.

Light-flyweight: Freddy Castillo (W.B.C), 1978, 1982; Amado Ursua, 1982.

OLYMPIC:

Featherweight: A. Roldan, 1968.

Flyweight: R. Dalgado, 1968.

*Born California, Mexican parentage.

## MIDDLEWEIGHT:

See under WEIGHT DIVISIONS.

## MILLER, Freddie:

German-American southpaw who was a boxer with real class. Miller showed amazing footwork and after becoming featherweight title-holder he was a busy champion not afraid to meet anyone.

He failed in his first bid for the world featherweight crown when he was outpointed by Battling Battalino in July, 1931, and his next meeting with the champion was declared "no contest" after three rounds.

The title was declared vacant soon after this until Tommy Paul emerged as champion in the eyes of the N.B.A. Miller then annexed this title by outpointing Paul at Chicago in January, 1933.

He defended his crown successfully several times, including two 15-round points victories over Nel Tarleton, but he lost it to Petey Sarron in May, 1936.

The following year Miller had two meetings with Sarron in South Africa. He won the first, a non-title bout, but lost the second.

## MILLIGAN, Tom:

Born Shieldmuir, Scotland, in 1904, Tommy Milligan won the Scottish welterweight title when he was 20.

Only two months after this victory he won the British and Empire welterweight championships and claimed the European title with a 20-round points victory over Ted "Kid" Lewis in Edinburgh.

Milligan relinquished these titles in 1925 and moved up into the middleweight division.

After an unsuccessful trip to America this Irish-Scot, whose real name was Mulligan, was matched with George West at the Holland Park Rink for the vacant British middleweight championship. Milligan stopped the ex-Guardsman in the 14th round.

On June 30, 1927, Milligan met Mickey Walker for the world middleweight title at Olympia. He put up a brave show but was badly punished and knocked out in the 10th round.

About this time Frank Moody was claiming the British middleweight title. He had beaten Roland Todd, who had been deprived of his title by the Boxing Board. Then, in March, 1928, Milligan was beaten by Alex Ireland in a non-belt match. The Boxing Board still acknowledged Milligan as champion, however, but when he was matched with Frank Moody at Glasgow in August, 1928, he was surprisingly knocked out in the first round and had to hand in his title.

## MILLS, Freddie:

Born at Bournemouth in 1919, Freddie Mills started boxing at the age of 14. He learnt the game the hard way in the travelling fairground booth where Gipsy Daniels gave him a lot of good advice.

Mills first hit the headlines when he outpointed Jock McAvoy over 10 rounds at Liverpool in August, 1940, and in June, 1942, he won the British and Empire light-heavyweight titles and gained recognition in this country as the world champion of that division by knocking out veteran Len Harvey inside two rounds.

The American world title-holder was Gus Lesnevich, and these two eventually met in London in May, 1946, Lesnevich stopping the popular British fighter in the 10th round.

In a return bout Mills gained undisputed recognition as world light-heavyweight champion with a 15-round points victory over the tough American.

That was in July, 1948, and Mills held on to the title until January, 1950, when he was knocked out by Joey Maxim and announced his retirement soon afterwards.

Due to the war, and also because this country was so poor in light-heavyweight talent, Freddie Mills was never called upon to defend his British title. So, although he was one of our most outstanding fighters, he never got a chance to make a Lonsdale Belt his own property.

Instead, this likeable fellow had to spend most of his time fighting heavyweights. He made two bids for the British heavyweight title but lost to Jack London and later to Bruce Woodcock.

Against these heavier men Mills proved that he had plenty of courage, and this, together with his swinging left hand punch, made him popular with the fans and helped him to become the first fighter to earn more than £60,000 in the British ring.

Freddie Mills was found shot dead in his car outside his night club in London in July 1965.

## MILSOM, George:

Another of those champions of the old prize ring who is not rated very highly because he reigned at a time when the sport was at a very low ebb.

Milsom took the title from George Meggs, a second-rater who had won the championship in a "fixed" contest. Milsom beat Meggs at Calne, Wiltshire, in July, 1762.

Three years later he lost it to Tom Juchau, who defeated him in 70 minutes at St. Albans.

## MINTER, Alan:

A former A.B.A. middleweight champion (1971) and Olympic bronze medallist (1972) who had his share of ups and downs after joining the paid ranks but shook off his tendency to swing wildly under pressure and matured into an accomplished and courageous world champion.

First won the vacant British middleweight crown in his twenty-fifth professional contest, outpointing Kevin Finnegan, in November 1975, but after making a Lonsdale belt his own property he was deprived of this title because of his inability to defend owing to commitment in Europe.

He captured the European title with a fifth-round k.o. of Germano Valsecchi in Milan in February, 1977, but lost it when the referee stopped his contest with Gratien Tonna in the eighth round for a harmless looking cut when the Crawley southpaw seemed on the way to victory.

In November 1977 Alan regained the British title with his third points victory over Kevin Finnegan, and in July 1978 re-captured the European title with a k.o. over Angelo Jacopucci which led to tragedy when the Italian fighter died.

After relinquishing the British and European titles Minter went for the world title and took this from Vito Antuofermo with a points win in Las Vegas in March 1980. He successfully defended it in a return bout, but in September, 1980, was beaten inside 3 rounds by Marvin Hagler. Minter retired the following year.

## MITCHELL, Charlie:

Born at Birmingham, Charlie Mitchell started his ring career in 1878 as a lightweight.

In April, 1882, he became middleweight champion of England by winning an open competition at Chelsea, and in December of that same year he gained recognition as heavyweight champion by winning another similar competition.

The following year Mitchell decided to try his luck in America, and on May 14 this game little fighter, who never scaled more than 160 lbs., met the powerful American champion, John L. Sullivan, at the old Madison Square Garden.

Mitchell floored Sullivan, the first man ever to achieve this, but the mighty Sullivan was quickly back on his feet and battered the cocky Briton so severely that the police stopped the fight in the third round.

Despite this hiding Mitchell still fancied his chance against Sullivan, and when the Boston Strong Boy crossed the Atlantic at the end of 1887 a match was made between these two to take place at Chantilly, France, March 10, 1888.

In this contest, Mitchell gave his finest display. He proved that he was something more than a boaster, for although he conceded the Irish-American 33lbs. he contrived to keep out of the way of that powerful hitter for more than three hours. It is true that Mitchell was doing all the back-pedalling but he was hoping to tire the bigger man out with these tactics before going on the offensive. The weather prevented the contest from reaching a decisive ending, for it was abandoned as a draw after 39 rounds.

Mitchell's claim to the heavyweight championship of England had lapsed during the time he was in America. In February, 1890, he was matched with Jem Mace in a contest which was billed as being for this title, but this was quite ridiculous, as Mace was then 58 years of age, and Mitchell won in three rounds.

Charlie Mitchell retired following his defeat by Jim Corbett in January, 1894. He died at Brighton in 1918.

## MITTEE, Sylvester:

Born St. Lucia and emigrated to Bethnal Green, London, he had a fine amateur record, including the A.B.A. lightweight championship in 1976, before turning professional as a light-welterweight. He was outpointed over 15 rounds in a bid for Clinton McKenzie's British title in March 1981 and temporarily retired after two more fights. In 1983 he came back under a different manager and as a welterweight winning his next seven fights inside the distance, including stopping Fighting Romanus to win the vacant Commonwealth title. In September 1985 he showed himself to have real class by outpointing Kostas Petrou for the British title.

A hard hitter Mittee, however, could not match Lloyd Honeyghan when they met in November 1985. It was a hard fight but Mittee was behind on points when it was stopped in the eighth round because of a cut over his right eye. This defeat cost Mittee his British and Commonwealth titles and enabled Honeyghan to retain his European crown.

## MIZLER, Harry:

Born St. George's, London, this Jewish boy had an outstanding amateur career before turning professional in 1933.

He was A.B.A. bantamweight champion in 1930, featherweight in 1932 and lightweight in 1933. He also won the Empire Games bantamweight championship in 1930.

Known as the "Iceberg," Mizler was a stylish boxer with a good left hand.

He won the British lightweight title from Johnny Cuthbert in January, 1934, and after defending it against Billy Quinlan he lost to Jack "Kid" Berg at the Albert Hall in October, 1934.

## MOIR, Gunner James:

Born at Lambeth in 1879, James Moir fought his earliest contests at Wonderland while serving in the Army, and was 27 before he won the British heavyweight title from Jack Palmer at the N.S.C. in October, 1906. Palmer was disqualified in the ninth round.

In 1907, when Tommy Burns came to this country, there were some people who fancied the Gunner's chances of relieving Burns of his world title, and the N.S.C. agreed to pay the Canadian £2,000 to meet the Englishman. That was quite a pile of money in those days, and moreover, Burns was actually handed that amount before he stepped into the ring.

Moir, however, was completely outclassed and was knocked out in the 10th round.

In April, 1909, he lost his British crown when he was knocked out in the first round by Iron Hague.

## MOLLOY, Tommy:

Born at Liverpool, Tommy Molloy a steel erector by trade, learnt the finer points of boxing with the St. Francis B.C.

While serving in the Army he won an I.S.B.A. light-welterweight title in 1953.

Molloy turned professional in 1955 and an unbeaten run of 31 contests earned him a match with Jimmy Newman for the vacant British welterweight title at Streatham, July 15, 1958. Molloy got the points decision.

After a successful defence against Albert Carroll he lost his title when outpointed by Wally Swift in February, 1960.

## MONAGHAN, John Joseph:

Born in Belfast in 1920, Rinty Monaghan is one of a family of 13 children. He was only 14½ when he had his first professional bout and knocked out his opponent in the fourth round.

Monaghan did not fight in London until he was 26, then he knocked out Terry Allen in one round. That was in March, 1947. Just under four months later he gave one of his best displays to date in outpointing the former French flyweight champion, Emile Famechon.

After the B.B.B.C. had deprived Jackie Paterson of his world flyweight title through his inability to make the weight for a match with Dado Marino, Monaghan stepped into the breach but was beaten on a foul in nine rounds. Subsequently he was matched with Marino in a contest recognised by the N.B.A. and Eire as for the world title and won on points.

Paterson was subsequently reinstated as world champion but Monaghan gained world-wide recognition as title-holder by stopping the Scotsman in seven rounds at Belfast, March 23, 1948. This victory also gave him the British and Empire titles.

The singing Irishman later annexed the European title by outpointing Maurice Sandeyron, and then, after being held to a draw by Terry Allen in September, 1949, he retired undefeated world champion.

## MONTANA, Small:

This little Filipino's real name is Benjamin Gan, and he started fighting professionally in 1931.

In September, 1935, he won the American flyweight title by outpointing Midget Wolgast, and also claimed the world title.

The championship of the flyweight division was in a state of confusion at that time, and it was not settled until January, 1937, when Montana came to London and was beaten by Benny Lynch.

## MONTGOMERY, Bob:

An American negro from South Carolina, Bob Montgomery became world lightweight champion, according to the N.Y.A.C., when he outpointed Beau Jack, another negro, over 15 rounds at Madison Square Garden in May, 1943.

He lost the title in a return with Jack six months later but regained it in a third meeting in March, 1944.

The N.B.A. subsequently recognised Ike Williams as world lightweight champion, and when these two met in August, 1947, Montgomery was beaten in six rounds.

## MONZON, Carlos:

One of the outstanding champions of modern times, Carlos Monzon was a clever middleweight with speed and real power who lost only three of his first 82 fights before winning the world title, and all of those defeats were avenged.

He took the world title from Nino Benvenuti in November, 1970, and subsequently defended it 14 times before retiring undefeated champion in 1977.

In a professional career which began in his native Argentina in 1963 he lost only three of his 102 fights and won 61 inside the distance.

## MOODY, Frank:

Lack of consistency marred the record of this rugged Welsh fighter, but he was popular on both sides of the Atlantic because of his aggressiveness and hard hitting.

Moody spent some time in the United States, where he had more than 30 fights and won two-thirds of them. In June, 1924, he met the world middleweight champion, Harry Greb, but was knocked out in six rounds, and while over there he was also outpointed by Greb's successor as champion, Tiger Flowers.

Moody claimed the British middleweight title following his points victory over Roland Todd in February, 1927, but Todd had previously been deprived of this title by the N.S.C. and the Welshman could not gain official recognition.

Even when Moody beat the official champion, Tommy Milligan, in one round at Glasgow in August, 1928, there was still some dispute about his claim, although he had every right to call himself champion. Six weeks later, however, he was outpointed by Alex Ireland. Moving up into the light-heavyweight division, Moody won that British championship by outpointing Ted Moore in November, 1927, but he lost it in his first defence against Harry Crossley, November, 1929.

## MOORE, Archie:

An American negro from Missouri, Archie Moore was a very experienced fighter by the time he won the world light-heavyweight title in December, 1952.

Moore took the crown from Joey Maxim with a 15-round points victory. At that time he was probably 39 years of age and he had been boxing for nearly 20 years.

A great personality, Moore practically managed his own affairs, although officially he probably had more managers than any other fighter.

He successfully defended his light-heavyweight crown in two return fights with Joey Maxim and, despite rumours about his inability to make the weight, he baffled everyone by shedding anything up to two stone for his various defences of his title.

Moore also had two world heavyweight title bouts. In September, 1955, he was knocked out by Rocky Marciano in nine rounds, and in November, 1956, Floyd Patterson stopped him in five.

Archie Moore was deprived of his world title, first by N.B.A. in 1960 and by N.Y.A.C. and E.B.U. in 1962.

## MOORE, Davey:

An American negro, born Lexington, Kentucky, Davey Moore met his death defending his world featherweight title against Sugar Ramos at Los Angeles in March, 1963. He retired at the end of the 10th round and four days later died of injuries to the brain.

A former American amateur champion, Moore had been a professional since 1954 and had won the world crown when he forced Hogan Bassey to retire with cut eyes at the end of 13 rounds at Los Angeles in March, 1959.

This fast, accurate puncher confirmed his superiority over Bassey in a return match, stopping him in 10 rounds, and successfully defended his title in four other contests before his tragic meeting with Ramos.

## MORRISON, Des:

A tall and skilful boxer, this immigrant from Jamaica won the British light-welterweight title by outpointing Joe Tetteh in November, 1973, but lost it when knocked out in 11 rounds by Pat McCormack in March of the following year.

He was subsequently beaten in two attempts to regain this title, losing to Joey Singleton and Colin Power.

## MORRISSEY, John:

This bare-knuckle prize fighter was born in Ireland but brought up in America.

He won the American championship by defeating John C. Heenan in 11 rounds at Long Point, Lake Erie, Canada, October 20, 1858.

Morrissey did not fight again after that but he made a great deal of money gambling on horse racing and also served two terms in the American Congress.

## MURPHY, Billy:

Born Auckland, New Zealand, in 1863, Billy Murphy was a very frail looking man, but his looks were deceiving, for when he took up boxing he soon became one of the toughest featherweights in the world.

He eventually became known as "Torpedo" Billy Murphy, and in addition to his fights in Australia he had many more in America.

After Dal Hawkins moved up into the lightweight division the featherweight title was claimed by Irishman Ike Weir, and in January, 1890, Murphy met him at the California Athletic Club and knocked him out in 14 rounds.

For this victory Murphy was presented with a featherweight championship belt by Richard K. Fox, American publisher of the *Police Gazette*, which was the most widely read paper covering prize fighting at that time.

Murphy's claim was never established throughout the world, however, and in September of the same year he was well beaten by Young Griffo in Sydney in a contest billed as being for the Australian title.

## NAMES:

Several boxers have adopted new names when embarking on a ring career. In most cases where this has happened you will find the boxer's real name mentioned in the biographies contained in this encyclopædia.

Most boxers have also been given nicknames during their careers and for those readers who wish to establish the identity of a boxer when only his nickname is known, I append below an alphabetical list of some of these names.

Ambling Alp ......... Primo Carnera.
Apollo of the Ring ...... Jem Belcher.
Astoria Assassin .... Paul Berlenbach.
Baby Face ........ Jimmy McLarnin.
Barbados Demon ....... Joe Walcott.
Basque Woodchopper
                    Paolino Uzcudun.
Belfast Spider ............. Ike Weir.
Benecia Boy........ John C. Heenan.
Black Cloud ......... Larry Holmes.
Black Panther .......... Harry Wills.
Black Uhlan ........ Max Schmeling.
Boilermaker............ Jim Jeffries.
Boston Strong Boy.. John L. Sullivan.
Boston Tar Baby ..... Sam Langford.
Boxing Marvel ........ Jack Britton.
Box O'Tricks........ Pedlar Palmer.
Brockton Blockbuster
                    Rocky Marciano.
Bronx Bull .......... Jake LaMotta.
Brown Bomber .......... Joe Louis.
California Grizzly Bear
                    James J. Jeffries.
Chicago Spider ...... Johnny Coulon.
Cinderella Man ... James J. Braddock.
Cleveland Rubber Man  Johnny Risko.
Cuban Bon Bon ...... Kid Chocolate.
Deaf Un .............. James Burke.
Durable Dane ....... Battling Nelson.
Fargo Express ........ Billy Petrolle.

Fighting Marine ....... Gene Tunney.
Flying Dutchman ....... Harry Greb.
Game Chicken ......... Hen Pearce.
Gentleman Jim .... James J. Corbett.
Georgia Deacon ...... Tiger Flowers.
Ghost with a hammer in his hand
                    Jimmy Wilde.
Globetrotter ............ Jeff Smith.
Gunboat............... Eddie Smith.
Hard Rock from Down Under
                    Tom Heeney.
Harlem Coffee Cooler ... Frank Craig.
Herkimer Hurricane.... Lou Ambers.
Hit Man ......... Thomas Hearns.
Homicide Hank ... Henry Armstrong.
Human Freight Car ... Ed Dunkhorst.
Human Punching Bag ..... Joe Grim.
Human Skyscraper... Henry Johnson.
Idol of Fistiana ....... Jack Dempsey.
Illinois Thunderbolt ..... Billy Papke.
Kansas Rube ............. Jim Ferns.
Kentucky Rosebud .. Walter Edgerton.
Knob Hill Terror ...... Monte Attell.
Little Artha .......... Jack Johnson.
Little Chocolate ...... George Dixon.
Livermore Larruper ....... Max Baer.
Louisville Lip ...... Muhammad Ali.
Madcap Maxie ........... Max Baer.
Manassa Mauler ...... Jack Dempsey.
Michigan Assassin ... Stanley Ketchel.
Michigan Wildcat ....... Ad Wolgast.
Mighty Atom ......... Jimmy Wilde.
Napoleon .............. Tom Sayers.
Nonpareil............ Jack Dempsey.
                    (Middleweight)
Old Chocolate...... George Godfrey.
Old Master .............. Joe Gans.
Old Smoke.......... John Morrissey.
Orchid Man..... Georges Carpentier.
Peerless Jim............ Jim Driscoll.
Phaintin' Phil ............. Phil Scott.
Pittsburgh Kid .......... Billy Conn.
Pottawatomie Giant .... Jess Willard.
Rochdale Thunderbolt. Jock McAvoy.
Saginaw Kid ....... George Lavigne.
Slapsie Maxie ... Maxie Rosenbloom.
Sugar Ray .......... Ray Robinson.
Sydney Cornstalk ...... Frank Slavin.
Terrible Terry ..... Terry McGovern.
Tipton Slasher ....... William Perry.
Toy Bulldog ........ Mickey Walker.
Two-ton ............. Tony Galento.
Tylerstown Terror ..... Jimmy Wilde.
Whitechapel Whirlwind
                    Jack "Kid" Berg.
Wild Bull of the Pampas .. Luis Firpo.

## NAPOLES, Jose:

An accomplished craftsman who has gone down in history as an all-time great, this Cuban exile residing in Mexico, first won the world welterweight crown in April 1969 when he battered Curtis Cokes into defeat in 13 round.

It was a real shock when Napoles was beaten by 9-1 underdog, Billy Backus, in December 1970, the referee intervening in the fourth round when Napoles sustained a cut eye, but Napoles regained the title when he stopped Backus with a cut eye in eight rounds six months later. This time Napoles was clearly the better fighter.

Napoles amply displayed his class before British fans when he knocked out Ralph Charles in the seventh round at the Empire Pool, Wembley, in March 1972.

It was another British fighter, John H. Stracey, who eventually deprived him of his world title in 1975 and Napoles never fought again.

## NASH, Charlie:

Irishman from Derry who in February 1978 won the British lightweight title (the first fighter from the Emerald Isle to do so) when he beat Johnny Claydon in a manner which caused a great deal of controversy but which was perfectly correct in accordance with the rules. The referee stopped the contest at the end of the twelfth round because Nash had a 10-point lead.

A good counter-puncher with a sharp left hook Charlie Nash won the vacant European lightweight title by outpointing Andre Holyk in June 1979. He successfully defended it against Ken Buchanan but then relinquished the crown to go after Jim Watt's W.B.C. world title. The referee stopped this fight in Watt's favour in Glasgow in March, 1980, but before the year was out Nash had regained the European crown by outpointing Spain's Francisco Leon. In May, 1981, his European title went in a surprise defeat by Italian Joey Gibilisco who gave Nash a thorough beating before knocking him out in the sixth round.

## NATIONAL SPORTING CLUB:

The old National Sporting Club probably did more to establish the sport of boxing in this country than any other organisation.

Indeed, it is not too much to say that this exclusive club, which opened at 43 King Street, Covent Garden, March 5, 1891, was a powerful influence for the good of the sport, not only in this country but on an international basis.

It was founded by John Fleming and A. F. "Peggy" Bettinson as a middle-class sporting club, and the Earl of Lonsdale was its first President.

"Peggy" Bettinson ruled the club with a rod of iron. The boxers had to behave themselves and so did the members. The contests, which took place after dinner before about 1,300 members and guests, were fought out in silence, for no talking was permitted during the rounds.

Over the years the N.S.C. built up a great tradition of sportsmanship and fair play. Nothing but the best in boxing was good enough for this club, as may be seen from the following bill which was staged there in June, 1902, as a grand Coronation Tournament.

That evening Jabez White (Birmingham) beat the American, Spike Sullivan. Another American, Eddie Connolly, beat Londoner Pat Daly. Ben Jordan (Bermondsey) knocked out American Kid McFadden in the 15th round. Joe Walcott, the "Barbados Demon," beat American Tommy West. Tommy Ryan stopped fellow American, Johnny Gorman, in the third round. Gus Ruhlin (America) beat Tom Sharkey (America), who retired in the 11th round.

But even that star-studded bill was surpassed on the occasion of Bettinson's benefit night in January, 1914. Then the members were treated to bouts featuring such famous fighters as Jim Driscoll, Jimmy Wilde, Ted "Kid" Lewis, Digger Stanley, Sam Langford, Billy Wells, Georges Carpentier, and Kid McCoy.

In the 1920s the sport grew too big for the club which had set it on its feet. The top-class men could draw bigger crowds and so demand larger purses than a club with limited seating capacity could afford. In an effort to stave off a threatened closure the N.S.C. opened its doors to the general public for the first time in October, 1928. But only 12 months later they had to put up the shutters at Covent Garden.

For a while they carried on at the Stadium Club, Holborn, before moving to 21 Soho Square, W.1, in January, 1930.

By now it was a real uphill struggle to keep the club going. A new company was formed in 1930 and there were various proposals for building new headquarters, but all of these fell through and the club was virtually extinct until 1936, when another enthusiast, John Harding, led a new committee which took over the Empress Hall to put on boxing shows.

In March, 1938, the N.S.C. opened new headquarters at the Hotel Splendide, Piccadilly, but then came the war and towards the end of 1940 the N.S.C. Ltd. went into voluntary liquidation.

A new N.S.C. Ltd. was formed in 1947 with a nominal capital of £50,000 in 1,000,000 shilling shares, and they took over the Empress Club in Berkeley Street in September, 1951.

This club really has no connection with the old N.S.C. but after moving to the Cafe Royal, Regent Street, in September, 1955, under the leadership of Charles Forte and John E. Harding, it caught something of the old atmosphere of its predecessor.

In 1982 the N.S.C. adopted Grosvenor House, Park Lane, as its HQ.

## NEEDHAM, Dave:

Only the third man in history to win both the British bantamweight and featherweight titles this classy Nottingham boxer has reached the top despite being prone to facial cuts. He won all his first 24 professional fights, including a points victory over Paddy Maguire in December 1974 which gave him the bantamweight title, before being held to a draw by Daniel Trioulaire in a bid for the Frenchman's European crown. In his next fight in October 1975 Needham lost the British championship when stopped because of cuts in a return with Maguire.

Dave Needham then turned to the featherweights and after being beaten by Alan Richardson (again because of cuts) for the British title in November 1976, he came back in April 1978 to take this title from Richardson with a points win in which Needham showed unusual aggression and also survived another bad cut over his right eye.

After failing in a bid for the European crown he lost his British title to Pat Cowdell in 1979.

## NEILL, Bobby:

Born at Edinburgh in 1933, Bobby Neill won a British title despite a lot of bad luck which would have been enough to stop the majority of fighters.

When he was an amateur he suffered a leg injury in a cycling accident. His boxing career seemed doomed, but he recovered, turned professional, and in September, 1956, he won the vacant Scottish featherweight title by stopping Matt Fulton in eight rounds. The following month he beat Raymond Famechon in five rounds, and in December of 1956 he beat the British featherweight champion, Charlie Hill, in a non-title bout. The referee stepped in to stop that contest when Hill was helpless after only 2 minutes 45 seconds.

Then came more bad luck. Neill was injured in a car crash and in September, 1958, he suffered a broken jaw in a contest with Aime Devish, of Belgium.

In April, 1959, however, Neill triumphed over all adversity and for the second time over Charlie Hill, relieving the fellow Scot of the British featherweight title. This time the referee stepped in and called a halt in the ninth round after Hill had been floored 10 times.

Neill secured a non-title bout with world champion Davey Moore, in October, 1959, but he had over-reached himself and was knocked out in 2 minutes 55 seconds.

In September, 1960, he lost his title to Terry Spinks, and announced his retirement after losing to Spinks in a return bout two months later.

## NELSON, Oscar "Battling":

They called him the "Durable Dane," and this fighter, who was born in Copenhagen in 1882, certainly was one of the toughest men ever seen in the ring.

Neilson or Nelson was no boxer but he was able to take everything most of his opponents could hand out and come back fighting as fast and as furiously as ever.

In well over 100 fights Nelson was only stopped twice. One man to beat him was the Englishman, Owen Moran, the greatest featherweight who never won a title.

As a boy Nelson broke his left arm and through lack of attention the arm was almost stiff when it healed, but he overcame this handicap in remarkable fashion.

Nelson's first world title bout is one of the epics of ring history. This was when he challenged Joe Gans and they fought 42 rounds before the Dane was disqualified, September 3, 1906.

At their second meeting Nelson beat the "Old Master" in 17 rounds to take the lightweight title, and he confirmed his superiority by beating Gans again in 21 rounds.

Nelson held the title until February 22, 1910, when he was beaten by Adolph Wolgast, the referee stopping the contest at the end of the 40th round. This was a real grudge fight and was a non-stop all-action battle.

The "Durable Dane" retired in 1923 and died in Chicago at the age of 71.

# NEW YORK STATE ATHLETIC COMMISSION:

This is the principal boxing authority outside the jurisdiction of the W.B.A. in America.

While the W.B.A. is a private organisation the N.Y.A.C. is a legal body originally set up in 1920 to enforce the stipulations of the new Walker Law.

It was re-organised in May, 1921, under the Simpson-Brundage Bill.

Since then this commission has done much to improve the game under its jurisdiction. For instance, they have made it compulsory for promoters to insure boxers appearing on their bills. They were also among the first to adopt a compulsory eight-count.

The headquarters of the N.Y.A.C. is 270 Broadway, New York City.

# NEW ZEALAND:

Apart from Bob Fitzsimmons, who was born in Cornwall but brought up in New Zealand, the best-known fighter ever to come out of these islands was probably Tom Heeney, born at Gisborne in 1898. Nineteen twenty-seven and 1928 were his best years, for then he went to America and leapt into the front rank with victories over Jim Maloney and Johnny Risko. He drew with Jack Sharkey in January 1928, and a victory over Jack Delaney two months later earned him a world title fight with Gene Tunney.

This fight failed to create much interest, for Heeney did not possess a killer punch to make him a real threat to the skilful Tunney. He put up a game show but he was outclassed before the referee stopped the contest in the 11th round to save the New Zealander from further punishment.

In recent years boxing has lost some of its popularity in New Zealand. For some reason or other it has become difficult to fill even a medium-size hall and more of their best men have deserted the home promoters for the bigger purses to be had in Sydney, Australia.

## Champions:

WORLD:—
Featherweight: Billy Murphy, 1890.
Empire:—
Middleweight: Bos Murphy, 1948; Tuna Scanlan, 1964; Monty Betham, 1975-78.
Welterweight: Barry Brown, 1954.
Lightweight: Manoel Santos, 1967.
Featherweight: Toro George, 1970-72.
Olympic:—
Welterweight: Ed Morgan, 1928.

# NICKNAMES:

See under NAMES.

# NIGERIA:

The first world title bout to take place in Nigeria was that between Dick Tiger and Gene Fullmer, at Ibadan, August 10, 1963.

## Champions:

World:—

Light-heavyweight: Dick Tiger, 1966-68.

Middleweight: Dick Tiger, 1962 (N.B.A. only), 1963, 1965-66.

Featherweight: Hogan Bassey, 1957-59.

Empire and Commonwealth:—

Middleweight: Dick Tiger, 1958-60, 1960-63.

Light-welterweight: Obisia Nwankpa, 1979-83; Billy Famous, 1983-86.

Lightweight: Jonathan Dele, 1975-77; Hogan Jimah, 1978-79.

Junior-lightweight: Billy Moeller, 1975-77.

Featherweight: Hogan Bassey, 1955-57; Eddie Ndukwu, 1977-80.

Flyweight: Ray Amoo, 1980.

## NOBLE, Tommy:

This Bermondsey, London, boxer's career began with a remarkable co-incidence. In his first fight at the Ring, Blackfriars, in 1915, his opponent was a George Noble, no relation.

Tommy Noble won the vacant British bantamweight title by outpointing Joe Symonds at the N.S.C., November 25, 1918.

In April, 1919, he knocked out the redoubtable Eugene Criqui in 19 rounds at the Holborn Stadium, but in June that year he lost his British title to Walter Ross.

The fact that Noble had fought a strenuous 20-round draw with Criqui in Paris only three days before his meeting with Ross may have had something to do with his defeat. At any rate the referee stopped the fight in the 10th round to save Noble from further punishment.

In 1920 he went to America to try and get a fight with Johnny Kilbane for the world featherweight title but Kilbane would not be drawn into a match. Tex Rickard decided to offer a "world featherweight title belt" of his own to a "fighting" champion (Kilbane was out of favour at that time), and Tommy Noble won this belt by beating Johnny Murray, who had already got the better of Kilbane in a "no decision" bout.

## "NO DECISION" BOUTS:

For 11 years before the Frawley Law came into effect in New York State in 1911 boxing had only been permitted in clubs to be witnessed by members. The Frawley Law allowed boxing for the general public, but one of its conditions were that all contests should be merely exhibitions with no decisions given.

Because of this no man could win a boxing match unless he did so by a knock-out, and so the champions were comparatively safe as long as they avoided hard-hitting opponents when putting their titles at stake.

During this period of "no decision" bouts there were "popular verdicts," the winner being decided by a majority vote of newspaper reporters, but these verdicts did not carry enough weight to deprive a champion of his title.

Decisions were not permitted in boxing matches in New York State until the Frawley Law was superseded by the Walker Law in 1920.

## NORWAY:

None of the Norwegian-born fighters won an international title among the professionals until Sven Erik Paulsen became European junior-lightweight champion in 1974.

Their only international champions before this had been among the amateurs, with the outstanding fighter being Otto Von Porat, who won both the Olympic and European heavyweight titles in Paris in 1924.

Although a Norwegian national, Von Porat was actually born in Sweden. He subsequently turned professional and had many fights in America. In New York he was twice beaten by Paolino Uzcudun.

Another amateur fighter, Christensen, won the European middleweight title in 1927.

Probably the best-known Norwegian boxer was Pete Sanstol. About 1930 he was a great favourite around New York and in Canada. In August, 1931, he was narrowly outpointed by world bantamweight champion, Al Brown.

## Champions:

EUROPEAN:—
Heavyweight: Steffen Tangstad, 1984-85, 1986.

Junior-lightweight: Sven Erik Paulsen, 1974-76.

Olympic:—
Heavyweight: Otto Von Porat, 1924.

## NOTICE, Horace:

Not big for a heavyweight but an aggressive all-action fighter who was A.B.A. champion in 1983, and captured the British and Commonwealth titles in only his 10th professional fight by stopping Hughroy Currie in the sixth round in April 1986. Notice was then nearly 29 years of age. He was born in Birmingham and taken to the West Indies as a child, not returning to West Bromwich until he was 21. Became first heavyweight for 20 years to win a Lonsdale belt after beating Dave Garside in five rounds and Paul Lister in three.

## O'BRIEN, Jack:

Joseph F. Hagan became known in the ring as Philadelphia Jack O'Brien. He was really little more than a middleweight but he fought several of the best heavyweights of his day, won the world light-heavyweight crown and also claimed the British middleweight title, although this last claim was never taken seriously.

He came to Britain in 1901 and here beat several of our best middleweights and heavyweights. He defeated George Crisp at a time when that Newcastle fighter was still claiming the British heavyweight title, and he also defeated our leading middleweight, Dido Plumb.

O'Brien won the world light-heavyweight title in December, 1905, when he knocked out the veteran Bob Fitzsimmons in 13 rounds.

O'Brien never really took much interest in this title after this, however. He preferred to go after the heavyweight crown, and in November, 1906, he fought a 20-round draw with the champion, Tommy Burns.

When these two met again in May, 1907, O'Brien's display was rather a disappointing one and he lost the decision.

After this O'Brien engaged mostly in "no decision" bouts and exhibitions before he retired in 1912, but one of these contests stands out. That was when he was challenged by the middleweight champion, Stanley Ketchel. O'Brien was knocked out in the last five seconds of that bout, but as he was saved by the bell and it was a "no decision" bout Ketchel never had the privilege of calling himself light-heavyweight champion.

## O'DOWD, Mike:

Born at St. Paul, Minnesota, of Irish parentage, in 1895, Mike O'Dowd became world middleweight champion in November, 1917, by knocking out Al McCoy in six rounds.

In May, 1920, he lost the championship when he was surprisingly outpointed by Johnny Wilson, but when they met again in a return match Wilson proved that this was no fluke by gaining another points victory.

When, in 1922, the N.Y.A.C. refused to acknowledge Wilson as champion, O'Dowd won their world title by defeating Dave Rosenberg on a disqualification in eight rounds, New York City, November, 1922. Four months later he was knocked out by Jock Malone and did not fight again.

## O'KEEFE, Pat:

This great-hearted London fighter had a remarkable record in the middleweight division. He first won the British title in 1906 and he won the same title for the last time nearly 12 years later.

O'Keefe's defensive work was particularly good, and he became British middleweight champion by outpointing Mike Crawley in March, 1906, but lost the crown to Tom Thomas two months later.

In April, 1913, he beat Frank Mantell over 20 rounds at a time when the German-American was claiming the world middleweight championship, but neither O'Keefe, nor Mantell were ever generally acknowledged as world titleholders.

In August, 1913, O'Keefe met Billy Wells for the British heavyweight title but was beaten on points over 15 rounds.

O'Keefe regained the middleweight crown in February, 1914, by outpointing Harry Reeve; lost it to Bandsman Blake in May, 1916, and regained it from Blake in January, 1918. He made the Lonsdale Belt his own property with this last victory over Blake. About a year later O'Keefe relinquished the British championship.

## OLIN, Bob:

A Golden Gloves champion in his amateur days, this American won the world light-heavyweight championship by outpointing Maxie Rosenbloom at Madison Square Garden, November 16, 1934. The referee's decision was hotly disputed, for it was very close.

In April, 1935, Olin was outpointed by John Henry Lewis in a non-title fight, and six months later he was again beaten by the negro fighter, and that time the title went with the decision.

## OLIVARES, Ruben:

Allowing for the confusion in World featherweight title claims this tough Mexican fighter won the world championship twice in both the bantamweight and featherweight divisions—a remarkable record.

Considering that he won something like 80 fights inside the distance there can be no disputing the claim that he was one of the hardest hitting men ever seen in the ring under 9 st. (126 lbs.). A study of the list of world champions towards the end of this book will show how he lost and won his titles but it is worth noting that after August 1969, when he first won the bantamweight crown by knocking out Lionel Rose in five rounds, Olivares engaged in 12 world title fights (including undisputed and W.B.A. or W.B.C.).

## OLSON, Carl:

Born at Honolulu of a Swedish father and a Portuguese mother, Olson put his age on to turn professional when he was only 15. The authorities found out and he quit Honolulu to fight in San Francisco, but his age was discovered again and he lost his licence for a while.

After Ray Robinson first announced his retirement in 1952 Olson beat Paddy Young to be recognised in America as middleweight champion.

On this side of the Atlantic Randolph Turpin was acknowledged as world middleweight title-holder, and so the two met on October 21, 1953, Olson winning on points.

Robinson returned to the ring in 1955 and in December of that year Olson lost his title to the coloured fighter, who knocked him out in the second round.

This rugged fighter, whose bobbing and weaving has upset so many opponents, announced his retirement more than once but kept coming back, and even when around 35 years of age he surprised many critics with wins over rated light-heavyweights.

## OLYMPIA:

The first big fight promotions in this country to be staged in the modern style were put on at Olympia in 1910.

Prior to this boxing was restricted to the smaller halls and clubs, but an Australian, Hugh D. McIntosh, altered all that.

McIntosh was a man with big ideas. Before coming to England from Australia he had built the Rushcutters Bay Stadium and staged the world title fight between Tommy Burns and Jack Johnson.

At Olympia in January, 1911, he put Bombardier Billy Wells in with Gunner Moir. A month later Sam Langford and Bill Lang topped the bill.

Charles B. Cochran continued these "big fight" promotions at Olympia. He brought Willie Ritchie over from America in 1914 to defend his world lightweight title against Freddy Welsh in this arena, and Welsh won this 20-round contest. In the same year Mr. Cochran also staged the Georges Carpentier—Gunboat Smith contest.

## OLYMPIC GAMES:

In the 18 Olympic Games boxing competitions held this century the country to win most titles has been the United States with a total of 42 gold medals.

The U.S.A. swept the board by winning all seven titles at St. Louis in 1904. The only other occasion that such a thing has occurred was in the London Olympics of 1908 when Great Britain captured all five of the titles put up for competition.

Great Britain made a great comeback to regain recognition as a power in the amateur boxing world when they won two gold medals, one silver, and two bronze medals in the 1956 Games at Melbourne. One hundred and fifty-one competitors took part that year, and Great Britain's success was the more remarkable because it was achieved with a team of only seven men.

The individual record for the most Olympic gold medals is held by Laszlo Papp and Teofilio Stevenson with 3 each. Papp, a railway clerk from Hungary, won the middleweight title in 1948 and the light-middleweight title in 1952 and 1956. Stevenson, from Cuba, won the heavyweight title in 1972, 1976 and 1980.

The only other men to win more than one Olympic title were O. L. Kirk (U.S.A.), who was feather and bantamweight champion in 1904; Harry W. Mallin (New Scotland Yard and Eton Manor B.C.), who gained the middleweight title at Antwerp in 1920 and again at Paris in 1924; B. Lagutin (U.S.S.R.) light-middleweight 1964 and 1968; J. Kulej (Poland), light-welterweight 1964 and 1968.

Here are the total number of gold medals won by each country in the Olympic games at St. Louis 1904, London 1908, Antwerp 1920, Paris 1924, Amsterdam 1928, Los Angeles 1932, Berlin 1936, London 1948, Helsinki 1952, Melbourne 1956, Rome 1960, Tokyo 1964, Mexico 1968, West Germany 1972, Montreal 1976, Moscow 1980, Los Angeles 1984.

U.S.A. 42, U.S.S.R. 13, Italy 13, Great Britain 12, Cuba 12, Hungary 9, Poland 8, Argentine 7, S. Africa 5, Germany 4, France 3, Czechoslovakia 3, E. Germany 3, Yugoslavia 3, Canada 2, Finland 2, Mexico 2, Bulgaria 2, E. Africa, Norway, Japan, Rumania, Holland, Belgium, Denmark, New Zealand, Venezuela, S. Korea and N. Korea, 1 each.

For Olympic champions who also won world professional titles see under AMATEUR TO PROFESSIONAL.

## ORTIZ, Carlos:

Born in Puerto Rico, but brought up in New York from the age of nine, Carlos Ortiz won national amateur titles before turning professional in 1955 and was unbeaten in his first 27 fights before losing to Johnny Busso.

Ortiz reversed this decision in a return, and in June, 1959, he became world junior welterweight champion by battering Kenny Lane into defeat in two rounds.

Lane had previously been the only other fighter, apart from Busso, to hold a decision over Ortiz, and, indeed, in his first 50 professional bouts only two more fighters were able to beat the hard-hitting Puerto Rican.

The first after Lane was Duilio Loi who relieved Ortiz of his world junior title and confirmed his superiority with another victory in a return bout. The second was Ismael Laguna, who, in April, 1965, took the world lightweight title from him, a title he had held for almost exactly three years since he had so clearly and surprisingly outpointed Joe Brown.

Ortiz regained the lightweight title from Laguna in November 1965, but after five more successful defences lost it to Carlos Teo Cruz in June 1968.

## ORTIZ, Manuel:

One of the hardest hitting bantamweights of all time, this Mexican won the world title from Lou Salica in Hollywood, August 7, 1942. He created a record in this division by defending the championship a total of 21 times.

Ortiz was not beaten until his 16th defence when he was outpointed by Harold Dade in January, 1947, and after regaining the crown from Dade in a return match two months later, he made another four successful defences before losing it to Vic Toweel in Johannesburg in May, 1950.

## O'SULLIVAN, Danny:

Born at King's Cross, London, Danny comes from a boxing family. His grandfather was a bare-knuckle fighter in Ireland and his father was a more than useful flyweight. Danny also has five brothers all of whom have been boxers.

Danny O'Sullivan won the A.B.A. bantamweight championship in 1947 just before turning professional. In December, 1949, he won the vacant British bantamweight title by stopping Teddy Gardner in nine rounds at the Albert Hall, but lost it five months later at Glasgow when he was knocked out in six rounds by Peter Keenan.

## OWEN, Johnny:

Nicknamed "skeleton" or "match-stick" because of his bony frame this lanky bantamweight from Merthyr worked at a terrific rate and picked his punches well. He won the British bantamweight title from Paddy Maguire in only his tenth professional contest in November 1977 and continued his unbeaten run to capture the vacant Commonwealth title 12 months later with a points win over Australian Paul Ferreri.

He added the European title in March, 1979, but when he attempted to win the W.B.C. world bantamweight crown from Guadalupe Pintor in Los Angeles in September, 1980, he was stopped in the 12th round and died later. It was a tragic loss of one of Britain's finest post-war boxers.

# P

which was billed as being for the heavyweight championship of England, and Palmer held on to this title until he was disqualified in the ninth round of a contest with Gunner Moir at the N.S.C. in October, 1906.

When world champion, Tommy Burns, visited this country in 1907-08, Palmer met him at Wonderland but he was no match for the stocky Canadian who knocked him out in the fourth round.

## PADDOCK, Tom:

Born at Redditch, Worcestershire, this champion of the old prize ring won some terrific battles. One of the most arduous fights in his record must have been his first battle with Aaron Jones. This lasted 121 rounds before Paddock was able to finish his opponent.

In a second meeting with Jones, Paddock won in 61 rounds and in his next battle he gained the championship by stopping Harry Broome in 51 rounds lasting 1 hour 3 minutes. The date was October 2, 1856.

Ill-health interrupted Paddock's career after this and he only fought two more contests, losing to Tom Sayers and Sam Hurst, before he died at the age of 39.

## PAINTER, Ned:

Born at Stretford, Lancashire, Ned Painter had one outstanding success and it won him the Championship of England. That was when he beat the scientific Tom Spring in 41 rounds at Russia Farm, Kingston, August 7, 1818.

Four months earlier, Painter had been beaten by Spring and he must have realised that in his subsequent victory he had caught the champion on an off-day, for when he was challenged by Spring for a return battle, Painter declined and forfeited his title.

## PALMER, Jack:

Jack Palmer of Newcastle claimed the British middleweight championship in 1902 but did not remain long enough in this division to really establish his claim.

In May, 1903, he stopped Ben Taylor in 12 rounds at Newcastle in a fight

## PALMER, Thomas "Pedlar":

Tom Palmer, of Canning Town, London, was without doubt one of the cleverest boxers this country has ever produced.

He made his debut at the N.S.C. in London at the age of 17 on February 27, 1893, and so enthralled the club's members with his effortless ease and his brilliant defensive work that he very soon became a great favourite at Covent Garden.

Eventually the boxing fraternity was to hold Palmer in such respect that later in his brilliant career he was presented with a gold and diamond belt worth more than £1,000, a great deal of money in those days. This belt was stolen from him some time later.

Palmer was not a heavy puncher but his hitting was so accurate and he was so clever at bobbing and weaving and riding his opponent's punches that he became known as "The Box o'Tricks."

Palmer won the world bantamweight title in November, 1895, with a victory over Billy Plimmer who was disqualified in the 14th round, but he was not recognised in America where Jimmy Barry was champion.

When Barry retired, Terry McGovern claimed the title and Pedlar Palmer went to New York to meet the Irish-American. It was quite a shock when the Cockney fighter was knocked out in 2 minutes 32 seconds of the first round.

In 1900 Palmer lost the British title, which he had also taken from Plimmer, when he was outpointed at the N.S.C. by Harry Ware, and in March, 1901, he was beaten by Harry Harris of Chicago for the vacant world bantamweight crown.

In 1904 and 1905, Palmer made two bids for the British featherweight title but lost to Ben Jordan and to Joe Bowker. The perky Cockney's contest with Bowker has seldom been surpassed for the skill exhibited by two boxers in the same ring. Palmer's seconds threw in the towel in the 12th round. Pedlar Palmer died at Brighton in 1949.

## PALOMINO, Carlos:

Born California of Mexican parents this welterweight was well known as a two-fisted puncher who rained blows on his opponents from all directions and was particularly vicious when hitting around the body. It was this body punching which put world champion John H. Stracey out of his stride when these two met at Wembley in June 1976 and enabled Palomino to take the welterweight crown when the referee intervened in the twelfth round.

In a subsequent visit to Wembley Palomino, a college graduate, successfully defended his title by knocking out Dave Green with a terrific left hook in the eleventh round, but in January 1979 he lost his crown when outpointed by Wilfredo Benitez.

## PANAMA:

Hungry fighters are often the best and in recent years Panama has again proved the truth of that old adage. The latest boxing boom in this country has produced so many first class fighters who have come up the hard way, even graduating from street fighting in the poorer districts to become world champions.

### Champions:

World:—

Light-middleweight: Roberto Duran, (W.B.A.), 1983-84.

Welterweight: Roberto Duran, 1980.

Junior-welterweight: Alfonso Frazier, 1972.

Lightweight: Roberto Duran, 1972-79.

Junior-lightweight: Alfredo Layne, 1986.

Featherweight: Rafael Ortega (W.B.A.). 1977; Eusebio Pedroza, 1978-85.

Light-featherweight: Rigoberto Riasco, 1976; Wilfredo Gomez (W.B.C.), 1977.

Bantamweight: Enrique Pinder, 1972-73.

Flyweight: Alfonso Lopez, (W.B.A.), 1976.

Light-flyweight: Jaime Rios, (W.B.C.), 1973-76; Hilario Zapata, 1980-82, 1982.

## PAPKE, Billy:

A German-American from Illinois, Papke was a really tough customer and they called him the "Thunderbolt." His four middleweight title fights with tearaway Stanley Ketchel remain among the hardest and bloodiest battles ever seen in the American ring.

Papke first met Ketchel in June, 1908, but was beaten over ten rounds.

Their second meeting, in September, 1908, was one of those ring epics and Papke handed Ketchel the biggest beating he ever had in the ring before the referee stopped the fight in the 12th round. This victory gave Papke the middleweight title.

In another gruelling contest, in November, 1908, Ketchel turned the tables on Papke and knocked him out in the 11th round.

After Ketchel's untimely death in 1910 Papke met Johnny Thompson for the vacant title at Sydney, February, 1911, but was beaten on points in 20 rounds.

Thompson relinquished the title and Papke again claimed it but he was eliminated through defeats by Bob Moha, Frank Mantell and Frank Klaus.

Papke retired in 1919. He committed suicide in 1936.

## PARET, Benny:

A game Cuban welterweight who took one beating too many and died 10 days after being battered to a standstill by Emile Griffith in the 12th round of a world title bout in New York, March 24, 1962.

Some say he should never have gone in with Griffith less than four months after attempting to wrest the N.B.A. world middleweight title from Gene Fullmer and being k.o'd in the 10th round.

Paret first won the world welter crown by outpointing Don Jordan in May, 1960. He lost it to Griffith when k.o'd by

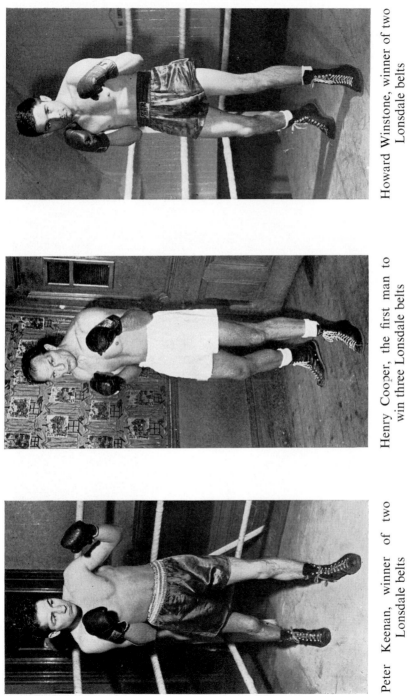

Peter Keenan, winner of two Lonsdale belts

Henry Cooper, the first man to win three Lonsdale belts

Howard Winstone, winner of two Lonsdale belts

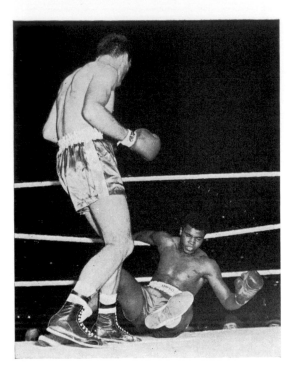

Henry Cooper's left-hook: (*left*) Cassius Clay survived one of the most dramatic moments in British ring history when dropped by Cooper in June 1963 and got up to win. But the left-hook that draped Joe Erskine over the bottom rope (*below*) ended this British heavyweight title bout in November 1959

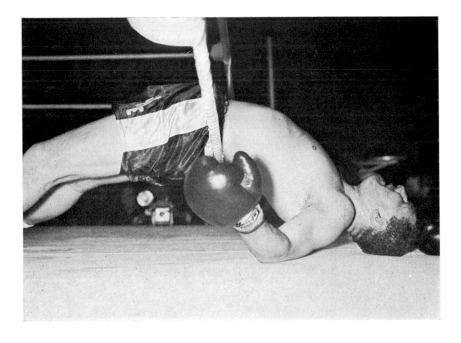

the American negro in 13 rounds, April, 1961, but regained the crown in a return only six months later with a surprise points victory.

The Cuban's last two contests followed this, his defeat by Fullmer and the tragic third meeting with Griffith.

## PASTRANO, Willie:

This good-looking well-dressed American lied about his age when he collected his first purse in the ring, for he was then only 15, and he had a long up-hill battle before becoming world light-heavyweight champion more than 12 years later.

Like so many fighters in this weight division he suffered set-backs when he became too ambitious and took on full-blown heavyweights; Brian London, Joe Erskine, Alonzo Johnson and Gregorio Peralta, were among those who defeated Pastrano.

Pastrano's speed and skill, however, gained him a points verdict and the world light-heavyweight title in June, 1963, when he met Harold Johnson, and he also proved that he can punch in his second successful title defence by stopping Terry Downes in 11 rounds.

Next time out, in March 1965, Pastrano couldn't keep out of trouble and lost his title to Jose Torres, the referee stopping the fight at the end of the 9th round.

## PATERSON, Jackie:

Born Springside, Ayrshire, in 1920, Paterson emigrated to the United States at the age of eight but returned five years later.

He turned professional in 1938 and in September of the following year he won the British flyweight title by stopping Paddy Ryan in 13 rounds. He added the Empire title to this in March, 1940, with a victory over Kid Tanner.

Paterson gained his greatest honour in June, 1943, when he knocked out Peter Kane in the first round of a contest at Hampden Park, Glasgow, to become world flyweight champion.

Paterson was deprived of this title in 1947 when he was taken ill and failed to appear at the weigh-in for a contest with Dado Marino. A subsequent Monaghan-Marino bout was recognised as for the world title by N.B.A. and the Eire Boxing Board, but Paterson brought an injunction against the B.B.B.C. preventing them from recognising the fight as for the title and after making an appeal the Scot had his title returned to him in November, 1947.

However, when he met Rinty Monaghan in March, 1948, he was knocked out in seven rounds.

Thereafter this southpaw fought mostly as a bantamweight. He had already won the British, Empire and European bantamweight titles. He lost his European title to Theo Medina in October, 1946, but held on to his British and Empire crowns until March, 1949, when he was outpointed by Stan Rowan at Liverpool.

He met a violent death by stabbing in November 1966.

## PATTENDEN, Alfred "Kid":

A Londoner, "Kid" Pattenden won the vacant British bantamweight title by stopping "Kid" Nicholson in 12 rounds at the N.S.C., June 4, 1928.

Soon after this the title was in dispute for it was also claimed by Teddy Baldock when he beat the previous champion, Johnny Brown, in August, 1928. Brown, however, had relinquished the title, and despite Baldock's protests it was Pattenden who got official recognition as Lonsdale Belt holder.

In May, 1929, the dispute was cleared up for Baldock and Pattenden met, and the former got the points verdict at the end of 15 rounds.

## PATTERSON, Floyd:

An American negro, Patterson has gone down in history as the first fighter ever to regain the world heavyweight title. Despite this achievement, however, he did not establish himself as a great champion because he failed to meet many of the leading contenders.

This was due largely to the policy of his manager, Cus D'Amato, who, for some time, carried on a feud with the I.B.C. of America and refused to allow Patterson to meet anyone connected with that organisation.

Patterson was a clever boxer and

although no great stylist he was a remarkably fast puncher who possessed very quick reflexes.

He had an outstanding amateur career, winning an Olympic medal in the 165 lbs. class when still only 17, and after turning over to the paid ranks he won the vacant heavyweight title in his 32nd contest by knocking out Archie Moore in 2 minutes 27 seconds of the fifth round at Chicago Stadium, November 30, 1956.

Patterson successfully defended his title four times before he was surprisingly defeated by Ingemar Johansson in New York, June 26, 1959. He was down seven times before the referee intervened and awarded the fight and the title to the Swede after 2 minutes 3 seconds of the third round.

It was only 12 months later that Patterson again surprised the critics and won back the title by putting Johansson out for the count in 1 minute 51 seconds of the fifth round, and in a third meeting he stopped Johansson inside six rounds.

His glory was shortlived, however, for when at last he was matched with leading contender, Sonny Liston, he was disposed of in only 2 minutes 6 seconds, and when these two got together again Patterson lasted only 4 seconds longer.

## PAUL, Larry:

This cheerful Wolverhampton fighter became the first holder of the British light-middleweight title in September 1973 when he k.o.'d the far more experienced former British welterweight champion, Bobby Arthur, in the 10th round.

A.B.A. light-middleweight champion in 1972 Paul had, therefore, reached the top of the tree in only his eighth professional bout, but after one successful defence he lost the title in November 1974 when stopped in eight rounds by Maurice Hope.

## PEARCE, David:

On the small side for a heavyweight but could pile on the pressure. David Pearce from Newport, Wales, won a novices competition in 1979; lost to Neville Meade for the Welsh heavyweight title the following year, but in September 1983 relieved Meade of the British heavyweight title. Pearce took all the veteran Meade could throw at him in the earlier rounds and came through to outpunch his opponent before the fight was stopped just before the end of the ninth round. Incidentally, this was the last British title fight scheduled for 15 rounds.

The brave Pearce took a lot of punishment when outpointed by the European champion Lucien Rodriquez in France in March 1984 and he did not fight again.

## PEARCE, Hen:

Born at Bristol in 1777, Hen Pearce was known to the fancy as "The Game Chicken."

He was one of the outstanding men of the old prize ring for he fought seven contests against six of the best men of his day and won all seven.

When Belcher relinquished the title, following the accident which cost him an eye in 1803, Pearce claimed the championship after beating Joe Berks in 15 rounds.

He subsequently defeated Berks a second time and followed this with victories over Elias Spray, Stephen Carter, John Gully, and Jem Blecher whom he beat in 18 rounds when the old champion was attempting a comeback.

## PELICAN CLUB:

This was a famous old boxing club for the aristocracy founded by William Goldberg, a racing journalist known as the "Shifter." It first opened at the Star Club in Denman Street, London, on January 19, 1887.

One of the outstanding personalities of old-time boxing in this country took charge of the boxing at this club. He was Ernest Wells, otherwise known as "Swears."

In 1889 the club moved to Gerrard Street and Wells was eventually succeeded by John Fleming, manager of Jem Smith, and another outstanding personality in ring history.

Fleming became co-founder of the National Sporting Club in 1891 and the Pelican Club faded out soon after this. Most of the committee of the Pelican Club followed Fleming to the N.S.C.

## PENDER, Paul:

A middleweight from Brookline, Massachusetts, Pender began his professional career in 1949 but brittle hands gave him a lot of trouble and slowed his climb to the top. There was one spell of five years in which he had only six fights.

However, in January, 1960, he was matched with the world middleweight champion, Ray Robinson, and upset the odds by outpointing the veteran negro fighter.

Five months later, Pender confirmed his right to the title by scoring a more convincing win over Robinson.

Pender had three meetings with British champion, Terry Downes. The American won the first in 7 rounds, lost his title in the second when stopped in 9 rounds, but regained the crown by outpointing Downes in their third bout.

In November, 1962, Pender was deprived of his title by all authorities except Massachusetts, and although the New York Supreme Court over-ruled the boxing authorities, Pender announced his retirement some six months later.

## PEP, Willie:

This skilled boxer had a run of 136 fights with only one defeat from the time he turned professional in 1940 until he lost his world featherweight title to Sandy Saddler in 1948. The single defeat was at the hands of Sammy Angott in an overweight match in March, 1943.

Pep won the world featherweight title from Chalky Wright in New York, November 20, 1942. There was still some dispute over this championship at that time for the N.B.A. favoured the claim of Sal Bartolo, but Pep settled this matter by stopping Bartolo in 12 rounds in June, 1946.

Pep had a short spell in the U.S. Navy after this but he returned still in top form and ran up another string of victories, beating such men as Manuel Ortiz, Chalky Wright (twice), and Phil Terranova, before joining the U.S. Army in March, 1945.

His service in the Army did not prevent him from continuing on the winning trail, and, amongst others, he beat Jackie Wilson, Sol Bartolo and Chalky Wright (all former world champions), before losing his title to Sandy Saddler by a knock-out in the fourth round, October 29, 1948.

An Italian-American, Pep regained his title in a return bout four months later with a 15-round points victory, but Saddler again got the better of him in their third meeting in September, 1950, when Pep was forced to retire after the seventh round.

Pep still fancied his chance against Saddler but in a fourth meeting he was stopped in nine rounds. He announced his retirement in January, 1959, following defeats by Hogan Bassey and Sonny Leon, but attempted a comeback in 1965. This ended the following year.

## PEREZ, Pascual:

This little Argentine fighter won the Olympic flyweight gold medal in London in 1948.

He did not turn professional until he was 26 years of age.

Standing only 4 feet 11 inches and scaling around 7 stone 8 lbs. (106 lbs.) he was, nevertheless, an extremely hard puncher.

He was the first Argentine boxer to win a world title when he captured the flyweight crown by outpointing Yoshio Shirai in Tokyo in November, 1954.

Perez had a remarkable undefeated run of 52 contests before being outpointed in a non-title bout by Japanese champion, Sadao Yaoita, in Tokyo in January, 1959.

Ten months later Perez avenged this defeat by scoring a 13th round k.o. over the Jap, but he lost his title to Pone Kingpetch in April, 1960.

## PEREZ, Victor "Young":

This Tunisian flyweight was recognised by I.B.U. as world champion when he beat the American champion, Frankie Genaro, in Paris in October, 1931.

Eight days later he came over to Manchester and fought a 15-round draw with Johnny King, but when he next visited Manchester, in October, 1932, he lost his claim to the flyweight title with a defeat by Jackie Brown. Perez took a hammering in that contest and the towel was thrown in in the 13th round.

Perez was murdered by Nazis in

Germany in 1942.

## PERRY, William:

Born at Tipton, Staffs, this bare-knuckle prize fighter was known as the "Tipton Slasher."

Following the retirement of Bendigo, William Perry claimed the championship after beating Tom Paddock on a foul in 27 rounds lasting 42 minutes at Woking, December 17, 1850.

However, in his very next fight, he was beaten on a foul in 15 rounds, 35 minutes, by Harry Broome, at Mildenhall, Suffolk, September 29, 1851.

In his last appearance in the ring William Perry was defeated in 11 rounds by Tom Sayers.

He died at Wolverhampton in 1881.

## PETERSEN, Jack:

This Welsh Carpentier had a phenomenal rise to fame. In 1931 he won the A.B.A. light-heavyweight title and before 1932 was a little more than half-way through, he had turned professional and won both the British light-heavyweight and heavyweight titles.

A courageous fighter, Petersen was always a big attraction wherever he appeared. He had the heart for the job but unfortunately he lacked the real physical strength necessary to make him a serious threat to world class heavyweights. The German, Walter Neusel, proved a stumbling block to Petersen on three occasions.

Born at Cardiff, Petersen intended becoming a doctor before the lure of the ring made him change his mind.

He won the British light-heavyweight title by outpointing Harry Crossley in May, 1932, but relinquished it almost immediately.

Within two months he had gained the heavyweight title from Reggie Meen with a second round knock-out and he went on to make the Lonsdale Belt his own property with victories over Jack Pettifer and Jack Doyle before he lost the title to Len Harvey in November, 1933.

Petersen regained the heavyweight crown together with the Empire championship when he defeated Harvey in a return bout six months later, and he held on to them until he was stopped in three

rounds by Ben Foord at Leicester in August, 1936.

Cut eyes were giving Petersen plenty of trouble at that time, and, following his third defeat by Neusel in February, 1937, he found that his sight was being affected and he wisely decided to retire from the game.

## PETROU, Kostas:

Born Birkenhead and fighting out of Birmingham, this welterweight lost to Lloyd Honeyghan in the early part of his career but improved with keeping and got a British title chance after outpointing dangerous Lloyd Christie. The British welterweight title had by then been vacated by Lloyd Honeyghan and Petrou, who fights from behind a high guard, went on to show a lot more aggression against Rocky Kelly stopping him in the ninth round at Darlington in April 1985 to take the British title. Unfortunately for Petrou he lost in his first defence only five months later, surviving some heavy punches from Commonwealth champion Sylvester Mittee but being clearly outpointed.

## PHILLIPS, Eddie:

Born Bethnal Green, London, Eddie Phillips was a classy boxer but too temperamental to attain world honours.

He had his first fight at East Ham Baths and in June, 1933, he was matched with Len Harvey for the vacant British light-heavyweight title but lost on points.

When Harvey relinquished this crown in 1934, Phillips took it over after outpointing Tommy Farr at Mountain Ash, February 4, 1935.

There was a real dearth of good cruiserweights in this country at that time and Phillips was not called upon to defend his title until middleweight champion, Jock McAvoy, met him in April, 1937. Phillips was knocked out in the 14th round.

After this Phillips put on weight fast until he was over 14 stone (196 lbs.). In 1938 he met Len Harvey for the vacant British heavyweight title but was beaten on a foul in four rounds.

## PLATTS, Gus:

In February, 1921, Gus Platts of

Sheffield became European middleweight champion with a victory over the Frenchman, Ercole Balzac, who was forced to retire in the seventh round.

The reigning British middleweight champion at that time was Tom Gummer, and, in March, 1921, Platts beat him at Sheffield, knocking him out in six rounds.

Naturally, Platts claimed the championship but although he was acknowledged by the vast majority of boxing fans in this country he did not receive the blessing of the N.S.C.

However, his reign did not last long for on May 31, at the Albert Hall, he was outpointed by Johnny Basham.

## PLIMMER, Billy:

This brilliant bantamweight from Birmingham was one of Britain's most successful fighters in the United States. Indeed, he was undefeated in about two dozen bouts on the other side of the Atlantic and made strong claims to the world bantamweight title.

Before sailing for America in September, 1891, Plimmer won the British title by stopping Jim Stevens in 15 rounds at the N.S.C.

While in America he beat Tommy Kelly at Coney Island in May, 1892, a victory which gave him good grounds for calling himself world champion.

In August, 1893, he added considerable strength to his claim by defeating the redoubtable George Dixon in four rounds in a catchweight bout.

Soon after returning to London in 1895 Plimmer lost his title to Pedlar Palmer. The "Box of Tricks" won on a disqualification in the 14th round of a contest at the N.S.C.

## PLUMB, Dido:

Crafty middleweight who was a great favourite at the old N.S.C. It was there in March, 1900, that he knocked out the Australian, Jem Ryan, inside eight rounds, a victory which encouraged Plumb to claim the British middleweight title.

Plumb's claim was never officially acknowledged and after this experienced booth fighter had suffered defeats at the hands of two visiting Americans, Charles McKeever and Philadelphia Jack O'Brien, he faded from the championship picture.

## POINTS, Awarding of:

The idea of awarding each contestant points as a method of adjudging the winner was first established in England by the Amateur Boxing Association.

Today there are several points systems throughout the world. In British amateur boxing the better man in each round must be given a maximum of 20 points and his opponent proportionately fewer.

For many years professional boxing in Britain preferred the 5-point system, but in 1973 the B.B.B.C. changed to the 10-point system which had been widely used in America for a considerable time. In the British system, however, half points are allowed whereas in most parts of the U.S.A. only whole points are given. The better man is given the maximum 10 points in each round, or, if judged to be equal, then both boxers must be given the maximum.

In New York State in 1948, Col. Eagan of N.Y.A.C. introduced a system of points and rounds. In this system up to four points are given to the winner of each round according to the margin of victory in that round. Then, if the contestants are equal on the number of rounds, points are taken into account.

Points are generally awarded for clean hits with the knuckle part of the glove delivered with the clenched fist to any part of the front or sides of the head or body, above the belt. Points are also awarded for good defensive work in guarding, slipping, ducking or getting away. "Belt" is an *imaginary* line across the body from the top of the hip bones.

Where contestants are equal in these respects then the maximum marks are given to the one who does the most leading off or displays the better style.

Professional boxing in this country is scored only by the referee. In most other parts of the world three judges score the fight and the decision is given on the majority vote.

In amateur international championship boxing the decision is left to a panel of five judges, the referee having no say in the awarding of the points.

The B.B.B.C. did not alter their rules to allow the announcing of the referee's score card until 1966 although this had been the practice for many years in other parts of the world.

## POWELL, Dennis:

Born Four Crosses, Monmouthshire. Dennis Powell began his professional career in 1946.

He won the vacant British light-heavyweight title by stopping George Walker in 11 rounds of one of the most gory fights seen in modern times at Liverpool in March, 1953, but after outpointing Albert Finch in a non-title bout, Powell was beaten in his first defence of his British crown in October, 1953. The man who took the title from him was Alex Buxton, the referee stopping the contest in the tenth round.

Powell retired from the ring in September, 1954.

## POWER, Colin:

Paddington fishmonger who proved to be a really good boxer after joining the paid ranks in 1975 and winning the British light-welterweight title from Des Morrison in October 1977. Morrison had previously been the only fighter to beat Power. In June 1978 when he relinquished the British title Power won the European crown in grand style by pounding Frenchman Jean-Baptiste Piedvache into defeat inside 11 rounds in Paris.

In September that year, however, Power was victim of one of those mysterious and controversial continental decisions which have plagued so many British fighters abroad when the referee surprisingly intervened to stop his contest with Fernando Sanchez "Chino" in the twelfth round and give the Spaniard the European crown.

Power regained the British light-welterweight title by outpointing Clinton McKenzie in February, 1979, but lost it in a return seven months later.

## PRITCHETT, Johnny:

An aggressive middleweight from Nottingham who surprisingly announced his retirement from the ring in 1969 after suffering only one defeat in a professional career of 34 fights. That defeat took place in Milan in February 1969 when he was disqualified for alleged butting in the thirteenth round when leading European middleweight champion Carlos Duran.

Pritchett had been A.B.A. welterweight champion in 1962 and 1963 and after turning professional took the British middleweight crown from Wally Swift in his sixteenth bout. That was in November 1965, and he went on to make the Lonsdale Belt his own property.

He added the Empire crown to his honours in October 1967, beating the Jamaican, Milo Calhoun, at Manchester, and retained both this and the British title until his retirement.

## PRITCHARD, Ted:

Another product of the fairground boxing booth this Lambeth, London fighter scaled only around 11 stone (154 lbs.) but most of his opponents were heavyweights.

On March 12, 1891, he knocked out Jack Burke in three rounds for the middleweight championship of England, a title which Pritchard held until he was beaten in four rounds by the Australian, Jem Hall, in August, 1892.

By that time, however, Pritchard was concentrating on the real big boys. In July, 1891, he had beaten the heavyweight champion, Jem Smith, in only three rounds at Jack Wannop's Gymnasium, New Cross. Pritchard conceded his opponent about 2 stone (28 lbs.) in that contest.

He held on to this title until Smith beat him in two rounds at Holborn, May 10, 1895.

Pritchard also regained the middleweight title, after Hall had lost interest in it, by stopping Dick Burke in two rounds in November, 1894. But following his defeat by Frank S. Craig the American negro, in December that same year, Pritchard faded from the scene.

## PROMOTERS:

The first big-time boxing promoter was Tex Rickard. Born in Kansas City, January 2, 1871, he was brought up in

Texas, where he began earning his living as a cowpuncher.

Tex Rickard later made a fortune in the Klondike gold rush but when he opened a gambling saloon he lost most of his money.

He eventually settled in Goldfield, Nevada, and it was there that he first turned his hand to promoting boxing. The first big fight he staged was that between Joe Gans and Battling Nelson for the world lightweight title. Gans won on a foul in the 42nd round.

Financially, this promotion was a success, for Rickard took nearly 70,000 dollars at the gate, but this was nothing to what he was to achieve later.

Rickard staged his first fights in New York at the Old Madison Square Garden, March 25, 1916. Jess Willard, the world champion, fought a ten-round "no decision" bout with Frank Moran. The receipts on that occasion were more than twice those of Rickard's first promotion.

Even that, however, was well below the standard Rickard eventually set, for he became famous as the first man to promote a fight which drew a million-dollar gate. This was the Dempsey-Carpentier contest at Jersey City in 1921. After that he promoted four other big fights which each drew million-dollar gates.

George L. Rickard had a reputation for honest dealing. He played fair with everyone, and it was a great loss to boxing in America when he died in January, 1929.

Other big names in America boxing apart from Rickard have included such men as Mike Jacobs, who was Rickard's right-hand man up to the time of that promoter's death, and subsequently became famous in his own right as founder of the Twentieth Century Sporting Club and promoter at the Madison Square Garden from 1937 to 1949; James J. Johnson, who promoted at the Garden in the early 1930s; Ray Arcel of New York City; James D. Norris of the International Boxing Club and Madison Square Garden, and Jeff Dickson, an American, who became famous as a promoter on the continent of Europe.

When Dickson promoted his first contest in this country at the Albert Hall, he met with opposition from the Board of Control, but on October 17, 1929, he staged a world flyweight title bout between Frank Genaro and Ernie Jarvis. On the same bill Primo Carnera met Jack Stanley.

The first man to promote boxing in a big way as a society occasion in London was an Australian, Hugh D. McIntosh. In Sydney he had built the Rushcutters Bay Stadium to stage the Burns-Squires and Burns-Johnson contests. He refereed the latter contest himself.

When he came to England in 1910 he promoted several big fights at Olympia (see under OLYMPIA).

Between the two wars Britain boasted such outstanding promoters as Major Arnold Wilson, Johnny Best (Liverpool Stadium), Sydney Hulls (Harringay), Arthur J. Elvin (Wembley), and Jack Callaghan (Holborn).

After World War II the promoter who put British boxing back on the map again was Jack Solomons. He had begun his promotions at the Devonshire Club, Hackney, as far back as 1931, but it was in 1946 that Mr. Solomons jumped right to the top of the list of British boxing promoters. Then he brought world light-heavyweight champion, Gus Lesnevich, over from America to meet Freddie Mills and Bruce Woodcock. Other Americans followed, including Joe Baksi, Lee Savold and Joey Maxim.

Apart from Jack Solomons, other British promoters who have done most towards keeping the game alive in this country since the last war include Jack Cappell, Sol Sheckman, Messrs. Ezra and Braitman, Harry Levene, Fred Bamber, Joe Jacobs, Alex Griffiths, Jim Windsor, Reg King, Gus Demmy, Mike Barrett, Micky Duff and Frank Warren.

## PUGILISTIC SOCIETY:

This was probably the first boxing society or club ever formed with the intention of exercising some control over the sport on a national basis.

The idea of such an organisation belonged to Gentlemen John Jackson, Champion of England in 1795. The club was founded in 1814 and it is on record that their first meeting was held at the

Thatched House Tavern, London, May 22, that year.

# PUNCHES:

There are so many punches or slight variations of the same punches that it would need a volume on its own with illustrations to describe them all, but the principal punches in boxing are as follows:

## The Hook:

The left hook, if properly delivered, is a much shorter punch than the straight left, but the essential difference is that as the hook lands the wrist is turned so that the blow is struck with the back knuckles. It can be delivered to the head or body.

The right hook is usually a shorter punch than that delivered with the left. More often than not it is delivered to the body only, for when it is used to the head it is usually termed a right cross.

## The Jab:

This is not normally a knock-out punch but it is a straight blow delivered with plenty of snap, usually from a distance. Joe Louis was considered to have been one of the best ever jabbers.

## The Straight Left:

If properly used this really is a punch. Quite often boxers seem to use the straight left like a feather duster, but it should be sent out straight from the shoulder with plenty of weight behind it on the point of impact.

## The Swings:

As the term suggests these are punches delivered with either hand from a long distance with all the body weight behind them.

## The Uppercut:

The right uppercut to the chin is probably the most popular knock-out blow. Moving inside the opponent's left lead and stepping slightly to one side bring the right up to the jaw. Jack Johnson was a specialist at uppercutting his opponents.

## Special Punches:

Certain boxers have been credited with inventing punches of their own. Lots of these claims can be discounted as most of the punches these boxers were said to have invented were being used long before their time. However, it would be true to say that the following men specialised or christened the punches they used:

Bolo Punch: This was a speciality of Ike Williams, world lightweight champion in 1947-1951. It is a wide swinging punch brought up almost from the canvas, and it is so named because the action is similar to that adopted by workers in the sugar plantations when cutting canes with the bolo knife.

Corkscrew punch: This is really a hook, but it is considered to have been invented by Kid McCoy who delivered it with his left hand. It landed with a twist of the wrist.

The one-two: This is the left lead followed immediately by the right cross to the jaw. In America it is considered to have been perfected first by Willie Lewis, a New York welterweight, who fought around 1908. It was later a speciality of Georges Carpentier the French champion.

Pivot blow: This is a foul blow. It is a back-handed swing with the boxer pivoting on his heel. It is said that this punch was first used in a title fight by George La Blanche when he knocked out Jack Dempsey (Nonpareil) in August, 1890. La Blanche's claim to the middle-weight title was not accepted because the blow was then declared to be illegal.

Solar plexus punch: This was the name given to the straight left to the mark with which Bob Fitzsimmons knocked out Jim Corbett to win the world heavyweight title, March 17, 1897. The only thing new about the punch at that time was the name. This stuck after a doctor had described the punch as one to the solar plexus. It was a Fitzsimmons speciality, and a paralysing blow.

# PURSES:

The situation regarding record purses is confused in modern times by the addition of all TV and film rights which often exceed any share of the live gate.

For instance Marvin Hagler was reported to have received $17 million when he was defeated by Sugar Ray Leonard for the world middleweight title in Las Vegas, April 6, 1987.

Below are listed a number of purses paid to boxers in important fights, but these are not necessarily the biggest purses.

£1,000 to Hen Pearce, bt. John Gully, October 8, 1805.

*$14,000 to J. L. Sullivan, bt. Herbert Slade, August 6, 1883.

£800 to Peter Jackson, bt. Jem Smith, November 11, 1889.

£1,750 to Peter Jackson, bt. Frank Slavin, May 30, 1892.

£8,000 to Bob Fitzsimmons, bt. Jem Hall, March 8, 1893.

£6,000 to Tommy Burns, btn. by Jack Johnson, December 26, 1908.

$120,000 to Jack Johnson, bt. Jim Jeffries, July 4, 1910.

‡$717,000 to Jack Dempsey, btn. by Gene Tunney, September 23, 1926.

$990,445 to Gene Tunney, bt. Jack Dempsey, September 22, 1927. This remained a record until well after World War II.

$175,622 to Max Schmeling, btn. by Joe Louis, June 23, 1938.

§§$625,916 to Joe Louis, bt. Billy Conn, June 19, 1946.

$720,000 to Sonny Liston, btn. by Cassius Clay, February 25, 1964.

£50,000 to Henry Cooper, btn. by Cassius Clay, May 21, 1966.

£600,000 to Jim Watt bt. Howard Davis, June 7 1980.

**$832,000 to Floyd Patterson, bt. Ingemar Johansson, Mar 13, 1961.

*Sullivan's record purse. ‡Dempsey's record purse. §Louis's record purse. **Patterson's record purse.

## No purse:

Frank Moran got nothing for his fight with Jack Johnson for the world heavyweight title, Paris, June 27, 1914. He should have got 40 per cent of the receipts, which worked out at about 8,000 francs, but Johnson took the lot.

John L. Sullivan got nothing when he lost his heavyweight title to Jim Corbett, September 7, 1892. It was winner take all.

Tommy Gibbons got nothing for going 15 rounds with Jack Dempsey at Shelby, Montana, in July, 1923.

## PYATT, Chris:

A speedy and determined fighter from Leicester (born London) who is a powerful puncher winning 11 of his first 16 fights inside the distance with only one defeat before beating the British light-middleweight champion Prince Rodney by a k.o. in the ninth round in February 1986. Rodney had blurred vision at the time and was counted out while resting on one knee, but Pyatt obviously had the better of him.

Pyatt, the A.B.A. welterweight champion in 1982, showed the power of his punching in one of the quickest European title bouts on record, stopping John von Elteren in only 97 seconds at the Albert Hall in September 1986. He was, however, outpointed by Gianfranco Rosi when defending this title in January 1987.

**QUEENSBERRY RULES:**
   See under RULES.

**QUICKEST K.O.:**
   See under KNOCK-OUTS (QUICKEST).

# R

## RAMOS, Mando:

Born in Mexico but brought up in Long Beach, California, Ramos became the youngest fighter ever to win the world lightweight title when he stopped Carlos Cruz with a cut eye in eleven rounds, February 1969. He was then aged 20 years 3 months.

However, he himself suffered cut eyes when defending his title against Ismael Laguna in March 1970 and was forced to retire in the ninth round.

In 1972 he was, for a brief spell, recognised by W.B.C. as world lightweight champion, and he eventually retired in 1975.

## RAMOS, Urtiminio (Sugar):

One of a family of 14 born in Cuba, this hard-hitting fighter was undefeated as an amateur and turned professional in 1957.

He won the Cuban featherweight title before fleeing the country and settling in Mexico City and it was from there that he ran up a string of victories which culminated in his fatal battering of world champion, Davey Moore, in Los Angeles in March, 1963.

Thereafter, Ramos had difficulty in making the featherweight limit when defending his title, and after losing it to Vicente Salvidar in September, 1964 (only his second defeat in 50 bouts) he moved up into the lightweight division. However, he twice failed to relieve Carlos Ortiz of that world title.

## REA, Des:

Liverpool Irishman who held the British Junior welterweight title for about a year 1968-69. When the division was created he became the first champion by outpointing Vic Andreetti; but lost it on points in a return and was k.o'd in 4 rounds by the same fighter in another contest before the division was abandoned.

## REACH:

A boxer's reach is the distance from finger-tip to finger-tip when the arms are extended sideways.

The longest reach of any gloved world heavyweight champion was that of Primo Carnera—$85\frac{1}{2}$ inches.

The shortest reach of any gloved world heavyweight champion was that of Rocky Marciano—68 inches.

## RECEIPTS:

The list of fights to have drawn million dollar gates has grown rapidly since the first edition of this encyclopaedia in 1960 showed only eight. The number has since nearly trebled and the record is $7m for the Leonard v. Hagler fight at Las Vegas in April 1987.

All the first five million dollar gates involved Jack Dempsey. A crowd of over 80,000 was drawn to a new arena built by the game's first great promoter Tex Rickard to see Dempsey defend his heavyweight title against the Frenchman Georges Carpentier. This was Boyle's Thirty Acres in Jersey City where originally Rickard arranged for 60,000 seats to be provided. The rush for tickets was so great that he subsequently increased this number by 50%. The receipts from the "live" gate amounted to $1,789,238.

Dempsey's other three opponents to help him draw million dollar gates were the Argentinian fighter, Luis Angel Firpo, Jack Sharkey and Gene Tunney (twice). The second fight with Tunney in 1927 drew over $2m and this remained the record for 49 years until less than one third of the number who paid that earlier record (104,953) went to the Yankee Stadium, New York, to see Muhammad Ali successfully defend his heavyweight title again Ken Norton over 15 rounds. The interest was great because Norton was the one of only two men (the other was Joe Frazier) to have beaten Ali.

Not surprisingly Muhammad Ali was involved in more million dollar gate fights than any other boxer—a total of six—v. Frazier (3), v. Norton, v. Leon Spinks, and v. Holmes.

## REESON, Samuel:

Battersea, London, southpaw cruiserweight who won his first 20 professional fights, including a points win over Stewart Lithgo in October 1985, which made him the first holder of the British cruiserweight title.

Reeson has a good right jab and this showed up well against Lithgo as well as when he became the first holder of the European cruiserweight crown by outpointing the veteran German fighter Manfred Jassman at the Albert Hall in April 1987. Reeson had previously relinquished his British title to go for the European crown and showed himself to be a thoughtful boxer in gaining this unanimous points victory.

## REEVE, Harry:

This popular fighter was born at St. George's-in-the-East, London, in 1893.

In February, 1914, he challenged Pat O'Keefe for the British middleweight title but was narrowly outpointed over 20 rounds.

In December that year he beat the up-and-coming Joe Beckett, who retired in the seventh round.

On October 30, 1916, Reeve won the British light-heavyweight championship from Dick Smith with a 20-round points decision. He relinquished the title the following year to campaign as a heavyweight but he did not do so well in this division.

In January, 1919, he was beaten in five rounds by Joe Beckett. He fought a draw with Phil Scott in 1924, and in 1927, when he was 34 years of age, he was stopped in three rounds by the British champion in a non-title bout.

## REFEREES:

The standard of refereeing in this country is jealously guarded by the Referee's Association, and any prospective referee has to pass a strict examination, both written and practical, before he is granted a referee's licence.

In Britain the referee in a professional contest is the sole judge of that fight, but in most other countries the referee controls the fight but he is assisted in arriving at a decision by judges who sit outside the ring, and the verdict is given on a majority vote.

Refereeing has now become a fine art and the good referee is a man to be respected. However, this has not always been the situation.

It would appear that in the old days the selection of the referee was not considered too important, and persons who had never refereed a contest in their lives before were often chosen to be the third man in some important bouts.

On occasions promoters have refereed their own contests. Two famous instances of this were the Jack Johnson-Tommy Burns fight, and the Jack Johnson-Jim Jeffries fight. The former contest at Sydney, December 26, 1908, was refereed by promoter Hugh D. McIntosh, when the principals would not agree to any other third man. In the other contest the fighters would only consent to promoter Tex Rickard acting as referee.

In the early 1920s it was the fashion in America for many champion boxers to employ their own referee and many of these men would not engage in a contest unless their opponent agreed to accept their man as referee. For instance, Jack Dempsey had his own referee, Jack Dougherty, for his fight with Tommy Gibbons at Shelby, Montana, July 4, 1923.

Many years later Jack Dempsey became a famous referee in his own right. In fact, he has been one of the highest paid men ever to referee a contest, for on two occasions his fee plus expenses reached the $10,000 mark.

With money values changing over the years it is difficult to compare amounts in one period with another, but Joe Louis received $10,000 for refereeing the Frazier v. Quarry fight, June 17, 1974.

Two of the best known referees in America were Arthur Donovan and Ruby Goldstein. Donovan officiated at more world heavyweight title contests than any other referee. His total was 14. Ruby Goldstein succeeded him as America's number one referee and officiated in 7 world heavyweight title bouts.

On this side of the Atlantic there have also been many famous referees over the years. It would be unfair to name any one as the outstanding man among them all, but there can be little doubt that one of the most popular was Mr. Eugene Corri, a stockbroker, who is said to have refereed over 1,000 contests in his time. Most of these contests were at the Ring, Blackfriars, where he was a great favourite during the period around World War I.

Eugene Corri ended his refereeing career with a world title fight. That was on June 30, 1927, when he was the third man in the ring for the middleweight bout between Mickey Walker and Tommy Milligan.

Another famous British referee was Jack Smith, a Lancastrian, who was also well known in the North of England as a promoter. In the 1930's Mr. Smith refereed many of the most important fights in this country.

Between the two wars a very popular referee was C. H. (Pickles) Douglas. He came from one of the best-known families in the game. His father was J. H. Douglas, a leading personality and referee at the old N.S.C. in Covent Garden, and his brother was J. W. H. T. Douglas, an amateur boxing champion and captain of Essex and England at cricket.

After mentioning J. H. Douglas and the N.S.C. we could not pass on without naming two of his contemporaries at the club, stern men who laid the foundations of the tradition of scrupulously fair refereeing in the country. They were Bernard John Angle and George Vize. These are names which do not mean much to the average boxing fan today, but they epitomise good refereeing. Both of these gentlemen were leading members of the Amateur Boxing Association.

One of Britain's best known post-war referees was Harry Gibbs O.B.E. who retired in 1986 after nearly 30 years as third man. He refereed over 30 British title fights as well as a large number of world title bouts.

In this country all professional referees are registered with the B.B.B. of C. They are divided into three classes, " A " Star, " A " and " B." On reaching the age of 65 years a referee is obliged to relinquish his licence.

The B.B.B. of C. has drawn up a scale of fees for all referees and this ranges from £30.00 when the cost of the programme does not exceed £1,000; up to £50.00 when the cost amounts to between £2,500 and £4,000. When the cost exceeds £4,000 a Class " A " referee's fee is settled by the board.

## Gun:

The famous occasion on which a referee is said to have drawn a gun on one of the contestants was when Bob Fitzsimmons met Tom Sharkey at the National Athletic Club, San Francisco, December 2, 1896.

This fight was believed to have been "fixed" so that Sharkey would be the winner. At any rate, Fitzsimmons was beating Sharkey all ends up when, in the eighth round, the referee, Wyatt Earp, stopped the fight and declared Sharkey the winner on a foul.

There was a terrific commotion and it was while Fitzsimmons was protesting to the referee that he drew the gun on the Cornishman and ordered him away.

## Inside the ring:

Probably the first occasion in the country when the referee controlled a contest from inside the ring was when Tommy Burns met Gunner Moir at the N.S.C., December 2, 1907. The third man was Eugene Corri. In America it had been the practice to referee inside the ring for some time before this date.

It was not until 1932 that the B.B.B. of C. made it a rule that contests should be refereed inside the ring.

## Knock-down or out:

Referee Max Pippow was floored by the former German middleweight champion, Pete Muller (Cologne) in the eighth round of a fight with Hans Stretz (Berlin) at Cologne, June 7, 1952. The German Boxing Association barred Muller for life.

Watford welterweight, Laurie Buxton, accidentally k.o'd referee Joey Walker who was unable to continue. Buxton won this contest with Mike DeCosmo on points over 10 rounds, Newark, New Jersey, May 18, 1948.

## Retired:

The famous American referee, Ruby Goldstein, had to retire from the ring at the end of the 10th round of a world light-heavyweight title contest between Joey Maxim and Ray Robinson at the Yankee Stadium, New York, June 25, 1952.

The contest took place in a heatwave and Goldstein was exhausted by pulling the men out of clinches.

## REGAINED TITLE:

See under WORLD CHAMPION-SHIP (Regained Title).

## REGISTRATION:

In British professional boxing every promoter, referee, boxer, boxers' manager, match maker, ring master, whip, trainer, timekeeper, second and M.C. is registered with and licensed by the B.B.B. of C.

A Referee's star licence costs £50.00 per annum, while at the other end of the scale a Ringmaster's, whips or second's registration fee is £10.00. The registration fee for a boxer is also £10.00.

## REILLY, Willie:

A speedy Scottish lightweight with style, but lacking in real punching power, Willie Reilly retired from boxing soon after being stripped of his British lightweight title in 1972 by the B.B.B.C. for refusing a purse offer for a title defence against Tony Riley.

Reilly had won the vacant title by stopping Jim Watt with a cut eye in 10 rounds in February, 1972.

## REVIE, Jimmy:

A hard jabbing southpaw, born Stockwell, London, who failed to win the British junior-lightweight title in 1968, when he was beaten in nine rounds by Jimmy Anderson, but went on to capture the vacant British featherweight championship by defeating John O'Brien, the referee calling a halt after five rounds in which Revie proved his punching power. This contest took place at the World Sporting Club, London, March 24, 1969.

In 1971, after being outpointed by the European champion, Jose Legra, Revie lost his British title when stopped in 12 rounds by Evan Armstrong.

## RHINEY, Henry:

It wasn't until this fighter took the European welterweight title with a tenth round k.o. of Austrian Josef Pachler in December 1978 that the boxing fraternity sat up and took notice of a previously under-rated champion. Rhiney, born in Jamaica, one of eight children, but settled in Luton, had won the British welterweight championship in December 1976 before his home crowd in Luton by stopping Pat Thomas in eight rounds, but three defeats the following year in non-title fights did nothing to enhance his reputation. He was alleged to be too cautious and to lack a big punch, although both Thomas and Pachler obviously thought otherwise.

At his best Rhiney showed that he had plenty of skill but in January 1979 he proved no match for the hard-hitting Dave Green who relieved him of his European title in five furious rounds.

In his next fight in April 1979 Rhiney lost his British title when beaten in 10 rounds by Kirkland Laing.

## RICE, Ernie:

Born Hull but brought up in the London area, this product of the fairground boxing booth who made his name at The Ring, Blackfriars, was a real fighter with an unorthodox style.

He won the vacant British lightweight title when he stopped Ben Callicott in seven rounds at the N.S.C., April 11, 1921, and annexed the European title a month later by knocking out Georges Papin, of France.

Rice then went to America to challenge Benny Leonard for the world title, but after beating one of the leading American lightweights, Richie Mitchell, in four rounds, he was prevented from gaining a title fight by a defeat at the hands of Sailor Friedman.

He lost his British and European titles when narrowly outpointed by Seaman Hall at the Liverpool Stadium in

September, 1922, and he was subsequently beaten on two further occasions when trying to regain the title from Hall.

In September, 1928, Rice was matched with Sam Steward for the vacant lightweight title but was knocked out in 12 rounds.

## RICHARDSON, Alan:

In seven years as a professional (1971-78) this fine boxer from Fitzwilliam, Yorkshire, always displayed an immaculate left hand in the finest tradition of a real stylist. A.B.A. featherweight champion in 1969 he won the British professional title in this division from Vernon Sollas in March 1977; failed in two bids for the Commonwealth title, losing on both occasions to Eddie Ndukwu, and then lost his British title to Dave Needham in April 1978. This was a hard fought contest which went the distance. Alan Richardson injured his left hand in the seventh round but refused to offer this as an excuse for his defeat. It was after only one more contest that he announced his retirement in October 1978.

## THE "RING" WORLD RANKING LIST:

The idea of rating fighters and publishing a ranking list annually originated with Mr. Nat Fleischer, former Editor and Publisher of *The Ring* magazine, and a widely respected authority on the game.

The first world ranking list appeared in *The Ring* magazine in February, 1925, and it was compiled by Tex Rickard.

## RING, The:

The term "ring" as applied to the roped square in which a boxing contest takes place is thought to have originated in the days of George I. In 1723, he ordered a piece of ground in Hyde Park to be fenced off and used as a place for "turn ups." This became known as the "ring."

A roped ring is first mentioned in the London Prize Ring Rules of 1838.

Padded rings as we know them today did not come into use until the early 1890's. Today it has become the general practice to cover the floor of the ring with a foam rubber or felt mat to protect

a fighter's head when falling.

In the old bare-knuckle days rings were from 20 to 24 feet square. Nowadays they are 16 to 20 feet square in professional contests, 12 to 20 feet square in amateur contests.

## RITCHIE, Willie:

An American born in San Francisco, Willie Ritchie took the world lightweight title from Adolph Wolgast on a foul in the 16th round of a contest at Daly City, in November, 1912.

Ritchie had had trouble in making the weight limit of 133 lbs. for this contest and as soon as he had taken the title he increased the limit to 135 lbs.

In 1914 he came to England and on July 7 met the British lightweight champion, Freddy Welsh, at Olympia. Welsh had already beaten Ritchie in Los Angeles before the American had won the world title, and he was able to repeat this performance and relieve him of his crown in their London meeting.

Ritchie put on more weight after this, and, in December, 1915, he met Ted "Kid "Lewis for the world welterweight title at Madison Square Garden. It was a "no decision" bout and it went the full distance, but Lewis got the newspaper verdict.

## ROBINSON, Ray:

Born in Detroit in May, 1920, this fighter's real name was Walker Smith, but he had his first contest with a licence borrowed from a fighter named Ray Robinson and he has stuck to that name ever since.

Robinson has been rated by some as the greatest fighter, pound for pound, of the present century. He created a record by winning the world middleweight title on five separate occasions.

As an amateur he was undefeated in 125 contests and won more than half these bouts inside the distance. He was also a Golden Gloves featherweight and lightweight champion.

The supreme stylist, Robinson won his first world title in December, 1946, when he outpointed Tommy Bell for the vacant welterweight championship. He successfully defended this crown five times before relinquishing it on winning the middleweight title in February, 1951.

Robinson lost his middleweight title for the first time when he visited London in July, 1951, and was outpointed by Randolph Turpin, but he stopped the British champion in a return bout in New York two months later.

Shortly after he had failed in a bid to wrest the world light-heavyweight title from Joey Maxim in June, 1952, Robinson announced his retirement and relinquished his middleweight crown.

He returned to the ring two years later and regained the middleweight championship from Carl Bobo Olson. He subsequently lost it to and won it back from Gene Fullmer, and lost it and won it back in two bouts with Carmen Basilio.

On the last occasion that he regained the crown from Basilio, Robinson was only 39 days short of his 38th birthday.

In 1959 the N.B.A. deprived him of his world title because of his delay in defending it. However, he was still acknowledged as champion by N.Y.A.C. until his defeat by Paul Pender in January, 1960.

## ROBSON, Frank "Spike":

Born North Shields, Spike Robson was a tearaway two-handed fighter who is sometimes named as a former British featherweight champion.

It is true he beat Johnny Summers at the N.S.C. on a foul in four rounds in December, 1906, and this was announced as a title fight, but the fact is that Joe Bowker was still claiming this title at that time and he had beaten Robson 14 months prior to the Northumberland fighter's match with Summers.

Robson was also beaten by Bowker's successor, Jim Driscoll, in two Lonsdale Belt matches in 1910 and 1911.

## RODERICK, Ernie:

Born at Liverpool in 1914, Ernie Roderick had a professional career which extended over 19 years and was a great favourite at the local Liverpool Stadium.

Roderick was an intelligent boxer and it was at Liverpool in March, 1939, that he won the British welterweight title by knocking out Jake Kilrain in the seventh round.

He gave the outstanding display of his career in his next fight when he went 15 rounds with Hurricane Henry Armstrong but failed to take the negro's world title, losing a points decision.

During more than nine years that he held the welterweight title Roderick made one Lonsdale Belt his own property and seemed all set to win another, but then lost a hotly disputed decision to Henry Hall in November, 1948.

Before this, Roderick had both won and lost the British middleweight title in two bouts with Vince Hawkins in 1945 and 1946.

## RODNEY, Prince:

Born London but fighting out of Huddersfield he had packed in plenty of experience before beating Jimmy Batten for the British light middleweight title vacated by Herol Graham who had earlier beaten Rodney inside one round. Former champion Batten was floored twice by Rodney before the referee called a halt in the sixth round at the Albert Hall in October 1983.

An injury received in training kept Rodney out of the ring for nearly a year during which time he relinquished the title, but in 1985 he regained it by knocking out Jimmy Cable in two minutes at Hastings.

Rodney has shown himself to be a tough competitor, often coming from behind to win contests, but in February 1986 his British crown went to Chris Pyatt who knocked him out in the ninth round.

## RODRIGUEZ, Luis:

This Cuban exile, resident in Miami, Florida, won his country's welterweight title before fleeing to the continent of America.

A feature of this fighter's career was the closeness of his four meetings with world champion Emile Griffith.

Griffith won their first meeting in New York before either of them had become world champions, but after Griffith had captured the title Rodriguez relieved him of it with a unanimous points win in March, 1963.

However, less than three months later, Rodriguez lost the crown with a split decision favouring Griffith, and in their fourth meeting in June, 1964, Rodriguez was again beaten by the narrowest of margins.

Towards the end of his career Rodriquez competed as a middleweight, but was beaten in 11 rounds when trying to wrest the world title from Nino Benvenuti in November 1969.

## ROOT, Jack:

Born in Austria but domiciled in America, Jack Root was a good boxer but he lacked a big punch.

He was the first man to claim the world light-heavyweight title when he outpointed the veteran Kid McCoy over 20 rounds in Detroit in April, 1903.

This division was established by the American, and Root's manager, Lou Houseman, was said to have been one of the prime movers in the introduction of this new class to bridge the gap between the middleweight limit of 158 lbs. and the heavyweights, many of whom weighed around 200 lbs. The limit for the new division was set at 175 lbs.

Root did not hold the title for long, however. In July, 1903, he was knocked out by George Gardner, but after beating Gardner (then no longer champion) in a return bout, and "Fireman" Jim Flynn, Root was one of the men selected by Jim Jeffries to fight for the vacant heavyweight title in July, 1905. Marvin Hart was the other contestant and he knocked Root out in the 12th round.

## ROSE, Lionel:

One of a family of nine children this Australian aborigine turned professional to support the home after his father had died of a heart attack at an early age.

Rose had won the Australian amateur flyweight title when only 16 and became professional bantam champion when he was 18.

In February 1968 he took the world bantam title with a unanimous points

decision over Fighting Harada, but he lost it to Ruben Olivares in August 1969, being k.o'd in five. He had had trouble making the weight.

Rose took the British Empire title from Alan Rudkin in Melbourne in March 1969, but he relinquished this crown to campaign as a featherweight.

## ROSENBLOOM, Maxie:

This Jewish-American was one of the comedians of the ring. He was discovered by film actor George Raft, who steered him through his earliest fights. Subsequently, Rosenbloom himself became a film actor and was well known in comedy and boxing roles in the 1930's and 1940's.

In the ring Rosenbloom was a good fighter at close quarters, but he lacked aggressiveness and his method of punching earned him the nickname "Slapsie."

After Loughran relinquished the light-heavyweight title in 1929 and it had been claimed by Jim Slattery, Rosenbloom beat Slattery in June, 1930, to gain N.Y.A.C. recognition.

Later the N.B.A. declared Lou Scozza champion, but Rosenbloom cleared up this dispute by outpointing Scozza in July, 1932, and held on to the title until losing to Bob Olin in November, 1934. That was a hotly disputed points decision.

Rosenbloom was one of the most active champions ever; 1932 was one of his busiest years when he fought 30 bouts.

He came to England in 1928 and was stopped in nine rounds by Tommy Milligan, the former British middleweight champion, at the Albert Hall.

Rosenbloom, who had his last fight in his 35th year, when he knocked out Al Ettore, a rated Italian-American heavyweight, in three rounds, also beat several other leading men in the top division. These included Leroy Haynes, King Levinsky, Lee Ramage and Lou Nova.

## ROSS, Barney:

In his amateur days this Jewish-American was a Golden Gloves champion.

A real fighting machine, he was one of the fastest welterweights ever seen in the ring and was the first man to hold both the lightweight and welterweight titles simultaneously. That was in 1934.

In June, 1933, he won the Junior welter and the world lightweight titles from Tony Canzoneri, but he was forced to relinquish the lightweight crown in 1935 through weight difficulties.

Before that, however, he had annexed the welterweight championship by outpointing Jimmy McLarnin in May, 1934

Ross lost this title in a return bout in September that year but regained it in a third meeting with McLarnin in May, 1935.

Ross then held on to the title until May, 1938, when he was outpointed by another all-action fighter, Henry Armstrong. He announced his retirement after this defeat.

During the last war he was decorated for gallantry with the U.S. Marines at Guadalcanal.

## ROSS, Walter:

Born Glasgow, July, 1898, Walter Ross took the British bantamweight title from Tommy Noble at the N.S.C. in June, 1919. The referee stopped that contest in the 10th round when Noble was in serious trouble.

Ross, however, relinquished this title soon afterwards without defending it.

## ROUMANIA:

Probably the best known Roumanian boxer of recent years was Lucien Popesco. As will be seen from their list of champions given below, he won European titles in three divisions over a period of 11 years.

## Champions:

World:—
None.
European:—
Featherweight: Lucien Popesco, 1939-41.
Bantamweight: Lucien Popesco, 1931-32; Aurel Toma, 1936-37, 1938-39.
Flyweight: Lucien Popesco, 1930-31.
Olympic:—
Welterweight: N. Linca, 1956.

## ROUNDS:

In most parts of the world, contests are generally limited to a maximum of 15 rounds duration, although in 1979 the E.B.U. cut many of their Championship contests to 12 rounds. In this country and in America 15 rounds was the stipulated distance for all championship contests and had been applied over here since the B.B.B. of C. made it a rule in February, 1929. It was not until 1983 that the Board cut the maximum to 12 rounds in line with the W.B.C., and the W.B.A. followed suit in October 1987. The I.B.F. have continued with 15-round title bouts.

The last 20-round contest to be fought in Britain was when Tommy Kirk outpointed "Tiger" Bert Ison, Leicester, September 13, 1932.

Contests scheduled for 20 rounds continued for many years in America, where the most recent title fight set for this distance was that between Joe Louis and Abe Simon in Detroit in 1941. Louis stopped Simon in the 13th round.

The last world title fight to be scheduled for 45 rounds was that between Jack Johnson and Jess Willard at Havana, Cuba, April 5, 1915. Willard won by a knock-out in the 26th round.

At the other end of the scale there have been world title bouts over a distance of only 10 rounds. The two Dempsey-Tunney contests were both fought over this shorter distance.

Most rounds under Queensberry Rules —77. Harry Sharpe k.o'd Frank Crosby, Nameoki, U.S.A., February 5, 1893.

The largest number of rounds ever fought in Britain in the days when a round ended with a fall was the 276 between Jack Jones and Patsy Tunney, Cheshire, 1825.

Because of the faulty electric clock used by the timekeeper Gerrie Coetzee was k.o.'d by Greg Page 50 seconds after the eighth round should have ended in a W.B.A. world heavyweight title fight, Sun City, December 1, 1984.

## ROUTIS, André:

The surprising thing about this Frenchman from Bordeaux was that he was never as good after he had won a world title as he was before.

Routis had been fighting about 10 years when he took the world featherweight title from Tony Canzoneri with a points victory at Madison Square Garden, September 28, 1928.

His career had been an up-and-down one before he achieved this distinction. He had been unable to get the better of Jack "Kid" Berg in three meetings and had lost to Harry Corbett, but he had fought a draw with Johnny Cuthbert and beaten Harry Lake and Charles Ledoux. However, after winning the title he won only one (knocking out Buster Brown) of his remaining nine fights, and soon after losing the title to Battling Battalino in September, 1929, at Hartford, he was forced to retire from the ring with eye trouble.

## ROWAN, Stanley:

Eldest of four brothers born in Liverpool, Stanley started boxing when he was only seven. He won over 100 contests as an amateur and turned professional in 1942.

Rowan caused quite a stir in fistic circles in September, 1947, when he floored Jackie Paterson six times before the referee intervened in the second round to save the former world champion from further punishment.

That was a non-title fight, but when these two met again in March, 1949, Paterson's British bantamweight title was on the line and Rowan took it with a 15-round points victory.

The Liverpool boy was forced to relinquish the crown in November, 1949, when he was no longer able to make the weight.

## ROWE, Mark:

Popular because of his aggressive style, this hard-hitting middleweight from Camberwell, London, won the British and Empire title when he beat Les McAteer in 14 rounds at Wembley, May 12, 1970.

His first defence was against Bunny Sterling 4 months later and cuts lost him the bout after 4 rounds.

## ROYALTY and BOXING:

It is difficult to say with certainty who was the first royal personage to patronise prize-fighting, but if we accept the assumption that the sport first came into its own in the days of James Figg, then King George I (1714-1727) was the first King to take an interest in what were popularly known at that time as "turn ups." The King did, in fact, order the erection of a small enclosure in Hyde Park where such bouts could take place.

George I and his only son (later George II) actually attended the first international prize fight ever seen in this country. That was when Bob Whitaker, a protégé of James Figg, fought and beat an Italian gondolier in London.

Another personage of Royal blood who took more than a passing interest in the sport was the third son of George II, whose title was Duke of Cumberland. He was the patron of the great Jack Broughton, and it is said that his greed and his confidence in Broughton cost him £10,000 when the champion was beaten by Jack Slack in 1750.

When George III was Prince of Wales he was patron of Daniel Mendoza and Tom Tring.

George IV formed a bodyguard of pugilists, headed by Gentleman John Jackson, to attend his Coronation ceremony at Westminster Abbey. It included such men as Tom Belcher, Tom Cribb and Tom Spring.

Turning to more recent times, the two young princes, Edward (later Duke of Windsor) and Albert (later George VI) were frequent visitors to the National Sporting Club.

Their grandfather, Edward VII, also took an interest in the sport, and it was to him, when Prince of Wales, that John L. Sullivan was introduced when visiting England in 1887. The meeting took place at the Prince's request at the Fencing Club in London. For many years afterwards the great John L. would boastfully remark, "Shake the hand that shook the hand of the prince of Wales."

October, 1918. Duke of York (later King George VI) visited N.S.C. and saw Sgt. Joe Beckett, R.F.C., win heavyweight competition.

March 31, 1919. Prince of Wales (later Duke of Windsor) attended N.S.C. and saw Jimmy Wilde outpoint Joe Lynch.

December 4, 1919, Prince of Wales (later Duke of Windsor) attended Holborn Stadium and saw Georges Carpentier beat Joe Beckett.

January 13, 1921. Prince of Wales (later Duke of Windsor) climbed into the ring at the Albert Hall and soothed an angry crowd the night Pete Herman beat Jimmy Wilde.

February 13, 1928. Prince of Wales (later Duke of Windsor) attended The Ring, Blackfriars, and saw Jack Hood outpoint Len Johnson.

November 18, 1936. The Duke of Gloucester attended Harringay to see Walter Neusel outpoint Ben Foord.

April 4, 1938. The Duke of Gloucester attended the Empress Hall to see Arthur Danahar k.o. Jim Cameron and Dave Crowley beat Pancho Martinez.

December 4, 1951. The Duke of Edinburgh was at Harringay to see Jim Slade beat Don Cockell in four rounds. The Duke has since attended professional tournaments on a number of occasions.

## RUDKIN, Alan, M.B.E.:

A rugged, aggressive fighter who was British bantamweight champion in two spells totalling over 5½ years before retiring undefeated in June 1972 following an eye operation.

He was also Empire and European champion for a time and went close to taking the world title when he was narrowly outpointed by Fighting Harada in Tokyo in November, 1965.

Born in Wales but brought up in Liverpool, Rudkin was especially popular with the fans because he always gave value for money and his two great battles with Walter McGowan will always be remembered.

After taking the British and Empire titles from Johnny Caldwell in 1965 Rudkin lost them with a controversial points decision going to McGowan when they met at Wembley in 1966. But in their return contest at Manchester in May 1968 Rudkin succeeded in reversing the decision.

He lost his Empire crown when attempting to wrest the world title from Lionel Rose in March 1969, and a third attempt at the world title came to an abrupt end when he was beaten in two rounds by Ruben Olivares later that same year.

Rudkin beat Franco Zurlo in 11 rounds for the European title in February 1971 but was outpointed by Agustin Senin when making his first defence six months later.

## RULES of BOXING:

The first rules of the prize ring were those drawn up by the Champion of England, John Broughton, 1743.

In February, 1741, Broughton had fought and beat one George Stevenson, a Yorkshireman. Stevenson died as a result of the injuries he received in this battle, and Broughton was so taken aback by this disaster that he swore he would never fight again.

Later, however, the champion relented, but not until he had made up his mind to produce a code of rules to control the game. Accordingly, Broughton went into a huddle with "several gentlemen" at his Amphitheatre, in the Tottenham Court Road, and on August 16, 1743, the following rules were published.

I. That a square of a Yard be chalked in the middle of the Stage; and on every fresh set-to after a fall, or being parted from the rails, each Second is to bring his Man to the side of the square, and place him opposite to the other, and till they are fairly set-to at the Lines, it shall not be lawful for one to strike at the other.

II. That in order to prevent any Disputes, the time a Man lies after a fall, if the Second does not bring his Man to the side of the square, within the space of half a minute, he shall be deemed a beaten Man.

III. That in every main Battle, no person whatever shall be upon the Stage, except the Principals and their Seconds; the same rule to be observed in bye-battles, except that in the latter, Mr. Broughton is allowed upon the Stage to keep decorum, and to assist Gentlemen in getting their places, provided always he does not interfere in the Battle; and whoever pretends to infringe these Rules to be turned immediately out of the house. Everybody is to quit the Stage as soon as the Champions are stripped, before the set-to.

IV. That no Champion be deemed beaten, unless he fails coming up to the line in the limited time, or that his own

Second declares him beaten. No Second is to be allowed to ask his man's Adversary any questions, or advise him to give out.

V. That in bye-battles, the winning man to have two-thirds of the Money given, which shall be publicly divided upon the Stage, notwithstanding any private agreements to the contrary.

VI. That to prevent Disputes, in every main Battle the Principals shall, on coming on the Stage, choose from among the gentlemen present two Umpires, who shall absolutely decide all Disputes that may arise about the Battle; and if the two Umpires cannot agree, the said Umpires to choose a third, who is to determine it.

VII. That no person is to hit his Adversary when he is down, or seize him by the ham, the breeches, or any part below the waist; a man on his knees to be reckoned down.

These rules governed the prize ring until 1838, when the British Pugilists' Protective Association introduced the London Prize Ring Rules or the New Rules of Prize-Fighting.

Broughton's "square of a yard" chalked in the middle of the stage was replaced by a "scratch" in the London rules. Kicking, gouging and head butting were ruled out, and, if a fighter went down deliberately without being hit or thrown, he was disqualified. Wrestling was permitted by these rules, and a round ended when one of the contestants was floored. A rest of 30 seconds was allowed between each round plus a further eight seconds to come up to scratch. The fight ended when either of the contestants failed to come up to scratch in time.

The London Prize Ring Rules were revised in 1853 and again in 1866.

These rules were eventually superseded by the Marquess of Queensberry Rules, which are believed to have been first published in 1866.

The original rules were compiled by the Marquess of Queensberry, Lord Lonsdale and Arthur Chambers, who later became lightweight champion of the world.

These rules were originally intended for amateur boxing but they were revised and adopted generally by professionals as well. Much of this revision and modification was probably carried out by journalists of the two famous sporting papers, *Referee* and *Sporting Life*.

The original Marquess of Queensberry Rules which applied to Contests of Endurance, read as follows:—

1. To be a fair stand-up boxing match in a 24 ft. ring or as near to that size as practicable.

2. No wrestling or hugging allowed.

3. The rounds to be of three minutes' duration and one minute's time between rounds.

4. If either man fall through weakness or otherwise, he must get up unassisted, 10 seconds to be allowed him to do so, the other man meanwhile to return to his corner, and when the fallen man is on his legs the round to be resumed and continued till the three minutes have expired. If one man fails to come to the scratch in the 10 seconds allowed, it shall be in the power of the referee to give his award in favour of the other man.

5. A man hanging on the ropes in a helpless state with his toes off the ground shall be considered down.

6. No seconds, or any other person, to be allowed in the ring during the rounds.

7. Should the contest be stopped by any unavoidable interference, the referee to name the time and place as soon as possible for finishing the contest, so that the match must be won or lost, unless the backers of the men agree to draw the stakes.

8. The gloves to be fair-sized boxing gloves of the best quality, and new.

9. Should a glove burst, or come off, it must be replaced to the referee's satisfaction.

10. A man on his knees is considered down, and if struck is entitled to the stakes.

11. No shoes or boots with springs allowed.

12. The contest in all other respects to be governed by the revised rules of the London Prize Ring.

These rules were subsequently revised until they included such regulations as the limiting of the number of rounds to 20; the minimum weight of the gloves to be six ounces; the defence, and the withholding of any prize from a fighter ruled out because of a deliberate foul.

About 1890 the Pelican Club produced a code of rules which were based on the Marquess of Queensberry's, and eventually these were taken over by the National Sporting Club, who revised them in 1909 and again in 1923. These rules were eventually adopted by the B.B.B. of C. upon its inception and remained in force until the Board issued their new and revised rules in November 1947. Here are the rules which control the game in the U.K. today:—

1. All Contests to be decided in a three-roped or four-roped ring with the ropes joined in the centre at each side, not less than 16 feet or more than 20 feet square and not less than 18 inches margin of ring floor outside the ropes. The floor to be covered with canvas over a safety mat approved by the Board. Corner posts to be padded from the top to the bottom rope with one whole length of padding not less than 2 inches thick and 6 inches in width.

Boxers must shake hands before the commencement of the Contest and at the beginning of the final round and must defend themselves at all times.

2. Contestants must be stripped to the waist, box in Regulation boots without heels or spikes, with Regulation shorts.

The gloves to be of a weight of six ounces each for Flyweights to Light Middleweights and eight ounces each for Middleweights to Heavyweights. (Breaking by twisting, removal of padding by fingering and thumbing from the potential part of the glove is prohibited). Contestants to weigh on the day of the Contest.

Bandages are permitted for the protection of the hands. If used, they must not exceed 18 feet of 2-inch soft bandage (W.C.W.) for all weights, and/or 9 feet of 1-inch zinc oxide plaster tape for weights up to and including Middleweights, and 11 feet of 1-inch zinc oxide plaster tape for light-heavyweights and heavyweights. In all cases these lengths are for each hand. The tape must not be applied over the knuckles.

3. In all Contests a Referee who must officiate inside the Ring and a Timekeeper shall be appointed.

In all contests no more than four persons acting as second shall be allowed in each corner.

The Seconds shall leave the Ring when ordered to so by the Timekeeper; the Referee to see this is carried out.

The Seconds shall give no advice or assistance to the contestants during the progress of any round.

4. Contestants shall be medically examined after the weigh-in or immediately prior to the commencement of the tournament.

In all Contests the number of rounds shall be specified. No Contest shall exceed 12 rounds nor be of less than 12 minutes' duration; except in the case of novice competitions which may be of eight minutes duration. Rounds shall be of three minutes duration, except in Contests of ten rounds and under when rounds may be of two minutes duration.

The interval between rounds shall be one minute.

5. The Referee shall award a maximum number of ten marks at the end of each round to the better man and a proportionate number to the other contestant or, when equal, the maximum number to each.

Marks shall be awarded for "attack"—direct clean hits with the knuckle part of the glove of either hand on any part of the front or sides of the head, or body above the belt (the belt is an imaginary line drawn across the body from the top of the hip bones); "defence"—guarding, slipping, ducking, or getting away. Where contestants are otherwise equal, the majority of marks shall be given to the one who does most part of the leading off or who displays the better style.

If a contestant is down he must get up unassisted within 10 seconds; his opponent meanwhile shall retire to the farthest neutral corner and shall not resume Boxing until ordered to do so by the Referee. A man is to be considered down even when he is on one foot or both feet, if at the same time any other part of his body is touching the ground, or when he is in the act of rising. A contestant failing to continue the Contest at the expiration of 10 seconds shall not be awarded any marks for that round, and the Contest shall then terminate.

In the event of the count being interrupted by the bell signifying the end of the round, the contest and count shall continue, either until the boxer who is down rises, or until the 'out' is reached, in which case the contest shall terminate.

The count shall not continue when the bell signifies the termination of the final round of the contest.

If at the conclusion of any round during the Contest one of the contestants should attain such a lead on points as to render it an impossibility for his opponent to win, he must then be declared the winner.

The referee shall decide each Contest in favour of the contestant who obtains the greater number of marks.

At the end of each contest which lasts the scheduled number of rounds the M.C. shall announce the Referee's final score.

(a) When ordered by the Referee to "break", both boxers shall immediately take one step back before recommencing to box. A boxer shall not strike or attempt to strike his opponent on the "break".

6. The Referee shall have power to disqualify a contestant for any of the following acts: (a) Hitting below the belt; (b) using the 'pivot blow'; (c) hitting on the back of the head or neck; (d) kidney punching; (e) hitting with the open glove, the inside or butt of the hand, or with the wrist or elbow; (f) holding, butting or careless use of the head, shouldering, wrestling, roughing; (g) not trying; (h) persistently ducking blow the waist-line; (i) intentional falling without receiving a blow; (j) failing to break when so ordered, or striking or attempting to strike an opponent on the break; (k) for deliberately striking an opponent when he is dropping to the floor or when he is down; (l) for ungentlemanly conduct; (m) for any other act or conduct which he may deem foul.

A contestant disqualified for any cause whatever shall not be entitled to any prize or remuneration, except in accordance with Regulation 20, Paragraph 15.

7. The Referee shall have power to stop the Contest if in his opinion a contestant is outclassed or accidentally disabled.

8. The Referee shall decide (1) any question not provided for in these Rules, (2) the interpretation of any of these Rules on matters arising during the time the contestants are in the Ring.

9. The Referee's decision shall be final.

The rules of boxing as laid down by the Amateur Boxing Association in this country are much lengthier than the professional rules but they include most of the same points.

They differ on certain specific points as follows:—

In Amateur boxing the ring can be as small as 12 feet square; competitors shall box in a vest completely covering the chest and back; gloves to be of a standard weight of eight ounces for boxers 67 kgs and below and 10 ounces for boxers over 67 kgs. If one boxer is over 67 kgs both will wear 10 ounce gloves; the length of bandages differ; each competitor is allowed only one second, although an assistant second may act, but shall not enter the ring to service the boxer; a maximum of 20 points are awarded a competitor in each round.

The Amateur Boxing Association's rules also include such additional points as that contained in rule 8 concerning the duration of rounds. This reads as follows:—

The number and duration of rounds for senior competitions and contests shall be as follows:—

Competitions: Novice—3 rounds of 2 minutes each.

Intermediate—3 rounds of 2 minutes each.

Open—3 rounds of 3 minutes each.

Contests:

Between open class boxers—3 rounds of 3 minutes each.

Between an open class boxer and an intermediate class boxer—3 rounds of 3 minutes each.

Between intermediate class boxers—3 rounds of 3 minutes each.

Between an intermediate class boxer and a novice class boxer—3 rounds of 2 minutes each.

Between novice class boxers—3 rounds of 2 minutes each. In every case there shall be an interval of one minute between the rounds.

The number and duration of rounds for junior boxers are laid down in a separate regulation.

## RUSSELL, Hugh:

Red-headed Belfast southpaw who became the first man to capture the British flyweight and bantamweight titles in reverse order. A clever box-fighter he took the bantamweight crown from John Feeney in January 1983 when the champion was disqualified in the 13th round for persistent use of the head. This was less than satisfactory in a closely fought contest.

The Irishman's reign lasted only 36 days before he was outpointed by veteran Davey Larmour. This was Russell's first defeat as a professional and by a man he had previously outpointed.

However, Russell got down to the flyweight limit and exactly a year and a day after winning the bantamweight crown he became Britain's 8-stone champion by relieving Welshman Kevin Smart of the title, forcing him to retire at the end of seven rounds. After becoming only the second Irishman to win a Lonsdale belt outright he retired undefeated champion in April 1985.

## RUSSIA:

There is no professional boxing in the Soviet Union but amateur boxing has a large following and well over 600 fighters compete annually for the National championships.

Russia entered the Olympic Games boxing tournament for the first time in 1952.

Two men who were born in Russia have won world titles, although neither of these actually did any boxing in that country. They were Louis "Kid" Kaplan, a Russian-Jew who went to America at the age of five and became world featherweight champion in 1925, and Benny Bass, another Russian-Jew, who has spent most of his life in America and was world featherweight champion in 1927-28.

Another world champion, light-heavyweight Gus Lesnevich, was born in America of Russian parents. He held the title from 1941 to 1948.

## Champions:

World:—
See two mentioned above.

Olympic:—
Middleweight: G. Chatkov, 1956; V. Popenchenko, 1964; Viateschev Lemeschev, 1972.

Light-heavyweight: D. Poznyak, 1968.

Light-middleweight: B. Lagutin, 1964 and 1968.

Light-welter weight: V. Jangibarian, 1956.

Featherweight: V. Safronov, 1956; S. Stepashkin, 1964; Boris Kousnetsov, 1972.

Bantamweight: O. Grigoryev, 1960; V. Sokolov, 1968.

## RYAN, Paddy:

Born in Tipperary, Ireland, in 1853, Paddy Ryan went to America and there, in May 1880, he won the championship of that country in what was his first proper contest in a ring.

This took place at Collier's Station, West Virginia, and Ryan beat an ageing Joe Goss in 86 rounds, lasting 1 hour and 24 minutes.

His title claim is now generally accepted but it is worth noting that Goss had been beaten less than two months earlier by John L. Sullivan in what was supposed to be merely an exhibition.

In any event, Ryan's reign as champion did not last long. On February 7, 1882, at Mississippi City, he was knocked out in nine rounds, 10 minutes 30 seconds, by John L. Sullivan.

These contests were fought with the bare knuckles. On two subsequent occasions, Ryan was well beaten by Sullivan in gloved contests, although in one of them the police intervened almost as soon as Sullivan had struck the first crushing blow and denied the "Boston Strong Boy" what was obviously going to be a clear-cut victory.

## RYAN, Tommy:

Born in America of an English mother and a French father, Tommy Ryan became one of the greatest middleweights of all-time. He won the world title at that weight and also in the welterweight division.

Ryan has been rated by Nat Fleischer as second only to the redoubtable Stanley Ketchel in a list of the finest middleweight fighters of all-time.

His real name was Joseph Youngs, and he started fighting in about 1887. When he was 24 he won the world welterweight title by outpointing Mysterious Billy Smith over 20 rounds in Minneapolis. The date was July 26, 1894.

He lost this championship to one of his former sparring partners, Kid McCoy, being surprisingly beaten by a knock-out in the 15th round, March 2, 1896.

Ryan claimed the middleweight title which had been vacated by Bob Fitzsimmons in 1895. Kid McCoy also considered himself to be champion of this division but he quickly moved up into the heavyweight class, leaving Ryan undisputed title-holder until his retirement from the ring in 1907.

# S

### SADDLER, Joseph "Sandy":
This hard-hitting negro featherweight from Boston was tall for his weight, and his long arms, and aggressiveness, gave most of his opponents plenty of trouble. In fact, Saddler was only beaten 16 times in over 160 contests.

He had a terrific left hook and there was one run in 1945 when he scored 14 consecutive knock-out victories.

Saddler finished Willie Pep with a left hook to the jaw to win the world featherweight championship in October, 1948.

Pep got a points victory in a return contest, but when these two met a third time, Saddler regained the title by forcing the Italian-American to retire after the end of the seventh round.

They had yet another meeting in September, 1951, but Saddler confirmed his superiority by stopping Pep in the ninth round of one of the roughest contests seen in America since World War II.

Sandy Saddler retired undefeated world champion in 1957 after being hurt in a motor accident.

### SALICA, Lou:
An Italian-American who was a Golden Gloves champion before turning professional in 1933, Lou Salica, was recognised as world bantamweight champion following his victory over Sixto Escobar in August, 1935.

However, he was beaten by Escobar in a return bout less than three months later, and lost a third meeting with the West Indian in February, 1937.

When the title became vacant in 1940 Salica again claimed it after outpointing Georgie Pace, and was recognised in New York State. He established world-wide recognition by outpointing Tommy Forte in January, 1941, but eventually lost the crown when beaten by Manuel Ortiz in August, 1942.

### SALAVARRIA, Erbito:
Filipino who won the world flyweight title in quick time when the referee called a halt to his fight with champion Chartchai Chionoi after only 1 min. 48 sec. of the 2nd round. Chionoi had been floored three times.

In some quarters Salavarria is considered to have lost his title in November 1971 after fighting a draw with Betulio Gonzalez and subsequently being disqualified for allegedly using illegal stimulant.

Elsewhere he was recognised as champion until being well beaten by Venice Borkorsor on points in February 1973.

### SALVIDAR, Vicente:
Rose from poverty-stricken surroundings in Oaxaca, Mexico to become world featherweight champion at the age of 21 and after only 21 professional fights.

It was in that 21st fight that he so battered the champion, Sugar Ramos, that the Cuban was unable to come up for the 12th round.

A really rugged fighter, Salvidar, who represented Mexico in the Rome Olympics of 1960, had lost only one of 34 professional fights when he announced his retirement and relinquished his title in 1967.

Two years later he began a comeback which culminated in his regaining the world title with a unanimous decision over Johnny Famechon, Rome, May 9, 1970, but he lost it to the Jap, Kuniaka Shibata in December that year.

### SANGCHILLI, Baltazar:
Born at Valencia, Sangchilli was the first Spanish-born fighter ever to have claimed a world boxing title.

In June 1935, in his home town, he outpointed Panama Al Brown to become bantamweight champion, but when he went to America for the first time in 1936 he was relieved of the championship by

Tony Marino, who knocked him out in the 14th round of a contest in New York.

Sangchilli's last important fight took place at Earl's Court, London, April 3, 1939, when he was outpointed by Peter Kane.

## SARRON, Pete:

Born in America of Syrian parentage, this whirlwind fighter represented the United States in the Olympic Games of 1924.

After turning professional he was beaten by Freddie Miller in his first bid for the N.B.A. world featherweight championship, but he took the title in a return bout which was fought in May, 1936.

Sarron and Miller had two more meetings, in South Africa in 1937, and Miller won the first, a non-title bout, but Sarron won the second.

When Sarron came to England that same year he lost to Harry Mizler on a disqualification in the first round and was also beaten on a ninth round disqualification in a match with Dave Crowley. However, when he met Mizler in South Africa, Sarron scored a first round knock-out.

He was relieved of his title when he was knocked out in six rounds by Henry Armstrong, October, 1937.

## SAXTON, Johnny:

As an amateur this American won a Golden Gloves title and entered the paid ranks soon after World War II.

In October, 1954, he took the world welterweight title from Kid Gavilan at Philadelphia but lost it in April, 1955, to Tony De Marco.

Saxton regained the championship from Carmen Basilio in March, 1956, with a 15-rounds points victory, a decision which was hotly disputed, but in a return bout in September that year he was stopped in nine rounds.

He made another bid for the crown in February, 1957, but this time Basilio beat him in less than two rounds.

## SAYERS, Tom:

Born Pimlico, Brighton, Tom Sayers was never more than a small middleweight but he fought and beat some of the heaviest and best men of his day.

According to contemporary reports, Sayers must have been one of the cleverest ring generals of all-time, and, of course, he had to be considering that he was conceding so much weight to the majority of his opponents.

In his great fight with the American heavyweight, John C. Heenan, at Farmborough, April, 1860, Sayers badly damaged his right arm in the fourth round but fought on gamely for 42 rounds before the battle had to be abandoned as a draw because the spectators had broken the ring. Sayers received a large testimonial and a silver belt after this contest, which was the first international championship match ever staged.

This son of a Sussex cobbler had won the championship by stopping the giant "Tipton Slasher," William Perry, in 10 rounds lasting 1 hour 42 minutes, June 16, 1857. Perry was five inches taller and more than 30 lbs. heavier than Sayers.

Sayers retired undefeated champion in 1860 after his battle with Heenan.

## SCALZO, Pete:

Another Golden Gloves champion who reached the top as a professional, Scalzo was born in New York City of Italian descent.

In December, 1938, he beat Joey Archibald (N.Y.A.C. world featherweight champion) in two rounds in an overweight match, but efforts to get these two into the same ring again for a title bout failed. Archibald was subsequently deprived of his title by the N.B.A. for his failure to meet Scalzo again and the Italian-American was installed as champion. He held on to this disputed crown until July, 1941, when he was eliminated through a knock-out by Richie Lemos.

During those 2½ years as N.B.A. champion Scalzo twice beat the Liverpool featherweight, Ginger Foran.

Scalzo retired in 1944 and became a boxing referee.

## SCHMELING, Max:

An examination of this German's record shows that he was by no means a great heavyweight. Nevertheless, he was extremely crafty and some of his best victories were gained through the care and thought he put into his preparation and his boxing rather than sheer brilliance.

An example of this can be found in his best remembered victory, when as a 14-1 underdog he caused one of the biggest upsets ever by knocking out an hitherto unbeaten Joe Louis in the 12th round of a contest in New York City, June 19, 1936.

Schmeling had laid plans for that bout when he had spotted a weakness in the negro's defence. That victory said much for the German's coolness and calculating brainwork.

Of course, Schmeling was smashed almost into oblivion when he fought Louis a second time in June, 1938. He was carried back to his corner after only 2 minutes 4 seconds of the first round.

Schmeling won the world heavyweight title in a most unsatisfactory manner. He won it on a foul, his opponent for the vacant title, Jack Sharkey, being disqualified at the end of the fourth round. The date June 12, 1930.

He also lost it in an unsatisfactory manner, for the points decision which gave Sharkey victory in a return bout on June 21, 1932, was one of the most bitterly disputed ever known in a world title bout. It was this decision which evoked the classic comment of Schmeling's manager, Joe Jacobs, "We wuz robbed."

Schmeling attempted a come-back after World War II when he was over 40. He won a couple of bouts but was beaten by another veteran, Walter Neusel, over 10 rounds at Hamburg, in May, 1948.

## SCHWARTZ, Izzy:

After the death of Pancho Villa in July, 1925, and the retirement in August, 1927, of Fidel La Barba, there was much confusion as to the rightful champion of the flyweight division.

Izzy Schwartz, a Jewish-American, was one of several men to stake a claim, and he was recognised by the N.Y.A.C. following his 10-round victory over Newsboy Brown in December, 1927.

However, following two defeats by Willie La Morte in 1929, Schwartz faded from the championship picture and retired from the ring.

## SCOTLAND:

Professional boxing in Scotland comes under the control of the B.B.B. of C., Scotland being the No. 1 Area of the Board.

## Champions:

World:—
Lightweight: Ken Buchanan, 1970-72.
Flyweight: Benny Lynch, 1935-38; Jackie Paterson, 1943-48; Walter McGowan 1966.

European:—
Middleweight: Tommy Milligan, 1925; Alex Ireland, 1928-29; John McCormack, 1961-62.
Welterweight: Tommy Milligan, 1924 (disputed).
Lightweight: James Hall, 1922-23; Ken Buchanan, 1974-75; Jim Watt, 1977-79.
Bantamweight: Jackie Paterson, 1946; Peter Keenan, 1951-52, 1953.
Flyweight: Elky Clark, 1925; Johnny Hill, 1928; Benny Lynch, 1935.

Empire and Commonwealth:—
Light-heavyweight: Chic Calderwood, 1960-63.
Middleweight: Tommy Milligan, 1926-27; Alex Ireland, 1928-29.
Welterweight: Tommy Milligan, 1924-25.
Featherweight: Johnny McGrory, 1936-37; John O'Brien, 1967; Evan Armstrong, 1974.
Bantamweight: Jim Higgins, 1920-22; Jim Brady, 1941-45; Jackie Paterson, 1945-49; Peter Keenan, 1955-59; Walter McGowan, 1966-68.
Flyweight: Elky Clark, 1924-25; Jackie Paterson, 1940-48; Frankie Jones, 1957; Jackie Brown, 1962-63; Walter McGowan, 1963-66; Johnny McClusky, 1970-71.
Olympic:—
Lightweight: R. McTaggart, 1956.

## SCOTT, Phil:

Like so many British heavyweights, Phil Scott (real name Suffling) fell short of world-beating class because he lacked the "killer" instinct.

A magnificent physical specimen, Scott stood 6ft. 3½in. in his socks and weighed around 14½ stone (203 lbs.).

In December, 1923, when he had been fighting for about five years, Scott knocked out Ike Ingleton in the first round to win a heavyweight competition at the Crystal Palace.

After that he beat some good men, including Gipsy Daniels, Tom Berry, Marcel Nilles, George Cook, Harry Reeve, Jack Stanley and Paolino Uzcudun.

In January, 1926, he won the Empire heavyweight title with his second victory over George Cook, and in March that year he took the British title from Frank Goddard with a third round knock-out.

Scott was quite a good boxer but in America he met with a mixed reception. In February, 1930, he was matched with Jack Sharkey in a final eliminator for the world heavyweight title but was beaten in three rounds. He claimed that he was fouled in that round and the referee allowed him time to recover but he was unable to continue.

Five months later, back in London again, he further disappointed his supporters when he was well and truly beaten in two rounds by Young Stribling.

Scott lost his Empire title to Larry Gains in June, 1931, his third consecutive knock-out defeat, and he retired from the ring. He died in Australia in 1983.

# SECONDS:

Under the rules of the B.B.B. of C. a boxer is allowed four seconds in his corner.

In amateur boxing in this country a competitor is allowed two seconds, only one of whom is permitted to enter the ring although the other can mount the platform.

Many seconds specialise as "cut men" and indeed this is one of the most important functions of a second. He should be able to treat any cuts his man may sustain, and an expert at this is worth a great deal to any fighter, especially if that fighter is liable to cuts over the eyes which may hamper his vision during the course of the bout.

Nowadays adrenalin is used for stopping the flow of blood in such cases. In the old days Monsell's solution was often used, but this is no longer permitted, for it can be dangerous used in these circumstances.

# SELLARS, Harry:

Harry Sellars won the championship when he stopped the Irishman, Peter Corcoran, in 38 rounds at Staines, October 16, 1775.

After beating Joe Hood and Bill Stevens, Sellars lost the championship to Duggan Fearns. This fight lasted only 1½ minutes, the shortest prize fight on record. There is no doubt that it was a "fix."

# SHARKEY, Jack:

The "Boston Cob" is not very highly rated among the men who have held the world heavyweight title. He had the build for the sport but his trouble was temperament. Sharkey had served in the U.S. Navy and after one or two of his shows of temperament in the ring he became known by another nickname— "Sobbing Sailor."

A surprise victory over the negro, Harry Wills, in October, 1926, put Sharkey on the boxing map. He actually got the decision on a foul in the 13th round, but although the finish was unsatisfactory there was no doubt that Sharkey was by far the better man in that particular contest.

In 1927, when Jack Dempsey was warming up for a return bout with Gene Tunney, he met Sharkey and knocked him out in seven rounds.

After beating the British champion, Phil Scott, in three rounds, Sharkey was matched with Max Schmeling for the vacant heavyweight title in June, 1930.

Sharkey got off to a good start in the bout but towards the end of the fourth round he hit Schmeling a low blow. The German's manager claimed a foul and pandemonium broke out. The bell had sounded for the fifth round before the referee made it clear that he had disqualified Sharkey.

After outpointing Primo Carnera, Sharkey took the world title with a hotly disputed points victory over Schmeling in June, 1932.

Sharkey lost the championship in his next fight, being knocked out in the sixth round with a right uppercut from Primo Carnera, June, 1933.

After that Sharkey faded fast, losing to King Levinsky, Tommy Loughran, and in his last fight, to Joe Louis in August, 1936.

## SHIBATA, Kuniaki:

The first Jap to win two world titles abroad, this terrific puncher punished featherweight champion, Vicente Salvidar, so severely that the referee intervened in the 12th round at Tijuana in December 1970, and when he moved up into the junior-lightweight division he gained a unanimous points decision over champion Ben Villaflor in Honolulu in March 1973.

Shibata lost the featherweight crown when k.o'd inside three rounds by Mexico's Clemente Sanchez, and the junior-lightweight title returned to Villaflor when he k.o'd Shibata in only 1 minute 56 seconds of the first round.

## SHORTEST FIGHT:
See under KNOCK-OUT (Quickest)

## SIBSON, Tony:

If somewhat erratic, Tony Sibson from Leicester has enjoyed one of the most active and successful careers in British post-war boxing. This stocky middleweight has one of the best left hooks in the business and it has caused a lot of damage, enabling him to win nearly half of his fights inside the distance. Turning professional in 1976 he has been reluctant to retire after over 60 contests.

Since 1979 Sibson has held the Commonwealth and European middleweight titles twice each, losing neither title in the ring. He has also held the British middleweight championship three times, only losing it in the ring the first time when he was outpointed by Kevin Finnigan. He regained this title for the third time as recently as September 1987 when, at the the age of 29, he stopped Brian Anderson.

In addition Sibson has contested both the world middleweight title and the W.B.C. version of the light-heavyweight crown. Unfortunately for this plucky fighter he had to meet one of the most talented of world middleweight champions in Marvin Hagler and was stopped inside six rounds. In the other contest he met the bigger and more powerful Dennis Andries in one of a small number of all-British world title fights and was overpowered in nine rounds after giving the fans their money's worth.

## SIKI, Battling:

A West African negro from Senegal, Louis Phail was originally taken to France to live near Nice as a bell boy. When his mentor died he became a washer-up in a hotel and took up boxing to augment his meagre income. Then came World War I and Phail served with distinction, winning the Croix de Guerre.

After the war he returned to France and took up boxing again, becoming known as Battling Siki.

He was still a comparatively unknown fighter when he was lucky enough to get a match with Georges Carpentier in September, 1922, and it was one of the biggest surprises in ring history when he stopped Carpentier in the sixth round to lift the world light-heavyweight title, which the French idol had held for nearly two years.

Although Siki was no boxer he wasn't exactly a novice either, for he was also good enough to beat the French and European middleweight champion, Ercole Balzac, and the Italian heavy weight champion, Ermino Spalla. As regards British fighters, Siki defeated an ageing Harry Reeve, on four occasions and also beat Tom Berry twice before that boxer had reached his peak.

However, when all is said and done, Siki was really little more than a good slogger, but in Dublin in 1923 he couldn't outslog the local hero, Mike McTigue. The Irishman got the referee's nod at the end of 20 rounds and also the world title.

Siki was often getting into trouble in the United States, and in December, 1925, he was involved in one fight too many—he was shot dead in the street.

## SIMS, Steve "Sammy":

A tough and durable Welsh fighter

who captured the vacant British feather-weight title with a 12th round k.o. of Terry McKeown in Glasgow in September 1982. Soon after this Sims relinquished the title to go after the European crown vacated by the retiring Pat Cowdell, and in April 1983 he was matched with the unbeaten Italian champion Loris Stecca.

About this time Sims was suffering from a persistent right-hand injury, but in this title fight it was a cut right eye which hampered him and although displaying great determination he was beaten in five rounds.

Sims failed to regain the British feather-weight crown in July 1986 being k.o.'d in five rounds by fellow countryman Robert Dickie.

## SINGER, Al:

This Jewish-American fighter, who was born and raised in the tough New York Bronx, both won and lost the world lightweight title with one-round knock-outs.

Singer won more fights than he lost, but his form was not to be depended upon. He was given a lot of coaching and encouragement by the great Benny Leonard.

He won the world title when he stopped Sammy Mandell in 1 minute 46 seconds in July, 1930, but lost it four months later when Tony Canzoneri knocked him out in 1 minute 6 seconds.

## SINGLETON, Joey:

A Liverpool Irishman from Kirkby who was one of Britain's most skilful boxers of recent years capturing the British light-welterweight title in November 1974 in only his eighth professional bout. In that contest he showed real class in outpointing the hard-hitting Pat McCormack after being floored in the first round.

Before losing his title to Dave Green in June 1976 Singleton had made a Lonsdale Belt his own property. A spell of inactivity followed before he made a come-back and eventually moved into the welterweight division. Here he gained a crack at the European title in 1980, but a bad cut hampered his chances and he was outpointed by the hard hitting Danish champion, Jorgen

Hansen, over 12 rounds.

## SLACK, Jack:

Born at Bristol, Jack Slack was a comparatively short but very heavily built prize fighter.

He won the heavyweight champion-ship in April, 1750, with a surprise victory over Jack Broughton at the latter's amphitheatre in London. Slack blinded the ageing champion and beat him in 14 minutes.

Slack subsequently met and beat the first French pugilist ever to appear in an English ring, one named Pettit. After holding the championship 10 years he lost it to Bill Stevens.

## SLATTERY, Jim:

An Irish-American, Jim Slattery was making a name for himself among the light-heavyweights when still in his teens.

He had an unusual style of fighting. More often than not he kept his arms hanging at his sides, but he didn't need a guard, for he was able to make his opponents miss with his clever bobbing and weaving.

Slattery won N.B.A's version of the vacant world light-heavy title in August, 1927, by outpointing Maxie Rosen-bloom.

A stronger claim to this title was made by Tommy Loughran following his victory over McTigue in October, 1927, and when Slattery and Loughran met in December that same year Loughran got the referee's nod at the end of 15 rounds.

Slattery gained a stronger hold on this title when he beat Lou Scozza in February, 1930, but unfortunately he never took his training seriously enough and less than four months later he was defeated by Maxie Rosenbloom.

## SMART, Kelvin:

Aggressive fly-weight from Caerphilly who proved to have a good left hook when he k.o.'d fellow Welshman, Dave George, to capture the British title vacated by Charlie Magri. That was in 1982, but although a strong body-puncher Smart was beaten in his first defence of the title 17 months later, being retired by his manager between the seventh and eighth rounds in an all-action fight with the former British bantamweight champion Hugh Russell in Belfast.

## SMITH, Amos (Mysterious Billy):

There has never been a tougher fighter than this Irish-American, who is generally considered the first welterweight champion of the world.

Mysterious Billy Smith laid claim to this title after stopping Danny Needham in 14 rounds in San Francisco, December 14, 1892, but after beating the Australian champion, Tom Williams, in two rounds, Smith lost his title to Tommy Ryan at Minneapolis, July 26, 1894.

Ryan was subsequently beaten by Kid McCoy, and, when the latter relinquished the title through weight difficulties in 1897, Smith claimed it once again and was accepted as champion until he was well beaten and disqualified in the 21st round of a contest at Buffalo with Rube Ferns, January 15, 1900.

## SMITH, Dick:

A stylish boxer who won a light-heavyweight Lonsdale Belt outright. In fact, he was the first holder of a Lonsdale Belt in this division, and won it by outpointing Dennis Haugh in what was only his third professional contest.

At that time, however, Smith was no novice. He had had a distinguished amateur career and been A.B.A. heavyweight champion in 1912 and 1913.

Smith, who was born in London in 1886, had been a soldier before he took up boxing for a living in 1913.

After winning the light-heavyweight title with his victory over Haugh, he defended it successfully against Harry Curzon, but was then outpointed by Harry Reeve in October, 1916.

When Reeve relinquished the title, Smith again became champion and got his third notch on the Lonsdale Belt by outpointing Joe Beckett. That was in February, 1918.

Soon afterwards, however, Smith also gave up the title and he went after Joe Beckett's heavyweight crown.

They met in December, 1919, but this time Beckett knocked Smith out in the fifth round. In another meeting over three years later Smith lasted 17 rounds before Beckett again applied the "finisher."

So Dick Smith had to retire without being able to achieve his ambition of becoming British heavyweight champion. Before meeting Beckett he had had three tries to lift the crown from the head of Billy Wells but had been beaten inside the distance on each occasion.

The closest Smith ever got to this title was when, in his second meeting with Wells, he had the champion down for what was alleged to have been a count of at least 16 seconds (see under COUNT, Long).

## SMITH, Jem:

A Londoner, Jem Smith fought during the transition period from the old Prize Ring to boxing under Queensberry Rules. He fought both with gloves and without, but at heart he was really one of the old school of bare-knuckle bruisers.

Smith first claimed the Championship of England after beating Jack Davies in a bare-knuckle contest in 1885, but he did not actually win this title in a gloved contest until September, 1889, when he beat Jack Wannop in 10 rounds.

This fighter's outstanding Prize Ring battle took place in France in 1887 when he went 106 rounds with the famous American pugilist, Jake Kilrain. This fight was abandoned as a draw when the light became too bad for them to continue.

In November, 1889, Smith was well and truly beaten by that great negro boxer, Peter Jackson, and in July, 1891, he lost his title when Ted Pritchard stopped him in three rounds.

Smith attempted a come-back in 1895 at the age of 32 and got his title back by beating Pritchard in two rounds, but a defeat by George Crisp in February, 1897, ended his career.

## SMITH, Roy:

Part-time fighter and bank alarm servicer from Nottingham, the stylish Smith has proved to be a useful tactician. After a good amateur career he had 13 wins and two defeats in professional bouts before taking the British cruiser-

Peter Kane, world flyweight champion, outpointing former world
bantamweight champion, Baltazar Sangchilli, at Earls Court,
London, in April 1939

Jimmy Wilde beating the American, Young Pal Moore, at Olympia,
London, in July 1919

A rare picture of an up and coming Len Harvey, still little more than a welterweight, on the way to a k.o. victory over Joe Rolfe in 1927

Freddie Mills seen applying the finishing touches to Len Harvey's career in 1942 when the Cornishman was beaten inside two rounds

weight title in February 1987, counter-punching his way to a points victory over Andy Straughn.

It was less than three months later that Smith was stopped in only 90 seconds to lose his title to Tee Jay.

## SMITH, Sid:

This clever Bermondsey flyweight started boxing when he was 17 and in December, 1911, he won the first Lonsdale Belt match in that division by outpointing Joe Wilson over 20 rounds.

Smith was not a hard hitter but he was a fast mover who always displayed outstanding footwork.

In September 1912, he outpointed Curley Walker, but after a dispute over the size of the purse offered by the N.S.C. he returned his Lonsdale Belt and went to Paris in April 1913 to beat the leading Continental flyweight, Eugene Criqui in a contest billed as being for both the European and world flyweight titles.

However, in June, 1913, he was knocked out in the 11th round by Bill Ladbury in a catchweight match, and immediately relinquished his titles.

Smith then went on the Music Halls and appeared all over the country with the famous stage personality, Harry Weldon.

## SMITH, Solly:

A Californian, Solly Smith was one of America's cleverest boxers towards the end of the 19th century.

During his career he beat five men who were at one time or another world champions. They were the feather-weights, George Dixon, Dal Hawkins and Billy Murphy, and the lightweights, George Lavigne and Frank Erne.

Smith won the world featherweight title by outpointing George Dixon at San Francisco in October, 1897, but he lost it in September, 1898, when he was forced to retire with a broken arm after five rounds against Dave Sullivan.

## SMITH, Wallace (Bud):

Cincinnati negro who won the world lightweight title from Jimmy Carter in June, 1955, and successfully defended it in a return bout four months later.

Smith was then 26 years of age and had reached his peak. He was never as good afterwards, indeed, following his first defence of the world championship he lost every one of his remaining 11 fights.

In May, 1956, he was beaten by the veteran Joe Brown in a non-title bout, and a little over three months later Smith had to hand over his crown when Brown beat him a second time.

Wallace Smith was shot dead in July 1973 when trying to intervene in an argument.

## SOLLAS, Vernon:

Until severe bruising of the brain had been diagnosed Sollas was one of the enigmas of recent British ring history. A Scot from Edinburgh who promised much and won the vacant British featherweight title in fine style by knocking out Jimmy Revie inside four rounds in March 1975, but on other occasions he disappointed either through lack of concentration or running out of steam when under pressure after six or seven rounds.

Typical of this kind of disappointment was when he was beaten by the European champion, Elio Cotena, in London in February 1976. After build-ing up a good lead he faded and was knocked out in the fourteenth round.

Sollas lost his licence in 1977 after being stopped three times in a row, including losing his British title when the referee halted his contest with Alan Richardson in the eighth round at Leeds.

It was then his illness forced him to give up.

## SOUTH AFRICA:

Professional boxing in South Africa was legalised in 1923. Today the most important centres for big fights are Johannesburg and Sun City.

The best known South African boxers over the years have probably been Ben Foord, who was the first man born outside the United Kingdom to become British heavyweight champion; their three world champions, Vic Toweel, Arnold Taylor and Brian Mitchell; and also Gerrie Coetzee who held the W.B.A. version of the world heavyweight title for a little over 14 months, 1983-84. Another South African, Piet Crous, held the W.B.A. version of the cruiserweight title 1984-85.

Other well-known South Africans were heavyweights George (Boer) Rodel, who fought in this country in 1912 and then went to America where he was twice defeated by the up-and-coming Jess Willard; Fred Storbeck, who, like Rodel, was knocked out by the British champion, Billy Wells; and Don McCorkindale, who was a Scotsman by birth but emigrated to the Union. He fought most of the best men in this country between the two World Wars; and Willie Smith, an Olympic champion who laid claim to the world bantamweight title after beating Teddy Baldock in London in 1927, but never gained much support for this claim.

Boxing is believed to have been introduced into South Africa by a Scotsman, J. R. Couper. A schoolmaster, Couper emigrated to the Union and settled in Basutoland.

The first black South African to take part in a world title bout was Norman "Pangaman" Sckgapane, beaten in nine rounds by W.B.A. light-welter champion, Antonio Cervantes, Bophuthatswana, August 26, 1978.

The first black South African to win a world title was Peter Mathebula who beat Taeshik Kim in Los Angeles to gain the W.B.A. flyweight crown in December, 1980.

## Champions:

World:—
Cruiserweight: Piet Crous (W.B.A.), 1984-85.
Junior-lightweight: Brian Mitchell, 1986.
Bantamweight: Vic Toweel, 1950-52; Arnold Taylor, 1973-74.
Flyweight: Peter Mathebula, 1980-81.
Empire and Commonwealth:—
Heavyweight: Ben Foord, 1936-37.
Welterweight: Gerald Dreyer, 1952-54; John Van Rensburg, 1958.
Lightweight: Laurie Stevens, 1936; Johnny van Rensburg, 1955-56; Willie Toweel, 1956-59.
Bantamweight: Vic Toweel, 1949-52.
Flyweight: Jake Tuli, 1952-54; Dennis Adams, 1957-62

British:—
Heavyweight: Ben Foord, 1936-37.
Olympic:—
Light-heavyweight: David E. Carstens, 1932; George Hunter, 1948.
Lightweight: Laurie Stevens, 1932; Gerald Dreyer, 1948.
Bantamweight: C. Walker, 1920; Willie Smith, 1924.

## SOUTHPAW:

A southpaw is a boxer who uses the unorthodox stance of right arm and right foot forward. Orthodox fighters are often troubled when they meet southpaws simply because of the differences in style, and the orthodox man usually has to change his tactics and keep moving to the right rather than to the left as he spars for an opening.

No southpaw has ever won the world heavyweight title, but there have been southpaw champions in each of the other divisions as follows:—

Light-heavyweight: Melio Bettina (N.Y.A.C. champion), 1939; Marvin Johnson (W.B.C.), 1978-79, (W.B.A.) 1979-; Mate Parlov (W.B.C.), 1978.

Middleweight: Al McCoy, 1914-17; Johnny Wilson, 1920-23; Tiger Flowers, 1926; Lou Brouillard (N.Y.A.C. champion), 1933; Alan Minter, 1980; Marvin Hagler, 1980-87.

Junior-middleweight: Ayub Kalule (W.B.A.), 1979-81; Maurice Hope (W.B.C.), 1979-81.

Welterweight: Lou Brouillard, 1931-32; Young Corbett III, 1933; Billy Backus, 1970-71.

Junior-welterweight: Sandro Lopopolo, 1966-67; Paul Fujii, 1967-68; Kim Sang Hyun, 1978-80; Johnny Bumphus (W.B.A.), 1984.

Lightweight: J. Watt (W.B.C.), 1979-81; Hector Camacho (W.B.C.), 1985-87; Jose Luis Ramirez (W.B.C.), 1987-.

Junior-lightweight: Flash Elorde, 1960-67; Yoshiaki Numata, 1967; Hiroshi Koboyashi, 1967-71; Ben Villaflor, 1972-73; 1973-76; Kuniaki Shibata, 1973.

Featherweight: Freddie Miller (N.B.A. and Europe), 1933-36; Vicente Salvidar, 1964-67, 1970; Cecilio Lastra (W.B.A.), 1977-78; Wilfredo Gomez (W.B.C.), 1984.

Junior-featherweight: Wilfredo Gomez (W.B.C.), 1977-83.

Bantamweight: Jimmy Carruthers, 1952-54; Johnny Caldwell, 1961-62 (E.B.U. and B.B.B.C. only). Masahiko Harada, 1965-68; Arnold Taylor, 1973-74.

Junior-bantamweight: Jiro Watanabe, 1984-85.

Flyweight: Jackie Paterson, 1943-48; Hiroyuki Ebihara, 1963-64; Venice Borkorsor, 1973; Shoji Oguma (W.B.C.), 1974-75; Luis Ibarra (W.B.A.), 1979-80; Koji Koboyashi, 1984; Gabriel Beral, 1984.

Light-flyweight: Netrnoi Sawvorasingh, 1978; Hilario Zapata (W.B.C.), 1980-.

## SPAIN:

Probably the best known fighter ever to come out of Spain was Paolino Uzcudun, a tough Basque, who never won a world title but was for many years one of the leading heavyweights.

Known as the "Basque Woodchopper", Uzcudun was rather short for a heavyweight and he did not have a real heavyweight punch, but he was a difficult man to hit and was as hard as nails.

In 1924 he stopped the British champion, Frank Goddard, in six rounds, and the following year he beat Phil Scott in the same distance. The same year he won the European title and then went to America where he had a fine run of success.

However, he was beaten by Max Schmeling and twice lost to Primo Carnera, once in a world title fight.

## Champions:

World:—

Light-middleweight: Jose Duran, 1976.

Featherweight: *Jose Legra, 1968-69, 1972-73; Cecilio Lastra (W.B.A.), 1977-78.

Bantamweight: Baltazar Sangchilli. (Not recognised by the N.B.A.), 1935-36.

European:—

Heavyweight: Paolino Uzcudun, 1926-28; Jose Urtain, 1970, 1971-72; Alfredo Evangelista, 1977-79, 1987.

Light-heavyweight: Martinez de Alfara, 1934.

Middleweight: Ignacio Ara, 1932.

Junior or Light-middleweight: Jose Hernandez, 1970-72; Jose Duran, 1974-75.

Welterweight: Alfonso Redondo, 1987.

Junior or Light-welterweight: Juan Sombrita, 1965; Pedro Carrasco, 1971; Toni Ortiz, 1973-74; Perico Fernandez, 1974; Jose Ramon Gomez Fouz, 1975; Fernandez Sanchez, 1978-79; Jose Luis Heredia, 1979; Antonio Guinaldo, 1980-81.

Lightweight: Luis Rayo, 1927-28; Pedro Carrasco, 1967-69; Miguel Velazquez, 1970-71; Perico Fernandez, 1976-77; Francisco Leon, 1980.

Junior-lightweight: Carlos Hernandez, 1979, 1979-82; Rodolfo Sanchez, 1979; Roberto Castanon, 1982-83.

Featherweight: Antonio Ruiz, 1925-28; Jose Girones, 1929-33; Fred Galiana, 1955-56; Jose Legra, 1967-68, 1970-72; Manuel Calvo, 1968-69; Gitan Jiminez, 1973-75; Nino Jiminez, 1976-77; Manuel Masso, 1977; Roberto Castanon, 1977-81.

Bantamweight: Carlos Flix, 1929-31; Luis Romero, 1949-51; Amed Mimun Ben Ali, 1963, 1965, 1966-68; Augustin Senin, 1971-72; †Bob Allotey, 1974-75; Juan Francisco Rodriguez, 1978-79.

Flyweight: Victor Ferrand, 1927-28; Young Martin, 1955-59.

*Naturalised Spaniard born in Cuba.

†Naturalised Spaniard born in Ghana.

## SPINKS, Leon:

One of seven children brought up in a St. Louis ghetto Leon Spinks gained a Gold Medal at the Montreal Olympics when he won the light-heavyweight competition and turned professional for the simple reason that he was out of work and needed the money. This is the kind of hungry background that has made champions and the young coloured boy soon proved that he was a determined all-action fighter. It was only after seven fights, including four first round k.o. victories, that he got a shot at Muhammad Ali's world heavyweight crown in Las Vegas in February 1978, and shocked the fight fraternity by punching his way to a split points victory. However, in a return only seven months later Ali showed his true mastery over this comparative novice and regained the title with a unanimous points victory. Spinks had held the world heavyweight crown for the shortest spell in ring history.

After this Leon frequently fought as a cruiserweight or junior heavyweight but was beaten in six rounds by Dwight Braxton in March 1986 when attempting to lift the W.B.A. version of the latter world title.

## SPINKS, Mike:

A fast mover with an upright style this American, a younger brother of Leon, has had something of a raw deal from the boxing authorities. In September 1985 he became the first world light-heavyweight champion to win the heavyweight title by outpointing Larry Holmes over 15 ducking and weaving rounds. It was two months after this that he actually relinquished his W.B.A. version of the light-heavyweight crown which he had won four years earlier by outscoring Mustafa Muhammad in what was Spinks' 17th win on the trot since turning professional in 1977.

In April 1986 Spinks confirmed his superiority over Holmes with another points victory but the judges' decision was much debated and, in any event, although undefeated Spinks was by that time only recognised as champion by the I.B.F. The authorities had confused even the heavyweight championship once again, but at the time of writing the man who won an Olympic middleweight gold medal in 1976 is still undefeated although denied world title recognition by W.B.A., W.B.C. and I.B.F.

## SPINKS, Terry:

This Londoner started boxing at an early age·and after winning schoolboy championships, the A.B.A. eight stone title and an Olympic Gold Medal, he turned professional soon after his 19th birthday.

Spinks won the British featherweight title in his 37th contest by defeating Bobby Neill in 7 rounds, September, 1960, but after successfully defending his crown against Neill in a return he lost it when forced to retire in 10 rounds against Howard Winstone, May, 1961.

## SPRING, Tom:

This Herefordshire prize-fighter was a protégé of Tom Cribb, and the old champion nominated Spring as his successor in 1817.

Spring, whose real name was Thomas Winter, beat Yorkshireman John Stringer, in 29 rounds, to win the approval of the Fancy as title-holder. That was in September, 1817, but six months later he was beaten by Ned Painter in 41 rounds at Russia Farm, Kingston.

Tom Spring was then only 23, young for a bruiser, and was still improving. After he had won a couple more fights, including one particularly gruelling battle of 71 rounds with Jack Carter, he again challenged Ned Painter, but the Lancashire man apparently thought better of it, for he did not accept and so forfeited his title to Spring.

## STANLEY, George Digger:

A gipsy, born in a caravan at Kingston-on-Thames, Digger Stanley could not read or write but he was a really clever boxer who developed in the best school—the fair-ground booth.

In 1903 he won the British eight-stone title by defeating Jack Walker but this cannot be rated as an official flyweight title as that division was not really established until 1909.

It was not until seven years later that Stanley won his first official title when he took the British and European bantamweight championships from Joe Bowker with an eighth round knock-out.

However, during those seven years Stanley actually claimed the world title in the bantamweight class. He made out quite a good case for himself in 1909, for then the American, Jimmy Walsh, gave up the title, and Stanley claimed it on the strength of his 15-round draw with Walsh in May of that year.

This claim faded in June, 1912, and he also lost his European title when he was knocked out by Charles Ledoux.

Stanley's British title went to Bill Beynon in June, 1913. He regained it in a return match with Beynon in October that year but finally lost it to Curley Walker in April, 1914. He died in poverty in 1919.

## STEELE, Freddie:

An Irish-American, Freddie Steele was recognised in the United States as world middleweight champion following his points victory over Babe Risko in July, 1936.

At that time, Marcel Thil was acknowledged as champion by the I.B.U.

In 1936 and 1937 Steele beat such men as Gus Lesnevich, Gorilla Jones, Babe Risko, Frankie Battaglia, and Ken Overlin, but in January, 1938, he was stopped in nine rounds by Fred Apostoli in an overweight match.

Apostoli claimed the championship but Steele continued as official American title-holder until July, 1938, when he was knocked out in the first round of a contest with Al Hostak.

## STERLING, Bunny:

This coloured Jamaican was the first immigrant to win a British title when he became British and Commonwealth middleweight champion in September 1970. His bout with Mark Rowe was stopped after only four rounds when the champion was cut on both eyes. Sterling had immigrated to London when he was seven and qualified for this title fight under the 10-year residence rule introduced by the B.B.B.C. in 1968.

A fast mover Sterling later confirmed his superiority over Rowe with a clear cut points victory, but lost his Commonwealth title to Tony Mundine in 1972 and his British title in a controversial points defeat by Kevin Finnegan in February 1974.

The following year he regained the British title by defeating Maurice Hope in eight rounds, then relinquished the crown to go after the European title. This he both won and lost during 1976.

## STEVENS, Bill:

Bill Stevens, "The Nailer," was born at Birmingham. He won the championship by knocking out Jack Slack in 27 minutes in June, 1760, but in March, 1761, he was beaten in 17 minutes by George Meggs, a protégé of Slack.

Stevens subsequently admitted that he had been bribed by Slack into "throwing" this fight.

## STEWARD, Sam:

Born at Lewisham, London, Sam Steward won the vacant British lightweight title by knocking out former champion, Ernie Rice, in 12 rounds, London, September 17, 1928.

An aggressive fighter, Steward's reign as champion lasted less than eight months, however, for he was outpointed by Fred Webster in his first defence of the title, May 2, 1929.

## STRACEY, John H.:

Cockney favourite from Bethnal Green who won the British welterweight title at the second attempt when he knocked out Bobby Arthur in a return bout in June 1973, and went on to take the European title by punching the tough Frenchman, Roger Menetrey, almost to a standstill in a devastating display in Paris in May 1974. The referee called a halt in the eighth.

It was obvious that Stracey was world class material and he got his chance to prove his ability when he met the top man, Jose Napoles, in Mexico City in December 1975. The experienced Cuban-born fighter was rated as a super-champion, having successfully defended his title 11 times since regaining it 4½ years earlier, but he proved no match for the hard-hitting Stracey and the referee had to intervene in the sixth round.

Officially Stracey was only a W.B.A. champion but his claim to world-wide recognition was certainly stronger than the W.B.A. champion at this time.

Stracey successfully defended his world title against Hedgeman Lewis at Wembley but lost it at the same venue in June 1976 when surprisingly outpunched by Carlos Palomino.

He was unbeaten both as British and European champion before relinquishing these titles in 1975.

## STRAUGHN, Andy:

Good class of boxer who won the A.B.A. light-heavyweight title in 1979, 80 and 81 before turning professional in 1982. He has a good variety of punches in his locker but lost both of his fights in America in 1984. However, after 18 professional contests this cruiserweight from Hitchin, Herts., captured the vacant

British title with a close points win over Tee Jay in October 1986.

Straughn suffered his first defeat in 20 fights when outpointed by Roy Smith in February 1987 and his championship reign ended after less than four months.

## SULLIVAN, Jim:

Another fighter from Bermondsey, Jim Sullivan took the British middleweight title from Tom Thomas in a hard contest at the N.S.C., November 14, 1910.

Sullivan broke two ribs in that bout but he fought on to gain a points decision at the end of 20 gruelling rounds.

Sullivan relinquished the title in 1911 and later went to Australia. On his return he beat Jack Harrison, who had been middleweight champion during his absence but had been deprived of the title by the N.S.C.

The same night Pat O'Keefe beat Harry Reeve for the official middleweight title, and when Sullivan met O'Keefe in May, 1914, he was outpointed over 20 rounds.

Sullivan made another bid to regain the championship after the war but he was stopped in 14 rounds by Tom Gummer.

## SULLIVAN, Johnny:

This Preston middleweight, who had his earliest fights in his father's fairground boxing booth, won the vacant British and Empire titles by knocking out Gordon Hazell in the first round, September 14, 1954. He had previously stopped the Bristol boy.

Sullivan was a good two-fisted fighter, but he was beaten in his first defence of his titles by Pat McAteer. In this contest at Liverpool, June 16, 1955, Sullivan was disqualified in the ninth round.

## SULLIVAN, John L.:

The "Boston Strong Boy" was probably the most idolised fighter in American ring history. Since his retirement Jack Dempsey has become the hero of the American fight fans, but during his ring career he was never held in such admiration as was the great John L.

This colourful character was born of Irish parents in Boston, Massachusetts, in October, 1858.

His first challenge to the American champion, Paddy Ryan, made in 1880, was rejected, so Sullivan went on a tour in which he took on all-comers, offering 40 or 50 dollars to anyone who could last four rounds with him. In a subsequent tour Sullivan increased this amount to a thousand dollars.

Sullivan won the American heavyweight championship from Paddy Ryan in a bare-knuckle contest at Mississippi City, February 7, 1882. Ryan was knocked out in 10½ minutes.

It is usually claimed that this made Sullivan world champion, but it is difficult to establish a clear-cut case on Sullivan's behalf. Ryan had beaten Joe Goss who had, in turn, beaten Tom Allen, but both of these men had lost to the British champion, Jem Mace. However, by the time Sullivan beat Ryan, Mace was virtually retired, and the British championship was claimed by both Jem Smith and Charlie Mitchell.

Now, Sullivan never met Smith, but he had two bouts with Mitchell. The first time he was giving Mitchell a thoroughly good hiding when the police intervened, and the second bout went 39 rounds before it was abandoned as a draw.

Because Sullivan was unable to win this battle he never established himself as an undisputed world champion, but on the other hand, there is no doubt that at his peak there was no contemporary fighter better than Sullivan (certainly not Mitchell), and therefore there is no reason why the Irish-American should not be acknowledged as a world champion.

In his prime Sullivan was a powerful hitter, and for his weight he was a surprisingly fast mover, but after about 1884 he took to drink and more often than not he was sadly out of condition.

Nevertheless, it was not until September, 1892, that he was beaten by a cleverer boxer, Jim Corbett, who knocked him out in 21 rounds. At that time Sullivan had not fought for 3 years 2 months, but had been on the stage appearing in a play "Honest Hearts and Willing Hands."

In his later years John L. Sullivan was a reformed character and he travelled around giving lectures on the evils of drink. He died in his 60th year.

## SULLIVAN, Mike (Twin):

This Irish-American claimed the world welterweight title at a time when the championship of that division was being hotly disputed.

Sullivan staked his claim by beating Honey Mellody on points over 20 rounds at Los Angeles in April, 1907, but he was never accorded world-wide recognition because of a counter-claim by the Dixie Kid.

He soon gave up his claim, for he became overweight, and he was then matched with Stanley Ketchel for the vacant middleweight crown in February, 1908, but was knocked out in the first round.

Mike's twin brother, Jack, was also a leading middleweight fighter.

## SUMMERS, Johnny:

In the six or seven years before World War I there were few better men in this country between nine stone and 10st. 7lbs. (126lbs.-147lbs.) than this Yorkshireman from Middlesbrough, who had been brought up in Canning Town.

He laid claim to the British featherweight championship in 1906 when he beat Spike Robson. The fight, which took place at the N.S.C., was billed as for the nine stone championship of England, but the featherweight championship was still claimed by Joe Bowker.

Bowker had won the title at 8st. 12lbs. (124lbs.) and had also beaten Robson, so that Summers could not be credited with the featherweight championship at that time.

In any event, Summers was beaten by Robson in a return match at the N.S.C. late in 1906, but then, in November, 1908, he claimed the British lightweight title after beating Jack Goldswain.

Goldswain had been acknowledged as lightweight champion before this, and the crown was passed on to Summers despite the fact that Goldswain weighed in at 10st. 4½lbs. (144½lbs.) for this contest.

When the N.S.C. presented their first Lonsdale Belt for competition in the lightweight division Summers was chosen to meet Freddy Welsh and was beaten on points. That was on November 8, 1909.

Still, Summers wasn't finished with championship fighting. In June, 1912, he took the British welterweight title from Arthur Evernden and held it until he was knocked out in nine rounds by Johnny Basham, in December, 1914.

When Welsh relinquished his British lightweight championship in 1917, the N.S.C. matched the 36-year-old Summers with Bob Marriott for this title. They met on June 23, 1919, and Summers was disqualified in the 10th round.

## SUNDAY:

Since the turn of the century only two British championship fights have ever taken place on a Sunday. That when Jackie Brown (Manchester) knocked out Bert Kirby (Birmingham) October 13, 1929, for the vacant British flyweight title, and when Chris Finnegan (Iver) took the British and Commonwealth light-heavyweight titles from Eddie Avoth (Cardiff) at the World Sporting Club, London, January 24, 1971.

Of course, outside of Britain many important contests are fought on Sundays.

The old International Athletic Club at 34 Windmill Street, London, was the first place where boxing shows were regularly staged on Sundays. This was in 1910 and the promoter was Bill Klein.

During the 1920's Sunday shows were popular at the Blackfriars Ring and Premierland, both in London.

## SWEDEN:

Until Ingemar Johansson won the world heavyweight title in 1959 Sweden had not made much of an impression in international boxing circles.

Their best men over the years have nearly all been in the heavier divisions and before Johansson, the best known Swedish fighters were Harry Persson, Arne Anderson, John Anderson, and Olle Tandberg. All except John Anderson were heavyweights.

Harry Persson fought in America during the 1920's and he also beat Phil

Scott in London.

Arne Anderson also went to America to try and make a name for himself but his career came to a tragic and abrupt end when he died after being knocked out by Lou Thomas in Chicago in 1941.

John Anderson, a light-heavyweight, had several fights in America in 1935 and 1936, and his victories included one over Mickey Walker, but when the "Toy Bulldog" was past his best.

Olle Tandberg became European heavyweight champion after outpointing Karel Sys, of Belgium, in May, 1943.

It was Tandberg, who put a stop to Joe Baksi's world title aspirations, surprisingly defeating the American in Stockholm in 1947, but when Tandberg went to America he was beaten by Joey Maxim.

### Champions:

World:—
Heavyweight: Ingemar Johansson, 1959-60.

European:—
Heavyweight: Olle Tandberg, 1943; Ingemar Johansson, 1956-59, 1962-63; Anders Eklund, 1985, 1987.

Light-heavyweight: John Anderson, 1933.

Junior-middleweight: Bo Hogberg, 1966.

Welterweight: Albert Badoud, 1915-16.

### SWIFT, Wally:

One of Britain's most popular fighters of the post-war era, this Nottingham favourite remained active for nearly 12 years, winning both the British welter and middleweight titles.

He took the welterweight crown from Tommy Molloy with a convincing points victory in February 1960 but lost it to the stylish Brian Curvis before the year was out.

Swift captured the middleweight championship in December 1964, outpointing Mick Leahy before a jubilant Nottingham crowd.

A clever counter-puncher, noted for his left-hand work, Swift lost his middleweight title when the referee stopped his fight with Johnny Pritchett in the twelfth round, November 1965.

### SWITZERLAND:

As one might suppose this small country has not produced many men who became world famous in the boxing ring. The only fighter ever born in Switzerland who won a world title was Frank Erne, born Zurich, but he went to America when still quite young and settled in Buffalo, where he started his professional career in 1893. Erne won the world lightweight title when he beat George Lavigne in July, 1899.

### Champions:

World:—
Lightweight: Frank Erne, 1899-1902.

European:—
Light-heavyweight: Louis Clement, 1924-25.

Welterweight: Mauro Martelli, 1987-.

Bantamweight: Maurice Dubois, 1935-36.

Flyweight: Fritz Chervet, 1972, 1973-74.

### SYMONDS, Joe:

A hard-hitting Plymouth flyweight who first claimed the British title in April, 1914, after he had stopped Percy Jones in the 18th round of a bout in the Devon seaport. However, this was never officially recognised because, unfortunately for Symonds, Jones had come in slightly over the weight limit, and, in any event, the N.S.C. would not recognise title fights outside their jurisdiction.

Symonds was eliminated as a title claimant when he was outpointed by Jimmy Wilde at the N.S.C. in November, 1914, but after Wilde was beaten by Tancy Lee, the Plymouth fighter came back to become the official champion by stopping Lee in 16 rounds at the N.S.C., October 18, 1915.

This victory also gave Symonds as good a reason as anyone to call himself champion of the world at this weight.

Symonds lost both these titles to Jimmy Wilde, who knocked him out in 12 rounds at the N.S.C. in February, 1916.

Symonds subsequently made two bids for the British bantamweight crown but he was beaten first by Joe Fox and later by Tommy Noble.

He died at Plymouth in 1953 aged 59.

## TARLETON, Nel:

This great Liverpool fighter was one of the most popular ring personalities this country has ever produced. He started boxing at the age of 12 and had his last fight at the age of 39 when he successfully defended his British featherweight title against Al Phillips over 15 rounds.

Towards the end of his career this remarkable boxer, who won two Lonsdale Belts outright, was fighting with only one lung. When you consider that and also his age, anyone who did not know Tarleton can imagine what ability he must have possessed to outpoint a 25-year-old "Tiger" such as Al Phillips.

Tarleton lacked a punch but his defensive work was astonishingly skilful.

During his career he took part in 10 British featherweight title bouts and won this crown on three separate occasions. He also fought twice for the world title but was beaten both times by Freddie Miller.

Tarleton was 41 when he finally decided to hang up his gloves and retire undefeated British featherweight champion in 1947. He died in 1956.

## TAYLOR, Arnold:

In a fine run during the first three years of his career this tough fighter won the South African light, feather, and bantamweight titles before he suffered a defeat in a non-title bout with world featherweight champion, Johnny Famechon.

Taylor enjoyed another good run after this, including a number of wins in Australia in 1971—his first fights abroad, and in November 1973 he took the world bantamweight title from Romero Anaya

in remarkable fashion. Taylor was floored four times and had his right eye shut, but in the 14th round, when he seemed destined for defeat, the game South African pulled out a knock-out punch to become his country's first world champion since Vic Toweel.

However, when called upon to defend his title against the South Korean, Soo Hwan Hong, Taylor weakened himself considerably in making the weight and was clearly outpointed.

Taylor was killed in a motorcycle accident in November, 1981.

## TAYLOR, Charles (Bud):

When Charlie Rosenberg relinquished the world bantamweight title in 1927 through weight difficulties, Taylor was matched with Tony Canzoneri for the N.B.A. version of the championship. They fought a draw over 10 rounds at Chicago, March 26, 1927, then Taylor won the return bout on points three months later.

This American was forced to relinquish the title when he became overweight in 1928, and, after he retired in 1931, he became a manager and boxing promoter.

## TAYLOR, George:

Some chroniclers do not include this fighter among their list of champions but he claimed that distinction during the 1730's following the retirement of James Figg. Indeed, if his claim is accepted then Taylor was the youngest-ever champion at 16 years of age.

Taylor, who was blind in one eye, had a boxing booth in the Tottenham Court Road, and here he reigned as champion until about 1734 (there is some doubt about this date for it may have been 1738) when he was beaten in 20 minutes by Jack Broughton.

Taylor eventually became totally blind and he died in 1758.

## TELEVISION:

The first boxing ever to appear on television was an exhibition bout arranged by Johnny Sharpe, which took place at Broadcasting House, London, August 22, 1933. The two principals were Archie Sexton (Bethnal Green) and Lauri

Raiteri (Stratford). But this was very much of an experiment and was not seen by many of the public.

Three exhibition bouts staged by the Alexandra A.B.C. of London were televised and seen by many more people on November 6, 1936, while on February 5, 1937, the same club was responsible for staging an Open Tourament on television, but the first top-class professional contest ever to be televised was that between Len Harvey and Jock McAvoy at Harringay Arena, London, April 4, 1938. This was on closed circuit.

The first professional fight televised for general viewing was that between Eric Boon and Arthur Danahar at Harringay Arena, London, February 23, 1939. This was also piped to three London theatres.

The first fight televised for public viewing in colour took place at Madison Square Garden, New York City, March 26, 1954. It was between Gustav Scholz (Germany) and Al Andrews (America). It was put out over 21 stations by the National Broadcasting Company.

## TERRANOVA, Phil:

A Golden Gloves champion in his amateur days, this Italian-American made a speedy rise to the top and won the N.B.A. version of the world featherweight title from Jackie Callura with an eighth round knock-out in August, 1943.

He also stopped Callura in eight rounds in a return bout but lost the championship when outpointed by Sal Bartolo, March, 1944.

In an attempt to regain the world title Terranova was outpointed by Willie Pep in February, 1945.

## THAILAND:

In recent years the Thais have developed real enthusiasm for boxing and their Royal Family attends most of the important contests.

CHAMPIONS:

World:—

Junior-featherweight:       Samarto Espinoza, (W.B.C.) 1986-

Super-flyweight: Payo Poon Tarat, 1983-84.

Flyweight: Pone Kingpetch, 1960-62, 1963-65; Chartchai Chionoi, 1966-69,

1970, 1973-74 (W.B.A.); Venice Borkorsor, 1972-73; Sot Chitalada, (W.B.C.), 1984-87.

Light-flyweight: Netrnoi Sawvorasingh, 1978.

## THIL, Marcel:

A tough French middleweight with a crouching style which bothered a lot of his opponents. He was a punishing body puncher but was handicapped because he lacked a really big punch.

Thil claimed the world middleweight title following a victory over Gorilla Jones in Paris, June 11, 1932. Jones was disqualified in the 11th round.

The title had previously been vacated by Mickey Walker and Jones was recognised as champion by the N.B.A.

The I.B.U. accepted Thil as titleholder and he continued to be recognised as such almost everywhere, except in the United States, until September, 1937. Then he met Fred Apostoli in New York and the referee was forced to stop the fight in the 10th round with the Frenchman suffering badly from cut eyes.

Apostoli was prevented from claiming the title because of an agreement with the N.Y.A.C., but Marcel Thil relinquished his claim after this defeat.

## THOM, Wally:

Southpaw from Birkenhead who started fighting professionally in 1949 and was unbeaten in his first 22 contests before losing to Jimmy Molloy in August, 1951.

In his next fight, however, Thom won the British and Empire welterweight titles from Eddie Thomas at Harringay.

That was in October, 1951, but when he made his first defence of these titles in July, 1952, he was knocked out in the ninth round by Cliff Curvis.

Thom regained British and Empire championships, after they had been relinquished by Curvis, by outpointing Peter Fallon in September, 1953, and he made the Lonsdale Belt his own property with a victory over Lew Lazar before he was stopped in five rounds by Peter Waterman in June, 1956.

Thom was also European welterweight champion during 1954-55. He retired shortly after his defeat by Waterman and became a boxing referee.

## THOMAS, Eddie:

A skilful, scientific boxer from Merthyr, Eddie Thomas won the A.B.A. lightweight championship in 1946.

After turning professional he became Welsh welterweight champion in 1948 and then took the British title from Henry Hall with a points victory at Harringay in November, 1949.

In January, 1951, he annexed the Empire title by stopping Pat Patrick, of South Africa, in 13 rounds, and the following month he won the European crown from Michele Palermo, of Italy.

Lack of aggressiveness was this clever Welsh boy's main weakness, and before 1951 was out he had lost his European title to Charles Humez and his British and Empire titles to Wally Thom.

More recently Eddie Thomas has made a name for himself as a manager steering two men, Howard Winstone and Ken Buchanan to world titles.

## THOMAS, Pat:

Born in St. Kitts but brought up in Cardiff this fighter became the first immigrant to win the British welterweight title when he knocked out Pat McCormack in 13 rounds at Walworth in December 1975. Thomas had then been fighting professionally for five years.

The new champion, who had taken over the title vacated by John H. Stracey, really looked good that night but he disappointed in a bid for the vacant European title, being knocked out in two by Marco Scano, and he also flopped against Jorgen Hansen when beaten in three rounds. He did better by defending his British title with a points win over Trevor Francis, but in December 1976 critics were advising him to quit the ring after losing his crown when beaten in eight rounds by Henry Rhiney, a fighter he had previously beaten on two occasions. Thomas, however, confounded his critics by moving up into the light-middleweight division and winning a Lonsdale belt after taking the British title from Jimmy Batten in 1979. He lost

this title to Herol Graham in March 1981.

## THOMAS, Tom:

Born Carncelyn Farm, South Wales, in 1880, this strongly built fighter with a good right-hand punch took the British middleweight title from Pat O'Keefe with a narrow points victory at the N.S.C., May 23, 1906.

Rheumatism began to bother Thomas soon after this and he did not fight again for nearly two years.

In December, 1909, this Welshman was matched with Charlie Wilson for the first middleweight Lonsdale Belt and he won on a knock-out in the second round, but in November, 1910, he lost his championship when outpointed by Jim Sullivan.

Chronic rheumatism really took a hold on Thomas after this and it killed him in 1911.

## THOMPSON, Billy:

Billy Thompson had nearly 500 contests as an amateur and won the A.B.A. lightweight title in 1944.

After entering the paid ranks he won the vacant British lightweight championship by stopping Stan Hawthorne in three rounds at Liverpool Stadium October 16, 1947.

Thompson won the Lonsdale Belt outright with victories over Harry Hughes and Tommy McGovern before the latter fighter took the title from him with a first round knock-out at Wandsworth, London, August 28, 1951.

Thompson had weakened himself in making the weight for that second contest with McGovern and he was suspended after this defeat by the B.B.B. of C.

Born at New Silksworth, Sunderland, Thompson, who retired in January, 1954, had also held the European lightweight title from February, 1948, to July, 1949.

## THOMPSON (Young) Jack:

An American negro, Jack Thompson quickly came to the fore as a welterweight, and when he had been fighting professionally for only two years he got a match with the world champion, Joe

Dundee, in August, 1928.

Dundee saw to it that Thompson came in over the welterweight limit for this bout, and the title did not change hands when the referee stopped the fight in Thompson's favour in the second round.

However, that victory was sufficient to persuade the N.B.A. to deprive Dundee of his title and to agree to a match between Thompson and Jackie Fields as being for the vacant championship. This contest took place in March, 1929, and Thompson lost on points.

Still, Thompson came back in May, 1930, and when he again faced Fields he took the title with a points victory.

In September, 1930, this hard-hitting welterweight lost the crown to Tommy Freeman, but in a return bout he became champion for the second time, Freeman being unable to come out for the 12th round.

Thompson finally lost the crown to Lou Brouillard in October, 1931, and he retired less than two years later.

## "THROWING A FIGHT" or "FIXED FIGHTS":

The first champion to "throw" a fight was probably Bill Stevens, "The Nailer."

He became Champion of England by beating Jack Slack in 1760, but in March, 1761, he was beaten in only 17 minutes by George Meggs.

It was said that Stevens had been given £50 by the former champion, Jack Slack, to lose this fight with Meggs.

A later champion, Bill Darts, was alleged to have been bribed with £100 to lose his fight with Peter Corcoran in May, 1771.

The worst period in boxing history was during the 1920's in America when gangsters ruled the game and boxers were forced to throw fights to suit the scheming of the betting fraternity under control of the mobsters.

One of the most controversial endings to a fight was when Jess Willard k.o'd Jack Johnson to take the hated negro's world title in 1915. Many believed that Johnson had thrown the fight, although if this was true it was surprising that he went 26 rounds before supposedly "lying down".

Even Battling Siki alleged that it had been agreed that he should be k.o'd in the fourth round of his world light-heavyweight fight with Georges Carpentier in 1922, but he changed his mind when he found that the French champion did not hit hard enough. Siki then went on to k.o. Carpentier in the sixth.

## TIGER, Dick:

A Nigerian who never failed to give the fans their money's worth in more than 17 years in the ring and had the satisfaction of holding both the light-heavy and middleweight world titles.

He steadily built up his reputation as a durable fighter after moving to Liverpool in 1955, and in 1958 he k.o'd Pat McAteer in nine rounds to take the Empire middleweight title. Tiger lost this title to Wilf Greaves in 1960, but only after the original decision of a draw had been changed when an error was discovered on one of the score cards.

Tiger made amends by battering Greaves into a ninth round defeat and went on to gain W.B.A. recognition as world champion with a points win over Gene Fullmer.

He was subsequently accorded world-wide recognition, and after losing and regaining his title in two gruelling bouts with Joey Giardello he finally lost the crown to Emile Griffith in April 1966.

Before the year was out, however, Tiger had won the world light-heavyweight championship by outpointing Jose Torres, and he saw active service in the Nigerian civil war before losing his title when k.o'd by Bob Foster in May 1968.

## TITLE FIGHTS:

The first occasion on which three British title fights were included in the same programme was on May 16, 1929, at Olympia, when the promoters were the N.S.C.

That evening Teddy Baldock outpointed "Kid" Pattenden for the bantamweight title; Johnny Cuthbert outpointed Harry Corbett for the featherweight title and Len Harvey knocked out Alex Ireland for the middleweight crown.

Four world title fights on one evening's programme was the record set up by the American promoter, Mike Jacobs, on September 23, 1937.

This ambitious programme, known as the "Carnival of Champions," was staged at the New York Polo Grounds. Welterweight champion, Barney Ross, retained his title with a points victory over Ceferino Garcia; Lou Ambers retained his lightweight crown by outpointing Pedro Montanez, Harry Jeffra took the bantamweight championship from Sixto Escobar with another points victory, and Fred Apostoli stopped middleweight champion Marcel Thil (I.B.U. recognition only) in 10 rounds.

## TITLE HOLDERS:

See also under BRITISH CHAMPIONS, EMPIRE TITLES, EUROPEAN BOXING UNION UNION (CHAMPIONS), and WORLD TITLES.

The fighter who held most National or International professional titles during his career was probably Ted "Kid" Lewis. His total was nine:— British featherweight title 1913-14. European featherweight title 1913-14. British welterweight title 1920-24. Empire welterweight title 1920-24. European welterweight title 1920-23. World welterweight title 1915-16, 1917-19. British middleweight title, 1920. Empire middleweight title 1922-23. European middleweight title 1921-23.

## TODD, Roland:

A Yorkshireman, Roland Todd outpointed the British, European and Empire middleweight champion, Ted "Kid "Lewis, at the Albert Hall, in February, 1923, and although the Boxing Board did not present him with the Lonsdale Belt after that victory, they did eventually acknowledge him as the top man in this division.

Todd had a useful left hand and was good at close quarters but he was usually a defensive boxer.

He lost his European title to the Italian, Bruno Frattini, in November, 1924, and later the following year the Boxing Board deprived him of his British and Empire titles because he was away in America and had not defended them.

Todd was twice beaten in non-title bouts by Len Johnson who was prevented from taking the British title because of his colour.

## TOKELL, Andrew:

This bantamweight took the British title from Harry Ware in 1901 but he was deprived of it by Joe Bowker in May, 1903.

Tokell's defeat by Bowker at the N.S.C. was not generally recognised as a title fight but it did serve to eliminate the Gateshead man from the championship, and a defeat by another leading contender, Owen Moran, in March, 1904, put Tokell right out of the running.

During the time that he had claimed the British title Tokell had visited America, and there, in February, 1903, he had been outpointed by the world bantamweight champion, Harry Forbes.

## TORRES, Efren:

The Thai fighter, Chartchai Chionoi, figures prominently in this Mexican flyweight's career. In their first meeting in January 1968 Torres, known as the "Scorpion," showed his tremendous spirit in a hard battle and needed 15 stitches in a cut over his left eye after the referee had called a halt in the 13th round with Chionoi retaining his world title.

One of the hardest hitters ever seen in the flyweight division, Torres battered Chionoi into defeat inside eight rounds to take the title in a return bout in February 1969, but when these two met for a third time in March 1970 the Thai fighter clearly outpointed Torres to regain the flyweight crown.

## TOWEEL, Vic:

South African, Vic Toweel, was the first man from the Union to win a world title, and he achieved this distinction only 18 months after turning professional by outpointing Manuel Ortiz in May, 1950. That was Toweel's 14th professional contest.

An all-action fighter, Toweel defended his world crown successfully against Danny O'Sullivan, Luis Romero, and Peter Keenan, but he was knocked out in 2 minutes 19 seconds by the

Australian, Jimmy Carruthers, at Johannesburg November, 1952.

Toweel failed to regain the championship in a return bout with Carruthers in March, 1953, being knocked out in the tenth round.

## TRAINER:

The finest trainers are excellent judges of human nature as well as first-rate men at the essential job of keeping their charges trained to the minute. A good trainer has to be a psychologist as well as a man who knows all the boxing skills and understands the needs and limitations of the human frame.

Among the best trainers in Britain over the years one would be bound to include such men as "Snowy" Buckingham, who trained Walter Neusel, Eric Boon and Larry Gains; Nat Sellar, trainer of Dave McCleave, Harry Mizler, Benny Caplan, Freddie Mills, etc.; Honey Francis, trainer of Henry Armstrong, Jack London, Tiny Bostock, and Dickie O'Sullivan.

The Gutteridge twins, Dick and Jack, were another two trainers highly respected for their knowledge of the game, as were Jack Goodwin and the famous London trainer, Wally May.

In America one of the most famous names among trainers was Whitey Bimstein, who handled such grand fighters as Lou Ambers, Rocky Graziano, James J. Braddock, Sixto Escobar, Paolino Uzcudun, and many more of the best men ever to have appeared in the ring.

Another man who made a name for himself as a trainer through his development of Joe Louis was Jack Blackburn who was himself an outstanding lightweight boxer in the early 1900's.

Since World War II Angelo Dundee has been tops among American trainers. Men who won world titles under his care—Willie Pastrano, Luis Rodriguez, Sugar Ramos, Ralph Dupas, Carmen Basilio, and Muhammad Ali.

The first Englishman ever to go out to America as a boxing trainer was probably George Thompson. He was invited to cross the Atlantic in 1843 specially to train Tom Hyer for his fight with Yankee Sullivan. Hyer won and became the first generally recognised heavyweight champion of America.

## TROPHIES:

See also under LONSDALE BELTS.

The first trophy ever awarded to a prize fighter was probably the championship belt presented to Jem Ward, the "Black Diamond" champion of England, in 1825. He received this belt after he had won the championship from Tom Cannon in 1825.

Ward received another championship belt in 1831 after he had regained the title with a victory over Simon Byrne. Ward had previously been deprived of the title by Peter Crawley who subsequently retired.

Following their epic fight in 1860, Tom Sayers and John C. Heenan were each presented with silver belts. The one given to the American is today in the possession of the B.B.B. of C. and has a place of honour in their Board Room.

One of the finest trophies ever presented to a fighter was "the ten-thousand-dollar belt" of solid gold "presented to the Champion of Champions, John L. Sullivan, by the People of the United States."

This remarkable belt which was studded with nearly 400 diamonds was presented to Sullivan in the theatre of his home town of Boston, August 8, 1887.

When, later in the same year, Sullivan arrived in England, he refused to pay duty of £120 demanded by the Customs and it remained in a bonded warehouse at Liverpool until he returned home.

## TUNNEY, James Joseph "Gene":

This unassuming fellow was a cool, skilful boxer, who went to great pains to learn the game properly so that he could achieve a burning ambition of becoming the world heavyweight champion.

He first began to attract attention immediately after the Armistice of World War I when he won the light-heavyweight championship of the American Expeditionary Force in France, but it was not until January, 1922, that he really came into the top class. Then it was that he defeated Battling Levinsky for the American light-heavyweight title.

Tunney lost this title four months later

to Harry Greb in what proved to be the only defeat in his professional career. He subsequently beat Greb on two occasions for the same title.

In 1924 Tunney stopped the Idol of France, Georges Carpentier, in the 15th round of a contest at the Yankee Stadium New York City.

Tunney won the world title by outpointing Jack Dempsey over ten rounds at Philadelphia, September 23, 1926, and he again defeated the "Manassa Mauler" over the same distance in Chicago, a year later.

Afterwards, this straight hitting champion with a fast left jab had only one more championship fight. In that he outclassed the very game New Zealander, Tom Heeney.

It was only about a month after this victory that Gene Tunney, who had collected nearly a million and three-quarter dollars for three world title fights, announced his retirement as undefeated champion.

## TURPIN, Dick:

Born at Leamington Spa, Warwickshire, in 1920, Dick Turpin was the first coloured fighter to become a champion of Britain under B.B.B. of C. rules.

After winning the Empire middleweight title from the New Zealander, Bos Murphy, with a first round knockout in May, 1948, Turpin took the British title by outpointing Vince Hawkins at the Aston Villa Football Ground, June 28, 1948.

Dick Turpin was a particularly cool and skilful boxer but he was often criticised for being too cautious.

He lost his Empire title when he was knocked out in the first round by Dave Sands in September, 1949, and his British title went to Albert Finch who outpointed him over 15 rounds at Nottingham, in April, 1950.

## TURPIN, Randolph:

A younger brother of Dick Turpin, Randolph was certainly not as stylish as his brother, but he was definitely more aggressive and could hit from all angles with great force.

After an outstanding amateur career he turned professional at the age of 18

and won his first British title in October, 1950, when he knocked out Albert Finch in five rounds at Harringay. This brought the middleweight title back to the Turpin family, for Finch had taken it from Dick Turpin in April, 1950.

During 1951 Randolph Turpin held the world middleweight title for 64 days. He gave his finest ever display when taking the championship from Ray Robinson in London, July 10, but he was beaten by the American negro in the return match in New York, September 12.

Turpin was never quite as brilliant again after that ten-round defeat by Robinson.

However, when Robinson first retired from the ring in December, 1952, Turpin was again acknowledged as world champion outside of America following his win over Charles Humez on June 9, 1953.

In America, Carl "Bobo" Olson was recognised as Robinson's successor and when Turpin and Olson met in New York, October 21, 1953 Olson won on points.

Turpin relinquished his British and Empire middleweight titles in 1954 shortly after he had lost his European title on a one round knock-out by Tiberio Mitri in Rome.

In June, 1952 Turpin also won the British and Empire light-heavyweight titles by stopping Don Cockell in 11 rounds. He subsequently relinquished and later regained these titles on two separate occasions before finally giving them up on his retirement in October, 1958.

He was found shot dead at his home in May 1966.

## TYSON, Mike:

A tough kid fighter in Brooklyn's Brownsville ghetto who learnt to box when in a penal instruction establishment for young delinquents, Mike Tyson has all the right attributes to make a world champion. Built like a tank with a 20-inch neck, he has the killer instinct and devastating punching power. It was the late Cus D'Amato, who guided Floyd Patterson and Jose Torres to world titles, who spotted Tyson's potential and became the 14-year-old's legal guardian.

After winning the National Golden Gloves heavyweight title in 1984 Tyson turned professional the following year and won. his first 19 bouts inside the distance, including 12 in the first round, before being made to go the full 10 rounds to beat James Tillis and Mitchell Green. Six more inside-the-distance victories followed and then he was matched with Trevor Berbick in November 1986 for the W.B.C. version of the world heavyweight title. The Jamaican-born champion was battered by a series of sweeping rights and left hooks before the referee called a halt after only 2 minutes 35 seconds of the second round. Tyson had laid claim to a piece of the world heavyweight title at the age of only 20 years 145 days.

James "Bonecrusher" Smith the W.B.A. champion showed that Tyson still had something to learn but he couldn't prevent the youngster from outpointing him in March 1987. Less than five months later the busy Tyson was taken the distance by IBF champion Tony Tucker but did enough to claim that title. Tyson had chalked up 31 wins in a row and only Mike Spinks stood between him and the right to be recognised by all the fans as undisputed world heavyweight champion.

## UNDEFEATED:

One of the most remarkable records of any boxer belongs to an amateur, Harold W. Mallin, the New Scotland Yard and Eton Manor Boxing Club middleweight who was A.B.A. champion in 1919-23 and Olympic Champion in 1920 and again in 1924. Mallin was undefeated in over 300 bouts.

Among the professionals a record was created by Hal Bagwell the Gloucester lightweight. This boxer was undefeated in 183 consecutive contests which followed a fifth round knock-out at the hands of Johnny King, August 15, 1938. This remarkable run was broken on November 29 1948, when Bagwell was outpointed over ten rounds by Morry Jones (Liverpool) at Leeds.

There have been four men who became world champions and then retired without suffering a single defeat throughout their entire professional careers. They were Rocky Marciano (heavyweight champion 1952-56), Jack McAuliffe (lightweight champion 1886-96), Jimmy Barry (bantamweight champion, American version, 1894-1900), Jimmy Carruthers (bantamweight champion 1952-54). The latter, however, returned to the ring more than seven years after his original retirement and was beaten four times before giving up his comeback.

In addition to these the following boxers finally retired as undefeated world champions (they had been beaten before they became champions):—James J. Jeffries, Tommy Ryan, Gene Tunney, Benny Leonard, Marty Servo, Sandy Saddler, Rinty Monaghan, Joseph Becerra, Duilio Loi, John Henry Lewis, Carlos Monzon, Sugar Ray Leonard, Bernard Pinango.

## UNITED STATES OF AMERICA:

Jacob Hyer versus Tom Beasley, in 1816, was the first prize fight between white men on record in America. Before then the sport was generally reserved for the negro slaves of the Southern States who were forced into the game to provide entertainment for their masters, some of whom had first seen prize fighting when visiting this country.

An Englishman, William Fuller (who had been beaten by Tom Molineux in 1814) went to America in 1818 and did a great deal towards popularising boxing in that country.

Fuller opened a gymnasium in New York and imparted his knowledge of the noble art to many students during his six-year stay in the States.

The first champion of the United States is considered to have been Tom Hyer, son of the Jacob Hyer mentioned above. Tom was acclaimed champion after his defeat of Country McClusky at Caldwell's Landing on the Hudson River, September 9, 1841.

America has long since outstripped Britain in this sport, but they did, of course, learn the game from us. The earliest British champions to visit America and stimulate interest in the sport over there were Deaf Burke, who crossed the Atlantic in 1837 (he could not find any real opposition in America at that time) and Ben Caunt, who went out in 1840. They were soon followed by Yankee Sullivan (whose real name was James Ambrose, born in Ireland), Billy Bell and Chris Lilly.

The first native-born American to make a name for himself in the ring was the negro, Bill Richmond. He was brought to England in 1777 by General Earl Percy and fought several times, including one bout with the great Tom Cribb in 1805. Cribb won in an hour and a half.

The most successful British boxers in the United States among those who have had a large number of fights, there have been Ted "Kid" Lewis and Jack "Kid" Berg.

## Champions:

The Americans have supplied so many world champions that a complete list of all those born in the United States would be almost a duplication of the list of champions given elsewhere in this volume under WORLD CHAMPIONS.

For instance in the heavyweight division only five generally recognised champions have not been Americans—Bob Fitzsimmons, Tommy Burns, Max Schmeling, Primo Carnera and Ingemar Johansson.

In this section, therefore, to preserve valuable space, only American Olympic champions are listed.

OLYMPIC:—

Super-heavyweight: T. Biggs 1984.

Heavyweight: S. Berger 1904, E. Sanders 1952, P. Rademacher 1956, J. Frazier 1964, G. Foreman 1968, H. Thomas 1984.

Light-heavyweight: E. Eagan 1920, N. Lee 1952, J. Boyd 1956, C. Clay 1960, L. Spinks 1976.

Middleweight: C. Mayer 1904, C. Barth 1932, F. Patterson 1952, E. Crook 1960, M. Spinks 1976.

Light-middleweight: W. McClure, 1960, F. Tate 1984.

Welterweight: A. Young 1904, E. Flynn 1932, M. Breland 1984.

Light-welterweight: C. Adkins 1952; Ray Seales 1972, R. Leonard 1976, J. Page 1984.

Lightweight: H. J. Spangler 1904, S. Mossberg 1920, R. Harris 1968, H. Davis 1976, P. Whitaker 1984.

Featherweight: O. L. Kirk 1904, J. Fields 1924, M. Taylor 1984.

Bantamweight: O. L. Kirk 1904.

Flyweight: G. V. Finnegan 1904, F. Genaro 1920, F. La Barba 1924, N. Brooks 1952, L. Randolph 1976, S. McCrory 1984.

Light-flyweight: P. Gonzalez 1984.

# V

## VALDES, Rodrigo:

A courageous fighter with an all-action style this Colombian middleweight won the W.B.C. version of the world title when he knocked out Bennie Briscoe in Monte Carlo in 1974, but Carlos Monzon was more widely recognised as world champion at this time. When these two met in Monte Carlo in an exciting punch out in June 1976 it was Monzon who gained a narrow points victory, largely on account of putting Valdes down for a compulsory eight count in the fourteenth.

Monzon also won a return fight the following year before announcing his retirement. Valdes then captured the title by again beating Bennie Briscoe, this time on points, but neither fighter showed quite their usual power. This was not surprising with Valdes nearly 30 years of age and Briscoe 34.

Valdes lost his title to the Argentinian, Hugo Corro, on points in San Remo in April 1978.

## VILLA, Pancho:

This Filipino who started fighting professionally immediately after World War I, became world flyweight champion when he knocked out Jimmy Wilde in the seventh round in New York, June 18, 1923.

Prior to this he had won the American title from Johnny Buff in 1922 and lost it to Frankie Genaro three months before he beat Wilde.

Villa defended his world title only once before he died in 1925 of blood poisoning following a tooth infection.

## VILLAFLOR, Ben:

One of the youngest men ever to win a world title, this Filipino began fighting at the age of 14 and had still not reached his 20th birthday when he captured the junior-lightweight title in 1972 by outpointing Alfredo Marcano.

The following year he lost the title on points to Kuniaki Shibata but won it back in a return fight with a record breaking first round k.o. in only 1 minute 56 seconds.

Villaflor lost his title in his 6th defence in 1976 when he was clearly outpointed in a return bout with Sam Serrano. They had previously fought a draw—a decision which had been hotly disputed. Villaflor never fought again after losing the title.

## WALCOTT, "Jersey" Joe:

Joe Walcott had been boxing professionally for at least 20 years when he won the world heavyweight title by stopping Ezzard Charles in seven rounds at Pittsburgh, July 18, 1951, and he was then over 37 years of age, the oldest fighter ever to win this championship.

A deeply religious man whose real name is Arnold Cream, Walcott had a hard struggle against poverty before he achieved the highest honour in boxing.

A good counter-fighter, Walcott started boxing around 1930 but it was not until some time after World War II that he came into the top class.

Then he was 33 but he twice outpointed Joey Maxim, and also beat another leading title contender, Elmer Ray.

In December of that year Walcott gave champion Joe Louis one of the hardest fights he had had up to that time but Louis retained his title on a split decision.

Walcott again fought Louis, in June, 1948, but this time Jersey Joe was knocked out in 11 rounds. Then, after Louis had retired, Walcott was matched with Ezzard Charles for the N.B.A. title but was beaten on points.

It was in his third fight with Charles that Walcott won the title, and he subsequently defended his crown successfully in a fourth meeting with the Cincinnati negro.

Walcott lost the championship when he was knocked out by Rocky Marciano in the 13th round of a 15-round bout at Philadelphia, September 23, 1952, and he was knocked out in the first round of a return bout with the Brockton Blockbuster.

## WALCOTT, Joe:

Known as the "Barbados Demon" this West Indian was a physical freak but he was one of the most dynamic punchers in the history of the ring.

He stood only 5ft. 1in. and weighed a shade over 10 stones (140lbs.) but he had such a long reach and was so powerfully built across the shoulders that he was able to beat many of the best men of his time inside the distance.

Walcott was never fussy about weight limits. He fought men of any weight. In February, 1900, he knocked out Joe Choynski, one of the leading heavyweights of the day, in seven rounds at the Broadway Athletic Club. He gave Choynski over two stone in weight and nine inches in height.

He also defeated such men as Dan Creedon and Joe Grim, both top-line middleweights.

Walcott won the world welterweight title when he knocked out Rube Ferns in five rounds, December 18, 1901, but was beaten by the Dixie Kid on a disqualification in 20 rounds in April, 1904.

When the Kid did not press his claim to the championship and left the States for Europe, Walcott reclaimed the title. It was very much in dispute for some years, but Walcott was not really eliminated until he lost to Honey Mellody in October, 1906.

## WALES:

Professional boxing in Wales comes under the jurisdiction of the British Boxing Board of Control, the Principality being the No. 3 Area in the Board's constitution.

The Welsh have produced outstanding fighters in all divisions but they are probably best known for the number of top class men under 9st. 9lbs. (135lbs.)

### Champions:

World:—
Featherweight: Howard Winstone, 1968.

Lightweight: Freddie Welsh, 1914-17.

Flyweight: Percy Jones, 1914; Jimmy Wilde, 1916-23.

European:—

Heavyweight: Dick Richardson, 1960-62.

Middleweight: Johnny Basham, 1921.
Welterweight: Johnny Basham, 1919-20; Eddie Thomas, 1951; Colin Jones, 1982-83.
Lightweight: Freddie Welsh, 1909-11, 1912-13.
Featherweight: Jim Driscoll, 1912-13.
Bantamweight: Johnny Owen, 1980.
Flyweight: Percy Jones, 1914; Jimmy Wilde, 1914-23; Dai Dower, 1955.
Empire and Commonwealth:—
Heavyweight: Jack Petersen, 1934-36; Tommy Farr, 1937-38; Johnny Williams, 1952-53; Joe Erskine, 1957-58.
Light-heavyweight: Gipsy Daniels, 1927; Eddie Avoth, 1970-71.
Middleweight: Frank Moody, 1927-28.
Welterweight: Johnny Basham, 1919-20; Eddie Thomas, 1951; Cliff Curvis, 1952; Brian Curvis, 1960-66, Colin Jones, 1981-84.
Lightweight: Freddie Welsh, 1912-13.
Featherweight: Jim Driscoll, 1908-09; Llew Edwards, 1915-16.
Bantamweight: Johnny Owen, 1978-80.
Flyweight: Dai Dower, 1954-56.

## WALKER, Con "Curley"

This very fast box-fighter from Bermondsey took the British bantamweight title from Digger Stanley with a points victory at the N.S.C., October 17, 1913.

Walker never defended this title before he became overweight in 1915 and gave it up.

Prior to winning the bantamweight crown Walker had met Sid Smith for the flyweight title but had been outpointed.

## WALKER, Mickey:

They called Mickey Walker the "Toy Bulldog" and during his ring career he was just that—a great-hearted fighter, as tough as could be and not afraid to fight any man regardless of weight.

This Irish-American won the world welterweight title by outpointing Jack Britton in November, 1922.

In July, 1925, he tried to annexe the middleweight crown but lost a close points decision to Harry Greb.

Walker was putting on weight fast at about this time and he had trouble making 10st. 7lbs. (147lbs.) when he defended his welterweight title against Pete

Latzo in May, 1926. Latzo got the referee's nod at the end of 10 rounds.

About a month later Walker was knocked out by Joe Dundee and he practically made up his mind to retire. However, his manager, "Doc" Kearns, persuaded him to try again and concentrate on the middleweights. Before the year was out Walker had won the world championship of that division from Tiger Flowers.

Walker still put on weight after this and he was forced to relinquish the 11st. 6lbs. (160lbs.) title in June, 1931.

He then went after the heavyweights and although handicapped by lack of inches he beat such men as Johnny Risko, King Levinsky, Paolino Uzcudun, and fought a draw with Jack Sharkey. He was, however, knocked out by Max Schmeling, and also lost his two bids for the world light-heavyweight crown, the first against Tommy Loughran and the second against Maxie Rosenbloom.

## WALSH, Jimmy (United States):

An Irish-American from Massachusetts, Jimmy Walsh first laid claim to the world bantamweight title in March, 1905, when he knocked out Monte Attell.

At that time Joe Bowker was more generally accepted as bantamweight title-holder, but when the Lancastrian took to fighting featherweights and did not press his world title claim, Walsh became his successor and really established his right to the crown by beating another British fighter, Digger Stanley, on points over 15 rounds, Chelsea, Mass., October, 1905.

Walsh relinquished the title when he became overweight in 1909.

## WALSH, Jimmy (England):

Born at Chester in 1913, Jimmy Walsh was a great favourite at the Liverpool Stadium, where he won the British lightweight title in April, 1936, by stopping Jack "Kid" Berg in nine rounds.

Walsh was an accomplished boxer and he successfully defended his title against another ring artist, Harry Mizler, in October, 1936, but in May, 1938, less than a month before he was due to meet Dave Crowley in his second title defence,

Walsh made the mistake of agreeing to meet a practically unknown 18-year-old named Eric Boon.

The latter caused a big upset by outpointing the experienced champion, and in his next fight Walsh lost his title to Dave Crowley, June 23, 1938.

## WARD, Jem:

By all accounts this prize fighter from Bow was a great deal more skilful than the average bare-knuckle bruiser of his day.

He became champion of England and was the first man to be presented with a championship belt when he beat Tom Cannon in 10 minutes at Stony Stratford, Warwickshire, in July, 1825.

In his next fight Ward, known as the "Black Diamond," was beaten by Peter Crawley, but when Crawley decided not to fight again, Ward reclaimed the championship, and after defeating Jack Carter and Simon Byrne, retired undefeated title-holder in 1832.

## WARD, Nick:

A younger brother of Jem Ward, Nick won the championship in September, 1840, when he beat Deaf James Burke on a foul after the crowd had broken the ring in the 17th round to save Ward from further punishment.

Ward successfully defended his doubtful right to the championship by beating Ben Caunt on a foul, but when these two met in a return fight at Long Marsden, Warwickshire, in May, 1841, Ward was beaten in 47 minutes.

## WARE, Harry:

Born at Mile End, London, Harry Ware started boxing in 1895 when he scaled only about seven stone (98lbs.)

In November, 1900, at the N.S.C., he became British bantamweight champion by outpointing Pedlar Palmer over 20 rounds, but in the following year he was defeated by the Gateshead bantamweight, Andrew Tokell.

## WATERMAN, Peter:

Born at Clapham, London, in 1934, Peter Waterman had a distinguished boxing career both as an amateur and a professional.

He started boxing at the age of 11 and lost only nine out of 130 amateur bouts. In 1952 he won the A.B.A. lightwelterweight championship and also represented Britain in the Olympic Games.

Later that year Waterman turned professional and he was unbeaten in his first 30 bouts before being outpointed in April, 1956, by Kid Gavilan, the former world welterweight champion.

Peter Waterman is a good scholar, and when he won the British welterweight title in June, 1956, by stopping Wally Thom in five rounds, it was said that he was one of the most intelligent and well-educated men ever to win a British boxing championship.

In January, 1958, Waterman took the European welterweight title from the Italian, Emilio Marconi, but following a defeat by the British lightweight champion, Dave Charnley, in April, 1958, Waterman relinquished his titles.

## WATSON, Robert Bertram "Curley":

This clever welterweight from Chatham died in 1910 when he was in his prime. That was when he was knocked out by Frank Inglis (West Indies) in a contest at Wonderland and never regained consciousness.

Watson first claimed the British welterweight title in December, 1906, after beating Charlie Knock over 10 rounds at Wonderland, but only three months later, in the same ring, he was knocked out in four rounds by Andrew Jeptha.

The welterweight championship became rather complicated after this, for Jeptha was beaten by Joe White, but the N.S.C. again acknowledged Watson as champion in November, 1907, after he had turned the tables on Jeptha in a return bout.

Even when Watson was himself beaten by Joe White at Liverpool in 1908 he still clung to the title.

Then came two fights with Jack Goldswain. The latter won the first and supposedly took the title. That was in May, 1909, but about a month later Watson won the return bout.

Also in June, 1909, Watson went to

Paris to meet Honey Mellody, a claimant to the world title, but the Chatham fighter was stopped in four rounds, in what was to be almost his last contest.

## WATSON, Seaman Tom:

Born at Newcastle in 1908, Watson joined the Royal Navy at 16 but later bought himself out to take up boxing seriously.

An all-action fighter, Watson outpunched Nel Tarleton to take the British featherweight title over 15 rounds at Liverpool in November, 1932.

He went to America in 1933 and beat Fidel La Barba, the former world flyweight champion, but when he went back again a few weeks later to meet the world featherweight champion Kid Chocolate, he lost on points.

In July, 1934, Watson lost his British title in a return bout with Nel Tarleton.

## WATT, Jim:

This Glaswegian southpaw revived boxing in that city during the 1970s. He twice won the vacant British lightweight title, first in 1972 and again in 1975, and after making a Lonsdale belt his own property he finally relinquished the title in 1977 rather than go to Northern Ireland to defend against Charlie Nash.

Thereafter, however, he got into the big-time, winning the vacant European lightweight title by stopping Andre Holyk with a cut eye in the first round, and becoming world (W.B.C.) lightweight champion by stopping Alfredo Petalua in Glasgow in April 1979. The title had been previously relinquished by Roberto Duran.

Watt then relinquished his European crown and successfully defended his world title four times in Glasgow before losing it when, boxing on the defensive, he was outpointed by Alex Arguello at Wembley in June 1981.

## WEBSTER, Fred:

Born Kentish Town, London, June 19, 1909, Fred Webster was one of a fighting family, and before turning professional he won the A.B.A. bantamweight championship in 1926, the featherweight title the following year,

and completed the treble in 1928 by taking the lightweight championship.

Webster was a good stylist but he lacked a real punch. He was too clever for Sam Steward and deprived him of the British lightweight title with a points victory in May, 1929, but in May, 1930, he was knocked out by Al Foreman in the first round of a contest at Premierland.

## WEIGHT:
### Heaviest:

These are some of the heaviest men ever to take part in professional or prize fighting.

Ewart Potgieter, South African fighter of the 1950's, 23 st. 13 lbs. (335lbs.).

Gogea Mitu, Rumanian fighter of the 1930's—23st. 5lbs. (327lbs.).

Charles Freeman, an American who fought William Perry in 1842, weighed 22st. 12lbs. (320lbs.).

Big Ben Moroz, of Philadelphia, who fought during the 1940's, weighed 21st. 8lbs. (302lbs.).

Ed Dunkhorst (The Human Freight Car), a German-American, 21st. 6lbs. ((300lbs.). He fought during the 1890's.

Ray Impellitierre, Italian-American, who fought during the 1930's, 19st. 4lbs. (270lbs.).

Primo Carnera, the Italian former world champion, 19st. 4lbs. (270lbs.).

Abe Simon, Jewish-American world title contender of the 1930's and 1940's, 18st. 8lbs. (260lbs.).

Henry Johnson, an American fighter of the 1890's, 18st. 8lbs. (260lbs.).

Jess Willard, who took the world title from Jack Johnson, 17st. 12lbs. (250lbs.).

The greatest aggregate weight of two contestants in a world title fight was when Primo Carnera, 18st. 7½lbs. (259½lbs.) met Paolino Uzcudun, 16st. 5¼lbs. (229¼lbs.). An aggregate of 34st. 12¾lbs. (488¾lbs.), Rome, October 22, 1933.

### Lightest:

Two of the lightest men ever to take part in first-class boxing—Jimmy Wilde (Wales) 6st. 12lbs. (96lbs.), and Pascual Perez (Argentine) 7st. 8lbs. (106lbs.).

The lightest boxer to win the world heavyweight title under Queensberry

Rules was Bob Fitzsimmons, 12st. 4lbs. (172lbs.).

## Conceding weight:

The greatest weight difference between two contestants in a world heavyweight title fight is 6st. 12lbs. (86lbs.). That was when Primo Carnera (270lbs.) met Tommy Loughran (184lbs.), March 1, 1934. Carnera won on points over 15 rounds.

According to the official ringside figures Jack Dempsey conceded Jess Willard 4st. 2lbs. (58lbs.) when he took the world title from the giant cowboy. Unofficially the figure has been placed as high as 5st (70lbs.).

The greatest weight difference in any top-line glove contest was 10st. (140lbs.) when Ed Dunkhorst, 22st. 4lbs. (312lbs.) was knocked out in two rounds by Bob Fitzsimmons, 12st. 4lbs. (172lbs.), April 30, 1900.

## WEIGHT DIVISIONS:

There was very little international or even national agreement about weight divisions until the early part of the 20th century. Indeed, back in the old prize ring days there were no weight divisions at all and men fought each other irrespective of their avoirdupois.

It is impossible to give any definite dates as to when weight divisions were established. In the 1850's and 60's the title of " middleweight " began to be used for all men below about 156lbs. Those above this limit were all considered to be heavyweights, but this is not to say that men on either side of that limit did not meet each other.

About the same period the term "lightweight " was introduced and generally considered to apply to all men below 9st. 7lbs. (133lbs.).

So it was that for several years only three classes existed, although there were occasional vague references to men who were welterweights. However, the next weight division to be really established was the featherweight with a limit of 8st. 3lbs. (119lbs.), and this was followed by the bantamweight division at 7st. 7lbs. (105lbs.).

It was not until the 1880's, after the widespread adoption of the Queensberry Rules, that a real effort was made to standardise weight divisions both at home and in America. An agreement was reached when the leading authorities of the game on both sides of the Atlantic got together in 1910. The result of their deliberations was the following scale.

Heavyweight—more than 12st. 7lbs. (175lbs.).

Light-heavyweight—not above 12st. 7lbs. (175lbs.).

Middleweight—not above 11st. (154lbs.).

Welterweight—not above 10st. 2lbs. (142lbs.).

Lightweight—not above 9st. 7lbs. (133lbs.).

Featherweight—not above 8st. 10lbs. (122lbs.).

Bantamweight—not above 8st. 4lbs. (116lbs.).

Flyweight—not above 8st. (112lbs.).

Paperweight—not above 7st. 7lbs. (105lbs.).

Even this scale was not adhered to in all quarters.

In recent years the various authorities have nearly doubled the number of weight divisions. This, in some cases, unnecessary proliferation, together with the added complication of the various names for the same weight divisions, serves to leave the average fight-fan quite bemused.

As recently as 1968 there were only eight divisions in British professional boxing—now there are 12. World-wide in 1968 there were 11 divisions—now they have increased to at least 15!

Here in brief are the histories of the various divisions showing the weight fluctuations. The years are as accurate as possible but by no means well established.

Cruiserweight—Created in 1979 by W.B.C. with a limit of 13st. 8lbs. (190lbs.) and raised in 1982 to 13st. 13lbs. (195lbs.).

Junior-heavyweight — created by W.B.A. in 1982 at 190lbs.

Light-heavyweight (some time in the past known as cruiserweight)—Started in America in 1903 by Lou Houseman, manager of Jack Root, who had outgrown the middleweight division. The limit was set at 12st. 7lbs. (175lbs.) and it remains at that figure today. This division was first recognised in Britain in 1913.

Super-middleweight—Introduced by I.B.F. in 1984 with a limit of 12st. (168lbs) but not widely recognised.

Middleweight—Men of a weight below 11st. 2lbs. (156lbs.) were classed as middleweights as far back as 1860.
1884 Canadian George Fulljames claimed title at 11st. (154lbs.).
1894 raised to 158lbs. by Bob Fitzsimmons.
1911 raised to the present limit of 11st. 6lbs. (160lbs.)

Junior or Light-middleweight: First recognised by W.B.A. in 1962 at 154lbs. First introduced into Britain as light-middleweight in 1973.

Welterweight—This class is mentioned in the records back in 1792 but it was not really established until the 1880's when the limit was 10st. 2lbs. (142lbs.).
1909 raised to present limit of 10st. 7lbs. (147lbs.).

Junior or Light-welterweight: Created in America around 1920 with limit of 140lbs. First recognised in Britain 1967-70 and reintroduced in 1973 as light-welterweight.

Lightweight — 1860's at 9st. 7lbs. (133lbs.).
Went as high as 140lbs. before the turnof the century but dropped back to 133lbs. soon afterwards.
1912 raised to present limit of 9st. 9lbs. (135lbs.) by Willie Ritchie.

Junior-lightweight — Created in America around 1920 with limit of 130lbs. Britain first recognised this division from 1967 to 1970 at 130lbs. It was re-introduced here in 1986. Also known in some parts as super-featherweight.

Featherweight—1867 at 8st. 3lbs. (115lbs.).
1888 at 8st. 6lbs. (118lbs.).
1897 at 8st. 8lbs. (120lbs.).
1901 at 9st. (126lbs.).

Junior or Light-featherweight or Super bantamweight—Created by W.B.C. in 1976 at limit of 8st. 10lbs. (122lbs.). A Junior-featherweight division was recognised in America 1921-22.

Bantamweight—1850's at 8st. (112lbs.).
1888 at 7st. 7lbs. (105lbs.).
1889 at 7st. 10lbs. (108lbs.).
1890 at 8st. (112lbs.).
1910 at 8st. 4lbs. (116lbs.) in America or 8st. 6lbs. (118lbs.) in Britain.
1920 at 8st. 6lbs. (118lbs.) both sides of Atlantic.

Super-flyweight—Introduced in 1979 by W.B.C. at 8st. 3lbs. (115lbs.). W.B.A. Junior-bantamweight from 1981.

Flyweight — Established in Britain in 1909 at 8st. (112lbs.).

Light-flyweight—Created by W.B.C. in 1975 at 7st. 11lbs. (109lbs.). W.B.A. Junior-flyweight from 1975.

Mini flyweight—Introduced in the Orient at 105lbs. and recognised by I.B.F. 1986.

From time to time there have been various attempts to introduce other weight divisions into professional boxing. These have included the following:—

Paperweight, 95lbs. or 105lbs.; heavy featherweight, 122lbs.; woodweights, 128lbs.; ironweight, 150lbs.; dreadnoughts, over 200lbs.
The weight divisions recognised in Britain at the present time in professional and senior amateur boxing are as follows:—

| Professional | | | Senior Amateur |
|---|---|---|---|
| Light-flyweight .................................................... | | | 48 kgs. (105lbs. 13oz. 2dr.) |
| Flyweight .............. | 8st. | (112lbs.) | 51 kgs. (112lbs. 6oz. 15dr.) |
| Bantamweight ......... | 8st. 6lbs. | (118lbs.) | 54 kgs. (119lbs. 0oz. 12dr.) |
| Featherweight ......... | 9st. | (126lbs.) | 57 kgs. (125lbs. 10oz. 9dr.) |
| Junior-lightweight .... | 9st. 4lbs. | (130lbs.) | |
| Lightweight ............ | 9st. 9lbs. | (135lbs.) | 60 kgs. (132lbs. 4oz. 7dr.) |
| Light-welterweight ... | 10st. | (140lbs.) | 63.5 kgs. (139lbs. 15oz. 14dr.) |
| Welterweight ........... | 10st. 7lbs. | (147lbs.) | 67 kgs. (147lbs. 11oz. 5dr.) |

|                  *Professional*        |                    | *Senior Amateur*                          |
| -------------------------------------- | ------------------ | ----------------------------------------- |
| Light-middleweight .. 11st.            | (154lbs.) ............... | 71 kgs. (156lbs. 8oz. 7dr.)        |
| Middleweight .......... 11st. 6lbs.    | (160lbs.) ............... | 75 kgs. (165lbs. 5oz. 8dr.)        |
| Light-heavyweight .... 12st. 7lbs.     | (175lbs.) ............... | 81 kgs. (178lbs. 9oz. 3dr.)        |
| Cruiserweight ........... 13st. 8lbs.  | (190lbs.) ...........................................................................  |  |
| Heavyweight ........... Any weight .................... | | 91 kgs. (200lbs. 9oz. 14dr.)      |
| Super-heavyweight ...................................................... | | over 91 kgs. (200lbs. 9oz. 14dr.) |

Weight divisions recognised by the leading authorities abroad at the time of writing are as set out below. This table also serves to indicate the complications arising out of so many different authorities. Obviously the European Boxing Union has metricated weights and the Americans use pounds. Stones and pounds are given here for the benefit of British fight fans:—

|                          | W.B.C.        | W.B.A.       | I.B.F.       | E.B.U.     |
| ------------------------ | ------------- | ------------ | ------------ | ---------- |
| 7st. 7lbs. (105lbs.)     | Strawweight   | —            | Mini Fly     | —          |
| 7st. 10lbs. (108lbs.)    | Lt. Fly       | Jnr. Fly     | Jnr. Fly     | —          |
| 8st. (112lbs.)           | Fly           | Fly          | Fly          | Fly        |
| 8st. 3lbs. (115lbs.)     | Super Fly     | Jnr. Btm.    | Jnr. Btm.    | —          |
| 8st. 6lbs. (118lbs.)     | Bantam        | Bantam       | Bantam       | Bantam     |
| 8st. 10lbs. (122lbs.)    | Super Bantam  | Jnr. Feather | Jnr. Feather | —          |
| 9st. (126lbs.)           | Feather       | Feather      | Feather      | Feather    |
| 9st. 4lbs. (130lbs.)     | Super Fthr    | Jnr. Lt.     | Jnr. Lt.     | Jnr. Lt.   |
| 9st. 9lbs. (135lbs.)     | Light         | Light        | Light        | Light      |
| 10st. (140lbs.)          | Super Lt.     | Jnr. Welter  | Jnr. Welter  | Lt. Welter |
| 10st. 7lbs. (147lbs.)    | Welter        | Welter       | Welter       | Welter     |
| 11st. (154lbs.)          | Super Weltr.  | Jnr. Midd.   | Jnr. Midd.   | Lt. Midd.  |
| 11st. 6lbs. (160lbs.)    | Middle        | Middle       | Middle       | Middle     |
| 12st. (168lbs.)          | —             | —            | Super Midd.  | —          |
| 12st. 7lbs. (175lbs.)    | Lt. Heavy     | Lt. Heavy    | Lt. Heavy    | Lt. Heavy  |
| 13st. 8lbs. (190lbs.)    | Cruiser       | Jnr. Heavy   | Cruiser      | Cruiser    |
| Any weight               | Heavy         | Heavy        | Heavy        | Heavy      |

## WELLS, Bombardier Billy:

This good-looking, debonair boxer, who was born in London in 1889, was an enigma of the ring. He had the build and the skill to become a world champion but he suffered the most amazing lapses, losing to men one day whom he might easily have beaten on another occasion.

What it really boiled down to was that Wells had everything but the temperament to make a world beater. He simply didn't have the "killer" instinct to go in and finish a man when he had him beaten.

That doesn't mean that he never stopped an opponent, no, far from it. In all but two of his professional contests he knocked his opponent out or was himself counted out. He was never beaten on points.

Wells won the All-India championship in 1909 when he was serving in the Army. He had his first fight in London the following year, and a defeat by Gunner Moir marred his early career, but after taking the British heavyweight title from Iron Hague in 1911, he went to America.

There he was knocked out by Al Palzer with a punch to the stomach and he was also stopped by Gunboat Smith, but he knocked out Tom Kennedy and Boer Rodel.

Returning home, he was knocked out by Georges Carpentier at Ghent in four rounds, a performance which the Frenchman was to repeat inside one round at the N.S.C. before the year was out.

Wells made the first heavyweight Lonsdale Belt his own property and created a record by defending this British title 14 times before losing it to Joe Beckett in 1919. Beckett stopped him in the fifth round, and beat him in three rounds when they met again the following year.

## WELLS, Matt:

This Jewish boy from London was outstanding both as an amateur and as a professional.

In the unpaid ranks he won the A.B.A. lightweight championship four times, 1904-05-06-07, then, when he turned professional in 1909, he went to America and gained some good experience.

In February, 1911, he beat Freddie Welsh at the N.S.C. to become British and European lightweight champion, but he lost these titles in a return bout in November, 1912.

Wells put on weight, and in March, 1914, after beating Tom McCormick in Sydney, he claimed the world and Empire welterweight titles.

This Londoner failed to clinch his claim to the world title when he went to America again in 1915, for he was beaten by Mike Glover, and he lost his Empire crown to Johnny Basham in November, 1919.

Wells had his last contest in 1922 at the age of 36 when he beat Jack Hart over 15 rounds.

After retiring he became a referee and an inspector of the B.B.B. of C. He died in 1953.

## WELSH, Freddie:

Born at Pontypridd, South Wales, Freddie Welsh (real name Thomas) is generally acknowledged as one of the gentlemen of the ring, although in some quarters he was considered to be a little too bombastic and his supreme self-confidence upset some of his friends.

Welsh was an intellectual and his brains and intelligence helped to make him one of the finest defensive boxers ever seen in the lightweight division. Apart from being a difficult man to hit, Welsh was also a great in-fighter.

When the N.S.C. presented their first Lonsdale Belt for competition in the lightweight division, Welsh, recently returned from America, was elected to meet the man who was acknowledged as the British champion at that time, Johnny Summers.

In a contest at the N.S.C. Welsh won over 20 rounds and so added the British title to the European title he had won a couple of months earlier.

He lost these titles to Matt Wells in February, 1911, but regained them in a return bout in November, 1912.

One of the bitterest contests in which Welsh was involved was his meeting with Jim Driscoll. They fought at the Westgate Street Rink, Cardiff, in December, 1910, and feelings ran so high that " Peerless " Jim was disqualified for butting in the 10th round.

After that the crowd got out of hand and the police had to clear the hall.

Welsh won the world lightweight title in a real needle contest at Olympia in July, 1914. The Pontypridd fighter was so sure that he could win the championship that he fought for his training expenses only. His opponent was Willie Ritchie, and Welsh got the referee's nod at the end of 20 rounds, although it was so close that they said there couldn't have been more than half a point between the two fighters.

Welsh did not fight again in this country after that. He relinquished his British title the same year and went back to America, where he retained the world crown until he was knocked out in nine rounds by Benny Leonard, May, 1917.

Following this defeat Freddie Welsh had very few fights. He retired in 1922 and died only five years later at the age of 41.

## WEMBLEY:

Wembley Stadium, Wembley Arena and the Wembley Conference Centre have staged many important fights in the last 50 years.

The first to draw a really big crowd in the Stadium was Jack Petersen's second fight with Walter Neusel in 1935. There were 50,000 in attendance on that occasion, and the following year not only saw Petersen beating Len Harvey in a British heavyweight title fight but a World title bout when John Henry Lewis outpointed Len Harvey in a defence of his light-heavyweight crown.

Wembley Pool, now known as Wembley Arena, seating 12,000 staged its first World title bout in January 1937 when Benny Lynch beat Small Montana, and since it was reopened for boxing in 1956 other world title bouts have included such stars as Terry Downes, Emile Griffith, Walter McGowan, Johnny Caldwell, John Conteh, Bob Foster, Marvin Hagler, Alan Minter, Maurice Hope and Barry McGuigan.

## WEST INDIES:

With the tremendous influx of West Indians into Britain since World War II the majority of the fighters listed below learnt the game over here and might well be listed under England or Wales.

## Champions:

World:—
Light-heavyweight: Leslie Stewart (W.B.A.), 1987.
Light-middleweight: Maurice Hope (W.B.C.), 1979-81; Mike McCallum (W.B.A.), 1987-
Welterweight: Joe Walcott, 1901-04; Lloyd Honeyghan 1986-87.
European:—
Light-middleweight: Maurice Hope, 1976-78.
Welterweight: Henry Rhiney, 1978-79; Lloyd Honeyghan, 1985-86.
British:—
Heavyweight: Bunny Johnson, 1975; Neville Meade, 1981-
Light-heavyweight: Bunny Johnson, 1977-81.
Middleweight: Bunny Sterling, 1970-74, 1975.
Light-middleweight: Maurice Hope, 1974-76.
Welterweight: Pat Thomas, 1975-76; Henry Rhiney, 1976-79; Sylvester Mittee, 1984-85; Lloyd Honeyghan, 1985-86; Kirkland Laing, 1979-80, 1987-
Light-welterweight: Des Morrison, 1973-74; Tony Laing, 1986.
Empire and Commonwealth:—
Heavyweight: Joe Bygraves, 1956-57; Trevor Berbick, 1981-86.
Light-heavyweight: Leslie Stewart, 1985-87.
Middleweight: Gomeo Brennan, 1963-64, 1964-66; Bunny Sterling, 1970-72; Roy Gumbs, 1983.

Light-welterweight: Tony Laing, 1987-
Lightweight: Ivor Germain, 1954; Bunny Grant, 1962-67; Percy Hayles, 1968-75; Lennox Blackmore, 1977-78; Claude Noel, 1982-84.
Featherweight: Percy Lewis, 1957-60; Tyrone Downes, 1986-
Bantamweight: Ray Minus, 1986-
Flyweight: Richard Clarke, 1987.
The great Peter Jackson was also a West Indian, but he learnt his boxing in Australia, where he lived for the greater part of his life, and he is generally considered to have been an Australian boxer.

## WHITE, Jabez:

Born at Birmingham in 1877, Jabez White was a scientific boxer who held the British lightweight title for a number of years around the turn of the century. The precise length of time he was champion is very much in dispute; this is how it happened.

In November, 1899, White beat Harry Greenfield at the N.S.C. in a bout that was described as being for the 9st. 2lbs. (128lbs.) Championship of England. The lightweight title was vacant at that time, having been relinquished by Dick Burge, so White claimed this crown and beat Bill Chester to prove his right to the title.

In April, 1906, he was surprisingly beaten by Jack Goldswain at the N.S.C., but in a bout at 10st. (140lbs.), and White quite rightly protested that he was still lightweight champion.

However, when Goldswain went on to beat another claimant to the title, Pat Daly, the *Mirror of Life* eventually acclaimed Goldswain as lightweight champion, and, when the N.S.C. selected two lightweights to fight for their first Lonsdale Belt, White was overlooked.

## WHITE, Joe:

This Cardiff fighter was much maligned by the boxing officials of his day. They refused to acknowledge him as British welterweight champion, although he beat the best men at that weight.

In August, 1907, he outpointed Andrew Jeptha over 15 rounds at Merthyr at a time when Jeptha was considered to hold the title.

In May, 1908, White beat another claimant to the crown, Curley Watson, in 20 rounds at Liverpool, but the N.S.C. still continued to name Watson as champion, and when Watson died, they matched Jack Goldswain with Young Joseph for the welterweight championship. By that time, however (it was 1910) White was fighting more as a middleweight.

## WHITE CITY, LONDON:

Many big fights took place at this West London open-air stadium up to 1958.

One of the earliest was the world middleweight title bout between Marcel Thil and Len Harvey, in July, 1932.

Harvey's second meeting with Jack Petersen for the British and Empire heavyweight titles, in June, 1934, was staged at the White City, as was the world light-heavyweight title contest between Harvey and Jock McAvoy in July, 1939.

Freddie Mills won the world light-heavyweight championship from Gus Lesnevich at the White City Stadium in July, 1948.

## WILDE, Jimmy:

This frail-looking Welshman from Pontypridd is generally acclaimed as one of the greatest little fighters ever seen in these islands.

A phenomenal puncher, Wilde scaled only about seven stone (98lbs.) but he carried a wallop which spelt curtains for most of his opponents.

Wilde was a boxing booth fighter in his early days and he really lost count of the number of contests he had but it must have been well over 800.

After beating Joe Symonds in a non-title bout, Wilde relieved the Plymouth fighter of his British flyweight championship in February, 1916, a victory which also gave him the right to call himself world champion.

However, the greater title was disputed by the Americans, but in December, 1916, when they sent over their champion, Young Zulu Kid, Wilde became undisputed world title-holder by knocking him out in 11 rounds at the

Central Hall, Holborn, December 18, 1916.

Wilde's best punch was his left hook, and it was Pedlar Palmer who said of him, "He is a ghost with a hammer in his hand."

Another of Wilde's nicknames was the "Tylorstown Terror," and when you consider that he conceded weight in nearly all of his contests yet lost only four times in well over 100 bouts not fought in the fair-ground booth, you can imagine how he came by that name. What is more, Wilde won nearly three-quarters of his contests by the knock-out route.

Wilde was way past his best when he lost his world title to Pancho Villa in June, 1923. The Filipino had him well beaten but the game little Welshman refused to give up and was knocked out in the seventh round. He never fought again after that.

## WILLARD, Jess:

The most amazing thing about this giant cowboy from Kansas was that he did not take up boxing until he was 28 and yet he went on to win a world title.

His was the era of the "white hope campaign" when everyone was seaching for a fighter to take the title from the hated negro, Jack Johnson.

Willard was not a good boxer, he would never train hard enough for that, but he had the height and the weight to carry him through, and, of course, he had the punch.

The truth is, however, that Willard was always reluctant to throw his biggest punch after he had knocked out Bull Young in 1913 and that fighter had died.

Willard was one of the tallest men to win the world championship. He stood 6ft. 5¼ins., and he became champion in April, 1915, when, at Havana, Cuba, he outlasted Jack Johnson and knocked the negro out in the 26th round. It will always be a matter for discussion as to whether or not Johnson "threw" this fight. Many good judges who were there say that Willard won fair and square.

No doubt, however, Johnson was past his best, and Willard was fitter then than he ever was for any other contest.

Willard only defended his title once,

and in that contest he was beaten in three rounds by Jack Dempsey. That was at Toledo in July, 1919, and after taking heavy punishment, including a fractured jaw, and going down seven times, Willard gave up at the end of the third session.

## WILLIAMS, Ike:

An American negro, Ike Williams first gained recognition as world lightweight champion in 1945 when he stopped Juan Zurita in two rounds at Mexico City.

This was only recognised by the N.B.A. The N.Y.A.C. champion was Bob Montgomery, but when these two negroes met on August 4, 1947, Williams won in six rounds.

Williams crossed the Atlantic to defend his N.B.A. title in September, 1946, against Ronnie James at Cardiff, and he stopped the British champion in nine rounds.

In 1950 he went after the world welterweight title but a defeat by George Costner prevented him from meeting Ray Robinson.

Weakened by making the weight, Williams lost his lightweight title to Jimmy Carter in May, 1951.

## WILLIAMS, Johnny:

Born at Barmouth, Wales, Johnny Williams was brought up at Rugby, Warwickshire, and was appearing in contests in that town when he was only 10.

He turned professional in 1946, and after losing only four contests in four years he was matched with Jack Gardner at Leicester in a final eliminator for the British heavyweight title.

Williams lost that contest and Gardner went on to take the title from Woodcock, but when Williams met him new champion again he outpointed him and became British and Empire titleholder.

That second meeting between Williams and Gardner took place at Earl's Court, March 11, 1952.

In May, 1953, Williams lost his title when he was outpointed by Don Cockell, but he went on winning contests until June, 1955, when he again met Gardner in a heavyweight title elimi-

nator. This time the Market Harborough fighter put Williams away in five rounds.

Williams had a chance to regain the British title in August, 1956, when he was matched with Joe Erskine, but he was outpointed in a hard contest.

## WILLIAMS, Johnny (Kid):

This Dane went to America at an early age and started his boxing career in Baltimore about 1910.

In June, 1914, he knocked out Johnny Coulon in three rounds and claimed the world flyweight title, but he was never recognised as champion outside of America.

Williams fought mostly as a bantamweight and his flyweight title was not considered for more than a few months.

However, he was recognised as world bantamweight champion. In January, 1914, he had knocked out Eddie Campi, who was acknowledged on this side of the Atlantic because of his victory over Charles Ledoux.

Williams confirmed his right to this title by beating Coulon in a contest which has been variously claimed as being either for the flyweight or the bantamweight crown, and he held on to the heavier title until January, 1917, when he was outpointed by Pete Herman.

Kid Williams continued boxing for several years after this. He retired in 1929, and in 1935, when he was 41, he decided to attempt a come-back, but this was not a success.

## WILLIS, Tony:

Skilful Birmingham-based Liverpudlian southpaw who was A.B.A. lightwelter champion in 1980 and again in 1981 and also won a bronze medal at the 1980 Olympics. Was stopped inside one round by George Feeney when making his first bid for the British lightweight title in 1983, but overcame that shocking set-back to capture the vacant title, after Feeney had retired, with a close decision over Ian McLeod in 1985. He won a Lonsdale Belt before losing his third title defence to Alex Dickson in September 1987.

## WINSTONE, Howard M.B.E.:

This talented Welsh featherweight from Merthyr Tydfil retired undefeated British featherweight champion in February 1969 after holding the title for nearly eight years, having won it when forcing Terry Spinks to retire at the end of ten rounds, May 2, 1961. During that period he won two Lonsdale Belts.

Displaying amazing boxing skill Winstone went on to take the European title from Alberto Serti in July 1963, but subsequently failed in three bids for the world crown, being twice outpointed by Vicente Salvidar, and then stopped in the twelfth round of a third meeting, when his manager, Eddie Thomas, threw in the towel after Winstone had taken heavy punishment.

Salvidar announced his retirement after that victory and when matched with Mitsunori Seki for the vacant title the Welshman beat the Jap in nine rounds, the referee stopping the fight.

Winstone lost his crown to Jose Legra in July 1968, suffering a cut eye in the first round before the referee stopped it in the fifth.

The Welsh Wizard forfeited his European title in 1967 when he failed to defend it within a stipulated time.

## WOLGAST, Adolph:

After running up a string of knock-out victories as an amateur Ad Wolgast turned professional in 1906.

An American of German descent, Wolgast was a devastating puncher, and in February, 1910, he engaged in one of the most gruelling lightweight contests ever seen. His opponent was another tough fighter, world champion Battling Nelson. It was scheduled to go 45 rounds, but at the end of the 40th round Nelson was in such bad condition that the referee stopped the contest and awarded it to Wolgast.

So this German-American was one of only two men ever to stop the "Durable Dane" inside the distance. (The other man was Owen Moran).

Wolgast himself knocked out Owen Moran in July, 1911, but after stopping Joe Rivers inside the distance he lost his world crown when he was disqualified in the 16th round of a bout with Willie Ritchie, November, 1912.

Freddie Welsh was the only man to stop Wolgast when he was in his prime. That was in November, 1914, in New York, and then it was because the German-American had broken a bone in his arm and had to give up in the eighth round.

Sad to relate, Wolgast spent many years in an asylum after his retirement from the ring and he died in 1955.

## WOLGAST, Midget:

Eldest of a family of six sons and four daughters, this Italian-American from Philadelphia was a real fighter who cared little for the finer points of the game.

In March, 1930, he outpointed Black Bill in New York and was recognised by the N.Y.A.C. as world flyweight champion.

He strengthened his claim to universal recognition when he beat Willie La Morte in six rounds in May, 1930, and in October, 1933, he came to London and gave an outstanding display in outpointing the British flyweight champion, Jackie Brown.

Wolgast clung to his claim as world champion for more than five years until he was beaten on points by Small Montana in September, 1935. This fight was officially designated as being for the American flyweight title.

## WOMEN IN BOXING:

Georges Carpentier is considered to have been the first boxer to draw women in any great number to watch the big fights. "The Orchid Man" was certainly an attraction for the fashionable women of Paris, and when he fought at Olympia in 1914 there were more women in the audience than there had been at any previous contest staged in this country.

That particular Olympia show was put on by Mr. C. B. Cochrane, and he did a great deal to make "big fight nights" occasions fit for women to attend. However, the man who was first to stage boxing in such a way that they attracted the fairer sex was the Australian promoter, Hugh D. McIntosh. It was his earliest shows at Olympia, London, which set the fashion.

Although boxing is truly a manly art and women are not encouraged to take part, several of the weaker sex have, in the past, attained great skill at boxing.

Probably the first woman to gain distinction in the ring was Elizabeth Wilkinson in 1722.

In June 1795 "Gentleman" Jackson seconded Mary Ann Fielding, of Whitechapel, in "a well-fought contest" against "a noted Jewess, of Wentworth Road, seconded by Dan Mendoza." Fielding was declared the winner in 1hr. 20 mins. after flooring her opponent "upwards of 70 times."

There is also on record mention of a fight between Martha Flaherty and Peg Carey over 14 rounds for a purse of £17 10s. in 1822.

In more recent years, between the last two wars, Miss Annie Newton, a relative of the blind boxer, Andy Newton, appeared in the ring at the old N.S.C.

Another woman who made a name for herself among the fairground fraternity as a skilful performer in boxing booths was Mrs. Polly Burns, who fought in these rings about the time of the First World War.

Among the women who have earned the respect and admiration of the boxing world as promoters, none ranks higher than Mrs. Dick Burge. This lady succeeded her husband as the promoter at The Ring, Blackfriars, London, after his death during World War I. Bella Burge then kept things going at The Ring until it was destroyed by German bombers during World War II.

In her dealings with boxers Mrs. Burge will always be remembered for her strictness and for the honest and fair way in which she carried out all her business arrangements. No boxer was ever able to say that he had not been properly treated by this much-loved boxing promoter.

In December 1969 Mrs. Beryl Gibbons of Bermondsey became the first woman promoter to be granted a licence by the B.B.B.C.

Ireland also had a famous woman promoter. She was Mrs. Clara Copley, who was known as the Grand Old Lady of Ulster boxing.

In Australia Mrs. Art Mawson has figured among promoters of that continent.

In Los Angeles Mrs. Aileen Eaton kept the fight game alive with regular shows at the Olympic Auditorium until 1980.

The first woman to officiate as a judge at a world title fight — Mrs. Emma De Urrunga — Duran v. Thompson, light-welterweight title, Panama City, June 2, 1973.

# WONDERLAND, LONDON:

This was one of the most famous boxing venues in the history of the sport in this country.

Situated in Whitechapel Road in the East End of London, it had once been known as the Effingham Music Hall before a Professor Joe Smith decided to put on occasional boxing tournaments there.

However, Wonderland is best remembered as being under the control of Harry Jacobs, one of the ablest of match-makers.

World champion, Tommy Burns, fought only two contests in London while he held the title and one of these, versus Jack Palmer, was staged at Wonderland in February, 1908.

On Sunday, August 13, 1911, this popular boxing arena with an atmosphere and a tradition all of its own, where so many great fights had taken place and so many jellied eels had been consumed at the ringside, was lost forever—destroyed by fire.

# WOOD, Tim:

Born Camden Town, but residing in Leicester, Tim Wood won the A.B.A. heavyweight title in 1972 and made a good start to his professional career by winning eight and drawing one of his first nine fights, but after losing three in a row in 1974 he dropped into the light-heavyweight division.

He was considered rather lucky to have become British light-heavyweight champion in 1976. Chris Finnegan had been forced to give up the title when he retired with eye trouble and Wood was beaten by Roy John in a final eliminator. However, Roy John also had to drop out with eye trouble and Wood then outpointed Phil Martin to take the title

John H. Stracey (*left*) defeating a great champion, Jose Napoles, to capture the world welterweight title in Mexico City, December 6th, 1975

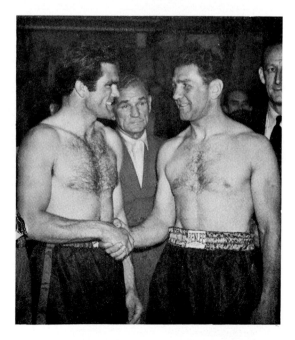

British champion Freddie Mills (*left*) and world light-heavyweight champion Gus Lesnevich at weigh-in for their return fight which Mills won in July 1948. Mills' manager Ted Broadribb (*centre*) was the only English fighter ever to stop Georges Carpentier

Jack Petersen's biggest stumbling block was Walter Neusel who defeated him three times. Here the British heavyweight champion is shown (*left*) in 1935 suffering his second beating by this tough German

Jim Driscoll's comeback in 1919 ended with defeat by the Frenchman, Charles Ledoux, seen slipping momentarily to the canvas in April 1976. In his first defence in March 1977 Wood, who was not a heavy puncher, was knocked out by Bunny Johnson in only 1 min. 43 secs.

## WOODCOCK, Bruce:

Born at Doncaster in 1921, this quiet, unassuming Yorkshireman had won the A.B.A. light-heavyweight championship three years before he turned professional in 1942.

Then, after only 19 fights, all of which he won, he met and defeated Jack London to become British and Empire heavyweight champion.

Woodcock knocked the veteran London out in the sixth round of that contest which took place at Tottenham, July, 1945.

Twelve months later Woodcock became European champion following a six-round victory over the Frenchman, Albert Renet.

In September, 1949, Woodcock was matched with Lee Savold for the world title (as recognised by B.B.B. of C.). A road accident caused a postponement, and when the fight eventually took place in June, 1950, the British champion was forced to retire in the fourth round with a badly cut eye.

The man who really upset Woodcock's ambitions of being a world beater was big Joe Baksi, for the Yorkshireman was never quite as good after he had gamely taken a beating from the American in April, 1947. In that contest Woodcock suffered a fractured jaw in the first round but fought on for six more rounds before retiring.

Woodcock was deprived of his European title by the E.B.U. in September, 1949, and he lost his British titles in a ferocious contest with Jack Gardner in November, 1950.

Woodcock threw all his best punches at Gardner that evening but after 11 rounds of the hardest fighting seen for many years in a British heavyweight title fight it was Woodcock who had to retire.

## WORLD BOXING ASSOC.:

This organisation which controls boxing throughout the greater part of the United States was formed as the National Boxing Association in 1920 after a meeting at the Flatiron Building in New York City. The title was changed to W.B.A. in August, 1962.

The original meeting was called by an Englishman, William A. Gavin, whose real interest at the time was in a project to build an International Sporting Club in New York City to be run on lines similar to that of the N.S.C. in London. The building never materialised but the N.B.A. came into being.

At the start it had a membership of 13 States. Today it has a membership of more than three times that number including boxing commissions and federations from outside the United States, mostly in North and South America, but also in the Far East.

## WORLD BOXING COUNCIL:

While the W.B.A. is largely American, the World Boxing Council is a truly international organisation which was formed in February 1963 and includes the European Federation, B.B.B.C., Latin American Union, and Oriental Federation. Its membership includes well over 100 nations.

## WORLD CHAMPIONS:

To avoid misunderstanding readers are asked to refer to this book's Introduction before studying this list of champions.

*Heavyweight*

JAMES J. CORBETT bt. John L. Sullivan, k.o. 21, New Orleans, Sept. 7, 1892.

BOB FITZSIMMONS bt. Corbett, k.o. 14, Carson City, Mar. 17, 1897.

†JAMES J. JEFFRIES bt. Fitzsimmons, k.o. 11, Coney Island, June 9, 1899. Jeffries retired 1905.

MARVIN HART bt. Jack Root, k.o. 12, Reno, July 3, 1905.

TOMMY BURNS bt. Hart, pts. 20, Los Angeles, Feb. 23, 1906.

JACK JOHNSON bt. Burns, r.s.f. 14, Sydney, Dec. 26, 1908.

JESS WILLARD bt. Johnson, k.o. 26, Havana, Apl. 5, 1915.

JACK DEMPSEY bt. Willard, rtd. 3, Toledo, July 4, 1919.

GENE TUNNEY bt. Dempsey, pts.

10, Philadelphia, Sept. 23, 1926. Tunney retired 1928.

MAX SCHMELING bt. Jack Sharkey, disq. 4, New York, June 12, 1930.

JACK SHARKEY bt. Schmeling pts. 15, Long Island, June 21, 1932.

PRIMO CARNERA bt. Sharkey k.o. 6, Long Island, June 29, 1933.

MAX BAER bt. Carnera, r.s.f. 11, Long Island, June 14, 1934.

JAMES J. BRADDOCK bt. Baer pts. 15, Long Island, June 13, 1935.

JOE LOUIS bt. Braddock, k.o. 8, Chicago, June 22, 1937. Louis retired 1949.

EZZARD CHARLES bt. Jersey Joe Walcott, pts. 15, Chicago, June 22, 1949. (Recognised by N.B.A.).

EZZARD CHARLES bt. Joe Louis, pts. 15, New York, Sept. 27, 1950.

JERSEY JOE WALCOTT bt. Charles, k.o. 7, Pittsburgh, July 18, 1951.

ROCKY MARCIANO bt. Walcott, k.o. 13, Philadelphia, Sept. 23, 1952. Marciano retired 1956.

FLOYD PATTERSON bt. Archie Moore, k.o. 5, Chicago, Nov. 30, 1956.

INGEMAR JOHANSSON bt. Patterson r.s.f. 3, New York, June 26, 1959.

FLOYD PATTERSON bt. Johansson, k.o. 5, New York, June 20, 1960.

SONNY LISTON bt. Patterson, k.o. 1, Chicago, Sept. 25, 1962.

CASSIUS CLAY bt. Liston, rtd. 6, Miami, Feb. 25, 1964.

Clay, who had changed his name to Muhammad Ali, deprived of titles by W.B.A. and N.Y.S.C. in 1967 and rest of the world in 1969.

JOE FRAZIER bt. Jimmy Ellis, rtd. 5, New York, Feb. 16, 1970.

GEORGE FOREMAN bt. Frazier, r.s.f. 2, Kingston, Jamaica, Jan. 22, 1973.

MUHAMMAD ALI bt. Foreman, k.o. 8, Kinshasa, Zaire, Oct. 30, 1974.

LEON SPINKS bt. Ali, pts. 15, Las Vegas, Feb. 15, 1978.

MUHAMMAD ALI bt. Spinks, pts. 15, New Orleans, Sept. 15, 1978.

Muhammad Ali announced his retirement in 1979 and LARRY HOLMES, who had been W.B.C. champion since 1978 became most popularly recognised, especially when he subsequently beat Ali, making another come-back, forcing him to retire in 10 rounds, Las Vegas, Oct. 10, 1980.

Larry Holmes relinquished W.B.C. title Dec. 1983.

MIKE SPINKS bt. Holmes, pts. 15, Las Vegas, Sept. 22, 1985.

Mike Tyson bt. Trevor Berbick, r.s.f. 2, Las Vegas, Nov. 22, 1986 (W.B.C.).

Mike Tyson bt. Bonecrusher Smith, pts. 12, Las Vegas, Mar. 7, 1987 (W.B.A.).

Mike Tyson bt. Tony Tucker, pts. 12, Las Vegas, Aug. 1, 1987 (I.B.F.).

†The first man to establish a clear-cut claim to the world championship.

*Cruiserweight*

Marvin Camel drew Mate Parlov, 15, Split, Dec. 8, 1979.

MARVIN CAMEL bt. Parlov, pts. 15, Las Vegas, Mar. 31, 1980.

CARLOS DE LEON bt. Camel, pts. 15, New Orleans, Nov. 26, 1980.

S.T. GORDON bt. De Leon, r.s.f. 2, Cleveland, Feb. 27, 1982.

CARLOS DE LEON bt. Gordon, pts. 12, Las Vegas, July 17, 1983.

ALFONSO RATCLIFF bt. De Leon, pts. 12, Las Vegas, June 6, 1985.

BERNARD BENTON bt. Ratcliff, pts. 12, Las Vegas, Sept. 22, 1985.

CARLOS DE LEON bt. Benton, pts. 12, Las Vegas, Mar. 22, 1986.

*Light-heavyweight*

JACK ROOT bt. Kid McCoy, pts. 10, Detroit, Apl. 22, 1903.

GEORGE GARDNER bt. Root, k.o. 12, Fort Erie, Jul. 4, 1903.

BOB FITZSIMMONS bt. Gardner, pts. 20, San Francisco, Nov. 25, 1903.

PHILADELPHIA JACK O'BRIEN bt. Fitzsimmons, k.o. 13, San Francisco, Dec. 20, 1905.

O'Brien concentrated on the heavyweight division soon after this and the light-heavyweight championship was virtually vacant from 1906.

JACK DILLON claimed title in 1909 but was not accorded world-wide recognition until the retirement of O'Brien in 1912. Indeed, Tommy Burns was widely recognised as champion around this time although he never pressed his claim and was not very active after losing his heavyweight title in 1908.

BATTLING LEVINSKY bt. Dillon pts. 12, Boston, Oct. 24, 1916.

GEORGES CARPENTIER bt. Levinsky, k.o. 4, Jersey City, Oct. 12, 1920.

BATTLING SIKI bt. Carpentier, rtd. 6, Paris, Sept. 24, 1922.

MIKE McTIGUE bt. Siki, pts. 20, Dublin, Mar. 17, 1923.

PAUL BERLENBACH bt. McTigue, pts. 15, New York, May 30, 1925.

JACK DELANEY bt. Berlenbach, pts. 15, Brooklyn, Jul. 26, 1926. Delaney relinquished title 1927.

N.B.A. Jimmy Slattery bt. Maxie Rosenbloom, pts. 10, Hartford, Aug. 30, 1927.

TOMMY LOUGHRAN bt. Mike McTigue, pts. 15, New York, Oct. 7, 1927. Tommy Loughran gained worldwide recognition by defeating Slattery on points over 15 rounds, New York, Dec. 12, 1927. Loughran relinquished title August, 1929.

N.Y.A.C. Jimmy Slattery bt. Lou Scozza, pts. 15, Buffalo, Feb. 10, 1930.

Maxie Rosenbloom bt. Slattery, pts. 15, New York, Jun. 25, 1930.

N.B.A. George Nichols bt. Dave Maier, pts. 10, Chicago, Mar. 18, 1932.

Lou Scozza bt. Nichols, pts. 10, Buffalo (non-title) May 31, 1932.

MAXIE ROSENBLOOM bt. Scozza, pts. 15, Jul. 14, 1932.

BOB OLIN bt. Rosenbloom, pts. 15, New York, Nov. 16, 1934.

JOHN HENRY LEWIS bt. Olin, pts. 15, St. Louis, Oct. 31, 1935. Lewis relinquished title Jan., 1939.

America:—

Melio Bettina bt. Tiger Jack Fox, r.s.f. 9, New York, Feb. 3, 1939.

Billy Conn bt. Bettina, pts. 15, New York, Jul. 13, 1939. Conn relinquished title 1941.

Anton Christoforidis bt. Bettina, pts. 15, Cleveland, Jan. 13, 1941.

Gus Lesnevich bt. Christoforidis, pts. 15, New York, May 22, 1941.

Britain:—

Len Harvey bt. Jock McAvoy, pts. 15, London, Jul. 10, 1939.

Freddie Mills bt. Harvey, k.o. 2, London, Jun. 20, 1942.

GUS LESNEVICH bt. Mills, r.s.f. 10, London, May 14, 1946.

FREDDIE MILLS bt. Lesnevich, pts. 15, London, Jul. 26, 1948.

JOEY MAXIM bt. Mills, k.o. 10, London, Jan. 24, 1950.

ARCHIE MOORE bt. Maxim, pts. 15, St. Louis, Dec. 17, 1952. Moore forfeited title.

HAROLD JOHNSON bt. Doug Jones, pts. 15, Philadelphia, May 12, 1962.

WILLIE PASTRANO bt. Johnson, pts. 15, Las Vegas, June 1, 1963.

JOSE TORRES bt. Pastrano, r.s.f. 9, New York, Mar. 30, 1965.

DICK TIGER bt. Torres, pts. 15, New York, Dec. 15, 1966.

BOB FOSTER bt. Tiger, k.o. 4, New York, May 24, 1968.

Foster relinquished title Sept. 1974.

(W.B.C. version) John Conteh bt. Jorge Ahumada, pts. 15, London, Oct. 1, 1974.

(W.B.A. version) Victor Galindez bt. Len Hutchins, rtd. 12; Buenos Aires, Dec. 7, 1974.

John Conteh deprived of W.B.C. title May 1977.

Miguel Angel Cuello bt. Jesse Burnett, k.o. 9, Monte Carlo, May 21, 1977 (W.B.C.).

Mate Parlov bt. Cuello, k.o. 9, Milan, Jan. 7, 1978 (W.B.C.).

Mike Rossman bt. Galindez, r.s.f. 13, New Orleans, Sept. 15, 1978 (W.B.A.).

Marvin Johnson bt. Parlov, r.s.f. 10, Sicily, Dec. 2, 1978 (W.B.C.).

Victor Galindez bt. Rossman, rtd. 9, New Orleans, Apl. 14, 1979 (W.B.A.).

Matthew Saad Muhammad bt. Johnson, r.s.f. 8, Indianapolis, Apl. 22, 1979 (W.B.C.).

Marvin Johnson bt. Galindez, r.s.f. 11, New Orleans, Nov. 30 1979 (W.B.A.).

Mustafa Muhammad bt. Johnson, r.s.f. 11, Knoxville, Mar. 31, 1980 (W.B.A.).

Mike Spinks bt. Mustafa Muhammad, pts. 15, Las Vegas, July 18, 1981 (W.B.A.).

Dwight Braxton (became Dwight Muhammad) bt. Matthew Saad Muhammad, r.s.f. 10, Atlantic City,

Dec. 19, 1981 (W.B.C.).

MIKE SPINKS bt. Dwight Muhammad Qawi (formerly Braxton), pts. 15, Atlantic City, Mar. 18, 1983.

Spinks relinquished title Nov. 1985.
J.B. Williamson bt. Prince Mama Mohammed, pts. 12, Las Vegas, Dec. 10, 1985 (W.B.C.).

Marvin Johnson bt. Leslie Stewart, r.s.f. 7, Indianapolis, Feb. 9, 1986 (W.B.A.).

Dennis Andries bt. Williamson, pts. 12, Picketts Lock Leisure Centre, London, Apl. 30, 1986 (W.B.C.).

Thomas Hearns bt. Andries, r.s.f. 10, Detroit, Mar. 7, 1987 (W.B.C.).

Leslie Stewart bt. Johnson, r.s.f. 9, Port of Spain, Trinidad, May 23, 1987 (W.B.A.).

Hearns deprived of W.B.C. title Aug. 1987.

Virgil Hill bt. Stewart, r.s.f. 4, Atlantic City, Sept. 5, 1987 (W.B.A.).

*Middleweight*

JACK DEMPSEY bt. George Fulljames, k.o. 22, Toronto, Jul. 30, 1884.

BOB FITZSIMMONS bt. Dempsey k.o. 13, New Orleans, Jan. 14, 1891. Fitzsimmons relinquished title 1895.

TOMMY RYAN claimed title but was not universally recognised until he beat Tommy West, k.o. 14, New York, Jun. 18, 1898. Ryan retired 1907.

STANLEY KETCHEL bt. Mike Twin Sullivan, k.o. 1, Colma, Feb. 22, 1908.

BILLY PAPKE bt. Ketchel, r.s.f. 12, Los Angeles, Sept. 7, 1908.

STANLEY KETCHEL bt. Papke, k.o. 1·1, San Francisco, Nov. 26, 1908. Ketchel shot and killed Oct., 1910.

JOHNNY THOMPSON bt. Papke, pts. 20, Sydney, Feb. 11, 1911. Thompson relinquished title 1911.

Title claimed by Frank Mantell, Billy Papke, and Frank Klaus, but no one established a strong claim until—

GEORGE CHIP bt. Frank Klaus, k.o. 6, Pittsburgh, Oct. 11, 1913.

AL McCOY bt. Chip, k.o. 1, Brooklyn, Apl. 7, 1914.

MIKE O'DOWD bt. McCoy, k.o. 6, Brooklyn, Nov. 14, 1917.

JOHNNY WILSON bt. O'Dowd, pts. 12, Boston, May 6, 1920.

HARRY GREB bt. Wilson, pts. 15, New York, Aug. 31, 1923.

TIGER FLOWERS bt. Greb, pts. 15, New York, Feb. 26, 1926.

MICKEY WALKER bt. Flowers, pts. 10, Chicago, Dec. 3, 1926. Walker relinquished title June, 1931—overweight.

N.B.A. Gorilla Jones bt. Tiger Thomas, pts. 10, Milwaukee, Aug. 25, 1931.

I.B.U. Marcel Thil bt. Gorilla Jones, disq. 11, Paris, Jun. 11, 1932.

N.B.A. deprived Jones of title following defeat by Thil but restored it to him after he beat Sammy Slaughter, k.o. 7, Cleveland, Jan. 30, 1933.

N.Y.A.C. Ben Jeby bt. Chuck Devlin, pts. 15, New York, Nov. 21, 1932.

Lou Brouillard bt. Jeby, k.o. 7, New York, Aug. 9, 1933.

Vince Dundee bt. Brouillard, pts. 15, Boston, Oct. 30, 1933.

Gorilla Jones' claim no longer valid after defeats by Martinez and Rankin in 1934.

N.B.A. and N.Y.A.C. Teddy Yarosz bt. Vince Dundee, pts. 15, Pittsburgh, Sept. 11, 1934.

Babe Risko bt. Yarosz, pts. 15, Pittsburgh, Sept. 19, 1935.

Freddie Steele bt. Risko, pts. 15, Seattle, Jul. 11, 1936.

Europe:—

Marcel Thil relinquished title after defeat by Fred Apostoli, Sept. 23, 1937, but the latter did not claim title because of an agreement with N.Y.A.C.

Fred Apostoli subsequently claimed title after beating Steele in an overweight match, Jan. 7, 1938, and a win over Glen Lee, Apl. 1, 1938.

N.B.A.:—

Al Hostak bt. Steele, k.o. 1, Seattle, Jul. 26, 1938.

Solly Krieger bt. Hostak, pts. 15, Seattle, Nov. 1, 1938.

Al Hostak bt. Krieger, r.s.f. 4, Seattle, Jun. 27, 1939.

Tony Zale bt. Hostak, k.o. 13, Seattle, Jul. 19, 1940.

N.Y.A.C.:

Ceferino Garcia bt. Apostoli, r.s.f. 7, New York, Oct. 2, 1939.

Ken Overlin bt. Garcia, pts. 15,

New York, May 23, 1940.
Billy Soose bt. Overlin, pts. 15, New
York, May 9, 1941. Soose relinquished
this title November, 1941.
TONY ZALE bt. George Abrams,
pts. 15, New York, Nov. 28, 1941.
ROCKY GRAZIANO bt. Zale, k.o. 6,
Chicago, Jul. 16, 1947.
TONY ZALE bt. Graziano, k.o. 3,
Newark, Jun. 10, 1948.
MARCEL CERDAN bt. Zale, rtd. 11,
Jersey City, Sept. 21, 1948.
JAKE LA MOTTA bt. Cerdan, rtd.
10, Detroit, Jun. 16, 1949.
RAY ROBINSON bt. La Motta, r.s.f.
13, Chicago, Feb. 14, 1951.
RANDOLPH TURPIN bt. Robinson,
pts. 15, London, Jul. 10, 1951.
RAY ROBINSON bt. Turpin, r.s.f.
10, New York, Sept. 12, 1951.
Robinson retired December, 1952.
America:—
Carl "Bobo" Olson bt. Paddy
Young, pts. 15, New York, Jun. 19,
1953.
Europe:—
Randolph Turpin bt. Charles
Humez, pts. 15, London, Jun. 9, 1953.
CARL "BOBO" OLSON bt. Turpin,
pts. 15, New York, Oct. 21, 1953.
RAY ROBINSON bt. Olson, k.o. 2,
Chicago, Dec. 9, 1955.
GENE FULLMER bt. Robinson, pts.
15, New York, Jan. 2, 1957.
RAY ROBINSON bt. Fullmer, k.o. 5,
Chicago, May 1, 1957.
CARMEN BASILIO bt. Robinson,
pts. 15, New York, Sept. 23, 1957.
RAY ROBINSON bt. Basilio, pts. 15,
Chicago, Mar. 25, 1958.
N.B.A.:—
Gene Fullmer bt. Basilio, r.s.f. 14, San
Francisco, Aug. 29, 1959.
PAUL PENDER bt. Robinson, pts.
15, Boston, Jan 22, 1960.
TERRY DOWNES bt. Pender, rtd. 9,
London, July 11, 1961.
PAUL PENDER bt. Downes, pts. 15,
Boston, Apl. 7, 1962. Pender relieved of
title Nov., 1962.
DICK TIGER bt. Gene Fullmer, pts.
15, San Francisco, Oct. 23, 1962.
JOEY GIARDELLO bt. Tiger, pts.
15, Atlantic City, Dec. 7, 1963.
DICK TIGER bt. Giardello, pts. 15,
New York, Oct. 22, 1965.

EMILE GRIFFITH bt. Tiger, pts. 15,
New York, Apl. 25, 1966.
NINO BENVENUTI bt. Griffith, pts.
15, New York, Apl. 17, 1967.
EMILE GRIFFITH bt. Benvenuti,
pts. 15, New York, Sept. 29, 1967.
NINO BENVENUTI bt. Griffith, pts.
15, New York, Mar. 4, 1968.
CARLOS MONZON bt. Benvenuti,
k.o. 12, Rome, Nov. 7, 1970.
Monzon retired 1977.
RODRIGO VALDES bt. Bennie
Briscoe, pts. 15, Campione d'Italia, Nov.
5, 1977.
HUGO CORRO bt. Valdes, pts. 15,
San Remo, Apl. 22, 1978.
VITO ANTUOFERMO bt. Corro,
pts. 15, Monaco, June 30, 1979.
ALAN MINTER bt. Antuofermo,
pts. 15, Las Vegas, Mar. 16, 1980.
MARVIN HAGLER bt. Minter, r.s.f.
3, Wembley, London, Sept. 27, 1980.
SUGAR RAY LEONARD bt. Hagler,
pts. 12, Las Vegas, Apl. 6, 1987.
Leonard retired undefeated May 1987.
Sumbu Kalambay bt. Iran Barley,
pts. 15, Livorno, Italy, Oct. 23, 1987
(W.B.A.).
Thomas Hearns bt. Juan Domingo
Roldan, k.o. 4, Las Vegas, Oct. 29,
1987 (W.B.C.).

*Junior or Light-middleweight*
RALPH DUPAS bt. Dennis Moyer,
pts. 15, New Orleans, Apl. 29, 1963.
SANDRO MAZZINGHI bt. Dupas,
k.o. 9, Milan, Sept. 7, 1963.
NINO BENVENUTI bt. Mazzinghi,
k.o. 6, Milan, June 18, 1965.
KIM KI-SOO bt. Benvenuti, pts. 15,
Seoul, Jan. 25, 1966.
SANDRO MAZZINGHI bt. Ki-Soo,
pts. 15, Milan, May 26, 1968.
MAZZINGHI relinquished title.
FREDDIE LITTLE bt. Stan Hayward,
pts. 15, Las Vegas, Mar. 3, 1969.
CARMELO BOSSI bt. Little, pts. 15,
Monza, July 9, 1970.
KOICHI WAJIMA bt. Bossi, pts. 15,
Tokyo, Oct. 31, 1971.
OSCAR ALVARADO bt. Wajima,
k.o. 15, Tokyo, June 4, 1974.
KOICHI WAJIMA bt. Alvarado, pts.
15, Tokyo, Jan. 21, 1975.
JAE DO YUH bt. Wajima, k.o. 7,
Kitsakyushu, Japan, June 7, 1975.

KOICHI WAJIMA bt. Jae Do Yuh, k.o. 15, Tokyo, Feb. 17, 1976.

JOSE DURAN bt. Wajima, k.o. 14, Tokyo, May 8, 1976.

MIGUEL ANGEL CASTELLINI bt. Duran, pts. 15, Madrid, Oct. 8, 1976.

EDDIE GAZO bt. Castellini, pts. 15, Managua, Mar. 6, 1977.

MASASHI KUDO bt. Gazo, pts. 15, Akita City, Aug. 9, 1978.

AYUB KALULE bt. Kudo, pts. 15, Akita, Oct. 24, 1979.

SUGAR RAY LEONARD bt. Kalule, r.s.f. 9, Houston, June 25, 1981.

Leonard relinquished title Sept. 1981.

Wilfred Benitez bt. Maurice Hope, k.o. 12, Las Vegas, May 24, 1981 (W.B.C.).

Tadashi Mirhara bt. Rocky Fratto, pts. 15, Rochester, N.Y., Nov. 7, 1981 (W.B.A.).

Davey Moore bt. Mihara, r.s.f. 6, Tokyo, Feb. 2, 1982 (W.B.A.).

Thomas Hearns bt. Benitez, pts. 15, New Orleans, Dec. 3, 1982 (W.B.C.).

Roberto Duran bt. Moore, r.s.f. 8, New York, June 16, 1983 (W.B.A.).

Duran relinquished W.B.A. title June 1984.

Mike McCallum bt. Sean Mannion, pts. 15, New York, Oct. 19, 1984 (W.B.A.).

Hearns relinquished W.B.C. title Sept. 1986.

Duane Thomas bt. John Mugabi, r.s.f. 3, Dec. 5, 1986 (W.B.C.).

Lupe Aquino bt. Thomas, pts. 12, Bordeaux, July 12, 1987 (W.B.C.).

Gianfranco Rosi bt. Aquino, pts. 12, Perugia, Oct. 2, 1987 (W.B.C.).

*Welterweight*

PADDY DUFFY bt. Billy McMillan, k.o. 17, Vancouver, Oct. 30, 1888. Duffy died July, 1890.

MYSTERIOUS BILLY SMITH bt. Danny Needham, k.o. 14, San Francisco, Dec. 14, 1892.

TOMMY RYAN bt. Smith, pts. 20, Minneapolis, Jul. 26, 1894.

CHARLES "KID" McCOY bt. Ryan, k.o. 15, Long Island, Mar. 2, 1896. McCoy relinquished title 1897.

MYSTERIOUS BILLY SMITH reclaimed title. This was undisputed as he had gained a decision over Ryan in an overweight match, Nov. 25, 1896.

RUBE FERNS bt. Smith, disq. 21, Buffalo, Jan. 15, 1900.

WILLIAM R. MATTHEWS bt. Ferns, pts. 15, Detroit, Oct. 16, 1900.

RUBE FERNS bt. Matthews, k.o. 10, Toronto, May 24, 1901.

JOE WALCOTT bt. Ferns, k.o. 5, Fort Erie, Dec. 18, 1901.

DIXIE KID bt. Walcott, disq. 20, San Francisco, Apl. 30, 1904. Despite this decision Dixie Kid was not granted universal recognition. The Kid himself did not press the matter but left the United States to fight over here and in France where he was a great favourite.

Walcott reclaimed the title on strength of a draw with Dixie Kid, 20 rounds, San Francisco, May 12, 1904.

Honey Mellody bt. Walcott, pts. 15, Chelsea (U.S.A.), Oct. 16, 1906.

Mike Twin Sullivan bt. Mellody, 20, Los Angeles, Apl. 23, 1907. Sullivan relinquished title when he became overweight. Title was subsequently claimed by Harry Lewis, Mike Glover, and Jack Britton.

In 1915 Ted "Kid" Lewis established a stronger claim to the title by defeating both Glover and Britton.

TED "KID" LEWIS bt. Jack Britton, pts. 12, Boston, Aug. 31, 1915.

JACK BRITTON bt. Lewis, pts. 20, New Orleans, Apl. 24, 1916.

TED "KID" LEWIS bt. Britton, Pts. 20, Dayton, Jun. 25, 1917.

JACK BRITTON bt. Lewis, k.o. 9, Canton, Mar. 17, 1919.

MICKEY WALKER bt. Britton, pts. 15, New York, Nov. 1, 1922.

PETE LATZO bt. Walker, pts. 10, Scranton, May 20, 1926.

JOE DUNDEE bt. Latzo, pts. 15, New York, Jun. 3, 1927.

N.B.A. deprived Dundee of title after his defeat by Young Jack Thompson in a catch-weights contest, 1928.

JACKIE FIELDS bt. Young Jack Thompson, pts. 10, Chicago, Mar. 25, 1929.

YOUNG JACK THOMPSON bt. Fields, pts. 15, Detroit, May 9, 1930.

TOMMY FREEMAN bt. Thompson, pts. 15, Cleveland, Sept. 5, 1930.

YOUNG JACK THOMPSON bt.

Freeman, t.k.o. 12, Cleveland, Apl. 14, 1931.

LOU BROUILLARD bt. Thompson, pts. 15, Boston, Oct. 23, 1931.

JACKIE FIELDS bt. Brouillard, pts. 10, Chicago, Jan. 28, 1932.

YOUNG CORBETT III bt. Fields, pts. 10, San Francisco, Feb. 22, 1933.

JIMMY McLARNIN bt. Corbett III, k.o. 1, Los Angeles, May 29, 1933.

BARNEY ROSS bt. McLarnin, pts. 15, New York, May 28, 1934.

JIMMY McLARNIN bt. Ross, pts. 15, New York, Sept. 17, 1934.

BARNEY ROSS bt. McLarnin, pts. 15, New York, May 28, 1935.

HENRY ARMSTRONG bt. Ross, pts. 15, Long Island, May 31, 1938.

FRITZIE ZIVIC bt. Armstrong, pts. 15, New York, Oct. 4, 1940.

FREDDIE RED COCHRANE bt. Zivic, pts. 15, Newark, Jul. 29, 1941.

MARTY SERVO bt. Cochrane, k.o. 4, New York, Feb. 1, 1946.

Servo retired August, 1946.

RAY ROBINSON bt. Tommy Bell, pts. 15, New York, Dec. 20, 1946.

Robinson relinquished title February, 1951.

N.B.A.:—

Johnny Bratton bt. Charlie Fusari, pts. 15, Chicago, Mar. 14, 1951.

Kid Gavilan bt. Bratton, pts. 15, New York, May 18, 1951.

KID GAVILAN bt. Gil Turner, r.s.f. 11, Philadelphia, Jul. 7, 1952.

JOHNNY SAXTON bt. Gavilan, pts. 15, Philadelphia, Oct. 20, 1954.

TONY DE MARCO bt. Saxton, r.s.f. 14, Boston, Apl. 1, 1955.

CARMEN BASILIO bt. De Marco, r.s.f. 12, Syracuse, Jun. 10, 1955.

JOHNNY SAXTON bt. Basilio, pts. 15, Chicago, Mar. 14, 1956.

CARMEN BASILIO bt. Saxton, r.s.f. 9, Syracuse, Sept. 12, 1956.

Basilio relinquished title Sept. 1957.

VIRGIL AKINS bt. Vince Martinez, r.s.f. 4, St. Louis, Jun. 6, 1958.

DON JORDAN bt. Akins, pts. 15, Los Angeles, Dec. 5, 1958.

BENNY PARET bt. Jordan, pts. 15, Las Vegas, May 27, 1960.

EMILE GRIFFITH bt. Paret, k.o. 13, Miami, Apl. 1, 1961.

BENNY PARET bt. Griffith, pts. 15, New York, Sept. 30, 1961.

EMILE GRIFFITH bt. Paret, r.s.f. 12, New York, Mar. 24, 1962.

LUIS RODRIGUEZ bt. Griffith, pts. 15, Los Angeles, Mar. 21, 1963.

EMILE GRIFFITH bt. Rodriguez, pts. 15, New York, June 8, 1963.

GRIFFITH deprived of title 1966.

CURTIS COKES bt. Jean Josselin, pts. 15, Dallas, Nov. 28, 1966.

JOSE NAPOLES bt. Cokes, r.s.f. 13, Inglewood, Calif., Apl. 18, 1969.

BILLY BACKUS bt. Napoles, r.s.f. 4, Syracuse, Dec. 3, 1970.

JOSE NAPOLES bt. Backus r.s.f. 8, Inglewood, June 4, 1971.

JOHN H. STRACEY bt. Napoles, r.s.f. 6, Mexico City, Dec. 6, 1975.

CARLOS PALOMINO bt. Stracey, r.s.f. 12, Wembley, June 22, 1976.

WILFREDO BENITEZ bt. Palomino, pts. 15, San Juan, Jan. 14, 1979.

SUGAR RAY LEONARD bt. Benitez, r.s.f. 15, Las Vegas, Nov. 30, 1979.

ROBERTO DURAN bt. Leonard, pts. 15, Montreal, June 20, 1980.

SUGAR RAY LEONARD bt. Duran, rtd. 8, New Orleans, Nov. 26, 1980.

Leonard retired Nov. 1982.

Don Curry bt. Junsok Hwang, pts. 15, Fort Worth, Feb. 13, 1983 (W.B.A.).

Milton McCrory bt. Colin Jones, pts. 12, Las Vegas, Aug. 13, 1983 (W.B.C.).

DON CURRY bt. McCrory, k.o. 2, Las Vegas, Dec. 6, 1985.

LLOYD HONEYGHAN bt. Curry, rtd. 6, Atlantic City, Sept. 27, 1986.

Honeyghan relinquished W.B.A. title Dec. 1986.

Mark Breland bt. Harold Volbrecht, Atlantic City, Feb. 6, 1987 (W.B.A.).

Marlon Starling bt. Breland, k.o. 11, Columbia, S. Carolina, Aug. 22, 1987 (W.B.A.).

Jorge Vaca bt. Honeyghan, technical pts. win 7 rounds after clash of heads, Wembley, Oct. 28, 1987 (W.B.C.).

*Junior or Light-welterweight*

MUSHY CALLAHAN bt. Pinkey Mitchell, pts. 10, Vernon, Calif., Sept. 21, 1926.

JACK "KID" BERG bt. Callahan,

London, Feb. 18, 1930.
TONY CANZONERI bt. Berg, Chicago, Apl. 21, 1931.
JOHNNY JADICK bt. Canzoneri, Philadelphia, Jan. 18, 1932.
BATTLING SHAW bt. Jadick, pts. 10, New Orleans, Feb. 20, 1933.
TONY CANZONERI bt. Shaw, pts. 10, New Orleans, May 21, 1933.
BARNEY ROSS bt. Canzoneri, pts. 10, Chicago, June 23, 1933.
Title in disuse.
TIPPY LARKIN bt. Willy Joyce, pts. 12, Boston, Apl. 29, 1946.
Title in disuse.
CARLOS ORTIZ bt. Kenny Lane, k.o. 2, New York, June 12, 1959.
DUILIO LOI bt. Ortiz, pts. 15, Milan, Sept. 1, 1960.
EDDIE PERKINS bt. Loi, pts. 15, Milan, Sept. 14, 1962.
DUILIO LOI bt. Perkins, pts. 15, Milan, Dec. 15, 1962. Loi retired.
ROBERTO CRUZ bt. Battling Torres, k.o. 1, Los Angeles, Mar. 21, 1963.
EDDIE PERKINS bt. Cruz, pts. 15, Manila, June 15, 1963.
CARLOS HERNANDEZ bt. Perkins, pts. 15, Caracas, Jan. 18, 1965.
SANDRO LOPOPOLO bt. Hernandez, pts. 15, Rome, April 30, 1966.
PAUL FUJII bt. Lopopolo, rtd. 2, Honolulu, Apl. 30, 1967.
NICOLINO LOCHE bt. Fujii, rtd. 9, Tokyo, Dec. 12, 1968.
ALFONSO FRAZIER bt. Loche, pts. 15, Panama City, Mar. 10, 1972.
ANTONIO CERVANTES bt. Frazier, k.o. 10, Panama City, Oct. 29, 1972.
WILFREDO BENITEZ bt. Cervantes, pts. 15, San Juan, Mar. 6, 1976.
Benitez stripped of title for failure to defend against Antonio Cervantes.
Antonio Cervantes bt. Carlos Giminez, r.s.f. 5, Maracaibo, June 25, 1977 (W.B.A.).
Sang Hyun Kim bt. Saensak Muangsurin, r.s.f. 13, Seoul, Dec. 30, 1978 (W.B.C.).
Saoul Mamby bt. Kim, k.o. 14, Seoul, Feb. 23, 1980 (W.B.C.).
Aaron Pryor bt. Cervantes, k.o. 4, Cincinnati, Aug. 2, 1980 (W.B.A.).
Leroy Haley bt. Saoul Mamby, pts. 15, Cleveland, June 26, 1982 (W.B.C.).
Bruce Curry bt. Haley, pts. 12, Las Vegas, May 20, 1983 (W.B.C.).
Aaron Pryor retired Dec. 1983 (W.B.A.).
Johnny Bumphus bt. Lorenzo Garcia, pts. 15, Atlantic City, Jan. 22, 1984 (W.B.A.).
Billy Costello bt. Curry, r.s.f. 10, Beaumont, Texas, Jan. 29, 1984 (W.B.C.).
Gene Hatcher bt. Bumphus, r.s.f. 11, Buffalo, N.Y., June 1, 1984 (W.B.A.).
Ubaldo Sacco bt. Hatcher, r.s.f. 9, Campione D'Italia, July 21, 1985 (W.B.A.).
Lonnie Smith bt. Costello, k.o. 8, New York, Aug. 21, 1985 (W.B.C.).
Rene Arredondo bt. Smith, k.o. 5, Los Angeles, May 5, 1986 (W.B.C.).
Patrizio Oliva bt. Sacco, pts. 15, Monte Carlo, Mar. 15, 1986 (W.B.A.).
Tsuyoshi Hamada bt. Arredondo, k.o. 1, Tokyo, July 24, 1986 (W.B.C.).
Juan Martin Coggi bt. Oliva, k.o. 3, Ribera, Sicily, July 4, 1987 (W.B.A.).
Rene Arredondo bt. Hamada, r.s.f. 6, Tokyo, July 22, 1987 (W.B.C.).
Roger Mayweather bt. Arredondo, r.s.f. 6, Los Angeles, Nov. 12, 1987 (W.B.C.).

*Lightweight*
ARTHUR CHAMBERS bt. Billy Edwards, disq. 35, Squirrel Island, Canada, Sept. 4, 1872.
Chambers retired 1879.
JACK DEMPSEY claimed title in 1882 and then when he became overweight in 1884 he nominated JACK McAULIFFE as his successor. JACK McAULIFFE is generally considered to have established his right to the title by beating Bill Frazier, k.o. 21, Boston, Oct. 29, 1886.
McAuliffe relinquished title in 1893 and retired undefeated in 1896.
GEORGE KID LAVIGNE claimed title in 1894.
GEORGE KID LAVIGNE bt. Dick Burge, k.o. 17, N.S.C. London, June 1, 1896.
FRANK ERNE bt. Lavigne, pts. 20, Buffalo, Jul. 3, 1899.
JOE GANS bt. Erne, k.o. 1, Fort Erie, Canada, May 12, 1902.
BATTLING NELSON bt. Gans, k.o.

17, San Francisco, Jul. 4, 1908.
ADOLPH WOLGAST bt. Nelson, r.s.f. 40, Port Richmond, Feb. 22, 1910.
WILLIE RITCHIE bt. Wolgast, disq. 16, Daly City, California, Nov. 28, 1912.
FREDDIE WELSH bt. Ritchie, pts. 20, Olympia, London, Jul. 7, 1914.
BENNY LEONARD bt. Welsh, k.o. 9, New York, May 28, 1917.
Benny Leonard retired 1925.
JIMMY GOODRICH bt. Stanislaus Loayza, k.o. 2, Long Island, Jul. 3, 1925.
ROCKY KANSAS bt. Goodrich, pts. 15, New York, Dec. 8. 1925.
SAMMY MANDELL bt. Kansas, pts. 10, Chicago, Jun. 3, 1926.
AL SINGER bt. Mandell, k.o. 1, New York, Jul. 17, 1930.
TONY CANZONERI bt. Singer, k.o. 1, New York, Nov. 14, 1930.
BARNEY ROSS bt. Canzoneri, pts. 10, Chicago, Jun. 23, 1933.
Ross relinquished title April, 1935—overweight.
TONY CANZONERI bt. Lou Ambers, pts. 15, New York, May 10, 1935.
LOU AMBERS bt. Canzoneri, pts. 15, New York, Sept. 3, 1936.
HENRY ARMSTRONG bt. Lou Ambers, pts. 15, New York, Aug. 17, 1938.
LOU AMBERS bt. Armstrong, pts. 15, New York. Aug. 22, 1939.
LEW JENKINS bt. Ambers, k.o. 3, New York, May 10, 1940.
SAMMY ANGOTT bt. Jenkins, pts. 15. New York, Dec. 19, 1941.
Angott announced retirement in November, 1942, but started boxing again four months later. This threw the championship into a state of confusion.
N.Y.A.C.:—
Beau Jack bt. Tippy Larkin, k.o. 3, New York, Dec. 18, 1942.
Bob Montgomery bt. Jack, pts. 15, New York, May 21, 1943.
Beau Jack bt. Montgomery, pts. 15, New York, Nov. 19, 1943.
Bob Montgomery bt. Jack, pts. 15, New York, Mar. 3, 1944.
N.B.A.:—
Slugger White bt. Willie Joyce, pts. 15, Baltimore, Jan. 4, 1943.
Sammy Angott bt. White, pts. 15, Los Angeles, Oct. 27, 1943.

Juan Zurita bt. Angott, pts. 15, Hollywood, Mar. 8, 1944.
Ike Williams bt. Zurita, k.o. 2, Mexico City, Apl. 18, 1945.
IKE WILLIAMS bt. Bob Montgomery, k.o. 6, Philadelphia, Aug. 4, 1947.
JIMMY CARTER bt. Williams, r.s.f. 14, New York, May 25, 1951.
LAURO SALAS bt. Carter, pts. 15, Los Angeles, May 14, 1952.
JIMMY CARTER bt. Salas, pts. 15, Chicago, Oct. 15, 1952.
PADDY DeMARCO bt. Carter, pts. 15, New York, Mar. 5, 1954.
JIMMY CARTER bt. DeMarco, r.s.f. 15, San Francisco, Nov. 17, 1954.
WALLACE BUD SMITH bt. Carter, pts. 15, Boston, Jun. 29. 1955.
JOE BROWN bt. Smith, pts. 15, New Orleans, Aug. 24, 1956.
CARLOS ORTIZ bt. Brown, pts. 15, Las Vegas, Apl. 21, 1962.
ISMAEL LAGUNA bt. Ortiz, pts. 15, Panama City, Apl. 10, 1965.
CARLOS ORTIZ bt. Laguna, pts. 15, San Juan, Puerto Rico, Nov. 13, 1965.
CARLOS TEO CRUZ bt. Ortiz, pts. 15, St. Domingo, June 29, 1968.
ARMUNDO (MANDO) RAMOS bt. Cruz, r.s.f. 11, Los Angeles, Feb. 18, 1969.
ISMAEL LAGUNA bt. Ramos, rtd. 9, Los Angeles, Mar. 3, 1970.
KEN BUCHANAN bt. Laguna, pts. 15, San Juan, Sept. 26, 1970.
ROBERTO DURAN bt. Buchanan, r.s.f. 13, New York, June 26, 1972.
Duran relinquished title Jan. 1979.
Jim Watt bt. Alfredo Pitalua, r.s.f. 12, Glasgow, Apl. 17, 1979 (W.B.C.).
Ernesto Espana bt. Claude Noel, k.o. 13, San Juan, June 16, 1979 (W.B.A.).
Hilmer Kenty bt. Espana, r.s.f. 9, Detroit, Mar.2, 1980 (W.B.A.).
Sean O'Grady bt. Kenty, pts. 15, Atlantic City, Apl. 12, 1981 (W.B.A.).
O'Grady deprived of title by W.B.A.
Alexis Arguello bt. Watt, pts. 15, Wembley, London, June 20, 1981 (W.B.C.).
Claude Noel bt. Rodolfo Gonzalez, pts. 15, Atlantic City, Sept. 12, 1981 (W.B.A.).
Arturo Frias bt. Noel, k.o. 8, Las Vegas, Dec. 5, 1981 (W.B.A.).

Ray Mancini bt. Frias, r.s.f. 1, Las Vegas, May 8, 1982 (W.B.A.).

Arguello relinquished W.B.C. title 1982.

Edwin Rosario bt. Jose Luis Ramirez, pts. 12, San Juan, May 1, 1983 (W.B.C.).

Livingstone Bramble bt. Mancini, r.s.f. 14, Buffalo, New York, June 1, 1984 (W.B.A.).

Jose Luis Ramirez bt. Rosario, r.s.f. 4, Jan Juan, Nov. 3, 1984 (W.B.C.).

Hector Camacho bt. Ramirez, pts. 12, Las Vegas, Aug. 10, 1985 (W.B.C.).

Edwin Rosario bt. Bramble, k.o. 2, Miami, Sept. 26, 1986 (W.B.A.).

Camacho relinquished W.B.C. title 1987.

Jose Luis Ramirez bt. Terrence Alli, pts. 12, St. Tropez, July 19, 1987 (W.B.C.).

### Junior Lightweight

JOHNNY DUNDEE bt. George Chaney, dis. 5, New York, Nov. 18, 1921.

JACK BERNSTEIN bt. Dundee, pts. 15, New York, May 30, 1923.

JOHNNY DUNDEE bt. Bernstein, pts. 15, New York, Dec. 17, 1923.

STEVE KID SULLIVAN bt. Dundee, pts. 15, Brooklyn, June 20, 1924.

MIKE BALLERINO bt. Sullivan, pts. 10, Philadelphia, Apl. 1, 1925.

TOD MORGAN bt. Ballerino, k.o. 10, Los Angeles, Dec. 2, 1925.

BENNY BASS bt. Morgan, k.o. 2, New York, Dec. 19, 1929.

KID CHOCOLATE bt. Bass, r.s.f. 7, Philadelphia, July 15, 1931.

FRANKIE KLICK bt. Chocolate, k.o. 7, Philadelphia, Dec. 26, 1933.

Title in disuse.

HAROLD GOMES bt. Paul Jorgensen, pts. 15, Providence, July 20, 1959.

FLASH ELORDE bt. Gomes, k.o. 7, Manila, Mar. 16, 1960.

YOSHIAKI NUMATA bt. Elorde, pts. 15, Tokyo, June 30, 1967.

HIROSHI KOBOYASHI bt. Numata, k.o. 12, Tokyo, Dec. 14, 1967.

ALFREDO MARCANO bt. Koboyashi, r.s.f. 10, Aomori, Japan, July 29, 1971.

BEN VILLAFLOR bt. Marcano, pts. 15, Honolulu, Apl. 25, 1972.

KUNIAKI SHIBATA bt. Villaflor, pts. 15, Honolulu, Mar. 12, 1973.

BEN VILLAFLOR bt. Shibata, k.o. 1, Honolulu, Oct. 17, 1973.

SAM SERRANO bt. Villaflor, pts. 15, San Juan, Oct. 16, 1976.

YATSATSUNE UEHARA bt. Serrano, k.o. 6, Detroit, Aug. 2, 1980.

SAM SERRANO bt. Uehara, pts. 15, Wakayama, Japan, Apl. 9, 1981.

ROGER MAYWEATHER bt. Serrano, k.o. 8, San Juan, Jan. 19, 1983.

RICKY LOCKRIDGE bt. Mayweather, k.o. 1, Beaumont, Texas, Feb. 26, 1984.

WILFREDO GOMEZ bt. Lockridge, pts. 15, San Juan, May 19, 1985.

ALFREDO LAYNE bt. Gomez, r.s.f. 9, San Juan, May 24, 1986.

BRIAN MITCHELL bt. Layne, Sun City, Sept. 27, 1986.

### Featherweight

DAL HAWKINS bt. Fred Bogan, k.o. 91, San Francisco, Jun. 3-4, 1889. Hawkins became overweight.

AUSTRALIAN BILLY MURPHY bt. Ike Weir, k.o. 14, San Francisco, Jan. 13, 1890.

Murphy's claim was not taken seriously in America.

YOUNG GRIFFO bt. Murphy, pts. 15, Sydney, Sept. 3, 1890.

America:—

Cal McCarthy claimed title and drew with George Dixon, 70, Boston, Feb. 7, 1890.

George Dixon bt. McCarthy, k.o. 22, Troy, Mar. 31, 1891.

British Empire:—

Young Griffo's claim to the title was not as strong after he failed to meet Billy Murphy in January, 1892.

GEORGE DIXON now had the title to himself.

SOLLY SMITH bt. Dixon, pts. 20, San Francisco, Oct. 4, 1897.

DAVE SULLIVAN bt. Smith, rtd. 5, New York, Sept. 26, 1898.

GEORGE DIXON bt. Sullivan, disq. 10, New York, Nov. 11, 1898.

TERRY McGOVERN bt. Dixon, rtd. 8, New York, Jan. 9, 1900.

YOUNG CORBETT bt. McGovern, k.o. 2, Hartford, Nov. 28, 1901.

Both Corbett and McGovern became

overweight.

ABE ATTELL bt. Harry Forbes, k.o. 5, St. Louis, Feb. 1, 1904.

Attell strengthened claim by beating Tommy Sullivan, k.o. 4, San Francisco, Apl. 30, 1908.

JOHNNY KILBANE bt. Attell, pts. 20, Vernon, California, Feb. 22, 1912.

EUGENE CRIQUI bt. Kilbane, k.o. 6, New York, Jun. 2, 1923.

JOHNNY DUNDEE bt. Criqui, pts. 15, New York, Jul. 26, 1923.

Dundee relinquished title 1924—overweight.

LOUIS KID KAPLAN bt. Danny Kramer, k.o. 9, New York, Jan. 2, 1925.

Kaplan relinquished title 1927—overweight.

BENNY BASS bt. Red Chapman, pts. 10, Philadelphia, Sept. 19, 1927.

TONY CANZONERI bt. Bass, pts 15, New York, Feb. 10, 1928.

ANDRE ROUTIS bt. Canzoneri, pts. 15, New York, Sept. 28, 1928.

BATTLING BATTALINO bt. Routis, pts. 15, Hartford, Conn., Sept. 23, 1929.

Battalino relinquished title 1932—overweight.

N.B.A.:—

Tommy Paul bt. Johnny Pena, pts. 10, Detroit, May 26, 1932.

Freddie Miller bt. Paul, pts. 10, Chicago, Jan. 13, 1933.

Petey Sarron bt. Miller, pts. 15, Washington, May 11, 1936.

N.Y.A.C.:—

Kid Chocolate bt. Lew Feldman, k.o. 12, New York, Oct. 13, 1932.

Chocolate relinquished this title 1934.

Baby Arizmendi bt. Mike Belloise, pts. 15, New York, Aug. 30, 1934.

Arimendi relinquished title—overweight.

Mike Belloise bt. Everette Rightmire, k.o. 14, New York, Apl. 3, 1936.

Henry Armstrong bt. Belloise, pts. 10, Los Angeles, Oct. 27, 1936.

HENRY ARMSTRONG bt. Petey Sarron, k.o. 6, New York, Oct. 29, 1937.

Armstrong relinquished title 1938.

N.Y.A.C.:—

Joey Archibald bt. Mike Belloise, pts. 15, Oct. 17, 1938.

N.B.A.:—

Leo Rodak bt. Leoni Efrati, pts. 10,

Chicago, Dec. 29, 1938.

JOEY ARCHIBALD bt. Rodak, pts. 15, Providence, Apl. 18, 1939.

N.B.A. declared Pete Scalzo to be champion, May, 1940. He had beaten Archibald, k.o. 2, New York, Dec. 5, 1938, in an overweight bout, but Archibald would not meet him again at the stipulated poundage.

Richie Lemos bt. Scalzo, k.o. 5, Los Angeles, Jul. 1, 1941.

Jackie Wilson bt. Lemos, pts. 12, Los Angeles, Nov. 18, 1941.

Jackie Callura bt. Wilson, pts. 15, Providence, Jan. 18, 1943.

Phil Terranova bt. Callura, k.o. 8, New Orleans, Aug. 16, 1943.

Sal Bartolo bt. Terranova, pts. 15, Boston, Mar. 10, 1944.

HARRY JEFFRA bt. Archibald, pts. 15, Baltimore, May 20, 1940.

JOEY ARCHIBALD bt. Jeffra, pts. 15, Washington, May 12, 1941.

CHALKY WRIGHT bt. Archibald, k.o. 11, Washington, Sept. 11, 1941.

WILLIE PEP bt. Wright, pts. 15, New York, Nov. 20, 1942.

N.B.A. still recognised Bartolo as champion, until he was eliminated by Willie Pep, k.o. 12, New York, Jun. 7, 1946.

SANDY SADDLER bt. Pep, k.o. 4, New York, Oct. 29, 1948.

WILLIE PEP bt. Saddler, pts. 15, New York, Feb. 11, 1949.

SANDY SADDLER bt. Pep, rtd. 7, New York, Sept. 8, 1950.

Saddler relinquished title 1957.

HOGAN KID BASSEY bt. Cherif Hamia, r.s.f. 10, Paris, Jun. 24, 1957.

DAVEY MOORE bt. Bassey, rtd. 13, Los Angeles, Mar. 18, 1959.

SUGAR RAMOS bt. Moore, rtd. 10, Los Angeles, Mar. 21, 1963.

VICENTE SALVIDAR bt. Ramos, rtd. 11, Mexico City, Sept. 26, 1964.

SALVIDAR retired 1967.

HOWARD WINSTONE bt. Mitsunori Seki, r.s.f. 9, London, Jan. 23, 1968.

JOSE LEGRA bt. Winstone, r.s.f. 5, Porthcawl, July 24, 1968.

JOHNNY FAMECHON bt. Legra, pts. 15, London, Jan. 21, 1969.

VICENTE SALVIDAR bt. Famechon, pts. 15, Rome, May 9, 1970.

KUNIAKI SHIBATA bt. Salvidar, r.s.f. 12, Tijuana, Dec. 11, 1970.

CLEMENTE SANCHEZ bt. Shibata, k.o. 3, Tokyo, May 19, 1972.

JOSE LEGRA bt. Sanchez, r.s.f. 10, Monterey, Dec. 16, 1972.

EDER JOFRE bt. Legra, pts 15, Brasilia, May 5, 1973.

Jofre deprived of title by W.B.C. for failing to defend against nominated opponent. The W.B.A. version of title was also vacant at this time as their champion, Ernesto Marcal had retired.

Ruben Olivares won W.B.A. version beating Zensuke Utagawa, r.s.f. 7, Los Angeles, July 9, 1974.

ALEXIS ARGUELLO bt. Olivares, k.o. 13, Inglewood, Nov. 23, 1974.

Arguello relinquished title June 1977.

Danny Lopez bt. David Kotey, pts. 15, Accra, Nov. 6, 1976 (W.B.C.).

Rafael Ortega bt. Francisco Coronado, pts. 15, Jan. 15, 1977 (W.B.A.).

Cecilio Lastra bt. Ortega, Torrelavega, Dec. 17, 1977 (W.B.A.).

Eusebio Pedroza bt. Lastra, k.o. 13, Panama City, Apl. 15, 1978 (W.B.A.).

Salvador Sanchez bt. Lopez, r.s.f. 13, Phoenix, Feb. 2, 1980 (W.B.C.).

Sanchez killed in car accident Aug. 1982.

Juan Laporte bt. Mario Miranda, rtd. 10, New York, Sept. 15, 1982 (W.B.C.).

Wilfredo Gomez bt. Laporte, pts. 12, San Juan, Mar. 31, 1984 (W.B.C.).

Azumah Nelson bt. Gomez, r.s.f. 11, San Juan, Dec. 8, 1984 (W.B.C.).

Barry McGuigan bt. Pedrozo, pts. 15, Loftus Road, London, June 8, 1985 (W.B.A.).

Steve Cruz bt. McGuigan, pts. 15, Las Vegas, June 23, 1986 (W.B.A.).

Antonio Esparragoza bt. Cruz, r.s.f. 12, Fort Worth, Mar. 6, 1987 (W.B.A.).

### Junior-featherweight or Super-bantamweight

RIGOBERTO RIASCO bt. Waruinge Nakayama, rtd. 8, Panama City, Apl. 3, 1976.

ROYAL KOBAYASHI bt. Riasco, r.s.f. 8, Seoul, Oct. 1, 1976.

DONG KYUN YUM bt. Kobayashi, pts. 15, Seoul, Nov. 24, 1976.

WILFREDO GOMEZ bt. Yum, k.o. 12, San Juan, May 21, 1977.

Gomez relinquished title Apl. 1983.

Jaime Garza bt. Bobby Berna, r.s.f. 2, Los Angeles, June 15, 1983 (W.B.C.).

Loris Stecca bt. Leo Cruz, rtd. 12, Milan, Feb. 22, 1984 (W.B.A.).

Victor Callejas bt. Stecca, k.o. 8, Guaynabo, May 26, 1984 (W.B.A.).

Juan "Kid" Meza bt. Garza, k.o. 1, Kingston, N.Y., Nov. 3, 1984 (W.B.C.).

Lupe Pintor bt. Meza, pts. 12, Mexico City, Aug. 18, 1985 (W.B.C.).

Samart Payakarum bt. Pintor, k.o. 5, Bangkok, Jan. 18, 1986 (W.B.C.).

Callejas deprived of title Dec. 1986 (W.B.A.).

Louie Espinoza bt. Tommy Laley, r.s.f. 4, Phoenix, Jan. 16, 1987 (W.B.A.).

Jeff Fenech bt. Payakarum, r.s.f. 4, Sydney, May 8, 1987 (W.B.C.).

### Bantamweight

GEORGE DIXON bt. Nunc Wallace, r.s.f. 18, London, Jun. 27, 1890.

Dixon relinquished title 1892.

BILLY PLIMMER bt. Tommy Kelly, k.o. 10, Coney Island, May 9, 1892. (Kelly, had previously drawn with Dixon).

Plimmer strengthened his claim by beating Dixon in 4 rounds, catchweights, New York, Aug. 22, 1893.

PEDLAR PALMER bt. Plimmer, r.s.f. 14, London, Nov. 25, 1895.

Palmer was not recognised in America where Jimmy Barry claimed the championship after beating Caspar Leon, k.o. 28, Illinois, Sept. 15, 1894.

Barry retired in 1899.

TERRY McGOVERN bt. Palmer, k.o. 1, New York, Sept. 12, 1899.

McGovern relinquished title 1900.

HARRY HARRIS bt. Palmer, pts. 20, London, Mar. 18, 1901.

Harris relinquished title—overweight.

HARRY FORBES bt. Caspar Leon, pts. 15, Memphis, Apl. 2, 1901.

FRANKIE NEIL bt. Forbes, k.o. 2, San Francisco, Aug. 13, 1903.

JOE BOWKER bt. Neil, pts. 20, London, Oct. 17, 1904.

Bowker became overweight and in America the title was claimed by Jimmy Walsh.

JIMMY WALSH bt. Monte Attell, k.o. 6, Philadelphia, Mar. 29, 1905.
Walsh relinquished title 1909—overweight.
British Isles and European Continent:—
Digger Stanley claimed title. He had drawn with Walsh, 15, May 24, 1909.
Digger Stanley bt. Ike Bradley, Liverpool, Sept. 14, 1911.
Charles Ledoux bt. Stanley, k.o. 7, Dieppe, Jun. 23, 1912.
Eddie Campi bt. Ledoux, pts. 20, Vernon, Jun. 24, 1913.
Kid Williams bt. Campi, k.o. 12, Vernon, Jan. 31, 1914.
America:—
Frankie Conley bt. Monte Attell, k.o. 42, Vernon, Feb. 22, 1910.
Johnny Coulon bt. Conley, pts. 20, New Orleans, Feb. 26, 1911.
KID WILLIAMS bt. Coulon, k.o. 3, Los Angeles, Jun. 9, 1914.
PETE HERMAN bt. Williams, pts. 20 New Orleans, Jan. 9, 1917.
JOE LYNCH bt. Herman, pts. 15, New York, Dec. 22, 1920.
PETE HERMAN bt. Lynch, pts. 15, New York, Jul. 25, 1921.
JOHNNY BUFF bt. Herman, pts. 15, New York, Sept. 23, 1921.
JOE LYNCH bt. Buff, k.o. 14, New York, Jul. 10. 1922.
ABE GOLDSTEIN bt. Lynch, pts. 15, New York, Mar. 21, 1924.
EDDIE MARTIN bt. Goldstein, pts. 15, New York, Dec. 19, 1924.
CHARLIE ROSENBURG bt. Martin, pts. 15, New York, Mar. 20, 1925.
Rosenburg relinquished title 1927—overweight.
Bud Taylor bt. Canzoneri, pts. 10, Chicago, Jun. 24, 1927.
Taylor relinquished title 1928—overweight.
Bushy Graham claimed title after beating Izzy Schwartz, pts. 15, New York, May 23, 1928.
Bushy Graham became overweight.
AL BROWN bt. Vidal Gregorio, pts. 15, New York, Jun. 18, 1929.
Brown was deprived of his title by N.B.A. and N.Y.A.C. for not defending it in a reasonable time.
N.B.A.:—
Sixto Escobar bt. Baby Casanova,

k.o. 9, Monteal, Jun. 26, 1934.
Lou Salica bt. Escobar, pts. 15, New York, Aug. 26, 1935.
Sixto Escobar bt. Salica, pts. 15, New York, Nov. 15, 1935.
Europe:—
Baltazar Sangchilli bt. Al Brown, pts. 15, Valencia, Jun. 1, 1935.
Tony Marino claimed title after beating Sangchilli, k.o. 14, New York, Jun. 29, 1936.
SIXTO ESCOBAR bt. Marino, k.o. 13, New York, Aug. 31, 1936.
HARRY JEFFRA bt. Escobar, pts. 15, New York, Sept. 23, 1937.
SIXTO ESCOBAR bt. Jeffra pts. 15, San Juan, Feb. 20, 1938.
Escobar retired 1940 after losing to Jeffra in a non-title bout, but Jeffra was now overweight.
LOU SALICA bt. George Pace, pts. 15, New York, Sept. 24, 1940.
MANUEL ORTIZ bt. Salica, pts. 12, Hollywood, Aug. 7, 1942.
HAROLD DADE bt. Ortiz, pts. 15, San Francisco, Jan. 6, 1947,
MANUEL ORTIZ bt. Dade, pts. 15, Los Angeles, Mar. 11, 1947.
VIC TOWEEL bt. Ortiz, pts. 15, Johannesburg, May 31, 1950.
JIMMY CARRUTHERS bt. Toweel, k.o. 1, Jo'burg, Nov. 15, 1952.
Carruthers retired May, 1954.
ROBERT COHEN bt. Chamrern Songkitrat, pts. Bangkok, Sept. 19, 1954.
N.B.A.:—
Raton Macias bt. Songkitrat, r.s.f. 11, San Francisco, Mar. 9, 1955.
MARIO D'AGATA bt. Cohen rtd. 6, Rome, Jun. 29, 1956.
ALPHONSE HALIMI bt. D'Agata, pts. 15, Paris, Apl. 1, 1957.
Halimi confirmed his right to universal recognition by beating the N.B.A. champion, Raton Macias, pts. 15, Los Angeles, Nov. 6, 1957.
JOSE BECERRA bt. Halimi, k.o. 8, Los Angeles, July 8, 1959.
Becerra retired 1960.
N.B.A.:—
Eder Jofre bt. Eloy Sanchez, k.o. 6, Los Angeles, Nov. 18, 1960.
Europe:—
Alphonse Halimi bt. Freddie Gilroy, pts. 15, Wembley, Oct. 25, 1960.

JOHNNY CALDWELL bt. Halimi, pts. 15, London, May 27, 1961.

EDER JOFRE bt. Caldwell, rtd. 10, Sao Paulo, Jan. 18. 1962.

MASAHIKO HARADA bt. Jofre, pts. 15, Nagoya, May 18, 1965.

LIONEL ROSE bt. Harada, pts. 15, Tokyo, Feb. 27, 1968.

RUBEN OLIVARES bt. Rose, k.o. 5, Inglewood, Calif., Aug. 22, 1969.

CHUCHO CASTILLO bt. Olivares, r.s.f. 14, Inglewood, Oct. 16, 1970.

RUBEN OLIVARES bt. Castillo, pts. 15, Inglewood, Apr. 2, 1971.

RAFAEL HERRERA bt. Olivares, k.o. 8, Mexico City, Mar. 19, 1972.

ENRIQUE PINDER bt. Herrera, pts. 15, Panama City, July 29, 1972.

ROMEO ANAYA bt. Pinder, k.o. 3, Panama City, Jan. 20, 1973.

ARNOLD TAYLOR bt. Anaya, k.o. 14, Johannesburg, Nov. 3, 1973.

SOO HWAN HONG bt. Taylor, pts. 15, Durban, July 3, 1974.

ALFONSO ZAMORA bt. Hong, k.o. 4, Inglewood, Mar. 14, 1975.

JORGE LUJAN bt. Zamora, k.o. 10, Los Angeles, Nov. 19, 1977.

JULIAN SOLIS bt. Lujan, pts. 15, Miami, Aug. 29, 1980.

JEFF CHANDLER bt. Solis, r.s.f. 14, Miami Beach, Nov. 14, 1980.

RICHARD SANDOVAL bt. Chandler, r.s.f. 15, Atlantic City, Apl. 7, 1984.

GABY CANIZALES bt. Sandoval, r.s.f. 7, Las Vegas, Mar. 10, 1986.

BERNARDO PINANGO bt. Canizales, pts. 15, New Jersey, June 4, 1986. Pinango retired 1987.

Takayu Muguruma bt. Azail Moran, k.o. 5, Morigachi, Japan, Mar. 29, 1987 (W.B.A.).

Chang Young Park bt. Muguruma, r.s.f. 11, Morigachi, Japan, May 24, 1987 (W.B.A.).

Wilfredo Vasquez bt. Park, r.s.f. 10, Seoul, Oct. 4, 1987 (W.B.A.).

*Super-flyweight or Junior-bantamweight*

RAFAEL ORONO bt. Seunghun Lee, pts. 15, Caracas, Feb. 2, 1980.

CHULHO KIM bt. Orono, k.o. 9, San Cristobal, Jan. 24, 1981.

RAFAEL ORONO bt. Kim, r.s.f. 6, Seoul, Nov. 28, 1982.

PAYAO POONTARAT bt. Orono, pts. 12, Pattaya, Nov. 27, 1983.

JIRO WATANABE bt. Poontarat, pts. 12, Osaka, July 5, 1984.

GILBERTO ROMAN bt. Watanabe, pts. 12, Osaka, Mar. 30, 1986.

SANTOS LACIAR bt. Roman, r.s.f. 11, Reims, May 16, 1987.

SUGAR BABY ROJAS bt. Laciar, pts. 12, Miami, Aug. 8, 1987.

*Flyweight*

SID SMITH bt. Eugene Criqui, pts. 20, Paris, Apl. 11, 1913.
Smith relinquished title 1913.

PERCY JONES bt. Ladbury, pts. 20, London, Jan. 26, 1914.

Jones relinquished title 1914— overweight.

America:—
Johnny Coulon recognised as champion 1910.

Kid Williams bt. Coulon, k.o. 3, Los Angeles, Jun. 9, 1914.

Thereafter, Williams fought mostly in the bantamweight division and his flyweight title claim was not established. Young Zulu Kid claimed title in 1915.

Europe:—
Jimmy Wilde bt. Joe Symonds, k.o. 12, London, Feb. 14, 1916.

JIMMY WILDE bt. Young Zulu Kid, k.o. 11, London, Dec. 18, 1916.

PANCHO VILLA bt. Wilde, k.o. 7, New York, Jun. 18, 1923.
Villa died July, 1925.

Frankie Genaro claimed title on strength of a victory over Pancho Villa in March, 1923. Genaro was not generally recognised.

Fidel La Barba bt. Genaro, pts. 10, Los Angeles, Aug. 22, 1925.

FIDEL LA BARBA bt. Elky Clark, pts. 12, New York, Jan. 21, 1927. La Barba temporarily ret'd Aug. 1927.

N.Y.A.C.:—
Izzy Schwartz bt. Newsboy Brown, pts. 10, New York, Dec. 16, 1927.
Willie La Morte twice beat Schwartz in 1929 but was not recognised as champion, although this eliminated Schwartz from the championship.

Midget Wolgast bt. Black Bill, pts. 15, New York, Mar. 21, 1930.

Small Montana eliminated Wolgast with a 10 rounds pts. victory, Sept. 16,

1935. Officially designated as for American flyweight title.

N.B.A.:—
Albert Berlanger bt. Ernie Jarvis, pts. 10, Toronto, Dec. 19, 1927.
Frankie Genaro bt. Berlanger, pts. 10, Toronto, Feb. 6, 1928.
Emile Pladner bt. Genaro, k.o. 1, Paris, Mar. 2, 1929. (recognised by I.B.U.).
Frankie Genaro bt. Pladner, disq. 5, Paris, Apl. 18, 1929. (not generally recognised as a title fight).
Frankie Genaro regained N.B.A. recognition by beating Berlanger, pts. 10, Toronto, Jun. 10, 1930.
Young Perez bt. Frankie Genaro, k.o. 2, Paris, Oct. 27, 1931. (also recognised by I.B.U.).
Jackie Brown bt. Perez, r.s.f. 13, Manchester, Oct. 31, 1932. (N.B.A. and I.B.U.).

I.B.U.:—
Benny Lynch bt. Brown, r.s.f. 2, Manchester, Sept. 9, 1935.
BENNY LYNCH bt. Small Montana, pts. 15, London, Jan. 19, 1937. Lynch became overweight 1938.
PETER KANE bt. Jackie Jurich, pts. 15, Liverpool, Sept. 22, 1938.
JACKIE PATERSON bt. Kane, k.o. 1, Glasgow, Jun. 19, 1943. Paterson deprived of title by B.B.B. of C. July, 1947.

N.B.A. and EIRE:—
Rinty Monaghan bt. Dado Marino, pts. 15, London, Oct. 20, 1947.
Paterson reinstated as champion by B.B.B. of C., 1948.
RINTY MONAGHAN bt. Paterson, k.o. 7, Belfast, Mar. 23, 1948.
Monaghan retired April, 1950.
TERRY ALLEN bt. Honore Pratesi, pts. 15, London, Apl. 25, 1950.
DADO MARINO bt. Allen, pts. 15, Honolulu, Aug. 1, 1950.
YOSHIO SHIRAI bt. Marino, pts. 15, Tokyo, May 19, 1952.
PASCUAL PEREZ bt. Shirai, pts. 15, Tokyo, Nov. 26, 1954.
PONE KINGPETCH bt. Perez, pts. 15, Bangkok, Apl. 16, 1960.
MASAHIKO HARADA bt. Kingpetch, k.o. 11, Tokyo, Oct. 10, 1962.
PONE KINGPETCH bt. Harada, pts. 15, Bangkok, Jan. 12, 1963.

HIROYUKI EBIHARA bt. Kingpetch, k.o. 1, Tokyo, Sept. 18, 1963.
PONE KINGPETCH bt. Ebihara, pts. 15, Bangkok, Jan. 23, 1964.
SALVATORE BURRUNI bt. Kingpetch, pts. 15, Rome, Apl. 23, 1965.
WALTER McGOWAN bt. Burruni, pts. 15, Wembley, June 14, 1966.
CHARTCHAI CHIONOI bt. McGowan, r.s.f. 9, Bangkok, Dec. 30, 1966.
EFREN TORRES bt. Chionoi, r.s.f. 8, Mexico City, Feb. 23, 1969.
CHARTCHAI CHIONOI bt. Torres, pts. 15, Bangkok, Mar. 20, 1970
ERBITO SALVARRIA bt. Chionoi, r.s.f. 2, Bangkok, Dec. 7, 1970.
VENICE BORKORSOR bt. Salavarria, pts. 15, Bangkok, Feb. 9, 1973.
Borkorsor relinquished title—overweight.
MIGUEL CANTO bt. Shoji Oguma, pts. 15, Sendai, Jan. 8, 1975.
CHAN HEE PARK bt. Canto, pts. 15, Pusan, Mar. 18, 1979.
SHOJI OGUMA bt. Park, k.o. 9, Seoul, May 18, 1980.
ANTONIO AVELAR bt. Oguma, k.o. 7, Mito, May 12, 1981.
PRUDENCIO CARDONA bt. Avelar, k.o. 1, Tampico, Mar. 20, 1982.
FREDDIE CASTILLO, bt. Cardona, pts. 15, Merida, July, 24, 1982.
ELEONCIO MERCEDES bt. Castillo, pts. 15, Los Angeles, Nov. 6, 1982.
CHARLIE MAGRI bt. Mercedes, r.s.f. 7, Wembley, Mar. 15, 1983.
FRANK CEDENO bt. Magri, r.s.f. 6, Wembley, Sept. 27, 1983.
KOJI KOBAYASHI bt. Cedeno, r.s.f. 2, Tokyo, Jan. 18, 1984.
GABRIEL BERNAL bt. Kobayashi, k.o. 2, Tokyo, Apl. 9, 1984.
SOT CHITALADA bt. Bernal, pts. 12, Bangkok, Oct. 8, 1984.

*Light-flyweight*
FRANCO UDELLA bt. Valentin Martinez, disq. 12, Milan, Apl. 4, 1975.
LUIS ESTABA bt. Udella, k.o. 3, Caracas, July 18, 1976.
FREDDY CASTILLO bt. Estaba, r.s.f. 14, Caracas, Feb. 19, 1978.
NETRNOI SAWVORASINGH bt. Castillo, pts. 15, Bangkok, May 6, 1978.
KIM SUNG-JUN bt. Sawvorasingh, k.o. 3, Seoul, Sept. 30, 1978.

SHIGEO NAKAJIMA bt. Sung-Jun, pts. 15, Tokyo, Jan. 3, 1980.

HILARIO ZAPATA bt. Nakajima, pts. 15, Tokyo, Mar. 23, 1980.

AMADO URSUA bt. Zapata, k.o. 2, Panama City, Feb. 6, 1982.

TADASHI TOMORI bt. Ursua, pts. 15, Tokyo, Apl. 13, 1982.

HILARIO ZAPATA bt. Tadashi Tomori, pts. 15, Kanazowa, Tokyo, July, 20, 1982.

JUNG-KOO CHANG bt. Zapata, k.o. 3, Daejon, Korea, Mar. 26, 1983.

## WORLD CHAMPIONS (BARE-KNUCKLE, PRIZE RING):

Until about 1870 there was only one champion irrespective of weight. However, the names that follow may be considered as heavyweight champions of the world.

JAMES FIGG, 1719 until he retired undefeated 1730. Towards the end of Figg's career Tom Pipes, Gretting and George Taylor claimed the championship

JACK BROUGHTON bt. George Taylor, 20 mins., London, about 1734.

JACK SLACK bt. Broughton, 14 mins., London, Apl. 11, 1750.

BILL STEVENS bt. Slack, 27 mins., London, Jun. 17, 1760.

GEORGE MEGGS bt. Stevens, 17 mins., London, Mar. 2, 1761.

GEORGE MILSOM bt. Meggs, 40 mins., Calne, Wilts., Jul. 1762.

TOM JUCHAU bt. Milsom, 70 mins., St. Albans, Aug. 27, 1765.

BILL DARTS bt. Juchau, 40 mins., Guildford, May, 1766.

TOM LYONS bt. Darts, 45 mins., Kingston, Jun. 27, 1769. Lyons retired.

PETER CORCORAN bt. Darts, 1 rnd., Epsom, May 10, 1771.

HARRY SELLARS bt. Corcoran, 38 rnds., Staines, Oct. 10, 1776.

DUGGAN FEARNS bt. Sellars, 1½ mins., Sept. 25, 1779.

TOM JOHNSON acknowledged as champion after beating Jack Jarvis, Sept., 1783 and the Croydon Drover, Mar., 1784.

BIG BEN BRAIN bt. Johnson, 20 mins., Jan. 17, 1791. Brain died 1794.

DANIEL MENDOZA bt. Bill Warr, 17 mins., Bexley Heath, Nov. 12, 1794.

JOHN JACKSON bt. Mendoza, 10½ mins., Hornchurch, Essex, Apl. 15, 1795. Jackson retired without defending championship.

JEM BELCHER bt. Andrew Gamble, 5 rnds., Wimbledon Common, Dec. 22, 1800. Belcher relinquished title after losing an eye while playing racquets, July, 1803.

HEN PEARCE bt. Joe Berks, 15 rnds., London, Aug. 12, 1803. Pearce retired undefeated 1806.

JOHN GULLY bt. Bob Gregson, 36 rnds., Newmarket, Oct. 14, 1807. Gully retired.

TOM CRIBB bt. Bob Gregson, 23 rnds., Moulsey Hurst, Oct. 25, 1808. Cribb retired and nominated Tom Spring.

NED PAINTER bt. Spring, 41 rnds., Russia Farm, Aug. 7, 1818. Painter declined a return with Spring and so the latter became recognised as champion. Spring was never again defeated and he retired in 1824.

TOM CANNON bt. Josh Hudson, 16 rnds., Warwick, Nov. 23, 1824.

JEM WARD bt. Cannon, 10 mins., Stony Stratford, July 19, 1825.

PETER CRAWLEY bt. Ward, 26 mins., Royston Heath, Herts., Jan. 2, 1827. Crawley retired almost immediately and Ward reclaimed the championship, holding it until his retirement in 1832.

DEAF JAMES BURKE bt. Simon Byrne, 186 mins., Noman's Land, St. Albans, May 30, 1833.

BENDIGO (Wm. Thompson) bt. Burke, 24 mins., Heather, Leicestershire, Feb. 12, 1839. Bendigo retired and Burke again claimed championship.

NICK WARD bt. Burke on a foul after crowd broke up fight in 17th rnd. to save Ward further punishment. Lillingstone Level, Oxon., Sept. 22, 1840.

BEN CAUNT bt. Ward, 47 mins., Long Marsden, Warwick., May 11, 1841.

BENDIGO bt. Caunt on a foul in 93 rnds., 130 mins., Lillingstone Level, Oxon., Sept. 9, 1845. Bendigo finally retired.

AMERICAN CHAMPIONS:
Tom Hyer bt. Yankee Sullivan 16 rnds., Rock Point, Feb. 7, 1849. Hyer retired.

John Morrissey bt. George Thompson, 11 rnds., Mare Island, California, Aug. 31, 1852. Morrissey retired in 1859 and was succeeded as American champion by John C. Heenan.

BRITISH CHAMPIONS:
William Perry bt. Tom Paddock, disq. 27 rnds., Woking, Dec. 17, 1850.

Harry Broome bt. Perry, disq. 15 rnds., Mildenhall, Sept. 29, 1851.

Tom Paddock bt. Broome, 51 rnds., Bentley, Suffolk, Oct. 2, 1856. Paddock forfeited title when he failed to accept a challenge from William Perry.

Tom Sayers bt. Perry, 10 rnds., Isle of Grain, Kent, June 16, 1857.

TOM SAYERS drew with JOHN C. HEENAN, 42 rnds., 2 hrs. 20 mins., Farmborough, Apl. 17, 1860. Sayers retired from the ring.

BRITISH CHAMPIONS:
Sam Hurst bt. Tom Paddock, 5 rnds., 9½ mins., Berkshire, Nov. 5, 1860.

Jem Mace bt. Hurst, 8 rnds., Medway, June 13, 1861.

Tom King bt. Mace, 21 rnds., Medway, Nov. 26, 1862.

TOM KING bt. John C. Heenan, 24 rnds., Wadhurst, Kent, Dec. 10, 1863. King forfeited title when he failed to accept a challenge from Jem Mace.

JEM MACE bt. Tom Allen, 10 rnds., Kennerville, La., May 10, 1870. Mace retired in 1871.

TOM ALLEN bt. Mike McCoole, 7 rnds., St. Louis, Sept. 23, 1873.

JOE GOSS bt. Allen, disq. 21, in two rings, Kenton and Boone Counties, Kentucky, Sept. 7, 1876.

PADDY RYAN bt. Goss, 87 rnds., West Virginia, May 30, 1880.

JOHN L. SULLIVAN bt. Ryan, 9 rnds., 10½ mins., Mississippi City, Feb. 7, 1882.

Jake Kilrain drew with Jem Smith (British champion), Ile des Souverains, France, 106 rnds., 2 hrs. 30 mins., Dec. 19, 1887.

JOHN L. SULLIVAN bt. Kilrain, 75 rnds., Richburg, Miss., July 8, 1889.

## WORLD CHAMPIONSHIP:

See under the various countries for world title-holders of particular nationalities.

With so many different versions of the World Championships it is impossible to give clear-cut records in many instances. The following records are for the most part based on the lists set out in this volume under WORLD CHAMPIONS. The U.S.A. have produced the most world title-holders. After dividing these Americans into sections according to the nationality of their parents, it will be found that the greatest proportion of American world title-holders born of foreign parents were the Italian-Americans.

Next to America, although a good way behind, in the number of gloved world title-holders, come England, Italy, Japan, France and Ireland in that order.

### Fewest fights:

Leon Spinks holds the record for winning a world title after the fewest professional fights. He had only 7 contests before he beat Muhammad Ali for the heavyweight championship.

James J. Corbett and James J. Jeffe-ries each won the world heavyweight title in their 13th professional contest.

The Thai fighter Saensak Muangsurin actually won the world Junior-welterweight title in only his third contest in July 1975, but this was the W.B.C. version not generally recognised, and Muangsurin had formerly been a champion kick-boxing champion.

Davey Moore (New York) won the W.B.A. light-middleweight title in his ninth professional fight in February 1982.

Vic Toweel won the world bantam-weight title in his 14th professional contest.

Fidel La Barba claimed the world flyweight championship after beating Frankie Genaro in his 11th professional contest but he was not universally recognised at that time.

### First:

There is some dispute as to the first contest ever fought which could rightly claim a world championship label. But favourite for this distinction was the first fight between Tom Sayers (Champion of England) and John C. Heenan (Champion of America) which took place at Farnborough, Hants., April 17, 1860.

The ring was broken into on the arrival of the police in the 37th round, and after five more rounds, which were fought amid absolute chaos, the fight was stopped and declared a draw.

There are various claimants to the distinction of being the first ever world title-holder, but the man with the strongest claim to this honour was Tom King, who was born at Stepney, London, in 1835.

After winning the championship of England by beating Jem Mace in 21 rounds, November 26, 1862, King defeated John C. Heenan in a contest at Wadhurst, Kent, December 8, 1863.

Heenan was still claiming the championship of America at that time and this contest was considered to have been for the world title. King won in 24 rounds.

## Longest Reign:

The longest reign of any world champion at any weight was that of Joe Louis.

He held the heavyweight title for 13 years 97 days, June 22, 1937, to September 27, 1950.

Louis actually announced his retirement in March, 1949 but he did not lose his title in the ring until, when making his come-back, he was beaten by Ezzard Charles, September 27, 1950.

The longest reign in the other divisions:—

Cruiserweight: Carlos De Leon, July 17, 1983 to June 6, 1985, 1 year 10 months.

Light-heavyweight: Archie Moore, December 17, 1952, to February 10, 1962, 9 years 2 months.

Middleweight: Tommy Ryan, June 18, 1898, to March, 1907, 8 years 9 months.

Junior or Light-middleweight: Thomas Hearns, (W.B.C.) December 3, 1982 to September 1986, 3 years 9 months.

Welterweight: Freddie Cochrane, July 29, 1941, to February 1, 1946; Jose Napoles, June 4, 1971, to December 6, 1975, 4 years 6 months.

Junior or Light-welterweight: Antonio Cervantes, October 29, 1972, to March 6, 1976, 3 years 4 months.

Lightweight: Jack McAuliffe, Oct. 29, 1886, to 1896, 10 years.

Junior-lightweight: Flash Elorde, March 16, 1960 to June 30, 1967, 7 years 3 months.

Featherweight: Johnny Kilbane, February 22, 1912, to June 2, 1923, 11 years 3 months.

Junior-featherweight: Wilfredo Gomez, May 21, 1977 to April 1983, 5 years 1 month.

Bantamweight: Panama Al Brown, June 18, 1929, to June 1, 1935, 5 years 11 months.

Super-flyweight: Chulho Kim, January 24, 1981, to November 28, 1982, 1 year 10 months.

Flyweight: Jimmy Wilde, February 14, 1916, to June 18, 1923, 7 years 4 months.

Light-flyweight: Jung-Koo Chang, June 26, 1983, to date, over 4 years.

## Longest world title fight:

The longest under Queensberry Rules was between Joe Gans and Battling Nelson for the lightweight title, at Goldfield, Nevada, September 3, 1906. Gans won on a foul in the 42nd round.

## Most defences of title:

Joe Louis holds the record for the highest number of official world title defences. He put his title at stake in the ring on 26 occasions.

Manuel Ortiz defended his world bantamweight crown a total of 22 times. This was during two spells as champion.

Henry Armstrong defended his world welterweight title 20 times and the lightweight title on one occasion.

George Dixon had 19 or 20 title fights when he was holder of the featherweight crown. However, his claim to the title was often in dispute and therefore it would be difficult to establish a definite figure.

## Most titles:

The first man to claim world titles in as many as four weight divisions is

Thomas Hearns. He held the W.B.A. version of the welterweight title 1980-81; W.B.C. version of light-middleweight title 1982-86; W.B.C. light-heavyweight title 1987, and then won the W.B.C. middleweight title in October 1987. This record of four world titles cannot be taken too seriously in the present confused state of world titles because Hearn's claim to be world welterweight champion was not accepted outside the W.B.A. with Sugar Ray Leonard the rightful champion over the same period. Indeed, Leonard beat Hearns in 1981.

The first man to win three world titles was Bob Fitzsimmons. He won the middleweight crown from Jack Dempsey, January 14, 1891; heavyweight title from J. J. Corbett, March 17, 1897, and light-heavyweight title from George Gardner, November 25, 1903.

Another man to win three world titles at different weights is Henry Armstrong who was feather, light, and welterweight champion. He had the added distinction of holding all three of these titles simultaneously for about four months in 1938.

Armstrong nearly added a fourth title, for in March, 1940, he held Ceferino Garcia to a draw in a bout recognised by N.Y.A.C. as being for the world middleweight championship.

Wilfred Benitez, Alexis Arguello, Roberto Duran, Wilfredo Gomez and Sugar Ray Leonard have each held three world titles at different weights. Benitez was W.B.A. Junior-welterweight champion 1976; welterweight champion 1979, and W.B.C. light-middlweight champion 1981-82. Arguello held the W.B.A. featherweight title 1974-77; W.B.C. junior-lightweight title-holder 1978-80, and W.B.C. lightweight champion 1981-82. Roberto Duran was lightweight champion 1972-79, welterweight 1980, and W.B.A. light-middleweight 1983-84. Gomez held the junior-featherweight title 1977-83, W.B.C. featherweight 1984-, junior-lightweight 1985-86, and Leonard was welterweight champion 1979-80, 1980-82, light-middleweight 1981, and middleweight 1987.

Barney Ross held the world lightweight and welterweight titles simultaneously for nearly four months during 1934. He was also junior-welterweight champion from June 1933 but never defended this title before the class was abandoned.

Tony Canzoneri was featherweight champion 1928; lightweight 1930-33, and junior-welterweight 1931, 1935-36.

Sugar Ray Robinson may be said to have held the world welter and middleweight titles simultaneously in February, 1951, although, officially, he was deprived of his welter championship immediately after winning the heavier title.

Carmen Basilio achieved the same distinction as Robinson by winning the middleweight championship in September, 1957, when he still held the welterweight crown.

Other men who have won two different world titles are:—

Sugar Ray Leonard: welterweight 1979-80, 1980-; light-middleweight 1981.

Johnny Dundee: featherweight 1923-24, junior lightweight 1921-23; 23-24.

Nino Benvenuti: junior-middleweight 1965-66, middleweight 1967, 1968-70.

Freddie Castillo: light-flyweight, 1978, flyweight, 1982.

Jack Dempsey (Nonpareil): lightweight 1882-84, middleweight 1884-91.

George Dixon: bantamweight 1890-92, featherweight 1894-97, 1898-1900.

Emile Griffith: welterweight 1961, 1962-63, 1963-66, middleweight 1966-67, 1967-68.

Masahiko Harada: flyweight 1962-63, bantamweight 1965-68.

Soo Hwan Hong: bantamweight 1974-75 (W.B.A.), light-featherweight 1977-78 (W.B.A.).

Harry Jeffra: bantamweight 1937-38, featherweight 1940-41.

Eder Jofre: bantamweight 1962-65, featherweight 1973-74.

Terry McGovern: bantamweight 1899-1900, featherweight 1900-01.

Ruben Olivares: bantamweight 1969, 1971-72, featherweight 1975 (W.B.A.).

Carlos Ortiz: Junior-welterweight 1959-60, lightweight 1962-65.

Barney Ross: lightweight 1932, welterweight 1934, 1935.

Tommy Ryan: welterweight 1894-96, middleweight 1898-1907.

Kuniaki Shibata: featherweight 1970-72, junior-lightweight 1973.

Mike Spinks: W.B.A. light-heavyweight 1981-85, W.B.C. light-heavyweight 1983-85, heavyweight 1985-87.

Dick Tiger: middleweight 1962-63, 1965-66, light-heavyweight 1966-68.

Mickey Walker: welterweight 1922-26, middleweight 1926-31.

Hilario Zapata: light-flyweight 1980-82, 1982-83, flyweight W.B.A. 1985-87.

## Most world title fights on one bill:

There were four world title fights on Mike Jacobs' bill at the New York Polo Grounds, September 23, 1937. Harry Jeffra v. Sixto Escobar, bantamweight; Lou Ambers v. Pedro Montanez, lightweight; Barney Ross v. Ceferino Garcia, welterweight; Fred Apostoli v. Marcel Thil, middleweight.*

* This should be ranked as a world title fight although Apostoli had signed a contract to the effect that he would not claim the title if he beat Thil.

## Regained title:

Sugar Ray Robinson regained the world middleweight title on four separate occasions. This is a record.

James Carter (lightweight), Emile Griffith (welterweight), Pone Kingpetch (flyweight), Muhammad Ali (heavyweight), Carlos De Leon (cruiserweight), Marvin Johnson (light-heavyweight) and Koichi Wajima (light-middleweight), have each regained the world title twice.

Other men who have regained a world title which they had previously held in the same weight division:—

Heavyweight: Floyd Patterson.

Light-heavyweight: Marvin Johnson (W.B.A.).

Middleweight: Stanley Ketchel, Tony Zale, Paul Pender, Dick Tiger, Nino Benvenuti, Emile Griffith.

Junior or Light-middleweight: Sandro Mazzinghi.

Welterweight: Billy Smith, Rube Ferns, Joe Walcott, Ted "Kid" Lewis, Jack Britton, Young Jack Thompson, Jackie Fields, Jimmy McLarnin, Barney Ross, Johnny Saxton, Carmen Basilio, Jose Napoles, Sugar Ray Leonard.

Junior or Light-welterweight: Duilio Loi, Eddie Perkins, Antonio Cervantes.

Lightweight: Tony Canzoneri, Lou Ambers, Jimmy Carter, Carlos Ortiz, Ismael Laguna, Mando Ramos, Edwin Rosario, Jose Luis Ramirez.

Junior-lightweight: Ben Villaflor, Sam Serrano.

Featherweight: George Dixon, Willie Pep, Sandy Saddler, Joey Archibald, Vicente Salvidar, Jose Legra, Ruben Olivares.

Bantamweight: Pete Herman, Joe Lynch, Sixto Escobar, Manuel Ortiz, Ruben Olivares.

Super-flyweight: Rafael Orono.

Flyweight: Pone Kingpetch, Chartchai Chionoi*, Shoji Oguma (W.B.C.), Freddie Castillo (W.B.C.).

Light-flyweight: Hilario Zapata.

No fighter has yet succeeded in regaining the world light-heavyweight, junior-featherweight titles after losing it in the ring.

In the flyweight division Frankie Genaro was only recognised as titleholder by the N.B.A. when he was beaten by Emile Pladner. Pladner was given I.B.U. recognition, but when Genaro subsequently beat Pladner he was still not accorded world-wide recognition.

*Chartchai Chionoi could also claim to have regained the world flyweight title twice, but the second time he was merely declared champion by the W.B.A. after the previous champion had relinquished the title.

## Shortest reigns:

The shortest time a boxer has held a world championship in each division is as follows:—

Heavyweight: Leon Spinks, February 15, 1978, to September 15, 1978, 212 days.

Cruiserweight: Alfonso Ratcliff, June 6, 1985, to September 22, 1985. 108 days.

Light-heavy: Jack Root, April 22, 1903, to July 4, 1903, 73 days.

Middleweight: Randolph Turpin, July 10, 1951, to September 12, 1951, 64 days.

Junior or Light-middleweight: Jose Duran, May 18, 1976, to October 8, 1976, 143 days. Tadashi Mihara held the W.B.A. version for 87 days in 1981-82.

Welter: Johnny Bratton, March 14, 1951, to May 18, 1951, 65 days.

Junior-welterweight: Tony Canzoneri, May 21 1933 to June 23, 1933, 33 days.

Light: Al Singer, July 17, 1930, to November 14, 1930, 120 days.

Junior-lightweight: Alfredo Lane, (W.B.C.) May 24, 1986, to September 27, 1986, 126 days.

Feather: Dave Sullivan, September 26, 1898, to November 11, 1898, 46 days.

Light-feather: Royal Kobayashi, October 1, 1976, to November 24, 1976, 54 days.

Bantam: Takuya Muguruma, March 29, 1987, to May 24, 1987, 56 days.

Super-flyweight: Payo Poon Tarat, November 27, 1983, to July 5, 1984, 221 days.

Fly: Emile Pladner, March 2, 1929, to April 18, 1929, 47 days.

Light-fly: Amado Ursua, February 6, 1982, to April 13, 1982, 66 days.

## WORMALD, Joe:

This London-born prize fighter is not listed among former British champions by all the boxing chroniclers, but the fact is that he did receive the Heenan-Sayers championship belt after beating Andrew Marsden in 18 rounds at Horley, Surrey, January 4, 1865.

At that time, however, Jem Mace was more generally recognised as champion, having regained that distinction when Tom King had failed to accept his challenge for a return bout.

The confusion might have been cleared up when Mace and Wormald contracted to meet other in September, 1865, but Wormald was forced to withdraw through illness and he forfeited £120 to Mace.

Soon after this Wormald went to America, and he died in Canada in 1871 when he was only 31.

## WRESTLER v. BOXER:

In Paris, December 31, 1908, Sammy McVey knocked out Tano Matsuda, a ju-jitsu expert, in 10 seconds.

Also in Paris, November 28, 1913, Jack Johnson knocked out Andre Sproul, a Russian wrestler, in two rounds.

In September, 1901, the heavyweight boxer, Frank Slavin, was challenged to a fight with gloves by the wrestling champion, Frank Gotch. The fight took place at Dawson City, September 25, 1901, and Slavin was declared the winner after giving the wrestler a hammering. Gotch had preferred to wrestle and he had succeeded in throwing Slavin out of the ring.

Packey O'Gatty k.o'd Shimakado with one punch in only 4 seconds, Yokohama, January 12, 1918.

Bob Fitzsimmons, wearing gloves, k.o'd Ernest Roeber in 1st round, Carson City, January 3, 1897.

Several boxers have also met each other in wrestling contests. Bob Fitzsimmons once wrestled Gus Ruhlin. The Cornishman had beaten Ruhlin with the gloves on, but in the catch-as-catch-can contest the Akron giant got the better of Fitzsimmons.

Joe Louis engaged in wrestling bouts after his retirement from boxing, and Primo Carnera made much more money as a wrestler than he ever did as world champion boxer.

The multi-million dollar contest between Muhammad Ali and Japanese wrestling champion, Kokichi Endo, in Tokyo in June 1976, was a bitter disappointment. It resulted in a draw after 15 farcical rounds of relatively little real contact.

## WRIGHT, Albert (Chalky):

Born at Durango, Mexico, but domiciled in California, this negro featherweight had a long career of over 20 years in the ring.

He started fighting professionally about 1928 and in a very short time he was highly rated on the American west coast, but in February, 1938, he was stopped in three rounds by Henry Armstrong.

Wright decided to hang up his gloves following this defeat, but after a few months he was persuaded to try again.

In 1939 he came to England and beat Dan McAllister, Kid Tanner, and George Daly, and in September, 1941, he became world featherweight champion after stopping Joey Archibald in 11 rounds at Washington.

Wright's title claim was not universally recognised, however, for the N.B.A. considered Richie Lemos to be the rightful champion.

In February, 1942, Wright beat Lemos, but even that did not clear up the dispute because Lemos had by that time lost his N.B.A. title to Jackie Wilson.

Still Wright was given wider recognition than the N.B.A. line of champions about this time and he held the title until November, 1942, when he was outpointed by Willie Pep.

# Y

## YAROSZ, Teddy:

This Polish-American from Pittsburgh won the American version of the world middleweight title when he outpointed Vince Dundee over 15 rounds in his home town, September 11, 1934.

Soon after this, however, an unfortunate injury was to mar his championship career. In a non-title bout with Babe Risko at Scranton, Yarosz tore a cartilage in his right leg in the first round, and, after staggering around in great pain, he was knocked out in the seventh round.

Following an operation his leg seemed better, but just before he was due to meet Risko in a return bout for the title it gave out again.

Yarosz gave a game display, hobbling about on one leg, but he was clearly outpointed by Risko and lost his claim to the world championship.

That was in September, 1935, and although the fighting career of this Polish-American appeared to be at an end when his leg was put into irons, he made a come-back after enduring months of painful treatment.

In 1936 he beat Risko, but that fighter had lost his title to Freddie Steele just months previously, and although Yarosz never regained the title, he remained one of America's leading middleweights until his retirement in 1942.

# Z

## ZALE, Tony:

The early career of this tough middle-weight from Gary, Indiana, was not too good, but when he came under the management of Sam Pian and Art Winch his fortunes began to change.

In July, 1940, he was acknowledged by the N.B.A. as world middleweight champion following his 13-round knock-out victory over Al Hostak.

At that time the N.Y.A.C. recognised Ken Overlin as champion.

Zale was beaten by Billy Soose in a non-title bout in August, 1940, and Soose went on to become the N.Y.A.C. middleweight champion, but when Soose relinquished that title in November, 1941, it left Zale undisputed champion, and he gained official world-wide recognition by outpointing Georgie Abrams.

Zale was beaten by Billy Conn in a non-title bout in 1942 and then served in the U.S. Navy for the remainder of the war until he came back in 1946 and ran up a string of knock-out victories which lasted until July, 1947, when he was himself stopped by Rocky Graziano in six rounds.

Zale was now a veteran of 34 but nearly 12 months later he regained the middleweight title by putting Graziano away inside three rounds.

In September, 1948, Zale had his last fight. It was a gruelling contest with Marcel Cerdan and after 11 hard rounds Zale was unable to come up for the 12th. So at the age of 35 Zale had lost his title and he wisely decided to hang up his gloves.

## ZAMORA, Alfonso:

A Mexican bantamweight whose short arms packed tremendous punching power and whose aggressive all-action style overwhelmed most of his opponents. Nearly all of his victories were well inside the distance and he knocked out Soo Hwan Hong inside four rounds to take the world title (W.B.A. version) in March, 1975.

He subsequently defended this crown successfully with wins in 4, 4, 2, 2, 3 and 12 rounds before he was himself knocked out by Jorge Lujan in 10 rounds in Los Angeles in November 1977.

## ZIVIC, Fritzi:

One of a family of five brothers, all of whom were fighters, Fritzi Zivic started his ring career in Pittsburgh in 1931, and was something of an experienced veteran when he won the world welterweight title from Henry Armstrong in October, 1940. Zivic was then 27 years of age and his victory over Armstrong surprised most of the critics.

Armstrong demanded a return bout and this took place at Madison Square Garden in January, 1941. This time Zivic stopped Armstrong in 12 rounds.

Zivic's next defence of the title was against Freddie Cochrane, who beat him on points over 15 rounds.

Soon after this Zivic was twice beaten by Ray Robinson, then he outpointed Cochrane in a non-title bout in September, 1942.

This Croatian-American was one of the busiest fighters in the ring about this time, but any hopes he may have had of regaining the title were shattered in October, 1942, when he was outpointed by Henry Armstrong, who was then making a come-back.

## ZULU KID, Young:

This stocky Italian started fighting in America just before World War I. By 1915 he was claiming the world flyweight title but he was not recognised on this side of the Atlantic.

In December, 1916, the Zulu Kid came to London to meet Jimmy Wilde at the Holborn Stadium in what was the first generally accepted world flyweight title fight. The Italian was knocked out in the 11th round.

## ZURITA, Juan:

Mexican lightweight who won the N.B.A. version of the world title from Sammy Angott in March, 1944, when he had been boxing as a professional for about 10 years.

He was beaten by Beau Jack in his next fight, a non-title bout, and when he was called on to defend his N.B.A. crown against Ike Williams in April, 1945, he was knocked out in the second round.

Zurita announced his retirement immediately after this defeat.

# Addenda

**AMATEUR to PROFESSIONAL:**
Wilston, T. A.B.A. (L.H.) 1983-84. . . .
British (L.H.) 1987-

## BRITISH CHAMPIONS:
*Light-heavyweight*
Collins relinquished title 1987.
Tony Wilson bt. Blaine Logsden, r.s.f.
6, Cardiff, Dec. 15, 1987.

## EUROPEAN BOXING UNION (Champions):
*Heavyweight*
Francisco Damiani bt. Eklund, r.s.f.
6, Aosta, Italy, Oct. 9, 1987.
*Light-middleweight*
Rosi relinquished title 1987.
*Bantamweight*
Gomis relinquished title 1987.

## WILSON, Tony:
Hard-hitting Wolverhampton light-heavyweight who is always dangerous and shows plenty of boxing talent. When making his professional debut in February 1985, after winning the A.B.A. title in 1983 and 1984, he stopped Blaine Logsden in four rounds. Two years 10 months later he beat the same fighter in six rounds to capture the vacant British title. Between times Wilson had suffered only one defeat.

## WORLD CHAMPIONS:
*Light-heavyweight*
Donny Lalonde bt. Eddie Davis, r.s.f.
2, Port of Spain, Nov. 27, 1987 (W.B.C.).
*Light-middleweight*
Mike McCallum relinquished W.B.A. title 1987.
Julian Jackson bt. In-Chul Baek, r.s.f.
3, Las Vegas, Nov. 21, 1987 (W.B.A.).
*Lightweight*
Julio Cesar Chavez bt. Rosario, r.s.f.
11, Las Vegas, Nov. 21, 1987 (W.B.A.).
*Super-bantamweight*
Jeff Fenech relinquished W.B.C. title 1987.
Julio Gerracio bt. Espinoza, pts. 12, San Juan, Nov. 28, 1987 (W.B.C.).
*Bantamweight*
Miguel Lora recognised by W.B.C. since outpointing Daniel Zaragoza in Aug. 1985, i.e. before Pinango retired.

# Index